WAR CRIMES
of the
Deutsche Bank
and the
Dresdner Bank

SCIENCE AND HUMAN RIGHTS SERIES
Christopher Simpson, Editor

Comfort Women Speak
Testimony from Sex Slaves of the Japanese Military
Edited by Sangmie Choi Schellstede
Photographs by Soon Mi Yu

War Crimes of the Deutsche Bank and the Dresdner Bank
Office of Military Government (U.S.) Reports
Edited and with an Introduction by Christopher Simpson

Forthcoming

The Politics of Historic Memory
Human Rights and Discourse in Chile Since Pinochet's Coup
By Hernán Vidal
Translated by Stacey Alban Skar

Satellite Technologies and Human Rights
Edited by Christopher Simpson

WAR CRIMES
of the
Deutsche Bank
and the
Dresdner Bank

OFFICE OF MILITARY
GOVERNMENT (U.S.) REPORTS

Edited and with an Introduction by

CHRISTOPHER SIMPSON

HOLMES & MEIER
NEW YORK / LONDON

Published in the United States of America 2002
by Holmes & Meier Publishers, Inc.
160 Broadway • New York, NY 10038

This book has been printed on acid-free paper.

designed by Brigid McCarthy
typesetting by JoAnne Todtfeld

Library of Congress Cataloging-in-Publication Data

The war crimes of the Deutsche Bank and the Dresdner Bank: the OMGUS reports/
edited by Christopher Simpson.
    p. cm.
Includes index.
ISBN 0-8419-1407-9 (alk. paper)
  1. Banks and banking—Corrupt practices—Germany—History—20th century. 2.
Deutsche Bank (1870–1945) 3. Dresdner Bank. 4. Business and politics—Germany. 5.
World War, 1939–1945—Confiscations and contributions—Germany. 6. Jewish
property—Germany—History—20th century. 7. World War, 1939–1945—Economic
aspects—Germany. I. Simpson, Christopher. II. Germany (Territory under Allied
occupation, 1945–1955: U.S. Zone). Office of Military Government.

D810.C8 W37 2001
364.16'8—dc21

                                     2001039596

Manufactured in the United States of America

Contents

PART TWO

OMGUS Report: The Dresdner Bank

Acknowledgments

My thanks to Marilyn Henry and Michael Pinto-Duschinsky whose advice was generously offered and gratefully received. Manfred Pohl, Saul Kagan, Ervin Staub, Ron Goldfarb, Ben Ferencz, and the late Telford Taylor were of great help at key junctures in the development of this project. Particular thanks go to my colleagues from the *Universities and Empire* project, as well as to Elizabeth Noelle-Neuman and H. M. Kepplinger for the insights they spurred concerning communication theory and academic self-deception. I am grateful to Holmes & Meier, particularly Miriam Holmes, Publisher, and Maggie Kennedy, Executive Editor, whose careful work and confidence gave me the push to complete this project.

A Note on Editing

The original manuscripts of the OMGUS reports reproduced here were prepared by teams of authors working under considerable deadline pressure. One result was inconsistencies in spelling, particularly of German names. For example, there is one instance in the original in which three different spellings of Reichmarshall Hermann Goering's name appear on a single page: 'Göring,' 'Goring,' and 'Goering.' Similarly, the city Koeln appeared variously as Cologne, Köln, and Koeln. This book has normalized the spellings with modern German usage throughout, removing the umlauts and spelling ö as oe, ä as ae, and so on.

The first version of the Deutsche Bank report appeared in late 1946. Several months later the same investigative team added an approximately fifty page Annex of newly discovered information. Together they remain the most complete of the OMGUS Finance Division dossiers on German banking during the Third Reich. The Deutsche Bank study also includes more than 430 exhibits, most of them captured bank records, totaling more than 1,500 pages. Dresdner Bank exhibits and the U.S. Counterintelligence Corps (CIC) reports on Dresdner executives total well over 1000 pages.

Because the Deutsche Bank Report Annex is structured to correspond to the main report—that is, Chapter VII, part 2 of the Annex corresponds directly to Chapter VII, part 2 of the main report, and so on—this book has the Annex pages inserted at the appropriate places in the main report, rather than maintaining the Annex as a separate document. To make it clear to the reader where that has taken place, each insert is introduced with "From the Annex to the Report" and set off from the regular text.

The original investigative reports are frequently repetitive, as would be expected in dossiers prepared for prosecutors handling large, complex war-crimes cases. The reports, in effect, sought to indict the banks as institutions as well as certain of their officers as individuals. That led to descriptions of particular crimes—Aryanization of Jewish property and the bankrolling of companies engaged in slave labor and looting, for example—being presented in two places, nearly verbatim: first in the discussion of the bank's own operations and again in the presentation of evidence concerning the individual bank officer's role in the crime.

In this volume, some of that duplication has been retained in order to provide context. More frequently, however, the reader is referred to the earlier, complete discussion by a short editor's note in square brackets that reads "[As detailed in Chapter VII], Carl Goetz signed," or words to that effect. This editing has permitted trimming the manuscript without removing the documentation of the central crime of which both the Dresdner Bank and Mr. Goetz stood accused.

Similarly, the original OMGUS Finance Division investigation teams designed their bank reports to stand alone as separate, book-length texts. That meant, for example, that in each study there is an essentially identical chapter that reviews the general structure of German corporations. There was little reason to subject modern readers to covering the same material twice (and in depth), so instead this information has been summarized in the introduction to this edition. Even so, those chapters have not been eliminated altogether, because there is information about the banks themselves that must be kept easily available to readers.

Considerable attention has been paid to preserving the substance of the OMGUS reports on the Deutsche Bank and Dresdner Bank, while at the same time reducing materials that are repeated verbatim in the two documents. Nothing of substance has been cut from either report.

Where editor's notes have been inserted, they appear in square brackets: e.g., "[The documents show that. . . . .]" Where a repetitive sentence or phrase has been trimmed, it is noted by four ellipses (. . . .). If a paragraph or more has been cut, as in the case of the verbatim repetition of the general aspects of German corporate structure, it is noted by this symbol: ❏ ❏ ❏. In a handful of instances, space has been reduced without eliminating content by placing tangential discussions in a footnote, rather than in the main text.

Specialists and those who wish to review the captured German records preserved as exhibits are urged to consult the original archival manuscripts, which are available at:

- U.S. Office of Military Government for Germany (U.S.) [OMGUS], Finance Division, Financial Investigation Section, "Report on the Investigation of the Deutsche Bank," November 1946, in file: "Deutsche Bank," box 229, RG 260, National Archives, College Park, Maryland.
- U.S. Office of Military Government for Germany (U.S.) Finance Division, Financial Investigation Section, "Report on the Investigation of the Dresdner Bank," 1946, box 235, RG 260, National Archives.

Additional OMGUS Finance Division investigations found in the papers of the OMGUS Office of Economic Affairs, OMG Berlin Sector, Finance Division, Box 461, RG 260 National Archives include profiles of Reichs-Kredit-Gesellschaft (Box 461, RG 260); Baron Kurt von Schroeder (same series, Box 230; available here only as offset printing plates); Kurt Schmitt – Allianz Insurance (same series, Box 233); and Hjalmar Schacht (same series, Box 236).

CHRISTOPHER SIMPSON

INTRODUCTION

Buried Records and Modern Controversies

After World War II, the Allies divided the land that was Germany into occupied zones, and the U.S. Military began a systematic documentation of German war crimes. The Office of Military Government—(U.S.) (OMGUS) Finance Division investigated the Deutsche Bank's, the Dresdner Bank's, and other financial institutions' involvement in the Holocaust and war crimes of the Third Reich. This investigation produced a series of reports totaling more than 10,000 pages, including original correspondence and records.

Today these reports are at the center of two bitter, intertwined controversies. The first concerns the extent of responsibility of the most powerful German banks implicated in Nazi crimes during the Third Reich, and, by extension, whether these institutions should be legally obligated to compensate those who suffered at their hands. Simple justice is at stake in that dispute. So is the possibility that these companies may be forced to pay billions of dollars to avoid lawsuits, sanctions, and damaging publicity.

The second, closely connected controversy involves how the facts of what the banks did during those years are to be established. All of the parties to the dispute rely on historians, archival records, and (to a much lesser degree) eyewitnesses to make their case. Given that, what are the standards for ethical behavior and accountability for the historians and other experts who are today employed by the institutions involved in these disputes? The issue is particularly pressing when academics hired by the companies enjoy exclusive access to parts of the banks' archives or other types of evidence.

This is the first time the OMGUS investigative records of German banks have been published in English.[1] This introduction recaps the origin of the OMGUS investigations, the strange history of the report's suppression during the early Cold War years and the deceit and power politics that accompanied the decision to bury the information they contained. It examines how declassified OMGUS Finance Division records have returned to center stage in disputes over the compensation of survivors of Nazi concentration camps, as well as in today's highly charged debates over the role of German finance and industry in Nazi crimes during the Holocaust.

The investigative reports published here were drawn up by OMGUS Finance Division staff in 1946 and 1947. Led by Gen. Lucius Clay and administered largely by the U.S. Army, OMGUS was the occupation government in the U.S. sector of

---

[1] An annotated German translation is available: OMGUS, Ermittlungen gegen die Deutsche Bank. Nordingen: Greno, 1986. On Dresdner Bank, see OMGUS, Ermittlungen gegen die Dresdner Bank. Nordlingen: Greno, 1986.

Germany in the first years following the war. OMGUS established its headquarters near Frankfurt in the sprawling, modern IG Farben corporate management complex, which had survived the war almost entirely intact. The new military government kept IG Farben's desks and heavy black telephones, boxed its records for storage, and soon filled the company's filing cabinets with U.S. government paperwork. OMGUS also maintained major offices in Berlin and Nuremberg.

The OMGUS Finance Division compiled investigative reports and other evidence concerning the activities of Germany's largest banks, insurance companies, and other financial institutions during and after the Third Reich. Their studies were intended to help prosecutors draw up formal indictments for war crimes and crimes against humanity by the hundred or so top German corporate officials who had been most deeply involved with the Nazi regime. U.S. prosecutors also sought to break up the giant Deutsche Bank and Dresdner Bank into smaller, more competitive units— a process that was known as decartelization. The OMGUS Finance Division reasoned that breaking up Germany's financial nerve centers would eliminate or substantially weaken the system of cartels and tightly interlocking directorships among Germany's largest corporations.

The OMGUS financial investigations are in this sense unabashedly partisan. They do not mince words; each opens with a blunt recommendation to bring criminal charges against senior officers and directors of these banks, and to rapidly liquidate the Deutsche Bank and Dresdner Bank empires.

In their investigative summaries, the American banking experts first explain the formal structure of German corporations and the extent to which various corporate officers are responsible for the activities of the institutions they lead. Put most simply, no major activity of either the Deutsche Bank or the Dresdner Bank was undertaken without specific authorization from senior management (the Vorstand), who in turn reported their decisions and activities at regular intervals to the supervisory board of directors which is known as the Aufsichtsrat.

These tightly knit economic and political power centers proved to be remarkably resilient. During the 1930s, the National Socialist (Nazi) Party and the Third Reich under Hitler had attempted—and largely failed—to break up the tightly interwoven web of German financial and corporate institutions by limiting the number of interlocking corporate boards on which a director could serve. (The Nazis, as always, were determined to undermine any possible rival for power.) The Nazi Party's failure to achieve that goal even at the height of its power casts an intriguing new light on the character of Hitler's state. For one thing, the failure of Nazi "reform" illustrates the real power of the major banking and industrial blocs *within* Nazi Germany and shows their ability to act in their own interest when they chose to do so.

The Nazi Party's failure to significantly reorganize the most senior levels of German capital is particularly significant when considered in the context of the Holocaust. It provides further evidence that many major German businesses voluntarily exploited opportunities created by the Nazis. Contrary to their post-war protestations that the German state or the National Socialists had forced their hand, the Deutsche Bank and Dresdner Bank's Aryanization and theft of Jewish property, as well as their role in bankrolling the joint SS–private-sector concentration camp system, became in most instances opportunistic forms of what was viewed at the time as clever entrepreneurship.

The OMGUS Reports document that major companies intensified their persecution of innocent people in order to win favor with the regime and accumulate enormous corporate assets, despite a variety of official restrictions on war profiteering. Said another way, German financial and industrial blocs proved that they were capable of evading Nazi edicts when it came to what corporations perceived as their central interests, particularly the maintenance of private sector control of key corporate assets. Active corporate cooperation with the Nazi-led disenfranchisement and the eventual attempt to exterminate Jews, on the other hand, proved to be both a business opportunity and a means of demonstrating political loyalty to the regime.[2]

Both major banks assigned some of their most talented officials to organize private sector profiteering from Nazi Aryanization of Jewish property, according to the post-war U.S. government investigation. The international departments of both institutions—led most notably by Hermann Abs of the Deutsche Bank and Carl Goetz at Dresdner—took as their tasks money laundering for the Nazi Party and the SS, and gold smuggling and collecting intelligence on behalf of the regime. They exploited the German military conquest to absorb rival banks across Europe. The OMGUS Finance Division reported that both institutions traded in hundreds of kilograms of concentration camp gold, and that both underwrote the activities of the SS and the construction of concentration camps. We know today that this included Deutsche Bank financing of construction of IG Farben facilities at the giant manufacturing and mass-murder camp complex known as Auschwitz-Birkenau.[3]

Both banks assigned their most senior officers as liaisons with the SS and the Nazi Party. Their "Circle of Friends of Reichsfuehrer SS Heinrich Himmler" meetings, for example, emerged as a key node in an informal yet brutally effective network that coordinated policy concerning private sector exploitation of slave laborers. By the end of the war, substantially all surviving concentration camp inmates had spent at least part of their captivity "leased out," so to speak, by the SS to private German companies.

The postwar OMGUS investigations documented this devastating pattern of corporate and individual complicity in many of the most heinous crimes of the century. If the prosecutions and corporate antitrust actions recommended by the OMGUS financial investigators had actually been carried out in the first years after the war, they could well have been successful, notwithstanding the deepening Cold War. The handful of corporate officials who were prosecuted at the time—the Krupp and IG Farben trials at Nuremberg, for example[4]—brought to light voluminous evidence of corporate complicity in genocide. Had U.S. attorneys carried out the prosecution of

---

[2] Christopher Simpson, *The Splendid Blond Beast: Money, Law, and Genocide in the Twentieth Century* (Monroe, ME: Common Courage Press, 1995) 68–69, 85–86, 151–57. Harold James discusses at length the necessity to demonstrate corporate loyalty to the regime, but draws different conclusions concerning its significance; see Harold James, *The Deutsche Bank and the Nazi Economic War Against the Jews* (Cambridge: Cambridge University Press, 2001).

[3] On Nazi gold, see page 151 in the Deutsche Bank report that follows. On Auschwitz, see Edmund Andrews, "German Bank Opens Files on Financing of Auschwitz," *New York Times*, February 5, 1999.

[4] See John Alan Appleman, *Military Tribunals and International Crimes* (Westport, Conn.: Greenwood Press, 1971) and Adalbert Rueckerl, *The Investigation of Nazi Crimes, 1945–1978*, trans. Derek Rutter (North Haven, Conn.: Archon Books, 1980) for a summary of these trials.

the Deutsche and Dresdner Banks at the time it was recommended, the information on looted Nazi gold and slave labor profiteering that has been revealed by the highly publicized scandals of the 1990s might well have come to light fifty years earlier, when the evidence was fresh. Instead, however, the U.S. government buried the OMGUS Deutsche Bank and Dresdner Bank reports in classified files, where they lay undisturbed and largely forgotten for the next four decades.

Today, specialists can establish with certainty that during that interregnum, the Deutsche Bank, Dresdner Bank, and certain other major German corporations purged their files of damning evidence concerning the Holocaust. The West German government, for example, appears to have destroyed key records concerning so-called Melmer gold—that is, the gold taken from the mouths of Jews murdered at extermination centers, as well as from eyeglasses, wedding rings and similar deeply personal objects. (The name "Melmer" refers to Hauptsturmfuehrer Bruno Melmer, the chief between 1942 and 1944 of the SS accounting unit responsible for management of *Zahngold*—"tooth gold"—as well as precious metals and other valuables seized during SS operations against Jews. Melmer's name often appears on the handful of surviving Deutsche Bank ledger sheets as the source of gold purchased for the bank's own accounts.)[5]

Important records concerning Melmer gold transactions were last reported to be in the hands of the Bundesbank, the ponderously respectable state bank of the West German government, which eventually took control of many Reichsbank (the state bank during the Third Reich) archives after the war. "Mysteriously all 26 files [known to concern this gold] disappeared during the 1970s, and have never been found," reports historian Jonathan Steinberg.[6] We know today that in 1976, the Bundesbank purged some 900 surviving Reichsbank record groups in 1976—thousands of documents, most of which were irreplaceable—and that the lost Melmer files were almost certainly among them.[7]

On the American side, the strange fate of the OMGUS financial investigation records of the 1940s became one element in a factional struggle within the U.S. government. Put briefly, the presidential administration of Franklin Roosevelt, his treasury secretary Henry Morgenthau, and parts of the U.S. War Department regarded Germany as the principal threat to peace after 1945. From this it followed that the United States should seek to maintain relatively normal diplomatic and military relations with its wartime ally, the USSR, and that U.S. occupation forces should pursue a strict approach to denazification of the U.S. zone in Germany. This meant implementation of a series of wartime U.S.-USSR agreements reached at the Moscow Conference, the Yalta Conference, and the Potsdam Conference. Each of these agreements emphasized that the allies would cooperate in a sweeping denazification of German society, including the dismissal and prosecution of the German financial and industrial leaders.

The Roosevelt administration was particularly determined to break up the power blocs and interlocking company directions between war industries, on the one hand,

---

[5] Jonathan Steinberg, *The Deutsche Bank and Its Gold Transactions during the Second World War* (Munich: Verlag C. H. Beck, 1999), 33, 112–119.

[6] Ibid., 35, fn 63.

[7] *Recherchenbericht zum Verbleib der Akten der Deutscher Reichsbank,*" July 28, 1998.

and the Deutsche Bank, Dresdner Bank, and a handful of other major financial institutions, on the other. Treasury Secretary Morgenthau viewed Germany's financial and industrial infrastructure as something akin to the Japanese system of Keiretsu corporate empires. The Mitsubishi Keiretsu, for example, used in-house banks to underwrite and attempt to coordinate the business activities of a sprawling empire that embraced automobile and aircraft manufacturing, weapons production, electronics, consumer products, construction, real estate, shipping, mining and much more. Mitsui operated a rival Keiretsu, as did Sumitomo. (They still do today.)

The German parallel was not exact, but it was close enough. The Siemens family of electronics fame had founded the Deutsche Bank, for example. Siemens, Deutsche Bank, Mannesman Steel, BMW, Daimler Benz, and the powerful Holtzmann construction companies had functioned as a de facto German Keiretsu for decades by the time Hitler took power. For many critics, the Siemens industrial combine, along with those of Krupp, Friedrich Flick, and similar magnates, constituted a "cauldron of wars," as the expression of the day went. Morgenthau and others argued that if the German cartels and combines were not dismantled, they would soon lead Europe into a third world war.

The economic and political realities of German business were considerably more complicated and paradoxical than any simple slogan, of course. The political coalitions, splits, betrayals, and reconciliations among the Nazis, Germany's business elite, and the Wehrmacht—to name only three examples—have been well documented. German industry's murderous exploitation of forced labor and slave labor at Auschwitz and other corporate-run concentration camps, and the continentwide looting of Jewish property are regarded by many to this day as evidence of the intrinsically criminal character of the alliance between the Nazi Party and the senior levels of Germany's economic power structure.

In early 1945, with Roosevelt still in the White House, the U.S. Joint Chiefs of Staff drew up an official directive for denazification and decartelization of German industry. This was the Commanders' Order no. 1067, better known as JCS 1067. President Roosevelt promulgated the directive shortly before his death. On paper, at least, the relatively hard-line policies of JCS 1067 provided the framework for American activities in occupied Germany throughout the first, crucial years after the collapse of the Hitler regime.

Harry S. Truman significantly altered Roosevelt's geopolitical strategy when he assumed the presidency after Roosevelt's death in April 1945. Truman quickly shuffled aside his predecessor's allies in the government, including Treasury Secretary Morgenthau. Within weeks of assuming the presidency, he quietly adopted many policies for dealing with Germany and the USSR that Roosevelt had explicitly rejected only months earlier.

Key U.S. State Department officials told Truman that a new war with the USSR "is as certain as anything in this world can be certain," as acting Secretary of State Joseph Grew commented in a presidential briefing only weeks after Hitler's suicide.[8] It would likely come soon, he continued. Grew and much of the senior staff at the State Department contended that the United States should encourage rapid

---

[8] Daniel Yergin, *Shattered Peace: The Origins of the Cold War and the National Security State* (Boston: Houghton Mifflin, 1977), 90–91.

economic reconstruction of Germany, limiting punitive measures to prosecution of a relative handful of die-hard National Socialists whose guilt was too grotesque to ignore. Meanwhile, Grew argued, Germany's financial and industrial elite should be reinstalled in positions of responsibility as soon as possible.

Grew and his political allies stressed that there had been significant splits between the Nazi Party and much of Germany's corporate elite. Most orthodox National Socialists viewed themselves as "revolutionaries" who favored Party rule throughout the private sector, as the attempted corporate law reforms of the late 1930s illustrated. Many favored a form of national-socialist syndicate such as the sprawling Hermann-Goering-Werke arms manufacturing combine or the Party-run VIAG holding company, which looted financial institutions across Europe and controlled the Reichskredit Gesellschaft (RKG) bank. Much of Germany's traditional economic elite remained suspicious of the Nazis, even though they were willing enough to profit from Hitler's government programs, the Aryanization of Jewish property, and the looting of Europe in the wake of the Nazi juggernaut.

Late in the war, much of Germany's corporate elite understood that their country was headed for catastrophe—the question was how soon it would come and at what cost. Many began quiet preparations for personal and corporate survival following the defeat of the regime. Such preparations could be dangerous, however, because they smacked of defeatism to orthodox Nazis determined to fight to the end for the Fuehrer. In retrospect, it is clear that ongoing active or tacit cooperation with the Nazis' campaign to exterminate Jews became for certain business leaders a means to demonstrate loyalty to the Nazi regime, even as they prepared for its eventual defeat. From BMW to Krupp to Volkswagen, much of corporate Germany maintained its "respectability" in the Nazis' eyes by exploiting slave labor supplied by the SS; continued looting of assets in Nazi-occupied territories; and continued complicity in the regime's *Endloesung* campaign to exterminate Jewry at any cost.

Men like Hermann Abs at the Deutsche Bank and Carl Goetz at Dresdner traded in death camp gold, for example.[9] Yet these two were not Nazis in a simplistic, ideological sense of that term, particularly during the last months of the regime. This tension between their ongoing criminal acts, on the one hand, and their plans to survive the war, on the other, provided the basis for their postwar claims that they had never "really" been Nazis, and instead had been forced to cooperate with policies determined by someone else.

The documentary records available today makes clear that U.S. diplomats such as Joseph Grew and George Kennan embraced such claims almost without question. By the end of 1945, they had succeeded in reframing many American policies toward occupied Germany. Where previously the problem faced by U.S. occupation forces was how to go about denazifying German industry under the terms of JCS 1067, the new orientation focused on fixing problems said to be *caused* by the modest denazification that had taken place.

---

[9] On corporations, see Simpson, *Beast,* 71–73, 157, 289–310. On Abs, see Chapter XIII: "Foreign Operations of the Deutsche Bank" (141ff) in the OMGUS manuscript that follows. On Goetz, see "Profiles," 358–64.

President Truman nevertheless found it opportune to maintain the appearance of observing JCS 1067, even as his administration dismantled it. There were at least two reasons for this institutionalized double-think. First, American public opinion strongly backed harsh measures against Germany and those responsible for Nazi atrocities, including the economic and political chiefs who had abetted those crimes. Second, maintaining reasonably stable relations with the USSR as it demobilized its armies in Eastern Europe required publicly embracing the fiction that the United States remained open to the Roosevelt-style unity of purpose that had underpinned the wartime alliance between East and West, at least for the moment. The Soviets, for their part, had much to gain from avoiding a military confrontation with the United States and from stabilizing cooperative governments in the Eastern European countries occupied by the Red Army.

Meanwhile, Stalin believed that he could read the Western Allies' fulfillment of their promises to dismantle German power as an important barometer, so to speak, of the West's intentions toward the USSR. Earlier, Stalin's belief that he would be betrayed by a British-German separate peace at the expense of the Soviets led directly to Stalin's decision to strike his own deal with Nazi Germany in the Hitler-Stalin Pact, for example. When the Nazis later betrayed Stalin and invaded the USSR, the Soviet leader's suspicion that his British and U.S. allies would also doublecross him in a deal with the Germans fueled wartime debates over the opening of a second military front in Western Europe. Once the Allies defeated Nazi Germany in 1945, Stalin regarded any indication of a 'soft' Western line on denazification as an indicator that new intrigues against the USSR were underway.[10]

This is not the place to rehash arguments concerning who cast the first stone in the Cold War. More relevant to the present discussion is that the Truman administration and the U.S. occupation government in Germany under Gen. Lucius Clay claimed to the American public and the world at large that they were implementing the relatively harsh, anti-Nazi policies of JCS 1067, when in reality they were seeking a politically palatable means to quickly bring it to an end. The OMGUS Finance Division's investigations of the wartime role of the Deutsche Bank and the Dresdner Bank took place on the cusp of that change.

In the summer of 1945, Gen. William Draper became chief of economic policy for the U.S.-administered zone of Germany. Draper was an imposing, broad-chested man with a bald pate and dark, bristling eyebrows that emphasized his high forehead. Prior to the war, he had served as corporate treasurer of Dillon, Read & Co., a private bank deeply involved in U.S.-German trade, and an officer of the German Credit and Investment Corporation of New Jersey, a holding company that specialized in international investments in Hitler-era Germany prior to the outbreak of World War II.[11] Though it was rarely stated directly, Draper's holding company served as a financial vehicle through which American investors had sought long-term profits from German businesses' Aryanization of Jewish property and the country's booming arms industry. He surrounded himself with like-minded aides to the extent

---

[10] Simpson, *Beast* 117ff; 199ff, 279ff.
[11] Ibid., pp.199ff; on Draper, see pp. 248–50.

that he could, and together they often succeeded in ending reform and denazification of the Germany economy before it began. Draper's steel industry chief in the U.S. occupation zone of Germany, for example, was Rufus Wysor, the president of the Republic Steel Corporation, which itself had a long history of cartel agreements with the German steel companies whose reconstruction he was now overseeing.

"What's wrong with cartels, anyhow?" Wysor replied when confronted with his lack of progress in denazifying and breaking up German steel and coal combines. "Why shouldn't these German businessmen run things the way they are used to? . . . German business is flat on its back. Why bother them with all this new stuff?"[12] Other senior Draper aides shared roughly similar backgrounds and perspectives.

In an interview given during his later years, Draper contended that,

> It became evident to us very quickly that . . . the United States would have to support Germany for the rest of time, or as long as that policy [JCS 1067] stayed in effect.
>
> And so, we had to wiggle here and waggle there and do the best we could without openly breaking our directive to permit the German economy to begin to function. We argued with this one and argued with that one here in Washington and in Germany . . . and bit by bit, we revised or recouped the situation.
>
> We didn't pay as much attention to [JCS 1067] as perhaps we should from the point of view of military discipline. There were several efforts to pull me back [to Washington] and have me charged with not carrying out the directive. [But] General Clay always defended me. He knew perfectly well that such a policy couldn't last just as well as I did."[13]

Critics pointed to the tough language in JCS 1067 and to U.S. international commitments made at the Potsdam Conference in August 1945, arguing that Draper had failed to implement the letter and the spirit of U.S. denazification policy. But what the critics did not understand was that the hard-line declarations were not the core of U.S. policy at all, regardless of what was said on paper.

Gen. Lucius Clay, the U.S. Military Governor in Germany, explained how he saw things at the time in an interview he gave some years later. "JCS 1067 would have been extremely difficult to operate under. . . . It was modified constantly; not officially, but by allowing this deviation, that deviation, et cetera."

Clay was convinced that President Truman was on his side. "We had . . . a change of administration [after Roosevelt]. The people who had had the greatest influence and developed the occupation powers went out, and Mr. Truman's administration came in," Clay remembered. Truman never supported the hard-line approach, Clay continued. "He had nothing to do with its creation and I don't think he ever believed in it."[14]

---

[12] James Stewart Martin, *All Honorable Men*, (Boston: Little, Brown, 1950), 164, 173.
[13] General William H. Draper, Jr., Oral History Interview, January 11, 1972, Harry S. Truman Library, Independence, MO., pp.32–33.
[14] Lucius Clay, Oral History Interview, July 16, 1974, Harry S. Truman Library, Independence, MO., 15–16 (on JCS 1067), 13 (on Truman).

Thus, the context within which the OMGUS Finance Division undertook its investigation into war crimes by German banks and bankers was a tough American policy on paper that was useful for pacifying public opinion in the West, for making promises to the Soviets, and for general public-relations purposes. But in reality, the upper echelons of the U.S. occupation government agreed at least as early as the summer of 1945 that a thorough denazification and decartelization of the German economy would never be attempted, regardless of what might be said for public consumption.

Draper's administrative techniques from the summer of 1945 forward provide a classic example of bureaucratic maneuver. He announced tough anti-Nazi measures in accordance with the official policy. Shortly after that, he proclaimed success in carrying out those measures while at the same time undermining the very policies he publicly professed to support.

That autumn, for example, Draper subordinates in the Finance Division attempted to initiate a program to arrest and interrogate about thirty top German bankers and financiers concerning the roles they had played in the Holocaust and the war. The interrogation effort focused only on those businessmen who had thrived under National Socialism or who had played a direct, personal role in Nazi expropriation and looting. The action did not call for criminal trials of these suspects, rather, its aim was to investigate, while the evidence was still fresh, what leading bankers had actually done under the Third Reich.

Draper blocked the measure as soon as it came to his attention, contending it would interfere with German economic recovery. When his Finance Division subordinates complained to sympathetic senators in Washington, Draper allies Robert Murphy (then the State Department's senior U.S. Political Advisor for Germany) and Col. Clarence Adcock (General Clay's most senior aide and long-time colleague) issued a series of reports in October 1945 stating that the main work of denazifying the German economy had already been completed, so there was no need to go ahead with further investigations. "What [U.S. banking investigators] are doing here through denazification is nothing less than a social revolution," Murphy's top aide Charles Reinhardt complained. "If the Russians want to bolshevize their side of the Elbe that is their business. But it is not in conformity with American standards to cut away the basis of private property."[15]

GERMAN BANKING UNDER MILITARY OCCUPATION

During the military occupation of Germany, the Deutsche Bank was for a time separated into three ostensibly competitive institutions by the occupation governments of the victorious Allies. From the Nazi-era Deutsche Bank, for example, sprang the new Norddeutsche Bank A.G., Rheinisch-Westfalische Bank A.G. and the Sueddeutsche Bank A.G. in the British, French and U.S. zones of occupied western German.[16] The

---

[15] Senate Committee on Military Affairs, *Elimination of German Resources for War*, Part II, 79th Congress, 187 Session, 1945, Y4.M59/2:G31, 1545–46.

[16] For a concise and accessible summary, see Lisa Mirabile, ed., *International Directory of Company Histories*, II, (Chicago: St. James Press, 1988), 278.

socialist government of the Soviet zone in eastern Germany nationalized the bank altogether. (They eventually used the Deutsche Bank's largest branch building in East Berlin to store the archives of the German Communist Party; its vault protected the Party's collection of the papers and original works of Karl Marx, Rosa Luxemburg, and other early leaders of European social-democratic and communist movements.)

In reality, however, the three separate parts of the old Deutsche Bank in the West functioned as a single unit, notwithstanding occupation government regulations requiring separation. The divided bank organized a shadow managing and a clandestine courier service that illegally crossed the borders of the various occupation zones with impunity.[17] (These supposedly competitive banks seamlessly reunited into a single, renewed Deutsche Bank shortly after West Germany joined NATO and assumed new national authority in the mid-1950s).

Hermann Abs, whom the OMGUS investigations consistently identified as a central figure in many of the bank's most egregiously criminal activities of the Nazi era, organized the semi-clandestine reconstruction of the institution and served as its principal strategist and spokesman after 1945. During the Nazi era Abs had been the Deutsche Bank's most important executive for international affairs, including the Aryanization of Jewish-owned banks and companies outside of Germany. He also oversaw Deutsche Bank negotiations with Himmler and other Nazi leaders concerning economic strategy for the Third Reich. Exercising influence through interlocking boards of directors, overlapping stock portfolios, and similar mechanisms, Abs became one of the most important private-sector coordinating points for German finance and industry from the invasion of Poland in 1939 through the collapse of the Nazi regime.

Nevertheless, the occupation government under Gen. Clay frequently promoted Abs's career from 1945 forward, despite the evidence collected by OMGUS investigators and their recommendation that Abs be tried as a war criminal.[18]

"We were never able to make Hermann Abs the financial minister [of Germany] as we would have," Clay remembered in the same interview quoted earlier, because the American and German public would likely refuse to accept a man who had been so deeply compromised during the Hitler years. But not to worry, Clay continued. "We were able to finally put him in charge of the Reconstruction Finance Corporation, which was somewhat outside the government." This agency was instrumental in distributing Marshall Plan funds for Germany.[19]

---

[17] OMGUS Office of the Financial Advisor, Financial Intelligence and Liaison Branch Field Investigation Section, *Report on the Investigation of Law 52 in the US Zone* (Restricted), May 1946. My special thanks to Louis Madison for bringing these records to my attention. See also OMGUS "Law 52: Blocking and Control of Property," (n.d.) four pages, in the same collection.

[18] Recommendations and data concerning Abs can be found at pp. 3, 65ff, and Chapter XIII in the OMGUS Deutsche Bank report that follows; "Herman Abs" in archival file *Nazis Dismissed from German Banking*, n.d. (1946), OMGUS/FINAD, box 234, RG 260, National Archives, College Park, MD. Abs was eventually barred from entering the United States due to his wartime record; see "Abs darf nich in die USA," Reuters news dispatch, May 7, 1990.

[19] Clay, Oral History Interview, 25–26. Abs's name is mistranscribed in the oral history as "Hermann Epps."

In 1952 and 1953, Abs represented Germany in the London Debt Settlement negotiations. The London meetings stabilized Germany's international trade and set a schedule for German national payments for damage to other countries stemming from World War II and Nazi crimes.

One result of the 1953 agreement is that today, German government representatives seem to have acquired the habit of greeting journalists with a handshake, a smile, and the highly questionable claim that the former West German state has paid about DM 100 billion to persons victimized by the Nazis and expects to pay about another DM 20 billion during the next several years. About three-fourths of the total has gone to Israel or surviving Jews, the German government reported recently.[20] A relative handful of individuals of many nationalities have also received some benefits.[21]

But the operative word here is German *state*. That is, whatever one may think of the debate over the numbers and the adequacy of the Bundesentschaedigungsgesetz (BEG) payments outlined above, these costs have been carried primarily by German taxpayers, regardless of their role in the Nazi regime (if any) or whether the taxpayer was born two or even three decades after Hitler's death. It is ironic but true that while German politicians reject any form of collective German guilt for Nazi crimes, they have meanwhile imposed precisely that "guilt"—or responsibility, if one prefers—through taxation of the general population.

Meanwhile, German finance and industry—arguably the principal financial beneficiaries of the Nazi era who survived the war—have enjoyed some fifty years of de facto legal immunity from being held accountable for the damage they *did* do to innocent people.[22] This can be traced quite directly to two giant loopholes that Hermann Abs engineered in the 1953 debt agreement.

"Two sizeable groups were not included in the system of State compensation paid by the Federal Republic [in the wake of the agreement]: prisoners of war and forced laborers," writes Lutz Niethammer, a mustachioed, aggressive academic who has emerged in recent years as a key adviser to the German chancellor on elimination of legal claims against German corporations implicated in Nazi-era murder, extortion,

---

[20] Lutz Niethammer, *Policy Paper for the Chef des Bundeskanzleramtes Relating to Current Questions of the Compensation of Forced Workers—Confidential!* (translation by Comprehensive Language Center, Inc.), January 1999, p.8.

[21] Ibid. The total does not include what today's German government asserts was DM 70 billion extracted by the USSR from the Soviet occupation zone in Eastern Germany. That figure is subject to dispute, and in any case does not come close to matching the cost of the destruction that Germany wrecked upon the USSR during the war. Nevertheless, it is true that the Soviets, like each of the other Allied governments, stripped valuable industrial and intellectual assets totaling billions of Deutschemarks from the German territories they controlled.

[22] Prior to 1953, the de facto immunity was not absolute. A handful of Krupp, IG Farben, and Flick executives were tried for war crimes and crimes against humanity in the "Subsequent Proceedings" phase of the Nuremberg trials during the late 1940s. Those prosecutions resulted in nineteen convictions and fourteen acquittals. All of the convicted executives were given amnesty within months by the new U.S. High Commissioner for Germany, John McCloy. See Appleman, *Military Tribunals,* for a summary of these trials. On McCloy's amnesty, see Office of the U.S. High Commissioner for Germany, Office of Public Affairs, "Landsberg: A Documentary Report," *Information Bulletin,* February 15, 1950.

Aryanization, and forced labor. In 1953, POWs and forced laborers were "assumed," as Niethammer put it, to have been "created by the war effects" and would only be compensated later by government-to-government arrangements at the time of an eventual peace treaty between Germany and the victorious allies.[23]

"At the time, the [West German] federal government protected the German industry," he notes with considerable understatement, "because it was feared that the wage claims of foreign workers would have an excessively negative impact on reconstruction and the impending defense expenditures" characteristic of the Cold War. [24]

As many Holocaust survivors see things, the 1953 agreements effectively legalized the forced labor, slave labor, and the company-run concentration camps characteristic of corporate life under the Nazis, at least to the extent that corporations were immunized from any responsibility to make good the crimes committed against their former prisoners. It is worth noting that negotiator Hermann Abs's own Deutsche Bank was and is among the largest single shareholders of many of the companies that most directly benefitted from the 1953 agreement.

In the years following that agreement, surviving forced laborers and Jewish slave laborers[25] brought several path-breaking lawsuits to German courts seeking redress. All have been dismissed.[26] Much the same has been true of lawsuits in other countries.

The Jewish Restitution Successor Organization (JRSO), and the Conference on Jewish Material Claims Against Germany (a coalition of major Jewish organizations active in restitution issues) have waged a protracted legal and political struggle on behalf of surviving Jewish slave laborers. They enjoyed some success, particularly considering the tenor of the times.[27] Long before the explosive political

---

[23] Contrary to popular belief, there was no formal peace treaty for more than fifty years between Germany and the countries on which it waged war, notwithstanding the unconditional surrender of German armed forces in 1945 and the collapse of Hitler's government. Germany's government and courts have long contended that no legal peace treaty meant there were no treaty obligations. Some experts argue that even the "Two-plus-Four" agreement of 1990 that reunited East and West Germany and ended the nominal Allied military occupation of Berlin should not be regarded as a peace treaty, technically speaking. The present German government sometimes refers to the "Two-plus-Four" agreement as the peace treaty ending World War II, yet in other circumstances avoids directly saying so.

[24] Niethammer, 8.

[25] The tiny fees paid by companies for *slave labor* by Jews and many Soviet POWs went into the coffers of the SS, not to the slaves. German corporations also exploited millions of non-Jewish *forced laborers*, but on terms somewhat different than those faced by the slaves. Early in the war, for example, foreign "guest workers" laboring in Germany from France, Belgium, Italy, and a handful of other countries were actually paid small amounts for their work. By late 1943, however, the large majority of those workers had been imprisoned, in effect, by the companies that "employed" them. Most were forbidden to return home, and the salaries said to be sent home to their families often ended up in German government hands. "Employees" caught attempting to escape corporate concentration camps faced death through labor at the hands of the SS.

[26] Benjamin Ferencz, "West Germany: Court Bars Claims of Forced Laborers," *American Journal of Comparative Law* 1967 15, no.3, 561–66.

[27] For a first-person account of more than a dozen such negotiations, see Benjamin Ferencz, *Less Than Slaves* (Cambridge, Mass.: Harvard University Press, 1979). The Jewish Restitution

(Footnote continued on next page)

and economic controversies of the late 1990s over Nazi slave labor, lawyers for these organizations extracted small "humanitarian" payments to former slave laborers from a half dozen or so major German companies that wished to avoid negative publicity.

One revealing aspect of these small victories has reappeared in recent negotiations between German corporations and surviving prisoners. Each of the companies specifically rejected any legal responsibility for forced labor and slave labor. Meanwhile, every "humanitarian" payment to an aging or infirm survivor came with a ream of legal documents whereby the laborer was forced to abandon all rights to make a legal claim against the company.

READING OMGUS RECORDS TODAY

The OMGUS Finance Division studies were never intended to be the type of bland, uncontroversial historical accounts that some historians find comfortable.

Nevertheless, the OMGUS investigations have proven to be quite strong from a strictly academic point of view. No scholarship on Nazi-era banking produced in any language for almost forty years matched the OMGUS work in its scope, overall accuracy, or depth of documentary evidence. It is true that war crimes trial records, academic research, and various biographies have filled in details and added nuance to the account that the first investigators outlined only in broad strokes. Nevertheless, as recently as the late 1990s, several of the most prominent academics of the Gesellschaft fuer Unternehmensgeschichte e.V. (GUG), or the Society for [German] Business History, have been forced to rewrite their semiofficial histories of the Deutsche Bank to take into account evidence that OMGUS investigators and Nuremburg prosecutors had brought to light more than fifty years earlier.[28] It has been a bitter pill for the GUG to swallow, but the fact remains that few historical studies of business in Nazi Germany have stood the test of time quite as well as the partisan OMGUS investigations. That includes a substantial fraction of the academic output of their own professional club.

Recent scholarship suggests that the scope, method, and subtlety of German bank looting was even greater than that which the OMGUS Finance Division discovered in its initial investigation. A preliminary report on the subject prepared in 1999 by Michael Hepp of the *Stiftung fuer Sozialgeschichte* (Institute for Social History)

(Footnote continued from previous page)

Successor Organization (JRSO) was founded in 1947. It later joined the Conference on Jewish Material Claims Against Germany, a coalition of major Jewish organizations active in managing restitution matters. JRSO also helped establish the United Restitution Organization to provide legal aid to individuals and families seeking restitution. The legal teams challenging the German government and corporations from 1947 through 1990 varied from case to case. For details on these organizations, see Ibid., p. xvi–xvii.

[28] The Deutsche Bank's sponsorship of massively detailed in-house histories is discussed below. See Lothar Gall, Gerald Feldman, Harold James, Carl-Ludwig Holtfrerich, and Hans Bueschgen, *The Deutsche Bank, 1870–1995* (London: Weidenfeld and Nicolson, 1995).

of Bremen, State Department historian William Slany's studies for the Eizenstat commission, and the Swiss Bergier Commission report concerning looted gold have each involved a major investigation in its own right.[29]

Hepp's modern summary of the evidence concludes that the Deutsche Bank and Dresdner Bank extracted at least the equivalent of some DM 1.9 billion (1999 currency values) from indisputably predatory, anti-Semitic and in many instances transparently criminal activities that had been "legalized" during the Nazi regime. His estimates of the amount of funds looted, currency exchange rates, mechanisms for extortion, and similar technical data are in each instance as conservative or more conservative than that which the U.S. government or the banks themselves have since admitted was actually the case.

Hepp's DM 1.9 billion total, moreover, does not include the profits to be reaped from fifty-five years of interest, which—assuming a very modest three percent interest rate compounded but once per year—comes to DM 9.87 billion (or about $4.7 billion) in criminal gains, when interest is included, for these two banks.[30]

Thus, conservatively estimated, Deutsche Bank and Dresdner Bank *alone* derived more from Nazi-era profiteering as the total amount all German corporations have presented (and the U.S. government accepted) as their final offer to settle all outstanding damage claims stemming from *any* Nazi-era crime by *every* German corporation, partnership, or individual.

Hepp reports that most of the funds looted by the Deutsche Bank and the Dresdner Bank were derived from profits on Aryanization of Jewish property

---

[29] Michael Hepp, *Preliminary Report Related to Damages Attributable to 1933–1945 Activities of Deutsche Bank and Dresdner Bank Only,* Stiftung fuer Sozialgeschichte Bremen, 1999. Marked "confidential," Hepp's study was compiled on behalf of plaintiffs in the *Watman et al. V. Deutsche Bank et al.* lawsuit 98 Civ. 3938 (SWK).

William Slany, *U.S. and Allied Efforts to Recover and Restore Gold or Other Assets Stolen or Hidden by Germany during World War II — Preliminary Report,* U.S. Department of State, May 1997. To download this text, access http://www.state.gov/ www/regions/eur/rpt_9705_ng_links.html. For more comprehensive access to report updates, errata, press statements and related material, see http://www.state.gov/www/regions/eur/holo-causthp.html.

The Independent Commission of Experts ("Bergier Commission"), *Gold Transactions in the Second World War: Statistical Review with Commentary,* December 4, 1997 is available at http://www. swissembassy.org.uk/news/news5.htm.

For a summary of that study presented from the point of view of the U.S. Department of State, see Stuart Eizenstat press briefing, June 28, 1998: http://www.state.gov/www/policy_remarks/ 1998/980602_eizenstat_nazigld.html.

The key archival reference to U.S.-held records derived from these and related studies is Greg Bradsher's massive compilation, *Holocaust-Era Assets: A Finding Aid to Records at the National Archives in College Park, Maryland* (Washington, D.C.: National Archives and Records Administration, 1999).

[30] Calculated by the author from figures compiled in Hepp, Preliminary Report, p. 9. The common wisdom in the United States is that the ultimate defeat of Hitler's government, the terrible human and material losses of the war, and the substantial reparations that West Germany paid to some victims led to a net loss for German finance and industry, despite its accumulation of wealth during the Nazi years. But recent scholarship raises significant questions about that preconception. For a sophisticated case study of Nazism's long-term advantages for the owners of Germany's multibillion dollar auto industry, for example, see Simon Reich, *The Fruits of Fascism: Postwar Prosperity in Historical Perspective* (Ithaca, N.Y.: Cornell University Press, 1990).

(approximately DM 850 million at current exchange rates, not including interest) and "capital blending" (DM 749 million). Capital blending is a technique through which assets that have been confiscated from Jews or purchased at fire-sale prices in Nazi-occupied territories are blended with existing bank investments to leverage the institution's ability to control target companies or to invest in businesses most likely to be economically or politically profitable under the new regime. In most cases, Nazi-era capital blending amounted to giant, never-to-be-repaid "loans" or outright extortion used to open up new business opportunities in territories under German control. Hepp's totals, moreover, do not include profits from Aryanizations in Poland, Greece, Yugoslavia (the occupied Balkans), and Romania, where he concludes reliable estimates remain unavailable.[31]

Similarly, the Preliminary Report does not include indirect profits or other benefits derived from exploitation of slave labor or forced labor at manufacturing and construction companies owned by or closely allied with these two banks. It does calculate the pfennigs-on-the-mark service charge collected for transferring fees owed to forced laborers, which was something like a check processing charge. The Nazi-era service charges can be calculated with considerable reliability based on captured bank records. These alone come to the equivalent of over DM 45 million in modern currency.

Calculating the profitability of slave labor and forced labor at major German companies remains controversial. Business economists have discovered, not surprisingly, that workers who toil at gunpoint tend to be less efficient than those who choose their employment. This revelation has led to—this is not a joke—bitter academic squabbling over the accounting standards best used by modern corporations to calculate the value of various forms of involuntary servitude.[32] Scholars do agree, however, that some ten million slave laborers and forced laborers toiled for the Reich during the war, and that millions lost their lives as a result.[33]

OMGUS investigators established more than fifty years ago that the Deutsche Bank and Dresdner Bank underwrote slave labor or forced labor business projects for familiar German corporations such as Siemens, IG Farben, Volkswagen, BMW, Mercedes, Krupp, Flick Steel, and the Philip Holzmann international construction combine. The banks also financed the Hermann-Goering-Werke armament empire and shared ownership of Kontinental Oel (Konti), which was a particularly murderous

---

[31] Many experts would agree that the Nazi Aryanization and theft of Polish property alone was equal to or greater that taken from the rest of Europe combined. The percentage of that loot that ended up in Deutsche Bank or Dresdner Bank coffers remains unclear, however. See United Nations War Crimes Commisssion, *Poland v. Dr. Paersch, Reichsbank Berlin, et. al.,* case No.7347 (Polish case No.1366) (February 1948) UNWCC Archives, New York, N.Y.; or as an attachment to Springer to Secretary of State, February 27, 1948, 740.00116EW2-2748, box 3628, RG 59, National Archives, College Park, Md.

[32] Among the more insightful recent overviews on the subject are Ulrich Herbert, "Zwangsarbeiter im Dritten Reich—ein Ueberblick" in Barig, Seethaff, and Weyde, ed., *Entschaedigung fuer NS-Zwangsarbeit: Rechtliche, historische und politische Aspekte* (Baden-Baden: Nomos Verlag, 1998); and Mark Spoerer, "Profitierten Untrenehmen von der KZ-Arbeit?" *Historische Zeitschrift*, February 1999, 61–95.

[33] Edward Homze, *Foreign Labor in Nazi Germany* (Princeton, NJ: Princeton University Press, 1967), 152–53; or dicussion in Simpson, *Beast*, 83–90, 335–38.

joint venture established by private-sector German banks and chemical companies. Konti relied on slave laborers supplied by the SS—most of whom died as laborers or were eventually murdered by the SS—to do the punishing labor necessary to exploit petroleum assets captured in Eastern Europe.[34]

LEGAL VERSUS MORAL OBLIGATIONS

Determining who should pay for these abuses and establishing an appropriate level and form of restitution remains much more than a historical exercise. Despite the heavily publicized deal finalized by U.S. negotiators during the summer of 2000, sharp disputes remain over who shall make restitution to the survivors of corporate-run Nazi concentration camps, as well as over how to account for the billions of dollars worth of gold, precious metals, stocks, bonds, real estate and private businesses seized by the Nazis and by Germany's private sector during the Nazi years.

Dozens of Germany's most prominent companies have since 1999 tentatively agreed to make what they characterize as a "humanitarian" contribution totaling about DM 5 billion to survivors of Nazi concentration camps operated by German corporations during World War II. The German government has offered a matching DM 4.5 billion. The same companies also made a joint declaration acknowledging the "moral responsibility of German firms in the area of the use of slave labor, Aryanization and other injustices from the time of the Nazi regime."[35]

The corporate acknowledgment of an undefined moral responsibility for Nazi crimes has the look and feel of a meaningful gesture, and no doubt for some German executives that is the case. The more closely one examines the rhetoric surrounding the corporations' gesture, however, the less convincing it becomes. The highly publicized acceptance of "moral" responsibility for Nazi crimes by major corporations announced by Minister Otto Graf Lambsdorff, for example, carried with it the tacit disavowal of any legal responsibility for the same crimes. Lambsdorff succeeded in sidestepping that issue in his statement to the press; nevertheless, corporate exploitation of purported morality as a device to avoid legal liability for a company's actions

---

[34] For details on the banks' interlocking supervisory boards, loans, securities investments, and similar aspects of their relationships with Siemens, BMW, Kontinental Oel. and other companies mentioned here, see the OMGUS reports reproduced in this volume. To cross-reference that list with data on corporate centers for slave labor and forced labor, see Martin Weinmann, ed., *Das nationalsozialistische Lagersystem* (Frankfurt: Zweitenausendeins), 1990 and International Red Cross, International Tracing Service (Internationaler Suchdienst), *Verzeichnis der Haftstaetten unter der Reichsfuehrer-SS, 1933–1945,* (Arolsen: International Red Cross, 1979). An initial list of corporations reported by survivors to have exploited slave labor has been compiled in Simpson, *Beast,* 289–310. The law firm Cohen, Milstein, Hausfeld & Toll provided details and documentation of specific crimes committed by corporations in addition to operating slave labor camps per se (such as "medical" experiments, forced abortions, infanticide, and forced sterilizations); see http://www.cmht.com/slave_labor/otherwrongs.htm (downloaded August 3, 1999). The law firm represented plaintiffs in actions against more than a dozen German companies.

[35] "Lambsdorff: 'Moral und Geschaeft dicht beineinander,'" *Spiegel* Online (http://www.spiegel.de), October 8, 1999; "Lambsdorff: Entschaedigung fuer Zwangsarbeiter geringer als gefordert," *Deutsche Presse Agentur,* October 2, 1999.

had already emerged as the core value of the German government's and private sector's negotiating position concerning slave labor matters at the time of Lambsdorff's announcement, and it remains so to this day.[36]

U.S. President Bill Clinton personally praised what appeared to be a completed agreement in December 1999, and U.S. Secretary of State Madeleine Albright remarked at ceremonies in Berlin, "This agreement will take U.S.-German relations to new heights in the new millennium."[37] That deal soon unraveled due to new demands from the German side for a binding commitment from the U.S. government to quash any state-level challenges to German corporations stemming from criminal acts during the Nazi years.

The U.S. representative to the negotiations delivered. In July 2000, then Assistant Secretary of State Stuart Eizenstat announced an extraordinary pledge from the U.S. Department of State that henceforth it would intervene in U.S. courts to suppress any legal action taken against any German corporation by Holocaust survivors who remained independent and stubborn enough to reject the pending settlement. Given U.S. legal precedent and a recent Supreme Court decision that strengthened executive branch authority in such matters, the State Department's intervention would almost certainly result in any survivor's case being summarily dismissed.

Eizenstat (speaking for the U.S. government), the German companies, and a battalion of attorneys, then announced a new "final" agreement in July 2000. Few funds have actually been distributed at this writing, however, and it remains an open question whether several of the German companies who have promised contributions will actually pay into the promised fund.

Even the July 2000 agreement may not be enough for today's corporations. The companies now contend that even though survivors are shut out of U.S. courts, Holocaust survivors might succeed in convincing state-level regulators or legislators in important markets—New York or California, for example—to publicly sanction or through some other means bring pressure to bear on German corporations. Their negotiators now argue that the U.S. federal government must bring elected state-level officials and representatives to heel using the terms of the World Trade Organization agreements, GATT, or similar trade treaties to do so.

Similarly, a new lawsuit filed in 2001 against U.S. computer giant IBM for alleged collaboration with the Nazis has renewed threats from the German government and corporations to refuse to make good on their "humanitarian" commitments. "The whole compensation program is now at risk," said German negotiator Wolfgang Gibowski during February, "The German firms involved will not make payments unless they are assured legal peace preventing further claims being made against them. The IBM lawsuit shows this is patently not the case."[38] Facing heavy U.S.

---

[36] The use of public claims of morality to avoid legal liability was the central theme of Neithammer's outline of negotiating tactics for German Chancellor Schroeder some ten months before Lambsdorff's statement, for example.

[37] Marilyn Henry, "Report on Pending Reparation and Restitution Actions," June 2000, 27. My thanks to Ms. Henry for sharing this manuscript with me and permitting me to quote from it.

[38] Tony Paterson and David Wastell, "IBM Sued as 100 US Firms Are Accused of Nazi links," *Telegraph* (London), February 18, 2001.

government pressure, the plaintiffs with claims against IBM dropped their case within a month.

Assuming for the moment that this settlement is eventually carried through, the principal beneficiaries are almost certain to be German corporations, who are guaranteed a much smoother entry into global markets; attorneys who engineered the settlement, whose fees are already measured in the tens of millions of dollars; and, not least, Mr. Eizenstat himself, who appears to have emerged as a publicly respected (yet often privately despised) hero for both the corporate leadership of Germany and a large number of Jewish leaders in the United States—a remarkable achievement, really, considering what is at stake.[39]

There is plenty of fine print in the pending agreement, and it remains to be seen whether these funds will actually be distributed, and if so on what basis. The promised sum averages out to about U.S. $4,000 per labor camp survivor who has managed to remain alive until today. The families of slave laborers who have died in the intervening fifty-plus years receive nothing. The share paid to groups of survivors depends on their ethnic background, the amount of time served in the camps, and similar factors.[40]

In any case, even the most generous version of the promised "humanitarian" gesture is roughly comparable to the costs many elderly patients incur during a two day stay in an American hospital.

A growing number of survivors have stated that the conditions attached to these funds demonstrate the fundamentally corrupt character of the pending settlement. As noted, the corporations insist that they have no legal responsibility to the former slaves, and that these monies instead should be viewed as "humanitarian" or charitable contributions. The survivors, meanwhile, must sign agreements abandoning any legal claims against the corporations that once enslaved them. This remarkable bit of double-think has the perpetrators disavowing legal liability while at the same time stripping victims of the rights to redress in the courts and judicial review that every other citizen enjoys.

The proposed settlement is widely referred to as the "slave labor agreement." Importantly, however—and almost entirely unreported by the American news media—the terms of the agreement sets out to terminate every dispute over law, property, human-rights abuses, destruction of synagogues and cemeteries, slavery, murder, and any other grievance of any sort stemming from the Nazi era that remains at issue between survivors, on the one hand, and German companies or the German state, on the other. Further, the plan sets out to extinguish the claims of all

---

[39] Mr. Eizenstat is also an attorney, so to avoid confusion it is important to note that he will not receive multimillion dollar fees from this particular settlement. Eizenstat's benefit is his enhanced reputation as a "fixer" for complex international financial negotiations, and that is a longer-term and in some respects considerably more valuable asset.

[40] The July 2000 version of the 'Final Settlement' asserts that slave labor survivors may receive the equivalent of $7000, while surviving forced laborers are to receive about $2400. See CNN, "Germany Signs Agreement to compensate Nazi slave laborers," http://www.cnn.com/2000/world/europe/07/17/holocaust.germany.03/index.html; or Roger Cohen, "German Industry Clears Way to Pay Nazi Slave Workers," *New York Times*, May 23, 2001.

afflicted persons and institutions of any sort at a single blow. Whether they know it or not, Jews, Romanis and Sinti (Gypsies), Slavs, Polish Catholics, Russian or American POWs, Jehovah's Witnesses, homosexuals, Orthodox Christian churches, Romanian bankers—everyone—will have but one opportunity to secure the justice that has been deferred since 1945.

Communists, a principal target of Nazi persecution who in the Nazi mind were indistinguishable from Jews, are not accorded the dignity of even being discussed as potential plaintiffs in the negotiations concerning the pending agreement. But the language of the deal is such that their grievances will be extinguished as well.

Under U.S. law, the survivors themselves need not, and in most cases will not, be consulted at all concerning whether they agree to these arrangements before the final deal is struck. Here is how the German chancellor's senior adviser on Holocaust settlements, Lutz Niethammer, summarized the strategy in a confidential report to Chancellor Gerhard Schroeder: Examination of damage claims and any transfer of funds to individuals should be "expedited," Niethammer wrote, by "aggregating the claims, through (1) the Jewish Claims Conference, (2) through the respective institutions, funds and foundations in Kiev, Minsk, Moscow, Prague, Warsaw (including those [persons] who live in the Baltic states and other GUS states), and (3) for non-Jewish former forced workers through appropriate organizations, assuming they are agreeable to handle this task."[41]

Negotiations over the terms of the pending deal have been carried out by a crazy quilt of representatives: from Germany, Poland, the Czech Republic, and other countries; from the Jewish Claims Conference; from charitable organizations (whose intentions are no doubt honorable, yet which are responsible only to their own board of directors and make no pretense of democratic consultation with their clients); and from attorneys for German companies or for plaintiffs who have brought lawsuits in U.S. courts. The U.S. government has presented itself as a nonpartisan mediator among these players. Everyone else has been denied participation, and individual plaintiffs are not even informed, much less consulted, about the tradeoffs and compromises made in their names.[42]

The pending plan also has noteworthy tax advantages for the companies. "Humanitarian" contributions of this sort are tax-deductible under enough countries' laws that any multinational corporation with a competent accounting department can readily make good use of these credits when toting up the year's profits.

Then think that through: The national taxes that are *not* paid by, say, BMW, Volkswagen, German construction companies, or other former concentration camp

---

[41] Niethammer, 16. The parenthesis and brackets in the quoted statement are those that appear in the English translation circulated among negotiators. "GUS" in this context is the German-language acronym for the Confederation of Independent States created in the wake of the collapse of the USSR.

[42] Romani and Sinti leaders have logged formal protests about such treatment. They contend that U.S. officials did not even read, much less respond to, legal correspondence from leaders and attorneys representing major Romani organizations. See International Romani Union and Roma National Congress, "Letter of Protest and Complaint of the IRU and RNC on the Holocaust U.S. Court Decision," December 19, 2000, *RomNews,* http://www.RomNews.com (Hamburg, Germany). (Romani and Sinti peoples are often termed "Gypsies," which is an ethnic slur.)

operators must sooner or later be paid by someone else, of course. As a practical matter, that most likely means that the middle classes and ordinary people will almost certainly be left to pick up most of the tab for absolving the corporations of responsibility for forced labor and slave labor. Considering the interlocking, multinational character of these companies and the specifics of U.S. tax law, it is not unreasonable to suspect that many Americans, including American Jews, may end up indirectly underwriting at least part of German companies' campaign to gain "legal peace" from Holocaust claims during the twenty-first century.

In almost any context other than the Holocaust, this merry chain of evasion might almost seem like comic opera, at least among those who take the trouble to trace out how the pending scheme could work. But the context is the Holocaust, and there is nothing funny whatever about cheating elderly men and women who live each day with concentration camp numbers tattooed on their arms.

Lest anyone think too hard about such matters, there is a unique clause calling for "cultural engineering" of public attitudes, as Niethammer put it,[43] which is attached to the pending settlement. The companies state they will agree to the token "humanitarian" restitution only when they can themselves draw on their payment to survivors to establish an additional DM 700 million public relations-oriented foundation that in the final analysis will be run by the German government and companies. This institution is presently named the "Foundation [for] Responsibility, Remembrance and the Future,"[44] and it appears it will also become tax deductible. Journalist Marilyn Henry, who has followed the negotiations closely for the *Jerusalem Post*, calls this unusual foundation the *sine qua non* for German cooperation in any settlement.[45] That is to say, without this seemingly innocuous goodwill project, nothing else will move forward.

The Foundation's supporters contend it is a demonstration of sincerity and corporate responsibility. Niethammer's report outlines a broad range of programs for the institution, ranging from care of memorial sites and museums to funded professorships, payments to scholars for Holocaust-related research projects, and "scholarships for . . . journalists, cultural workers, technicians, etc." engaged in "cross-boundary cooperation," so long as the project includes a pre-approved German partner.[46]

The Foundation for Responsibility, Remembrance and the Future seems to carry the same strange psychological markings as the rest of the "humanitarian" settlement program. In the latter situation, German corporations insist on formally stripping survivors of legal rights in a situation where the companies contend they have no legal liability in the first place.

Meanwhile, at their required academic foundation, "cultural engineering" projects that pay specialists to contextualize and research the Holocaust for the general public emerge as the German companies' prerequisite to agree to any sort of settlement at all. Presumably, the corporations that operated concentration camps would have

---

[43] Niethammer, 4.
[44] Henry, correspondence with the author, February 26, 2001.
[45] Ibid.
[46] Niethammer, 17–19.

little to gain from stirring up these ashes. Why, then, is this foundation so central to their demands?

The academic foundation presents a classic study of tactics usually associated with political warfare or, to put it more politely, manufacturing public consent for a particular version of history and society.[47] The emerging German foundation might be better understood as a particularly sophisticated, twenty-first century counterpart to the Turkish government's well known campaign to endow professorial chairs for paper-trained, pet historians who in one way or another deny the Armenian genocide and attempt to re-write the history of the mass deportations and killings of a million or more Armenians during World War I.[48]

What distinguishes the German from the Turkish public relations campaigns is that the objective of the German foundation is *not* Holocaust or genocide denial in the crude sense—far from it. It might be better described as Holocaust spin doctoring, or astutely engineered mass communication calculated to divorce the well known brand-names of German corporations from any substantive responsibility for Nazi crimes.

The academics who enjoy project funding from the proposed German foundation will in all likelihood derive more money for their modest services than, say, the large majority of families of the Russian, Ukrainian and Polish forced laborers who toiled and died in all of Nazi Germany's corporate concentration camps taken together, for almost without exception those families received little or nothing from corporate Germany for their loss. The academics will also quite likely collect more for the preparation of a short manuscript in a comfortable library than the average settlement payment made to Jewish slaves who survived Auschwitz, Gross Rosen, or other camps, assuming that the promised "humanitarian" payments are made at all.

Given these realities, it will be enlightening to observe who agrees to serve on the board of an academic foundation of this sort, and who it is that lines up for grants.

It is worth noting that the U.S. Department of State some time ago opened discussions with the Japanese government to engineer much the same sort of settlement in that government's dispute with survivors of World War II rape camps organized by the Japanese military (euphemistically termed "Comfort Women" by the

---

[47] Paul A. Smith, Jr., *On Political War* (Washington DC: National Defense University Press, 1989). For a historical overview of German corporate public relations programs concerning Nazism, see Jonathan Wiesen, "Overcoming Nazism: Big Business, Public Relations and the Politics of Memory," *Central European History* (1996) 206.

[48] See, in relation to chairs at Princeton and Harvard, John Yenna, "Turkish Largess Raises Questions," *Boston Globe*, November 25, 1995; at Princeton, Gwen Florio, "Princeton's use of funding from Turkey draws criticism," *Philadelphia Inquirer*, November 30, 1995; at Harvard, Princeton, Georgetown University, and University of Chicago, Associated Press, "Critics say Turkey is using money to 'change' history," *Newark Star-Ledger*, November 26, 1995; at Princeton, Nathaniel Herzberg, "Bernard Lewis condamné pour avoir nié la réalité de génocide arménien: Selon le tribunal, l'historien a commis une 'faute'," *Le Monde*, June 23, 1995; at UCLA, Georgetown University, University of Chicago, Harvard, Indiana University, and Portland State University, Kenneth R. Weiss, "Strings on Foreign Aid Trouble Colleges," *Los Angeles Times*, November 24, 1997; and at UC-Berkeley, Lewis Gray, "Controversy Over Grant Proposal Seeking Turkish Funds," *Daily Californian*, February 19, 1998.

Japanese), Allied POWs, and the victims of horrific medical experiments used to develop Japanese biological weapons. The American proposals to the Japanese government are nearly identical with those of the pending German settlement. In both cases, they include the perpetrators' rejection of legal responsibility for war crimes and crimes against humanity, token payments for selected victims, U.S. State Department assistance in suppressing legal challenges, and creation of a foundation to underwrite studies and publications by vetted intellectuals.[49]

In both the German and the Japanese cases, the explicit goal of U.S. policy is to close off the possibility of successful lawsuits against corporations or other former Axis entities responsible for war crimes and crimes against humanity during World War II. Though rarely stated directly, that policy is driven at least in part by globalization and "New World Order" trade policies, on the one hand, and a quite realistic concern that if German and Japanese corporations can be successfully sued for gross violations of human rights, U.S. multinational corporations are likely to be the next ones in the dock. There is no shortage of potential plaintiffs with well-founded claims.

"CONTEXTUALIZING" THE HOLOCAUST

It is obvious why many powerful institutions wish to bury their unresolved liabilities from World War II once and for all, and would prefer that the records of the OMGUS investigations drop from sight along with them. The OMGUS financial investigations demonstrate that good documentation and a solid knowledge of facts are particularly powerful tools for exposing and disarming the spin campaigns, corporate image advertising, studies by complacent scholars, and similar public relations ploys that virtually every powerful institution today utilizes to present itself to the public.

The core of the present debate among historians and Holocaust scholars is over who shall define the context within which historical facts concerning the corporate role in the Holocaust shall be presented. For example, the organized "contextualization" of the Holocaust, and especially of the role of major German companies in that crime, is the central thread of the Niethammer report to German Chancellor Schoeder, discussed earlier.

Some historians are quite frank about what is at stake. The companies want their actions to be "contextualized" or "historicize[d]," writes Gerald Feldman, who is both a scholar of German business history and a leading contract academic for German financial giants such as Allianz Insurance and the Deutsche Bank.[50] (Feldman refers to the Deutsche Bank as a "shining example" of a post-Holocaust,

---

[49] U.S. Department of State, from U.S. Mission Geneva to Secretary of State, Washington D.C., "Japan, Korea and the 'Comfort Woman' Issue at the U.N. Human Rights Commission," Doc. number 96Geneva02203 (Confidential), obtained via Freedom of Information Act request 9603084.

[50] For Feldman's own detailed presentation of his role in these controversies, see Gerald D. Feldman, "The Business History of the 'Third Reich' and the Responsibilities of the Historians: Gold, Insurance, 'Aryanization,' and Forced Labor," *Occasional Paper* (January 1999). Quotations here are from *Occasional Paper*, 12, 13. Feldman's specialty is generally recognized to be the German inflation crisis of the early 1920s, not the Holocaust.

modern corporation.) German corporate problems "are not simply legal, but also political and moral," he continues. German companies fear American regulatory agencies, loss of customers, bad publicity, and deteriorating employee morale.

> They also fear the media, which often reports on new findings in archives and elsewhere in ways that are very damaging. They thus turn to historians for a number of reasons. . . . [Companies are] often ill equipped to defend themselves against charges in the courts and the media, especially the latter. They need to recover their history, and they need to do so in a hurry. . . . They have a choice between having information appear in the media as a series of hammer blows on their heads or having the entire story, however unpleasant, come out in a sober and *contextualized manner.* They need professional help and this can only come from historians who understand something about economics and business."[51] [my italics]

More than cash is at stake: Reputation, tradition, and cultural cohesion are crucial to mobilizing popular acceptance of the systemwide functions (courts, taxation, police, and bread-and-circus holiday seasons, for example) upon which the stability of commodity-based, consumer societies depend. Spin-doctoring the Holocaust facilitates social and moral re-integration of particular German multinational corporations, just as Japan's government and multinationals are today attempting to spin-doctor evidence of their role in organizing mass rape camps and other atrocities in the Pacific theater. More fundamentally, critics contend, what is actually at stake is protecting the claim to legitimacy of key corporate and national power centers integral to the corporate "new world order" that is envisioned in some circles for the twenty-first century.

Thus, some historians have "suddenly found their services in great demand," echoes Jonathan Steinberg, Holocaust historian funded by the Deutsche Bank for a study of the bank's gold trading. Many companies, "having denied for years that they had records or archives from the Second World War, miraculously discovered they had been there all the time. The largest and most powerful multi-national businesses had to recognize how vulnerable they or their subsidiaries were to waves of emotion and agile lawyers in their biggest market, the United States of America. Such considerations generated an urgent demand for historians, to explore the records and reconstruct the troubled past of governments and companies. They had to answer complex questions in the 'sound-bites' available to modern journalism."[52]

THE DEUTSCHE BANK AND ITS HISTORIANS

The Deutsche Bank probably has had more experience with contextualization or spin doctoring the Holocaust than any other major German corporation. Its experience illustrates broader and deeper trends.

---

[51] Feldman, *Occasional Paper,* 12.
[52] Steinberg, *The Deutsche Bank and Its Gold Transactions,* 10.

During the last two decades the Deutsche Bank has undertaken a "major expansion of its foreign operations," as a standard commercial review of the bank's activities has put it, including large-scale "operating and trading in Japanese, British and American securities." By opening new branches and taking over existing commercial banks, merchant banks, and stockbrokers, the Deutsche Bank began to play a far more important role in the British and American capital markets than ever before. Industrial and consumer-goods corporations owned or closely interlocked with the Deutsche Bank—Siemens and Daimler Benz (now Daimler-Chrysler), for example—have invested heavily in winning market share in the United States.[53]

Rewriting the corporate history of the Nazi years has remained a major project since this expansion began. Among the largest—and most troubled—projects in this effort was a massive study written by Lothar Gall, Gerald Feldman, Harold James and two other prominent business historians, and published in German and English in 1995.[54]

Despite the voluminous detail of that text, the study has come to be known primarily for its relative silence concerning central questions about the Nazi years. The bank's trade in concentration camp gold, its underwriting of the construction of synthetic petroleum works at the Auschwitz concentration camp, its role as a central financial coordinating point for the Eastern-Front slave labor giant Kontinental Oel, even most of the story of its investment of hundreds of millions Reichsmarks in Aryanization of Jewish property—all projects central to Deutsche Bank business history even by the most narrow economic definition—received no mention at all or, in the case of some aspects of Aryanization, a brief treatment. Silence reigns despite the fact that historical evidence and leads to evidence concerning these affairs were readily available for researchers willing to confront the record, including the evidence gathered by the OMGUS financial investigations team.

The business historians sponsored by the bank did not lie, exactly; rather they interpreted the evidence and "contextualized" the truth in such a way that they presented what many historians today agree was a misleading picture of what the Deutsche Bank and its principal international agent, Hermann Abs, had actually done during the Third Reich. For example, the 1995 text goes so far as to imply that Abs was something of an underground anti-Nazi resistance leader. The exceedingly slim basis for this claim has three parts. Early in the war, Abs and much of Germany's economic elite recommended a different strategy for conquest than that of orthodox Nazis. Abs favored Germany reentering world markets after grabbing as much as possible through conquest, while orthodox Nazis favored a self-sufficient, National Socialist regime stretching from the Atlantic to the Ural mountains. In the meantime, these two factions found common cause in seizure and exploitation of Europe's wealth.[55] Second, Abs attempted to keep intact under Deutsche Bank administration two or three of the industrial and banking empires of Europe's very richest Jews, such as Czechoslovak Petschek family, rather than dispersing those

[53] Mirabile, *International Directory of Company Histories,* 280.
[54] Lothar Gall, et. al., *The Deutsche Bank,* 1870–1995.
[55] Simpson, *Beast,* 68–73.

assets to rival German economic interests.[56] (Abs meanwhile led Deutsche Bank's effort to systematically dispossess the property of thousands and quite likely tens of thousands of middle class and prosperous Jews in Vienna, Prague, Belgrade, Belgium and France—a campaign that in many cases led in short order to the deportation of entire families to extermination camps. He was also among the corporate supervisors resposible for IG Farben operations at Auschwitz.)[57] Finally, as will be discussed in a moment, during the last disastrous months of the war, Abs turned to concealing Deutsche Bank wartime assets in Swiss banks, rather than fighting to the death for the Fuhrer.[58]

In short, Abs's participation in Nazi crimes—like that of many of his peers in Germany's economic elite—is best understood at least in part as an opportunistic or entrepreneurial effort to secure political and economic influence with the regime while simultaneously preparing for postwar careers. This is not the same as the straightforward brutality and murder characteristic of the Gestapo or the SS, yet in the larger scheme of things it was fully as deadly. The Deutsche Bank historians' willingness to characterize these activities as "resistance" to Nazism is a semantic dodge worthy of George Orwell's *1984*.

The 1995 history of Deutsche Bank organized facts and events in exhaustive detail and prioritized story elements in order to present the authors' version of reality in the form of a historical narrative. But the inexorable corollary to remembering and legitimizing some events is organizing the forgetting or delegitimizing of others. The 1995 project rallied almost a thousand pages of organized memory processing of the bank's history. Even so, some truths about its role in the Holocaust simply would not go away.

For a short time after it was published, the 1995 history fared well. The bulk of the text did not concern the Nazi years, which were in a thematic sense set off in brackets, figuratively speaking, as an aberration quite separate from previous or subsequent bank behavior. Much of the 1995 work featured new or reinterpreted information about the bank's first years or its more recent history. The volume enjoyed general acclaim, at least among the few hundred members of the highly specialized and in-bred community of German business historians. It even won a history prize from a British newspaper.

But unfortunately for Gall and his colleagues, the social and political situation that had given rise to their project was changing even as the book rolled off the printing presses. In the mid-1990s, political campaigns in the United States, news media reports, and especially lawsuits against the Deutsche Bank and other German companies drew attention to their activities during the Nazi years. International scandals over Swiss and German bankers' failure to return Nazi victims' accounts and their trade in concentration camp gold were erupting. Thousands of concentration camp survivors, their families, and surviving forced laborers brought lawsuits against

---

[56] Wilhelm Treue, "Widerstand von Unternehmen und Nationalokonomen" in Juergen Schmadeke, *Der Widerstand gegen den Nationalsozialismus,* Munich: Piper, 1986, 917–37.

[57] OMGUS Deutsche Bank, 122–29, below; and Hans Safrian and Hans Witek, *Und kleiner war dabei: Dokumente des alltaglichen Antisemitismus in Wein 1938.* Wein: Picus Verlag, 1988, 95–157 passim; Simpson, *Beast,* 68–9. Abs's role at Auschwitz is detailed below.

[58] Steinberg, *The Deutsche Bank and Its Gold Transactions,* 59–66.

Deutsche Bank and against companies owned by, or closely interlocked with, Deutsche Bank or the Dresdner Bank.

Against the backdrop of these controversies, the Deutsche Bank was engaged in the expansion noted above. It made a $9.5 billion bid for U.S.-based Bankers Trust in 1998, and announced an estimated $30 billion merger of Deutsche Bank and its former rival Dresdner Bank in late 1999.

To close the Bankers Trust deal, they needed the permission of the New York State Banking Department, which is responsible for licensing and regulating most banking and financial institutions in that state.[59] The department had established a Holocaust Claims Processing Office in June 1997, and had already blocked expansion of certain Swiss banks into the New York market pending a settlement of Holocaust-era financial claims.[60] State Insurance Superintendent Neil Levin let it be known that the Deutsche Bank acquisition of Bankers Trust and similar deals could expect close scrutiny as well. In addition to the questions of simple justice at stake, some critics argued that the rash of lawsuits spreading against the bank and its corporate partners in a half-dozen countries raised reasonable doubts as to whether Deutsche Bank would be able to afford to buy or operate Bankers Trust at all.

By 1997, the flaws of the Deutsche Bank's 1995 effort to "reconstruct" its history, to use Jonathan Steinberg's term, had become so obvious that even the bank's management tacitly conceded that the 1995 opus had failed to present a credible account of the bank's activities under National Socialism. In 1997, Deutsche Bank's in-house historian, Manfred Pohl, hired an Independent Historical Commission (IHC) to write a new and more credible account of Deutsche Bank activities during the Nazi years. Gerald Feldman, Jonathan Steinberg, Harold James, Avraham Barkai, and Lothar Gall made up the core of the team. With the exception of Steinberg and Barkai, it was the same group that had been generously funded to write the 1995 version of Deutsche Bank history. The IHC continues to produce new texts today.

The "new" IHC group, Pohl emphasized in dozens of public statements, would truly enjoy open access to bank records and independence from corporate pressure. The available evidence suggests that Pohl has kept his word. Nevertheless, substantially the same assurances had been made about the same group of men concerning their 1995 effort. If the professed independence had been true when writing the 1995 volume, why were such aggressive public reassurances needed just two years later?

The official explanation for the creation of the IHC was that new evidence, not available in 1995, had recently come to light, and this that had prompted the renewed study.[61] It was true that some new evidence had come to light, particularly a handful of newly released American archives that the first group of sponsored historians had failed to request under the Freedom of Information Act. Meanwhile, lawsuits and national investigations into Swiss, Swedish, Vichy French, and other banks had brought attention to newly discovered records, as well as new attention to documents

---

[59] See *State of New York Banking Department Weekly Bulletin* for December 12, 1998; April 16, 1999; April 23, 1999; May 7, August 24, 1999; and September 10, 1999 for a paper trail of the procedures by which this was effected.

[60] See http://www.claims.state.ny.us/hist.htm for a brief history, policy statements, processing forms, speeches by officials, and similar materials concerning this office.

[61] Steinberg, *The Deutsche Bank and Its Gold Transactions*, 11.

that had in many cases been available all along—many of them in the publicly accessible sections of Deutsche Bank's own archives[62]—that the "old" historians group had presumably combed for clues.

The claims of newly discovered evidence are true, up to a point, but they are also misleading. In reality, about 90 percent of U.S. archives concerning Nazi gold (including many captured German records) had already been declassified when work on the 1995 volume began.[63] More to the point in the present context, substantial evidence of some of the most damning aspects of the Nazi-era activities of the Deutsche Bank existed in the pages of the OMGUS investigations and in the thousands of pages of exhibits that accompanied them. Courts in a half dozen countries had found this already-available evidence sufficiently compelling to permit thousands of plaintiffs to file damage claims against the bank and its associated companies.

The real problem with the 1995 study was not a lack of evidentiary leads. It was, rather, the set of preconceptions among the bank-sponsored historians of that period that led them to dismiss the OMGUS investigations and to interpret the remaining record through a lens that extended every benefit of the doubt to their sponsor, the bank itself. What was at work here was not deceit or gross irresponsibility on the part of the authors of the 1995 study, at least not in the usual sense of those terms. The 1995 work was, rather, a practical example of the powerful yet almost invisible means through which talented academics had been led into a morass by their internalized framework of preconceptions defining the supposed context of business life in Nazi Germany.

Many Holocaust survivors regard the 1995 opus as an apologia for corporate crimes committed during the Third Reich. At the time the book was published, their views were dismissed as naive and ill-informed by the community of professional business historians. It is certainly true that professional historians sponsored by German corporations often can cite the academic literature and archival references with greater fluency than can their critics. But in at least this one instance, it was the "naive" survivors who held a fundamentally more accurate view of the activities and moral character of the Deutsche Bank, Dresdner Bank and their corporate partners than the experienced and talented scholars who had been hired to "reconstruct" company histories.

Whether Pohl himself or the historians he hired understood it or not, from the standpoint of the Deutsche Bank public relations managers, the true tasks of expert commissions such as the IHC come down to two main objectives. The first is to quickly produce a credible account of company actions that puts the best possible face on the situation, even if some of the news is negative. This elementary public relations tactic dates back at least as far as the seminal work of Edward Bernays and Ivy Lee in the first decades of the twentieth century.[64] The second, closely related

---

[62] Manfred Pohl, E-mail to author, August 2, 2000.

[63] Feldman, *Occasional Paper*, 9.

[64] For an unusually frank example of crisis management strategy that has been leaked to the press, see Ketchum Public Relations, *Crisis Management Plan for the Clorox Company* (1991), published as appendix to John Stauber and Sheldon Rampton, *Toxic Sludge is Good for You: Lies, Damn Lies and the Public Relations Industry*, (Monroe, Me.: Common Courage Press, 1995), 209–12. The tactic of employing third-party experts to lend credibility to corporate objectives is examined in depth in Stauber and Rampton, *Trust Us, We're Experts* (New York: Jeremy Tarcher, 2001).

mission is to compile a thorough historical archive for company attorneys, who quite naturally wish to avoid nasty surprises when they go into court on behalf of their client.

Today's disputes over the corporate spin on the Holocaust at times concern specific facts. For example, did the Deutsche Bank finance construction of the IG Farben factory complex at the Auschwitz concentration camp, as critics have often asserted based on the OMGUS investigations and other evidence, or did it not, as the bank's team of historians long argued?[65]

Several IHC scholars publicly insisted that there was nothing to the story. But they ended up with egg on their face in 1999, when company management issued a press statement admitting that the substance of the allegation had been true all along.[66] Deutsche Bank did indeed bankroll IG Farben's construction of a synthetic oil production plant at Auschwitz. It also knew at the time that much of the construction work would be carried by slaves and forced laborers "leased" from the SS. In the end, the project killed thousands of inmates through heavy labor, starvation, disease, freezing working conditions, the dangers inherent in clearing bomb damage left by Allied bombing raids, brutality by guards, and deportation of sick or injured workers to the SS gas chambers down the road. (Indeed, from the SS point of view, the objective of leasing Auschwitz slave laborers to IG Farben was to extract work from them that would lead to their deaths.[67] Whether that fate arrived through brutal labor or in the Auschwitz/Birkenau gas chambers was a tactical question.) Deutsche Bank's acknowledgment that it underwrote slave labor at the IG Farben plant has special importance to Auschwitz survivors, who have at last seen their experiences and knowledge publicly confirmed.

CENSORSHIP AND TRUTH

For the broader public, the dispute over who financed the IG plant at Auschwitz reveals a side of corporate-sponsored historical study that professors generally

[65] World Council of Orthodox Jewish Communities, "Deutsche Bank Sued for Participation in Nazi Campaign to Destroy Jewish and Cultural Property in Europe," *PR Newswire*, October 5, 1999.

[66] John Marks, "Loans for Auschwitz: Deutsche Bank Says It Financed the Camp," *U.S. News and World Report*, February 15, 1999.

[67] Hermann Abs's knowledge of, responsibility for, IG Farben war crimes at Auschwitz is demonstrated in Nuremberg trial records NI-6099 and NI-600. These are extracts of the minutes of the companies Aufschitsrat meetings of July 11, 1941, and May 30, 1942, respectively, which discuss the use of Russian POWs and other forced labor at Farben's Auschwitz plant. Abs ws a member of the Farben supervisory board when it unanimously ordered company managers to "make all efforts" to obtain foreign workers and POWs for exploitation at Auschwitz. Farben's weekly reports to its Vorstand and Aufsichsrat committees meanwhile documented that this labor was killing thousands of Farben's prisoners. See the war crime trial record *U.S. v. Krauch, et al,* (the Farben case) at: Germany/Territory Under Allied Occupation, 1945–1955, U.S. zone, Military Tribunals, *Trials of War Criminals Before the Nuremberg Military Tribunals Under Control Council Law No. 10,* Washington DC: USGPO (1952), Vol. VII and VIII with cited documents at vol. VIII, 391 and 434. Quotation is at 391.

prefer to deny: Many experts internalize the values and preconceptions of the institutions they favor to the point that they become nearly blind to evidence that is inconsistent with those values. Judging from their writings and speeches, the censorship of the Deutsche Bank-sponsored historians, in 1995 as today, comes from within the men themselves, not from ham-handed pressure by the institution that supports them. The bank's money does play a role, of course, even if only to ensure their historians international visibility, travel and expense account comforts. But if money really was all there was in it for the members of the commission, they would have more likely pursued careers as bankers themselves, rather than as historians of banking.

Academic censorship in this instance is *self*-censorship. When internalizing values of the institutions they describe, the Deutsche Bank historians turn to ideology to defend their presentations and to attack critics. For example, Princeton's Harold James attributes the failure of many mainstream business histories even to address the question of forced labor to his old nemesis, the New Left of the 1960s and 1970s. He contends they view Hitler as little more than a tool of major corporations.[68] (James is forced to cite propaganda pamphlets from 1937 and 1939 to support this thesis.) James' partner on the IHC, Gerald Feldman of the University of California, makes much the same argument.[69] Thus, two scholars of German business history appear to justify to themselves their own failure to aggressively investigate German business's role in the Holocaust by pointing to purported ideological errors in the work of others—however imperfect that work may have been—who actually took up the task.

CONTEXTUALIZING THE HOLOCAUST

Here is a more subtle example of how this phenomenon operates. Among the first publications of the IHC at Deutsche Bank has been a study by Jonathan Steinberg of the bank's Nazi era dealings in gold, including concentration camp gold. The study is based largely on records of the Reichsbank, DEGUSSA (the German gold and silver combine of concentration camp gold infamy), and a previously unknown cache of fragmentary ledgers from the Istanbul branch of Deutsche Bank, each of which Steinberg has carefully dissected.[70]

The text provides more detail than was available to OMGUS investigators. Yet with one important exception, substantially all of the important points that Steinberg elaborates first appeared in the OMGUS investigation report fifty years earlier. For example, the OMGUS investigation identified the Istanbul branch of the bank as a key route for smuggling Nazi gold out of Europe; pinpointed Hermann Abs' senior assistant Alfred Kurzmeyer as the bag man for the transfer of assets—including hundreds of kilos of Nazi gold of highly questionable origin—into Swiss banks accounts;

---

[68] James, *The Deutsche Bank and the Nazi Economic War Against the Jews*, 2–3.
[69] Feldman, *Occasional Paper*, 6–8.
[70] Steinberg, *The Deutsche Bank and Its Gold Transactions*, 83–173.

documented that Abs served as the central figure in every aspect of Deutsche Bank's international strategy, from the benign to the horrific; proved that Deutsche Bank profited at the expense of Jews deported to extermination centers; and outlined the complex politics of the alliance between the National Socialists and Germany's corporate elite.

True, the OMGUS financial investigation was but a sketch. Even so, it is reasonable to suspect that had a trial of, say, Hermann Abs or his top aides gone forward as recommended, a far more complete and well documented picture of banking under the Nazis would have emerged in the 1940s, rather than as a result of political and social scandal fifty years later. Surviving slave laborers and their families would have enjoyed considerably more leverage to force companies to pay the compensation due them.

In any event, as a result of General Draper and his aides burying the OMGUS investigation's facts and investigative leads after 1947, the proposed prosecution of Abs and other key bank officials never took place.

The most explosive bit of information Steinberg discovered is that Hermann Abs maintained a secret cache of almost 700 pounds of Deutsche Bank gold in a Swiss bank account throughout his life.[71] OMGUS had discovered that Abs and his second-in-command, Alfred Kurzmeyer, had smuggled hundreds of kilos of gold into Switzerland in 1945, most likely via Istanbul. Steinberg provides new details about how the scheme worked and reveals that the bank kept SS gold on ice in Switzerland for more than forty years after 1945.

Briefly, he outlines what appears to have been a three-sided scheme through which the SS would put its wealth under the stewardship of Kurzmeyer and a Deutsche Bank subsidiary in Switzerland, which in turn guaranteed that the SS could withdraw an equivalent sum from the Deutsche Bank branch in Berlin, even if the Swiss or Turks blocked German accounts in the final, disastrous months of the war.[72] The Abs "foreign exchange reserve," as he called it in postwar interrogations, provided the guarantee that the Deutsche Bank would eventually collect on any funds advanced to the SS in Berlin.

Circumstantial evidence strongly suggests that the "foreign exchange reserve" gold cache was looted from the dead. The timing and method of Abs's acquisition of the gold; Kurzmeyer's clandestine transfer of this and other loot to Swiss banks; this gold's use to guarantee international transfer of the SS's criminal assets; and Abs's postwar secrecy about the existence and true function of a supposed "foreign exchange reserve" for wartime Deutsche Bank subsidiaries that had long since passed into oblivion, taken together, all point to that conclusion.

Similarly, the Deutsche Bank finally sold off the gold cache on the international market after Abs retired and kept the proceeds for itself. But when the world's attention focused during the mid-1990s on looted Nazi wealth hidden in Swiss banks, the Deutsche Bank rethought that gold sale and quickly donated an equivalent sum

---

[71] Ibid., 65–66.
[72] Ibid., 63–64.

(about DM 5.6 million) to Jewish charities and a foundation specializing in rehabilitating Germany's international reputation.[73]

Here is where the "contextualization" or spin-doctoring of the Holocaust presents itself in its most evolved form. Steinberg has indeed traced Abs's and Kurzmeyer's involvement with this cache of gold in greater detail and with more documentation than any previous author. He also chose to bury that information deep in his text, where it has passed into something approaching oblivion without substantive coverage in any general-circulation news media that could be located using Lexis/Nexis and Internet searches. He then followed his breakthrough concerning Abs with what many readers may consider to be an extended apologia for corporate criminality.

The fact that Deutsche Bank executives possessed detailed prior knowledge of the Jewish extermination campaign and related crimes against humanity has no bearing on evaluating the bank's operations during the Holocaust, Steinberg contends. "[W]hat does knowing mean?" he asks. "The fact is that knowing [the truth of the Holocaust while it was underway] meant little." A large part of the German population was uninterested in the fate of the Jews, he continues, and "the board of the Deutsche Bank did not escape this decline in human values."[74]

In reality, however, knowing means a great deal. From a legal standpoint, for example, it marks the difference between premeditated murder and acting negligently or even more or less innocently under difficult circumstances. "Knowing" is the hallmark of *mens rea*, "a guilty mind," as *Black's Law Dictionary* puts it: "a guilty or wrongful purpose; a criminal intent."[75]

Further, "knowing" has a very substantial impact on how modern historians evaluate the inherently ambiguous traces left by past events. That in turn shapes the particular forms of organized remembering and organized forgetting that the Deutsche Bank and the Foundation for Responsibility, Remembrance and the Future is today attempting to engineer. Just as it would in a more conventional criminal case, the World War II-era bank executives' prior knowledge of the deadly consequences of their actions cuts away the presumption of innocence that these officials would otherwise enjoy. For example, the Deutsche Bank's decision to underwrite Kontinental Oel activities on the Eastern Front means one thing if it is interpreted as a naïve but more or less routine bank investment in an expanding business. It means quite another if Hermann Abs and other key executives involved realized they were bankrolling a dozen corporate concentration camps that had been dedicated since their inception to slavery and death through labor. All of the available evidence points to the latter conclusion.

Steinberg's conclusions on such matters lead him into extraordinary self-contradictions. At various points he lays out quite precise evidence concerning the bank's role in the Holocaust and then asks, "is the charge . . . that Abs, Kurzmeyer and their colleagues collaborated with the regime justified?" The answer would seem to be obvious, considering the deal with the SS outlined earlier. But Steinberg's own

---

[73] Ibid., 63–66.

[74] Ibid., 69.

[75] *Black's Law Dictionary,* revised 4th edition, St. Paul: West Publishing, 1968, 1137.

answer is that "layers of foggy language, bureaucracy (uniformed and civilian) to process and sanitize" information separated the "respectable people" of the bank's executive board from the "brutes" who packed people into gas chambers. In the case of gold looted from the mouths of the dead, he continues, "the further the gold gets from the victims the more the moral responsibility seems to dissipate and the [gold] transactions normalize themselves. . . . [the Deutsche Bank] only entered the chain at six or seven removes from the victim's body."[76]

Later Steinberg poses the realities of bank culpability for crimes against humanity as rhetorical questions, which he then answers with explanations—or rationalizations, as some would call them—that in each instance exculpate the Deutsche Bank and its senior executives from any substantive responsibility for the crimes of the Nazi era and, it seems, from even collaborating with Nazi Party leaders. In the end, Steinberg's fog of doublespeak had embraced Feldman and James's approach to the discredited 1995 study. There, they concluded that self-blinding "political culture" of top industrialists (Feldman) and their "moral shortsightedness" (James) constitute the beginning and the end, the alpha and omega, of the executives' or the Deutsche Bank's corporate responsibility for any outrage.

No one need doubt Steinberg's personal integrity, competence as a historian, knowledge of the Holocaust, or accomplishments in documenting new details of the Deutsche Bank's wartime or postwar history. What his published study illustrates, however, is that even an academic of his background and qualifications can be drawn into the highly compromised position of simultaneously condemning Nazi crimes, on the one hand, and exonerating the single most powerful economic institution of the era from any substantive responsibility for its direct role in them, on the other. Whether Steinberg realizes it or not, this evasion is the very heart of modern Germany's spin-doctoring of the Holocaust.

The OMGUS financial division investigation, in contrast, concluded that the Deutsche Bank and its Nazi-era rival, the Dresdner Bank, committed specific crimes for which they should be held legally accountable. For this reason the OMGUS investigations have taken on considerable new importance in recent years. They are one key to understanding the highly questionable settlement that the U.S. government engineered between those who profited from Nazi Germany, on the one hand, and those who paid the price for Nazi crimes.[77]

The OMGUS financial investigation's conclusions ended up buried in U.S. government files. Neither Deutsche Bank nor Dresdner Bank executives faced prosecution for criminal activities during the Nazi years, although a handful of executives such as the Dresdner Bank's Karl Rasche were prosecuted and convicted for other Nazi crimes. Rather than holding the German economic elite to account for its important role in Nazi initiatives, including in key economic aspects of the Holocaust,

---

[76] Steinberg, *The Deutsche Bank and Its Gold Transactions,* 71–72. For more on the significance of "knowing," see the recently released transcripts of British Intelligence's bugging of the jail cells of high ranking German POWs: Ed Vulliamy, "Jail small talk reveals Holocaust guilt," *The Observer,* May 20, 2001.

[77] For an overview, see Ludolf Herbst, *Der Totale Krieg und die Ordnung der Wirtschaft,* (Stuttgart: Deutsche Verlags-Anstalt, 1982).

Western governments for the most part helped reorganize and re-establish what George Kennan termed "the present ruling class of Germany,"[78] especially after the escalation of the Cold War with the Korean conflict.

Today, new public attention to the Holocaust and the economic imperatives of a globalized economy have combined to create intense pressure on Germany's most powerful economic groups. They fear sanctions, boycotts and lawsuits. German companies are willing to pay out a fraction of what they once looted to those survivors who are still alive, only on the conditions that survivors abandon every damage claim against any German corporation, regardless of its merits, and that hundreds of millions Deutsche Marks of the settlement funds go toward propaganda projects ultimately overseen by the companies themselves. Despite the relentlessly publicized claims of humanitarian intent, these deals have little to recommend them from the standpoint of surviving slave laborers, forced laborers, or anyone else with a legitimate damage claim stemming from Nazi crimes.

If a German corporation's support of slave labor and attempted extermination of identifiable groups of people more than fifty years ago is a crime against humanity, should not a comparable standard be set for other perpetrators as well? Major Japanese corporations and the Japanese government also fear legal responsibility for slave labor, organized rape, and grotesque "medical" experimentations whose systematic character has only recently begun to be recognized in the United States.[79]

U.S.-based multinational corporations could easily find themselves the subjects of claims on the part of Vietnamese, Cambodians, Laotians, Kurds, East Timorese, Guatemalans, ethnic Hawaiians, and enemies-of-the-moment such as Iran, Iraq, and Libya.

This perspective does not suggest that the Holocaust is "the same as" other gross violations of human rights, nor that human suffering should be, in some banal sense, measured along a yardstick for pain. It does indicate that realistic international standards defining gross violations of human rights need to be articulated, and that there is no morally defensible reason why the United States or any other country should exclude itself from meeting these standards.

Given these realities, the current demand for vetted historians to assist in the "reconstruction" of the past is likely to continue. The media-saturated environment that has helped incubate this corporate crisis has simultaneously brought forward increasingly sophisticated tools to attempt to manage public perceptions. Selective sponsorship of approved historical scholarship and other third-party experts are central to these tactics. If the scholars involved have achieved fine reputations, so much the better; it improves their credibility. Frequently, overt censorship of an expert's work is unnecessary and may even be counterproductive. A much better approach is to cultivate friendships with cooperative scholars, meanwhile easing out troublemakers and making a point of not inviting them back. Word soon gets around

---

[78] George F. Kennan, *Memoirs 1925–1950* (Boston: Little, Brown, 1967), 175–77.

[79] U.N. Commission on Human Rights, *Contemporary Forms of Slavery, Systematic Rape, Sexual Slavery, and Slavery-like Practices During Armed Conflict: Final Report*, Gay McDougall, Special Rapporteur, 1998, reproduced in Sangmie Choi Schellstede and Soon Mi Yu, *Comfort Women Speak: Testimony from Sex Slaves of the Japanese Military* (New York: Holmes & Meier, 2000), 136–52.

concerning who is "reliable," "sensible," or "fair" from a company's point of view, and who is not.

The British political scientist, Michael Pinto-Duschinsky, who chairs the International Political Science Association's Research Committee on Political Finance and Political Corruption, put his finger directly on the problem in an article for the *Times Literary Supplement:*

1. Since it is the client firms which select the historians, the participants are unlikely to include scholars known to be critical of them. . . .
2. Academics invited to join highly-paid historical commissions do not need to be told to tow the line. The hope of lucrative work in the future may be enough to tempt them to alter their wording and emphasis. . . .
3. When pressed for time, [these selected] historians tend to rely on the selection of documents by company archivists.
4. Official historians are often drawn into a web of secrecy; [and]
5. Dons and academic administrators have every motive to avoid offending gigantic enterprises such as VW, Siemens and Deutsche Bank, whose educational foundations finance university fellowships and grants.

Most of all, Pinto-Duschinsky continues, the "propaganda element" in sponsored histories "potentially distort research, writing and teaching" throughout an academic field, which in this instance is the history and legacy of the Holocaust. "Suppose an academic has a choice between two subject areas or countries," he asks. "For one of them, research costs will be paid, grants will be awarded and teaching posts will be available; for the second, there will be no such provisions. Naturally, all but the most devoted or the most talented dons will go where the money goes."[80]

These long-buried works open up new questions and new avenues for inquiry into the history of the Holocaust, and into the nexus between major corporations and the academy. As these studies open new and more subtle perspectives, they will have achieved their purpose.

CHRISTOPHER SIMPSON
Washington, D.C.
August 2001

---

[80] Michael Pinto-Duschinsky, "Selling the Past," *Times Literary Supplement,* October 23, 1998.

PART ONE

OFFICE OF MILITARY GOVERNMENT FOR GERMANY (U.S.)

Finance Division
Financial Investigations Section
APO 742
Report on the Investigation of the DEUTSCHE BANK
November 1946

The following personnel participated, for varying periods, in the investigation of the Deutsche Bank:

Sidney L. Klepper	Paul J. Brand
Saul Kagan	Charles B. Bancroft
Emil Lang	Elizabeth J. Koblenzer
Ernest Mehlman	Hans Moses

CHAPTER I

Recommendations

It is recommended that:

1. The Deutsche Bank be liquidated.

2. The responsible officials of the Deutsche Bank be indicted and tried as war criminals.

3. The leading officials of the Deutsche Bank be barred from positions of importance or responsibility in German economic or political life.

CHAPTER II

Summary

Investigation of the Deutsche Bank has revealed it to be an excessive concentration of economic power and a participant in the execution of the criminal policies of the Nazi regime in the economic field.

The Deutsche Bank was the largest of all the German commercial banks and it made itself, during the war, the largest bank on the European continent. It held in 1942 some 21 percent of the total deposits and 18.5 percent of the total assets of all the 653 commercial banks of the Greater Reich. It established and maintained, in addition, a far-flung network of branches and affiliates not only throughout Germany, but also in the annexed, occupied, and satellite countries of Europe. At the peak of its power, in 1942, it maintained some 490 branches and agencies, some one-third more than its closest competitor, the Dresdner Bank.

The Deutsche Bank, like the other Berlin Grossbanken, had no American counterpart. It was a universal bank combining in its operations commercial as well as investment banking, and it wielded an influence and control over industry to a degree unparallelled in modern American banking. It transacted some 30 percent of all stock transfers of the major German corporations, it was the acknowledged leader in the flotation of huge stock and bond issues for German industry and in consequence of its position in the securities field it came to dominate the leading stock exchanges. Through the peculiar German system of proxy voting it controlled and voted in key industrial enterprises large blocks of shares, without owning more than a minor fraction of them. Within a single year it voted 28 percent of the stock represented at the annual meeting of the Allgemeine Elektrizitaets Gesellschaft, 38 percent of that of the I.G. Farben, 49 percent of that of the Deutsche Maschinenfabrik (Demag) and 53 percent of that of the Mannesmann Roehrenwerke.

The most tangible medium of influence and control exercised by the Deutsche Bank over German industry assumed the form of an extensive system of interlocking directorships. The principal representatives of the bank—the members of the *Vorstand*,[1] the Aufsichtsrat[2] Chairman and the fourteen general agents—joined the *Aufsichtsraete* of some 379 industrial enterprises. The eleven Vorstand members alone

---

[1] *Editor's note:* The *Vorstand* is the senior management of a German enterprise. It is typically made up of six to twelve members, meets daily, and is most directly responsible for day-to-day decision-making. The Vorstand is roughly comparable to the president, chief executive officer, chief financial officer, and similar senior management in U.S. corporations.

[2] *Editor's note:* The *Aufsichtsrat* is similar to the board of directors of a U.S. corporation. In German business custom, however, the Aufsichtsrat chairman, vice-chairman and key committees typically play a larger role in the enterprise's day-to-day affairs than is found in U.S. corporations of comparable size. Similarly, representatives of the boards of ostensibly competing corporations (BMW and Daimler Benz, for example) often can be found in the Aufsichtsraete of banks and key suppliers.

held between them some 76 Aufsichtsrat chairmanships and vice-chairmanships in other corporations.

The application of the various means of control over industry at the disposal of the bank revealed itself in the virtual domination it exerted over various industrial enterprises. Foremost among them were the Mannesmann Roehrenwerke, Germany's leading tube and sheet metal manufacturer, Daimler Benz, the country's second largest automobile manufacturer and the Bayerische Motoren Werke which, together with Daimler Benz manufactured during the war for the Luftwaffe some two-thirds of all airplane engines. In this connection the Deutsche Bank played a role far out of proportion to its position as merely the largest of the German commercial banks.

The Deutsche Bank showed the way to all German commercial banks with its contributions to the rearmament program. It provided the Reich with vast funds for rearmament purposes. Thus in the prewar year of 1938 it already invested some 35 percent of its total assets in Reich paper. It acted as the leader or co-leader of virtually all of the major credit syndicates whose operations made possible the financing of the entire rearmament program. It guided the industries, which it controlled directly, into the channels of production desired by the Government and the Party.

The Deutsche Bank played a leading role among the commercial banks in the exploitation of the economic resources of the countries of annexed, occupied, and satellite Europe. Beginning with the Anschluss in 1938 it proceeded, with great aggressiveness, to expand its banking empire outside of the old German borders. It acquired control of the Creditanstalt Bankverein, Wien, the largest commercial bank in Austria, which had more than 40 branches in that country. It acquired control of the Boehmische Unionbsank of Czechoslovakia and incorporated some 23 of the latter's branches into its own branch network. It obtained, after the fall of France and Belgium, the bulk of the extensive holdings in Balkan banking and industry of the Société Générale de Belgique, one of the largest holding companies in Europe, and thereby won for itself a dominant position in the banking structure of the Balkan countries. So extensive did the foreign acquisitions of the Deutsche Bank become that between the years 1938–1941 the number of its branches and affiliates outside of Germany showed a sixfold increase.

The Deutsche Bank also acted on a number of occasions as a spearhead institution for the German Government in the economic penetration of the annexed, occupied, and satellite countries of Europe. The Kontinentale Oel A.G. which was established by Goering in March 1941, so as to create a German oil monopoly in Europe, acquired the core of its initial holdings—the majority control of the two largest Romanian oil companies—from the Deutsche Bank. The latter in its own turn had previously, following the German victory in the West, taken over these shares from the former French and Belgian holders.

The Deutsche Bank participated in numerous Aryanization transactions in Germany as well as in the countries of annexed, occupied, and satellite Europe and profited extensively from them. It took over in 1938, without compensation, the entire clientele of the very prominent non-Aryan banking house of Mendelssohn & Co., Berlin, and it established a new banking house, during the same year, to take over the business of the large private and non-Aryan Simon Hirschland Bank of Essen. It extended to its customers a great volume of credits to assist them in acquiring and financing non-Aryan business properties. It also supplied new "purchasers" for properties of this description and it became a competitor of the Dresdner Bank, whose aggressiveness in this field had become a byword in Germany, in a race for commissions and profits out of Aryanization transactions.

The Deutsche Bank's great expansion program, during the twelve years of the Nazi regime, came to be realized, in considerable degree, through the closeness of its connections with Government Ministries as well as with Party and affiliated agencies. Emil Georg von Stauss, the leading member of the Vorstand between 1920–1933, was an early supporter of Hitler, with whom he maintained a close and continuing relationship. Von Stauss was also on excellent terms with Goebbels and Goering and was appointed in 1934 to the vice-presidency of the Nazi Reichstag. Three reliable Party men were invited, during the Nazi regime, to join the Vorstand—SA Oberfuehrer [General] Ritter von Halt, a member of the notorious Keppler Circle,[3] Heinrich Hunke, Gauwirtschaftsberater [district economic adviser to the Nazi Party] of Berlin and Robert Frowein whose appointment received the personal endorsement of Minister Funk.

The Deutsche Bank's Aufsichtsrat fairly bulged with strong Party men and sympathetic fellow travelers. A full third of the membership bore the title of Wehrwirtschaftsfuehrer [war economic leader], in recognition of the role they played in fulfilling the demands of the war economy. A majority of the Aufsichtsrat's steering committee, the Arbeitsausschuss, were outspoken Party men. The Aufsichtsrat vice-president, Albert Pietzsch, was an old Party activist, an economic adviser to Rudolf Hess and president of the Reich Economic Chamber. Among the other influential Aufsichtsrat members were numbered Philipp Reemtsma, a principal financial supporter of Goering, Wilhelm Zangen and Rudolf Stahl, president and vice-president respectively of the powerful Reichsgruppe Industrie in the Reich Economic Chamber and Otto Fitzner, Gauwirtschaftsberater of Lower Silesia.

The Deutsche Bank was also a contributor during the Nazi regime of large sums to a variety of political funds. During a period of some six years, beginning in 1939, the bank contributed the sum of RM 75,000 per year to a special fund for the personal use of Heinrich Himmler. The bank also contributed, during an even longer period, an average of some RM 300,000 per year to the Adolf Hitler Spende, for the use of the Party and its affiliated agencies.

The Deutsche Bank employed its excessive power in the German economy to participate in the execution of the criminal policies of the Nazi regime in the economic field. The responsibility for these actions rests with the Vorstand members who directed them, with the Aufsichtsrat members who sanctioned them, and with the officials and employees of the bank who executed them.

---

[3] *Editor's note:* The Keppler Circle became a focal point for business and SS cooperation throughout the Third Reich. Business leaders sought influence outside official channels with the increasingly powerful SS chief; Himmler in turn sought the political and economic support of the business elite. Key participants included Siemens general director Rudolf Bingel, Unilever and Kontinentale Oel director Karl Blessing, steel industrialist Friedrich Flick and about two dozen other senior officers and directors of Germany's most powerful corporations. The then highly secret series of meetings is better known today as the Himmlerkreis or "Circle of Friends of Reichsfuehrer SS Heinrich Himmler." The term "Keppler Circle" refers to the Himmler adjutant who arranged the gatherings.

CHAPTER III

History

The history of the Deutsche Bank, Germany's largest commercial bank, is one of expansion—expansion in the sense of ever increasing volume of operations and of ever increasing geographical spread. This expansion was accomplished by the absorption of numerous other banking institutions and, in later years, by close coordination of the bank's moves and policies with the expansionist objectives of the leaders of the Third Reich.

The year of the bank's foundation, 1870, was the beginning of the "founders' years" in Germany, a time when numerous new industrial and financial enterprises were established. It was a year of historical importance in the Greater Germany movement, in that it saw German unification under Chancellor Bismarck and ushered in an era of German imperialism. The primary purpose of the bank at its inception was to finance German foreign trade and to make that foreign trade, as well as German industry, increasingly independent of foreign banks. The initial capital of the bank was RM 15 million. Its principal founder was Georg von Siemens, and up to the present the bank has maintained especially close ties with the Siemens family and the Siemens industrial enterprises.

❏ ❏ ❏

Emil Georg von Stauss, who became a leading executive of the bank around the turn of the century, was similarly instrumental in promoting the bank's industrial interests. It was he who, after the First World War, succeeded in preserving the German aircraft industry. In 1924–1925 he took a firm hand in the reorganization of two large producers of motors, Bayerische Motoren Werke (BMW) and Daimler Benz, and subsequently he remained the decisive man in their management. These companies have continued to be under Deutsche Bank domination ever since. During World War II, they produced two-thirds of all German airplane engines.

The method most consistently and successfully applied by the Deutsche Bank in its drive for expansion was the absorption of other banking institutions. In each series of mergers, the bank not only profited by an increase of resources and clientele but attained a greater density and more complete territorial coverage in its network of branches throughout Germany.

❏ ❏ ❏

The greatest merger occurred after the monetary stabilization in 1929, when the Deutsche Bank joined forces with the Direction der Disconto-Gesellschaft, then

41

Germany's second largest bank. The capital of the Deutsche Bank at that time was RM 150 million, ten times its original size, to which Disconto-Gesellschaft added RM 135 million. Open reserves were RM 90 million for the Deutsche Bank, RM 66.5 million for Disconto-Gesellschaft. Thus, in capital and reserves as well as total resources (RM 5.5 billion), the consolidated bank far outdistanced any other bank in Germany. Into this huge combine the Disconto-Gesellschaft brought not only its own facilities and clientele but also those of its important subsidiaries, the A. Schaffhausenscher Bankverein, with an old established business in the industrial Rhineland, the Rheinische Creditbank and the Sueddeutsche Disconto-Gesellschaft, prominent in Baden and Wuerttemberg, and the Norddeutsche Bank in Hamburg, one of the most reputable banks in Germany's international trading center. The combined institutions had some 800,000 accounts, almost twice the number carried by the old Deutsche Bank. [Some] 289 branches made up its network as against the 181 of the Deutsche Bank prior to the merger.

❑ ❑ ❑

For some years after the merger, the institution styled itself "Deutsche Bank and Disconto-Gesellschaft," but in 1937 it reverted to the old name of Deutsche Bank.

In the same year, 1929, and in 1930, the Deutsche Bank absorbed a number of private banking houses: L. Pfeiffer in Kassel, J. Frank & Cie in Krefeld, Doertenbach & Cie in Stuttgart, and E. Ladenburg in Frankfurt.

The size of the sprawling institution called for a measure of technical local autonomy. Hence, the country was divided into geographical districts provided with regional advisory boards, and certain decisions such as the granting of loans up to RM 50,000 or RM 150,000 (depending on the size of the branch), could be made on a district level without prior reference to Berlin. Stringent supervision on all major loans, however, was retained in Berlin. Moreover, under the leadership of Hans Rummel, a member of the Vorstand who came to be known as a pace-maker in his field, the bank developed an elaborate system of branch cost accounting which allowed closer supervision and direction of branch operations from the center.

The position of the Deutsche Bank was sufficiently strong to enable it to weather the banking crisis of the early 30s with far less government support than the other big banks. The government did take over some RM 50 million of the bank's capital which was then, after two readjustments in 1932, RM 144 million. During this period the bank freely availed itself of the extremely close ties by which certain large industrial concerns were bound to it. It succeeded in placing sizable blocks of its stock with Mannesmann, Rheinische Braunkohlen, and the Reemtsma Konzern. In the years from 1933 to 1937 the bank was gradually "reprivatized," that is, the shares held by the government were again placed into private hands.

The era of Nazi rule provided the Deutsche Bank with an opportunity to direct its expansive force into entirely new channels. In close coordination with the aggressive moves of the Third Reich, the bank spread its influence and its network into the invaded territories. This phase of its expansion will be dealt with in some detail in a subsequent chapter. Following the First World War, the bank's foreign business had dwindled to relative insignificance, particularly after the "Standstill Agreements" of

1931. Prior to 1938, the Deutsche Bank had but few participations in banking institutions abroad, such as in Handel-Maatschappij H. Albert de Bary & Co. in Holland, and in the Deutsche Ueberseeische Bank, the largest German bank in Latin America and Spain. As German aggression progressed, the bank rapidly expanded its foothold in foreign countries. It was quick to capitalize on the "Anschluss" by gaining control of Austria's largest bank, the Creditanstalt Bankverein. This acquisition brought a system of over 40 branches into the Deutsche Bank fold. It also provided the Deutsche Bank with a repository into which it placed some of the interests in Southeastern Europe which it successively acquired. In Czechoslovakia, the bank followed the pattern of the Reich's official foreign policy by converting the 21 Sudetenland branches of two Czech banks into branches of Deutsche Bank. In the rest of Czechoslovakia, the branches were retained under the name of the native institutions which, in turn, were brought under the control of the Deutsche Bank. By the time Germany reached the climax of her expansion, the Deutsche Bank had branches in Czechoslovakia, France, the Baltic states, Poland, Turkey, and Danzig, and subsidiaries in Austria, Czechoslovakia, Romania, Bulgaria, Yugoslavia, Luxembourg, Holland, Spain, and Latin America.

It also made a bid for extension of its influence in the Far East by participating with other German banks in the creation of two German institutions for the financing of Far Eastern trade: the Deutsch-Asiatische Bank with its head office in Shanghai and branches in China and Germany, and the Deutsche Bank fuer Ostasien, a government sponsored creation, set up in 1942 to further the exchange of goods and operation of the clearing between Germany and Japan.

The Nazis' anti-Jewish program further served the Deutsche Bank's constant drive for extension of its power. In 1938 it took over the clientele of the dissolved firm of Mendelssohn & Co., Berlin, which had been the largest private banking house in Germany. In the same year the bank participated in the Aryanization of the well-known private banking house of Simon Hirschland, Essen, and acquired control of its successor, Burkhardt & Co. The bank participated in numerous other "Aryanizations" of industrial and financial enterprises.

It took the impact of the Allied breakthrough and an air bombardment to divert the Deutsche Bank, for a short period, from its policy of centralized management.

In late 1943 and in 1944, evacuation offices ("Ausweichstellen") were set up in Wiesbaden (to cover the branches in the Frankfurt and Kassel region and in Wuerttemberg and Bavaria), in Hamburg (for the northwestern, western and southwestern branches), and in Erfurt for the eastern branches.

How the Deutsche Bank has endeavored since V-E Day to reverse even this modest measure of decentralization, forced upon it by the military situation, will be discussed in a subsequent chapter.

CHAPTER IV

Scope of the Institution

Through the expansive and aggressive policy which has been described, the Deutsche Bank well maintained its position as the largest commercial bank in Germany. This section is intended to provide some yardsticks for the actual size of the bank's business and the pace of its expansion.

Table I shows the spectacular growth of the bank's total resources. Its assets grew from some RM 3 billion in 1933 to RM 7.5 billion in 1942 and 11.4 billion in 1944. During the same period, deposits, excluding interbank deposits, rose from RM 2.1 billion to RM 10.2 billion. In other words, assets nearly quadrupled, deposits quintupled from the Nazis' accession to power to the last year of the war. This growth in itself demonstrates that the bank fully participated in the rapid credit expansion which was generated by Reich financing of preparations for a war of aggression and later the conduct of it. The part the bank played in this development becomes even clearer by an examination of its direct stake in government financing. The third column of Table I shows the rise of the bank's investment in Reich and Laender obligations insofar as they are identified as such in the bank's published statements. The

Table I
DEUTSCHE BANK:
TOTAL ASSETS AND HOLDINGS OF TREASURY PAPER, 1933–1944.

Year	Total assets in million RM	Treasury paper in million RM[a]	Ratio of treasury paper to total assets (%)	Ratio of total treasury paper and other public obligations to total assets (%)
1933	3,038	259	8.5	NA
1934	2,962	233	8	NA
1935	3,017	358	12	NA
1936	3,064	354	11.5	NA
1937	3,300	376	11.5	NA
1938	3,748	817	22	NA
1939	4,184	1,312	31.5	44[b]
1940	5,315	2,652	50	63[c]
1941	6,573	3,835	58	71[b]
1942	7,504	4,430	59	73[b]
1943	8,703	5,115	59	73[c]
1944	11,374	7,914	70	82[c]

[a] Reich and Laender
[b] Source: Report of Vorstand to AR 30 March 1943
[c] Estimate

ratio of such disclosed investments in government paper to total assets rose from 8.5 percent in 1933 to 70 percent in 1944. An analysis of the bank's balance sheets for the war years (cf. Table II) further reveals that some 90 percent of the increase in deposits from 1938 to 1944 (RM 7.694 million) was placed into government securities.

Investigation has revealed, however, that the published statements do not tell the full story. At a meeting held on March 30, 1943, the Board of Managers [Vorstand] informed the Board of Directors [Aufsichtsrat], that the total investment in "public obligations" amounted to 73 percent of the total assets in 1942, as against the 59 percent disclosed in the statements under Reich and Laender obligations. For 1941 and 1939, the Vorstand named a figure of 71 percent and 44 percent, respectively, compared with the 58 percent and 31.5 percent apparent from the balance sheets. On the basis of these figures and additional information obtained (see below), it can be estimated that the peak figure of 70 percent shown in the financial statements for 1944, startling as it is, must be increased by some 12 percent to give a true picture of the bank's stake in the government and its instrumentalities.

It has been found, for instance, that in 1944 the Deutsche Bank held about RM 900 million promissory notes of the Deutsche Golddiskontbank (Dego), a subsidiary of the Reichsbank. This investment, which constituted about 8 percent of the total assets, was listed in the balance sheet under commercial bills. These "Dego" bills represented about 90 percent of the total commercial bill position shown.

In addition to its own huge investment in government securities, the bank, of course, was one of the outstanding agents for the placement of government paper among the public. In 1942, it distributed RM 1.4 billion worth of treasury and industrial bonds (Source: MG Handbook M 356-5, *Money and Banking*). While no accurate breakdown is available, it is clear that treasury bonds made up a sizable part of the amount.

Due to the vast government financing program reflected in the above figures, it is true that the direct lending business of the banks was relegated to a secondary role measured in terms of overall growth of assets. It is totally unwarranted, however, to say, as most German bankers do, that the loan business of the bank died and was of but negligible importance in the financing of the Nazi Reich's war effort. Table III shows the number and total amount of new loans extended by the Deutsche Bank in each year from 1932 to 1943. It shows that, almost without exception, a new peak was reached in each successive year. In 1943, over RM 2 billion new loans were extended by the bank, almost four times the amount of 1932. Even more interesting is the entirely uninterrupted increase in the ratio of large loans (over RM 100,000) to the total of new loans granted. This aspect will be discussed in more detail in Chapter IX, "Rearmament and War Financing."

The significance of the Deutsche Bank becomes even clearer by a comparison with other credit institutions. Its RM 11.4 billion total resources in 1944 exceeded those of the Dresdner Bank, second largest commercial bank in Germany, by about RM 2.8 billion. Thus it led its closest rival by about 33 percent. As to number of branches and agencies, the ratio (in 1941) was Deutsche Bank 489, Dresdner Bank 368.

Table II
DEUTSCHE BANK:
SUMMARY OF BALANCE SHEETS, IN MILLION RM, 1937–1944

	1937	1938	1939	1940	1941	1942	1943	1944
ASSETS								
Cash items[a]	151	189	240	304	371	420	540	671
Due from credit institutions[b]	57	55	46	38	53	59	83	50
Bills	1,086	836	770	806	846	886	941	957
Treasury bills	203	530	1,149	2,079	2,909	3,951	4,635	7,503
Treasury notes	173	288	163	573	927	479	480	412
Other securities	157	173	189	191	150	127	102	90
Syndicate holdings[c]	35	35	25	31	18	27	20	23
Debtors:								
Credit institutions[d]	24	44	34	46	43	37	38	50
Others	1,147	1,310	1,323	996	1,042	1,281	1,628	1,435
Advances against merchandise	136	143	95	89	64	84	84	49
Stock exchange loans	4	3	9	2	3	6	5	2
Participations	37	51	50	70	64	70	70	55
Other assets	90	92	91	89	84	78	77	77
Total	3,300	3,748	4,184	5,315	6,573	7,504	8,703	11,374
LIABILITIES								
Capital	130	130	130	160	160	160	160	160
Reserves	55	75	83	99	103	114	117	121
Deposits:								
Savings deposits	309	409	496	668	939	1,309	1,719	2,183
Credit institutions	212	257	269	301	401	368	481	600
Others	2,239	2,509	2,897	3,804	4,705	5,285	5,978	8,086
Own acceptances	216	234	214	185	173	164	145	113
Acceptances abroad	105	102	72	66	66	65	64	64
Other liabilities	34	33	24	31	27	39	39	47
Total	3,300	3,748	4,184	5,315	6,573	7,504	8,703	11,374

[a] Includes cash in vault, balances on Reichsband giro and postal checking accounts, dividend and interest coupons, and checks.

[b] Deposits with other credit institutions falling due not later than 3 months and made at the initiative of the depositing bank.

[c] Securities held subject to agreements (especially underwriting agreements) with other credit institutions and which may be disposed of only with consent of the syndicate members.

[d] Current account advances, at short or long-term, made at the initiative of the borrowing bank.

Table III
DEUTSCHE BANK

New loans granted, in amounts up to and above 100,000 RM 1932–1943

	Up to 100,000 RM			Above 100,000 RM			
Year	Number of loans	Amount	Ratio to loan total (%)	Number of loans	Amount	Ratio to loan total (%)	Total Amount in RM
1932[a]							436,000,000
1933	117,299	425,780,000	62	947	281,190,000	38	706,970,000
1934	94,015	429,821,200	51	1,144	399,388,400	49	829,209,600
1935	91,853	442,283,233	49	1,211	447,394,268	51	889,677,501
1936	96,943	493,762,438	47	1,424	551,956,555	53	1,045,718,993
1937	103,965	548,624,030	45	1,732	682,027,536	55	1,230,651,566
1938	109,236	608,760,989	41	2,098	874,287,217	59	1,483,048,206
1939	106,562	626,700,181	37	2,361	1,046,024,766	63	1,672,724,947
1940	94,282	531,000,801	34	2,026	999,630,498	66	1,530,631,299
1941	81,250	538,327,995	34	2,115	1,037,530,217	66	1,575,858,212
1942[a]							1,876,700,000
1943[a]							2,107,000,000

[a] No breakdown available.

Measured in terms of the total German commercial banking system consisting of 653 banks, the Deutsche Bank in 1942 held 21 percent of the total deposits (excluding interbank deposits) and 18.5 percent of the total assets of all these credit institutions. It also owned 21 percent of the long-term and short-term Reich securities held by these 653 banks.

The Deutsche Bank held virtually unchallenged leadership in the field of investment banking and underwriting. This is an activity, of course, on which the balance sheet furnishes no clues. The annual report for certain years, however, contains some information on the subject. In 1941, for example, the Deutsche Bank participated in the underwriting and floating of four public issues, the floating and stock exchange introduction of 31 industrial bond issues and of 57 new stock issues and stock conversion operations. In how many instances Deutsche Bank headed the syndicates formed for these operations was not disclosed, and no files are available to assemble this data for successive years. The confidential report to the Board of Directors referred to earlier, however, gives some information on the subject of new issues introduced on the stock exchange. It states that Deutsche Bank had the syndicate leadership in 14 stock issues out of a total of 28 and in 12 bond issues out of a total of 18 so introduced. As to the volume of securities trading carried on by the Deutsche Bank during 1942, the same report says:

The securities trading business transacted through the Deutsche Bank in 1942, reached the following amounts:

in fixed interest bearing securities   RM 3,698,000,000
in stock   RM   395,000,000

A former deputy manager of the Deutsche Bank's securities trading department has estimated, after consultation with stockbrokers, that the Deutsche Bank's transactions accounted for 35–40 percent of the total volume of trading on the Berlin stock exchange. The Dresdner Bank was the second largest securities dealer and the two institutions combined were responsible for about two-thirds of the turnover in stocks and bonds on the Berlin exchange. The Berlin stock exchange handled a volume of business far greater than that of all other German exchanges combined.

❑ ❑ ❑

CHAPTER V

Management and Organization

CORPORATE BODIES AND FUNCTIONAL ORGANIZATIONS

This discussion treats the governing bodies of the Deutsche Bank less with regard to their legal position within the corporate structure, than in appreciation of their actual importance for the operations of the bank. The system of checks and counter-checks legally provided in the division of power among the *Hauptversammlung* (General stockholders' meeting) Aufsichtsrat (Board of Directors) and the Vorstand (Board of Managers). [But this] had small significance in a corporation like the Deutsche Bank, where the Aufsichtsrat and Vorstand were so closely identified, that in joining forces they held the key to any such system with their control over a majority of the voting stock. The introduction of the German corporation law of 1937 with its far reaching changes had but little consequence on the direction of the bank's business. While, for instance, the power of the Aufsichtsrat was severely reduced by the new law, the Aufsichtsrat of the Deutsche Bank asserted itself as before. The personalities on the Aufsichtsrat continued to exert their influence. The particularly close relationship between Aufsichtsrat and Vorstand found its outward expression in a general extension of Aufsichtsrat and Vorstand mandates from term to term. The leadership of the bank was fully self-perpetuating.

THE HAUPTVERSAMMLUNG

The Hauptversammlung, as a rule, was convened once a year. Its relative importance was negligible, as the Deutsche Bank leadership, working in unison, was always assured of a majority in the voting.

❑ ❑ ❑

[In 1943, the largest blocks of privately held Deutsche Bank stock included:]

Mannesmann Roehrenwerke		RM 2.2 million
Reemtsma	about	RM 8 million
Siemens Konzern		RM 4 million
Johann P. Vielmetter	about	RM 2.5 million

These holdings remained a safety margin of control in the years when the Deutsche Bank management could not count on controlling the majority of [shareholder] votes by representing the scattered share holdings of the many smaller customers of the bank.

❑ ❑ ❑

THE AUFSICHTSRAT

The Aufsichtsrat of the Deutsche Bank was elected by the Hauptversammlung. Its members were appointed for a four-year term, but were immediately eligible for re-election upon its expiration.

The main duties of the Aufsichtsrat were the appointment of the Vorstand members and the supervision of their conduct of the bank's business.

In the last few years, the Aufsichtsrat consisted of about 30 members, after authority had been granted to maintain it at more than the 20 members, stipulated by the corporation law of 1937. Even so, the bank which sent its executives into the Aufsichtsrat of hundreds of enterprises, could accommodate on its own board only a very limited number of its most important customers, outstanding business leaders, and politically influential men. Due to this limitation, those Aufsichtsrat members, who were not in close business connection with the bank, could be only few in number, carefully selected for their political and social standing. It was of political advantage to the bank to have Albert Pietzsch on its board, and it added to its standing to have the backing of men like Hugo Eckener or Guenther Quandt. In joining the bank's board, these men thus took over not only a legal responsibility, but also a moral one.

The whole body of the Aufsichtsrat met only about twice a year. Really active participation was taken only by about one-third of the members who were elected into the working committee. The remaining members were satisfied to appoint the working committee to which they delegated their function between Aufsichtsrat meetings.

The [Aufsichtstrat] working committee, meeting usually once every month, through conferences with the Vorstand members and through access to the files, kept itself fully informed and maintained a close watch on policy and operations. New loans were singled out for particularly close scrutiny; loans between RM 1 and 3 million were subject to the approval of the "Praesidium" (presidency) of the Arbeitsausschuss, meeting almost daily; those in excess of RM 3 million could be granted only with the approval of the Arbeitsausschuss in its entirety. Table IV [gives] the composition of the working committee from 1935 to 1944.

It is obvious that the Aufsichtsrat members found their relationship to the bank an advantageous one as no resignation took place. Members could have resigned from office with a month's notice, even without an important reason (art. 11 sec. 5 of the by-laws). Aside from those Aufsichtsrat members eliminated in 1933/34 in connection with the Aryanization of the Aufsichtsrat, members were separated usually only upon their death or incapacity.

THE BEIRAT

This body was not a legal requirement of the corporate structure. However, it came under the jurisdiction of the Aufsichtsrat according to article 14 of the by-laws, leaving

Table IV
MEMBERS OF THE WORKING COMMITTEE OF THE DEUTSCHE BANK AUFSICHTSRAT, 1935–1944

Name	1935	36	37	38	39	40	41	42	43	44
Franz Urbig, Berlin	x	x	x	x	x	x	x	x	x	died 9/28 1944
Dr. Ernst Enno Russell, Berlin	x	x	x	x	x	x	x	x	x	x
Gustav Hardt, Berlin	x	x	x	x						
Carl Friedrich v. Siemens, Berlin	x	x	x	x						
Dr. Joh. P. Vielmetter, Berlin	x	x	x	x	x	x	x	x		
Dr. Wilhelm de Weerth, Wuppertal	x	x	x	x	x	x	x	x		
Oskar Schlitter, Berlin	x	x	x	x	died 11/30 1939					
Dr. Emil Georg von Stauss, Berlin	x	x	x	x	x	x	x	died 12/11 1942		
Dr. Jacob Hasslacher, Essen	x	x	x	x	x	died 7/16 1940				
Hans Oesterlink, Berlin	x	x	x	x	x	x	x	x	x	x
Dr. Wolfgang Reuter, Duisburg	x	x	x	x	x	x	x	x	x	x
Philipp F. Reemtsma, Hamburg	x	x	x	x	x	x	x	x	x	x
Wilhelm Zangen, Duesseldorf					x	x	x	x	x	x
Eduard Mosler, Berlin				x	died 8/22 1939					
Franz Hasslacher, Wien							x	x	x	x
Dr. Karl Kimmich, Berlin								x	x	died 10/9 1945
Otto Fitzner, Breslau									x	x
Dr. Albert Pietzsch, Muenchen									x	x

it to the Aufsichtsrat to form "Beiraete" (advisory boards) for the Central Office at Berlin and the branches. The Beiraete were to advise and to support the managers in the conduct of the bank's business and to promote close cooperation between branch management and local customers. They served the dual purpose of strengthening the local position of the bank's branches, emphasizing their services in competition with the local and regional banks, and of providing a means to connect with the bank a vast number of prominent businessmen, industrialists, and politicians, for whom there was no room on the small Aufsichtsrat.

The Deutsche Bank had Beiraete in 21 districts with a total membership of 423 (in 1940). The Beirat for Rheinisch-Westphalia was by far the most numerous with 122 members, underlining the importance of the bank's interest in that district.

THE VORSTAND

Management responsibility for operations of the bank as a whole was vested in the Vorstand. In practice it made most of the current policy decisions. It selected the lesser officials, responsible for operations, requiring the approval of the Aufsichtsrat, however, for all appointments down to "Prokurist" (confidential clerk).

The Vorstand varied from 7 to 11 members; the last Vorstand had 11 members. Its composition in the years 1932 to 1944 is contained in Table V.

❑ ❑ ❑

As has been pointed out, Vorstand and Aufsichtsrat maintained close liaison for running the business of the bank. If necessary, the Vorstand, just as members of the Aufsichtsrat, had the right to demand a meeting of the entire Aufsichtsrat within two weeks. For practical purposes, the work of the individual Vorstand members was divided according to the functional divisions of the bank. Responsibility, however, was placed on the Vorstand in its entirety. Article 13 of the *Geschaeftsordnung* [operational code; by-laws] states:

> The bank's business is conducted by the Vorstand as a whole. The distribution of the work does not relieve a member of the Vorstand from the common responsibility for the conduct of the entire business.

This common responsibility required that all Vorstand members were at least informed about the activities of their colleagues, even if their express approval was not always required. Individual Vorstand members, for instance, had the right to extend credits in amounts up to RM 1 million. A vital part of the work of the Vorstand members was also the representation of the bank [as members of the Aufsichtsrat in other] industrial and commercial enterprises in Germany and abroad. The impact on the operations of the bank of this function, in which even the lesser Berlin executives and the branch managers were made to share, is discussed in Chapter VIII, "Influence and Control over Industry."

Table V
MEMBERS OF THE VORSTAND OF THE DEUTSCHE BANK, 1932–44

Name	1932	33	34	35	36	37	38	39	40	41	42	43	44
Theodor Frank	x												
Oscar Wassermann	x												
Alfred Blinzig	x	x											
Peter Brunswig	x	x											
Georg Solmssen	x	x											
Gustav Schlieper	x	x	x	x	x								
Eduard Mosler	x	x	x	x	x	x	x						
Karl Kimmich		x	x	x	x	x	x	x	x	x			AR
Oswald Roesler		x	x	x	x	x	x	x	x	x	x	x	x
Hans Rummel		x	x	x	x	x	x	x	x	x	x	x	x
Karl Ernst Sippel		x	x	x	x	x	x	x	x	x	x	x	x
F. Wintermantel		x	x	x	x	x	x	x	x	x	x	x	x
Hermann J. Abs							x	x	x	x	x	x	x
Karl Ritter von Halt							x	x	x	x	x	x	x
Johannes Kiehl							x	x	x	x	x	x	x
Clemens Plassmann									x	x	x	x	x
Erich Bechtolf										x	x	x	x
Robert Frowein												x	x
Heinrich Hunke												x	x

From the Annex to the Report

The Vorstand members of the Deutsche Bank treated with great seriousness the financial responsibilities which they contracted when acting in other companies as Aufsichtsrat members. Thus, when the Government's Office of the Four Year Plan requested the approval to a particular transaction of the Aufsichtsrat of the Suedost-Montan-Gesellschaft, [Hermann] Abs, who was a member of that body, voted his assent only after obtaining a legal opinion of his responsibilities in the case. This legal opinion emphasizes that Aufsichtsrat members are responsible for the exercise of prudent supervision over the management as well as for the careful examination of transactions for which their particular approval is required. The document points out, in addition, that Aufsichtsrat members who vote this approval upon the request of a government official, in this instance Reichsmarschall Goering, are not relieved thereby of their liability. This transaction is described in greater detail in [the report's] section devoted to the Mines de Bor and the Suedost-Montan-Gesellschaft (see Chapter XII).

❏ ❏ ❏

The last [Deutsche Bank] Vorstand divided among its members the duties and responsibilities for the functional and geographical distribution of bank operations in the following fashion:

Oswald Roesler
Speaker of the Vorstand
Member of the Vorstand since 1933
Responsible for the following departments:
General secretariat (Kessler)★
Economic Research (E.W. Schmidt)★★
Liquid funds (Ermisch)★★
Securities trading & placement (Adam)★★
Reich customers banks and Reich customers nonbanks (Boehnert)★★
Responsible for the following regions of Germany:
Hannover, Hildesheim, Braunschweig
Responsible for the following regions outside Germany:
Boehmische Union Bank
Creditanstalt Bankverein, Sudeten-branches (Reichenberg)

Erich Bechtolf
Member of the Vorstand since 1941
Responsible for the following department:
Secretariat (Benz)★★
Responsible for the following regions of Germany:
Duesseldorf, Duisburg, Essen, Saxony

Hermann J. Abs
Member of the Vorstand since 1937
Responsible for the following department:
Foreign Department.
Kurzmeyer★: Swiss business, agencies in Paris, Brussels. General
Bank Luxembourg and other foreign transactions of a special nature
Haeussler★★: foreign correspondence
Pollems★★: foreign syndicate loans
Responsible for the following regions of Germany:
Cologne, Frankfurt (Main), Saarbruecken
Responsible for the following regions outside Germany:
Deutsche Bank branch Istanbul (Turkey)
Deutsche Ueberseeische Bank (South America)
Creditanstalt Bankverein, Vienna and all foreign affiliates

Dr. Karl Ritter von Halt
Member of the Vorstand since 1938
Responsible for the following department:
Personnel (Raeffner)★★

★ General agents (Direktoren der Bank mit Generalvollmacht fuer saemtliche Niederlassungen)
★★ Department heads and/or managers of main office, Berlin.

Responsible for the following regions of Germany:
Thuringia, Siegen

Robert Frowein
Member of the Vorstand since 1943
Responsible for the following department:
None
Responsible for the following region of Germany:
Silesia

Clemens Plassmann
Member of the Vorstand since 1940
Responsible for the following department:
Main Office Berlin (Wieland)★★
Responsible for the following regions of Germany:
Elberfeld, Bielefeld, Osnabrueck, Aachen, Krefeld

Fritz Wintermantel
Member of the Vorstand since 1933
Responsible for the following department:
Main Office Berlin (Wieland)★★
Responsible for the following regions of Germany:
Hamburg, Bremen, Stettin, Koenigsberg
Responsible for the following region outside Germany:
Danzig

Karl Ernst Sippel
Member of the Vorstand since 1933
Responsible for the following department:
Legal department (Simon)★
Responsible for the following regions of Germany:
Magdeburg, Halle, Baden, Pfalz

Hans Rummel
Member of the Vorstand since 1933
Responsible for the following departments:
Auditing department (Ulbricht and Ahlborn)★★
Employees accounts department (Herzog)★★
Main bookkeeping department (Ulbricht)★★
Organizational department Real Estate (Guenkel)★★
Responsible for the following regions of Germany:
Bavaria and Wuerttemberg

Heinrich Hunke
Member of the Vorstand since 1943
Responsible for the following department:
No special assignment. Political contact man.

★ General agents (Direktoren der Bank mit Generalvollmacht fuer saemtliche Niederlassungen)
★★ Department heads and/or managers of main office, Berlin.

CHAPTER VI

Political Connections

The Deutsche Bank was able to assert and retain its unchallenged leadership in German finance and to accelerate its program of expansion during twelve years of Nazi rule. It could not have done so had it not known how to maintain, through its leading executives and directors (and by suitable additions to its top staff), excellent connections with the new ruling class and had it not eagerly carried out the political operations it was called upon to undertake. Deutsche Bank willingly engaged in "Gleichschaltung" (coordination), a key word in the Third Reich.

PERSONAL POLITICAL TIES

The most important participants in that personal liaison were the members of the Aufsichtsrat, the Vorstand, and the more important department heads.

DEUTSCHE BANK'S LEADER BETWEEN THE WARS

One of the earliest links between the bank and the Nazi movement was Dr. Emil Georg von Stauss, a man whose ideology ran toward extreme nationalism and militarism long before National Socialism was born. Von Stauss was the decisive man in Deutsche Bank from about 1920 until his retirement from the Vorstand in 1933.

❑ ❑ ❑

Von Stauss joined the Deutsche Bank in 1898. His pre–World War I activities in support of Germany's oil policy in Romania and his wartime oil activities in the Middle East were rewarded by elevation to the nobility. Among German businessmen he became known as the "political banker," and often after the 1914/18 war the political motives guiding his management of the Deutsche Bank became even more pronounced.

In cooperation with the German government, von Stauss proceeded to use the financial power at his disposal to rehabilitate the German aircraft and aircraft engine industry which had been reduced to ineffectiveness following Germany's defeat. At his instigation the Deutsche Lufthansa was founded as an outlet for the production of the German aircraft industry and as a means of developing German aviation. As chairman of the board of directors of both the Bayerische Motoren Werke and Daimler Benz since 1925, von Stauss developed the aircraft engine and airframe factories and laid the foundation for Hitler's rearmament in the air.

Elected to the German Reichstag in 1930, von Stauss, still the leading Vorstand member of the Deutsche Bank, identified himself with the reactionary group of industrialists and financiers who supported Hitler financially before his rise to power and then helped to lift him into the saddle. Even then von Stauss was a member of the NSDAP [Nazi Party, Nationalsozialistische Deutsche Arbeiterpartei]. He had personal contact with Hitler, Goebbels, and Schacht, and was a good friend of Hermann Goering who shared his interest in aviation. Hitler not only made von Stauss vice president of the Reichstag, but later heaped other honors and titles on him.

In 1933 Stauss retired from the Vorstand of the Deutsche Bank and became a member of the bank's Aufsichtsrat and of the credit committee.

He died in 1942. Upon his death, Hermann von Siemens, then ruler of the world-wide electric combine, eulogized him as "a man whose economic undertakings were full of political consideration."

CONNECTIONS WITH NATIONALIST ASSOCIATIONS

Stauss was not the only one of the Deutsche Bank's executives who had affiliations with super-nationalistic and expansionist causes. Kurt Weigelt, a manager in the foreign department of the Deutsche Bank, Berlin, played an especially important part in the "Greater Germany" movement. He was a close friend of Ritter von Epp of the SA who became Nazi governor of Bavaria and the head of Hitler's "Kolonial-politisches Amt" (Office for Colonial Policy). He was a member of the advisory council of the "Bund der Auslandsdeutschen" (Bund of Germans Abroad) which, after it was brought under the fifth column inspiring "Auslands-Organisation" of the NSDAP in 1933, spread Nazi propaganda and financed fascist minorities in foreign countries. The Bund was headed by an SS Lt. General (Obergruppenfuehrer) Lorenz and maintained its bank account with the Deutsche Bank.

Weigelt was an officer in two other organizations also, whose very names betrayed their expansionist objectives: the "Deutsch-Ostafrikanische Gesellschaft, Berlin" (German East Africa Society) and the Deutsche Orient Verein. The latter association was founded in 1934 in the presence of representatives from the Reich ministries of Propaganda and Economics, the Foreign Office of the NSDAP and other political offices of the Nazi Reich. Weigelt was chosen chairman of the Verein's Committee on Turkey.

❑ ❑ ❑

With his numerous offices in associations championing German territorial ambitions, Weigelt was the logical man to head the "Gruppe Deutscher Kolonialwirtschaftlicher Unternehmungen, Berlin" (group of German colonial economic enterprises), the overall group uniting German economic enterprises in Germany's former colonies.

❑ ❑ ❑

NAZIFICATION OF MANAGEMENT

In "coordinating" its policy-making bodies with the requirements of the "New Order," Deutsche Bank sought to, and succeeded in, reconciling two objectives: to have on these bodies a sufficient number of men who had good connections with the party and were generally endorsed by it and at the same time to maintain a certain nonpolitical element so as not to undermine the confidence the bank enjoyed abroad. This dual objective was accomplished by an immediate infusion of "new blood" into the Aufsichtsrat and working committee and by the retention, at least for the time being, of the "old guard"on the Vorstand.

THE AUFSICHTSRAT

The "rejuvenation" of the Aufsichtsrat was carried out in the course of a structural reorganization of the bank's supervisory organs.

❏ ❏ ❏

Some of these newcomers were:

Carl Eduard Herzog von Sachsen-Coburg und Gotha. "*Wer ist's?,*" the German *Who's Who,* gives the following information about this new member:

> 1928—Reichsstaffelfuehrer (general) in the Stahlhelm, militaristic organization of veterans of World War I, which became an early sympathizer of the NSDAP, helped it to power and merged with the SA during 1933/34.
> 1929—President of the "Bund der Auslandsdeutschen" described earlier.
> 1930—Member of Vorstand of "Stahlhelm."
> 1932—Reprimanded by Stahlhelm for excessive support of Hitler.
> March 1933—Reich Plenipotentiary for Motor-Traffic-System.
> Aug. 1933—SA Major General on the Staff of the Supreme Command of the SA.
> Dec. 1933—President of the German Red Cross. (Leading posts in the German Red Cross were given only to men and women considered reliable by the Nazis.) The duke chose for his deputy Professor Grawitz, an SS General. The Nazis bestowed several other honorary positions and titles upon the duke, who formally joined the NSDAP in May 1933.

Philipp Reemtsma. The cigarette tycoon Reemtsma was "persona grata" with many top Nazi officials and his membership on the board of directors of the Deutsche Bank was to become a valuable political contact for the bank.

Reemtsma first met Goering in August or September 1933; shortly after this meeting, Reemtsma's name was removed from the "Corruption" list previously published by the Nazis. At that time Reemtsma contributed an initial RM 4 million to "special projects close to the heart of Marshall Goering"; this amount was followed by an annual contribution of RM 1 million. About Reemtsma's relationship to Goering, Georg Eidenschnik, a Munich banker, stated:

> He (Reemtsma) had a particularly favorable relationship to Hermann Goering, who probably also received valuable presents (pictures). . . . Through Goering, Reemtsma obtained large woods in Slovakia, for the exploitation of which one of the largest European wood processing works was established in Turnay in Slovakia.

❑ ❑ ❑

The title of *Wehrwirtschaftsfuehrer* (Leader of War Economy) was conferred upon Reemtsma in 1939. Reemtsma's political connections, by his own admission, were extensively used for the benefit of the Deutsche Bank. Here is his own testimony:

> In view of the fact that in 1935 or 1936 I joined the Aufsichtsrat of the Vereinigte Glanzstoff [VGF] . . . upon the request of the Deutsche Bank, I was called by the Deutsche Bank to intervene in a problem concerning the VGF and Goering. . . . I saw Goering and he agreed to abandon the scheme. . . .

> In addition to the VGF, I joined, upon the personal request of Mr. Kimmich, the Aufsichtsrat of the Henkel Company, Duesseldorf, the largest soap manufacturer of Germany . . . I believe it was in 1942 and I was asked to join the Aufsichtsrat of Henkel in order to use my connections with Goering to intervene on behalf of the company who had some difficulties with Goering . . . the Deutsche Bank was the main banking connection of the Henkel Company—since many years . . .

Albert Hackelsberger. Hackelsberger, in July 1933, became the liaison official between the former Centrist representation in the Reichstag and the NSDAP. He also was the official "Hospitant" (guest) of the NSDAP representation in the Reichstag.

❑ ❑ ❑

Hermann Schmitz. Schmitz was a member of the Nazi Reichstag and head of the I.G. Farbenindustrie trust, [and] an early supporter of Hitler.

Wolfgang Reuter. Reuter too was an official member of the NSDAP and, in April 1934, became president of the Reich Bund of German Industry. He was a powerful man in heavy industry and received several honorary positions in the many associations the Nazis established. He is said to have had particularly strong connections with the German Labor Front.

Fritz Springorum. This industrialist also had very early ties with the party and was chosen a member of the Nazi Reichstag.

Carl Friedrich von Siemens. Siemens was then the head of the Siemens combine and a very close friend of Emil Georg von Stauss. The Siemens complex aided Hitler with substantial contributions, had many of its executives in Nazi key positions, used its foreign branches for spy activities, and employed considerable slave labor.

❑ ❑ ❑

The above are only some of the more outstanding men of the new Aufsichtsrat. As time went on and the Nazis tightened their grip, the number of German industrialists "converted" to Nazi ideals increased, and more Nazi "old timers" were appointed to the board of directors of the Deutsche Bank.

In 1944, the Aufsichtsrat of the Deutsche Bank consisted of 31 members, one-third of whom were Wehrwirtschaftsfuehrer; they were Pietzsch, Brecht, Fitzner, Freudenberg, Kreibich, Quandt, Reemtsma, Stahl, Schmitz, and Schirner. The task of a Wehrwirtschaftsfuehrer is defined as follows in a German encyclopedia:

> It is the duty of the "Wehrwirtschaftsfuehrer" to cooperate in fulfilling the war armament demands to be made on German Economy. (*Der Neue Brockhaus* 1938, Vol. IV).

Most of the newcomers were men with important political ties. [Following] are some of them.

Albert Pietzsch. Pietzsch met Hitler in 1925 and became a member of the NSDAP on 16 February 1927. Hitler's ardent follower and personal friend, he has supported the "Fuehrer" and the party since 1925.

Pietzsch became Hess' economic adviser in 1934. As president of the Reich Economic Chamber since 1936, he held one of the highest positions in German economy. This position also involved him in armament planning long before the war. Pietzsch became a member of the Aufsichtsrat of the Deutsche Bank in 1939. Pietzsch himself described the background of this appointment in an interrogation as follows:

> Q. — Now Mr. Pietzsch—you were the head of the Reich Economic Chamber?
>
> A. —Yes.
>
> Q. — And you had very close ties with the National Socialist Party, didn't you?

A. — Yes.

Q. — You were appointed to certain positions in business, such as the board of directors of the Deutsche Bank because of your close ties with the party and your position in the governmental agency I have just mentioned.

A. — That is correct . . . .

Q. — . . . you were generally considered the link between the party and the bank?

A. — . . . I was taken in as the man who, in the opinion of the directorate, could speak with the party about the problems of the bank.

Mr. Pietzsch became vice-chairman of the board and of the important Working Committee. A more detailed sketch of Pietzsch is contained in a later chapter.

Emil Kreibich. Kreibich held the following political positions:

> Wehrwirtschaftsfuehrer
> Head of Heeres Kraftfahrpark Reichenberg (Army Motor Pool for the Reichenberg district, Sudetenland)
> Head of Chamber of Economics for Sudetenland
> Head of Industrial Department of the Chamber of Economics for Sudetenland
> Head of Foreign Trade Office for Sudetenland
> Head of District Group Sudetenland for the Trade Association for Cotton, Reichenberg
> Advisory Councillor of Reich Office for Cotton, Bremen
> Advisory Councillor of Reich Office for Cotton Yarns and Cotton Textiles, Bremen
> Advisory Councillor of the General Association for the Sudetenland (Schulze Delitsch), Inc.
> Advisory Councillor of Reich Chamber of Economics
> Member of Inner Advisory Council of the Reichsgruppe Industry
> Advisory Councillor of Reichsbank for Sudetenland District
> Advisory Councillor of Resettlement Association (Siedlungs- gesellschaft) Reichenberg
> Vice-President of the Southeast-Europe Association, Vienna, headed by Baldur von Schirach.

Kreibich also was the vice-chairman of the board of directors of the Boehmische Unionbank, Prague, and a member of the board of directors of the Creditanstalt Bankverein, Vienna, both subsidiaries of the Deutsche Bank.

Wilhelm Zangen. Zangen was appointed general manager of the Mannesmann combine by the men of the Deutsche Bank, who were shaping the policies of this worldwide enterprise.

Zangen had good connections with the Party, of which he was an official member. As head of the Reichsgruppe Industry, he had the most powerful position of control over German industry and industrial planning. As Rudolf Stahl, also a member of the Aufsichtsrat of the Deutsche Bank, was vice-president of this group, the link between industry and the Nazi government (Funk) was made up solely of members of the Aufsichtsrat of the Deutsche Bank, namely, Pietzsch, Zangen, and Stahl.

In 1942 the "Ruestungsrat" (Armament Council) was formed as an advisory body to the Speer Ministry. Its purpose was to establish even closer collaboration between the Ministry of Armaments and War Production, the armed forces and industry. Presided over by Speer himself, the council was composed of top-ranking officers of the armed forces, such as Generals Milch, Thomas, and Leeb, and a small select group of men representing industry. Among the latter was Wilhelm Zangen.

Zangen held the following additional political posts:

> Vice-president of Chamber of Economics (which Pietzsch headed)
> Vice-president of Chamber of Economics, Duesseldorf.

Zangen too was a member of Deutsche Bank's Working Committee.

Otto Fitzner. Fitzner was a high official of the NSDAP. He held the following political appointments:

> Gauwirtschaftsberater (Gau Economic Adviser—a position given only
>   to highly trusted Party members) of Lower Silesia
> Wehrwirtschaftsfuehrer
> President of Chamber of Commerce, Breslau
> Head of Wirtschaftsgruppe Metal Industry
> Head of Chamber of Economics for Lower Silesia, Breslau
> Advisory Councillor of Reich Economic Chamber.

Fitzner also was elected to the Working Committee of the Deutsche Bank.

VORSTAND

The old members of the Vorstand of the Deutsche Bank officially remained aloof from the Party. They agreed, however, to admit into the Vorstand three Party members and ardent disciples of Hitler, at least two of whom were men of prominence in the Party: von Halt was appointed in 1938; Hunke and Frowein in 1943.

Carl Ritter von Halt. With the admission of von Halt to the Vorstand, Deutsche Bank obtained the services of a man with deep roots and strong standing in the Nazi Party. According to the statement of von Halt's secretary, he had been a member of the Nazi Party since 1933 and had attained the high rank of "Oberfuehrer" (General) in the SA.

About von Halt's appointment, Hans Cesterlink, vice-chairman of the Aufsichtsrat, stated:

From 1934 I was a member of the Board of Directors. In 1938 von Halt was elected to the Board of Managers at their own free will because of his good connections with the Party. . . .

❑ ❑ ❑

The Party had every reason to consider von Halt "well placed" as the head of the Personnel Department of the largest German bank. His appointment to such a key position served to strengthen the ties of the bank with the Nazis.

Baron von Schroeder, the liaison man between big business and the Party, commented on von Halt's appointment as follows:

Q. — Was von Halt of the Deutsche Bank a strong Party man?

A. — Yes.

Q. — Did he have much influence in the Deutsche Bank?

A. — Yes. He devoted his time and interest largely to problems of organization and to the employees. In both of these activities he served the interest of the Party as well as the bank.

❑ ❑ ❑

Ritter von Halt was one of the members of the notorious "Freundeskreis der Wirtschaft beim Reichsfuehrer SS Himmler," the small circle of industrialists and bankers gathered around Keppler and Himmler. One of the functions of this circle was to solicit funds for Himmler. The contributions were collected annually and deposited in the "Special Account S" with the bank J. H. Stein, Cologne, of which SS General Baron Kurt von Schroeder was a partner. The Deutsche Bank annually, at least since 1939, contributed RM 75,000 to this fund, much more than any other German bank.

From the Annex to the Report

Von Halt in 1937 was invited by the Reichsfuehrer SS to inspect the concentration camp at Dachau. Von Halt and the other Circle members under the guidance of Heinrich Himmler and SS Obergruppenfuehrer Pohl inspected the SS factories and installations during the time that the concentration camp prisoners were at work. In 1939 v. Halt and the other "Freundeskreis" members paid a similar visit, under the guidance of Heinrich Himmler, SS Obergruppenfuehrer Karl Wolff and SS Obergruppenfuehrer Pohl, to the concentration camp at Oranienburg.

❑ ❑ ❑

Heinrich Hunke. In 1943, shortly after the formation of the Martin Bormann Committee on Banking, it named Heinrich Hunke to its Vorstand.

Bormann, head of the Party Chancellery and chief "Wirtschaftspolitiker" (economic policy maker of the Party), was keenly interested in the Nazification of German business, and had launched an intensive drive in this direction in 1941. In 1943 the head of the Party's Economics Department, Froehling, set up a Committee on Banking under Bormann.

According to von Schroeder, there were about twelve members on this committee. All of them were "Gauwirtschaftsberater" (regional economic advisers), the Party representatives who acted as deputies and advisers to the Gauleiter in the execution of general Nazi policy and specifically of Aryanization in their regions.

Hunke was a member of the Martin Bormann Banking Committee. As Gauwirtschaftsberater of Berlin, he was the most important of them all. When he was placed on the Vorstand of the biggest bank in Germany, the mutual benefits inuring to the Nazi Party and to the Deutsche Bank were huge. The only other link the bank had with the committee was Walter Rafelsberger, an Aufsichtsrat member of its Austrian subsidiary, the Creditanstalt Bankverein, Wien.

Hunke was not much of a banker, technically. Hans Pilder, Dresdner Bank Vorstand member, says Hunke:

> joined the Deutsche Bank in 1943; supposedly an authority on economics, he had no banking background, and his entry into the Deutsche Bank was sponsored by the Party.

Soon after Hunke's appointment to the Vorstand, he became a member of the Advisory Board of the Reichsbank where he, together with [Hermann] Abs, represented the Deutsche Bank and could exercise his influence for the benefit of the bank.[1] Before he was appointed to the Deutsche Bank, Hunke had shown how a Gauwirtschaftsberater could manage to use his official function with respect to Aryanizations for his own personal enrichment. In 1938 or 1939 he acquired the controlling interest in the Jewish-owned Erste Berliner Rosshaar Fabrik, and in order to finance this acquisition obtained a loan of RM 100,000 from one of the big Berlin banks.

---

[1] Hunke was well-established as a Nazi politician. In addition to the powerful position of Gauwirtschaftsberater, he held the following political posts:

> Hauptlektor der Parteiamtlichen Pruefungskommission zum Schutze des N.S. Schrifttums (Chief Lecturer of the Official Party Examination Committee for the Protection of National Socialist Literature)

> Leiter der Auslandsabteilung im Reichsministerium fuer Volksaufklaerung und Propaganda (Head of Foreign Department in Goebbels' Propaganda Ministry)

> Member of Gesamtvorstand der deutschen Handelskammer in Uebersee (Board of Managers of the German Chamber of Commerce Overseas)

Robert Frowein. By appointing Robert Frowein to the Vorstand in 1943, the Deutsche Bank redeemed a promise given Reich Minister Funk to supplement the Vorstand with another Party member in addition to Hunke. Funk had consented that the new man need not be an outsider but might be drawn from the ranks of Deutsche Bank's staff if he met with the Party's approval. The Deutsche Bank chose Frowein who until then had been the head of the bank's Frankfurt branch. The Party approved. Frowein was given regional supervision over the bank's business in Silesia.

The old members of the Vorstand, who kept out of Party limelight, nevertheless managed to maintain excellent connections with leading Nazis and were entrusted with positions as confidential advisers to government committees. In these positions, they contributed their knowledge of finance and their experience in banking and offered the many domestic and foreign connections which were at the disposal of the Deutsche Bank. The Deutsche Bank received ample compensation in return. Even the fractional evidence uncovered, without access to the bank's records and without interrogation of the two most important Vorstand members, Hermann Abs and Oswald Roesler, shows close cooperation between the Deutsche Bank and the Nazi controlled German government. Baron Kurt von Schroeder, head of the Fachgruppe Private Banking, gave recognition to this close cooperation in saying:

> They (the banks) had a very powerful influence with the Party and with the Government. The big banks were consulted by the Party and the Government, which was dominated by the Party, on every economic and financial question that arose. In fact, the officials of the big banks would be consulted on practically every issue by the Reichsbank and other Government officials and very often what they said was considered the last word on the subject. Men like Abs, Roesler, Kimmich, and Urbig of the Deutsche Bank were continuously consulted by Government and Party leaders; . . . In the last few years the relations between the big banks and the Party were strengthened even further by the appointment of important Party men to the Vorstand of these banks.

Because of his phenomenal rise to prominence within the Vorstand, Hermann Abs' political connections deserve closer attention.

Hermann J. Abs. Until 31 December 1937, Abs was a partner of Delbrueck, Schickler & Co., a well-known private banking house in Berlin. It was a favorite of the Nazi leaders, and Hitler, Rosenberg, and the former chief of the Gestapo, Daluege, kept their personal accounts with it.

Upon Gustav Schlieper's death in 1937, Eduard Mosler, then speaker of the Vorstand of Deutsche Bank, invited Abs to take Schlieper's place in the Vorstand, and especially to take charge of the bank's foreign business. Perhaps Hjalmar Schacht, who knew Abs personally and had much confidence in his ability, first suggested the appointment of Abs to Mr. Mosler. Mosler, as "primus inter pares" of the bank's Vorstand, had frequent contact with Schacht as he represented the Deutsche Bank in its dealing with the Ministry of Economics and the Reichsbank.

Within a short time after his entry into the Vorstand of the Deutsche Bank on 1 January 1938, Hermann J. Abs became the bank's brilliant and most energetic member. He also became the bank's most adept contact man in its dealings with the Reich government. Together with Hunke he represented the bank in the advisory council of the Reichsbank.

Abs' influence with the government was described as "tremendous" by von Schroeder, who was a specialist in watching over relations between big business and the political powers. Von Schroeder further said:

> His [Abs'] influence was mainly with the Reichsbank and with the Ministry of Economics. Abs proved very valuable to the Party and to the Government by using his bank to assist the Government in doing business in the occupied countries and in other foreign countries. Abs enjoyed excellent relations with Funk, who was both president of the Reichsbank and head of the Ministry of Economics in recent years.

Abs' importance in German economy was so great that both Hjalmar Schacht and Walter Funk independently stated that "Abs from the Deutsche Bank" was one of the few men in Germany who might be able to clarify for the Allied authorities some of Germany's past financial operations.

Abs acted as the representative of the German economy as a whole in international negotiations. He played an important part in Germany's conferences regarding the Standstill Agreement. He discussed these problems with Schacht and Funk as early as 1937 (before he entered Deutsche Bank) and was asked to represent Germany in her negotiations with foreign creditors in December 1937. In the spring of 1938, Schacht sent Abs to London. He carefully briefed Abs as to the arguments he was to use in advancing the German case in the Standstill negotiations, and Abs was perfectly willing to present these arguments as facts regardless of his own belief in their veracity, although Abs has since admitted that he doubted at the time that Germany held only RM 77 million in gold. But he freely used this figure as a statement of fact in arguing that the foreign exchange position of the Reichsbank did not allow it to repay certain credits which according to the agreement had to be repaid at that time in foreign exchange.

It is now known that Germany's actual gold holdings at the time amounted to RM 500 million in 1937.

Abs was also consulted by Schacht about the "New Order" of the Austrian economy in connection with the annexation of Austria by Germany which was then in the making.

But Abs' principal activities concerned the foreign operations of the Deutsche Bank, which are discussed in a later chapter. The spectacular expansion of Deutsche Bank's own interest in foreign countries as well as its participation in the German penetration into foreign industries had the consent and sponsorship of the Nazi authorities.

Emil Puhl, vice-president of the Reichsbank, has stated that Abs' personal standing in leading government circles was the reason why "the competent government officials favored to a great extent the expansion of the Deutsche Bank."

Abs himself admits that the government, and Funk in particular, instructed the bank "to buy certain foreign securities which were to the interest of Germany."

Abs reciprocated the favors bestowed upon him and his bank by taking an active part in various economic committees and circles established by the Nazis.[2]

Abs was on the board of directors of some of the most important industrial and financial organizations in Germany and in countries dominated or occupied by the Nazis. Abs held more than 40 directorships during 1941–42.

Abs' compliance with the pattern of the government's internal and foreign operations was reflected in his personal affairs as well. His confidential secretary and assistant was SS-man Ulrich (now in British custody). He actively participated in the Aryanization of the firm Adler and Oppenheimer. By personal acquisition of former Jewish property, he became an even more direct beneficiary of the Nazi regime. Part of the briquette works of the Czech Petschek family were acquired by the Abs family after their sequestration and Aryanization though the major part of the other Petschek properties was incorporated into the huge combine built up under Nazi protection by Goering's friend Friedrich Flick.

Nazification of affiliates. The foreign subsidiaries and affiliates of Deutsche Bank, which were Abs' primary responsibility, were also in step with the "Coordination" movement initiated in the Reich. As the most important one of the subsidiaries in the countries overrun by the Nazis, the Creditanstalt Bankverein, Vienna, has been

---

[2] Some of them are listed here:

Beirat fuer Auslandswirtschaft (Advisory Council for Foreign Economy of the federations of commerce and industry). This organization was founded by Funk in 1944.

Handelspolitischer Ausschuss der Reichswirtschaftskammer (Trade Policy Committee of the Reich Chamber of Economics). Former Secretary of State Dr. Trendelenburg was the chairman of this committee, which was established before 1941, under Pietzsch's Reichswirtschaftskammer.

Mittel-Europaeischer Wirtschaftstag (Central European Economic Council). It was founded sometime before 1940. I.G. Farben's Max Ilgner became vice-president of the board of directors of this clandestine committee which was generously supported by industry and finance.

Committee headed by President Kehrl of RWM. On 8 May 1944, this committee invited Abs (and Aufsichtsrat members Reemtsma and Schmid) to a meeting. The letter of invitation contains the following language:

> Mr. President Kehrl expressed the desire that our work will be carried out in this direction, finding for each individual country some qualified personalities with whom problems concerning the leadership of production and economy on a universal European base can be discussed currently. . . . We intended to invite such personalities to the Reich to have discussions here with leading persons concerning economy problems.

Leading personalities invited included steel magnate Hugo Stinnes, Secretary of State Lindemann, Major Momm from the rearmament office, Dr. Koester from the planning department, Dr. E. R. Fischer from the raw material department, etc.

selected as an illustration. Its Aufsichtsrat too was staffed on the principle of maximum utilization of political contacts and connections.[3]

As to the Vorstand, unlike in the case of Deutsche Bank, no effort was made in the Creditanstalt Bankverein to present an appearance of continuity of management. In the years following the "Anschluss," the Vorstand was almost entirely restaffed. Three Party members, Hans Friedl, Ludwig Fritscher, and Rudolph Pfeiffer, were

---

[3] Following are the political affiliations, as far as ascertained, of some of the members of the Aufsichtsrat of the Creditanstalt Bankverein:

Dr. Alfred Olscher
  Ministerialdirektor in the Reich Ministry of Finance (on leave to Reichskredit-
    Gesellschaft)
  Vice-chairman of the Court of Honor of the German Economy (Stellvertretender Vorsitzer
    des Ehrengerichtshofs der Deutschen Wirtschaft)
Prof. Dr. Ing. Arnim Dadieu
  Regional Captain and Chief of Regional Office of Steiermark, Graz (Gauhauptmann und
    Gauhauptamtsleiter)
Karl Gerland
  Commissioner of the State (Staatskommissar)
  Minister of Agriculture
  Chief of Group for Nutrition and Agriculture with Reich Protector for Bohemia and
    Moravia (Leiter der Gruppe Ernaehrung und Landwirtschaft beim Reichsprotektor
    fuer Boehmen und Maehren, Prag)
Franz Langoth
  Member of the German Reichstag
  Head of Gau Office, Linz on the Danube (Gauamtsleiter)
Dipl. Ing. Walter Rafelsberger
  Gauwirtschaftsberater (cf. above)
  City Councillor of the Municipal Administration of the Reich Gau of Vienna
  Member of the Bormann Committee on the "Reform of Banking" (see above)
Dr. mont. h.c. Philipp von Schoeller
  Alderman of the City of Vienna
  President of the Regional Chamber of Economics (Gauwirtschaftskammer), Vienna
  Member of Reich Chamber of Labor (Reichsarbeitskammer), Berlin
  Advisory Councillor of Reichsgruppe Industry, Berlin
  Advisory Councillor of Wirtschaftsgruppe for Iron Manufacturing Industry, Berlin
  Advisory Councillor of Bezirksgruppe Southeast of Wirtschaftsgruppe for Iron Producing
    Industry, Vienna
Max Ilgner
  Head of I.G. Farbenindustrie's N.W. 7 Office, which acted as an economic espionage
    agency for the Wehrmacht (cf. I.G. Farben report to Kilgore Committee)
  Advisory Councillor of the German Group of the International Chamber of Commerce,
    Berlin
  Vice-President of the Central European Economic Council, German Group
    (Mitteleuropaeischer Wirtschaftstag, Deutsche Gruppe)
Dr. h.c. Ing. Karl Innerebner
  Head of Chamber of Economics (Wirtschaftskammer) Alpenland
  President of Chamber of Industry and Commerce for Tyrol, Innsbruck
  Holder of Knight's Cross of the F.J.O. (Ritterkreuz des FJO)
Hermann Rhomberg
  Vice-President of the Chamber of Economics (Gauwirtschaftskammer)
  The chairman of the Aufsichtsrat was Franz Hasslacher, member of the Nazi Party, who
    also was on the Working Committee of the Deutsche Bank.

appointed, and a fourth one, Richard Buzzi, was made chairman of the Vorstand upon the specific joint recommendation of Gauwirtschaftsberater Rafelsberger and the Deutsche Bank. Josef Joham was the only hold-over from the old Vorstand who remained throughout the years. He was "acceptable" to the Nazis. That a "New Order" was put into effect in a similar fashion in the bank's other affiliates throughout German-controlled Europe can be taken for granted.

❏ ❏ ❏

ACCOUNTS OF POLITICAL SIGNIFICANCE

It would be revealing to go through the books of the bank and to determine how many high Nazi dignitaries and organizations kept their accounts with it. Goering knew very well that by placing his account with a certain bank he was committing a political act and putting his stamp of approval upon the institution. Even without access to the books, a few accidental bits of intelligence have produced the following wholly incomplete list of accounts maintained with the Deutsche Bank:

Individuals
Hermann Goering
Field Marshall Keitel
Foreign Minister Ribbentrop
Reich Minister and Head of the Reich Chancery Lammers
Reichsleiter Alfred Rosenberg
Air Force General K. H. Bodenschatz (chief of staff to Goering)
Chief of the Reich Press Dietrich
Staatsrat Gritzbach (head of Goering's "Stabsamt")

Associations
Reichswirtschaftskammer
Reichsleitung der NSDAP (head office of the Nazi Party)
Bund der Auslandsdeutschen (cf. above)
Deutsch-Weltwirtschaftliche Gesellschaft e.V. (cf. above)
Reichskolonialbund (cf. above)

❏ ❏ ❏

From the Annex to the Report

Political Contributions

On 27 May 1933 representatives of the Berlin Big Six Banks assembled to discuss the collection of a large fund for political purposes. Although the other banks were represented by a single member each, the Deutsche Bank had two representatives in attendance, Dr. Mosler and Dr. Abshagen. Dr. Mosler acted as chairman and informed his colleagues that it was planned to raise from industry the sum of RM 25 million and from credit institutions RM 5 million. A partial payment of RM 6 million, in addition, was to be prefinanced before the end of August 1933, and a syndicate under the leadership of the Deutsche Bank was to finance an advance payment of RM 2 million from industry. The loan syndicate was not to engage in operations unless the plans received the approval of the highest political leaders. To this end, Otto Christian Fischer of the RKG and Friedrich Reinhart of the Commerzbank were instructed by the syndicate to consult with Rudolf Hess so as to determine whether the enterprise would receive the personal endorsement of Hitler.

By the beginning of June 1933, all contributions to the Party from the German economy were coordinated into the "Adolf Hitler Spende der Deutschen Wirtschaft" (Adolf Hitler Fund of the German Economy). The Central Organization of German Banking, on 6 June 1933, informed the Deutsche Bank that for the period 1 June 1933–31 May 1934 it was expected to contribute to the fund the sum of RM 141,084.

The document proceeds to state that:

> The management of the Fund is in the hands of a Kuratorium which is composed of representatives of the participating branches of the economy.

> We emphasize particularly that information is not to be given to the Press (underscoring copied from original text).

The Deutsche Bank's contribution increased in 1934 to RM 160,000 and continued to grow until in 1942–1943 it came to RM 325,000. Mosler was already a member of the Kuratorium in 1935 and may have received the post even earlier.

The RM 75,000 contributed each year to the Himmler group has already been discussed in connection with Ritter von Halt.

❑ ❑ ❑

All contributions of any size to the Party and other political organizations required the approval of the entire Vorstand. The important annual contribution to the SS fund, which has been mentioned, was dispatched with a letter of transmittal signed by two Vorstand members, usually von Halt, the sponsor of the arrangement, and Hans Rummel. All the members of the Vorstand not only knew of the bank's large contributions to Himmler's SS-fund, to the Adolf Hitler Fund, and to other agencies which served the Nazi Party at home and abroad. They approved of these contributions. They were accomplices in the growth and strengthening of Nazi power.

CHAPTER VII

Influence and Control over Domestic Financial Institutions

The Deutsche Bank controlled or influenced a considerable number of other financial institutions in Germany. To the extent [that] these institutions were not established and owned by the bank, they were brought into its sphere of influence through capital participations or simply through services the most powerful among the German commercial banks was able to render. The Deutsche Bank's influence found its expression in the delegation of one or more of the bank's officials into the Aufsichtsrat of the institution in question. The importance of interlocking directorships as a measure of control and influence over industry will be fully discussed [later in] this report. Exchange of directors between the bank and financial institutions, or the unilateral delegation of bank officials to the boards of financial institutions, as a rule presupposed an even greater mutuality of interests, primarily because of the homogeneous and complementary nature of the two businesses. In this connection directorships held by Deutsche Bank officials in financial institutions in which the bank had only a small or no capital participation assume added significance. An outstanding example of this is the bank's ties to mortgage bond institutions.

Financial institutions in the Deutsche Bank sphere of influence, excepting a small number which served the financial community as a whole and which are omitted from this discussion even if the Deutsche Bank held a certain capital participation or maintained directorships in them, are grouped as follows:

> Local commercial banks
> Regional commercial banks
> Banks for overseas operations
> Mortgage bond institutions
> Insurance companies
> Holding companies
> Financing companies
> Special administrative companies

LOCAL COMMERCIAL BANKS

The three banks in this category are located in the Rhineland. They are subsidiaries whose names and outward independence were continued. They have the character of medium-size branches of the bank.

J. Wichelhaus P. Sohn A.G., Elberfeld. The entire capital of RM 1.5 million of this bank is in the possession of the Deutsche Bank.

❑ ❑ ❑

C. G. Trinkaus, Duesseldorf. The Deutsche Bank participates with RM 345,000 in the capital of RM 2 million.

❑ ❑ ❑

Burkhardt & Co., Essen. This bank was founded in 1938 to take over the Aryanized banking firm of Simon Hirschland. The Deutsche Bank participated with RM 2.5 million in the capital of RM 6.5 million. Control was established through its financing the paid-in capital of the two personally liable partners, that of Dr. Freiherr von Falkenhausen, a former branch manager of the Deutsche Bank, in the amount of RM 500,000, and part of the capital participation of Mr. Burkhardt, amounting to over RM 250,000. In addition the Deutsche Bank acquired a RM 250,000 participation which had been sold by one of the other founding firms.

REGIONAL COMMERCIAL BANKS

Niederlausitzer Bank A.G., Cottbus. The Deutsche Bank participates with RM 231,000 in the RM 2.2 million capital of this bank, mainly serving the textile industry in the Lausitz area.

❑ ❑ ❑

Mecklenburgische Depositen- und Wechselbank, Schwerin. The Deutsche Bank exercises the controlling influence with a participation of RM 900,000 in the RM 3 million capital together with the state of Mecklenburg, which holds RM 1 million.

❑ ❑ ❑

Allgemeine Deutsche Creditanstalt, Leipzig (Adca). . . . Close relationship was maintained by the Deutsche Bank, although it did not hold a capital participation in the Adca. For important financing operations the Adca resorted to the Deutsche Bank who in turn enabled the Adca to participate in loan and securities syndicates.

The leading manager of the Adca, Dr. Ernst Schoen von Wildenegg, was a member of the Deutsche Bank board of directors and Fritz Wintermantel, a Deutsche Bank manager, was on the board of directors of the Adca. Rudolf Stahl was a common director of both institutions.

❑ ❑ ❑

BANKS FOR OVERSEAS OPERATIONS

Two Deutsche Bank affiliates were engaged in banking operations in the Far East.

The Deutsch-Asiatische Bank, Shanghai-Berlin. Founded in 1889 under the leadership of the Disconto-Gesellschaft for the financing of German trade in Asia; it was fully controlled by the Deutsche Bank after its merger with the Disconto-Gesellschaft.

The Deutsche Bank fuer Ostasien, Berlin. Founded in 1942 to handle all banking transactions in connection with the German-Japanese trade agreement of 1941. Thus during the short period of its existence its operations were primarily of a governmental nature. Deutsche Bank leadership in this bank was personified in Hermann J. Abs who became chairman of its Aufsichtsrat.

THE DEUTSCHE UEBERSEEISCHE BANK, BERLIN (DUB)

Deutsche Bank subsidiary founded in 1886. Incorporated in Germany and endowed with a capital of RM 36 million, it was the largest and most influential German bank for South America and Spain with a total of twenty-one branches in these countries. The bank received a severe blow in 1942, when Brazil, Peru, and Uruguay broke off relations with the Axis powers. . . . In the succeeding years the branches in Brazil, Argentina, Chile, and Peru were liquidated upon orders of the respective governments. According to a newspaper report of October 1945, the three branches in Spain continued operating, but under increased supervision.

The DUB properties in Spain and the proceeds from the liquidation of the South American branches constitute important German external assets. A detailed statement in this connection was made by Albrecht Seeger, a former manager of the DUB, according to which working capital and reserves of the branches in Spain represent German property equivalent to about $2,200,000, whereas about $12,400,000 resulting from the liquidation of the South American branches are held by the respective South American governments.

MORTGAGE BOND INSTITUTIONS

The German commercial banks with but few exceptions were excluded from the field of mortgage banking by law. However, Deutsche Bank influence on mortgage banks has always been considerable due to its outstanding placement power of mortgage bonds. The Deutsche Bank was affiliated with thirteen of the twenty-six German incorporated mortgage banks through stock ownership and/or interlocking directorships.

Hans Oesterlink [to name only one example], was the leading manager of the Deutsche Centralbodenkredit A.G., which was by far the largest German mortgage bond institution . . . and at the same time a leading figure in the Deutsche Bank, occupying the position of vice-chairman of the board of directors.

❑ ❑ ❑

INSURANCE COMPANIES

The Deutsche Bank maintained close relationships with a number of the most important German insurance companies. While participating in the capital of only one company, the bank's executives were delegated to the Aufsichtsrat of twenty-two additional insurance companies. There was a great community of interest between the Deutsche Bank and these companies; the bank was in a position to direct substantial business to its insurance friends, whereas the latter kept considerable funds on deposit with the bank and made extensive use of other banking services.

HOLDING COMPANIES

Of the four companies in this group, three were subsidiaries of the Deutsche Bank and served to conceal assets of the bank or its customers. Operations of the two institutions fulfilling these functions abroad are discussed in greater detail in a later chapter.

A.G. fuer Vermoegensverwertung. This corporation was founded in 1911 for the financing of building companies. Equipped with a capital of RM 1.2 million, it is a wholly owned subsidiary of the Deutsche Bank. By the 1930s it began to be employed as a straw man in securities transactions, and became the Deutsche Bank's agency for the cloaking of its own and customers' holdings of securities in foreign countries at the outbreak of war.

Export-Kreditbank A.G., Berlin. This corporation was founded by the Deutsche Bank together with its main foreign subsidiary, the Deutsche Ueberseeische Bank, and the Allgemeine Deutsche Creditanstalt (see above), in September 1939. In the capital of RM 1 million, the Deutsche Bank participated with 70 percent, the DUB with 20 percent, and the Adca with 10 percent. The purpose of the new bank was the concealing of foreign credit balances and deposits to safeguard them from attachment or seizure abroad. In addition it developed into the main agency for the liquidation of Poland's foreign trade balances. In December 1939, the RWM (Reich Ministry of Economics) commissioned the Export-Kreditbank to collect all claims of German exporters against firms in the part of Poland which had been taken over by Russia and in the part which had been annexed by Germany. Even exporters in neutral countries used the bank to collect their claims in Poland. Upon instructions of the *Haupt-Treuhandstelle Ost*, in charge of confiscated Polish enterprises, the

Export-Kreditbank in turn collected Polish export claims in neutral countries. The bank, however, still holds about RM 15 million, collected in Poland for the account of American, British, and French exporters. Total assets of the bank as of 31 December 1944 amounted to RM 22.2 million, consisting mainly of short-term advances to credit institutions (RM 16.3 million) and accounts receivable (RM 5.2 million). Georg Graf von der Goltz was the leading personality in the Export-Kreditbank until 1943 when he became the Deutsche Bank representative in Sweden.

Bank fuer Industriewerte G.m.b.H. (formerly A.G.). A general agent of the Deutsche Bank, Dr. J. Kessler, was chairman of the bank's board of directors. In later years the bank was used exclusively as a securities holding company. It held preferred stock with special voting privileges and blocks of shares of industrial corporations, close to the participating banks.

Allgemeine Transportmittel Finanzierungs A.G., Berlin. The Deutsche Bank participated with 11.4 percent in the capital of RM 4.2 million. Other blocks of the capital were held by the Berliner Handelsgesellschaft and Belgian financial institutions. It is a holding company for participations in the transportation field. It owns over 25 percent of the capital of the Eisenbahnverkehrsmittel A.G.

FINANCING COMPANIES

The Deutsche Bank participated in the few companies developed in Germany to finance the marketing of such durable goods as agricultural machines, tractors, and trucks. Volume of the companies discussed became insignificant during the last years of the war after reaching a peak around 1939/40.

Finanzierungsgesellschaft fuer Landmaschinen A.G., Berlin. . . . The Deutsche Bank participation was 12 percent. The company held a 26.1 percent participation in the [following company].

Finanzierungsgesellschaft fuer Industrielieferungen A.G. (Maschinenbank), Berlin. This company, established in 1928, concentrated on the financing of heavy trucks and specialized equipment. The Deutsche Bank shared with 30 percent in the RM 1 million capital.

Gefi G.m.b.H., Berlin. This company was a sole venture of the Deutsche Bank into the field of financing purchases on the installment plan. . . .

Deutsche Beamten-Zentralbank G.m.b.H., Berlin. This institution does not strictly belong to the group of financing companies. It was founded in 1922 [for] granting loans to civil servants, particularly in the lower brackets. The Deutsche Bank acquired a 76 percent participation in the RM 500,000 capital in 1930. . . . The Nazi regime absorbed [it] into the "Reichsbund der Deutschen Beamten." . . . Customers' deposits with the company were guaranteed by the Deutsche Bank.

SPECIAL ADMINISTRATIVE COMPANIES

The Deutsche Bank founded eleven different companies in Berlin with a total capital of RM 2,521,500 for the purpose of administering its own and customers' real estate holdings. . . . The two auditing companies controlled by the Deutsche Bank also acted as trustees or custodians of customers' properties.

Deutsche Treuhand-Gesellschaft, Berlin. The Deutsche Bank holds 46 percent of the RM 2.4 million capital and the Berliner Handelsgesellschaft about RM 100,000. . . .

Schwaebische Treuhand A.G., Stuttgart. The Deutsche Bank holds a 49 percent participation in the capital of RM 800,000. Its Stuttgart branch manager was a member of the company's board of directors.

CHAPTER VIII

Influence and Control over Industry

It has always been axiomatic to say that the Grossbanken wielded a decisive influence in German industry. Some observers prefer to speak of the "control" of the German banks over the most important sectors of German industry. The terminology is really of little importance since there are instances of varying degrees, from an intimacy of relations barely transgressing normal bank-customer relationships, to a hand-in-glove collaboration in which the influence is a more or less mutual one, to instances of practically complete control by the bank over certain industrial complexes. There is also general agreement among those familiar with German finance that the bank with the most solidly entrenched and most far-flung industrial connections and ties was the Deutsche Bank. In this respect, the Deutsche Bank had a lead far out of proportion with its position as Germany's largest bank measured in terms of general size. In other words, the Deutsche Bank was a "specialist" in the field of industrial relations and influence on industrial combines. The purpose of this chapter is to show by facts and illustrations that these general beliefs are not a mere myth or fiction and to explain some of the means used to establish and maintain the bank's influence in the industrial life of Germany.

It will be found that the extent of its hold on German industry coupled with the weight of its own importance as a bank, the vastness of its resources and of its branch network, made the Deutsche Bank easily the greatest concentration of economic power among German banks and one of the outstanding examples of concentration of economic power in the whole German economy.

MEANS OF INFLUENCE OR CONTROL

The instruments employed to secure a bank's influence in industrial enterprises include interlocking directorships, proxy voting of stock, stock ownership, securities trading, and syndicate operations. They are, of course, coextensive, and it is not uncommon for all of the elements named to exist between the bank and one of its "industrial friends." They must, however, be considered separately.

INTERLOCKING DIRECTORSHIPS

The most important single element of influence or control probably is that of personal ties in the form of interlocking directorships. In saying "the most important," reference must be made to what has been said about the coextensiveness of the elements of influence. Obviously an Aufsichtsrat membership does not arise out of a vacuum. It must be preceded by some form of relationship, be it the extension of considerable loan facilities or the existence of a substantial voting power. Nevertheless, it is only through representation on the Aufsichtsrat that a high degree of influence is attained, and no corporation will be found to be "within the sphere of influence" of a bank without the existence of one or more interlocking directorships. The presence of more than one representative of one bank on an industrial board of directors is invariably a sign of very strong influence and often of control, and so is the occupancy of the chairmanship by an official of the bank. Interlocking directorship relations run in both directions but the mutuality is obviously limited: the bank sends its representatives to the boards of a multitude of industrial corporations, but it can accommodate only its most intimate and most important industrial "relatives" on its own Aufsichtsrat.

The number of positions in other corporations held by the top personalities of Deutsche Bank is charted in Table VI. It covers the members of the Vorstand, the Aufsichtsrat, and the General Agents (Direktoren der Bank) who form the management level directly below the Vorstand. Their interlocking positions add up to the impressive total of 707. Yet the chart gives but an inadequate picture of the spread of the bank's influence through this method alone. First, it is based on incomplete data since smaller corporations were generally not listed in the sources available, and the bank's Secretariat records, which alone could furnish complete data, were not accessible. Second, officials below the levels charted, i.e., branch managers, department heads, held an additional sizable number of directorships (see below). Third, organizations other than *Aktien-Gesellschaften* (corporations), such as G.m.b.H.s and *Kommanditgesellschaften,* are not completely covered. The chart, nevertheless, shows 197 directorships held by the 11 Deutsche Bank Vorstand members and the chairman of the Aufsichtsrat, a former prominent Vorstand member. [There are at least] 194 enterprises on whose boards of directors there was at least one Vorstand member of the Deutsche Bank. In 76 of these cases the Deutsche Bank men were chairmen or vice-chairmen of the board. These surely were not routine or courtesy positions. The chairman of the Aufsichtsrat in particular exercises supervision over the major policies of the company and often over the minor ones as well, as is evidenced by correspondence files maintained by Hans Rummel, Vorstand member of Deutsche Bank, in connection with his chairmanship of Daimler and Bayerische Motoren Werke. These files contain correspondence concerning the minutest details of the company's affairs, on which the chairman was regularly consulted.

Hans Rummel himself, who has been interrogated, occupied Aufsichtsrat positions in 18 corporations, in a number of which he admitted to "having taken active interest." . . .

Of the general agents' 182 Aufsichtsrat mandates, 72 are chairmanships and vice-chairmanships. The members of the Deutsche Bank Aufsichtsrat, on the other hand, are managers of 31 industrial corporations, among them I.G. Farben, Mannesmann, Rheinisch-Westfaelisches Elektrizitaetswerk, Hoesch, and Rheinische Braunkohlen. They further maintained 297 interlocking directorships in other corporations, in 164 cases as chairmen or vice-chairmen.

Aufsichtsrat membership of a Deutsche Bank official was not his personal affair—it was strictly the bank's business. No member of the Vorstand or any other employee was permitted to accept a position on any board of directors without express

Table VI
DEUTSCHE BANK—NUMBER OF POSITIONS HELD BY DEUTSCHE BANK MANAGERS AND DIRECTORS IN OTHER CORPORATIONS BY TYPE OF BUSINESS.*

Deutsche Bank position / Position with other corporations	Management and chairman of board of directors (12 persons)				Member of board of directors (30 persons)				General agents** (14 persons)				TOTAL
	Manager	Board of directors — Chairman, Vice-Chairman	Board of directors — Member	Board of directors — Total	Manager	Board of directors — Chairman, Vice-Chairman	Board of directors — Member	Board of directors — Total	Manager	Board of directors — Chairman, Vice-Chairman	Board of directors — Member	Board of directors — Total	
TYPE OF BUSINESS													
Banking, finance	–	3	9	12	3	5	15	23	–	6	5	11	46
Banking, foreign	–	8	6	14	–	–	2	2	–	–	2	2	18
Insurance	–	–	10	10	1	13	15	29	–	–	10	10	49
Coal, mining, petroleum	–	3	22	25	2	19	19	40	2	4	9	15	80
Iron, steel, metals	–	6	14	20	2	7	7	16	–	4	7	11	47
Machinery, metal, products	–	15	7	22	2	14	22	38	–	12	16	28	88
Aircraft	–	7	–	7	1	2	2	5	–	–	–	–	12
Electrical	–	3	4	7	1	4	6	11	–	–	1	1	19
Chemicals, rubber	–	4	11	15	1	11	10	22	–	1	5	6	43
Textiles, paper	–	6	6	12	7	20	14	41	–	15	8	23	76
Food, beverages	–	3	6	9	–	2	6	8	–	6	13	19	36
Construction, building materials	–	3	5	8	1	1	1	3	–	7	7	14	25
Transport, communication public utilities	–	4	10	14	1	16	27	44	–	7	9	16	74
Commercial, service, trade	–	1	4	5	–	6	7	13	1	2	3	6	24
Misc.	–	10	7	17	9	13	11	33	1	8	11	20	70
Total	–	76	121	197	31	133	164	328	4	72	106	182	707

Source: OMGUS, Finance Division, Financial Intelligence & Liaison Branch, 15 May 1946.

**Direktoren der Bank mit Generalvollmacht fuer saemtliche Niederlassungen.

permission of the Deutsche Bank Vorstand. The reason for this rule was, as Hans Rummel expressed it, that

> membership of any employee on a board of directors meant a moral responsibility of the bank, and the public came to think in such cases that the Deutsche Bank would look after things in that corporation.

Hence when the corporation law of 1937 limited the number of Aufsichtsrat mandates any one individual could hold to twenty (with certain exceptions to be granted by the competent Reich ministry), it was the bank's affair and the bank met the challenge. It met the challenge by redistributing the directorships of its Vorstand members, many of whom had more than the permissible numbers and by passing the excess mandates down to junior officials—to the Direktoren der Bank (general agents), and more frequently, to the branch managers. Some industrial corporations did not like this down grading of the Deutsche Bank representation on their Aufsichtsrat, but, as Hermann Kaiser, one of the Deutsche Bank's general agents, expressed it, "since the law made redistribution necessary, it had to be done." The men of Deutsche Bank never even considered the possibility of an actual reduction of the total directorships held by the bank. It was too important to hold on to all of them. Some positions were too important even to be delegated to anyone less than a Vorstand member, particularly those involving the bank's acquisitions in Austria. The bank, therefore, obtained governmental permission for Oswald Roesler and Hermann J. Abs to retain, at least for the duration of the war, directorships in excess of the legal limit.

The men of Deutsche Bank knew that each directorship meant a position of influence. They knew that their accumulation meant a position of tremendous power for the bank as an institution.

They also knew, though they are not so ready to recall it, that a place on an Aufsichtsrat means a responsibility as well, that it is membership in the highest policy-making and supervisory body of a corporation, in the body which alone has the power to hire and fire the executive officers of the corporation. This is a point which cannot be ignored in assessing the responsibility of the officials of the bank.

PROXY VOTING

Of course, the voting of corporate stock is the most important, or, theoretically, the only means of ultimate control of a corporation. Since this power, the vote of the share of stock, is exercised at only infrequent intervals, it is not quite so important as the continuing personal influence that is implied in interlocking directorships. It is nevertheless the indispensable means of securing and maintaining directorships. And, in Germany, the banks have for many years been the biggest stock voters. In fact, the largest blocks of stock voted in all industrial enterprises of any substantial size, with the possible exception of family-controlled businesses, were almost invariably voted by the banks. This stock voting strength of the banks derives almost exclusively from the practice of proxy voting. As will be seen later, outright ownership is an insignificant factor.

The Deutsche Bank voted the largest blocks of shares of the largest industrial giants in Germany, some of them the largest in the world. It voted 38 percent of the total stock voted in I.G. Farben, the largest chemical combine in the world; 19 percent in Vereinigte Stahlwerke, the largest iron and steel concern in Europe; 28 percent in AEG and probably well over 20 percent in Siemens & Halske, the two largest electrical cartels in Germany; and sizable blocks in Rheinisch-Westfaelisches Elektrizitaetswerk, one of the largest public utility trusts. The following table [Table VII] contains detailed information on capitalization and voting and interlocking directorships in some selected big business enterprises of Germany.

This exercise of the power of the vote does not necessarily mean that the Deutsche Bank controlled and wholly dominated all these industrial complexes. It means, at least, that the bank had sufficient influence to assure that the policies of the industrial enterprise were never inconsistent with its own; it means, at least, that there was always a mutuality of operations of the bank and the industrial corporation, which is what constitutes the hand-in-glove relationship.

It is evident that a conflict between management and stock voters could hardly be expected to arise under these circumstances. If ever such a conflict might occur, it would be ironed out in the intra-corporation and industry-bank politics before the election. When asked for any instances of a split between industry-management and its bank at a stockholders' meeting, Karl Schmoelder, a prominent banker and corporation lawyer, stated that he knew of no such case.

Hans Rinn, formerly head of the Syndicate Department of the Dresdner Bank, amplified the explanation of the motives for the banks' control of proxy voting. The banks, he said, desire to maintain their voting strength in order to retain the corporation as a customer and to retain their quota in syndicate transactions. The industrial corporation similarly desires the banks to control proxy voting because they were generally considered friendly to the management.

The banks may desire to control the proxy votes of an industrial corporation for a variety of special reasons. The important point is that the banks will desire a maximum of control, and have developed a series of practices to secure it. The contention that proxy voting is merely a service to the stockholder customer is belied by the evidence. For instance, at a time when Deutsche Bank controlled RM 11.8 million of the capital of Schering, and the Dresdner Bank only RM 6.2 million, the Dresdner planned to secure the voting control over a large block outside of Germany for the purpose of upsetting the Deutsche Bank's dominant position. In a memorandum, the chief of the Syndicate Department of the Dresdner made a careful analysis of the voting situation of the Schering stock at the last meeting, and assessed the effects on the relative voting strength of the acquisition by the Dresdner Bank of proxy representation for an additional RM 1.5 million which were changing hands. He concluded that with this shift in voting strength, the Dresdner Bank would be in a position to press for "a closer tie, possibly a directorship with Schering."

Moreover, the banks made considerable efforts to vote all the individual shares and small blocks owned by their customers. Formerly, authority to vote was part of the uniform general agreement between a bank and its customers. (Individual proxies were not necessary because all stocks were unregistered bearer shares.) Later, when the law required individual proxies to be signed by each customer, and their

Table VII
PROXY VOTING BY DEUTSCHE BANK IN SOME LARGE INDUSTRIAL CORPORATIONS

Corporation	Type of business	Capital	Face value of stock represented at shareholders' meeting	Face value of stock voted by Deutsche Bank at meeting	% of D. Bank to total represented	% of total capital voted by D.B.	Member of Deutsche B. Vorstand and branch managers on Anfeichterat of Deutsche Bank	Member of Vorstand of corporation on Aufsichterat of Deutsche Bank	Deutsche Bank member of AR on AR of corporation
I.G. Farben Industrie A.G.	chemicals	1,400 Mill.	850 Mill.	324 Mill.	38.1	23.1	Abs	Hermann Schmitz	
Vereinigte Stahlwerke A.G. Duesseldorf	steel	460 Mill.	351.7 Mill.	66.3 Mill.	18.8	14.4	Kiehl		v. Siemens, H. Schmitz
Allgemeine Elektrizitaets Gesellschaft (AEG)	electric	264 Mill.	142.7 Mill.	39.8 Mill.	27.7	15.0	Wintermantel		Quandt, Zangen, Vielmetter
Mannesman Roehrenwerke A.G.	tubes and sheet metals	180 Mill.	105.7 Mill.	56.9 Mill.	53.9	31.3	Roesler, Wuppermann (General Agent)	Zangen	H. v. Siemens, P. v. Siemens
Rheinische Stahlwerke A.G.	steel	180 Mill.		21.6 Mill.		12			H. Schmitz
Hoesch A.G.	coal and steel	122 Mill.		33.3 Mill.		27.3	Bechtolf, Kimmich	Tgahrt	
Schering A.G.	mining and chemicals	48 Mill. (1941)	29.5 Mill.	11.8 Mill.	40	24.5	Plassmann		
Kloeckner Werke A.G. Duisburg	steel	105 Mill.	88.2 Mill.	10.7 Mill.	12.2	10.1	Kimmich		Kloeckner
Demag A.G. Duisburg	machinery	42.4 Mill.	28.4 Mill.	14.0 Mill.	49.5	33.0	Kiehl, Kimmich	W. Reuter	Carp, R. Stahl, Zangen

						Abs	Koepchen	
Rheinisch-Westfaelische Elektrizitaets-werke A.G.	electricity, gas, water	246 Mill.	23.3 Mill.		9.5			
Gelsenkirchner Bergwerke A.G.	coal	200 Mill.	28.8 Mill.		14.4			
Deutsche Erodel A.G.	oil	100 Mill.	30 Mill.		30	Sippel, Bechtolf, Kimmich	Schirner, R. Ullner, H. Groeber (Reg. Adv. Board)	
Bayerische Motoren Werke (BMW) Munich	airplane motors	100 Mill.	about 50%	about 50%	about 50%	Rummel, v. Rintelen (Munich)	Popp (Reg. Adv. Board)	Max H. Schmid
Daimler Benz A.G., Stuttgart	airplane motors, trucks	120.2 Mill.	about 50%	about 50%	about 50%	Rummel		Carp, Schmid, Quand; Reg. Adv. Board: Popp, Jahr
Siemens & Halske A.G.	electrical equip-ment	251 Mill.	42 Mill.		16.7	Roesler	F. Jessen (Reg. Adv. Board)	H. v. Siemens, Muench-meyer
Hamburg Amerika Linie (Hapag)	shipping	46.37 Mill.	majority	majority	majority	Bechtolf		Reemtsma

Koepchen

renewal at fifteen-month intervals, the banks meticulously proceeded to print proxy forms and circularize their clients with letters of solicitation.

Furthermore, the bank, as investment counsel, was able to assure that the stockholdings of its customers were in the corporations in which the bank was interested. It is not a coincidence that the Deutsche Bank voted more than 80 percent in Mannesmann in certain years and about 50 percent in Daimler Benz and Bayerische Motoren Werke, although it owned very little stock. (A subsequent section shows how these three corporations are peculiarly and completely dominated by the Deutsche Bank.)

Since the Deutsche Bank did practically all the securities trading of its customers, almost all the stock so purchased remained with the bank, and the proxy-getting procedure described above followed as a matter of course. As the biggest bank in Germany, the bank maintained an unequaled proxy control. Its leading position as a securities dealer and underwriter has already been shown by some figures in Chapter IV. For example, in 1942, the bank traded and sold RM 395 million worth of stock to its customers. Its share in total trading on the Berlin stock exchange was estimated to be as high as 40 percent. The same leading position was held by the bank in the distribution of new issues.

When a significant block of stock was to be sold by one customer, the bank saw to it that it was sold to its own customers. In this way it maintained its voting control despite trading and changes in legal ownership.

STOCK OWNERSHIP

A thorough study of the subjects leads to the inevitable conclusion that in the influence exercised by the banks on industry, ownership of stock by the banks themselves is of only secondary importance. Outright stock ownership is too obvious a means of control and therefore most readily subject to criticism, particularly since it ties up depositors' funds in an investment whose liquidity and safety might frequently be questioned.

It is especially true in the case of some of the larger corporations most closely linked with Deutsche Bank, such as Mannesmann, Daimler, and Bayerische Motoren Werke, the bank's ownership of stock was of a minor proportion measured by the total capital. Nevertheless, as will be shown later, Deutsche Bank not only influenced but effectively controlled these corporations. It is equally true, however, that the German banks have always held considerable amounts of industrial stocks. Such stockholdings, in the case of medium-size and smaller corporations, are sometimes sufficient in themselves to spell out control; in other instances, they merely add weight to the other factors described above (interlocks, proxy voting, etc.) to assure a measure of influence or control.

The balance sheet of the Deutsche Bank for 1944 showed the book value of stocks owned as RM 82.7 million, of which RM 66.7 million were listed on exchanges. This figure does not include the bank's participations in financial institutions, which amounted to an additional RM 88 million in 1944.

Other corporations where the [Deutsche Bank] holding amounts to 10 percent or more of the total capital [. . . include] 33 industrial corporations in all. There are 9 corporations in which Deutsche Bank owns an equity interest of 50 percent or more. It is a well-known fact that considerably less than a 50 percent stock interest will be sufficient to control a corporation, except where another block of similar size is in one hand, which is comparatively rare. Going one step further, then, one finds that in 23 corporations Deutsche Bank owns an interest of 20 percent or more. Furthermore, because of the casual relationship between the bank's "interest" and its customers' securities holdings, which has been discussed above (under Proxy Voting), it will generally occur that where the bank holds a substantial minority interest in a corporation, its customers will have additional holdings on deposit with it. These customers' holdings which the bank votes by proxy combined with the shares it owns will frequently make up a solid majority block. Such was the case, for instance, with the Krauss-Maffei A.G., Munich, and the Heinrich Lanz A.G., Mannheim, both producers of heavy machinery and important war producers. Of the latter company's capital stock, Deutsche Bank owned 26 percent but voted an additional 50 percent for customers. In the Krauss-Maffei corporation the ratio was 38.5 percent stock owned, 20–25 percent held for depositors. In both corporations the Deutsche Bank effectively controlled the management by heavy representation on the Aufsichtsrat. The Aufsichtsrat chairmanship in the hands of a Deutsche Bank Vorstand member was not considered sufficient in view of the Vorstand's far-flung activities. To assure more effective supervision, the manager of the Deutsche Bank branch near the location of the company was added to its board in both instances.

❑ ❑ ❑

Some of these industrial interests came to be owned by the Deutsche Bank as the result of corporate reorganizations, particularly in the crisis years of the early thirties. Others represented Deutsche Bank's share in the spoils of German territorial expansion. The holdings of Heinrichthaler Papierfabrik A.G. and Neudecker Wollkaemmerei A.G., for instance, were taken over from the Boehmische Unionbank when Deutsche Bank acquired control of that bank following the German occupation of Czechoslovakia. The 34 percent interest in Butzkewerke A.G. was obtained by Deutsche Bank in the process of "Aryanization" of the firm (cf. Chapter X, "Aryanization").

It is clear from the above illustrations that bank ownership of corporate stock is a factor which cannot be ignored in the study of the "tie-in" between the German Grossbanken and industry. While it is, on the whole, of lesser importance than interlocking directorships, proxy voting, and loans, it is in some instances a decisive element, in others a complementary one in clinching the bank's influence on certain industries.

Regardless of the original acquisition, once the bank was entrenched in a commanding position in an "interesting" concern, it was reluctant to part with its stockholding. This is borne out by a memorandum from the files of the [Friedrich] Flick concern. The company under discussion was the above-mentioned Krauss-Maffei A.G. Flick was eager to acquire the Deutsche Bank's interest in the concern and, in June 1942, had discussed the matter with Kiehl, [a] Deutsche Bank Vorstand member. Kiehl explained the bank was carrying the holding on its books at a rather attractive figure and enjoyed certain tax privileges on it (Schachtelprivileg)—in brief, the bank was not interested in disposing of it.

There are instances, where, notwithstanding a relatively small investment, the significance of stock ownership was magnified because of the practice of having a class of stock with multiple voting power. In the case of Daimler Benz, for instance, Deutsche Bank owned the entire issue of RM 259,200 preference shares. This preference stock had thirtyfold voting power in matters of the greatest importance, such as the appointment of the directors, changes of by-laws, or dissolution. Since Deutsche Bank generally controlled a majority of the common stock of this corporation by proxy, as shown in the preceding section, the multiple voting rights represented a marginal and potential means of control, and, in fact, may never have been exercised. The corporation law of 1937 aimed at eliminating such multiple voting privileges, but it appears that Daimler Benz received special permission to continue and even increase this class of stock. (Hans Rummel, chairman of the board of Daimler Benz, was unable to give definite information on this point.)

LOANS AND SYNDICATES

The extension of loans as the means of securing control or influence over industry is most clearly part of a normal banking business. It may serve at least as the means of introducing the bank and borrower to each other and, if the investment is obviously sound and the bank has no wish to influence the borrower, the relationship may stop at the simple debtor-creditor relationship. It is of significance outside normal banking only when it is used in conjunction with one of the other means of influence, as when it either reflects or precedes interlocking directorships or control over voting by either proxy-held or owned shares. A quick check over a list of corporations in which the Deutsche Bank was the leader of loan syndicates reveals that almost every single one was under other means of Deutsche Bank influence, and that in the overwhelming majority there were interlocking directorships between the bank and the corporation. A similar check of a list of the biggest loans of the bank would undoubtedly reveal similar relationships, although probably not quite of the same magnitude due to the fact that these loans might represent participations in syndicates led by other banks.

As an example of large credits, there is the brown coal and lignite system, components of which were interlocked with the Deutsche Bank by mutual directors and participations in a rather complicated fashion. Of a RM 50 million bank syndicate loan in 1940 to Rheinische A.G. fuer Braunkohlen, one of the companies in the system, the Deutsche Bank participated with a quota of 32.25 percent. Of a RM 60 million bank syndicate loan to Roddergrube in 1941, another company in the system, the Deutsche Bank took a quota of 29.75 percent. Of syndicate loans given to the important synthetic fuel manufacturer Union Rheinische Braunkohlen Kraftstoff

A.G., a third company of the system, the Deutsche Bank participated with the following quotas:

Year of Loan	Amount	Deutsche Bank Quota
1940	RM 60 million	33.375%
1942	RM 40 million	33.375%
1943	RM 50 million	25.8%

And more impressive are the cases of Bayerische Motoren Werke A.G. and Daimler Benz, discussed in other sections of this report. It becomes apparent that general reform measures designed to separate the banks from influence over industry should include provision for examination of credits with a view toward preventing their extension where they are designed primarily as a means of exercising control.

SPECIAL INDUSTRIAL TIES

There are innumerable instances where a strong combination of the factors which have been described, often coupled with other circumstances (political contacts, or a link arising from the corporation's foundation), brings about a "special situation." They are either situations of extraordinary intimacy, where industrial corporations of substantial scope are, for all practical purposes, "run" by the bank management, or situations of less complete control where the bank-industry connection has some other angle of peculiar interest. Again it was the Deutsche Bank which had an unusually large number of such special situations.

By way of illustration, some of the industrial concerns and complexes falling into this category by reason of their relations with the bank are individually discussed below. Among them are three industrial concerns, Mannesmann, Rheinische Braunkohlen A.G., and Reemtsma, which took part in a transaction typical of that hand-in-glove cooperation between banking and industry in the pursuit of which the bank often strayed off the banking field and the industry in turn stepped out of the bounds of its own business. The transaction in question was the purchase by each of the three concerns (and presumably a few others) of sizable blocks of Deutsche Bank stock (several million each). It took place in the early 1930s, shortly after the German banking crisis when Deutsche Bank was anxious to escape "outside" influence (and increased government influence). It therefore arranged to place these large blocks of stock safely among the "circle of friendly or dominated industrial enterprises," as the *Berliner Tageblatt* termed it. As far as the latter were concerned, the deal was obviously not in the "usual course of business," and it was far from being a safe and sound investment as evidenced by the subsequent decline in the price of the stock.

Max Steinthal, then a ruling force in both Mannesmann and Deutsche Bank, tried to explain the transaction at a stockholders' meeting. He stated that one of its purposes was to prevent the bank being forced into extension of more small loans by the government's acquisition of a decisive stock interest. In other words, by the acquisition of large capital interests, the "affiliated" industrial concerns wanted to make sure that credit facilities would be confined to big business, and, more specifically they would thus assure to their own concerns any loans they might desire in the future.

Even among the German financial community, so much more accustomed than the outside world to the integration of banking and industry and to monopolistic arrangements among them, this operation caused a considerable stir. The *Berliner Tageblatt,* leading liberal daily of pre-Nazi days whose financial section was particularly prominent, devoted a full-page article to an extremely critical analysis of the whole transaction and of Steinthal's explanation. The article referred to "capitalistic solidarity" and pointed particularly at the fact that at least two of the large stock purchasers belonged to the heavy industry of the Rhineland. It concludes:

> Perhaps they simply wanted to secure for themselves the position of economic power which obviously lies in influence on one of the two largest German banking institutions. Such influences and friendships need not bear fruit only in the realm of one's own credit needs. Their object may also be the treatment of loans to competitor firms, the exercise of the influence on the bank in manifold operations. Such motives, coupled with feelings of solidarity and friendship, may have carried more weight than a calculation in sober figures.

To be sure, in the case of Mannesmann, as will be seen, the weight of the influence was clearly on the side of the bank, and the stock purchase deal could, at best, have brought about a slightly greater mutuality of relations. But in the other instances, the scales were more evenly balanced—relationships were more of the "hand-in-glove" nature which has been mentioned before. These various shadings in the picture of the bank's influence on industry are well worth some study and consideration.

MANNESMANN ROEHRENWERKE A.G.

The Mannesmann Roehrenwerke A.G. with its affiliates is probably the one individual complex which, for two generations, has been most closely identified with the Deutsche Bank. Anyone familiar with German finance and industry, when asked about Mannesmann, will say: "That's the Deutsche Bank." But such statements are made even in a less casual fashion. The German banking periodical *Die Bank* wrote in its issue of 3 May 1940: "Whoever knows even a little history of Mannesmann, knows it is a child of the Deutsche Bank."

Mannesmann Roehrenwerke A.G., Duesseldorf, is Germany's foremost producer of seamless tubes. It is also prominent in the production of sheet metal and has important coal interests, blast furnaces, rolling mills. Its present stock capital amounts to RM 180 million. It sold approximately half of the tubes produced in Germany and employed over 71,000 people in 1943. Mannesmann has over twenty domestic and many foreign establishments, some of which were acquired through Aryanization, some in the wake of Germany's aggression. It had sales agencies in Zuerich, Stockholm, Copenhagen, Oslo, London, Cracow, Rotterdam, Belgrade, Bucharest, and Sofia, and manufacturing subsidiaries in Argentina, Brazil, England,

France, Holland, and many other countries. Its foreign representatives faithfully submitted to the mother company not only information on sales, but also sent data on political and industrial espionage, acted as cloaks and aided in camouflage activities when the war broke out.

The domination of Deutsche Bank over the activities of Mannesmann goes back to 1890 when Deutsche Bank men reorganized the enterprise established by the Mannesmann brothers for the exploitation and development of their seamless tube process. . . .Within a few years thereafter, the Mannesmann brothers were forced out of the company. They brought suit, which was settled by a payment of RM 2 million on the part of Deutsche Bank. [But] Deutsche Bank's hold on Mannesmann . . . was not weakened. It was reaffirmed in the appointment to the post of Oskar Schlitter, former Vorstand member and then chairman of the Aufsichtsrat of Deutsche Bank. Upon Schlitter's death, Oswald Roesler, speaker of the Vorstand of Deutsche Bank, succeeded to the Mannesmann chairmanship. In other words, from 1896 to the present the chairmanship of the Mannesmann board of directors was, without interruption, in the hands of top executives of Deutsche Bank. . . . [The] Deutsche Bank had three and at times four of its officials (Roesler entered the Aufsichtsrat in 1935) in the Aufsichtsrat of the Mannesmann parent company alone, not counting two or three men (like the Siemens') who were on the Aufsichtsrat of both the bank and Mannesmann.

With such powerful representation on the Mannesmann Aufsichtsrat, the men of the Deutsche Bank throughout the years functioned as policy makers and, what is more, as "kingmakers" in the Mannesmann complex. The most recent example of the latter was the appointment of Wilhelm Zangen to the Vorstand of Mannesmann in 1934 and his elevation to the post of general manager a year later. . . .

Here is how Zangen's appointment came about: Bierwes, the previous general manager, had to be replaced, according to general belief, because he was persona non grata with the Nazi Party. Oskar Schlitter [of Deutsche Bank] suggested Zangen [. . . whom he had known] for many years from his work on the Vorstand of two companies which were closely connected with Deutsche Bank: Schiess A.G., Duesseldorf, and later Demag A.G., Duisburg. Schlitter was chairman of the Demag Aufsichtsrat and Schiess was a subsidiary of Demag.

❑ ❑ ❑

Zangen certainly was not subject to the political handicaps which had brought his predecessor to fall. He was head of the powerful Reichsgruppe Industrie, [the] top supervisory organ (directly under the Reichswirtschaftskammer) of all German industry in the Nazi corporate setup. He was close enough to Hitler, Goering, and Funk to receive their personal greetings on his birthday though he became an official Party member only in 1937. Promptly upon his appointment, a program of Nazification was carried through in the Mannesmann concern. Within one year Zangen radically changed the staff. By 1940, the "rejuvenation," as Zangen called it, had established in a Vorstand of eleven men, six longtime Nazis (including one of the founders of the Gestapo) and five men who had been with the company less than six years. It was a young, powerful group, which united the Nazi Party's new goals of world domination with the old imperialistic interests of the Ruhr industrialists. (Cf. Report by Joint Special Financial Detachment, U.S. Group CC, Control Com. for Germany, British Element, Duesseldorf.)

In 1938 Zangen was elected to the Aufsichtsrat of the Deutsche Bank. Deutsche Bank, in addition to its domination of the board of the parent company, was represented on the boards of a multitude of domestic and foreign subsidiaries of Mannesmann. An incomplete list furnished by the company shows thirty individuals connected with Deutsche Bank who, over a period of years, have held one or more positions in Mannesmann companies in Germany and abroad. In which direction the weight of the influence was exercised is shown by the fact that, during the same period, only three Mannesmann executives sat on the boards of Deutsche Bank and its affiliates.

To illustrate the extent to which Deutsche Bank's influence reached out into the worldwide subsidiary network of Mannesmann, the positions in Mannesmann companies of only three top executives of Deutsche Bank and Deutsche Bank subsidiaries are charted. *(See following page.)*

As usual, the strong personal representation was supported by a corresponding voting strength at stockholders' meetings. To assure that control would not slip out of its hands, Deutsche Bank saw to it always to "put" a sufficient number of its customers "into" Mannesmann and to obtain their proxies. Thus Deutsche Bank invariably voted the largest single block, in fact always voted more than half, and in some years about 80 percent of the total stock represented at the annual meetings. . . .

How much of the stock so represented was owned by Deutsche Bank itself has not been ascertained. It is believed, however, that in the maintenance of controlling influence over Mannesmann, outright stock ownership by Deutsche Bank has played a minor part, at least in recent years.

Mannesmann, on the other hand, acquired a sizable block of Deutsche Bank stock in 1932. It was one of the "individual friends" who cooperated with the Deutsche Bank at the time of its "reprivatization" when the bank was anxious to have its stock placed in friendly and "reliable" hands. The amount purchased by Mannesmann was RM 3 million and at least some of the shares are still on deposit with the Aachen branch of Deutsche Bank. On this stock purchase deal, as far as it involved Mannesmann, the trade journal *Ostdeutscher Maschinenmarkt* in its issue of 30 July 1932, commented as follows:

> The Mannesmann Roehrenwerke rendered the Deutsche Bank a special favor because the demand for the new shares of the consolidated banks is not regarded as very great. The friendly relationship between the Deutsche Bank and the Mannesmann Roehrenwerke is known to be very old.

Naturally the Deutsche Bank was the "house bank" of Mannesmann. It was the leader of all syndicates for new capital issues, acquisitions of new affiliates, bond issues and loans.

❏ ❏ ❏

Name	Position in D.B.	Position in D.B. foreign subsidiary	Position in M/W	Position in M/W foreign subsidiary
Oswald Roesler	Speaker, Vorstand, D.B., Berlin	Chairman, Vorstand, Boehmische Unionbank, Prague	Chairman, AR, M/W, Duesseldorf	Vorstand, Prager Eisenindustrie Ges., Prague
		AR, Credit-anstalt Bank-verein, Wien	Vice-chairman AR, M/W Stahlblechbau A.G., Berlin	Vice-chairman, AR, M/W Komotau
		AR, Boehmische Unionbank, Berlin	AR, Kriegs-wohlfahrtsstif-tung of the M/W	
Walter Pohle		Manager, Boehmische Unionbank, Prague		Chairman, AR, Ostdeutsche Metallwerke
				Chairman, Vorstand Metall-walzwerke Maehrisch Ostrau
				Chairman, AR Zinkwalzwerke, VAc, Hungary
				AR, M/W, Komotau
Alfred Hermann		Manager, Banco Alemán Transatlantico, Buenos Aires, and head of all Argentinian branches of same		Vice-Chairman, AR, Sociedad Tubos Mannesmann, Buenos Aires
				AR, Sidapar, São Paulo, Brazil

Straight bank loans were given to Mannesmann as well as to its foreign subsidiaries by the Deutsche Bank and its foreign affiliates. One of the more recent ones was a RM 5 million loan extended by Deutsche Bank, Duesseldorf branch in 1938, when Germany's war preparations were reaching their peak. When Germany went to war in 1939, this loan was doubled. It was canceled in August 1945.

In December 1945 Deutsche Bank extended a new loan of RM 10 million to Mannesmann. Evidently V-E Day has not severed the intimate relationship between the two concerns. [This includes] export and import loans in various currencies and foreign exchange futures given by Deutsche Bank to the Mannesmann parent company. As to Mannesmann foreign subsidiaries, they were served with loans both by Deutsche Bank itself and by its foreign branches and affiliates. Among the latter, the following were active in financing Mannesmann subsidiaries: in Czechoslovakia—the Boehmische Unionbank, Prague and branches, and Gewerbebank, Prague; in Holland—H. Albert de Bary & Co., Amsterdam; in Austria—Creditanstalt Bankverein, Vienna; in France—Deutsche Bank, Strasbourg; in Yugoslavia—Bankverein A.G., Belgrade, and in South America—the Banco Alemán Transatlantico, Buenos Aires and Rio de Janeiro.

Clearly the bonds which bound Mannesmann to the Deutsche Bank were such that Mannesmann was, in effect, an industrial affiliate of the bank. Hence, the responsibility for the activities of Mannesmann rests as much on the Deutsche Bank as on the management of Mannesmann itself. Mannesmann was a war producer of tremendous importance. Mannesmann grasped control of numerous foreign industries in the wake of Germany's aggression. Mannesmann amply availed itself of the opportunities offered by the Aryanization of Jewish property. Some of these activities, in which Deutsche Bank and Mannesmann worked as a team, will be discussed in more detail in subsequent chapters.

DAIMLER BENZ AND BAYERISCHE MOTOREN WERKE (BMW)

Domination as complete as in the case of Mannesmann was exercised by the Deutsche Bank over two other industrial complexes: Daimler Benz A.G. (Daimler) and Bayerische Motoren Werke A.G. (BMW). The type of business of the two concerns, the history of the acquisition, and the methods of control by the Deutsche Bank are similar.

While the Deutsche Bank did not rear these two concerns practically from the cradle, as in the case of Mannesmann, it did take a firm hand in their affairs in their 1925–26 reorganizations and never loosened its grip since. In the Daimler reorganization the Deutsche Bank succeeded in bringing about the merger of the former Daimler Motoren Gesellschaft and Benz & Cie., both prominent, if not financially strong, companies in the automotive field since its early development stage. While the Deutsche Bank had had some ties with the predecessor companies of Daimler and BMW, it is from the time of their reorganizations on that its relationship could be called domination, a domination continued through good years and bad and undiminished by the spectacular growth of both corporations. It was Emil Georg von Stauss of the Deutsche Bank who carried out the reorganizations and subsequently piloted the companies for many years. With remarkable "foresight" Stauss, [whose political background was discussed in Chapter VI], recognized the potentialities of Germany's power in the air, always with an eye on early rearmament and war. He was largely responsible for directing the productive efforts of both BMW and Daimler, previously engaged in the production of peacetime automotive vehicles, into the manufacture of airplane engines long before the outbreak of war.

Stauss was chairman of the Aufsichtsrat in both complexes until his death and made these corporations his primary interest, so much so that in 1933 he shifted from the Vorstand of the Deutsche Bank to its Aufsichtsrat in order to be able to devote almost exclusive attention to the Deutsche Bank's industrial interests. Upon von Stauss's death in 1942, Hans Rummel, Vorstand member of Deutsche Bank, and having previously been vice-chairman under Stauss, took over the two chairmanships. Hence, Deutsche Bank men have held these key posts for twenty years without interruption. The chairman, as Rummel himself describes it, "took an active interest" in the affairs of these industrial concerns. He made regular visits to the companies' headquarters about once a month. In the interim, company officials paid frequent visits to him to discuss the affairs of the company. Correspondence files disclose that the chairman was also kept currently informed and consulted on many details such as current production figures, problems of relocation of plants, questions of personnel and internal conflicts, in addition to the usual financial reports.

When Hermann Kaiser, General Agent of Deutsche Bank, was asked:

> Can it be said that von Stauss, and later on Rummel, were actually more than chairmen of the board—that they were actually running these two corporations, BMW and Daimler Benz?

[Kaiser] answered,

> Yes, that can be said . . . [until his death] von Stauss maintained an office in the Deutsche Bank, Berlin, which he used to handle the affairs of BMW and Daimler Benz. He took a great deal of interest in these companies and was responsible for extension of large credits to them. The other members of the Kredit Ausschuss were not in favor of these credits but could not intervene as von Stauss was obviously collaborating with the Reich government in these matters.

To assure an even closer day-to-day supervision, the managers of Deutsche Bank's local branches in the cities of the main offices of the corporations were also placed on their boards of directors. Max H. Schmid, another member of Deutsche Bank's Aufsichtsrat, also sat on the Aufsichtsrat of both Daimler and BMW. But Max Schmid represented the Deutsche Bank in a more specific way than is indicated by his Aufsichtsrat position. Back in the early 1930s, he was an industrial consultant for Deutsche Bank and in that capacity he assisted in carrying through the reorganizations of industrial concerns. It is to this activity that his election to the boards of Daimler and BMW can be traced.

Additional members of the Aufsichtsrat of Daimler were also on the Aufsichtsrat of the Deutsche Bank. As of a recent date, the Deutsche Bank representation was made up as follows:

Daimler Benz
Hans Rummel (Chairman)—Vorstand of Deutsche Bank
Hermann Koehler—Manager of Deutsche Bank, Stuttgart Branch
Carl Jahr—Chairman of Deutsche Bank's Advisory Council for Baden
    and Palatinate
Max H. Schmid—Aufsichtsrat of Deutsche Bank

Guenther Quandt—Aufsichtsrat of Deutsche Bank
Werner Carp—Aufsichtsrat of Deutsche Bank
The total membership of Daimler's Aufsichtsrat was fourteen.

BMW

Hans Rummel (Chairman)—Vorstand of Deutsche Bank
Victor von Rintelen—Manager of Deutsche Bank, Munich Branch
Max H. Schmid—Aufsichtsrat of Deutsche Bank
Membership of the Aufsichtsrat of BMW was ten.

The important Working Committees were similarly staffed with Deutsche Bank men. First Stauss, then Rummel, were the ex-officio chairmen of the Working Committees of both Daimler and BMW. In Daimler the Working Committee consisted of Stauss, Rummel, and two others, and, after Stauss's death, of Rummel, Jahr (see above), and two others, so that a 50 percent representation of the Deutsche Bank was maintained.

In the subsidiaries the chairmanships were held by the same Deutsche Bank Vorstand members. These subsidiaries included Daimler's important Genshagen plant and the various subsidiaries BMW set up for the development of the aircraft production in the form of G.m.b.H.s for reasons of secrecy, as shown in more detail in Chapter IX, "Rearmament and War Financing."

Interlocking relations running in the opposite direction, that is from the industrial enterprises to the Deutsche Bank, were established in the person of Franz Popp, onetime Vorstand member of BMW and later on the Aufsichtsrat of BMW and Daimler. Popp was on the Bavarian Advisory Council of Deutsche Bank. Wolfgang von Hentig, of the Daimler Vorstand, was a member of the bank's advisory council for Berlin-Brandenburg.

Deutsche Bank's managerial and personal control was supported by a corresponding voting power. It voted about 50 percent of the stock in each corporation by proxy for its customers. (The Dresdner Bank voted about 15 to 22 percent in each of them.) As an added protection of its position, Deutsche Bank owned the entire issue of RM 259,200 preference shares of Daimler. The thirtyfold voting power of this stock in certain important matters has already been mentioned.

The rapid expansion of these two industrial complexes in preparation for and in the pursuit of Germany's aggressive aims meant big-time financing and investment business for Deutsche Bank. The BMW parent company raised its capital from a prewar RM 15 million to RM 100 million in 1944, with Deutsche Bank, of course, heading the syndicates for the distribution of all of the stock. The same was true of Daimler, whose capital rose from RM 40 million to RM 120 million during the same period. In the field of bond issues, Daimler floated RM 40 million bonds in 1942; BMW RM 55 million in 1942–43. Deutsche Bank's syndicate quota was 50 percent and 60 percent, respectively. Deutsche Bank's leadership was also well established in connection with straight bank loans. Even in October 1944, Deutsche Bank had credit lines for BMW and its subsidiaries on its books for about RM 63 million out of total facilities of about RM 175 million then at the disposal of the concern, though at that time a large share of this type of financing was carried by government-sponsored institutions such as the Bank der Deutschen Luftfahrt. As far as the loans were syndicate loans, Deutsche Bank's quota was one-third, one-half, and two-thirds in individual transactions. In Daimler syndicate loans the Deutsche Bank had a 50 percent quota in the bank syndicate in which the Dresdner and Commerz banks shared the rest. Commitments as of June 1944 were RM 27.5 million.

The real importance of Daimler and BMW, which rose under the tutelage of Deutsche Bank to a position where their contribution was indispensable to the Luftwaffe's success, however temporary, will be shown in a succeeding chapter. Combined they accounted for two-thirds of Germany's aircraft engine production during the war.

I.G. Farbenindustrie A.G.

The I.G. Farben complex was obviously too huge and too powerful to be controlled by any one bank. It had among its subsidiaries a bank of its own, the Deutsche Laenderbank, which together with the I.G. Farben Central Finance Administration was able to take care of routine banking matters and the shifting of excess funds within the combine. For an enterprise of the size of I.G. Farben, however, there was need for cooperation and close connection with one or more of the really large banks. And it was above all the Deutsche Bank with which a peculiarly intimate relationship developed. This relationship, according to Hermann Schmitz, president of I.G., dates back to the days prior to the organization of the Farben combine when Deutsche Bank was the main banking connection of the Badische Anilin and Soda-Fabrik, the largest constituent unit of I.G.,

> when the I.G. Farben was created in 1925 it was natural that the Deutsche Bank continued relations with the I.G. Farben.

The closeness of these ties is demonstrated by a number of factors. Although I.G. Farben obviously had substantial dealings with all the big banks, Deutsche Bank was the only one that was invited to place a representative on the board of directors of I.G. Deutsche Bank was last represented on the Farben board by Hermann J. Abs, who succeeded Oskar Schlitter. Both were Vorstand members of the Deutsche Bank. The arrangement was reciprocal in that Hermann Schmitz sat on the Aufsichtsrat of the Deutsche Bank. Similarly, interlocking directorships existed between subsidiaries of I.G. Farben and the Deutsche Bank and its affiliates. In the early 1930s, for instance, when Max von Schinckel was still honorary chairman of the Deutsche Bank and Disconto-Gesellschaft, he was also chairman of the board of Dynamit A.G. formerly Alfred Nobel & Co., one of Germany's outstanding producers of explosives and one of the most important subsidiaries of I.G., which controls it by stock ownership (45 percent) plus stock exchange and option agreements. Karl Kimmich, the last board chairman of the Deutsche Bank, was also on the Aufsichtsrat of Rheinische Stahlwerke in which I.G. Farben similarly holds the controlling stock interest. In turn, shortly after the invasion of Austria, Max Ilgner, member of the Vorstand and head of the Central Finance Administration of I.G., joined the board of directors of the Creditanstalt Bankverein, Vienna, Austria's largest bank, over which Deutsche Bank was then steadily tightening its control. The same Max Ilgner was elected in 1941 to the board of directors of the Deutsche Ueberseeische Bank, which was 51 percent owned by the Deutsche Bank and which played such an important part in promoting German interests in Spain and Latin America (cf. in Chapter XII, Expansion of Foreign Subsidiaries and Affiliates).

The close connection which existed between the two concerns was further reflected in the voting power Deutsche Bank exercised in the stockholders' meeting of I.G. Farben. At the stockholders' meeting of 30 July 1943, Deutsche Bank voted on behalf of customers RM 324.0 million, that is 38.1 percent of the total RM 850 million stock represented at the meeting, a truly impressive percentage considering the size of the I.G. Farben capitalization and the wide distribution of its stock. The Deutsche Bank was represented at the stockholders' meeting by Louis May and Dr. Georg Stein, both managers of the Frankfurt branch of the Deutsche Bank.

That Deutsche Bank was able to assemble such a large percentage of I.G. Farben's stock under its voting control was in part due to the bank's prominent part in the distribution of I.G. Farben securities and in all other important financing transactions of the chemical combine. . . . In the capital increase of RM 235 million which was effected in 1942, the Deutsche Bank headed the underwriting syndicate and itself took a quota of 27.5 percent plus 1.5 percent for Creditanstalt Bankverein, Deutsche Bank's Austrian subsidiary, compared with Dresdner Bank's 19.5 percent and the 15 percent of the Deutsche Laenderbank. In several previous capital increases, the new stock was reserved for exchange against stock of subsidiary companies and for the conversion of convertible debentures. While no underwriting syndicate was thus required, the Deutsche Bank headed the banking syndicates which signed the prospectus filed in connection with application for stock exchange listing. It therefore assumed the primary liability of the *Prospekthaftung* (prospectus liability). The Deutsche Bank managed the syndicate which underwrote an issue of RM 100 million 4.5 percent bonds of I.G. in 1939. The proceeds of this loan were to be used for expansion of plants.[1] The Deutsche Bank quota in this syndicate was 28.5 percent plus 1.5 percent for its Austrian subsidiary as against the 28.5 percent of the Dresdner Bank and 15.5 percent of the Deutsche Laenderbank. Deutsche Bank also was appointed trustee for this issue. In February 1944, when Schmitz for the first time deemed it wise to resort to a large straight bank loan to tide I.G. over the contingencies he saw ahead, Deutsche Bank again was called upon to take the lead of the banking syndicate which stood ready to provide a loan of RM 170 million. In this instance, the quotas of the Deutsche, Dresdner, and Laender Banks were equal (RM 30 million), but the additional RM 5,000,000 taken by Creditanstalt again secured the Deutsche Bank interests the lead over Deutsche Laenderbank.

The above illustrations show that in its relation with the I.G. Farben complex the Deutsche Bank more truly performed the functions of a "house bank" than even I.G.'s own Deutsche Laenderbank.

Exhaustive investigations have been conducted by United States agencies into the activities of I.G. Farbenindustrie. They have revealed the tremendous efforts made

---

[1] *Editor's note:* Later investigations established that a substantial portion of these bonds were used to finance the I.G. Farben synthetic fuel plant at the Auschwitz concentration camp. See John Marks, "Loans for Auschwitz: Deutsche Bank Says It Financed the Camp," *U.S. News and World Report,* February 15, 1999.

by I.G. in preparing for war, its indispensable part in making Germany's aggression possible, its subversive activities abroad, its cloaking of external assets. Because of the importance of the subject and the peculiar relationship between the Deutsche Bank and the Farben concern, the report submitted by the War Department to the Subcommittee on War Mobilization of the Committee on Military Affairs of the United States Senate (Kilgore Committee) is hereby incorporated by reference.

H. F. AND PH. REEMTSMA

Philipp Reemtsma stated, under interrogation, that in 1929, when several smaller cigarette manufacturing enterprises were merged into the Reemtsma Konzern, "the Deutsche Bank became the leading single bank in the cigarette industry." In so stating, Mr. Reemtsma not only properly circumscribed the connection between the Reemtsma firm and the bank but unwittingly furnished a general characterization of the integration of German banks, most prominent among them the Deutsche Bank, with certain industries—banks that were "in industry."

After the merger referred to, the Reemtsma interest controlled between 40 and 45 percent of all German cigarette production. In later years, by successive absorptions of other manufacturing companies, their share rose to 80 percent of total production.

The relationship between the bank and Reemtsma was indeed a peculiar one, and one which provides another striking illustration of the perfect "hand-in-glove" collaboration carried out between the bank and certain industries. The connection goes back to Deutsche Bank's leadership of a banking syndicate which controlled 75 percent of the capital of the Jasmatzi company which became one of the constituent units of the Reemtsma concern in 1925. From that year on, Deutsche Bank had two Vorstand members on Reemtsma's board of directors: Kiehl and Millington-Hermann. This representation was continued even after 1935 when the Reemtsma firm changed its legal structure from a corporation to a *Kommanditgesellschaft* (similar to a limited partnership). The Deutsche Bank men took their places on the newly created advisory council (Beirat). After the death of Millington-Hermann, Schlitter took his place, and upon the latter's death, Abs entered the advisory council of the Reemtsma firm.

Philipp F. Reemtsma, principal owner and executive of the Reemtsma firm, in turn, was elected to the board of directors of Deutsche Bank in 1934. In so further strengthening its ties with Reemtsma, the Deutsche Bank wisely sought to use Reemtsma's excellent connections with the new rulers of Germany (cf. Chapter VI, "Political Connections").

In implementing the hand-in-glove policy, Philipp Reemtsma strayed far afield from the cigarette business. In 1935 or 1936, he joined the Aufsichtsrat of the Vereinigte Glanzstoff Fabriken A.G., the great German rayon combine with international ramifications, in which the Deutsche Bank had a decisive stake. The sole purpose was to secure the bank added influence in the rayon trust. How little personal interest Reemtsma had in Glanzstoff's actual business is evidenced by his own admission that he, though a director, devoted one half day every two days to the affairs of that company.

Similarly, upon the personal request of Kimmich, then the leading man in Deutsche Bank, Reemtsma had himself elected to the Aufsichtsrat of Heinkel & Cie., the largest soap manufacturer in Germany. The Heinkel company was wholly owned by the Heinkel families, and Reemtsma could enter its board only as the representative of the Deutsche Bank, which was the company's principal banking connection. Again, one of the objectives was to use Reemtsma's influence with Goering in behalf of one of the bank's industrial protégés.

In the 1931 crisis, when Deutsche Bank was anxious to have sizable blocks of its stock placed securely among its special friends, the Reemtsma Konzern was one of the industrial concerns which stepped into the breach. It purchased RM 5 million Deutsche Bank stock to which it later added another 3 million. Reemtsma deposited that stock with Deutsche Bank and authorized the bank to have it represented at meetings.

The Deutsche Bank in turn performed valuable—and profitable—services for Reemtsma and his enterprises. It took care, of course, of their legitimate financing needs at home and abroad. As a cigarette manufacturer, Reemtsma had need for substantial advances and guarantees for customs and tax obligations. Deutsche Bank provided these facilities.

❑ ❑ ❑

Deutsche Bank figured prominently in syndicate transactions for Reemtsma, such as a foreign loan of 7.5 million Dutch florins floated for the purpose of acquisition by Reemtsma of the Dutch Caland Tobacco Company. In this particular transaction Deutsche Bank ranked on a parity basis with the Amsterdamsche Bank. Generally, however, the distribution of quotas in Reemtsma's syndicate transactions was: Deutsche Bank 50 percent, Dresdner Bank and Commerzbank 25 percent each.

The Deutsche Bank Istanbul branch played an important part in the financing and clearing settlements of tobacco imports, particularly when the Reemtsma firm was appointed by the Reich government as sole agent for all tobacco purchases in Turkey for the entire German industry. The Reich Economic Ministry, [in a letter] dated 10 July 1941, authoriz[ed] issuance of a blanket foreign exchange permit to Deutsche Bank up to RM 20 million for Reemtsma tobacco purchases.

In Bulgaria, the Kreditbank, Sofia, a subsidiary of the Deutsche Bank, was "instrumental in establishing" a Reemtsma agency. Naturally, the Kreditbank became the subsidiary's main banking connection, and the stock of the Bulgarian company was deposited with it.

The transactions in which the Deutsche Bank procured Reemtsma sizable blocks of stocks, either from its own portfolio or through its agency, conformed even less to orthodox commercial banking practice. Around 1940, when Reemtsma was interested in gaining a foothold in the shipping trade, Deutsche Bank sold him RM 5 million, or 42 percent of the total capital, stock of the Hansa Steamship Co., which Deutsche Bank had held for a few years. Subsequently, Philipp Reemtsma acquired RM 19 million (over 40 percent of the total capital) stock of the Hamburg America Line (HAPAG) and RM 12.5 million (28 percent) stock of the North German Lloyd. Philipp Reemtsma's brother Hermann owned another RM 4 million North

German Lloyd stock, and the holdings of the brothers were pooled with the 12.5 million of one Hermann Ritter to form a clear majority. Similarly, a majority block was created by a pooling arrangement in HAPAG. Philipp Reemtsma became a director of these, the biggest two German shipping corporations, in 1942.

Again from its own holdings, Deutsche Bank allowed Reemtsma to purchase "several million" RM of stock of the Niederschlesiche Bergbau A.G. (total capital RM 24 million). A Vorstand member and a branch manager of Deutsche Bank sat on the Aufsichtsrat of that corporation. The bank knew that transfer of the stockholding to as close an industrial "relative" as Reemtsma would not jeopardize its influence in the company. In fact, in practically all, if not all, of these cases, the shares acquired by Reemtsma remained on deposit with the Deutsche Bank and Deutsche Bank was permitted to exercise the voting rights.

From the Annex to the Report

Reemtsma Loans to Nazi Party Affiliates

The Deutsche Bank extended to the Hamburger Tageblatt, a Party-owned newspaper and publishing house which issued National Socialist and National Socialist-approved newspapers, magazines, and books, two loans totaling RM 700,000. The first loan, RM 300,000, was granted in 1935 and guaranteed by Philipp Reemtsma. The second loan, RM 400,000, was granted in 1938 and guaranteed by the Standarte, a Party-owned publishing house. The Standarte guarantee, in its turn was guaranteed by Philipp Reemtsma.

SIEMENS COMBINE

The close relationship between the Deutsche Bank and the Siemens concern was based on tradition and on the great mutual advantages that could be derived for both partners from an association of the largest bank and one of the largest industrial combines in Germany. Intercorporate influence in Germany was generally secured and maintained through stock "ownership or proxy" voting, extension of credit facilities, interlocking directorships, and the like. All these elements were present in the Siemens–Deutsche Bank relationship, but rather as an outgrowth of the cooperation between the industrial giant and the bank, than to wield influence.

Siemens was the third largest industrial complex in Germany, ranking only after I.G. Farben and Vereinigte Stahlwerke. It was the largest electrical engineering firm in Europe and the second largest in the world.

Siemens & Halske, the parent company with a capital of RM 400 million, was both a producing and a holding company with direct and indirect interest of 25 percent or more in over one hundred firms within Germany and with direct and indirect interests in 196 foreign firms. In 1944, Siemens & Halske and its wholly owned subsidiaries employed a total of 250,000 people and reached a production of RM 2 billion. Devoting 85 percent of its manufacturing capacity to products directly or indirectly connected with rearmament in 1937, an even higher percentage of the Siemens output went into armaments during the war. The Siemens Combine was ruled by the Siemens family through its control over Siemens & Halske. The family and two foundations hold a minimum of 22.8 percent of the total share capital outstanding and a minimum of 50.6 percent of all voting rights. This divergence is caused by the plural voting rights of RM 19 million preferred shares which formed the core of the entire capital structure. Their 114,000 votes in the hands of a single trustee (31.2 percent of the total voting rights) constituted in themselves virtual control.

The relationship between the Deutsche Bank and the Siemens Combine was very close and manifold. Tied to the House of Siemens from the day of its inception, the Deutsche Bank has perpetuated a close relationship with the Siemens concern through generations. Some of its manifestations were interlocking directorships, representations of eight-figure amounts of stock by the Deutsche Bank at Siemens stockholders' meetings, Siemens ownership of Deutsche Bank stock, and the extensive use by Siemens of the facilities of the Deutsche Bank, its branches and affiliates, domestic and foreign.

The relationship began in 1870, when Georg Siemens, nephew of Werner Siemens, the original founder of Siemens & Halske, participated in the establishment of the Deutsche Bank and became its leading manager. . . . [Siemens was also] instrumental in establishing the Mannesmann works. While Mannesmann developed into what may be called an industrial affiliate of the Deutsche Bank, the ties between Siemens and Mannesmann remained very close through the years. Siemens owns Mannesmann stock and two members of the Siemens family, Hermann von Siemens and Friedrich Siemens, were on the board of directors of Mannesmann. The triangular relationship among the Deutsche Bank, Siemens, and Mannesmann was highlighted by the minutes of the 1937 stockholders' meeting of Mannesmann, which listed Friedrich Siemens as "Representative of the Deutsche Bank." Like Mannesmann, the Siemens concern in the 1932 crisis responded to the Deutsche Bank's request to acquire and hold some of its stock. Siemens & Halske took over RM 2 million Deutsche Bank shares in that year; another RM 2 million were acquired by Siemens & Halske and RM 1 million by Siemens-Schuckert in 1937, when the Deutsche Bank wanted to place among its friends the balance of that part of its stock which had been taken up by the German government during the 1932 crisis.

Thus Siemens first aided in limiting the amount of Deutsche Bank stock which was to come under government control, and finally in the reprivatization of stock actually acquired by the government.

On the other hand, the investment and commercial banking resources of the Deutsche Bank were always at the disposal of the Siemens concern. . . . The Deutsche Bank led the various syndicates for the placement of Siemens bond issues and those of Siemens shares in connection with capital increases, such as the issue of new stock of [the Siemens holding company], Elektrische Licht- und Kraftanlagen A.G., in 1943. Due to their liquid position, both Siemens & Halske and Siemens-Schuckert maintained large credit balances with the Deutsche Bank during the last ten years. Whenever required, however, the Deutsche Bank extended substantial loans to Siemens subsidiaries, for example, a RM 50 million loan to the Telefunken radio company during the war years. The Deutsche Ueberseeische Bank, a Deutsche

Bank subsidiary, served as the principal banking connection for the Latin American business of the Siemens concern. It facilitated the transfer of funds for purchases in Argentina and extended credit facilities for the same purpose as well as guarantees for Siemens delivery contracts.

The Deutsche Bank controlled the largest block of Siemens & Halske stock which was not family held. At the general meeting of 23 March 1943 for example, out of a total of RM 176,066,000 voting shares represented, the Deutsche Bank represented RM 42,050,000 shares for the account of its customers. It is obvious that stock represented by the Deutsche Bank was never voted in opposition to the Siemens management. Siemens-held Deutsche Bank stock in turn simply went to increase the votes controlled by the bank's management. In the bank's general meeting in April 1942, for instance, the Siemens-held stock was represented by proxy by one of the bank's employees together with other customer holdings.

The ties between Siemens and the Deutsche Bank were strengthened and received their outward manifestation through the mutual exchange of executive personnel to serve on each other's board of directors. While the Deutsche Bank delegated top personnel to the board of Siemens & Halske and its subsidiaries, there always was a member of the Siemens family on the board of the Deutsche Bank and several other executives on the boards of Deutsche Bank affiliates and advisory councils. . . .

Without attempting to record all of the many interlocking directorships between Siemens and the Deutsche Bank and their subsidiaries and affiliates, a chart of such directorships on the last boards of the Deutsche Bank, Siemens & Halske, and Siemens-Schuckert may serve as an illustration for the close personal ties between Siemens and the bank. *(See chart below.)*

	Deutsche Bank	**Siemens & Halske**	**Siemens-Schuckert**
Oswald Roesler	Vorstand	Aufsichtsrat	—
Hermann v. Siemens	Aufsichtsrat	Chairman	Chairman
Albert Pietzsch	Vice-chairman	—	Aufsichtsrat
Hermann Muenchmeyer	Aufsichtsrat	Aufsichtsrat	—
Oskar Sempell	Aufsichtsrat Deutsche Ueberseeische Bank	Vorstand	Vorstand
Ernst Kraus	Aufsichtsrat Creditanstalt Bankverein, Vienna	Vorstand	—
Hermann Reyss	Aufsichtsrat Deutsche Ueberseeische Bank	—	Vorstand
Fritz Jessen	Advisory council, Berlin-Brandenburg district	Vorstand	Vorstand

RHEINISCHE A.G. FUER BRAUNKOHLENBERGBAU UND BRIKETTFABRIKATION (RHEINBRAUN)

The Deutsche Bank has been associated with the Rheinische A.G. fuer Braunkohlen-bergbau und Brikettfabrikation (Rheinbraun) through interlocking directorships, and by serving as leader of banking syndicates.

Rheinbraun produces briquettes, electric power, and 10–11 percent of all German lignite, and until 1939/40 was the largest single lignite producer in Germany. It owns six large lignite mines with briquette factories and workshops and has substantial stockholdings in other lignite concerns, notably the Braunkohlen und Brikettwerke Roddergrube A.G. (Roddergrube), its parent company, which in turn is a subsidiary of the Rheinisch-Westfaelisches Elektrizitaetswerk A.G. (RWE). The stock capital of RWE amounted to RM 246 million in 1942, that of Rheinbraun to RM 120 million, and Roddergrube's to RM 72 million. According to [Gustav] Brecht, general manager of Rheinbraun and member of the Aufsichtsrat of the Deutsche Bank, RWE, Roddergrube, and Rheinbraun:

> were legally independent companies, but economically held together by mutual capital interests, dividend guarantee contracts, the same chairman of the board of directors in all three companies.

Rheinbraun and Roddergrube represent an influential part of an intricate network of lignite mines, briquette factories, electric works, synthetic fuel plants, shipping lines, in which they hold substantial participations and subparticipations.

Deutsche Bank ties with RWE and Roddergrube are evident through interlocking directorships. Hermann J. Abs (Vorstand, Deutsche Bank) was on the board of RWE and Roddergrube, Arthur Koepchen (Vorstand, RWE and Vorstand chairman, Roddergrube) and Gustav Brecht (Aufsichtsrat, Roddergrube) were on the Deutsche Bank's board.

Abs, Koepchen, and Brecht represent the interlocking links also for Rheinbraun. Abs, whose family owns about 1 percent of Rheinbraun's share capital, was the fifth successive Vorstand member of the Deutsche Bank in the Rheinbraun Aufsichtsrat during the thirty-eight years since Rheinbraun has been known under its present name.

Brecht stated that the Deutsche Bank has been the leader of all banking syndicates for Rheinbraun during the past twenty-five years. During the last fifteen years, Deutsche Bank and its syndicate granted a RM 50 million loan to Rheinbraun in 1930 and again in 1940. Even though the banking syndicate for the last loan was composed of thirteen members, Deutsche Bank participated with as much as 32.25 percent. Rheinbraun proved itself a loyal Deutsche Bank friend when it purchased a substantial block of Deutsche Bank stock immediately following the banking crisis of 1931 (Handelszeitung of *Berliner Tageblatt*, 17 July 1932). Rheinbraun owned [nominal] RM 2 million Deutsche Bank shares until 1935/36.

Rheinbraun is in possession of the majority block of 41.2 percent of the share capital of Union Rheinische Braunkohlen Kraftstoff A.G. (UK), a synthetic fuel corporation founded in 1937 as another step in the Nazi rearmament program. In 1940 the Deutsche Bank headed, with a participation of 33.375 percent, a banking syndicate of fourteen members for a bond issue of RM 60 million and in 1942 an additional one of RM 45 million. In 1943 fifteen banks, headed by Deutsche Bank's grant of RM 12,900,000, subscribed to a loan of RM 51,950,000 to UK.

A list of Deutsche Bank loans shows that the bank granted RM 60 million to Roddergrube in 1941, heading a banking syndicate composed of eleven with a participation of 29.75 percent.

The report on Gustav Brecht (cf. Chapter XIV) contains an account of his position in industry and the part Deutsche Bank played in that branch of German industry with which he is associated.

The companies and complexes which have been discussed in the preceding pages are illustrations of the very unusual relationship existing between the Deutsche Bank and certain industries which, at least in some of the cases, amounts to virtual control by the bank. They do by no means represent a complete listing of such "special situations." There are a number of other industrial enterprises which would seem to fall into the same category but which have not been specifically studied. A few of them are listed below with some of the indices of their special relationship to the Deutsche Bank:

VEREINIGTE GLANZSTOFF FABRIKEN AND ITS DUTCH ASSOCIATE AKU

A report on this powerful rayon combine has been prepared by the Decartelization Branch of the Economics Division. Deutsche Bank's position is indicated by a substantial stock interest, voting control, numerous interlocks (von Stauss, Kiehl, Schlitter, and Abs were on the board of directors at different times), syndicate operations, and manipulation of stock.

DEUTSCHE ERDOEL A.G.

This concern, engaged in the exploitation of petroleum and lignite deposits with important holdings in Romania and Austria, has three top executives of the Deutsche Bank on its Aufsichtsrat: Kimmich as chairman, and Bechtolf and Sippel as members. Carl Schirner, Vorstand of Deutsche Erdoel, was on the Deutsche Bank Aufsichtsrat. Richard Ullner was a common Aufsichtsrat member in both corporations. The Deutsche Bank voted 30 percent of the stock.

DEMAG A.G.

Vorstand members Kiehl and Kimmich of Deutsche Bank were on the Aufsichtsrat of Demag, one of the most important producers of heavy machinery. Demag's chairman of the board and former general manager, Wolfgang Reuter, was on Deutsche Bank's Aufsichtsrat. In addition there were three common directors including Zangen of Mannesmann, whose particularly close connection with Deutsche Bank is explained in other parts of this report. Deutsche Bank held proxies for 50 percent of the Demag stock.

HOESCH A.G. AND ITS SUBSIDIARIES

Two Deutsche Bank top officials were on the Aufsichtsrat of this large coal and steel combine—Kimmich as chairman and Bechtolf as a member. Erich Tgahrt, general manager of Hoesch, on the other hand, was on the Deutsche Bank Aufsichtsrat. Deutsche Bank voted over one quarter of the Hoesch stock. In this connection [there is] an interesting document from the files of the Flick concern [presenting] a grievance to be discussed with Kiehl and Kimmich of Deutsche Bank. The bank had apparently arranged for the majority block of stock of an industrial corporation (Maschinenbau und Bahnbedarf frueher Orenstein und Koppel) to pass into the hands of the Hoesch concern. The Flick people felt that they should be given the preference in acquiring control of that corporation and accordingly stated:

> The procurement of the MBA majority for Hoesch was a most unfriendly act of the Deutsche Bank toward us. The transaction was not justified by the factual situation since MBA has been, in the Berlin and Central German market, essentially one of the natural and important customers of the Mittelstahl group (one of the units of the Flick combine).

This statement illustrates another important aspect of the bank's power in directing the course of industrial organization. By its eminent position as a securities dealer and as a result of its far-flung contacts in industry and finance, the Deutsche Bank was frequently in a position to decide single-handedly who was and was not to acquire and to hold a majority interest or a decisive minority interest in a given industry. This is an aspect of the influence of the Grossbanken in German industry which may well be worth further exploration.

CHAPTER IX

Rearmament and War Financing

The operations of the Deutsche Bank in the years after 1933 were geared to an ever increasing degree to support Germany's preparation for, and conduct of, a war of aggression. For Germany's economic mobilization for war demanded, in an ever increasing measure, a total effort. It engulfed the whole economy, and it engulfed, not least of all, the financial community, which, by and large, was responsible for the direct or indirect financing of the whole venture.

This is not to say that the bank had no choice. Basically, from 1933 on, it had to choose between two alternative courses: to continue operations along traditional lines as far as possible without making a special effort to assist the government, or to throw in the full weight of its organization in support of Party and state. The former course would undoubtedly have meant a drastic reduction in the relative importance of the bank, a consequence the bank's officials did not relish. The latter course was much more in line with their nationalist-militaristic outlook. This basic agreement in philosophy far outweighed any misgivings which may have existed if the distorted anticapitalist aims of a faction of the early Nazis seemed a bit strange to some of the old-line bankers. Above all, full cooperation with the new regime afforded the bankers an opportunity for themselves and for the bank as a whole not only to retain their power and influence, but to increase it. The individual choices the bank had to make all along the road will be illustrated in subsequent pages.

All the evidence indicates that the Deutsche Bank did, in fact, choose the road of all-out cooperation, notwithstanding the protestations of its officials that, on the contrary, they were desperately struggling to stay on the "conservative" side.

From the Annex to the Report

None of the principal Deutsche Bank officials has admitted having had knowledge before the war of secret rearmament. A file note, prepared on 24 March 1937 by Karl Sippel for the information of his colleagues on the Vorstand, presents the case in another light. The document describes a visit to the Deutsche Bank of a representative of the Office of the Four Year Plan, Dr. Kraenzlein, who informed Sippel of the intention to construct a series of plants for the production of explosive materials for armament purposes. Dr. Kraenzlein requested the assistance of the Deutsche Bank for the establishment of a holding company of which the bank, in the name of the Reich, was to acquire the majority of the capital stock. The bank, which was to receive prompt reimbursement from the Reich for moneys it expended, would, in this fashion, be secured against all risk. The entire arrangement was conceived so as to camouflage the interests of the Reich.

The principal Deutsche Bank officials also informed themselves, via the Mefo bills,[1] of the character of rearmament financing. [Eduard] Mosler circulated among his Vorstand colleagues a file note written by him on 25 February 1938 directly following a visit to Reichsbankdirektor Huelse. Huelse had informed Mosler that the issuance of Mefo bills would on 31 March 1938 be discontinued and that future orders for rearmament as well as for the creation of an autonomous supply of raw materials were to be financed out of the Reich budget. Huelse added, that the Reichsbank, which previously had placed Mefo bills with the Deutsche Bank and the Girozentrale alone, would extend the practice thereafter to all members of the Reichsanleihe Konsortium (Syndicate for government loans).

An internal bank report prepared for Karl Kimmich on 17 February 1941 reveals that the credits and loans extended by the Deutsche Bank for armament purposes were greater in volume than the fragmentary evidence heretofore available had indicated. Credits for Four Year Plan purposes, narrowly defined, came to RM 488,100,000 of which only the fourth part was guaranteed by the Reich. Credits to firms in the aircraft industry attained the enormous figure of RM 178,100,000, only 5 percent of which was guaranteed by the Reich.

The Deutsche Bank was the exponent of a strong German banking system, the kind of system needed by the Nazis to build up a war potential both rapidly and smoothly. Three main groups of activities make up the contribution the Deutsche Bank, as the most important commercial bank in Germany, made to the efficient development and maintenance of this war potential: providing the Reich with funds; financing war industry through loans and distribution of new securities; and directing the industries controlled by the bank into "appropriate" channels of production.

Loans were extended by the bank increasingly to meet the demands of the rearmament program. With the beginning of the war, of course, practically all financing was concentrated on enterprises connected in one way or another with the war effort. As an investment house, the bank placed shares and bonds of the same type of enterprise with the public. Financing of the Reich became the bank's broadest and most important function. Its scope and some of its special aspects will, therefore, be discussed first.

FINANCING OF THE REICH

TREASURY PAPER

In financing the Reich, the Deutsche Bank, like the other commercial banks, concentrated mainly on the purchase of treasury bills *(Schatzwechsel und unverzinsliche Schatzanweisungen des Reichs und der Laender),* which were short-term instruments and as such most suited for investment of funds derived from customers' demand

---

[1] "Special bonds" for covert financing of government-backed, war-related industries and corporate acquisitions.

deposits. The longer-term treasury notes and bonds *(Anleihen und verzinsliche Schatzanweisungen des Reichs und der Laender)* were taken up mostly by savings banks and insurance institutions, and to a smaller extent, by commercial credit institutions, industry, and commerce, and the general public. The amount absorbed by non-banking institutions and individual purchasers, however, was substantial and Deutsche Bank with its huge organizations and network was admirably suited to act as the Reich's agent in the placement of large amounts with its customers. The following remarks, taken from the bank's annual report for the year 1937, are pertinent:

> Total funding of the Reich debt . . . now reaches the sum of about RM 8.75 billion. This financial success, and a very considerable one for the progress of the entire economy, was substantially aided by the commercial credit banks. Again and again the close contact of the bank with its large number of customers from all spheres of the economy has proved to be an instrument which is essential for the necessary long-term financing of Reich expenditures.

In the following year, 1938, an additional RM 8 billion of government paper could be placed. In 1942, the Deutsche Bank alone was able to place over RM 1 billion of treasury bonds with the public. The bank itself retained RM 479 million in its portfolio, a holding representing 11.8 percent of the treasury notes and bonds held by all German commercial banks. The bank's proportionate share of treasury bills was even larger. It amounted to 23.1 percent (RM 3,951 million) of all commercial bank holdings.

While up to 1937 the bank's holdings of treasury bills fluctuated between RM 200 and 300 million, a huge increase took place in the succeeding years, as shown in the following tabulation:

```
1937—RM   202,880,532
1938—RM   529,674,690
1939—RM 1,148,758,779
1940—RM 2,079,256,329
1941—RM 2,908,564,808
1942—RM 3,950,696,413
1943—RM 4,635,278,845
1944—RM 7,502,694,558
```

[As reported in Chapter IV], in 1944 this meant an investment of 66 percent of the total assets of the bank (RM 11,374 million) in treasury bills. Adding to this figure treasury notes and bonds (RM 412 million), promissory notes of the Deutsche Golddiskontbank (RM 873 million), and loans extended with Reich guarantee for special Reich projects (about RM 560 million), one finds that over 82 percent of the Deutsche Bank assets were employed in direct and indirect financing of the government at the end of 1944. . . .

The steadily increasing emphasis on financing the Reich by direct investment of the bank's assets was a deliberate policy. In its report for the year 1940, the bank proudly points out its achievements in saying:

In this year, in which Germany's armed forces gained victories of historic proportions, the German war economy has measured up to what had been expected of it. The credit banks have contributed particularly in the successful execution of the short-term financing of the Reich.

But apart from the above-mentioned financing activities the bank gave invaluable assistance to the government by absorption of various species of special financing instruments of the Reich.

WORK CREATION BILLS AND TAX REMISSION CERTIFICATES

In addition to the issue of treasury paper, the Nazi state, from the very beginning, relied heavily on special bills and certificates for the financing of the tremendous requirements first of the so-called re-employment, and later of the rearmament program. The Deutsche Bank played an important part in the success of these programs, granting an ever increasing volume of credit on the various short-term instruments. Hitler's Four Year Plan of 1933 contemplated an outlay of RM 4.5 billion for public works and the construction of the strategic *Reichsautobahnen* (Reich motor roads). This "re-employment" program, of course, was only the first stage of remilitarization—and preparation for war. Financing was accomplished through the issue of *Arbeitsbeschaffungswechsel* (work creation bills), which were bills drawn by the contractors on special financial institutions of the Reich, and which when due were extended again and again. The use of these bills declined after 1934, as did the circulation of tax remission certificates, which had been continued from the period immediately preceding the Nazi rule.

MEFO BILLS

After 1935, when Hitler announced the withdrawal of Germany from the disarmament conference and the reintroduction of conscription, the public works program as a stimulus to employment was tapered off and replaced by a program of direct production for rearmament. The new program was financed by bills issued from February 1936 until the end of March 1938 under the innocuous name of *Sonderwechsel* (special bills). They later came to be known as "Mefo bills." In a letter dated 27 January 1936 from the Reichsbank directorate to all Reichsbank branches and credit institutions, the German banking world received an outline of this new scheme. The following is an extract:

> With regard to the intermediate financing of Reich expenditures for purposes of work creation with particular emphasis on the building up of the Wehrmacht, we confidentially inform you of the following. We request that you treat this communication as strictly confidential and that you see to it particularly that no part of its contents will get into the newspapers. From 1 February 1936 on, industrial enterprises executing Reich orders will mainly receive 6 months' acceptances of the Metallurgische Forschungsgesellschaft m.b.H. [Institute for Metallurgical Research, Ltd.] in place of the usual cash

payment. These bills carry the signature of the industrial firm as drawer and first endorser, and a further endorsement of the Handelsgesellschaft fuer Industrie-Erzeugnisse G.m.b.H. [Industrial Products Trading Company, Ltd.].

The Metallurgische Forschungsgesellschaft (Mefo), was nothing but a camouflaged financial tool of German rearmament under the Four Year Plan. It acted as a straw man for the Reichsbank and the Reich Ministry of Finance, with no other function than to lend its name for the acceptance of special armament bills. By accepting these Mefo bills for discount, the Deutsche Bank, like the other commercial banks, knowingly gave Germany's rearmament its financial backing and helped to keep the volume of such financing, and hence the extent of the rearmament effort, a well-guarded secret. In reality nothing but an advance of money to the Reich, the use of Mefo bills for the financing of Reich expenditures enabled the Reichsbank to exceed by many billions the RM 400 million it was permitted by its charter to lend to the government. Dr. [Otto] Schniewind, member of the Reichsbank Directorate at the time, when interrogated regarding the Mefo bills, stated:

> We believed that the Mefo bills would be paid in cash when due, and we were convinced that by throttling this financial source the whole national-socialist spook would be made to disappear suddenly.

Such was the importance of this financing instrument.

The Deutsche Bank started to take in Mefo bills for discount in 1936. Hans Rummel, member of the Deutsche Bank Vorstand, states that the bills were discounted with the Deutsche Bank by companies engaged in filling orders for the German armed forces. He remembered Daimler Benz and possibly Maschinenfabrik Augsburg-Nuernberg (MAN) as outstanding depositors of such bills. A check of the Mefo-bill transactions of the Mannesmann Roehrenwerke, Duesseldorf, and some of its subsidiaries reveals that they alone discounted more than RM 3 million of such bills with the Deutsche Bank in 1936, and a total of some RM 12.5 million from 1936 to 1938. Conscious of the significance of its role in this type of financing, the Deutsche Bank included in its report for the year 1936 the following remark:

> For the purchase of special bills of the Reich, substantial amounts were made available. As in the preceding years, the banks have thus put themselves at the disposal of the Reich, for the financing of expenditures, which could not be covered by increased tax revenues.

Mefo bills had an initial tenure of six months, but were renewable indefinitely; three months after issuance, they were eligible for rediscount with the Reichsbank [that is, redeemed at a profit]. In addition to discounting Mefo bills from customers, the Deutsche Bank also bought them in the open money market and from the Reichsbank. [Captured records show] acquisition of a block of RM 20 million Mefo bills from the Reichsbank.

In a drive to consolidate the Reich short-term indebtedness, the issue of Mefo bills to suppliers was discontinued on 31 March 1938. All bills were to be presented to the Reichsbank, as the agent of the Reich, for redemption during the following six months. Of the total amount of some RM 12 billion outstanding, about 90 percent were produced by the commercial banks. Actually the Reich did not redeem the bills at that time. The Reichsbank acquired them as trustee for the Reich and retained them as the basis for the issuance of so-called *Mefo-Wechsel-Bescheinigungen* (Mefo bill certificates) issued in round denominations with maturities varying from three months to a year. This new paper was promptly placed by the Reichsbank with credit institutions, who were willing buyers. The main attraction for the banks was the fact that they could show these certificates (like the Mefo bills) under "commercial bills" in their financial statements. Thereby their true character of a government obligation was concealed and the bank's total investment in the Reich understated. From the point of view of the Nazi government, this technique allowed the concealment of total Reich expenditures and particularly of those applicable to Germany's rearmament and treaty violation. The Reich started redemption of Mefo bills in 1941 and the issue of Mefo bill certificates was discontinued by the Reichsbank in July 1943.

The importance of the Mefo bills in the German rearmament economy is manifested by the fact that they constituted 12 percent of the total German public debt in 1940. At a meeting of the board of directors of the Deutsche Bank, it was disclosed that in 1940 the total public debt, according to Secretary of State Reinhardt, was made up as follows:

Disclosed debts of the Reich including tax remission certificates	RM 79,000 million
Mefo bills	RM 12,000 million
Debts of the "Laender"	RM 2,300 million
Debts of the "Gemeinden"	RM 8,000 million
	RM 101,300 million

The entire volume of transactions in Mefo bills by the Deutsche Bank cannot now be ascertained. However, the amount of Mefo bills or certificates held at the end of each year from 1936 to 1943 (none was held at the end of 1944) is shown in the following tabulation:

end of 1936—RM 405,055,500
1937—RM 572,810,200
1938—RM 241,357,200
1939—RM 212,143,900
1940—RM 349,528,300
1941—RM 510,241,800
1942—RM 617,840,300
1943—RM 341,621,000

DELIVERY NOTES

After the issue of Mefo bills was discontinued, a new instrument for short-term financing of armament expenditures was created by the Reich. Suppliers were given so-called *Lieferungsschatzanweisungen* (delivery notes) in payment for deliveries. These delivery notes, unlike the Mefo bills, were not eligible for rediscount at the

Reichsbank. They were redeemed, without renewal, at the end of six months by the Reich Treasury.

The Deutsche Bank acquired Lieferungsschatzanweisungen from customers and in the open market, thus throwing in its weight in support of this new means of armament financing. Transactions reached a substantial volume, according to Deutsche Bank officials, but accurate figures could not be obtained. Delivery notes were included in the balance sheet under "Treasury bills and noninterest-bearing treasury notes of Reich and Laender." In its report for the year 1938, the Deutsche Bank explains its own contribution and that of the other commercial banks as follows:

> Banks participated in the financing of deliveries since the spring of 1938 by taking over from the various enterprises the Lieferungsschatzanweisungen, which had been issued by the Reich. The introduction of this new instrument has strongly influenced the development of bank balance sheets in general and also of our balance sheet for the past year; the reduction in bills of exchange, resulting from the maturity of special bills [Mefo], was offset by a sharp increase in treasury bills [Schatzanweisungen].

According to the tabulation shown above, Mefo bills dropped RM 331 million between 1937 and 1938. Annual balance sheets, on the other hand, show an increase in treasury bills of RM 327 million in the same year.

DEGO PROMISSORY NOTES

With the redemption of Mefo bills, promissory notes *(Solawechsel)* of the Deutsche Golddiskontbank (Dego) gained considerable importance. They had previously been in circulation only in small volume. The Deutsche Bank assisted the Reich by substantial purchases of such promissory notes *(Degowechsel)*. The following tabulation shows the Deutsche Bank's holdings at the end of each year from 1937 to 1944:

1937—RM	12,300,000
1938—RM	39,600,000
1939—RM	107,400,000
1940—RM	160,000,000
1941—RM	138,000,000
1942—RM	83,500,000
1943—RM	422,500,000
1944—RM	872,950,000

The promissory notes of the Dego, like the Mefo bills, offered the Deutsche Bank an opportunity to "dress up" its balance sheet. According to the Reichsbank's instructions, they could be listed as commercial paper. Such window dressing was indeed needed since, as a result of increasing financial involvement with the government, the Deutsche Bank's holdings of true commercial bills of exchange had dwindled to about RM 84 million at the end of 1944. By adding to this amount the holdings of Dego notes, the Deutsche Bank was able to boast a commercial bill portfolio of RM 957 million for that year.

The unrestrained efficiency with which the Deutsche Bank directed the bulk of its resources into the pool from which the Reich financed its expenditures, largely military in nature, is indicative of the bank's basic agreement with the policy underlying these expenditures. The more direct procurement of funds to "strategic" industries, in the form of loans and syndicate operations, though second in size to government financing, and the operations of bank-controlled war industries, are even more conclusive proof of the bank's readiness to serve the Nazi "cause"—the cause of forcing Germany's will upon the world at the point of a gun.

As early as 1934, the Deutsche Bank was appraising its economic activities in terms of *Wehr-Politik* (armament economy). In a memorandum sent to the Deutsche Golddiskontbank (Dego) in February 1934, the bank sought to enlist the Dego's support for the financing of a German syndicate headed by Deutsche Bank and engaged, jointly with Turkish interests, in the exploitation of a copper ore deposit in Asiatic Turkey. The Deutsche Bank syndicate was striving to have all orders for machinery needed in this mining venture placed with German manufacturers. As to the importance of the enterprise, the Deutsche Bank said:

> The enterprise constitutes a valuable asset to German economic activity abroad. Considering its propagandistic effect as a model of German industrial achievement, and also considering that this copper mine not only has excellent prospects, but is the only one in Turkey, it assumes great significance in general and, more particularly, for our armament economy *(Wehrpolitische Bedeutung)*. It appears to us to be extremely important to secure and to strengthen the German influence in the enterprise.

This statement showed true foresight. Especially during the war years Turkey became a most valuable source of vital raw materials for Germany. Though such early foreign undertakings of the Deutsche Bank proved important for the success of German war planning, the bulk of the bank's activities in support of German rearmament was domestic business, at least in the initial stages. Domestic loans were extended by the bank increasingly to meet direct or indirect armament requirements, such as the establishment and development of the new raw material industries and the development and expansion of armament manufacturing industries of all kinds.

In its annual report for the year 1937, the Deutsche Bank said:

> Frequently the capital requirements of Four Year Plan projects and plant extensions connected therewith exceeded available funds and made the use of loan grants necessary. This resulted in an increase in loans granted in comparison with the previous year, especially in the higher brackets. . . .We have granted substantial loans for the erection of facilities for the manufacture of new basic materials.

The steady increase in the number of large individual loans granted can be seen from a tabulation of new loans above RM 1 million measured by their ratio to the total amount of new loans granted. (See Table VIII.)

The consistent growth of loans in the higher brackets was in line with the trend towards industrial concentration. This growth expressed itself not only in the

Table VIII
NEW LOANS ABOVE RM 1 MILLION

Year	Number of loans	Amount in RM	Percentage of total amount of loans granted
1933	35	58,112,600	8
1934	51	114,025,100	14
1935	65	147,987,731	16
1936	73	223,379,061	21
1937	99	245,663,918	20
1938	129	328,500,481	22
1939	136	434,282,889	26
1940	153	508,198,843	33
1941	160	544,387,928	35

number of loans over RM 1 million but also in their average amount, which rose from RM 1.7 million in 1933 to RM 3.4 million in 1941.

There is no doubt that large loans to munitions makers continued to increase, both in number and average size, in the years following 1941, for which no detailed breakdown is available. War industries had until then relied heavily upon advance payments on Reich contracts as a source of working capital. When during the winter 1942–1943 the government imposed severe limitations—at least temporarily—on these advance payments, the Deutsche Bank enjoyed a further increase in the demand for loans. The Deutsche Bank itself made this point in its annual report for the year 1943:

> In the past year 70,331 loans, amounting to a total of RM 2,107 million, were drawn on or granted. This increase does not indicate a higher demand for loans on a broad basis. Additional money requirements were concentrated in a limited number of loan users, mainly those of the armament industry, which was depending on the use of loan capital for the fulfillment of new tasks, or due to the discontinuance of advance payments by the state.

FINANCING OF SPECIFIC WAR INDUSTRIES

The most direct contribution the bank could make to Germany's rearmament race consisted, of course, in the direction of the productive effort of industrial enterprises under its influence or control. The following corporations have been selected for discussion:

> Daimler Benz A.G., Stuttgart-Untertuerkheim
> Bayerische Motoren Werke A.G., Munich
> Mannesmann Roehrenwerke A.G., Duesseldorf
> Krauss-Maffei A.G., Munich-Allach

DAIMLER BENZ A.G.

As has been shown in Chapter VIII Daimler Benz was one of the largest enterprises essentially controlled by the Deutsche Bank. A peacetime producer of automobiles, trucks, and motors, the company took up the production of airplane motors in 1935, when the first shift of industrial capacity toward rearmament occurred in Germany. The plant at Untertuerkheim was enlarged and a new plant was built at Berlin-Marienfelde for this purpose. In the following years, production was almost exclusively confined to orders of the German armed forces. The Daimler corporation produced tanks since 1937. Manufacturing facilities were expanded through the erection of plants at Sindelfingen, Mannheim, Gaggenau, and Koenigsberg. During the war years, subsidiaries were acquired in Genshagen, Germany, as well as in the occupied territories of France, Poland, and Hungary. Daimler Benz A.G. won special recognition and awards for its achievements from the Nazi government. On its letterhead it boasted a gold-embossed swastika, with the words *National-Sozialistischer* Musterbetrieb (National Socialist Model Enterprise). With a 1933 output valued at only RM 100 million, production figures developed as follows during the crucial period:

> 1939— about RM 250 million
> 1942— about RM 844 million
> 1943— about RM 951 million
> 1944 (1st 8 mos.)—about RM 657 million

Such an increase in output could be accomplished only by investments in plant and machinery. For the ten-year period ending in 1943 these investments amounted to RM 305 million. The Deutsche Bank ran a very considerable risk in its advances to the company, but it was too deeply involved to relinquish control once the company had been launched on its production program even had it so desired. In 1943 the Deutsche Industriebank and the Bank der Deutschen Luftfahrt stepped in with substantial amounts; but as of June 1944, the Deutsche Bank was still engaged with RM 27,477,000 credits open on its books. . . . [Daimler Benz] was entirely occupied with orders for the armed forces. It was producing, in the order of RM volume, airplane engines, spare parts, trucks, and tanks. Here are some of the delivery figures for the first eight months of 1944:

> 8,493 airplane engines—value RM 242 million
> 5,294 trucks—value RM 77 million
> 796 special vehicles (tanks)—value RM 68 million
> parts and repairs—value RM 156 million

Unfilled war orders as of 31 August 1944 amounted to RM 1,131,076,000. At its peak in 1944, the company with its subsidiaries employed 70,300 workers, 40 percent of whom were foreign laborers (including 3,300 prisoners of war).

BAYERISCHE MOTOREN WERKE A.G. (BMW), MUNICH

Like Daimler Benz, BMW has been under Deutsche Bank domination since its reorganization in 1925 when von Stauss, for all practical purposes, became its managing head (cf. Chapter VI). Von Stauss's early efforts toward the resurrection and preservation of a German aircraft industry have also been previously discussed. In this resurrected, and then steadily growing German aircraft industry, BMW came to be the largest manufacturer of engines. Particularly with the advent of Hitler, production was rapidly expanded mainly through the establishment of subsidiaries until BMW became one of the keystones of German rearmament in the air. The following subsidiaries were established:

> BMW Flugmotoren G.m.b.H., Munich and Munich-Allach
> BMW Flugmotorenwerke Brandenburg G.m.b.H., Berlin-Spandau
> BMW Flugmotorenfabrik Eisenach G.m.b.H., Eisenach
> Giesserei und Maschinenfabrik Bitschweiler G.m.b.H., Bitschweiler

These subsidiaries were set up in the form of *Gesellschaften mit beschraenkter Haftung* (G.m.b.H.s, limited liability companies) for one primary reason: to keep the volume and nature of their output, geared entirely to preparation for war, a well guarded secret. Unlike Aktiengesellschaften (A.G.s, corporations) G.m.b.H.s were not required by law to publish annual reports. If any further proof be needed to establish this fact, it can be found in a report rendered by the Vorstand to the Aufsichtsrat in May 1944 when a change of the organizational structure was proposed. On page 5 of this report, the Vorstand says:

> Considerations of camouflage and risk which guided the separate establishment of the aircraft engine business in 1934 and the foundation and taking over of further subsidiaries could be discarded already in 1942.

For this very reason of camouflage, production was increasingly shifted to the subsidiaries until in 1943 the parent company's, BMW A.G.'s output amounted to less than 10 percent of the total. Value of production, which had only been RM 65 million in 1933, was quadrupled during the rearmament period; it further increased during the war years as follows:

> 1939—RM 280 million
> 1941—RM 385 million
> 1942—RM 561 million
> 1943—RM 653 million

Ninety-five percent of the 1943 production consisted of engines for the German air force. For the year 1944, the firm envisaged a production of engines valued at RM 1,200 million; a goal which, however, was not reached, mainly due to bombing attacks and the shifting of plant and machinery away from danger zones. The Deutsche Bank could hardly consider its interests in BMW a sound investment, yet it did not withdraw when huge financing demands of the works had to be met. According to a Deutsche Bank memorandum, expansion of plant facilities alone required an outlay of RM 205 million from 1940 to 1943. The same memorandum shows the Deutsche Bank's commitment in loans to BMW as of October 1944 as amounting to RM 63 million plus RM 3,500,000 to the Niederbarnimer Flugmotorenwerke G.m.b.H., in which BMW held a participation.

When Deutsche Bank's von Stauss back in the 1920s engineered the rehabilitation of the German aircraft industry and in subsequent years drove BMW (and Daimler) ever deeper into the production of airplane engines, he knew and his bank knew that the development of such productive capacity could only be justified by military objectives. For clearly any substantial aircraft engine production could find an outlet only in Germany's rearmament demands. It could not possibly be absorbed by civil aviation requirements.

Hence the men of BMW and Daimler Benz can hardly have experienced any surprise when Goering gave formal notice that war was in the offing. That notice came at a secret conference held at Karinhall on 8 July 1938, in a speech made by Goering, in which he also extolled BMW's contribution to rearmament in the air. The following are quotations from the minutes of the conference, as shown in the translation of document R-140, Office of U.S. Chief of Counsel:

> We are fully embarked on the way to mobilization capacity and shall not be able for years to deviate from it.

> This is why I again beg of you with all my heart, gentlemen, consider yourself an industry which has the duty to create an Air Force and which is most intimately connected with that Air Force. . . .

> The same applies in general to the airplane motor industry. Here the main task will be to produce Mercedes "GOIs" in large numbers. As to BMW, I put great hopes on the future . . . as an enormous step forward. Until then the most intensified production of the present type has to be continued of course.

That secret conference was attended by BMW's general manager Popp, Daimler Benz' general manager Wilhelm Kissel, and other leading men of the aircraft industry as well as high officials of the air ministry.

MANNESMANN ROEHRENWERKE A.G., DUESSELDORF (M/W)

Mannesmann was the largest of the Deutsche Bank–controlled enterprises. A very detailed report about its operations has been compiled by the Joint Special Financial Detachment USGCC, Control Commission for Germany, from which the following extract is quoted:

> From 1933 onwards M/W was one of the small group of very large, vital German industries which, management-controlled, and under the autocracy of the Vorstand, Chairman and a few chosen advisers, operated autonomously, under the self-imposed discipline of the cartels, in the sphere of one or more of the largest banks and in cooperation with the Nazi Government it helped to power. Oversimplifying these elements,— (1) the man is Wilhelm Zangen, (2) the cartel is the Roehrenverband, (3) the bank is the Deutsche Bank.

In 1935 the Deutsche Bank passed the direction of M/W into the hands of Wilhelm Zangen, whose powerful political position has already been described (cf.

Chapter VI). In the following years M/W became one of the most important suppliers of iron, steel, and semifinished products for the German armament program. A comparison of production figures (excluding coal and allied products) for the years 1932 and 1943 of the works located in Germany proper indicates a growth matched only by a very few other concerns in heavy industry. (Figures from Joint Detachment report mentioned above.)

M/W Production (in tons)

	1932	1943
Limestone	57,000	265,000
Pig iron	168,000	727,000
Raw steel	218,000	1,100,000
Semifinished products	131,000	514,000
Heavy plate	49,000	188,000
Thin sheets	43,000	168,000
Plates and sheets	98,000	471,000
Tubes	77,000	532,000

This growth was accomplished through a policy of plant extension and through the acquisition of competing or allied enterprises. Not considered is the production added by ruthless expansion into the countries surrounding Germany. Almost in every case with the advice, assistance, or financial banking of the Deutsche Bank or of a Deutsche Bank subsidiary, M/W expanded into the territories annexed or occupied by Germany. A case in point is that of the Metallwalzwerk A.G. Maehrisch-Ostrau, which with its subsidiaries was brought into the M/W fold in 1940 by the Boehmische Unionbank (a Deutsche Bank subsidiary) with the approval of the Nazi authorities. The importance of M/W as a producer of armaments is borne out by the fact that Zangen, its leading official, was one of the handful of leading industrialists who were called into the Ruestungsrat, the coordinating committee between the armed forces, the Speer Ministry, and war industry.

KRAUSS-MAFFEI A.G., MUNICH-ALLACH

This Deutsche Bank–controlled corporation is of less impressive size than the enterprises discussed above. Nevertheless as a manufacturer of locomotives it was essential to German armament and the conduct of the war. Little conversion was required for the production of tractors and heavy engineering equipment for the German armed forces. The firm employed a labor force of about 8,000 workers and reached an output of RM 100 million in 1943. The financial statement as of 15 November 1944 shows advance payments by the *Oberkommando des Heeres* (OKH, German Army High Command) amounting to RM 3,100,000.

AIR REARMAMENT

Deutsche Bank's activities in the field of rearmament in the air were not confined to the two complexes under its control. A partial list of loans extended by the bank at the end of 1939, titled "Larger commitments in the aircraft industry," shows the following additional companies and the amounts loaned to them:

Messerschmitt A.G., Augsburg—	RM 3,464,000
Vereinigte Deutsche Metallwerke A.G., Frankfurt—	RM 2,572,000
Ardeltwerke, Eberswalde—	RM 10,643,000
Ernst Heinkel Aircraft Works, Berlin	RM 1,087,000

After the impact of actual warfare made itself felt, naturally considerably larger amounts were required and the number of borrowers increased.

Hans Rummel, Vorstand member, stated that the Junkers Werke had loans up to RM 10 million, the Dornier Werke received RM 6 million in 1943 and a "large loan" was extended to the Frankfurt affiliate of the Vereinigte Deutsche Metallwerke A.G., Frankfurt.

In a tabulation of the largest accounts receivable, the Deutsche Bank branch in Frankfurt lists a loan of RM 24,380,000 to the Continentale Metall A.G., Bad Homburg, and a loan of RM 7,550,000 to the Matra Werke G.m.b.H., Frankfurt/Main. The Continentale Metall A.G. was the successor of the VDM Luftfahrtwerke A.G., the above-mentioned affiliate of the Vereinigte Deutsche Metallwerke A.G., whose aircraft-works holdings were combined in it. The Matra Werke manufactured special tools and machinery for automobile and aircraft repair work.

From the questioning of the Deutsche Bank officials available and from the few files accessible, little information could be obtained on loans granted to many of the smaller aircraft or aircraft accessory makers. However, in addition to the loan to "Matra," files were located concerning another substantial engagement with an aircraft accessory maker, the "Gema" *(Gesellschaft fuer elektroakustische und mechanische Apparate G.m.b.H., Berlin-Koepenick)*. The Gema, which was founded in 1934, was occupied from its inception almost exclusively with production for the German rearmament program. According to the statement of an official of the Deutsche Industriebank, which had subparticipations in some of the loans extended to Gema by the Deutsche Bank, the latter was the "house bank" of the concern and handled all its more important financing operations. The company manufactured equipment for signal communications and for the interception of communications and the measuring of impulses (apparently similar to radar).

From 1936 on, Deutsche Bank financed Gema's Wehrmacht orders by discounting Mefo bills in amounts up to RM 800,000. In addition, the bank granted short-term loans beginning with RM 100,000 in 1937 and increasing to RM 1.5 million by 1942. In 1943, when Gema was engaged in filling huge orders for the Luftwaffe, Deutsche Bank extended a RM 20 million loan to finance the expanded operations. In the following year, even this amount proved inadequate, and a RM 50 million loan was arranged. Half of this amount was supplied by the Deutsche Bank with two minor subparticipants, the other half was provided by the Luftwaffe's own "Bank der Deutschen Luftfahrt." As of 30 April 1945 Gema still owed the Deutsche Bank RM 20,200,000 on this loan.

In view of the size of a single commitment such as the above and the others already considered, it is reasonable to assume that Hans Rummel understated the

Deutsche Bank's total engagement in the aircraft industry in naming a figure of about RM 150 million.

In any event, the bank assumed risks in this field such as no other commercial bank, with the possible exception of the Dresdner Bank, was willing to take. Only the Bank der Deutschen Luftfahrt, which was government sponsored, surpassed the two commercial banks in this field.

FINANCING OF SYNTHETIC FUEL PRODUCTION

As a major shortcoming in Germany's war potential, the lack of natural fuel received early consideration by the Nazi government. The only solution was seen in the extension of existing facilities and the construction of a series of new plants for the production of synthetic gasoline and fuel. Since coal is the basic raw material for such production and the Deutsche Bank had long been close to the large coal mining interests, it was natural for the bank to turn its attention to the development of the growing hydrating industry. True, it seemed a risky business, but it offered an opportunity to earn big profits, and at the same time to demonstrate the bank's loyalty to the Nazi program of self-sufficiency. However, the Deutsche Bank soon found that it had a rival in the synthetic fuel field in the smaller, but aggressive Dresdner Bank.

Thus the Dresdner Bank had the edge over Deutsche Bank when the lignite industry, upon government initiative, organized a special corporation in 1934 for the development of synthetic fuel. The corporation was called the Braunkohle-Benzin A.G. (Brabag). Its initial capital of RM 100 million was provided by the major lignite producers through a *Pflichtgemeinschaft der deutschen Braunkohlen Industrie* (Duty Association of the German Lignite Industry). A banking syndicate was called upon to supply additional funds. SS General Baron von Schroeder, who was on the Brabag board, explained that Reichsbank President Schacht, who had conceived the original idea of setting up the Brabag, turned to the Dresdner Bank for the forming of a banking syndicate to provide a RM 25 million loan to the Brabag. The Dresdner and the Deutsche Bank each participated to the extent of 20 to 25 percent, but the Dresdner Bank led the syndicate. According to Gustav Brecht, top official of the Rheinbraun A.G. and deputy chairman of the Brabag board of directors, loans totaling about RM 130 million were raised by a large banking syndicate, again headed by the Dresdner Bank. Though the Deutsche Bank was not the syndicate leader, its quota equalled that of the Dresdner Bank. Brabag's various installations came into production in 1936; for the first full year of operations, 1937, production reached a total of about 320,000 tons. This figure increased substantially in later years.

On the whole, however, the Deutsche Bank could not be relegated to second place in the financing of synthetic fuel production. As already pointed out, the Deutsche Bank had cultivated a close relationship with the large coal mining interests for many years. It was the main banking connection of this industry and had been supplying them with capital and operational funds for some time, mainly through the floating of stocks and bonds. By the same method most of the financing of synthetic fuel production was effected.

In October 1935, the Ruhrbenzin A.G., Oberhausen-Holten, was founded upon the Reich's request for the production of synthetic fuel and lubricants. Founders were firms prominent in Ruhr coal mining and which were within the Deutsche Bank's sphere of influence, headed by the following:

Vereinigte Stahlwerke A.G.
Harpener Bergbau A.G.
Hoesch-Koeln-Neuessen A.G.
Friedrich Krupp A.G., Essen
Essener Steinkohlen Bergwerke
Haniel Konzern
Mannesmann Roehrenwerke

The Ruhrbenzin A.G. was to have an initial capacity of 30,000 tons per annum. For the construction of the plant a syndicate, headed by the Deutsche Bank, granted a RM 9 million loan, to be repaid in installments by 1940. The syndicate quotas were:

Deutsche Bank—	RM 4,000,000
Dresdner Bank—	RM 2,800,000
Commerz- & Privat-Bank—	RM 1,700,000
Berliner Handelsgesellschaft—RM	500,000

In 1936 an additional loan for extension of plant facilities was granted in the amount of RM 12 million. Again the Deutsche Bank led the syndicate, this time with a quota of 50 percent or RM 6 million. Out of its quota the bank gave a subparticipation of RM 3 million to the Bank fuer Deutsche Industrie Obligationen (later renamed Deutsche Industriebank). The Reich bought the entire synthetic fuel output at a guaranteed price. When the Ruhrbenzin late in 1937 requested a one and half year extension on one of the amortization installments, the syndicate agreed "in view of the scope of this enterprise and the special tasks assigned to it within the framework of the Four Year Plan."

In December 1936 the Vereinigte Stahlwerke, together with its subsidiary the Gelsenkirchener Bergwerke A.G., organized the Gelsenberg Benzin A.G., Gelsenkirchen, for the production of synthetic gasoline. As in the case of the Ruhrbenzin A.G., the Deutsche Bank took over the leadership in supplying the required funds. For plant construction RM 30 million was made available by a banking syndicate consisting of:

Deutsche Bank (in charge)—	RM 10,050,000
Dresdner Bank—	RM 10,050,000
Commerz- & Privat-Bank—	RM 3,300,000
Berliner Handelsgesellschaft—RM	1,800,000
Five others—	RM 4,800,000

Here again the Reich took over the entire output at a guaranteed price. In July 1939 the Gelsenkirchener Bergwerks A.G., Essen, was substituted for the Gelsenberg Benzin as the debtor on this engagement. The above loan was repaid in 1940 and replaced by a bond issue of the Gelsenberg Benzin A.G.

In January 1937 the Union Rheinische Braunkohle Kraftstoff A.G., Cologne (UK), was founded by the Rhineland lignite companies for the production of synthetic fuel. Its initial capitalization of RM 45 million was raised to RM 90 million in 1940. Like the above-mentioned firms, it was set up by order of the Nazi government as another step in the rearmament program. The Deutsche Bank was particularly close to UK from the outset by virtue of its ties with the Rheinische A.G. fuer Braunkohlen- und Brikettwerke Roddergrube A.G., and the Braunkohlen-Industrie A.G., Zukunft, Eschweiler (cf. Chapter VIII). In addition to old-established business relations, interlocking directorships exist[ed] between Deutsche Bank and each of the three lignite corporations. These three companies together provided 82 percent of the initial capital of the UK, which in turn took over their combined holdings in the Brabag, that is, close to 30 percent of the latter's share capital. It was a foregone conclusion that the Deutsche Bank was to take charge of the necessary financing operations. It headed the syndicates which granted a RM 50 million loan in 1943 and floated a RM 60 million bank issue in 1940 and another one of RM 45 million in 1942.

The last hydrating company to be discussed in some detail is the Oberschlesische Hydrierwerke A.G., Blechhammer (Upper Silesia). This corporation was founded in December 1939 with a capital of RM 50 million. Among the participating Silesian mining interests, two government-owned enterprises formed a substantial minority:

Bergwerksverwaltung Oberschlesien G.m.b.H.
    der Reichswerke "Hermann Goering," Kattowitz—26.81   percent
Preussische Bergwerks und Huetten A.G., Berlin—   17.619 percent

The capital was later increased to RM 250 million by distribution of RM 120 million common stock pro rata among the founding interests and the issue of RM 80 million preferred stock, which was floated in November 1942 by a syndicate headed by the Deutsche Bank. The syndicate consisted of:

Deutsche Bank (in charge)—   28.50 percent
Dresdner Bank—   28.50 percent
Commerzbank—   11.75 percent
Bank der Deutschen Luftfahrt— 7.75 percent
Berliner Handelsgesellschaft— 7.75 percent
Reichs-Kredit-Gesellschaft— 7.75 percent
Bank der Deutschen Arbeit— 6.00 percent
Delbrueck Schickler & Co.— 2.00 percent

As indicated by its capitalization, the Oberschlesische Hydrierwerke was as important an object as the Brabag. Accordingly, the leadership in the banking syndicate was coveted also by the Dresdner Bank. But here the Deutsche Bank refused to yield to the ambitious competitor. With a letter dated 30 December 1941 to the Dresdner Bank the Deutsche Bank agreed to let the Dresdner share with an equal quota in the syndicate, but it firmly refused to share the syndicate management. The main argument advanced by Deutsche Bank was that "the great mass of participants in the hydrating works consists of enterprises in which we have the leading bank position."

The Deutsche Bank leadership was maintained in the underwriting of another RM 200 million "Hydrierwerke" bonds in 1942, another RM 150 million in 1943, and a Reich-guaranteed loan of RM 100 million in 1944. According to a statement of Dr. H. Jannsen of the Reichskredit-Gesellschaft additional funds were provided by the Reich air ministry and the Navy High Command, the principal purchasers of the output. Production was to reach 1 million tons of fuel per annum. Jannsen also stated:

> The earning power of the hydrating works was decidedly questionable as they were experimenting with processes untested in quantity production. In spite of this fact, the banks agreed to place large bond issues with their customers.

The Deutsche Bank's final commitment in this venture amounted to RM 27,408,431. Other hydrating plants, in whose financing the Deutsche Bank played a leading role, were the Hydrierwerke Poelitz A.G., Stettin, and the Hydrierwerk Scholven A.G., Gelsenkirchen. Deutsche Bank's leadership in the I.G. Farben syndicate financing operations (cf. Chapter VIII) should also be mentioned here since a considerable part of Farben's production was concentrated on synthetic fuel.

The Deutsche Bank's importance in the financing of synthetic fuel production is but an illustration which shows how the bank threw the weight of its resources into an unorthodox venture to promote a new industry whose existence was solely predicated upon Germany's preparation for war.

That Deutsche Bank's financing services were equally important to the war production of more established industries, heavy industry in general as well as the chemical, machinery, motor, and weapons industries, need hardly be emphasized. The thoroughness of the bank's application to the task of rearmament and war financing can be understood only in the light of the basic attitude of the bank's managing officials, a mixture of exaggerated nationalism, the urge for greater power and influence, and the desire for increased earnings regardless of their source.

Frequent mention has been made above of banking syndicates formed for financing operations. This financing method became of increasing importance in Germany during the past decade. Normally, the Deutsche Bank would have attempted to provide for its customers' financial needs without recourse to other credit institutions. However, demands for individual loans during the rearmament and war period were often of such size, the terms of repayment so extended, and the risks involved so unusual that it became advisable to an increasing extent to let other institutions participate in such transactions.

As to the increasing extension of long-term loans, Hans Rummel stated:

> When intermediate term loans became imperative for continued operation of German industries, the Deutsche Bank decided to grant such credits to some of its old customers for terms up to five years. Later on it became necessary to extend commitments to eight- or ten-year terms.

As an illustration, a RM 10 million loan might be mentioned which was granted by the Deutsche Bank to the Braunkohlen- und Brikett-Industrie A.G., "Bubiag," Berlin, one of the important producers of lignite of the Niederlausitz region. This loan was made available in December 1941 for a term of eight years. The Deutsche Bank formed a syndicate to which it contributed 50 percent; the Berliner Handelsgesellschaft and the Deutsche Industriebank participated with 25 percent each. Most of the large loans granted in the same year, and even earlier, were of a long-term investment character, involved very large sums, and made the use of banking syndicates advisable. Very frequently these syndicates were under the leadership of the Deutsche Bank, which was thus charged with the overall responsibility for the management and negotiation of the whole operation.

Also on a syndicate basis were the large loans for the importation and storage of foodstuffs and raw materials, which were granted either to one of the Reich agencies *(Reichsstellen)* or to firms or groups of firms entrusted by a Reichsstelle with carrying out the transactions. These loans and some of those granted for the economic reorganization and exploitation of the annexed territories were secured by Reich guarantees. Some of the large commitments of the Deutsche Bank of this type were:

Reich agency for eggs and fats—	RM 70–90 million
Reich agency for grains—	RM 60 million
Central storage association for clothing—	RM 35 million
Various Saar mines—	RM 100 million

Reich-guaranteed loans made by the Deutsche Bank, according to Mr. Hermann Kaiser, a general agent of the Deutsche Bank, started in the prewar period and increased substantially later on, until they reached an amount of between RM 550 and RM 600 million at the end of 1944.

Syndicates were also widely employed by the Deutsche Bank acting as an investment house in the floating of stock and bond issues for its customers in industry and commerce. Frequently long-term bank loans of an investment character were converted into bond issues. The following are a few illustrations of the Deutsche Bank's part in this type of financing for rearmament and war purposes:

I.G. Farbenindustrie. The RM 100 million bond issue floated in 1939 under Deutsche Bank management has already been mentioned (cf. Chapter VIII).

Steinkohlen-Elektrizitaet Aktiengesellschaft. The Deutsche Bank led the syndicate which underwrote a RM 25 million bond issue in 1939. Its quota was 35 percent.

Accumulatoren-Fabrik Aktiengesellschaft. With a quota of 28 percent, the Deutsche Bank headed the syndicate for a RM 20 million bond issue in 1940.

Eisen- und Huettenwerke Aktiengesellschaft, Koeln. The Deutsche Bank led the syndicate for a RM 20 million bond issue in 1940. Its quota was 41 percent.

Maschinenfabrik Augsburg-Nuernberg (MAN). A RM 20 million bond issue was floated in 1943 by a syndicate under Deutsche Bank leadership. The bank's quota was 35.5 percent.

Of all the major bond and stock issues introduced to trading with Deutsche Bank sponsorship in the period from 1936 on, a very substantial portion served its customers in the mining, synthetic materials, electric power, and heavy industries, that is, the industries essential in the rearmament and war program. This is substantiated by the following chart compiled from the annual reports of the bank.

Year	Total number of issues	Issues to armament industries in number	percentage	
		Bonds		
1936	21	17	81	
1937	41	29	71	
1938	30	19	63	
1939	40	26	65	
1940	55	42	76	
1941	31	25	81	
		Stocks		
1936	35	20	60	
1937	36	21	58	including
1938	28	12	60	stock
1939	41	24	60	conversions
1940	43	28	65	
1941	57	33	58	

To measure the relative importance of bond and stock issues in the bank's activities, it must be considered that the amounts involved in bond issues exceeded those in stock issues in a ratio of about ten to one. The bank accordingly spoke with particular emphasis of the distribution of bond issues in its reports to prove the important role it played as an investment banker in providing funds for the heavy industries.

In the annual report for 1940 the Deutsche Bank said:

> Through private bond placements, long-term funds totaling approximately RM 1 billion could be made available for the improvement and extension of industrial facilities.

In the early days of rearmament the bank was even more eloquent. The 1936 report states:

> Lately numerous industrial bond issues serving to implement the Four Year Plan could be placed with great success in the new issue market without disturbing in the least the steady price structure in the bond market. Again we found that the circle of our business friends, which extends over all parts of the country and through its entire economy, enables us to play a decisive role in the placement of issues of all types. With our work in this connection in the past year we believe to have proved once more that the German banking structure, combining the features of the commercial deposit bank with those of an investment bank, conforms in a most happy manner with German conditions.

When the future looked bright, the Deutsche Bank made no secret of its tremendous power to direct the funds of the nation and to direct them into channels where they would "serve to implement" a program the bank then deemed fitting and proper.

CHAPTER X

Aryanization

The elimination of Jewish citizens from the German economy started with the National Socialist advent to power. At first, Jews were removed from positions in publicly owned enterprises, later on from all positions in the economy, whether as employees or owners of enterprises or as holders of property.

Frequently contracts of ownership transfer were accomplished under pressure or under circumstances constituting ordinary duress. In the course of the Nazi regime the legal and sociological atmosphere that had been encouraged served to prevent the formation of true contracts of ownership transfer wherein there was a free and voluntary meeting of the minds of the participants and a possibility of genuine mutual gain. Transfers of ownership became simple means of expropriation in behalf of the Reich or the new holders.

The Deutsche Bank had three reasons for active participation in the Aryanization program. It gained politically by its demonstrations of loyalty to the Nazi program. It reaped immediate and tangible extra profits. It preserved customers' accounts which it might have lost had it not participated in the Aryanization; it also happened that new accounts were actually gained by the bank as a result of such participation.

The Deutsche Bank indicated a very early interest in Aryanization.

In 1935 a manager of the Dresdner Bank pointed out to his associates that the Deutsche Bank had reportedly set aside an amount of RM 5 million for the transfer of "non-Aryan" enterprises into "Aryan" hands at special terms.

Keeping pace with the disfranchisement of the Jews, Aryanization of enterprises was stepped up in the following years, until it reached a climax in 1938 with the pogrom in November of the same year. By then the Deutsche Bank had made a name for itself in this shady business. But the bank's leading Vorstand member wanted to give it a further boost. Hermann Kaiser of the bank's branch supervisory office stated:

> Now I recall that Dr. Kimmich more than the rest of the Vorstand was interested in that type of business with a view to earning commissions. He repeatedly asked branch managers to what extent the branches had taken part in Aryanization transactions and what profits had been made on them. I do not know whether the question was ever raised in the form of a circular letter, but I do know that Kimmich, who in a sense was our general manager, repeatedly raised it with branch managers visiting Berlin.

Ehrhardt Schmidt, a manager of the Berlin head office of the Deutsche Bank, added to this:

> I recall that letters regarding Aryanizations were sent by the Vorstand of the Deutsche Bank to the individual main branches around the end of 1938. I do not remember the exact contents of these communications, but they stated first of all that Aryanizations were now quite common and then pointed out that the Dresdner Bank was deriving appreciable profits from such transactions. For the same reason, the Deutsche Bank in its own interest would have to take advantage of all opportunities along these lines.

The Aryanization activities of the bank consisted of acquisitions for its own account, the financing of customers' transactions, the selection and appraisal of objects for Aryanization and the search for parties interested in their acquisition.

For its own account the Deutsche Bank picked up, among other objects, several private banks. The firm of Simon Hirschland, Essen, was Aryanized in 1938 and its property transferred to the newly established banking house of Burkhardt & Co. The new firm, which was endowed with a capital of RM 6,500,000, was controlled by the Deutsche Bank. It participated with RM 2,500,000 directly and secured the majority by financing the two personally liable partners, one of whom was a branch manager who entered the new firm.

In the same year, the Aryanization of Mendelssohn & Co., Berlin, the leading German private bank, was initiated. After the resignation of its Jewish partners the firm entered into liquidation and the Deutsche Bank took over all customers' accounts without compensation.

In assisting in the Aryanization of Wolf, Netter & Jacobi by Mannesmann in 1938, the bank acquired the majority in Butzke Bernhard Joseph A.G. previously held by Wolf, Netter & Jacobi.

The most common means whereby the Deutsche Bank participated in Aryanization transactions was the extension of credits to the new purchaser. Because the sales price was usually far below the real value of the business, this constituted a sound and profitable undertaking for the bank. The situation in Breslau may be regarded as fairly typical for the bulk of Deutsche Bank Aryanization transactions. This situation has been described by Felix Theusner, a Deutsche Bank general agent and a manager of the Breslau branch, as follows:

> Aryanizations in my district as a rule were effected by our granting to [ethnic German] branch managers or other leading employees of Jewish enterprises those loans that were required for the taking over and continuing of the business. These men had the technical knowledge, but usually not the funds to take over the enterprises.

He then described the positions of the Deutsche Bank liaison men:

> Mr. Klose was chief of the bookkeeping department at Breslau and was later promoted to department manager at Katowice. He is reported to have been the Ortsgruppenleiter of Katowice at the same time.

> Mr. Jacob was "Gauwirtschaftsberater" at Breslau and was later transferred in this capacity to Katowice. There he was appointed to the Deutsche Bank *Beirat* (Advisory Committee).

Mr. von Schirach is the cousin of the former Reich Youth Leader and Gauleiter of Vienna. At the Deutsche Bank branch in Breslau he was in charge of the personnel department and of liaison with the Deutsche *Arbeitsfront* (Nazi labor organization).

Eugen Kretschmar, a manager of the Berlin head office, in charge of the Eastern branches of the Deutsche Bank, had the following to add on this subject:

Breslau always was a center of the garment industry (in third place), which was preponderately in Jewish hands. Most of the (Aryanization-) business was brought to us by Gauwirtschaftsberater Dr. Jacob, who was a friend of Mr. Klose, one of our department chiefs who had close ties to the NSDAP. According to my information there were no cases in the RM million category, rather a greater number of small and medium-size firms. As a rule, these enterprises were taken over by managers or buyers who did not have larger funds at their disposal and who initially obtained a short-term loan against the cheaply acquired stock on hand. Through the sale of the stock at increased prices, they were in a position to repay or substantially reduce such loans in a relatively short period.

The Breslau district was also covered by a member of the Deutsche Bank Aufsichtsrat, Otto Fitzner, who was president of the Breslau Chamber of Commerce, head of the Chamber of Economics for Lower Silesia, and Gauwirtschaftsberater of Lower Silesia.

The biggest Aryanizations in which the Deutsche Bank participated as a financier or confidential agent were in behalf of its industrial affiliates and clients such as Mannesmann and Siemens.

In 1936 the Kronprinz A.G., Solingen-Ohligs, a Mannesmann subsidiary, wanted to acquire the Jewish-owned Roehrenwerk Coppel, Hilden. The Deutsche Bank through its Elberfeld branch extended a RM 1,500,000 loan to Kronprinz to enable it to make this purchase.

In the Aryanization of the M. Stern A.G., Essen (later renamed Eisen- und Metall A.G.), in 1937, the Deutsche Bank took a very active interest, as it did not want to lose this lucrative account. Managers von Falkenhausen and Spengler of the Essen branch of the bank intended to make sure that the shares of Stern A.G. would change over into the hands of industrial enterprises, which were close to the bank, or which at least had no other banking preferences. Mr. Kimmich, then the leading figure in the Deutsche Bank Vorstand and a member of the Aufsichtsrat of the Hoesch A.G., Dortmund, took great personal interest in the negotiations, which finally resulted in the acquisition of the Stern A.G. for RM 3,100,000 by Mannesmann, Hoesch, and Rheinmetall in equal parts.

When the Deutsche Bank acquired shares it did not hesitate to take advantage of the expropriation and confiscation measures of the Reich. Thus the Deutsche Bank served as the main collecting agency for a special levy imposed upon the Jewish population of Berlin after the November 1938 pogroms. This account held in the branch office of the Deutsche Bank was called *Wiedergutmachungskonto fuer die Schaeden Berlins* (Compensation Account for the Damages of Berlin). This account was opened by Werner Waechter and Erwin Koehnen, who served as trustees of the Reich for the collection of this fine. This fine was paid by the Jewish population in cash and partly with securities later sold by the Deutsche Bank. According to the manager of branch office H of the Deutsche Bank, in the first two weeks over RM 5,000,000 in cash and securities were deposited with the Deutsche Bank. Partial records of this account show other banks (even the Reichsbank) forwarded payments toward this fine to the Deutsche Bank. The bank received its customary commission, and obviously enjoyed priority in the purchase of the Jewish-owned securities among which there were sizable blocks of Mannesmann, I.G. Farben, and shares of other industrial concerns.

It also availed itself of similar opportunities in behalf of its industrial friends. For example, in 1939, when Mannesmann wished to consolidate and buy up a few remaining minority holdings in its subsidiary Kronprinz A.G., it offered the holders of Kronprinz shares Mannesmann shares instead. The source of these shares was neither Mannesmann nor the Deutsche Bank, which controlled it; the source was the Preussische Staatsbank, which acted as a depository for stock holdings confiscated from Jews. The following is quoted from the report on Mannesmann by the Joint Special Financial Detachment USGCC, Exhibit II, page 42:

> The carrying through of the offer of conversion was based on the possibility of purchasing Mannesmann shares from the Preussische Staatsbank (called "Seehandlung") out of a special deposit. This was a deposit of such shares as were delivered by Jewish proprietors according to the first and second order of delivery of the Reich.

The Deutsche Bank bought nominal RM 1,500,000 Mannesmann shares from this source.

The taking over of the non-Aryan Hahnische Werke A.G., Berlin, by Mannesmann in 1938 was also in part effected through an exchange of shares. The Deutsche Bank procured the required Mannesmann shares in the amount of nominal RM 2,472,000 (page 67 of the above-mentioned report).

The assistance rendered Mannesmann by the Deutsche Bank and its affiliates in the annexed and occupied countries in extensive acquisitions of Jewish-owned properties outside the old Reich boundaries is discussed in Chapter XII, "Foreign Operations."

The Siemens concern also exploited the opportunities for expansion presented in Aryanizations. It availed itself of the services of the Deutsche Bank in the acquisition of the Aronwerke Elektrizitaets A.G., Berlin, manufacturers of electric meters and radio receiving sets. Manfred Aron, owner of the majority of the nominal RM 8 million share capital, had been put under great pressure by the Party. Several times arrested by the Gestapo, he finally, in August 1935, consented to sell out. The Deutsche Bank took over the nominal RM 7,464,000 shares of the Aron family and resold them partly to Siemens, partly to the Siemens holding company, Elektrische Licht- und Kraftanlagen A.G. The name of the Aryanized firm was changed to Heliowatt Werke A.G.; Hans Rummel of the Deutsche Bank Vorstand became a member of the Aufsichtsrat of Heliowatt.

In addition to Aryanizations supported by such large industrial complexes as Mannesmann and Siemens the Deutsche Bank actively engaged in the Aryanization of small businesses. The value and distribution by size of Jewish holdings in Germany prior to 1933 cannot now be ascertained. They are, however, known to have been substantial, particularly in the fields of the manufacture and distribution of consumer goods and private banking. Instances in which the Deutsche Bank extended financial support to the new owners are set forth below.

Old Firm	Place	Year	Taken Over by	Approximate Purchase Price (RM)	Loan Extended by D.B.
A. Baum	Berlin		Dr. E. Hering	250,000	250,000
Gebr. Cassel	Mannheim	1938	Koppel & Temmler	220,000	120,000
Cellulose-fabrik Okrif-tel Ph. Oppenheimer	Okriftel	1938	Friedrich Minoux	4,600,000	1,084,000
Frankfurter Asbestwerke KG vorm. L. Wertheim	Frankfurt	1938	Paul Kind K.G.	1,132,735	1,154,171
Gustav Lustig G.m.b.H	Berlin		Joh. Bartmann	428,000	330,000
Rud. Milchner & Co.	Goerlitz	1938	H. Dietmeier	1,075,000	800,000
Louis Rosenthal & Co., A.G.	Berlin		E. Grahl	100,000	100,000
Tannwalder Textilwerke A.G.	Tannwald		Denk Brothers	4,800,000	2,320,000

In addition to supplying financial assistance to the buyer of an enterprise being Aryanized, the Deutsche Bank frequently acted as a broker to bring buyer and seller together and to extract thereby an additional fee for broker services. The interests of the old owners usually suffered considerably. The bank gained through the collection of clients' commissions and it established good relationships with the new owners.

According to Mr. Ladenburg, an official of the Frankfurt branch of the bank, the bank acting for the Deutsche Textilgesellschaft, Berlin, approached the Jewish textile firm Aumann & Rapp for the sale of their enterprise in early 1938. Upon the consummation of the transaction at a price of somewhat below RM 1 million, the bank received a commission of RM 2,000. In the taking over of the Frankfurter Asbestwerke in September 1938 by Paul Kind for a price of RM 1,132,735, the

Deutsche Bank received a commission of 1 percent for bringing the parties together. The transaction was financed through a loan of RM 1,004,171 of the Wuppertal branch and one of RM 150,000 of the Frankfurt branch of the bank.

The Deutsche Bank acted as the agent of the buyers also in the sale of the Frankfurt shoe-manufacturing firm Bernhard Schulenklopper to the firm Freitag and Bodenstedt in December 1938. The firm which had a yearly production of about RM 700,000 was sold for RM 93,568, a fraction of its value. The following is taken from a statement by the Frankfurt branch of the bank:

> The taking over (of the business) was arranged by us. The old firm had not been in business connection with us. In this instance the price, according to the files, favored the purchasers. At least with respect to the machinery, which first had been appraised at RM 90,000 by an expert, and which on the basis of another appraisal was reduced to RM 30,000. As we recall, an auditor named Hoehne was introduced into the negotiations at the instigation of the authorities, probably the "Gauwirtschaftskammer." It should also be emphasized that Mr. Schulenklopper was put into a concentration camp during the "November-Aktion" 1938 while the negotiations were going on. He was released after a few weeks and presumably signed the final contract.

In November 1938 the firm Franz Mueller & Kramer, Greiz, weavers of woolen and silk fabrics, was Aryanized. The majority holdings of the Jewish partners were taken over by Alfred Schuetz at a price which amounted to fraud, according to the statement of Kramers' legal representative. The real value of their share in the firm was about RM 1,500,000, but all they received was RM 500,000. According to the Deutsche Bank, whose Poessneck branch managers participated in the sales negotiations, the firm had a yearly sales volume of RM 7 million. Schuetz was an SS leader, president of the "Gauwirtschaftskammer" for Eastern Thuringia in Gera and chairman of its Aryanization committee. The Deutsche Bank financed Schuetz with a RM 550,000 loan and made an additional RM 550,000 available for the repayment of a loan in like amount which had been granted by the Commerz- & Privat-Bank to the old firm. Both loans were repaid already by the middle of 1940.

The process of Aryanization required close liaison with Party offices at local level, for all sales of Jewish enterprises required the approval of the Chamber of Commerce or in more important cases that of the Gauwirtschaftskammer (District Economic Chamber) and the Gauwirtschaftsberater (District Economics Adviser of the NSDAP).

The Gauwirtschaftsberater of Berlin, Heinrich Hunke, was a member of the Deutsche Bank Vorstand. The bank also had on the Aufsichtsrat such personalities as the following: Otto Fitzner, who is previously mentioned as president of the Breslau Chamber of Commerce; Emil Kreibich, president of the Reichenberg Chamber of Commerce and head of the Chamber of Economics for the Sudetenland area; Albert Pietzsch, president of the Munich Chamber of Commerce and head of the Reich Economic Chamber; Philipp F. Reemtsma, the behind-the-scenes economic adviser of Gauleiter Kaufmann in Hamburg; Wilhelm Zangen, vice-president of the Duesseldorf Chamber of Commerce.

This chapter is concerned only with Aryanization as an institutional matter. The personal acquisition of the Jewish-owned Erste Berliner Rosshaarfabrik by Hunke was mentioned in a previous chapter. Von Stauss also profited in personal transactions; for instance, he acquired a RM 500,000 participation from Dr. J. Koerfer, the Goebbels-sponsored purchaser of a participation in Garbaty, one of the important cigarette manufacturers in Germany.

This chapter represents a wholly incomplete report on Deutsche Bank participation in Aryanization. It was prepared without recourse to the files and records. The part played by the bank was concealed as much as possible by the bank in order to avoid reactions from abroad, at least in the early days of Nazism. And finally, the available officials of the bank were most reluctant to discuss the subject.

More accurate testimony could be furnished by those who were deprived of their property in the years following 1933. The collection of such testimony would, however, be a practically impossible task due to the now almost complete unavailability of evidence and because of the resettlement in other countries of those victims of the Aryanization program who were able to escape extinction in German-dominated Europe.

From the Annex to the Report

Recently discovered documents reveal that the Aryanization plans and policies of the Deutsche Bank not only were circulated among the Vorstand members, but also became the subject of discussion with other banks, notably the Dresdner Bank. A file note of July/August 1938 confirms previous information that in this field Kimmich played a particularly active role. On 23 July 1938 he discussed Aryanization problems with Carl Goetz of the Dresdner Bank, whom the RWM had requested to conduct a survey of all Jewish properties in Germany available for Aryanization. Kimmich informed Goetz that the Deutsche Bank "had already successfully Aryanized a great number of enterprises" though it was careful not to expose itself in Aryanization cases lest it jeopardize its foreign credits.

In the same document Kimmich tabulated the accomplishment as well as the difficulties encountered by the Deutsche Bank in Aryanization cases:

> Out of 700 Jewish enterprises under the jurisdiction of the central office some 250 were Aryanized by the end of August 1938. Negotiations for numerous other enterprises are under way. Reports are coming in daily about objects that have been Aryanized. In some branches of business the supply of really good objects has diminished greatly. Demand is far greater, for example in the metal and chemical branches, and it is not always possible to divert buyers to other lines of business. An acceleration of the Aryanization process may be looked for when permits are granted more rapidly. Two months frequently will elapse until all the appropriate authorities have expressed their approval.

Deutsche Bank officials have uniformly denied the existence of a special Aryanization department at their bank. The above document makes it clear, however, that a department of this description was unnecessary since Aryanization cases were transacted by Karl Kimmich and were his responsibility. Kimmich was assisted in these cases by Gerhard Elkmann, who also maintained liaison with the Section for Jewish Affairs in the Reich Economics Ministry.

The Deutsche Bank was ready to profit at the expense of absentee Jewish property owners. The Deutsche Bank branch at Karlsbad in the Sudetenland territory desired to acquire two hotels, valued at RM 200,000, the Jewish owners of which had, following the German occupation of the Sudetenland, fled to Prague. When the absentee owners rejected a proposal providing for the payment to their account of only one half of the reduced sales price and of the remainder to blocked Reichsmark accounts, the bank instituted forcible Aryanization proceedings for which the sanction of the local Gauleiter was sought.

Aryanization of Personnel. On 30 May 1933, the two Jewish members of the Deutsche Bank Vorstand, Theodor Frank and Jacob Wassermann, informed Wilhelm Keppler, the economic adviser to Hitler in the Nazi Party, that they were resigning from the bank. The resignations were accepted by the Deutsche Bank management without questions, and Karl Kimmich and Fritz Wintermantel were appointed to the vacancies. The Aryanization of personnel became, in later years, the first order of business wherever the Deutsche Bank or its subsidiaries obtained a controlling interest in a foreign bank.

Adler and Oppenheimer A.G. (A & O). During the course of the Aryanization of the Adler & Oppenheimer A.G., one of the key leather manufacturing companies of Germany, the Deutsche Bank acquired control of more than 75 percent of the capital shares of the company, a portion of which it disposed of afterward at an excellent profit. It also acquired control of the foreign affiliates of A & O in Holland, France, and Luxembourg.

Corporate Structure of A & O. The Adler & Oppenheimer A.G. was established in 1872 at Strassbourg, Alsace, as a wholesale leather company, and soon after the foundation it branched out into the manufacture of leather as well. . . .

The capital stock of A & O, which, in 1938, had a par value of RM 18,000,000, was owned by members of the Adler and Oppenheimer families. Other members of these families owned and managed an enterprise in Holland, the N.V. Amsterdamsche Ledermaatschappij, Amsterdam, which engaged in the same field of business. This company held the entire share capital of factories in Holland (N.V. Amsterdamsche Ledermaatschappij, Oisterwijk) and Luxembourg (Lederfabrik Wiltz) as well as a trading company in France (Le Cuir Modern, Paris). By 1939, the Dutch holding company owned RM 16,000,000 (89 percent) of the A & O share capital. Otto Weigel, the Aufsichtsrat chairman of the Norddeutsche Lederwerke, the Aryanized and reorganized version of A & O, has stated that the transfer to Holland began only in 1933 and that the balance sheets prior to that year revealed no Dutch holdings.

Aryanization of A & O Shares Held in Germany and Repatriation of A & O Shares Held in Holland. Deutsche Bank, acting upon the request of the RWM, which had an active interest in the case, effectuated the transfer into Aryan-German out of Dutch and non-Aryan possession of the majority of the A & O capital shares. For its efforts in this so-called repatriation, the Deutsche Bank netted a handsome profit and became at the same time the dominant influence in one of the key leather manufacturing companies of Germany. The firm name, after the completion of the Aryanization in 1941, was altered to Norddeutsche Lederwerke AG.

During the course of the repatriation the Deutsche Bank came into possession of the following capital shares:

a. RM 617,000. A banking syndicate, in which the Deutsche Bank as leader held a 50 percent participation and the RKG one of 30 percent, acquired these shares from a number of non-Aryan owners. The sales price, which in the original agreement of September 1938 was fixed at 135 percent of par, was reduced afterward to 106 percent (RM 654,020), and the reduced sum came, in fact, to be paid only in December 1939. The syndicate some fifteen months afterward disposed of the shares at 161 percent of par (RM 997,553) at a profit of RM 343,523. Out of this latter sum the Deutsche Bank retained some 55 percent as its share of the profit.

b. RM 9,528,000. In February 1940, several months prior to the German campaign in the West, the Deutsche Bank sought the permission of the RWM for its efforts to obtain at 106 percent of par this block of A & O shares which was held in Holland. On 3 May 1940 Gerhard Elkmann of the Deutsche Bank reported to Abs of a visit he had made to Regierungsrat von Coelln of the Judenreferat (Section for Jewish Affairs) in the RWM, to whom he had explained the bank's interest in bringing the transaction to a speedy close. The Judenreferat in consequence extended to the Deutsche Bank oral permission, and promised its subsequent written approval as well, to carry out the Aryanization of the A & O shares held in Holland. One week afterward, on 10 May 1940, the Deutsche Bank acquired the entire share block for its own account. It thereupon on 20 June 1940 organized a syndicate, in which as leader it held a 62 percent participation and the RKG one of 25 percent, for the disposition of the shares. These shares remained in its possession and control, however, until they were finally sold in 1941.

c. RM 3,239,000. On 13 August 1940 the Deutsche Bank, in a letter signed by Roesler and Elkmann, requested of Minister Funk the permission of the RWM for the purchase of this particular share block, which also was held in Holland. With these shares in its possession, the communication stated, Deutsche Bank would hold 75 percent of the A & O capital stock, and would be enabled, under the provisions of existing Nazi law, to have the company declared an Aryan enterprise. The letter stated furthermore that ever since the reopening of the German-Dutch system of clearing payments, the German Commissioner General for Finance and Economics at The Hague (Dr. Hans Fischboeck) had made means available for the acquisition of participations which were in Dutch possession. The Deutsche Bank therefore desired a priority for the repatriation to Germany of the A & O shares. The RWM, on 29 August 1940, approved the petition; the price paid for the shares was 94.7 percent of par and the syndicate mentioned in the preceding paragraph participated in the subsequent distribution of these shares as well.

The total profit to the syndicate out of the sale of the shares acquired in Holland came to RM 4,492,726, of which the Deutsche Bank, as syndicate leader, retained RM 2,749,544.

The Influence of the Deutsche Bank in the Norddeutsche Lederwerke (NDL). Hermann J. Abs became Aufsichtsrat Chairman of A & O in 1938 in order to expedite the Aryanization of the enterprise, and he came to play in the company the principal role. Ernst Steinbeck, a member of the NDL Vorstand, has described this role in the following terms:

> Abs . . . probably controlled the corporation (NDL) to a much greater extent than it was necessary for him to do as chairman of the Aufsichtsrat. Even though Mr. Abs had so many other Aufsichtsrat positions he took great pains in keeping constantly informed about the management of our firm. I do not believe any other Aufsichtsrat chairman would have taken as much interest as Mr. Abs showed.

Franz Heinrich Ulrich, an assistant to Hermann J. Abs at the Deutsche Bank and an Aufsichtsrat member of the NDL, has supplied a number of corroborative details. He has stated that between the years 1941–1943 Abs had participated in negotiations and concluded agreements on behalf of the NDL which went "far beyond the scope of activities of the board of directors." These activities included:

a. participation in negotiations with Dutch and German authorities for the acquisition of A & O affiliates in Holland and France,
b. participation in the Aryanization and reorganization of one of these affiliates, and
c. the temporary purchase, in the name of the Deutsche Bank, of RM 1 million of the NDL shares, so as to prevent their falling, as a minority block, into the hands of a Dutch company.

CHAPTER XI

Slave Labor

The control exercised by the Deutsche Bank over certain large corporations was of such an all-inclusive nature that the use of slave labor, concentration camp labor, and prisoners of war by those corporations warrants a special discussion in connection with the operations of the Deutsche Bank.

Mistreatment of slave labor, abuse of concentration camp inmates, and employment of prisoners of war in armament industries constitute war crimes.

Chapter VIII of this report analyzes and establishes the decisive role that the Deutsche Bank played not only as the financier but as the policy maker, production, and personnel manager of Mannesmann Roehrenwerke, Bayerische Motoren Werke, and Daimler Benz, and to a considerably lesser degree of Siemens. In the first three corporations, Vorstand members of the Deutsche Bank headed the boards of directors and were assisted by several representatives from the Deutsche Bank.

Mannesmann was in fact an industrial affiliate of the Deutsche Bank, fully controlled and directed by its leading Vorstand members. Thus the conclusion of the report of the Joint Financial Detachment of the U.S. Group Control Council (Duesseldorf) on employment of foreign labor in Mannesmann plants is applicable to the Deutsche Bank as well. It states:

> All instances of mistreatment, abuse and criminal neglect mentioned in this memorandum (and this cannot be emphasized too much) were taken from reports prepared by M/W and their own field managers. It cannot even be guessed how much more incriminating evidence independent research would turn up. Nevertheless, the picture drawn on M/W's summary and extracts from the reports, which are attached, will show conclusively that Mannesmann, and this includes the Vorstand, the directors of subsidiaries and their employees in charge of foreign workers, are guilty of: murder by starvation, forcible use, inhuman treatment, gross criminal neglect, and abuse of foreign labor.

Individual reports [have been] submitted by MW plants within the British zone of occupation. Following are a few extracts of these reports.

1. *Neanderthal lime quarries (Kalkwerke Neanderthal).* In 1939 50 Polish prisoners were employed, who were replaced by 98 French prisoners. They in turn were replaced in 1941 by Russian POWs . . .

   The food of the prisoners was insufficient, in particular those POWs suffering from famine-edema could not be nourished sufficiently. My remonstrances in this matter were refuted with the argument that the general food situation was bad, and that it was impossible to obtain any additional allotments from the food office. A number of POW fell ill, suffering from stomach and intestinal troubles together with an increasing collapse of strength, so that I ordered food to be administered in a finely minced state (often entire vegetable leaves were found in the soup), if it was impossible to supply additional food. The camp leader at that time promised to obtain a mincing machine. The above-mentioned POW, in a grave state and suffering from a complete collapse, could not be helped by medicaments. Under increasing signs of a weakening heart and circulation system a number of them died. No signs of any infectious diseases could be noted.

s/ Dr. Gilhaus, Specialist for internal diseases

2. *M/W Mines Consolidation and Unger, Fritz, Gelsenkirchen.* . . . an average of 1,849 Russian POW and 156 French POW were employed in this period. For a short time, some 60 Italian POW were also used. Furthermore, about 350 Polish civilians, 40 Dutch civilians, 340 Russian civilians, and some 100 miscellaneous foreign workers were employed in this period.

   Most of the French POW, whose rate of illness was the highest, were employed on surface jobs, while Russians and Poles were almost invariably used below grounds . . . . analyses of meals made by a chemist, Dr. phil. habil. Strohecker, Gelsenkirchen. In one case, a noonday meal of carrots and potatoes was found to contain 615 calories, instead of the 639 provided for by regulations; in another, soup with noodles, 405 calories instead of 560 per liter of soup; and in the third analysis presented a supper of sauerkraut and potatoes, only 384 calories instead of the 460 required by Gestapo regulations. . . .

   Average disease rates were: Russian POW 6–7 percent, French POW 10–11 percent, free foreign workers (Belgian, Dutch, etc.) 4–5 percent, Poles 5–6 percent.

3. *M/W Dept. Grossenbaum, Duisburg-Grossenbaum.* Duisburg, 27 March 1944. We should like to give you a brief report on our experiences with the use of IMI (Italian Military Internees), in order to advise you in time of the dangerous trend in the use of labor.

   Since October, 1943, Grossenbaum employs 150 IMI. Most of these men came from Southern Italy, and with few exceptions are built on rather weak lines. We could not take this into consideration in using them, and were forced to use them in all departments, even in jobs demanding great physical exertions. Shortly after their arrival the percentage of illness was 13 percent, but today it has mounted to 17 percent. While in the beginning most of the sick suffered from harmless diseases, this situation has lately been changing dangerously. According to examinations of the company physician more than 40 IMI lost from 10–15 kg. According to the physician most of the IMI have no muscular tissue left, so that most of them are no longer able to do any heavy labor, particularly warm labor. Their recovery, according to the doctor, would take several months, so that a considerable number of workers would be missing for our essential war production. Although all IMI get workers rations, most of them suffer from actual hunger-edema. [From] letter written by Baare, labor department of the Grossenbaum plant to Thelen, head of foreign labor department of Mannesmann in Duesseldorf)

4. *Grillo-Funke, Gelsenkirchen.* From 1942–45 the company employed about 150 Italians, 220 Russian workers and some 60 civilians of miscellaneous nationality, together with an average of 550 Russian, French and Italian POW.

    . . . solitary confinement punishment "for civil Russians only . . . perhaps 10–12 times" . . .

    Between 1943–45 the disease rates for Western workers averaged around 22 percent, that of the Eastern workers around 8 percent . . .

    Discipline of foreign workers is deeply interlocked with their treatment, the food they are supplied, and the type of work they are used for. Flights are the result of bad treatment, bad nourishment or of the wrong use of labor. While the other plants have scarcely any cases of escapes, Grillo-Funke, f.i., has frequent escapes. (Report by Thelen on 31 August 1943)

5. *Heinrich Bierwas Huette, Duisburg-Huckingen.* . . . began using foreigners in 1940, when a first shipment of 200 French POW arrived . . . . Depending on the size of the family, up to six families were lodged in one room. . . .

    Disciplinary measures used against workers included withdrawal of tobacco, withdrawal of permission to leave camp and up to three days arrest in solitary confinement cells built into an air raid shelter. These cells were located in the toilet of the transportation department. In case of severe infractions the Gestapo was informed and the slave workers turned over to them.

    Since the Gestapo has often sent escapees from other camps, who were picked up again, to us as penal laborers, they requested in 1943 that we place part of our large camp area at their disposal for use as a penal camp.

    From April, 1943, to February, 1945, average sickness rates were: for French POW 10 percent, French civilians 7 percent, Belgian civilians 10 percent, Dutch civilians 10 percent, Polish civilians 11 percent, Russian civilians 8 percent, and Italian POW 20 percent, Italian civilians 15 percent.

    A total of 72 slave workers died. 59 of these were Russians, 18 were killed by air raids (no shelter), 16 by accidents.

    The large percentage of death by accident of the Eastern workers is explained by the fact that Eastern workers in many cases did not have the right shoes for the work they performed, so that wooden shoes instead of leather ones were worn at work.

The Mannesmann Roehrenwerke with its affiliates is probably the one individual complex which for two generations has been most closely identified with the Deutsche Bank.

The Deutsche Bank dominated as fully as in the case of Mannesmann two other industrial complexes, Daimler Benz A.G. and the Bayerische Motoren Werke A.G.

During the past 20 years two members of the Deutsche Bank Vorstand, Emil Georg von Stauss and Hans Rummel, led Daimler Benz and BMW as the chairmen of the boards of directors of both companies. They decided upon matters of production, finance, personnel, and internal organization of these corporations.

Employment of slave labor, of prisoners of war, and of inmates of the Dachau concentration camp was common practice at BMW. That this employment was not a matter which never came to the attention of the Deutsche Bank management is amply borne out in the statement of E. Woerner, who served as secretary to Rummel. Woerner was in charge of all matters pertaining to the South-German companies with which Hans Rummel was connected. He states:

> The first time I learned of the employment of concentration camp inmates by the BMW was in the middle of 1943 from the so-called concern reports, which the BMW sent monthly to Mr. Rummel and which in addition to statistical material on the financial situation, turnover, orders, etc., contained data on the personnel; one day in these reports appeared "concentration camp inmates and SS prisoners." I cannot tell whether the number of these prisoners was stated in the reports or if it was occasionally mentioned by one of the managers. In any case I recall the number of 3–5,000, and I believe once having heard mentioned the number 6,000.
>
> In February–March 1944 after a meeting of the board of directors the members visited the works at Allach and saw at this occasion a fitting shed where concentration camp inmates and SS prisoners were put up. I cannot recall anymore who the members of the board of directors were that visited the works. I seem to remember that Mr. Rummel was present.
>
> According to what I was told the inmates and prisoners did not receive any cash payment from the SS.

Guenther, plant manager at BMW, adds the following:

> When I took over the Allach plant on 1 August 1942, there were 1,200 French and about 8,000 prisoners. In March 1943 I was informed by my superior Dr. Zipperich that in Allach . . . will be brought in concentration camp inmates. Upon my retort that in Allach are being employed already members of 23 nationalities, I was informed that the new arrivals will be utilized in new additional plants. From June 1943 concentration camp inmates were put to work and by August 1944 when I left the Allach plant there were about 3,000 at work. The chief of the camp was SS Sturmfuehrer Jarolin who was transferred here from Dachau.

On 29 March 1945 BMW concluded an agreement with the Reichsfuehrer SS to sell the inmates camp to the SS for 7.5 million RM.

This transaction was concluded in consultation with Hans Rummel. On 14 March 1945 the Vorstand of the BMW dispatched the following letter to Hans Rummel:

> Dr. Kessler, whom I sent to Berlin to get some basic clarification re our war damages at the Ministry of Economics or at the Ministry of the

Interior, and to conduct preparatory negotiations with the Main Office of the SS regarding their buying and taking over of our concentration camp, will pass through Krautheim and bring to you copies of my letters addressed to you.

Daimler Benz, a sister corporation of BMW, employed according to Hans Rummel, chairman of the Aufsichtsrat, 15,000 foreign workers. This number constituted over 25 percent of the total labor force of this corporation.

The ties between the Deutsche Bank and the Siemens Combine, although not as intimate as with the three corporations discussed, are sufficiently close to deserve examination from the slave labor aspect as well (cf. Chapter VIII and Siemens profile). Tied to the house of Siemens from the day of its inception the Deutsche Bank has perpetuated a close kinship with the Siemens Combine through generations. Hermann von Siemens, the last head of the Siemens Combine, was a member of the board of directors of the Deutsche Bank.

The Siemens Combine made extensive use of concentration camp inmates and foreign labor. Special work halls were set up in Berlin where several hundred Jewish women worked for Siemens until their deportation by the Gestapo. This was only a small portion of the concentration camp labor exploited for the profits of Siemens. There were "Siemens Kommandos" in Buchenwald, Oranienburg, Auschwitz, and in Ravensbrueck. According to Hermann von Siemens

> the prisoners had been glad at the possibility to work. Nothing has been reported to me about signs of insufficient nourishment and rude treatment of the people working for us.

Quite different is the picture given by a recipient of the Siemens benevolence. This affidavit by an inmate of the concentration camp Ravensbrueck gives us some idea of the working conditions in the Siemens department of the camp.

> In these Siemens barracks about 1,500 female concentration camp inmates were working guarded by SS women and supervised by civilian personnel. . . . We had to work 12 hours a day. . . . For this the best workers received every few months a bonus of RM 0.50 to RM 3. Prisoners who did not accomplish the required amount of work because of their poor condition were forced to work another three hours at night. When a prisoner did not do [her] work in the right way but had to retain the material given out, Mr. Boehnke or Miss Venske, a foreman, made a report of sabotage to the SS supervisor. The result was that the prisoner involved was taken away from Siemens & Halske and sent to the penitentiary.

> There were workshop supervisors who requested a new SS guard every day because the one they had was not strict enough. They liked to see that the prisoners were reported at least once a day and beaten.

Another affidavit adds some additional information in regard to the conditions in the Siemens branch of the Ravensbrueck concentration camp.

This firm "Siemens" distinguished itself, because all the inmates, mostly women of all nationalities, looked especially miserable and were in a very poor condition. There was a possibility for Siemens to intervene with the camp management in order to get better food and decent barracks for the prisoners. . . . The gentlemen from Siemens did not care how many lives were lost. . . . Whenever the required job was not finished in time, the prisoners were beaten cruelly and this beating was ordered by Siemens.

The affidavit of Wilhelm Martinkat, chief of the Siemens plant I in Ravensbrueck, bears out the accusations leveled at Siemens by the inmates of the concentration camp and lists the principal accomplices who served and are still in the employ of Siemens.

The Siemens Combine maintained a plant at the infamous Auschwitz extermination camp. According to the report of the International Labor Office titled *Exploitation of Foreign Labor by Germany:*

Inside the camp (Auschwitz) were several factories, a war production plant (Deutsches *Aufruestungswerk)*, a factory belonging to the Krupp-Werke, and others belonging to the Siemens concern. . . . Thus, to the end, exploitation was combined with extermination. (page 255)

In addition to the employment and mistreatment of concentration camp inmates the Siemens Combine extensively used slave labor and prisoners of war. According to Hermann von Siemens:

The number of foreign workers rose gradually from about 35,000 in 1942 to about 40,000 at the end of 1944. This goes for the main firms of Siemens & Halske and Siemens-Schuckert.

The largest number of foreign workers came from the East. They were called "Ostarbeiter."

Prisoners of war, especially Russians, were also offered. . . . The Siemens firms always refused to guard prisoners of war. They only put the working places at their disposal and instructed them in the work. Payments for work were made to the prison camp.

This last statement attains special significance in view of the fact that the Siemens Combine was almost totally a war producer, and already in 1939 50 percent of all U-boat motors came from Siemens.

CHAPTER XII

Foreign Operations of the Deutsche Bank

Deutsche Bank's foreign interests and operations expanded from a relatively moderate size to a tremendous scope after the Nazi accession to power. With this expansion the bank helped to carry out the well-planned economic scheme which the Nazis had designed to make them the undisputed overlords of a greater Europe. In the period preceding the territorial expansion of Germany, the Deutsche Bank played a leading part in the execution of the current aims of the Nazi foreign policy, which, in preparation for the planned war, desired to arm Germany's potential allies and to utilize her entire foreign trade for the stockpiling of strategic raw materials.

The principal acquisitions of the Deutsche Bank in foreign banking came as a result of the political and military subjugation of Europe by Germany (Table IX). Prior to the Nazi accession to power Deutsche Bank's foreign affiliates were but few, consisting primarily of the Handel-Maatschappij Albert de Bary and the Deutsche Ueberseeische Bank's branches in South America and Spain. From 1938 on the Deutsche Bank pursued a most aggressive policy of increasing its network outside the borders of Germany. The aggressiveness of the Deutsche Bank in the foreign field evidenced itself in the battle it fought for the control of the Creditanstalt Bankverein, the largest commercial bank in Austria, and for the control of the holdings of the Société Générale de Belgique, the largest bank and holding company in Western Europe. The [Reich] Ministry of Economics, the agency directing the foreign expansion of German finance and industry, consistently supported all efforts of the Deutsche Bank to attain the standing of the largest bank in Europe.

The expansion of foreign affiliates served primarily the bank's own ambition, but it was also made necessary to carry out more conveniently the intent of the German government's aggressive policies in the economic field, which were defined by Walter Funk and implemented through subsequent directives from the Ministry of Economics.

The task assigned to the Deutsche Bank as Germany's largest bank in carrying out the Nazi scheme of economic penetration was outlined clearly in the statement of policy by Funk to Goering on 6 August 1940, titled "Continental Economy and Economy for Large Areas." The following excerpts are self-explanatory:

> My basic assumption is that the incorporation of the occupied territories into the Greater German Economy, and reconstruction of a European Continental Economy under German leadership, cannot take place through a single act of state policy. . . .

141

Table IX
EXPANSION OF FOREIGN SUBSIDIARIES AND AFFILIATES*

Country and name of bank	Amount of participation (nominal)	% of total capital	Acquired
I. Affiliates prior to 1938			
South America Deutsche Ueberseeische Bank, Berlin	RM 18,665,000	51	1886
Bulgaria Deutsch-Bulgarische Kreditbank, Sofia	Leva 32,063,700	64	1905
China Deutsch-Asiatische Bank, Berlin	RM 42,000 (preferred shares)	60	1890
Holland Handel-Maatschappij H. Albert de Bary & Co., N.V., Amsterdam	hfl 14,323,000	95	1919
II. Acquisitions of affiliates after 1938			
Austria Creditanstalt Bankverein, Vienna	RM 36,057,000	51	1938/42
Czechoslovakia Boehmische Unionbank, Prague	Kc 89,258,000	59	1938/39
Poland Creditanstalt A.G., Cracow	Z 1,200,000	20	1940
Luxembourg Generalbank Luxembourg A.G.	luxfrs 6,049,000	30	1941
Romania Banca Comerciala Romana, Bucharest	Lei 176,372,000	58	1941
Yugoslavia Bankverein A.G., Belgrade	Din 12,864,400	12	1941
Bankverein fuer Kroatien, A.G., Zagreb	Kuna 18,750,000	15	1941
Japan Deutsche Bank fuer Ostasien, Berlin	RM 2,000,000	20	1942

* Excluding foreign participations of principal subsidiaries (cf. special sections)

. . . all measures which are nonessential from the point of view of our own Greater German interests can be left undone . . .

Interlacing under German leadership of European national economics with the Economy of Greater Germany in the following fields . . . Financial domination of the most important European economic enterprises . . .

Control of the economic and finance policies of the European countries . . .
through agreements between nations, arrived at through a showing of
German might (unter Einsatz der deutschen Machtmittel). (Document No.
1093-PS—Office of U.S. Chief of Counsel)

On 17 August 1940 Goering fully accepted the entire program of Funk and added:

As I explained already at the conference about it in Karinhall, I take special
interest in a most intensive penetration of the Dutch and Belgian . . . economy by German capital on the broadest possible basis even before the end of
the war. . . . Furthermore I beg you to promote with all means the acquisition of dominating economic positions in third countries from French,
Dutch, Belgian, Danish, or Norwegian ownership by the German economy,
and this already during the period of war. (Document No. 1093-PS—Office
of U.S. Chief of Counsel)

A series of directives implementing the above-mentioned policies was issued in
September of 1940 by the Ministry of Economics. Several outlined the task of
German banks in the execution of the Funk-Goering program. One decreed:

Berlin will have to be the center of the European money and capital market,
as well as of the insurance market, too. Germany must infiltrate the
European banks as strongly as possible with capital and personnel.
(Document No. 1093-PS—Office of U.S. Chief of Counsel)

The basic directive for the acquisition of banking and industrial holdings held by
French, Belgian, and Dutch interests to fulfill Goering's demand was issued on 20
September 1940:

In order to bring about a clear interlacing *(Verflechtung)* of capital between
the Dutch, Belgian, and French economies on one hand and the German
economy on the other, and in order to strengthen the influence of German
capital in Holland and Belgium, I deem it necessary for German capital to
participate in Dutch, Belgian, and French enterprises which are important
from an economic point of view. It is furthermore desirable that participations in foreign enterprises of considerable size which are in Holland,
Belgium, and France are taken over by Germany. This applies especially to
participations in enterprises operating in the Balkans. I, therefore, plan to
enable German banks to acquire these participations in the form of securities for their own account and registered in their name in Holland, Belgium,
and the occupied territories of France.

The far-flung network of foreign branches and affiliates of the Deutsche Bank
built up during the three-year period from 1938 to 1941 was harnessed to the
achievement of the Funk-Goering aims. Subsequent sections of this chapter describe
the organization of the Foreign Department of the Deutsche Bank, which served as
the general staff for the bank's foreign expansion; trace the chronological growth of

the bank's foreign branches, subsidiaries, and affiliates; and discuss some phases of the bank's operations covering the implementation of Nazi foreign policy in the field of foreign trade and finance; the role of the Deutsche Bank in the economic penetration and spoliation of German-dominated Europe, and its activities in neutral countries.

Information dealing with the foreign operations of the Deutsche Bank is rather fragmentary due to the unavailability of records of the Foreign Department and inaccessibility of Hermann J. Abs, head of the Foreign Department of Deutsche Bank, for systematic interrogations. The information available, however, is sufficiently diversified and significant to show the leading part played by the Deutsche Bank in furthering the expansionist aims of the Nazi regime and its major industrial backers.

THE FOREIGN DEPARTMENT OF THE DEUTSCHE BANK

The Foreign Department of the Deutsche Bank, located in Berlin, was responsible for the direction of the foreign activities of the Deutsche Bank. This involved all matters pertaining to the foreign network of branches controlled by the Deutsche Bank and of banks in which Deutsche Bank had vested interests. Table X represents this foreign network of the Deutsche Bank, which covered 123 branches of banks controlled by Deutsche Bank in ten European countries, in Asia and in Latin America, 26 branches or representations which Deutsche Bank itself maintained in 8 European countries and 3 banks in whose stock capital Deutsche Bank or one of its subsidiaries participated, which were located in Yugoslavia, Czechoslovakia, and Japan.

The operations of the Deutsche Bank, the largest German bank, in the foreign field were complex and manifold. They embraced the financing of export and import trade, the acquisition of foreign banking institutions, the extension of German industrial control over foreign corporations, the participation in transactions of the German government in foreign countries, the responsibility for all administrative matters pertaining to the branches and affiliates and the cooperation with Nazi Party organizations abroad.

This complex department was managed by four individuals under the direction of Hermann J. Abs. Since 1938, the responsibility for the Foreign Department of the Deutsche Bank has been in the hands of Hermann J. Abs, whose phenomenal rise within the Nazi economy was discussed in greater detail in Chapter VI, "Political Connections." Within four years (1938–1942) he rose from partnership in a private banking house, Delbrueck & Schickler, to the position of one of the three outstanding German bankers in foreign finance. The extraordinary expansion of the Deutsche Bank in the foreign field in the wake of German aggression is closely identified with the energy and resourcefulness of Hermann J. Abs and his intimate connections with the Ministry of Economics and the Reichsbank. Within those four years he became member and often chairman or vice-chairman of the board of directors of over forty banking and industrial enterprises in Germany and abroad,

Table X
FOREIGN NETWORK OF THE DEUTSCHE BANK

Country	Deutsche Bank branches	Branches of banks controlled by Deutsche Bank	Banks with participation of Deutsche Bank or its subsidiaries
Argentina		3	
Austria		43	
Belgium	1*		
Brazil		6**	
Bulgaria		7	
Czechoslovakia	9	22	1
Chile		6**	
China		6	
France	5***		
Hungary		2	
Japan			1
Latvia	1*		
Lithuania	1		
Luxembourg		3	
Netherlands		1	
Peru		2	
Poland	7	6	
Romania		8	
Spain		3	
Sweden	1*		
Turkey	1		
Uruguay		1	
Yugoslavia		4****	1
Total	26	123	3

* representation
** reported liquidated in 1942
*** representation in Paris and 4 branches in Alsace-Lorraine
**** including branch in Ljubljana

including the Reichsbank, the Creditanstalt Bankverein Wien, I.G. Farbenindustrie A.G., the AKU, Libby Owens, and Zeiss Ikon A.G. From the day Hermann J. Abs became a member of the Vorstand of the Deutsche Bank and its Foreign Department, he devoted all his efforts to the expansion of German economic domination over Europe.

Hermann J. Abs was assisted by three "Direktoren der Bank," managers of the bank below the Vorstand level: Alfred Kurzmeyer, Richard Haeussler, and Helmuth Pollems. Of these three men, Alfred Kurzmeyer is of greatest interest and importance because he figured prominently in all Deutsche Bank acquisitions of foreign banks with Belgian-French interest, starting with the time of the Sudeten crisis (September 1938) through the war to the post–V-E Day period. He negotiated with the Société Générale de Belgique, the Banque de l'Union Parisienne, and the Banque de Paris et des Pays-Bas to bring about the transfer into the hands of the Deutsche Bank of French and Belgian holdings in Czechoslovakia, Luxembourg, Yugoslavia, and Romania. Kurzmeyer had close ties with Swiss business and, at the end of 1943, he acquired Swiss citizenship, thus gaining the status of a neutral. As such he was able to maintain contact between the Deutsche Bank and its branches and affiliates in Argentina, Spain, and Turkey. At the present time he is in Zuerich, and there are indications that he was closely associated with operations pertaining to the concealment of German funds and the spreading of risks by transferring such funds from Switzerland to countries like Argentina and Spain.

The other two assistants of Hermann J. Abs divided between themselves the current management of the foreign activities of the Deutsche Bank. Richard Haeussler was in charge of the four correspondence subdivisions and the Zentralstelle und Auslandsvertretungen of the Foreign Department. Helmuth Pollems was in charge of all foreign credits, primarily syndicate credits, the Deutsche Bank fuer Ostasien and the Export-Kreditbank. Even though both of these men had their own, distinctive field of work, they had to be able to represent each other in their respective job. Richard Haeussler is still in Berlin, Helmuth Pollems allegedly in Soviet custody.

The *Zentralstelle und Auslandsvertretungen* (Central Section of the Foreign Department and Foreign Representations) was competent for management and policy problems of Deutsche Bank's foreign agencies and affiliations and all business pertaining to foreign countries as a whole which did not come within the jurisdiction of the correspondence subdivisions. The section was managed by Dr. Feske who now heads the Foreign Department of the Fuehrungsstab of the Deutsche Bank in Hamburg.

The current correspondence and the routine business of the Foreign Department was distributed among four subdivisions according to geographical areas [as shown in Chart I].

The files of the Foreign Department of the Deutsche Bank were kept in Berlin but after the intensive air raids over Berlin, copies of current correspondence were also forwarded to Goerlitz and Dresden. When Hermann J. Abs left Berlin for Hamburg in January 1945, he took with him the Vorstand files dealing with the activities of the foreign subsidiaries and affiliates of the Deutsche Bank.

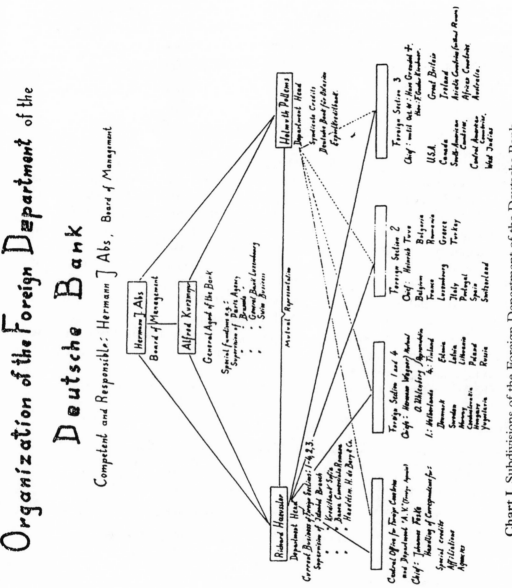

Chart I. Subdivisions of the Foreign Department of the Deutsche Bank

EXPANSION OF FOREIGN SUBSIDIARIES AND AFFILIATES

DEUTSCHE UEBERSEEISCHE BANK

Sixteen years after its establishment, the Deutsche Bank turned to the field of foreign banking. In 1886 it founded the Deutsche Ueberseeische Bank (DUB) which, in a very short time, extended its operations to Latin America and then to Spain and soon became the largest and most important German bank for the Ibero-American countries.

❏ ❏ ❏

Between 1887 and 1930, the DUB opened branches in Buenos Aires, Córdoba, Rosario de Santa Fe (Argentina); in Valparaiso, Santiago, Concepcion, Valdivia (Chile); in Barcelona, Madrid, Sevilla (Spain); in Lima, Arequipa (Peru); in Rio de Janeiro, São Paulo, Santos, Curityba, Bahia, and Porto Alegre (Brazil).

The operations of the Deutsche Ueberseeische Bank were directed from Berlin and Hamburg; although Berlin was the official seat of the Vorstand and Aufsichtsrat, Hamburg played a much greater part in the direction of current business in view of the fact that this city was the center of German export and import trade. In that connection it is significant to note that the Hamburg offices of the Deutsche Bank and the Deutsche Ueberseeische Bank had a joint management.

The Deutsche Bank exercised its control over the DUB by placing Deutsche Bank executives in the most important positions of the Aufsichtsrat and by deciding upon the composition of the Vorstand.

The Aufsichtsrat of the Deutsche Ueberseeische Bank in 1943 consisted of:

Name	Position in AR of DUB	Main Business Connection
Hermann J. Abs	Chairman	Vorstand Deutsche Bank
Oswald Roesler	Vice-Chairman	Vorstand Deutsche Bank
Martin Arndt	Member	Vorstand Philipp Holzmann A.G.
Peter Brunswig	Member	Partner of C.G. Trinkaus, banking house with DB interest
Alfred Busemann	Member	Manager of Krupp A.G.
Hugo Eckener	Member	Chairman Luftschiffbau-Zeppelin G.m.b.H. (member of AR of Deutsche Bank)
Walter Graemer	Member	—
Paul Henrichs	Member	Management Carl Zeiss
Oscar R. Henschel	Member	Chairman of AR of Henschel & Sohn G.m.b.H.

Max Ilgner	Member	Vorstand I.G. Farben
Adolf Friedrich Herzog zu Mecklenburg	Member	—
Erich Neumann	Member	Gen. Manager Deutsches Kali-Syndikat G.m.b.H
Hermann Reyss	Member	Vorstand Siemens-Schuckertwerke A.G.
Gustav Schmelz	Member	Vorstand Continentale Gummiwerke A.G.
Karl Freiherr von Schroeder	Member	Partner of Staudt & Co., Berlin
Ricardo W. Staudt	Member	Staudt & Co., Buenos Aires
Fritz Wintermantel	Member	Vorstand Deutsche Bank

The Vorstand of the Deutsche Ueberseeische Bank in 1943[1] consisted of Albrecht Seeger, Willy Haerter, and Alfred Russel.

The DUB accounted for 2,231 employees in Germany and its branches abroad in 1939. The influence of the Nazi Party over the bank was strong, especially abroad. According to the testimony of Albrecht Seeger, member of the Vorstand of the DUB, NSDAP member since 1936, the Party insisted on prominent bank representatives abroad being members of the Nazi Party.

In that connection it is significant to note that the DUB dismissed its Jewish manager in Buenos Aires, as early as 1935, and thus set the pace for the Nazification of German banking personnel abroad. . . .

---

[1] Department heads and managers of Deutsche Ueberseeische Bank branches as of 1940:

Berlin, Hamburg: Bernhard Croissant, Walter Czech, Carl Girr, Walter Lachmann, Franz Metz, Urban Schlueter

ARGENTINA
Buenos Aires: Alfred Hermann (simultaneously manager of all Argentine branches) Deputies: Paul Petersen, Jorge Schmidt

Córdoba: Alfred Buerklin
Rosario de Santa Fe: Alfred Metzger

BRAZIL
Rio de Janeiro: Hermann Sthamer (simultaneously manager of all Brazilian branches), Richard Bamberger
Deputies: Hermann Boumann, Theodor Ewes

Bahia: Rudolf Abendroth
Curityba: Hans Moeller
Porto Alegre: Johannes Naumann
Santos: Ewald Selke
São Paulo: Martin Spremberg
Deputies: Edgar Cramer, Bernhard Pritze

(Footnote continued on following page)

DEUTSCH-ASIATISCHE BANK

The Deutsch-Asiatische Bank (DAB), like the Deutsche Ueberseeische Bank, was founded during the last quarter of the nineteenth century, the principal period of economic expansion of the First Reich. It was to fulfill the same mission in the Far East which DUB was to accomplish in Hispano-America.

The DAB soon operated and maintained branches in all important ports of China and also in British India and Japan. During World War I, the Deutsch-Asiatische Bank was liquidated, but it was reopened on a somewhat smaller scale in 1921. The new DAB maintained head offices in Berlin and Shanghai and branches in Hamburg, Tientsin, Peking, Tsingtau, Hankau, Canton, and Kobe (the last named was closed in 1935).

The Deutsche Bank controlled the DAB. With Franz Urbig, Hermann J. Abs, and Kurt Weigelt on the board of directors of the DAB, the Deutsche Bank had more representatives than the other banks interested in DAB. Deutsche Bank also represented 60–65 percent of the share capital of the DAB. The share capital was expressed in Chinese silver dollars and fluctuated between 5–10 million RM depending upon the foreign exchange value of the Chinese dollar.

In order to have complete German control over the Deutsch-Asiatische Bank, 1,000 preferred shares, carrying 50 votes each, were distributed among the German banks with the Deutsche Bank retaining 600 of them, the Dresdner Bank 200, and the Berliner Handelsgesellschaft 100, the remainder being distributed among smaller banks and private individuals.

This bank served as the Deutsche Bank agent for business in China and until 1942, when the Deutsche Bank fuer Ostasien was created, it [DAB] was the only bank for the Far Eastern operations of the Deutsche Bank.

(Footnote continued from previous page)

CHILE

Santiago:	Hans Kratzer (simultaneously manager of all Chilean branches)
Antofagasta:	Heinz Wichmann
Concepcion:	Georg Maerz
Temuco:	Hans Bonert
Valdivia:	Erich Karcher
Valparaiso:	Hans Kratzer

PERU

Lima:	Albrecht Seeger (simultaneously manager of Arequipa branch)
	Deputies: Manuel Moncloa y Ordoñez
	Eberhard von Oldershausen (simultaneously deputy manager of Arequipa branch)
Arequipa:	Fritz Volkert

URUGUAY

Montevideo:	Otfried Duernhoefer
	Deputy: Jost Tegtmeyer

SPAIN

Barcelona:	Josef Euwens (simultaneously manager of all Spanish branches)
Madrid:	Leonhard Dangers (simultaneously deputy manager of all Spanish branches)
Sevilla:	Georg Maurer

DEUTSCHE BANK BRANCH IN TURKEY

During the period of the expansion of German economic influence prior to World War I, the Deutsche Bank established strongholds not only in Latin America, Spain and the Far East, it also followed the path of German penetration into the Near and Middle East by creating a branch in Istanbul, Turkey, in 1910. This branch was prominently identified with the financing of railroad construction (the then famous Berlin-Baghdad railroad)[2] and with placing Turkish loans in Germany. From 1918 until 1923 the branch was closed. When it reopened, it remained in operation until August 1944, when Turkey severed diplomatic relations with Germany.

The two important representatives of the Deutsche Bank in Turkey were Hans Weidtmann, manager of the Istanbul branch since 1931, and Kurt Hausmann, manager since 1938. Both managers are supposed to have been interned in autumn 1944 and the management of the branch turned over to Messrs. Jatrou, Caracelar, and Celal Sofu, Turkish nationals who were previous employees of the bank.

In conformity with Turkish law, the capital of the branch amounted to Ltq. 1,200,000 which had to remain untouched. Richard Haeussler, deputy manager of the Foreign Department of the Deutsche Bank and in charge of its operations in Turkey, estimated that the branch had at its disposal in August 1944 cash amounting to between Ltq. 3.5–5 million. This large amount had accrued because Turkey had obstructed the transfer to Germany of the profits the bank had made in Turkey. Information from U.S. agencies in Turkey indicates, however, that immediately before and following the severance of Turko-German relations, numerous and sizable withdrawals of funds were made from the Istanbul branch of the Deutsche Bank for concealment purposes.

Because gold trading was not restricted in Turkey, the Deutsche Bank branch in Turkey handled considerable amounts of gold. Richard Haeussler claims not to know whether and how the Istanbul branch disposed of the gold on hand. He points out that if the branch was given the opportunity to sell the gold on the open market and not compelled to turn it over to the Turkish National Bank at the official rate, a considerable sum would have been realized.

The Deutsche Bank, Berlin, attempted to retain contact with its Turkish branch from August 1944 to April 1945 through the mediation of Alfred Kurzmeyer, then residing in Switzerland. The last telegram Kurzmeyer is supposed to have received from Istanbul indicated that the Turkish government prohibited the continuation of bank operations, directed that past affairs be settled and current accounts transferred to a Turkish bank, in other words, ordered the liquidation of this branch of the Deutsche Bank.

---

[2] *Editor's note:* The Baghdad railway project played an important role in the Armenian Genocide of World War I. The "Young Turk" military junta worked thousands of Armenian men to death on the project during 1915–1916, then shot the survivors. See Christopher Simpson, *The Splendid Blond Beast: Money, Law and Genocide in the 20th Century* (Grove, 1993), p. 28. For detailed discussion of evidence concerning German complicity in the Armenian Genocide, see Vahakn Dadrian, *The History of the Armenian Genocide,* Berghahn Books, 1997, pp. 248–300.

From the Annex to the Report

The last two managers of the Deutsche Bank branch in Istanbul, Kurt Hausmann and Hans Weidtmann, were recently repatriated to Germany from internment in Turkey and are currently in U.S. custody. They have [recently] supplied additional information about the political connections of the Istanbul branch, its principal business transactions, its relations with Swiss banks, and its status after the severance of diplomatic relations between Turkey and Germany.

Political Connections. The good relations which von Papen had previously maintained with the Deutsche Bank in Germany were continued in Turkey after his appointment as ambassador to that country. Hence manager Weidtmann came to be on excellent terms with the German embassy, which enabled him to form the acquaintanceship of high ranking members of the Turkish government. Weidtmann believes that von Papen intervened with the Turkish authorities on behalf of Imhoff, a Swiss citizen, whom the Deutsche Bank desired to retain in Turkey as the custodian of German corporations, in the event of a rupture of diplomatic relations between the two countries. The bank also supplied speculative tips to General Rohde, German military attaché to Turkey, who was "forever in financial distress."

The German consulate general in Istanbul engaged the Deutsche Bank to conduct a considerable portion of the consulate's financial business, which, by Weidtmann's estimate, amounted during the war to some 5 million Swiss francs. Weidtmann claims to have maintained social relations with all the higher officials of the German consulate as well as with officials of the other German offices in Istanbul with the exception of the Gestapo and the NSDAP organizations. Among his personal friends he listed the diplomat Freiherr Kurt von Lersner, a close friend of von Papen and the I.G. Farben adviser in Turkey.

Weidtmann never joined the NSDAP. Hausmann has stated in his Fragebogen that in May 1933 he became a Party member, that he was an SA Scharfuehrer (noncommissioned officer) as well as Berater der Wirtschaftsstelle der Ortsgruppe Istanbul (Adviser of the Economics Office of the Istanbul branch of the NSDAP).

Principal Business Transactions. Transactions in gold during the war years, and especially during 1942/43 became to the bank a profitable source of income. The salaries of the German diplomats in Turkey were paid in unblocked Reichsmarks, which, through the agency of a Swiss bank, the Schweizerische Kreditanstalt, were converted into gold. This gold was shipped by air freight to Istanbul and was sold on the local stock exchange. The turnover during this period, according to Weidtmann's estimate, amounted to some 10 million Swiss francs.

The principal task of the Istanbul branch, however, was the promotion of German–Turkish trade. It supplied the necessary documents for making exports, attended to the collection of bills and the extension of loans and credits to German purchasing companies, and established an information service for business opportunities in the country. . . . Since most of the tobacco smoked in Germany was of Turkish or of blended Turkish origin, Philipp Reemtsma maintained a purchasing agency in Turkey which "basically managed all purchases of tobacco for Germany." Reemtsma, whose connections with the Deutsche Bank [were described earlier], was one of the foremost customers of the Istanbul branch. The Deutsche Bank, Berlin, urged the management of the Istanbul branch to carry out the new "Blanco-Refinanzierung" (unsecured refinancing) of Reemtsma purchases, notwithstanding any mental reservations of the business that they might entertain. . . .

Relations with Swiss Banks. With the exception of certain smaller accounts in Sweden, the Istanbul branch of Deutsche Bank concentrated virtually all of its external assets in the Schweizerische Kreditanstalt Zuerich, where it maintained three accounts:

1.   Current account for current business, the gold business in particular. The account usually fluctuated in the neighborhood of 500,000 Swiss francs.
2.   Special account (Sonderkonto), which usually varied between 200,000–250,000 Swiss francs.
3.   Separate account and separate deposit for currency and gold, which the Deutsche Bank, Berlin, had extended to the Istanbul branch to afford it additional backing. This account was carried on the books of the Istanbul branch as the property of the central office, Berlin. Weidtmann believes that the account amounted to 700,000 Swiss francs. Hausmann on the other hand maintains that it may have risen during 1944 to 1,100,000 Swiss francs, and that the repository contained some 311 kilos of gold. [Captured documents] indicate that on 3 October 1944 the Schweizerische Kreditanstalt Zuerich held 1,150,000 Swiss francs, and its Interlaken branch held some 310 kilos of gold as the property of the Istanbul branch.

Hausmann has stated that the Istanbul branch maintained an additional account at the Schweizerische Bankverein, Zuerich, which never amounted, however, to more than 30,000 Swiss francs.

Status upon Breach of Diplomatic Relations. Upon the severance of diplomatic relations with Germany, the business of the Istanbul branch together with its assets and deposits were given over to Sofu, a Turkish lawyer, who was appointed by the Vorstand of the Deutsche Bank, Berlin. Selected to assist him were:

Jules Imhoff (Swiss)—   Adviser
Vehby Karaon (Turkish)— Prokurist
Antoine Jatrou (Greek)—   Prokurist
Alfons D'Orfani (Italian)—Secretariat Chief
Louis Rosoiato (French)— Chief Accountant

These persons were instructed to extend financial support, upon request, to members of the Deutsche Bank staff, their friends, and customers during the period of internment. They were instructed, in addition, to pay all creditors and collect from all debtors of the bank but to accept no new business.

As the Istanbul branch in general followed a policy of high liquidity (some 85 percent of its assets in 1944 were in liquid form), its depositors in Turkey could withdraw their funds and nevertheless leave to the bank a cash and gold balance of some Ltq. 1,800,000 and debits of approximately the same amount. The assets of the branch are at present in the custody of the Turkish State Bank. Both, Weidtmann and Hausmann, profess their ignorance, however, of the present whereabouts of the gold, which, at the time of their internment, was in the possession of the Istanbul branch.

❑ ❑ ❑

DEUTSCH-BULGARISCHE KREDITBANK, SOFIA

The Deutsche Bank maintained a branch in Sofia prior to World War I. When the Deutsche Bank amalgamated with the Disconto-Gesellschaft in 1929, the Bulgarian-branch of the Deutsche Bank also merged with the Bulgarian subsidiary of the Disconto-Gesellschaft, the Kreditbank, Sofia, which had been founded in October 1905. The new bank maintained branches in six Bulgarian cities and was renamed Deutsch-Bulgarische Kreditbank, in 1942.

The share capital of the Deutsch-Bulgarische Kreditbank amounted to Leva 50 million in 1942. Of this amount the Deutsche Bank held 94 percent, that is, 64 percent in its own name and 30 percent through the Creditanstalt Bankverein, Wien, the Austrian subsidiary of the Deutsche Bank.

With Germany's steadily growing economic domination over the Balkan countries, the DBK also increased in size and scope. The total assets of the Deutsch-Bulgarische Kreditbank amounted to Leva 2,033,834,855 on 31 December 1942 as compared to Leva 1,353,353,914 in 1941. In 1943 it took over the Sofia branch of the Prager Kreditbank.

The Deutsche Bank supervised the operations of the Deutsch-Bulgarische Kreditbank through its representatives in the Aufsichtsrat. The last Aufsichtsrat of the Deutsch-Bulgarische Kreditbank consisted of the following members:

Name	Position in AR of DBK	Main Business Connection
Hermann J. Abs	Chairman	Vorstand Deutsche Bank, Berlin
Marco Riaskov	Deputy Chairman	Bulgarian Finance Minister
Iwailo Danev	Member	—
Theodor Dimanow	Member	Bulgarian consul in Berlin
Nikola Geschow	Member	—
Richard Haeussler	Member	Department head of the Deutsche Bank, Berlin

| Josef Joham | Member | Vorstand Creditanstalt Bankverein, Wien |
| Eduard Naudascher | Member | German consul in Sofia |

In addition to the Bulgarian manager, the Foreign Department of the Deutsche Bank assigned a German manager to the Deutsch-Bulgarische Kreditbank to be directly represented in its management. The last German manager was a Mr. Eble, who, to quote Hermann J. Abs:

> Reported regularly in writing to me as President of the Board on current business.

The Deutsche Bank utilized its Bulgarian subsidiary for the training of bank personnel in foreign business. Richard Haeussler, Heinz Osterwind, Hermann Kaiser, and other executives of the Deutsche Bank received their early training and experience at this Deutsche Bank subsidiary in Sofia.

HANDEL-MAATSCHAPPIJ H. ALBERT DE BARY & CO., N.V., AMSTERDAM

This bank, HADB, is the principal affiliate of the Deutsche Bank in Western Europe, one of its oldest foreign footholds in the West, and, at the same time, one of the most important of Holland's numerous foreign-controlled banks.

❏ ❏ ❏

In 1936, the Deutsche Bank made an attempt to give this bank a Dutch façade through nominal transfers of stock into Dutch hands. In this connection Hermann J. Abs stated in his report on HADB:

> The capital structure underwent certain changes between 1937 and 1940, but Deutsche Bank always owned the majority of shares and controlled de Bary.

These camouflage attempts became especially important in September 1939 when the German government and the Deutsche Bank decided to retain beneficial ownership and yet camouflage HADB to prevent its being blacklisted by the Allied powers. The section Cloaking, describes in greater detail the methods Deutsche Bank used to accomplish this objective. A number of Germans were dismissed from the staff of the HADB at that time but all non-Aryan Dutch members of the staff were removed as well. When Germany occupied Holland, the Deutsche Bank openly reestablished its control and retained 95 percent of the share capital of HADB, which amounted to florins 15 million.

Between September 1939 and September 1942 HADB's total assets increased from florins 51,591,392 to florins 83,347,715.

In September 1939 the deposits and current accounts of HADB amounted to florins 29,113,281 and in 1941 to florins 61,777,468. The doubling of these items during the period of occupation clearly indicates the growth of Deutsche Bank's importance in Holland during that time.

The Deutsche Bank exercised control and influence over the policies and activities of HADB by retaining the leading position on the board of directors for its representatives prior to the outbreak of World War II and again after May 1940 when Germany occupied Holland.

In 1939, three out of the seven members of the board of directors were Germans: Hermann J. Abs, Ernst Enno Russel of the Deutsche Bank, and Robert Pferdmenges from the Aryanized private banking house Pferdmenges & Co., Cologne.

During the period of occupation the number of members on the Aufsichtsrat was reduced from seven to four and that of the Vorstand from six to one.

In 1941 the board of directors of HADB consisted of Hermann J. Abs, chairman, Erich Bechtolf, J. M. Honig, and K. H. Twignstra. The two first named were members of the Vorstand of the Deutsche Bank. J. M. Honig, a Dutch Nazi, had not been connected with HADB prior to the German occupation of Holland. He was a member of the Committee of Industrial Organizations, which was formed in November 1940 to organize Dutch industry to become an integral part of the Nazi economic program for Europe. The fourth member, K. H. Twignstra, a pro-Nazi Dutchman, also became a member of this board of directors at the time of the occupation. He, too, was closely identified with the above-mentioned Dutch Nazi committee.

E. M. Braendlin was the only former Vorstand member who was retained after the reorganization. He was the man who had executed the plans [for] the Deutsche Bank and the German assets in Holland when World War II broke out. For this purpose Braendlin had founded in September 1939 a holding company called N.V. Gemeenschappelijk Bezit van Aandeelen Maatschappij H. Albert de Bary & Co.

Through HADB Deutsche Bank controlled several finance and holding companies, which enabled it to influence Dutch industry.

The HADB owned all ordinary and 85 percent of the preferred shares of the N.V. Capital Beleggings Societeit. The share capital of this general investment and finance company amounted to florins 5 million. The HADB also had vested interests in the Internationale Accountants en Trustee Kantoor, which acted as custodian and administrator of securities in the international market. It was headed by van Vlissingen, a close friend of Hermann J. Abs. It should be mentioned in this connection that both van Vlissingen and Abs were prominently associated with the management of AKU, a German-Dutch rayon combine.

From the Annex to the Report

[New information has surfaced] about the degree of control which the Deutsche Bank exercised over the HADB. In September 1940 the Deutsche Bank owned more than 87 percent and by May 1943 more than 95 percent (florins 14,323,000) of the total share capital of the HADB. The shares were retained in the Berlin vaults of the Deutsche Bank.

Through the HADB, the Deutsche Bank extended its control in 1940 over the Banque de Commerce, Antwerp. The capital stock of this bank was florins 30 million, of which slightly less than one half was held by British, French, and Dutch interests. In September 1940 the HADB owned 5,842 shares or 19.5 percent of the share capital, the bulk of which it had acquired during 1935/36; Barclays Bank, London, held some 27 percent, for which a custodian was appointed in 1940 by the German occupation authorities. The Credit du Nord, Paris, held some 2 percent.

Director Kurzmeyer of the Deutsche Bank, working in close cooperation with the German occupation authorities in Belgium, arranged for the elimination of the Anglo-French interests in the Banque de Commerce in order to bring it under complete German control. The managers of the bank were ordered to arrange a general meeting at which the two representatives on the board of directors of Barclays Bank were to be replaced by two nominees of the Deutsche Bank. The Barclays Bank participation was to be divided between the HADB and the Deutsche Bank and the latter alone was to obtain the participation of the Credit du Nord. In order to obtain an absolute majority of the capital shares of the Banque de Commerce, Kurzmeyer instructed the Banque de Paris et des Pays-Bas, Brussels, via the German banking commissioner, to purchase in the open market some 400–500,000 additional shares. The shares taken over by the Deutsche Bank were to be transferred afterward to the HADB through which bank it would continue to exercise control over the Banque de Commerce.

CREDITANSTALT BANKVEREIN, WIEN [VIENNA, AUSTRIA]

The dynamic expansion of the Deutsche Bank in the foreign field gained momentum with the Anschluss (annexation) of Austria (15 March 1938) and the succeeding economic penetration and domination of Austria by Germany.

In preparation of the annexation of Austria, the German authorities made extensive, minute plans for the penetration of Austria's economic structure. The Ministry of Economics coordinated the demands of German banks for their share in Austrian banking. Emil Puhl, vice-president of the Reichsbank, stated:

> Starting with the period preceding the Anschluss of Austria the big banks made known to department 4 of the RWM their intention and interests in Austrian banking and so the Deutsche Bank (Roesler and Abs) expressed their desire to acquire control of the CABV, the Dresdner Bank stated the same intentions to the Laenderbank, Wien.

August Rohdewald, chief of the foreign department of the Reichs-Kreditgesellschaft, the banking subsidiary of Vereinigte Industrieunternehmungen (VIAG), stated:

> At the time of the Anschluss it was the desire of the RWM to integrate the Austrian economy into the German economy. The intentions of the banks in

acquiring interest in the Austrian banks were in harmony with the intentions of the RWM.

The Deutsche Bank chose control of the Creditanstalt Bankverein, Wien, the largest Austrian bank and the most important bank in the Balkans.

❑ ❑ ❑

The Creditanstalt Bankverein, Wien, was founded in 1855. . . .

As a result of extensive merger movements the Creditanstalt Bankverein, Wien, grew to become the principal Austrian bank whose influence extended into the countries of Southeastern Europe. Due to its size, its network of branches and affiliates and its industrial participations, it has been a dominating factor in Austrian economic life. In 1941 CABV's share capital amounted to RM 70,700,000. Its total assets grew from RM 542,689,654.81 as of 1 April 1938 (the date of the conversion from the Schilling to the Reichsmark system) to RM 780,693,854.14 as of 31 December 1940.

The bank maintained thirty-two offices in Vienna, thirteen branches in Austria, and a branch in Hungary (Budapest). The activities of these branches became so extensive that, between 1935–1940, the number of CABV's employees grew from 1,688 to 2,300. In addition to its branches, the Creditanstalt Bankverein, Wien, controlled three regional banks in Austria:

1. Bank fuer Kaernten A.G., Klagenfurt (with share capital amounting to RM 3 million and total assets to RM 21 million in 1943)
2. Bank fuer Oberoesterreich und Salzburg, Linz, later named Bank fuer Oberdonau und Salzburg (with share capital amounting to RM 6 million and total assets to RM 75 million in 1943; the bank had 18 branches)
3. Bank fuer Tirol und Vorarlberg, Innsbruck (with share capital amounting to RM 1 million and total assets to RM 39 million in 1943)

Business relations between the Deutsche Bank and the CABV had already existed for several decades as both institutions were the most important commercial banks of their respective countries. Prior to the Anschluss Deutsche Bank held a minority interest in the CABV and a seat on its board of directors. Until September 1937 this position was held by Schlieper, the head of the Foreign Department of the Deutsche Bank, and after his death, Hermann J. Abs, his successor, became a member of the board of directors of the Creditanstalt Bankverein, Wien; he attended his first CABV meeting on 5 March 1938, ten days prior to the Anschluss. According to the report Hermann J. Abs wrote regarding the CABV, Deutsche Bank's desire to acquire control and interest in the CABV was not even discussed at that time. However, CABV's first memorandum after the Anschluss shows that the Deutsche Bank had already prepared ground in its own sphere when German troops marched into Austria. The memo, dated 26 March 1938, was signed by Abs and Pollems on behalf of the Deutsche Bank and Joham and Heller on behalf of CABV, and stated the following:

After conversations held on March 4–5 and on invitation of Creditanstalt on March 17–26 in Vienna, the undersigned agree in the following points:

Deutsche Bank is prepared—subject to the approval of the Ministry of Economics—to take over

1. up to about 120,000 ordinary shares of Creditanstalt now held by the state of Austria;
2. up to 20,000 ordinary shares of Creditanstalt now held by the Oesterreichische Nationalbank;
3. up to 50,000 ordinary shares of Creditanstalt now held by Oesterreichische Industrie-Kredit A.G.;
4. 43,032 preferred shares of Creditanstalt now held by the pension institute of the Oesterreichische Creditanstalt—Wiener Bankverein.

❏ ❏ ❏

Most significant is the final paragraph of the memorandum:

The two contracting parties are of the opinion that Vienna ought to achieve special importance for greater German industrial and commercial activities in Southeastern Europe. Consequently the Deutsche Bank would, if feasible—provided appropriate relations with the Creditanstalt are established—direct its Southeastern European business via Vienna with due regard to the particular credit relations to Berlin.

[However,] the Deutsche Bank was not able to put into effect the provisions of the above agreement with the CABV since the majority of the capital of the CABV belonged to the Austrian state and thus passed into the hands of the [German] Ministry of Finance automatically which, in turn, entrusted it to VIAG, Vereinigte Industrieunternehmungen A.G., its industrial holding subsidiary, and to the Reichs-Kredit-Gesellschaft, which was the only bank controlled by the Ministry of Finance. Thus the VIAG became custodian of 76 percent of the stock of the Creditanstalt Bankverein, Wien, on March 1938.

❏ ❏ ❏

From the Annex to the Report

[Newly recovered documents] testify to the vigor with which the Deutsche Bank prosecuted its efforts to win control of the CABV. Although opposition arose from many quarters, it was ultimately overcome in great measure, through the tenacious efforts of Hermann Abs and through the exploitation of the excellent connections he enjoyed with high-ranking Reich ministry officials.

Directly following the Anschluss Abs led a group of Deutsche Bank officials to Vienna to open negotiations for the acquisition of the CABV. On 19

March 1938 he received the following telegram from Dr. Mosler, his colleague on the Deutsche Bank Vorstand:

> Two neighbors, Goetz (Dresdner Bank) and Fischer (RKG) have registered claims upon the object. Final decision as to the share capital is said to rest with the "Wilhelmplatz" here. [RWM] President Schacht will be there on Monday and has been informed by us. He expects your visit Monday afternoon at the Nationalbank. Announce yourself at once. Consider whether you cannot secure very soon an option on the preferred shares, the pension fund shares and shares owned by the CABV.

In view of the pressure of banking rivals, the Deutsche Bank representatives in Vienna applied themselves to the task with such energy that by 26 March the CABV was prepared to sign a so-called friendship agreement. It was clearly stated in the agreement that the Deutsche Bank intended to acquire a minimum of 75 percent of the CABV capital stock. But Abs's ambitions proved more boundless than even the Reich ministries and the Party were willing to accept. A burst of indignation in official quarters in Austria greeted the news of the negotiations. SS Brigadefuehrer Hans Kehrl of the RWM explained to Abs that he had been compelled to defend him against the strong misgivings of his group and that he could not consent to the acquisition by the Deutsche Bank of the CABV share capital and with it the control over the entire structure of Austrian industry. State Secretary and SS Obergruppenfuehrer Wilhelm Keppler expressed himself even more bitingly:

> The Deutsche Bank wants to rob; it came to Vienna with twenty men to take over the CABV.

The friendship agreement was disapproved, in consequence of this opposition, and the Deutsche Bank was informed that closer relations with the CABV would be unwelcome.

Directly following the Anschluss, the VIAG, acting as trustee for the Finance Ministry, acquired some 75 percent of the CABV shares. It thereupon exerted every effort to obtain for its own subsidiary, the Reichs-Kredit-Gesellschaft (RKG), a leading position in the CABV. The Deutsche Bank opposed this ambition by every means. Its hopes of gaining complete control, in time, of the CABV never diminished; in the meantime, however, it strove to prevent other institutions from obtaining participations in that bank. In a conversation on 14 May 1938 with Dr. Joham, a leading Vorstand member of the CABV, Abs explained:

> For us to share with others is simply out of the question. However, one can very well discuss mutual limitations and common transactions. Otherwise we shall have to go our own way.

Abs also pointed out to State Secretary Brinkmann of the Economics Ministry that the Deutsche Bank would be in a better position to exploit the CABV for the benefit of the Reich if the RKG were not permitted to interfere. The CABV, Abs added, was in a position to reinforce German economic influence in Southeastern Europe, provided that its friendship with the

Deutsche Bank were further cemented. This result could best be achieved if the Deutsche Bank were permitted to influence the appointment of staff members to the CABV.

The VIAG and the RKG continued to act in the belief that they would triumph over the Deutsche Bank in the struggle for the control of the CABV. Hence August Rohdewald, a member of the RKG Vorstand, drafted a plan for the equal division of the 60,000 CABV shares administered by the VIAG among the Deutsche Bank, Commerzbank, and the RKG.

The Deutsche Bank succeeded in preventing the execution of this plan though it failed during the succeeding months to make headway in the acquisition of any substantial CABV participation. On 27 July 1938 Karl Kimmich complained to Abs by letter that too much valuable time had already been lost and recommended that to expedite matters he ought to enlist the assistance of Reichskommissar Buerckel (General of the SS and the principal Party representative in Austria following the Anschluss).

The Deutsche Bank, however, still owned less than 1 percent of the CABV capital when in November 1938 the VIAG expressed its readiness to negotiate for the transfer of a portion of the CABV shares which it held in trusteeship. The Deutsche Bank succeeded in obtaining a 25 percent participation. It thereupon commenced to exercise a leading role in the CABV although it finally acquired control over a majority of the CABV capital only in May 1942.

❑ ❑ ❑

The contract between the VIAG and the Deutsche Bank, which now held about 35 percent of CABV's share capital, was signed in Berlin in December 1938 and went beyond the mere transfer of 25 percent of the share capital of the CABV. The contract states:

> VIAG and Deutsche Bank formed a syndicate for the joint administration of their holdings of shares. . . . In the spirit of cooperation the parties agree that during the existence of this syndicate they will jointly exercise the voting rights and the influence resulting therefrom. . . . Consequently they will, before each general meeting, come to an understanding on how to vote . . . VIAG and Deutsche Bank will reach a preliminary understanding on the questions pertaining to the Aufsichtsrat . . . [and] to the appointment and removal of managers. In order that the parties should be represented on the Aufsichtsrat by representatives of their own firms, VIAG may appoint not more than three and Deutsche Bank not more than two representatives of their institutions.

The role of the Creditanstalt Bankverein, Wien, as a spearhead of German economic penetration was reaffirmed in article 3 of the same contract.

> They (the parties) agree that banking transactions in Southeastern Europe must be handled in the best possible order by German banks. They are

therefore anxious to achieve such an order and an adequate place for the Creditanstalt.

From then on the Deutsche Bank took a very active interest in the management of the Creditanstalt Bankverein through its two representatives on the board of directors, Hermann J. Abs (vice-chairman) and Hans Rummel, both from the Vorstand of the Deutsche Bank.

❏ ❏ ❏

From the testimony of Otto Neubaur, Vorstand member of the Reichs-Kredit-Gesellschaft and of the VIAG, who became chairman of the Vorstand of the Creditanstalt during the last part of 1941, it is apparent that the primary reason for the delay in transferring full control of the Creditanstalt Bankverein to the Deutsche Bank was a conflict between the Reich-German and Austrian NSDAP and governmental agencies:

> Serious differences of opinion originated in Vienna because of the block (controlling block of shares of the CABV) between the party and the ministry on one hand and between the Reich-German and the Austrian government offices on the other hand.

Otto Neubaur emphasizes the fact that the Deutsche Bank received the full support of the Ministry of Economics (RWM), particularly department 4 of RWM, in its efforts to expand into Austria. Neubaur states:

> Keppler informed Olscher that several proposals for the disposition of the CABV shares had already been made. Riehle of the Economics Ministry had urged that they be given to the Deutsche Bank which already held a 13 percent interest in the Creditanstalt.

After a series of industrial holdings of the Creditanstalt Bankverein were transferred from the bank to the Hermann-Goering-Werke, the conflict lost much of its intensity. The *Handbuch der deutschen Aktiengesellschaften 1941*, Volume 3, page 250 states:

> A number of participations of CABV was transferred to other hands. The Reichswerke Hermann Goering especially received the following participations of long standing: Steyrische Gusstahlwerke A.G., Kaerntnerische Eisen- und Stahlwerks-Gesellschaft, Fein-Stahl-Werke Traissen A.G., Steyr-Daimler-Puch A.G., Maschinen- und Waggon-Fabrik A.G. in Simmering, and Oesterreichische Donau Dampfschiffahrts-Gesellschaft.

In the course of the war the conflict between the Austrian and the Reich-German Nazi Party and governmental offices lost its importance and the persistent drive of the Deutsche Bank to bring its interest in the CABV to a full majority finally resulted in the transfer of another block of 25 percent of the share capital of the Creditanstalt from the VIAG to the Deutsche Bank. An agreement was reached on 4 May 1942, which provided for the sale of CABV shares nominal value RM 17,675,000 in exchange for important blocks of industrial shares in which the VIAG was particularly interested, namely, nom. RM 2,150,000 Rheinisch-Westfaelische Elektrizitaets-Gesellschaft shares and some smaller blocks of public utility shares which were in the portfolio of the Deutsche Bank. It further transferred to Reichs-Kredit-Gesellschaft nominal RM 460,000 I.G. Farben shares, nominal RM 140,000 Siemens ordinary shares and nom. RM 140,000 Siemens preferred shares. In addition to the transfer of nominal RM 6,127,000 Universale Hoch- und Tiefbau A.G. shares to the Alpen-Elektrowerke (the public utility subsidiary of the VIAG in Austria), the Deutsche Bank undertook the following mission, which throws specific light upon the relationship between the Deutsche Bank and industrial enterprises:

> In connection with this transaction we shall cause the Muerztaler Holzstoff-und Papierfabrik AG in Bruck on the Mur to sell three power stations to Alpen-Elektrowerke AG for the price of RM 1 million.

Although a number of industrial holdings of CABV were transferred to the Hermann-Goering-Werke and the VIAG, CABV remained the principal holder of industrial participations among Austrian banks. Thus it held 53 percent of the RM 5 million stock capital of the Martin Miller A.G., a producer of steel, iron, and metal goods, and 62 percent of the RM 1,200,000 stock capital of Schember & Soehne, a machine factory. It owned 75–77 percent of the stock capital of four Austrian textile corporations, Gebr. Enderling, Ebreichsdorfer, Guntramsdorfer, and Patria. It controlled 77 percent of the Muerztaler Holzstoff paper mills (capital RM 1,800,000) and of the Suedosteuropaeischer Getreidehandel (Southeast European Grain Trade), capitalized at RM 2 million. Sixty-nine percent of the shares of two leather factories was in the possession of CABV, Aeterna (capitalized at RM 3,200,000) and Delka (capitalized at RM 1,400,000).

Since 4 May 1942, the Deutsche Bank has been the majority shareholder of the CABV and fully controlled all operations of the Creditanstalt Bankverein. Besides Abs and Rummel, Oswald Roesler, the speaker of Deutsche Bank's Vorstand, also became a member of the Aufsichtsrat of the CABV. Later on, Rummel's seat was given to Ritter von Halt, [of the] Vorstand of the Deutsche Bank and member of the Keppler Circle, bringing the total of Deutsche Bank Vorstand members in the Aufsichtsrat of the Creditanstalt to three. This was the largest representation of Deutsche Bank Vorstand members on any of its subsidiaries. Walter Tron, the Leipzig branch manager of the Deutsche Bank, was brought into the Vorstand of the CABV. The political composition of the Aufsichtsrat and the Vorstand of the Creditanstalt Bankverein, Wien, is discussed in greater detail in Chapter VI, "Political Connections."

Now the Deutsche Bank was afforded the opportunity to fulfill the mission which originally had been designed for the Creditanstalt Bankverein in the foreign business of the Deutsche Bank: to act as the spearhead of its Balkan business. The Creditanstalt Bankverein was given important minority holdings in banks which the

Deutsche Bank controlled in various countries of Central and Southeastern Europe. This process started already in June 1940 when the Deutsche Bank transferred to the Creditanstalt the branch it had opened in Cracow, Poland. Subsequently this branch, together with the branch in Lemberg, was transformed into the Creditanstalt A.G. Krakau with a capital of RM 6 million. In 1940 the branch of the Boehmische Unionbank at Pressburg, Slovakia, was reorganized into the Union Bank, Pressburg, where the Creditanstalt received a majority interest of 55 percent of the share capital of kronen 15 million. When the Deutsche Bank had attained full control of CABV, Creditanstalt received a third of the share capital of the Boehmische Unionbank, the Deutsche Bank affiliate in Czechoslovakia, amounting to kronen 50 million. In addition, the Creditanstalt Bankverein, Wien, also received 30 percent of the share capital of the Deutsch-Bulgarische Kreditbank, Sofia, which amounted to Leva 15 million and 30 percent of the share capital (total amount Lei 90 million) of the Romanian subsidiary of the Deutsche Bank, the Banca Comerciala Romana, Bucharest.

The grant to CABV of minority participations in the foreign subsidiaries of the Deutsche Bank was followed by the addition of CABV representatives to the board of directors of the respective banks. Thus, for instance, the Deutsche Bank informed the Creditanstalt Bankverein, on 4 May 1942:

> In connection with our agreements we herewith guarantee you a seat on the board of directors of the Deutsch-Bulgarische Kreditbank, Sofia, and the Banca Comerciala Romana.

The Deutsche Bank also placed two representatives of the Creditanstalt Bankverein on the board of directors of the Boehmische Unionbank.

In relation to the Boehmische Unionbank, it should also be pointed out that the Deutsche Bank directed the Boehmische Unionbank to conduct its business in Southeastern Europe, principally in Hungary, Serbia, and Croatia, through the Creditanstalt Bankverein, Wien.

BOEHMISCHE UNIONBANK

Less than six months after the Anschluss of Austria, the Sudetenland became part of the Greater German Reich. This expansion of Germany again was the signal for new acquisitions by the Deutsche Bank. To quote from the bank's annual report of 1938:

> The historically memorable year 1938, which brought to our "Vaterland" an increase of 10 million people and an area of more than 110,000 sqkm with the return of the Ostmark and the Sudetenland, presented the German economy with a task of hitherto unknown magnitude. Our participation in the largest Austrian bank, the Oesterreichische Creditanstalt Bankverein, Wien, and the taking over of the Sudeten business of the Boehmische Unionbank created the organizational foundation for our cooperation in the solution of the banking and credit tasks which will serve as the basis for our activity in the new areas and, closely connected therewith, in the South-Eastern regions. . . . Through this (the acquisition of over sixteen branches of the BUB) our business connections in the Sudetenland received valuable addition.

Germany's conquest and dismemberment of Czechoslovakia in the following year and the creation of the Protectorate for Bohemia and Moravia enabled the Deutsche Bank to acquire the entire Boehmische Unionbank. How closely the Nazi victories were tied in with the expansion of Deutsche Bank is shown in the following comment from the annual report of the Deutsche Bank for the year 1939. It states:

> In connection with the creation of the Protectorate for Bohemia and Moravia we are extending our relations to the Boehmische Unionbank whose Sudeten business we took over in the fall of 1938. Upon the execution of the decisions of the general meeting held 12 December 1939, the majority of the share capital of the Boehmische Unionbank will be in our possession.

After listing the eleven branches of the Boehmische Unionbank which were added to the sixteen acquired previously, this annual report goes on to say:

> In cooperation with our Viennese friends, the Creditanstalt Bankverein, and with us, the Boehmische Unionbank will transform the already existing Pressburg branch into an independent bank in order that we may be thus represented in Slovakia.

The statements quoted above constitute the cryptic description of the events which brought the Deutsche Bank into possession of the control of the third largest commercial bank in Czechoslovakia.

The inaccessibility of the files located in Hamburg presents an obstacle in describing all details surrounding the acquisition of this Czech bank. It is known, however, that this acquisition followed a plan which the Reich Ministry of Economics had mapped out carefully in agreement with the large banks. This fact was expressed by Emil Puhl in the following statement:

> At the time of the Sudeten crisis and subsequent occupation of Czechoslovakia, the "Grossbanken" submitted to the RWM their intentions toward the major Czech banks. A very strong competition among the banks for the most favorable position within the RWM continually persisted. The banks were asked to submit their plans for the acquisition of control of Czech banking. On the basis of these proposals the RWM made the final decisions in cooperation with the Economic Department of the administration of the Protectorate.

From the Annex to the Report

Boehmische Unionbank, Prague (BUB)

Acquisition of the BUB Branches in the Sudetenland. Recently recovered documents show that within a few days after the signing of the Munich Agreement and the entry of the German armies into the Sudetenland, the principal Berlin Grossbanken commenced to stake out their claims within the newly acquired territory. A keen rivalry broke out between the Deutsche and the Dresdner Banks for the acquisition of the Sudeten branches of the Boehmische Escompte Bank & Creditanstalt (BEBCA). The acquisition of these branches was considered by the German banks to be more desirable than those of another leading institution, the Boehmische Unionbank (BUB), which had a "strong Jewish clientele" and concentrated its activities in the textile industry and in commerce. Abs, during the first week of October 1938, informed the Reich Commissioner for Banking, Dr. Ernst, who, in cases of this description, possessed a considerable measure of jurisdiction, that the Deutsche Bank had been the first to undertake negotiations with the BEBCA and hence "is unwilling to retreat a single inch."

The [competing] Dresdner Bank succeeded, nevertheless, in wresting control of the Sudeten branches of the BEBCA, whereupon the Deutsche Bank turned its attention to the acquisition of the Sudeten branches of the BUB. It informed the RWM on 24 October 1938 that it had entered into negotiations with the BUB for the transfer of the Sudeten branches as well as of participations in twenty-one industrial enterprises in the Sudetenland. During the first days of January 1939 the transfer to the Deutsche Bank of the twenty-three Sudeten branches together with the industrial participations of the BUB was consummated.

Acquisition of the BUB, Prague. The principal Berlin Grossbanken formed their plans for the acquisition of Prague banks even prior to the invasion of Czechoslovakia in March 1939. Thus, Hans Rummel, Vorstand member of the Deutsche Bank, had knowledge in February 1939 of pending negotiations by a syndicate composed of the Dresdner and Deutsche Banks as well as the Reichs-Kredit-Gesellschaft for the acquisition of the BEBCA in Prague. The day following the occupation Hans Rummel and Oswald Roesler wrote to the RWM:

> We assume that the economy of the newly acquired territory of the former Czech republic . . . will be completely incorporated into the German economy. To attain this aim it is particularly necessary to absorb the Czech banks through the banks of the Reich . . . so as to smash the dominating economic influence of the Czech national banking institutions and to replace them with German banks. . . .

> The Grossbanken alone have the necessary experience and financial power to accomplish the desired incorporation of the Czech economy into the German economic system. . . .

> Furthermore it is clear that some Czech banks must for racial reasons disappear. . . .

This document is in sharp contradiction to the statement made under interrogation by Mr. Christian, an official of the General Secretariat of the Deutsche Bank in charge of BUB affairs, and quoted in the principal report:

> In the spring of 1939 after the occupation of Czechoslovakia by the German troops, the Deutsche Bank was commissioned by the Ministry of Economics . . . to undertake the necessary support of the Boehmische Unionbank Prague.

The share capital of the BUB was distributed, at that time, in the following fashion:

> K 42,000,000, Boehmische Unionbank, Prague
> K 20,000,000, British Overseas Bank Ltd., London
> K 14,000,000, Société Générale de Belgique, Brussels
> K 74,000,000, Widely dispersed throughout Czechoslovakia. An estimated K 20,000,000 was in Sudeten-German possession.

The Deutsche Bank, with the endorsement of the RWM, secured control of the K 42,000,000 shares owned by the BUB. [It] prodded the latter at the same time to acquire the participations of the British Overseas Bank and the Société Générale de Belgique. The foreign shareholders, however, flatly rejected the BUB offer of 10 percent of the nominal value, payable in London out of a blocked sterling account, and declared that the so-called losses suffered by the BUB were of German manufacture entirely, created by the "undervaluation of accounts belonging to non-Aryans."

After the outbreak of war in 1939 the K 42,000,000 shares held by the BUB were transferred to the Deutsche Bank for 10 percent of the nominal value. The voting rights of the foreign-held shares were abolished; a fact which taken together with the widespread distribution within Czechoslovakia of the remaining K 74,000,000 shares enabled the Deutsche Bank, at the next general meeting in December 1939, to exercise majority control.

❏ ❏ ❏

As Hermann Abs put it:

> Deutsche Bank asked the British Overseas Bank, the Prudential Insurance Company and the Société Générale of Brussels, which had formerly been very important shareholders, to participate in the reorganization (of the BUB). They refused, however, and Deutsche Bank was left with approx. 80 percent of the capital on its hands.

After the occupation of Belgium in 1940, the Deutsche Bank acquired the interest of the Société Générale in the Boehmische Unionbank.

In 1942 the capital of the Unionbank was increased by kronen 50 million which were turned over to the Creditanstalt Bankverein, Wien; thus the CABV received a 33 percent interest. Following is the distribution of the share capital of the Boehmische Unionbank as of 1943: Deutsche Bank, Berlin, 58 percent; Creditanstalt Bankverein, Wien, 33 percent (British Overseas Bank, London); Société Générale, Brussels, 2 percent; miscellaneous 7 percent.

The Deutsche Bank exercised control over the operations of the Boehmische Unionbank through Oswald Roesler, chairman of the board of directors of the Boehmische Unionbank, through Emil Kreibich, vice-chairman of the board of directors of the Boehmische Unionbank, through Hermann J. Abs, and through managers of the Creditanstalt Bankverein, Wien, like Richard Buzzi, chairman of the

Vorstand of Creditanstalt Bankverein, Wien, and Ludwig Fritscher who joined the board of directors of BUB in 1942.

❏ ❏ ❏

As a result of declaring Slovakia an "independent" state, the Union Bank Pressburg was formed. This bank was operated jointly by the Creditanstalt Bankverein, Wien, and the Boehmische Unionbank. The Deutsche Bank was represented on the board of directors of the Union Bank Pressburg by Hermann Kaiser. Ludwig Fritscher, from the Vorstand of the Creditanstalt Bankverein, was the chairman of the Aufsichtsrat; Max Rohde, from the Vorstand of the Boehmische Unionbank, was deputy chairman. The capital of the Unionbank amounted to kronen 50 million.

❏ ❏ ❏

From the Annex to the Report

Deutsche Agrar- und Industriebank, Prague

The methods and tactics employed by the Deutsche Bank to obtain control of the Sudeten branches of the Deutsche Agrar- und Industriebank, Prague, viz. the use of political pressure upon Czech public authorities and the economic exploitation of the political situation created by the Nazi government, foreshadowed the activities and manipulations at a somewhat later date of the German occupation authorities in the countries of conquered Europe.

The Deutsche Agrar- und Industriebank, Prague, [DA] was one of the larger of the Czech commercial banks. Capitalized at koruna 48 million, its total assets in 1937 amounted to Kc 621 million. Its principal business was in the Sudetenland where it maintained twenty-four out of a total of twenty-five branches. These branches were transferred to the Deutsche Bank directly following the annexation in 1938 of the Sudetenland and the Bank at Prague passed out of existence altogether in 1940.

Already during the political crisis which preceded the Munich Agreement in 1938 the Deutsche Bank conferred with Victor Ulbrich, manager, of the DA, a Sudeten German, to explore the prospects for the taking over of the Sudeten branches of his bank in the event of the annexation by Germany of the Sudetenland. The Deutsche Bank promised Ulbrich a suitable position if he succeeded in bringing to it his own institution or the business of other Czech banks.

Directly following the annexation of the Sudetenland the Deutsche Bank proceeded to incorporate the Sudeten branches of the DA into its own branch system and sought, in addition, to acquire the capital shares of the bank in Prague together with the control of the last remaining branch at Brno. The Deutsche Bank explained its actions to the RWM in the following terms:

. . . a German bank in Prague could strengthen the German people remaining there. . . . It is particularly necessary that there exist in Prague one bank under Reich German influence which can look after the interests of Germany and to which all (Germans) can turn for advice and information. . . .

The transfer to the Deutsche Bank of the Sudeten branches created the need for the settlement of the claims of these branches against the head office at Prague. These claims in the sum of Kc 76 million arose principally out of previous transfers of deposit funds by the branches to the head office as well as of reserves kept at Prague for anticipated losses from customer accounts of the branches. The Deutsche Bank then imposed against the Prague office an additional claim for reserves of some Kc 23 million. No provision for such reserves had previously been contemplated. This additional claim made desperate the already precarious position of the head office of the DA which had to accept it nevertheless in view of the prevailing political situation. The Deutsche Bank demanded in settlement of the outstanding claims of the Sudeten branches. . . . The Deutsche Bank planned to use the [funds] to acquire at low prices the accounts and securities of Jews who were compelled to leave the country and anticipated that it would realize in this fashion the sum of RM 11,116,000.

After the occupation of Czechoslovakia, the Deutsche Bank discovered opportunities for obtaining even greater profits from the [Prague Bank] than had originally been contemplated. On 30 March 1939 it instructed its main branches by confidential letter:

> The RWM in agreement with the Golddiskontbank has suggested that we execute the blocked mark transaction ourselves and buy up securities of Jewish customers who are about to emigrate.
>
> The entire transaction must be kept strictly confidential, of course, and if necessary an intermediary for its execution will be used.
>
> We are interested to know which of your customers have declared any wish for emigration and how you judge the prospect of making these customers emigrate by virtue of our offer.

The RWM at the same time extended permission to the Deutsche Bank to buy up Jewish accounts at the rate of 6.5 percent of their normal value, payable in foreign currency. On 3 June 1939 the rate was reduced to 6.2 percent for cash and 6.1 percent for securities. The Deutsche Bank, in addition, deducted a service charge of 1–2 percent from the Jewish "client." In November 1939 the rates payable to Jewish clients were reduced a second time to 5.2 percent for cash and 5.1 percent for securities. By that date the Deutsche Bank had acquired some RM 12 million in Jewish accounts [for about 5 percent of their value, and] expected to acquire an additional RM 3.5 million of such accounts. These transactions were completed by the summer of 1940.

In exchange for the £80,000 [in Czech currency] the Deutsche Bank obtained RM 15,782,000 worth of Jewish-owned cash and securities. The net profit accruing out of this sum to the Deutsche Bank came to nearly RM 15 million.

The Deutsche Bank also sought to compel the shareholders of the DA, Prague, to sell out at low prices. By a variety of bookkeeping devices such as the undervaluation of customer accounts of the Sudeten branches the bank was declared to be insolvent, notwithstanding the fact that for the business year of 1938 the Sudeten branches had earned a profit of RM 369,065. Hermann Kaiser has admitted that undervalued accounts showed considerable improvement at a later date and various of them became completely sound.

In consequence of these tactics the Deutsche Bank was enabled to acquire the majority of the shares of the DA, Prague, from a Swiss company, the Agraria Industrie & Handels A.G., which held them on deposit. The purchase price was considerably less than 50 percent of par. In addition the Deutsche Bank also offered to buy out small shareholders at 50 percent of par. To avoid every possibility of resistance the Deutsche Golddiskontbank, a Reichsbank subsidiary, was to call in these shares as foreign values. "The capital of the DA will then be ours" Abs had previously explained to the RWM.

In 1940 the DA, stripped of its Sudeten branches, was merged with the BUB, a Deutsche Bank subsidiary.

The modus operandi employed by the Deutsche Bank in the various transactions described above reflect the readiness to exploit for its own profit the economic resources of occupied Czechoslovakia. The fact that the political setting in which these transactions were effected was the creation of Nazi government authorities and not of banking officials fails to lessen the responsibility of the Deutsche Bank for its collaboration in the program of exploitation.

❑ ❑ ❑

EXPANSION INTO LITHUANIA AND POLAND

The occupation of Czechoslovakia in March 1939 was paralleled by the annexation of the Memel area from Lithuania. The Deutsche Bank entered that area as well. In the Memel region a branch was opened after the Deutsche Bank had taken over the business of the Landschaftsbank in Memel and Heidekrug in 1939.

The outbreak of the war in September 1939, the incorporation of the western areas of Poland into the Reich, and the subsequent creation of the General Gouvernement gave the Deutsche Bank the opportunity to enlarge its network of branches in the areas of former Poland. In the region of the so-called Polish Corridor the Deutsche Bank opened a branch in Gdynia (Gotenhafen), which was integrated into Deutsche Bank branches of prewar days located in the free city of Danzig, Tiegenhof and Zoppot. The Deutsche Bank also opened new branches in Bielitz, Oderberg, and Teschen in Silesia, in Posen, the capital of the so-called Warthegau, and in Lodz and Cracow in the General Gouvernement. As has been pointed out already in connection with the Creditanstalt Bankverein, the Deutsche Bank transferred the business of its Cracow branch to the Creditanstalt Bankverein in 1940 and retained a 20 percent interest (zloty 1,200,000) in the Creditanstalt, Cracow.

THE DEUTSCHE BANK AND THE BANQUE DE LA SOCIÉTÉ GÉNÉRALE DE BELGIQUE

The period following the occupation of the Low Countries and France became the turning point in the extension of Deutsche Bank's influence into Luxembourg and the Balkan countries. The controlling interests which Franco-Belgian banking and industrial groups held in the banks and industries of Czechoslovakia, Romania, Yugoslavia, and Luxembourg became the stepping-stone for the acquisition of this control by German banking circles. The largest single holder of these industrial and banking interests was the Banque de la Société Générale de Belgique (Société Générale). Its capital and reserves amounted to bfrs. 650 million [Belgian francs], its total assets to bfrs. 6.85 billion as of 31 December 1939. Out of a total number of 1,095 branch offices of banks in Belgium, the Société Générale maintained a net of 311 branch offices. Everything considered, it was more than twice as large and important than the second largest Belgian bank, the Banque de Bruxelles.

The Société Générale held considerable interests in the following banks:

> Banque d'Anvers
> Banque Belge pour l'Etranger, Paris
> Banque Belge pour l'Etranger (overseas), London
> Banque Générale de Luxembourg
> Banque Belge et Internationale en Egypte
> Banque du Kongo-Belge
> Banque Commerciale du Congo

The Société Générale and its affiliates controlled substantial holdings in the Balkans. The Société Générale held interests under its own name in Yugoslavia in the Allgemeiner Jugoslawischer Bankverein, Belgrade, and in the Yugoslav Unionbank, Zagreb, while the Banque Belge pour l'Etranger and the Banque d'Anvers, its affiliates, had a joint interest in Romania, in the Banca Comerciala Romana, Bucharest.

The struggle for the control over these crucial positions resulted in [further] conflict between the Deutsche and the Dresdner Bank. In spite of the excellent political connections the Dresdner Bank had with the Party and SS, the influence of the Deutsche Bank, of Hermann J. Abs in particular, was strong enough to reverse the original decision the RWM had made in favor of the Dresdner Bank by giving the leading share of the Société Générale's holdings to the Deutsche Bank. An indication of the competition between the Deutsche Bank and the Dresdner Bank is given in the memorandum written by Carl Goetz, chairman of the board of directors of the Dresdner Bank, who fought to obtain the major share of the holdings of the Société Générale for the Dresdner Bank. On 20 September 1940 Goetz wrote to Minister Funk:

> Upon return from my last trip, I was informed by Ministerialdirigent Dr. Riehle, that Mr. Abs had called on you in the meanwhile in order to point out to you the relations of the Deutsche Bank to the Société Générale de Belgique, and in order to prove that his personal connections, respectively those of the Deutsche Bank were closer than ours. He wanted to reach a change in your decision, according to which the Deutsche Bank was to have first call on negotiations in the Netherlands and the first call in Belgium with

the Société Générale, so that the Deutsche Bank would be favored also in Belgium.

After citing some of the arguments that Abs probably represented to Minister Funk, Carl Goetz went on to say:

> The situation remains unchanged and both banks, our bank and the Deutsche Bank, have equal connections with the Société Générale. The fact is that we, on the basis of your decision, refrained from undertaking any steps in Holland and in this way undoubtedly lost opportunities for further development. Furthermore, we were asked to renounce in favor of the Deutsche Bank our claims on the Credit Industriel in connection with the negotiations for the establishment of branches in Alsace-Lorraine. All these steps which we have taken as result of the authorization for negotiations with the Société Générale should speak in our favor. In Holland the Deutsche Bank occupies a preferential position through its close relations with Herr Fischboeck (former chairman of the Vorstand of Creditanstalt Bankverein and subsequently Enemy Property Custodian of the German Military Government in Holland under Seyss-Inquart), whom you informed about your decision and through de Bary.

The protest by Goetz apparently had no effect. Regarding the standing of Abs and that of the Deutsche Bank with Minister Funk, it is significant that the RWM no longer was willing to give the Dresdner Bank a preferential status in Belgium since Abs had intervened with Funk. Upon the suggestion of Karl Kimmich of the Deutsche Bank, Minister Schacht was requested to arbitrate between the two banks. His findings, however, can hardly have been satisfactory to the Dresdner Bank; Schacht only pointed to the recalcitrant attitude of the Société Générale to enter into any sort of general and long-term agreement with German banks and refrained from any basic decision. In effect, whatever previous restriction had been imposed on the Deutsche Bank to consider the Dresdner Bank in its desire to extend its hold on the Société Générale and Belgian economy was no longer valid now.

The Dresdner Bank conceded its "defeat" and the Dresdner Bank representative in Brussels even acknowledged the preferential position of the Deutsche Bank. On 11 December 1940 Joachim Overbeck wrote to Carl Goetz from Brussels:

> in the course of our conversation Mr. Haven (manager of the Société Générale in Verviers) made a remark from which I conclude that the Société Générale is inclined towards the Deutsche Bank more than before. . . . When I asked Mr. Haven for more details and I told him that I personally was under the impression that the Deutsche Bank is receiving a preferential treatment from Société Générale which is apparent from the recent events.

Emil Puhl threw additional light on the circumstances surrounding the support for the preferential standing of the Deutsche Bank by the Ministry of Economics in regard to the Société Générale, when he stated:

In Belgium the Deutsche Bank was favored which was in close connection with the Société Générale. The nature of these connections were such that the Société Générale turned over the biggest part of its business to the Deutsche Bank. The transfer of Belgian interests to the Deutsche Bank came from joint action of the Deutsche Bank (Abs) and the Financial Division of the German Military Government in Belgium. The head of the Financial Division of the Military Government was Reeder. Under him worked as head of the Financial and Banking Division, Dr. Becker and his representative Hofrichter. This division exercised influence, after receiving the decision of the RWM, upon the Société Générale to increase their relations with the Deutsche Bank. The Dresdner Bank through the person of Mr. Goetz attempted very hard to receive preferential status in the control of Belgian banking. However, the competent authorities in Berlin as well as in Brussels decided in favor of the Deutsche Bank.

It is necessary to view the transfer of the holdings of the Société Générale de Belgique to the Deutsche Bank in connection with the basic policies of the German government in regard to the acquisition of German interests and ownership of Belgian, Dutch, and French participations. During the meeting at the Reich Ministry of Economics on 16 August 1940 on the subject of acquisitions of shares of important foreign enterprises in Southeastern Europe, Dr. Schlotterer of the Reich Ministry of Economics commented:

> Private economic penetration of the Southeastern area by German influence is desirable, likewise the supplanting of British and French interest in that territory. (Document of the Office of U.S. Chief of counsel No 43. Report on the meeting at the Ministry of Economics of 16 August 1940, page 1)

Between August and November 1940, the Deutsche Bank and its subsidiaries were well on the way of supplanting such non-German interests by acquiring considerable Belgian interests in the Balkans. In his report for November 1940 the German military governor for Belgium stated:

> Among the important business deals of this kind (transfer of Belgian investments) which have been concluded should be mentioned the taking over by the Creditanstalt Wien of an essential interest in the Allgemeiner Jugoslawischer Bankverein from the Société Générale (capital approximately RM 1 million) and the taking over by the Deutsche Bank of the overwhelming majority of the Banca Comerciala Romana from the Société Générale (capital approximately RM 2 million). The Deutsche Bank also succeeded in acquiring shares of the Creditanstalt Wien of approximately RM 800,000 nominally from the Société Générale and from one of its subsidiaries. Negotiations between the Deutsche Bank and the Société Générale on the transfer of approximately 25 percent of the capital of Banque Générale de Luxembourg are about to be concluded. Through this deal the Deutsche Bank together with the other German groups obtains the absolute

majority of the Luxembourger Bank (approximately 70 percent of the shares). The Deutsche Bank gets the right to acquire another 25 percent of the shares that for the time being remained with the Société Générale. (Document of the office of U.S. Chief of Counsel Ec 34. Report of the military commander of Belgium, 1 December 1940, page 1)

These transactions were handled by the Brussels office, which Deutsche Bank established shortly after the Nazis had occupied Belgium, while the payment for the acquisition of these interests in Luxembourg and the Balkans was made through the Belgian-German clearing.

From the Annex to the Report

Banque de la Société Générale de Belgique

During the first months following the occupation of Belgium, the Deutsche Bank proceeded to strengthen its influence in that country by securing the appointment of several of its own men to key positions in the Economics Division of the German Administration in Belgium. Karl Kimmich, who was informed of the fact that the Dresdner, the Commerz, and other banks were proceeding in similar fashion, wrote to Abs on 5 August 1940 as follows:

> I agree with what you said about the activities of our competitors;— it goes without saying that we enjoy the better connections to the important offices. On the other hand, let us not overlook that we should take still more of a hand in places where business opportunities arise daily.

The Deutsche Bank came to deal in Belgium with the Banque de la Société Générale de Belgique and its subsidiary holding company, the Société Générale de Belgique. Both institutions cooperated with it in the completest harmony. The two institutions are accordingly referred to . . . as the "Société Générale."

The particular significance to the Deutsche Bank of a close working relationship with the Société Générale lay in the diversified portfolio of participations held or controlled by the latter institution. In a number of instances the Deutsche Bank acquired from the Société Générale some of its prized holdings. In other instances the Deutsche Bank directed the transfer of industrial holdings into the hands of its own customers. . . . The following thumbnail summary illuminates the degree of influence in the Société Générale exerted by the Deutsche Bank:

1. **Allgemeiner Jugoslawischer Bankverein.** The Société Générale, on the strength of negotiations conducted by Kurzmeyer in September 1940, sold to the Creditanstalt Bankverein, Wien, 116,484 shares, or 37.5 percent of the capital stock of the Allgemeiner Jugoslawischer Bankverein.
2. **Banque Générale de Luxembourg.** The Société Générale in November 1940 sold to the Deutsche Bank 5,940 or 29.7

percent of the capital stock and granted it an option to purchase another block of the same size.

3. **Banca Comerciala Romana, Bucharest.** The Société Générale
   during the early months of 1941 sold to the Deutsche Bank
   205,821 shares, or 34 percent of the capital stock.
4. **Creditanstalt Bankverein, Vienna.** The Société Générale sold
   to the Deutsche Bank 7,875 shares, or some 1 percent of the
   capital stock.
5. **Boehmische Union Bank, Prague.** The Société Générale sold
   3,517 shares to the Deutsche Bank.
6. Société Générale prior to March 1941 also transferred to the
   Deutsche Bank several blocks of shares which the latter redis-
   tributed at a substantial profit among its affiliates and customers. These included:

58,643 shares, Oesterreichische Eisenbahnverkehrsanstalt, Vienna.
10,904 shares, Instituto Nazionale di Credito per il Lavoro al Estero.
25,000 shares, Banca Nazionale d'Albania.
 8,620 shares, Landesbank fuer Bosnien und Hercegovina.

The general agreement between the Deutsche Bank and the Société
Générale also provided for consultations in all important transactions concerning enterprises in which the latter had an interest. The Deutsche Bank
was thereby afforded the opportunity of influencing the distribution of
those participations which it did not desire for its own account. In a consultation of this nature on 16 November 1940 between Galopin and de Munck
of the Société Générale and Abs and Kurzmeyer of the Deutsche Bank . . . Abs
[approved] the sale of RM 1,500,000 shares of the Dahlbusch company out of
the portfolio of the Société Générale, as well as to preliminary negotiations
with the Société Générale for the acquisition by the Deutsche Bank of
its holdings in the ARBED, of Luxembourg (Acieries Reunies de Burbach-
Eich-Dudelange), the foremost steel trust in Europe next to the Vereinigte
Stahlwerke. The Société Générale owned 38,400 out of a total of 250,000
ARBED shares, the only large block said to be under single control. It was
proposed that the Société Générale transfer these shares to a holding company to be established in Luxembourg in which the Deutsche Bank would
acquire a 50 percent participation. The clash of conflicting interests in
Luxembourg, however, between the Deutsche and the Dresdner Banks, as well
as between the Gauleiter of Moselland and the Reichswerke Hermann Goering
brought the plan to nothing. A trustee was appointed in consequence by the
German Alien Property Custodian, who, aided by a staff of German officials,
took over the management of the ARBED.

❏ ❏ ❏

ACQUISITION OF CREDIT INDUSTRIEL D'ALSACE ET DE LORRAINE

After the defeat of France, the Deutsche Bank reopened its office in Paris, which was
concerned primarily with the purchase of industrial securities and similar transactions.

When the Alsace and Lorraine regions were incorporated into the Reich, the territorial integration of these provinces was followed by a concentrated effort to integrate the economy of these two regions with the German economy. Richard Haeussler, assistant to Abs in the Foreign Department of the Deutsche Bank, states the following:

> After the occupation of Alsace and Lorraine by German troops in the summer of 1940, a number of measures were taken by the German civil administration of this district. The aim of these measures was a fast and effective integration into the economic system of Germany. In the field of finance the French franc had to be replaced by the Reichsmark and the liquidation of the existing French banking system and its transfer into German possession . . . The German authorities ordered the influential Berlin big banks . . . to establish branches of their own in Alsace Lorraine as soon as possible.

As was stated in connection with the struggle between the Deutsche and the Dresdner banks for the control of the holdings of the Société Générale, the Deutsche Bank was given preference over the Dresdner Bank in the establishment of branches in Alsace and Lorraine.

❏ ❏ ❏

BANQUE GÉNÉRALE DE LUXEMBOURG

The Banque Générale de Luxembourg was the largest commercial bank in Luxembourg with a capital amounting to 20 million [Belgian francs]. It was an affiliate of the Banque de la Société Générale de Belgique in Brussels which owned 11,879 of its 20,000 shares, that is, more than 50 percent of the total share capital.

When the Deutsche Bank acquired Société Générale holdings the first major transfer of interests involved the participation of the Belgian bank in the Banque Générale de Luxembourg. According to the contract, the Deutsche Bank received half (about 25 percent of the total amount) of the shares which were in the hands of the Société Générale with the right of preemption for the second half of the shares in possession of the Société Générale. The report written by Hermann Abs and Richard Haeussler on 20 November 1940 to the Ministry of Economics, attention Ministerial-Dirigent Dr. Riehle (head of department 4 of the Ministry of Economics in charge of banking and foreign economic penetration) states in part:

> The remaining approximately 8,000 shares of Banque Générale de Luxembourg are in Luxembourgian, i.e., German possession, which has the effect that after the sale of the above mentioned first 50 percent of the Belgian group to us an amount of about 70 percent of the shares will be in German possession. It is further provided in the said contract that two representatives of our bank shall join the board of directors of the Banque Générale de Luxembourg, one of whom shall be vice-president. Furthermore, a representative of our bank shall be delegated to the management for

liaison purposes and the treasury of the Luxembourg bank shall be transferred to us.

Like the initial sales, the payment for this sale also went through the Belgian-German clearing; the Deutsche Bank stated:

> Payment shall be made through the German-Belgian clearing by crediting the above-mentioned amount (Luxembourgian francs 4,454,250) to the account No. 1,028 of the Emissions Bank in Brussels in favor of Banque de la Société Générale de Belgique and/or Société Générale de Belgique respectively.

Société Générale's agreement to sell 50 percent of its participation in the Banque Générale de Luxembourg and to render the right of preemption on its second 50 percent was followed by a syndicate agreement, signed by Alexander Galopin, manager of the Société Générale de Belgique, M. Willi de Munckh, president of the board of administration of the Banque Générale de Belgique on one hand, and Alfred Kurzmeyer and Helmuth Pollems, on the behalf of the Deutsche Bank. The purpose of the syndicate agreement was to act jointly in all matters pertaining to the management of the Banque Générale de Luxembourg.

The Deutsche Bank was represented on the board of directors of the Banque Générale by Hermann Abs and Alfred Kurzmeyer. Abs became vice-chairman and in 1943 its chairman.

BANCA COMERCIALA ROMANA, BUCHAREST

The Banca Comerciala Romana (COMRO) with a share capital of [Romanian] Lei 300,000,000 was the third largest commercial bank and the largest foreign controlled bank in Romania. It, in turn, controlled the smaller Banca Comerciala si Industriala. In addition to its head offices in Bucharest the bank maintained five branch offices in Romania.

The COMRO was controlled by the Banque de la Société Générale de Belgique and the Banque d'Union Parisienne (PARUNION). As a result of the support accorded Deutsche Bank in its dealings with Société Générale (cf. above), the Deutsche Bank first acquired control of the Banque Générale de Luxembourg, and then of the COMRO. The negotiations for the acquisition of COMRO coincided with the period when Germany started to bring Romania under her political, military, and economic domination.

Hermann J. Abs' report on COMRO shows clearly that the Nazi RWM was more than merely interested in the acquisition of COMRO by the Deutsche Bank:

> In August 1940 the Ministry of Economics desired that the German banks take a more extensive interest in the banking situation in Romania. The Deutsche Bank was asked to ascertain whether the Société Générale de Belgique was prepared to sell its shares of Banca Comerciala Romana.

In order to obtain full control of COMRO it was necessary to acquire the majority interest, which was in the possession of PARUNION (54 percent, Lei 156,959,000). Abs goes on to say:

Negotiations were thereupon carried out with both the Belgian and French shareholders and on the part of the Deutsche Bank, mostly through Mr. Kurzmeyer.

The official report by the French Ministry of Finance gives a good account of the atmosphere during these negotiations:

> Representatives of Deutsche Bank offered to purchase the Union Parisienne's (PARUNION) shares (of Banca Comerciala Romana).
>
> When the leaders of the bank informed the French Finance Ministry at the beginning of October 1940, they refused to allow the sale (Ministerial decision of November 1940).
>
> In the meantime the Germans tried to exert pressure in Romania to force Union Parisienne (PARUNION) to accept their offer.
>
> On the other hand, the measures taken by the Romanian government with regard to the administration of businesses were known by the Germans; the decree of October 21st, limiting the number of members of the Board of Managers in corporations to seven, in addition to the existing regulation which stated that two-thirds of the Board of Managers had to be of Romanian nationality, led to the elimination of most French board members, thus leaving them with no control over the situation.
>
> Finally, the occupation of Romania and the measures for Romanization made the situation of the French managers still more difficult.
>
> By the beginning of 1941, the Belgian shares had been sold to the Germans.

When questioned about the pressure Deutsche Bank exercised in acquiring the interests of the Banque d'Union Parisienne, Richard Haeussler, assistant to Abs, stated:

> I could imagine that the German Armistice Commission in Wiesbaden may have helped.
>
> Q. — What makes you think so?
>
> A. — When difficulties arose we occasionally wrote to them.

The acquisition of the interest held by the Banque d'Union Parisienne apparently constituted such "difficulty" because, according to the French Ministry of Finance:

> The question of the rest of the shares was to be regulated by the government and was made the subject of correspondence between March 7th and 10th, 1941 between the French delegation and the German Armistice Office for Economic Affairs in Wiesbaden as to whether the French government gave its consent to give away a certain number of shares, among which, those of Banca Comerciala Romana.

These statements by the French Ministry of Finance together with Haeussler's testimonial give an entirely different picture of the circumstances surrounding the penetration of Romanian banking by the Deutsche Bank than is contained in the interrogation of Hermann Abs on 22 September 1945, which reads:

> To give you an example of the country Romania where we, the Deutsche Bank, acquired on our own initiative the control of a banking institution . . . After the occupation of Belgium and France we had the idea of taking over the interests of Société Générale de Belgique and Banque d'Union Parisienne in the Banca Comerciala Romana. These negotiations ended in 1941 . . . By purchasing about 90 percent of the capital of the Banca Comerciala Romana.

Abs further claimed:

> As concerns the Belgian enterprise in the time of 1940 and 1941 the author-ities in Belgium and France preferred to liquidate their Romanian interest.

When asked about any pressure exercised, Abs answered:

> There was never and at no time any pressure exercised by the Deutsche Bank.

When asked whether he considered such sale to have been a free sale, he replied:

> I have said we must make a distinction in the case of Banque Générale de Luxembourg and also in the question of the Banca Comerciala Romana. I cannot think of any pressure exercised with any of them.

Thanks to the energetic efforts of Hermann Abs in Berlin and Alfred Kurzmeyer in Brussels and the pressure exercised in Romania, France, and Belgium, the Société Générale sold its interest in the Banca Comerciala Romana, which amounted to Lei 102,910,500 and covered 205,821 of the 600,000 shares of this bank. On 22 January 1941, the Reichskommissar fuer das Kreditwesen granted to the Deutsche Bank per-mission to acquire this participation.

❏ ❏ ❏

As soon as the Deutsche Bank acquired control of the Banca Comerciala Romana

> the Belgian and French members of the Board retired and were succeeded by me [Abs] as vice-president and three Romanians.

Later Hermann J. Abs became the head of the Aufsichtsrat and Albrecht v. Ressig was appointed by the Deutsche Bank to become the general manager of Banca Comerciala Romana. After the Deutsche Bank acquired full control of the

Creditanstalt Bankverein, Wien, it ceded to Creditanstalt Bankverein a 30 percent interest in the share capital of the Banca Comerciala Romana, and a representative of the Creditanstalt Bankverein joined the board of directors of the COMRO.

Germany was very eager to bring Romania under her domination, if only because of Romania's vast resources in raw materials. It is, therefore, interesting to read COMRO's first annual report after it had come under German control. The 1942 report states that the bank's export business had increased enormously; the export documents signed covered almost twice the sum as compared with the previous year. The report records a considerable increase in business in all departments of the bank between 1941–1942: the balance sheet increased by about 25 percent, investments in bills of exchange and debits by about 68 percent and assets rose from Lei 3,632,823,162 to Lei 4,531,824,427.

From the Annex to the Report

The RWM had a particular interest in the acquisition by German interests of the COMRO, the third largest bank in the country, because it was the house bank for the Romanian oil-companies. In August 1940 RWM officials made it clear that:

> The RWM desires to occupy even during the war those key-positions abroad, particularly in the South-East, which are of particular importance to Germany for future commerce and policy.

On 13 November 1940 Freiherr v. Falkenhausen, a former Deutsche Bank branch manager, was ordered by the Economics Division of the German Military Government in France to call on Director Letondot of the Banque de l'Union Parisienne and to obtain his views of proposals previously tendered by Kurzmeyer for the purchase of the COMRO shares held by the French bank. Letondot expressed his own agreement with the proposals but stated that the Vichy government had not, as yet, given its approval. On 22 January 1941 Abs informed Ministerial-Dirigent Riehle of the RWM that the approval of the Vichy government to the transfer of the shares was still lacking though the Banque de l'Union Parisienne was attempting to obtain it. Riehle thereupon instructed Abs that the Deutsche Bank should discontinue its efforts and that he himself would demand and obtain the approval on the following 1 February when he would travel to Paris.

❑ ❑ ❑

ALLGEMEINER YUGOSLAWISCHER BANKVEREIN

In its foreign penetration the Deutsche Bank pursued the policy of extending its influence into smaller countries through its principal affiliates. In regard to Southeastern and Central Europe, the Deutsche Bank controlled the major commercial banks in Austria, Czechoslovakia, Bulgaria, and Romania through a direct majority; in Polish, Hungarian, Slovakian, Yugoslavian, and subsequently in Croatian banking, however, the Deutsche Bank exercised its influence primarily through the Creditanstalt Bankverein, Wien, and the Boehmische Unionbank, Prague.

The Allgemeiner Yugoslawischer Bankverein had a share capital of Dinar 60 million in 1939, which was distributed in the following manner:

Creditanstalt Bankverein	50.3 percent
Société Générale de Belgique	38.8 percent
Basler Handelsbank, Basel	5.4 percent
Boehmische Unionbank, Prag	4.0 percent

The first step toward closer control and acquisition of the Allgemeiner Yugoslawischer Bankverein was made when the Deutsche Bank took over the majority of shares of the Boehmische Unionbank and Hermann J. Abs, as a result of that, became a member of the Aufsichtsrat of the Allgemeiner Yugoslawischer Bankverein. [Abs joined] there Josef Joham, who headed this board, and Ludwig Fritscher, both members of the Vorstand of the Creditanstalt Bankverein, Wien.

In 1939, a conflict developed within the management of the Allgemeiner Yugoslawischer Bankverein, when Fischboeck, [who was at the time] chairman of the Vorstand of the Creditanstalt Bankverein, demanded that Franz Neuhausen, the German consul general in Belgrade, be appointed to the Aufsichtsrat of the Allgemeiner Jugoslawischer Bankverein. Société Générale declined to support this appointment because Neuhausen was most closely identified with the Nazi political and economic domination of Yugoslavia. The Creditanstalt Bankverein then desired to acquire the interest of the Société Générale in the Yugoslav bank. But in winter 1940 Joham and Abs approached the Société Générale without attaining their aim.

After the occupation of Belgium, however, the Société Générale transferred its interest in this Yugoslav bank through the Deutsche Bank to the Creditanstalt Bankverein. Mr. Kurzmeyer of the Deutsche Bank, the roving assistant of Hermann Abs, negotiated this transfer.

❑ ❑ ❑

Thus 88 percent of the capital of the Yugoslawischer Bankverein was under Deutsche Bank influence by the end of 1940. Although the Yugoslav government protested against the change of ownership in the Allgemeiner Yugoslawischer Bankverein, it was unable to change the state of affairs.

From the Annex to the Report

[At that point Neuhausen obtained the board seat he had sought.] Franz Neuhausen, Special Plenipotentiary to Yugoslavia of Reichsmarschall Hermann Goering, accepted his appointment to the presidency of the Verwaltungsrat (board of directors) of the Allgemeiner Yugoslawischer Bankverein in the following terms:

> I fully realize that . . . I will have to take over this responsibility in the interests of the German economy in Yugoslavia. A German bank is a necessary instrument which I need if I am to supervise and manage the interests of the German economy in Yugoslavia according to the demands and instructions of Field Marshal General Goering. . . .
>
> It is in the interests of Germany and of the German economy in particular, that the bank, which we are now ready to introduce openly as an instrument of our economic policy (Wirtschaftsfuehrung), truly is powerful economically. I shall always strive for that.

Neuhausen, who was the Landesgruppenleiter of Yugoslavia in the Auslands Organization of the NSDAP, had, some years prior to the war, been appointed German Consul General at Belgrade. Ernst Wilhelm Bohle, the leader of the Auslands Organization, has described the nature of this appointment. Neuhausen, he stated, had been appointed by the (German) Foreign Office as Consul General for the express purpose of facilitating the performance of political tasks for the AO.

❑ ❑ ❑

As a result of the occupation of Yugoslavia by the German army in April 1941, the country was split into two separate states: Serbia and Croatia. The banks adapted themselves to the new situation and the Allgemeiner Yugoslawischer Bankverein was transformed into two separate units. In Serbia, it was called Bankverein A.G., Belgrade; the capital of this bank amounted to Dinar 100 million and the majority of the shares remained in the hands of the Creditanstalt Bankverein. The Deutsche Bank held a 12 percent interest in the bank also under its own name. The total assets of this bank amounted to Dinar 1,674,218,290 as compared to 972,679,423 in 1941. . . . Joham and Abs represent[ed] the combined Deutsche Bank–CABV interest [on its board].

The Bankverein fuer Kroatien was created in Croatia from the Zagreb, Zenum, and Ljubljana branches of the former Allgemeiner Yugoslawischer Bankverein. Since the Serbian unit retained the whole stock capital, the capital for the Croat unit had to be supplied in its entirety. The capital of the Bankverein fuer Kroatien was put at kunas 125 million and distributed among the Creditanstalt Bankverein (55 percent), the Deutsche Bank (15 percent), the Boehmische Unionbank (10 percent); thus 80 percent of the share capital of the bank was under Deutsche Bank control. The total assets of this new bank amounted to kunas 919,718,520 in 1942. Josef Joham was heading the Aufsichtsrat with Hermann Abs and Walter Pohle representing the Deutsche Bank and the Boehmische Unionbank, respectively.

The Landesbank fuer Bosnien and Hercegovina, Sarajevo, seems to represent a special case as a direct control of its capital is not apparent. The bank [had] . . . a share capital of kunas 20 million and total assets amounting to kunas 900 million.

Abs stated about this bank:

> I do not know who owned the shares of the bank, except for small holdings in the hands of the Creditanstalt and Bankverein fuer Kroatien. . . . Deutsche Bank had no interest in the bank.

According to the War Department Civil Affairs Guide on "German penetration of corporate holdings in Croatia" (War Department pamphlet No. 41-129 published 20 July 1944), however:

> this bank was controlled up to 1940 by the banking group which controlled the Allgemeiner Yugoslawischer Bankverein. However, in 1940 and 1941 the Deutsche Bank and the Creditanstalt Bankverein, Wien, increased their interest by acquiring the Belgian holdings.

The fact that Hermann J. Abs and Josef Joham represented the Deutsche Bank–CABV interest on the board of directors of the Landesbank fuer Bosnien and Hercegovina also indicates that this bank, too, was under the domination of the Deutsche Bank.

EXTENSION OF DEUTSCHE BANK INFLUENCE INTO GREECE

The penetration of the banking structure in Greece differed from the usual method of penetration and acquisition of banks followed in most of the occupied and satellite countries in Europe. Instead of acquiring the share capital of Greek banking institutes, so-called *Freundschaftsabkommen* (collaboration agreements) were concluded, which organized a close working relationship between a German "Grossbank" and a Greek bank.

The Banque National de Grece (Nationalbank) was the largest commercial bank in Greece. In 1939, its capital and reserves amounted to drachmas 1,205 million and its total assets to drachmas 12.5 billion. It maintained nintey-seven branches in Greece at that time and a subsidiary in New York City, the Hellenic Trust Company.

The Deutsche Bank first established contact with the Nationalbank through Richard Diercks in May 1941 immediately following the occupation of Greece by Nazis. Richard Diercks was a representative of the Siemens company, which was closely connected with the Deutsche Bank (cf. "Influence and Control of German Industry" and Profile of Hermann von Siemens). In his report of 6 June 1941 about his trip to Greece, Richard Diercks wrote:

> I had a conference, which lasted one hour and a half, with the leading heads of the National Bank of Greece.
>
> I had been told already before this conference started that I would be asked to support the project for collaboration between the Nationalbank of Greece and a German Grossbank. The trend of my conversation was a good transition for this problem and I promised to discuss the possibilities with Deutsche Bank in an informal manner upon my return to Berlin. The gentlemen from the Nationalbank explained that the bank was not in need of money, that it was very liquid and had deposits of about drachmas 11 billion (RM 225 million) at the present time. They rather had in mind a syndicate which was to participate in the economic reconstruction of Greece primarily in its industrialization, for which German capital probably would not even be necessary though, of course, it would have to be left to the German financial institutions and industries to pursue their own special interests. . . . Dr.

Jessen arranged for a conference in my office in Berlin with Mr. Abs and Mr. Kurzmeier [Kurzmeyer] of the Deutsche Bank which was then held on the 4th of this month. They immediately showed great interest in the project and planned to start negotiations with the Nationalbank. If possible, Mr. Abs intended to go to Greece personally about the 16th of this month, probably accompanied by Mr. Kurzmeier, and to send Mr. Heusler [Haeussler] to Athens in the meantime to make a first contact with the Nationalbank. Mr. Heusler is the present top official of the Deutsche Bank in Sofia. I was authorized to inform the Nationalbank accordingly, which I did.

On 21 June 1941, Diercks reported about the further progress of the negotiations between the Deutsche Bank and the Nationalbank. He wrote:

Mr. Abs from the Vorstand of the Deutsche Bank, who had flown to Athens on the 16th of this month, telephoned me yesterday to give me a short account . . . about the outcome of his conferences. . . . A verbal agreement has been reached regarding the formation of a syndicate between the Deutsche Bank and the Nationalbank of Greece for participating in the industrial reconstruction of Greece.

❏ ❏ ❏

The agreement between the Deutsche Bank and the Banque National de Grece was signed on 17 June 1941. It provided for the establishment of a syndicate committee composed of the following men:

Greek members:
   The Governor of the Banque National de Grece.
   Konstantin Goumarakis, head of Siemens telephone company in Athens
      (AETE) and member of Aufsichtsrat of Nationalbank of Greece
      (a known Germanophile, educated in Germany)
   Johannes Paraskevopoulos, professor of Economics at the University of
      Athens

German members:
   Hermann J. Abs, Vorstand, Deutsche Bank
   Helmuth Pollems, department head, Foreign Department, Deutsche
      Bank
   Richard Diercks, Vorstand, Siemens & Halske A.G., Berlin

This contract states:

The Banque National de Grece will submit to the Deutsche Bank Berlin memoranda on various projects especially concerning construction of hydroelectric plants, industrialization, production of bituminous coal and minerals.

In line with the policy of the Deutsche Bank to utilize the Creditanstalt Bankverein, Wien, as its main instrument for the penetration of the Balkan countries, the Deutsche Bank brought a CABV representative into the German-Greek syndicate. Upon acquiring the majority of the CABV, the Deutsche Bank informed the Creditanstalt Bankverein on 4 May 1942:

> In line with our increased interest in your bank we shall exert our influence to bring a representative of the Creditanstalt Bankverein into the German-Greek committee. This may be in addition or instead of the second representative of our bank.

DEUTSCHE BANK FUER OSTASIEN

The creation of a special bank for Japan afforded the Deutsche Bank a new and potentially important channel for its expansion in the Far East.

When a new German-Japanese trade agreement was concluded in 1941, Ministerial director Wohlthat, the German economic representative in Japan, instigated the establishment of a special bank whose sole function was to be the settlement and financing of all business resulting from this agreement which provided for a trade volume totaling about RM 600 million.

Upon the initiative of the government, a banking syndicate under the management of Deutsche Bank was formed to organize the new bank, the Deutsche Bank fuer Ostasien (DBO). Founded in November 1942, the share capital of the bank was guaranteed by the Reich up to 70 percent and set at RM 10 million, which were distributed in the following manner:

	Percentage
Deutsche Bank	20 (Manager)
Dresdner Bank	20
RKG	15
Commerzbank	10
Deutsch-Asiatische Bank	6
Berliner Handelsgesellschaft	5
Bank der Deutschen Arbeit A.G.	5
Allgemeine Deutsche Credit Anstalt	2
Bayerische Hypotheken und Wechselbank	2
Deutsche Laenderbank A.G.	2
C.H. Donner & Co. (Hamburg)	2
Hardy & Co. G.m.b.H.	2
Merck, Fink & Co.	2
Norddeutsche Kreditbank A.G.	2
Pferdmenges & Co.	2
Vereinsbank in Hamburg	2
Westfalenbank A.G.	1

The direction and management of the DBO was in the hands of the Deutsche Bank. Helmuth Pollems, Abs's right-hand man in Deutsche Bank's Foreign

Department, was business manager of the Vorstand and Abs chairman of the Aufsichtsrat of the DBO. Other members of the Aufsichtsrat included Hans Schippel (Dresdner Bank), August Rohdewald (Reichs-Kredit-Gesellschaft A.G.), Eugen Bandel (Commerzbank A.G.), Friedrich Bethke (Rowak Handelsgesellschaft m.b.H.), Herbert von Dirksen (German ambassador to Japan), Felix Kilian (Deutsch-Asiatische Bank), Staatsrat Karl Lindemann (Keppler Circle; Melchers & Co.—one of the most important German firms engaged in Far Eastern trade; Hamburg America Line and North German Lloyd), H. Waibel (I.G. Farbenindustrie A.G.), Dr. Otto Wolff (*Gauhauptstellenleiter,* Hamburg—Chief of Main Gau Offices, Hamburg), and so on.

Deutsche Bank's own offices officially served as business offices for the main branch in Berlin; another branch was opened in Tokyo, Japan.

Because the Deutsche Bank managed the syndicate, because Deutsche Bank men acted as business manager of the Vorstand of DBO and as chairman of its Aufsichtsrat, and because Deutsche Bank housed the DBO, the Deutsche Bank emerges as the dominant force within this bank even though other banks had vested interests in it.

From the Annex to the Report

The Japanese on their side named the Yokohama Specie Bank, Ltd., to act as the counterpart to the DBO, and on 8 June 1943 the two banks concluded a working agreement.

The banks participating in the German syndicate received the guarantee of the Reich against all possible losses beyond RM 3,000,000 arising out of risks which were financed with syndicate funds. This guarantee, which was extended on 27 August 1943 via the Deutsche Revisions- und Treuhand A.G., also provided that the Reich would take over credit balances of Yen 100,000,000 or more, whenever it proved impossible, during an entire year, to convert such funds into Reichsmarks.

FINANCING OF FOREIGN TRADE AS AN INSTRUMENT FOR FURTHERING NAZI POLITICAL OBJECTIVES

The period preceding the territorial expansion of the Third Reich was devoted primarily to the stockpiling of strategic raw materials and the strengthening of the Axis countries and their allies. The latter function continued through the war years especially as the satellite countries served as buffer states for Germany in the East and Southeast.

With the enactment in 1934 of Schacht's New Plan for the control of foreign exchange and foreign trade, Germany's import and export trade became part of the rearmament program.

The Deutsche Bank considered the financing of foreign trade as more than a commercial activity. The annual report of 1934 clearly states the bank's policy in this field:

Although this part of our activities which formerly prospered to a particular degree thus hardly is profitable anymore today, we regard it as a necessity and a duty not only toward our own interests, but also toward the interests of Germany in general, to devote our special attention continuously to German's foreign contacts even if incurring sacrifices.

In the 1937 annual report the Deutsche Bank further specifies the objectives of Germany's foreign trade:

To the abundance of work which resulted for industry and skilled labor from carrying out the great tasks of developing the domestic production of raw materials, of rearmament, and of public construction, an increased demand by the world market for goods of production and consumption of all kinds was added during the year covered by the report; this demand did, however, undergo a certain decline in the course of the second six month period. The increased export opportunities were used to the fullest and permitted an increase in the quantity of imports, from which profited the supply of raw materials as well as the import of food and forage. The increase in the export quota thus obtained is a process which retains high economic significance, even within the scope of increased domestic production of raw and working materials.

The Deutsche Bank actively participated in the implementation of the Nazi foreign policy in the field of finance. Whatever the policy was at the given moment, the Reich government received the full cooperation of the Deutsche Bank which stood ready to support each Reich venture with the wealth of its resources, experience and foreign connections.

DUB's Foreign Trade

It has already been pointed out that the Deutsche Ueberseeische Bank was the German bank which disposed over a larger number of branches, a larger stock capital, a larger amount of assets, and a larger number of employees in Hispano-American countries than did the Deutsch-Suedamerikanische Bank, the only other German bank in these countries.

Because DUB was the better established bank, it also transacted a larger percentage of business. The following table will indicate the distribution of business between the two banks as given by Albrecht Seeger, leading member of the Vorstand of DUB:

	DUB (percentage)	**DSB** (percentage)
Argentina	55	45
Brazil	60	40
Chile	70	30
Peru	100	—
Spain	60	40
Uruguay	100	—

DUB counted some of the most important corporations among its customers. World-known companies such as the I.G. Farbenindustrie, the Siemens Combine, the Mannesmann complex, Staudt & Co., the Zeiss concern, Holzmann and various South American firms such as Mauricio Hochschildt, the second largest tin producer in Bolivia, availed themselves of the banking facilities of the DUB and its Hispano-American net of branches.

The DUB financed the German export of finished products like machinery, chemicals, and photographic instruments for the import of raw materials such as rawhides, wolfram, cork, oranges, and fruit pulp, goods needed in Germany during the rearmament and war periods.

The annual report of the Deutsche Bank for the year 1934, the first year of Schacht's New Plan, already emphasizes the increase of the activities of the DUB for the German export and import trade:

> (1934) The Deutsche Ueberseeische Bank is able to report a gratifying stimulation of economy in almost all parts of its sphere of work. Beyond that the bank was able to extend valuable service to the cultivation and promotion of German foreign trade within the method in which international trade has been financed recently. It not only cooperated successfully in the unblocking of the claims German exporters had in the different South American countries, but was increasingly active also in the promotion of German export and particularly in providing Germany with raw materials by financing German purchases.

The annual reports for the succeeding years also claim a steady increase of both export and import transactions with South American countries and particularly stress the procurement of raw materials for Germany.

The fact that DUB was the best-established German bank in South America led to the designation of this bank to act as official clearing agent for all transactions resulting from the German-Uruguayan trade agreement concluded in November 1934. . . .

The full importance of designating the DUB, a private bank, as official clearing agent for the agreement between the two governments can be measured only by the realization that the Uruguayan state bank, the Banco de la República Oriental del Uruguay, was DUB's official partner in all resulting negotiations.

The benefit derived by DUB can be judged best by the fact that, during the first year already, the bank expected the volume of business to amount to RM 15 million.

Export of Arms. As part of the policy of the Nazi government to arm its potential allies and Axis partners, a series of credits was granted for the export of munitions from Germany. Credits of over RM 100,000,000 were extended between 1935–1942 for the export of arms to Portugal, Afghanistan, Turkey, and Bulgaria. An important exporter of arms to these countries was the Rheinmetall-Borsig, a munition factory controlled by VIAG and, since 1938, by the Hermann-Goering-Werke. The exports to Portugal took place between 1935–1944; to Turkey from 1936 until 1940; to Afghanistan from 1937–1942, and to Bulgaria from 1940–1942. The Deutsche, Dresdner, and RKG participated equally in the extension of these credits.

Credits to Bulgaria. The above-mentioned credits to Bulgaria concern only one phase of Germany's effort to fortify this Axis satellite country. The major credit, extended directly to Bulgaria to build there a strong army and an extensive defense system, amounted to RM 500 million. This loan was given in 1940–1941 by a banking syndicate under the leadership of the Deutsche and Dresdner Banks. Forty-eight percent of the goods exported from Germany to Bulgaria on the basis of this loan were aircraft, artillery, and ordnance.

Credits to Romania. With the political and military entrenchment of Hitler's Germany in Romania in the latter part of 1940 the German government embarked upon a ten-year program of expansion of the Romanian economy. The short-range aim was to transform Romania into a fighting ally of Germany and in the long-range to make Romania fully dependent upon Germany and her industry. To finance this ten-year program, a series of credits were extended by a banking syndicate headed by the Deutsche and Dresdner Banks, with the Deutsche Bank managing the syndicate. By 1944 this credit amounted to RM 1.05 billion to which the Deutsche Bank subscribed with 21.5 percent. The political nature of this operation becomes even more evident in the words of Richard Haeussler, assistant to Hermann J. Abs in the Foreign Department of the Deutsche Bank, who stated:

> and thereby express that they (the banks) were willing to cooperate in this kind of government business even though the margin for the banks was so unusually narrow for long-term business.

Credits to Japan. Nazi Germany with the assistance of the banks under the leadership of the Deutsche Bank extended weighty financial aid to Japan, its Axis partner in Asia. The overall decision to finance Japan was taken during a conference between Goering's office, the Ministry of Economics, the Ministry of Finance, the Foreign Office, and the banks on 24 November 1938. To help Japan wage war against China and to assist her in the preparations for war against the United States and Great Britain, Nazi Germany financed the transformation of Manchuria into the arsenal of Japan. The Japanese puppet government of Manchukuo set up a five-year program (1937–1942) for the development of coal mining, power, automotive and aircraft industries (statement by Manchurian minister Kishi as quoted in the *Boersen-Zeitung,* 15 July 1939). From 1938–1943 a banking syndicate dominated by the Deutsche Bank, which represented 47.5 percent of the total, with the Dresdner Bank retaining only a 15 percent share, supplied the Japanese with RM 155 million.

The largest sums, however, were supplied for the rearmament program in Japan proper. Starting with December 1938, when a RM 60 million loan under the leadership of the Deutsche Bank (DB's share: 33 percent) was extended for the export of weapons, precision instruments, chemicals, and aircraft to Japan, the financing of the Japanese war machine by Germany reached its climax in the 1941–42 period when a loan of RM 510 million was extended by a banking syndicate under the leadership of the Deutsche Bank and the Dresdner Bank.

[As noted earlier,] to direct the extension of the above credits a banking syndicate under the leadership of the Deutsche Bank established in 1942 the Deutsche Bank fuer Ostasien.

Credits to the USSR. The best illustration of the readiness of the bank to strengthen and support the foreign policy of the Nazi government financially is evidenced in the extension of credits to the USSR during the period (August 1939–June 1941) when it was in the interest of the Nazi regime to maintain friendly relations with the Soviet Union. On the basis of its agreement with the USSR of August 1939, the Reich government required RM 350 million to finance German exports to Russia. When there was the danger that the commercial banks would not be asked to participate in this credit, the Deutsche Bank registered its desire to retain its leading position in financing the extension of foreign loans. Hermann J. Abs, head of the Foreign Department of the Deutsche Bank, wrote to Emil Puhl, vice-president of the Reichsbank, and to the Vorstand of the Deutsche Golddiskontbank on the 25 August 1939:

> You will understand our desire not to be eliminated from participating in the new credit agreement with the Soviet Union of 19 August of this year.

Apparently the Reich government fulfilled the desire of the Deutsche Bank, because this bank managed the banking syndicate which extended the RM 350 million loans, itself covering 27.25 percent of this amount.

When Nazi Germany invaded the Soviet Union in June 1941, the Deutsche Bank fulfilled the current aim of the Nazi government, which now concerned the exploitation of the Russian industries for Germany. The Deutsche Bank participated in a syndicate which extended RM 100 million to the Berghuette Ost for the refitting of industries destroyed by the Russians in the Donets Basin. The Deutsche Bank's quota was 25 percent.

Credits to Turkey. As a result of negotiations concluded between the German and the Turkish governments in December 1942, Germany decided to export RM 100 million of armament to Turkey in exchange for chromium ores. Tanks, airplanes, and ammunition represented the major part of the German deliveries. To offset the overrated price between the Turkish chromium, the actual value of the German exports did not exceed about RM 50 million; the difference of the German evaluation and the invoiced foreign price was to be paid to the Treasury of the Reich. The financial transactions were handled by the Deutsche Revisions- und Treuhand A.G. (D.R.T.). This agency received RM 100 million in Turkish bonds, which it deposited with the Deutsche Bank. To finance the production of armament to be delivered, most of the German industrialists involved turned to commercial banks giving their claims against the Turkish bonds as security. The Deutsche Bank outdistanced all other banks by taking over claims amounting to about RM 9 million and by granting loans of more than RM 12 million. Due to the break in diplomatic relations between Germany and Turkey and the resulting stoppage of payments, Turkish government bonds of about RM 90 million should still be in the vaults of the Deutsche Bank.

ECONOMIC PENETRATION AND SPOLIATION OF GERMAN-DOMINATED EUROPE

The primary objective of the Deutsche Bank in accordance with the Funk-Goering program for economic penetration and spoliation of Europe was the acquisition of the major banking establishments of the occupied and satellite countries of Europe. The section, Expansion of Foreign Subsidiaries and Affiliates, in this chapter described each Deutsche Bank acquisition in the field of foreign banking.

Because of its widespread network of foreign branches and affiliates and because of its leading position in German and foreign banking, the Deutsche Bank emerged as an active agent, and often collaborator, of the German government and of large industrial corporations in their efforts to establish Germany's economic domination of the Continent.

A number of operations covering a wide variety of transactions is fully indicative of the role and importance of the Deutsche Bank in fulfilling these Nazi aims. Such operations ranged from assistance to I.G. Farben, Mannesmann, VGF, and similar outstanding German combines in obtaining the choice enterprises of conquered Europe to close collaboration with the Reich in establishing monopoly corporations for the exploitation of the mineral riches of Eastern and Southeastern Europe. These activities were complemented by the German efforts to repatriate foreign government bonds to the countries of their origin primarily in order to obtain foreign exchange. Remittances sent home by foreign workers in Germany gave the Nazi economists another fraudulent way to benefit from her clearing agreements with satellite countries.

I.G. Farben in Austria

Chapter VIII of this report dealt at some length with the special ties between I.G. Farben and the Deutsche Bank. The report on the investigation of I.G. Farben submitted by the War Department to the Subcommittee on War Mobilization of the Committee on Military Affairs of the United States Senate (Kilgore Committee) [also] supplies some information as to the part played by the Deutsche Bank in acquiring a plant in Austria for I.G. Farben after the Anschluss. According to this report:

> For years prior to the Anschluss of Austria, I.G. had tried to acquire the Pulverfabrik Skoda Werke Wetzler, a large chemical factory in Austria, from the Creditanstalt, one of the leading banks in Vienna, which was controlled by the Rothschild group. As soon as the Nazi troops moved in, the interests of the Rothschilds were confiscated, and the Deutsche Bank, Berlin, secured control of the Creditanstalt. By virtue of this Nazi plundering and in the full knowledge of what had happened, I.G. was able to obtain the long sought-after Skoda Werke Wetzler. Dr. von Schnitzler, a leading figure of I.G., has said himself "I.G. acquired the Skoda Wetzler works from the Deutsche Bank which had acquired the Skoda Wetzler works by participating with the Nazi government in a theft of the property."

Deutsche Umsiedlungs-Treuhandgesellschaft (DUT)

One of the principal instruments in the spoliation of occupied countries was the confiscation of property and the resettlement of Germans in areas which were considered a part of the Greater Reich.

In 1939 the Deutsche Umsiedlungs-Treuhandgesellschaft was formed in order to concentrate all "ethnic" Germans scattered in various countries of Southern and Eastern Europe in the area of the Greater German Reich. The DUT was under the jurisdiction of the *Reichskommissariat fuer die Festigung des deutschen Volkstums* (Reich Commissariat for the Strengthening of Germanism), headed by Heinrich Himmler. About 600,000 Germans from the Baltic states, Poland, France, and Russia were moved into areas incorporated by the Germans into the Reich after the occupation of Poland. In order to accommodate the German settlers, the DUT with the cooperation of the SS confiscated three-fourths of the commercial establishments and artisan shops belonging to Polish nationals in the so-called Wartheland. Millions of Poles were forcibly evicted from their farms, homes, and businesses in order to make room for the German settlers. Most of the Poles were taken to Germany for forced labor and the rest moved into the newly formed General Gouvernement. To finance the operations of the DUT the Deutsche Bank together with the Dresdner Bank headed the syndicate, which extended RM 100,000,000 for the resettlement operations of this organization.

THE BOEHMISCHE UNIONBANK AND THE HAUPT-TREUHANDSTELLE OST

The Deutsche Bank cooperated to a great extent with the HTO *(Haupt-Treuhandstelle Ost;* Chief Trustee Office, East). The Deutsche Bank acquired French interests in Polish enterprises for this government agency and it, in turn, also received assets from HTO which had been sequestered for political and racial reasons.

The HTO was established by Goering within that part of the Four Year Plan which dealt with the economic exploitation of Poland. It was responsible for the confiscation, administration, and liquidation of Polish property.

Since 1940 the Deutsche Bank, through the BUB, its Prague subsidiary, participated in the Nazi campaign to gain control over French enterprises in Poland for the HTO. In these negotiations, the Deutsche Bank cleared all necessary matters with the competent German ministries for the BUB.

On 19 October 1944, Pohle and Rohde (Vorstand BUB) stated in a letter:

> Since 1941 we have executed by order and for the account of HTO, Berlin, a number of transactions in France which were concerned mainly with the acquisition of French holdings of establishments in the iron industry and in coal mining in former Poland.

The transactions listed concern the French holdings in the following key industrial enterprises of Poland:

1. Acquisition of the invested and floating capital of Huta Bankowa.
2. Acquisition of the invested and floating capital of the A.G. der Dombrowaer Kohlengruben (Dombrow Coal Mines, Inc.).
3. Acquisitions of the shares of the Sosnowitzer Roehren und Eisenwerke (Sosnowitz Tube and Iron Works), as far as they were in French possession.

4. Acquisition of the Sosnowitzer Bergwerks- und Huetten A.G. (Sosnowitz Mining and Smelting Company), as far as they were in French possession.

5. Acquisition of the shares of the Galizische Bergwerksgesellschaft Kohlengruben Janina (Galician Mining Company Coal Mines Janina).

A report from the French Ministry of Finance regarding the acquisition of industrial shares by Germany during the occupation of France, lists the above transactions and shows that BUB acquired, in addition

1. 225 shares of the Société pour l'Industrie Metallurgique in Poland (Company for Metallurgical Industry in Poland)

2. 225 shares of the Société Comte Renard (Count Renard Company).

All these transactions undertaken by BUB were settled through the French-German clearing.

In turn, HTO sold several large enterprises of heavy industry in the Nazi-dominated Eastern regions to the Deutsche Bank. Among these were furnaces and iron works in Drzynietz, smelting works in the region of Kattowitz (Koenigshuette, Bismarckhuette, Falvahuette, Silesiahuette, and so on).[3] These enterprises, which had been confiscated by the HTO, were bought by the Deutsche Bank and its banking syndicate to become incorporated into the Berghuette-Konzern, a complex which was being built up by the Deutsche Bank into a large combine extending from Czechoslovakia into Poland.

The Berghuette-Konzern developed from the former Berg- und Huettenwerke-Gesellschaft, Prague, which had always been closely associated with BUB. Soon after BUB became a subsidiary of the Deutsche Bank, Mr. Pohle, Vorstand member of the BUB, became chairman of the board of directors of the Berg- und Huettenwerke-Gesellschaft. By 1941, he was able to purchase the sizable interest in the Berg- und Huettenwerke-Gesellschaft (almost 50 percent) which was held by the Union Européenne, the holding company of the industrial participations of Schneider-Le Creuzot, Paris.

According to the report by the French Ministry of Finance, the purchase was paid for by "francs of unknown origin," that is, banknotes stolen by the Germans. This purchase gave the BUB full control over the corporation.

In 1942 the company was moved to Teschen in the Olsa region and reconstructed according to the provisions of German law. The capital was set at RM 75 million and then increased by an additional RM 50 million which were taken over by the Deutsche Bank, Berlin. The block of RM 33 million, containing the shares obtained from the French and a small parcel of shares which had come into the hands of the BUB from the Gestapo (Vermoegensamt Prague), also became property of the Deutsche Bank, Berlin. These RM 83 million were sold to the public at 136 percent

---

[3] Information presented (above) on the basis of a file-note by Hermann Abs, dated 1 November 1938, contradicts statements of Otto Neubaur, Vorstand member of the RKG, which [are] incorporated into the principal Deutsche Bank Report. Neubaur repeatedly asserted that the Deutsche Bank was in possession of about 10 percent of the CABV capital prior to the Anschluss.

under the direction of the Reich Ministry of Economics. This placement represented the largest placement of shares during the last ten years and was undertaken by a banking syndicate formed and headed by the Deutsche Bank.

The RM 50 million invested in 1942 and two loans amounting to a total of RM 100 million extended by the Deutsche Bank and its banking syndicate during the years 1943–44 served for those acquisitions of holdings from the HTO which were discussed above.

The new acquisitions developed the Berg- und Huettenwerke-Gesellschaft into a huge combine, renamed Berghuette-Konzern, which was divided into the following corporations:

> Berghuette, Berg- und Huettenwerke-Gesellschaft, Teschen (only a holding company)
> Berg- und Huettenwerke-Gesellschaft Aktiengesellschaft, Teschen (all coal mines)
> Koenigs- und Bismarckhuette Aktiengesellschaft Koenigshuette (for iron mills and foundries)
> Osmag, Oberschlesische Maschinenbau-A.G., Kattowitz (for plants reworking iron)

and a number of additional subsidiaries.

Thus Deutsche Bank not only purchased assets by order and for the account of HTO, the Deutsche Bank also benefited from the "depolonization" and confiscation practices of the Haupt-Treuhandstelle Ost.

THE DEUTSCHE BANK AND THE ALGEMEENE KUNSTZIJDE UNIE N.V.

The Deutsche Bank has been closely associated with the history and the management of the huge international rayon cartel, the Algemeene Kunstzijde Unie-Vereinigte Glanzstoff-Fabriken ever since its establishment and thus was well able to utilize its power over it to further the materialization of the Nazi Reich's effort to gain full control of this international rayon combine.

The history of the cartel is briefly as follows: founded in 1899, the Vereinigte Glanzstoff-Fabriken, A.G. (VGF) developed into the largest individual rayon concern in Germany and, through stockholdings, license and cartel arrangements, was a center of worldwide rayon interests before World War II. The capital of VGF amounted to RM 19,500,000 in 1942.

[Following] 1929, the [joint German-Dutch company] Algemeene Kunstzijde Unie N.V. (AKU), entered into a cartel agreement with VGF and became its holding company. AKU also arranged cartel agreements with other rayon corporations in Germany, Holland, Austria, United States, Japan, England, Italy, and France and held participations in them. Through these companies it gained interests further in rayon concerns in Argentina, Spain, Czechoslovakia, Poland, Romania, and Belgium. The total stock capital of AKU amounted to nominal hfl. 230,048,000 (authorized shares) in 1942 of which nom. hfl. 104,375,500 had been issued. The most important block of shares was represented by 48 priority shares at hfl. 1,000 each, which were equally divided between the joint German-Dutch AKU and the German VGF.

The Deutsche Bank had always been the principal bank of VGF and had been a strong promoter of the rayon industry. Of eight members in the VGF Aufsichtsrat in 1942, for example, four were members of Deutsche Bank boards: H. J. Abs and Johannes Kiehl from the Vorstand, Werner Carp and Ph. F. Reemtsma from the Aufsichtsrat of the bank. Ernst Hellmut Vits was chairman of the VGF Vorstand; Abs had been instrumental in the initial nomination of Vits to this corporation's Aufsichtsrat, which soon resulted in his appointment to the Vorstand.

In view of the fact that VGF was a principal factor in AKU, the Deutsche Bank and its executives consequently assumed leading roles in AKU. The Deutsche Bank held up to three seats of its Aufsichtsrat, headed the German group in AKU, and had an important voice in voting the priority shares.

The Aufsichtsrat of [the parent company] AKU was set up on a parity basis with four representatives of the Dutch and the German groups respectively. Between 1935–1939, however, O. Schlitter from the Vorstand of the Deutsche Bank was considered a "neutral" member. Thus the board in fact was then composed of four Dutch and five German members; three of these five Germans were from the Deutsche Bank: von Stauss, Kiehl and Schlitter.

❑ ❑ ❑

According to the Dutch corporation law, a six-vote limitation was placed on all share holdings, that is, no matter how many shares a single owner held, his vote could not exceed six voices for his participation and six additional ones if he was acting as proxy. In the case of AKU, the corporation had vested all power in the forty-eight priority shares mentioned above, which were equally divided between the Dutch and the German groups. In case of a deadlock, spheres of interest were worked out. [At that time,] VGF [was] the real owner of twenty-four and AKU of the other twenty-four priority shares. Abs and his protégé E. H. Vits are two of the present holders of the legal title to six shares each of the German group.

Baron Kurt von Schroeder, head of the Cologne banking house J. H. Stein and most prominent SS banker, also holds the legal title to six priority shares of the German group at present. [He said,] "I believe the Deutsche Bank had finally a majority of the shares of AKU."

❑ ❑ ❑

The dominant position of the Deutsche Bank in relation to AKU attained pronounced importance during the occupation of Holland by Germany.

As part of the German scheme to penetrate and rule the European economy, the Nazi economists desired to obtain full control of this rayon cartel. Even though ownership of the common and preferred AKU shares legally did not carry much weight in controlling AKU, the RWM desired to bring the majority of AKU shares into German hands and commissioned the Deutsche Bank as the official agent to buy up AKU shares. H. K. F. Kehrl, head of the textile division of RWM who had built up the artificial fiber industry within the Four Year Plan, intimated that the Reich desired majority ownership of AKU shares because such majority in fact was able to dominate AKU.

> **A.** — The six-vote limitation provided for by Dutch law as to the common shares had been overcome hundreds of times in Holland as a matter of fact.

> **Q.** — In other words the Germans expected to gain a dominating position by the majority ownership of the common shares.

> **A.** — That was about the idea . . . the majority ownership of common shares gave more a strength of moral position than legal position.

In fact, the Nazis were playing with the idea of abrogating by law the six-vote limitation as soon as the majority of AKU stock was in German possession. They were also planning to sever VGF from AKU upon acquisition of a large majority of AKU shares, reorganize the two corporations as individual companies, repatriate all VGF shares to Germany, and control AKU by owning a majority of its stock capital.

❑ ❑ ❑

Deutsche Bank and its Dutch subsidiary, H.M.H. Albert de Bary & Co. N.V. (HADB) in Amsterdam . . . bought large amounts of AKU stock on the stock market.

By 30 September 1940 Deutsche Bank had purchased about hfl. 5 million AKU shares on the market through HADB. This brought the amount of AKU shares held in Germany to hfl. 31 million. For camouflage purposes the shares bought in Holland remained with HADB for the time being. Only one and a half years later, in 1942, Abs and Ulrich (Deutsche Bank) were able to inform the Dego, the Deutsche Golddiskontbank (Reichsbank subsidiary), that hfl. 52,598,000 shares, more than 50 percent of the AKU share capital, now were in German hands.

By 1942, . . . Vits estimated that there were then present in Germany at least hfl. 61,454,100 of common AKU shares. Deutsche Bank held hfl. 27,762,000, which were sold on the German market during April and May 1941 and placed in the form of deposit certificates. After the disposition of these shares, German AKU shareholders were asked by the banks to follow suit by depositing their AKU shares with the Deutsche Bank in return for certificates. The shares themselves could be claimed after 1 July 1946. When selling these certificates, the Deutsche Bank retained the voting right of the shares. Many Germans were induced by the Deutsche Bank to make such conversion because the certificates could be traded on the German stock exchange while the shares, being those of a foreign corporation, could not be so traded at that time. According to Mr. Sopp, chief accountant of the Deutsche Bank Secretariat, AKU shares in the amount of hfl. 27,762,900 with German stamp and hfl. 3,444,400 without German stamp are deposited with the Deutsche Bank branch in Hamburg *(Streifbanddepot)*.

Deutsche Bank always represented hfl. 8 million AKU shares in the annual AKU meetings in Holland for the Dego, which had come in possession of hfl. 11,514,900 shares between 1936 and 1940 when the Reich requested all Germans to offer their foreign securities to Dego. While other foreign securities were sold abroad, the AKU shares were kept at the disposal of the RWM. These securities were deposited in the Security Department of the Reichsbank, Berlin.

Even though the RWM made it a point that nobody should buy single blocks of shares exceeding RM 200,000 in value and that anyone desiring to subscribe more should be investigated, the Deutsche Bank, in 1942, sold hfl. 1.25 million AKU shares in certificates to Philipp Reemtsma, the tobacco tycoon and member of Deutsche Bank's Working Committee. Reemtsma had joined the VGF board of directors in 1935 or 1936 upon the request of the Deutsche Bank to intervene with Goering on behalf of this corporation and the bank. His intervention had been successful.

The Deutsche Bank and its executives also maintained excellent relations with the leader of the Dutch AKU group, F. H. Fentener van Vlissingen. His father had founded [a small rayon company] Enka and van Vlissingen himself has been the chairman of the AKU board of directors intermittently between 1929–1933 and continually since then and one of the most energetic and forceful personalities in the cartel. Van Vlissingen had good relations with Abs who had worked on the staff of Rhodius-Koenigs in Holland, a subsidiary of Delbrueck, Schickler & Co., for a number of years. In fact, Kehrl stated that Abs was appointed chairman of VGF and vice-chairman of AKU in 1939 partly because of his good relations with van Vlissingen.

> So Abs became chairman of the Aufsichtsrat of VGF and his person was very agreeable to the government as he had an international reputation and as far as I know good relations with van Vlissingen.

Kehrl characterized van Vlissingen's standing with Deutsche Bank with the following words:

> [H]e was a customer of the Deutsche Bank. They valued his account very much.

In addition to VGF, he also had considerable interests in German heavy industry mostly with corporations where the Deutsche Bank figured prominently (Hoesch, Harpener Bergbau, and so on). His ties with the leaders of German industry and state were strengthened through his family relation to Joachim von Ribbentrop, the Nazi foreign minister, and the Heinkel family. He was made a commander in the Hitlerite Order of the German Eagle and subsequently cooperated with the Germans during the occupation of Holland.

The Decartelization Branch of the Economics Division of the Office of Military Government for Germany (U.S.) is completing a detailed report on the AKU-VGF cartel.

From the Annex to the Report

Ernst Vits . . . was invited to join the VGF Vorstand and during the first months of 1940 was offered the chairmanship of that body. Vits expressed an unwillingness to accept this office but the persuasion of Abs and of President Hans Kehrl of the RWM produced in him a change of heart. . . .

[The goal was] elimination of [influence] by the Dutch group over the VGF [and simultaneously to extend] German control, under the leadership of the Deutsche Bank, in the parent company, the AKU.

By an agreement, dated 15 August 1939, the Internationale Accountants-en-Trustee Kantoor N.V. Arnhem (IAET), composed of a Dutch group headed by Fentener van Vlissingen and a German group headed by Hermann Abs, was named to act as trustee of the forty-eight priority shares which controlled the management of the AKU. From secondary sources it has been learned that the Deutsche Bank subsidiary in Holland, H. A. de Bary & Co. also held a participation in the Dutch group of the IAET, thereby increasing to an even greater degree the influence in the AKU of the Deutsche Bank.

After the outbreak of the war the AKU, in seeking to evade the restrictions of the Allied blockade applying to companies under German control, passed into nominal Dutch ownership. On 1 November 1939 the IAET transferred the trusteeship together with the forty-eight priority shares to the Nederlandsche Administratie-en-Trustkantoor N.V. but reserved to itself the privileges previously delegated by the priority shareholders.

In October 1940 Hermann Abs, as chairman of the German group in the AKU and acting in agreement with Hans Kehrl of the RWM and Hans Fischboeck, [at that time the] German Commissioner General for Finance and Economics in occupied Holland, pressed for the reelection of the four German members of the AKU Aufsichtsrat. Fentener van Vlissingen, Chairman of the Dutch group in the AKU, expressed objections to such a step stating that it would be a violation of the agreement of November 1939 between the two national groups in control of the AKU and would expose its U.S. properties to seizure under regulations of the American State Department. Abs thereupon proposed a "compromise" solution for the protection of these American properties whereby the AKU would be given the appearance of a Dutch-owned company. The German group would retain only three members on the Aufsichtsrat, in place of the previous four, and the Dutch group five. This arrangement was calculated to serve as mere window dressing, however, for one of the five "Dutch" members, Jansma, was to act, in fact, as a member of the German group, which would, in this fashion, retain its four memberships on the Aufsichtsrat. Van Vlissingen gave his consent to this arrangement on the insistence of Abs.

❑ ❑ ❑

The Deutsche Bank also obtained special access to the unpublished balance sheets of the AKU–VGF combine, which afforded it an unrivaled opportunity for stock exchange manipulations. According to captured records the

Deutsche Bank engaged in manipulations in the registration of customer shares and undertook the filing of dividend certificates in such a fashion that knowledge of the scope of its own holdings would be kept secret from the AKU.

THE DEUTSCHE BANK AND KONTINENTALE OEL A.G.

The Kontinentale Oel A.G. was formed in March of 1941 as a result of discussions between Hitler and Goering to establish a German oil monopoly for Europe. This corporation was sponsored by the government, but its management and financing was to a great extent done by private oil corporations and the banks. The Deutsche Bank, and Hermann J. Abs in particular, figured prominently in the financing and expansion of Kontinentale Oel. The Concordia and Columbia Oil Companies operating in Romania constituted the core of the holdings of Kontinentale Oel.

In the letter inviting the oil corporations, the banks, and prominent Nazi officials to the first meeting of Kontinentale Oel, Goering pointed out:

> The corporation will take over upon its foundation the majority of the shares of the Concordia acquired from the Belgians, and the majority of Columbia acquired from the French.

The Deutsche Bank acquired that majority control of the oil wealth of Romania from Belgian and French capital and subsequently turned it over to the Kontinentale Oel. Hermann J. Abs (in the interrogation of 22 September 1945) stated:

> The instructions we received (from Minister Funk) to buy certain foreign holdings which were to the interest of Germany concerned first the majority of Columbia oil which was at that time in French hands, and of Concordia oil which were at that time in Belgian possession. Both companies were Romanian joint stock companies with producing plants in Romania. The negotiations for sales of participations of oil industry in the case of France were started by myself. Both negotiations with France and Belgium were handled by various managers of the Deutsche Bank, a Mr. Osterwind in the case of Concordia, Dr. Pollems in the case of Columbia, and both of them with the assistance of Director Kurzmeyer.

When asked about pressure connected with any of the acquisitions Abs stated:

> I also do not believe that any pressure has been also on Belgian holders of the Concordia oil, but possibly the question of the sale of the Columbia oil in France may have been a part of political negotiations between Germany and France.

As late as June 1944, the Deutsche Bank was buying up all available Columbia and Concordia shares.

The report of the French Ministry of Finance listing the acquisitions of industrial shares by various German banks and enterprises lists 600,000 Columbia shares acquired by the Deutsche Bank for French francs 300 million, and 351,992 Concordia shares also acquired by the Deutsche Bank, for French francs 42 million.

The share capital of Kontinentale Oel amounting to RM 80 million was distributed among the newly organized Reich holding company Borussia (37.5 percent), German oil corporations (25 percent), and the banking syndicate led by the Deutsche Bank (37.5 percent).

The support of the banks in this enterprise was especially valued by Minister Funk:

> The banks not only took over purely the business risk by supplying a considerable part of the capital of the Kontinentale Oel, a corporation which was newly founded, and the liquidity of which is unforeseen, but undertook a general political risk.

The banking syndicate was under the leadership of the Deutsche Bank, which took over 35 percent of the syndicate commitment. The Dresdner Bank took a similar part followed by the Reichs-Kredit-Gesellschaft and the Berliner Handelsgesellschaft with 15 percent each.

The Deutsche Bank claimed leadership in view of its preliminary work.

The Deutsche Bank held the same share in the RM 40 million loan extended to the Kontinentale Oel by the banks.

The Aufsichtsrat was headed by Walter Funk who was assisted by Wilhelm Keppler and six other members of the Himmler Circle (Heinrich Buetefisch, Hans Fischboeck, Franz Hayler, Fritz Kranefuss, Karl Rasche, August Rosterg), as well as top executives of governmental agencies and the oil industry. Hermann J. Abs became an Aufsichtsrat member of Kontinentale Oel thus joining as representative a group of Nazi economic leaders as will ever be found. Kontinentale Oel was managed by Karl Blessing (another Himmler Circle member) and its operations in Romania were directed by Heinz Osterwind, mentioned above as the Deutsche Bank representative negotiating with the Belgians for the control of Concordia. Heinz Osterwind received his training in the Foreign Department of the Deutsche Bank. He worked during various periods in the Kreditbank Sofia, in the Istanbul Branch of the Deutsche Bank. Upon his return to Berlin in 1938 he worked in the Deutsche Bank as assistant to Kurt Weigelt (cf. Chapter VI). With the creation of the Kontinentale Oel and the considerable influence of the Deutsche Bank, Osterwind received leave of absence from the bank in order to manage the Concordia and the Columbia enterprises in Romania.

From the Annex to the Report

The Deutsche Bank was requested by the RWM in September 1940 to secure the transfer into German hands of the capital shares of two principal Romanian oil enterprises, the Columbia and the Concordia Oil Companies which were owned by French and Belgian shareholders. To this end Alfred Kurzmeyer opened negotiations with the Compagnie Financiére Belge des

Petroles (Petrofina), Brussels, for the acquisition of the shares of the Concordia Oil Co. An agreement was reached on 28 December 1940 for the transfer of 1,885,000 shares at a price of some bfrs 280,000,000. Negotiations for the acquisition of the Columbia Oil Co. shares were undertaken at the same time by the Deutsche Bank.

At a meeting of government officials and bankers on 23 January 1941 the Office of the Four Year Plan announced its intention of creating the Kontinentale Oel A.G. as a holding company for all foreign oil interests falling within the German sphere of influence. The Deutsche Bank, it was stated, had already, at a cost of RM 22,500,000 acquired some 45 percent of the capital shares of the Concordia Oil Co. and was continuing with its efforts to purchase in France and Belgium the additional shares needed to give it majority control. Abs participated in the meeting as the Deutsche Bank representative.

Negotiations for the acquisition of the Columbia Oil Company shares, in the meantime, made slow progress. The French owners, who held 650,000 out of a total of 760,000 shares, desired a price of RM 100,000,000 while the Deutsche Bank offered RM 15,000,000. The procedural suggestions which Abs received from Abetz at the German legation in Paris failed to speed up the negotiations. The political support extended by the RWM to the Deutsche Bank before the Wiesbaden Armistice Commission also failed to force the transaction to an immediate conclusion. However by April 1941, the French owners were persuaded to sell their shares to the Deutsche Bank for RM 16,250,000, a mere fragment of the previous asking price.

The Deutsche Bank claimed for itself the leadership in all future banking transactions of the Kontinentale Oel A.G. because of its part in the acquisition of the Columbia and Concordia shares. This view was accepted by the Reich, and thereafter the Deutsche Bank assumed the leading position in all syndicate financing of the company.

❑ ❑ ❑

MINES DE BOR AND SUEDOST MONTAN— DEUTSCHE BANK OPERATIONS IN YUGOSLAVIA

The Mines de Bor, founded in 1904 under the name Compagnie Française de Mines de Bor to exploit the copper riches of Yugoslavia, was the most important copper mining enterprise in Europe. Upon the occupation of France and later of Yugoslavia, the Nazi government considered the acquisition of ownership of Mines de Bor as a primary mission in the fulfillment of the Funk-Goering program. Consul Neuhausen, Gauleiter of Belgrade, who figured prominently in the Allgemeiner Yugoslawischer Bankverein, Deutsche Bank affiliate, was the instigator of action against the French owners of Mines de Bor.

Emil Puhl, vice-president of the Reichsbank, gave the following details on the circumstances surrounding the transfer of French ownership of Mines de Bor:

> With the occupation of Yugoslavia, German interests led by Neuhausen (Gauleiter of Belgrade) demanded the control of Mines de Bor. Pressure

was exercised on the French owners to transfer their control of Mines de Bor. After prolonged negotiations the shares were transferred to the German side. A German holding company was created to administrate the shares under control of Neuhausen.

The report of the French Ministry of Finance concerning acquisitions of French industrial participations by Germany during the occupation states that 500,000 shares of Mines de Bor were acquired by the German government and paid for in occupation costs.

In the administration of the Mines de Bor the Reich was represented by the Suedost Montan G.m.b.H. which was a Reich-owned company with a share capital of RM 30 million. This company was created in March 1943 for the purpose of exploiting the nonferrous mineral wealth of the Balkans on behalf of the Four-Year Plan. The Suedost Montan acquired control of the molybdenum fields located in Yugoslavia through the acquisition of Yugomontan, a corporation which held rights to sixty mining areas. Suedost Montan also mined chromium in Albania, lead in Yugoslavia, and ores in Greece.

To finance the operations of Mines de Bor and Suedost Montan the Reich Government called upon the Deutsche Bank. Hermann J. Abs became a member of the boards of directors of both corporations being one of the only two bankers on these boards.

The report of Richard Haeussler, assistant to Hermann Abs, on Mines de Bor emphasizes the important role played by the Deutsche Bank in this venture of Nazi economists. He states:

> In preliminary conferences between the Four Year Plan and the Deutsche Bank and in a meeting of the interministerielle Ausschuss (Interdepartmental Committee of the Ministry of Economics and Ministry of Finance) with the Deutsche Bank, the credit requirements of the Bor copper mines were marked as very urgent.

The Deutsche Bank took the leadership in providing loans for these corporations and enlisted the cooperation of all other Grossbanken in this affair.

Between 1943 and 1944, the banking syndicate formed and headed by the Deutsche Bank (initial participation 35 percent, upon enlargement of the syndicate 27 percent) extended to Mines de Bor five long-term credits of RM 25 million each, that is, amounting to a total credit of RM 125 million altogether, in addition to a short-term loan of RM 60 million. All grants, RM 185 million, were fully guaranteed by the Reich and utilized up to about RM 125 million by January 1945. The syndicate which granted these credits to the Mines de Bor also became responsible for large credits extended to Suedost Montan. Between 1943 and 1944 the syndicate extended several long-term credits totaling RM 67.5 million to this government owned corporation, which utilized these grants up to about RM 44 million.

The report of the first syndicate meeting of all six banks, written on 18 December 1943, by the representative of the Berliner Handelsgesellschaft gives a clear picture of the leading role played by the Deutsche Bank in providing the means to develop and extend German economic control and domination of the Balkans. The report relates the discussions of the syndicate participants regarding the grant of loans and credits to the newly acquired Mines de Bor as well as the recently founded Suedost Montan [company]. The report states:

> Upon the invitation of the Deutsche Bank a meeting took place on the 17 December of this year (1943). Mr. Abs, in the beginning, made various statements about the Mines de Bor, or the "Bergwerks-Gesellschaft Bor," under which name it will be known in the future.

During this meeting, Mr. Abs gave a short account of the acquisition in 1941 of Mines de Bor by Germany from the former French shareholders (Mirabaud).

The Reich resold the majority, which was divided equally between Mansfeld, Preussag and the Reich-owned Suedost Montan G.m.b.H.

Mr. Abs then explained that he expected a production of 24,000 tons of copper for 1943 with a labor force of 20,000 workers, half of whom were obtained from the Organisation Todt.

After giving a short outline of the newly founded Suedost Montan and credits extended, the report closes emphasizing that these loans are purely political:

> Mr. Abs and Dr. Schaeffer pointed out at the end, that under no circumstances it is possible to withdraw from this loan business as it is a political affair where a 100 percent Reichs-guarantee was given, but which is also the only justification for our participation.

❏ ❏ ❏

From the Annex to the Report

Under the preceding French management the Mines de Bor had been a highly profitable enterprise. . . . The Office of the Four Year Plan, however, pressed for the ruthless exploitation of the mines without consideration of cost. Vast investments had to be made, in consequence, and the danger of great financial losses loomed ahead. In this situation the Deutsche Bank, with the approval of the Finance Ministry and the Office of the Four Year Plan, proceeded to organize a banking syndicate for the extension of additional credits.

The Suedost Montan Gesellschaft under the sponsorship of the Office of the Four Year Plan acquired the control of another mining company, the Jugomontan Aktiengesellschaft. The Office of the Four Year Plan not only refused, however, to guarantee the risks connected with the transaction but requested the Aufsichtsrat members of the Suedost Montan Gesellschaft (among them Hermann Abs who had joined that body upon the request of the Finance Ministry) to agree that their company take over the Jugomontan at its own risk because the interests of the Reich "demanded" it. The scope of this risk was of such a magnitude that it could not be evaluated or even estimated in advance. The operation of the Jugomontan was carried on under the most difficult conditions imaginable and the Aufsichtsrat members were not informed of the details. An accurate balance sheet did not exist and the Office of the Four Year Plan itself stated that losses from the very outset were anticipated.

The transaction was of so dubious a character and so contrary to sound business principles that Hermann Abs expressed the fear that if he nevertheless voted his approval of it, he would expose himself to damage suits. In the end Abs voted his approval, however, and the Deutsche Bank, in consequence, participated in future syndicate credits to the Suedost Montan Gesellschaft with the largest quota.

❑ ❑ ❑

Schlesag and SAG

The Deutsche Bank transferred to German from foreign ownership a major industrial combine [through] . . . merger of the SAG (Schlesische Aktiengesellschaft fuer Bergbau und Zinkhuettenbetrieb, Lipine, Poland), a foreign-owned company, and the Schlesag (Schlesische Bergwerke- und Huetten A.G., Beuthen, Germany), a German-owned company, so as to eliminate the influence of the foreign owners of the former company.

In a file note Director Ulrich of the Deutsche Bank states:

> The Deutsche Bank was materially responsible for successfully preparing and concluding the merger of the SAG with the Schlesag. Special credit is due to Mr. Abs who went far beyond the normal responsibilities of an Aufsichtsrat chairman in participating during a period of several years in all of the manifold and difficult negotiations with the Chief Trustee Administration for the East (Haupt-Treuhandstelle Ost), the Economics Ministry, the Commissioner for Enemy Property, the Foreign Office, the Economics Adviser to the Gauleiter (Gauwirtschaftsberater) for Upper Silesia, the Commissioner for the Strengthening of Germanism (Reichskommissar fuer die Festigung deutschen Volkstums) and in the discussions with the French and Belgians. Abs has decisively influenced the result of all these negotiations.

The properties of the SAG consisted principally of coal and zinc mines, refineries and rolling mills, which were located in Poland and were controlled by the Banque de Neuflize & Cie., Paris, the Société Générale de Belgique, Banque de l'Union Parisienne, Paris, and the Banque Franco-Polonaise, Paris. The Vorstand was composed of three Poles but the Aufsichtsrat chairman was Jacques de Neuflize, Paris, and the vice-chairman, Amand Fleury, Brussels. Only two of the eighteen members of the 1937/38 Aufischtsrat maintained their domiciles in Germany.

The merger between the SAG and the Schlesag had a twofold purpose: To incorporate the SAG properties into the Upper Silesian industrial economy and to divest the non-German shareholders of their control of the company.

The latter goal was attained by the outright seizure of the shares of the Polish holders and by restricting the amount of the Franco-Belgian participation in the newly created enterprise to less than 25 percent. In addition, all non-German members of the Vorstand and the Aufsichtsrat, with the single exception of Prince Gerome Murat of Paris, were removed from their positions in the new company.

Although the Poles, prior to the war, had not held the controlling interest in the SAG, Polish interests had considerably influenced the preceding administration of the company. During the German occupation, however, the three Polish Vorstand members and the seven Polish Aufsichtsrat members were removed and when, in June 1943, the merger of the two companies took place "the nonregistered" (that is, Polish[4]) "shares of the formerly Polish SAG were declared void according to Paragraph 31 of the Decree for the Liquidation of Polish Claims and Obligations of 15 August 1941, and the shares passed into the possession of the German Reich." Shares with a face value of RM 1,750,000 were confiscated in the name of the Reich, by the Haupt-Treuhandstelle Ost.

The Deutsche Bank participated extensively in the enormously difficult negotiations which were conducted during a period of some three and one half years and finally led to the successful conclusion of the merger. It included an endless number of conferences with government ministries and political agencies, the reshuffling of share parcels, the maintenance of liaison with the French and Belgian shareholders, and the acquisition from a Swiss company of Schlesag shares in the amount of RM 2,176,000 for which the Deutsche Bank paid with valuable shares out of its own portfolio. The merger could never have been consummated without the assistance of the Deutsche Bank and of Hermann Abs in particular.

The Deutsche Bank's quota in the banking syndicate which had previously financed the Schlesag came to 20 percent while the Dresdner Bank had a 27.5 percent quota. As compensation for the services rendered by the Deutsche Bank, Abs requested that its quota in the Schlesag syndicate be increased to 27.5 percent so as to equal that of the Dresdner Bank. The request was granted and the Deutsche Bank, furthermore, looked forward to the receipt of an additional membership on the Schlesag Aufsichtsrat.

EXPANSION OF MANNESMANN IN EUROPE

The unusually intimate relationship between Deutsche Bank and the Mannesmann Roehrenwerke complex in Germany proper extended to foreign countries where the Deutsche Bank and Mannesmann acquired subsidiaries. The Deutsche Bank mobilized its extensive network of branches and affiliates in foreign countries for the

---

[4] Upon registering their SAG stock the shareholders had to furnish documentary proof that they were not numbered among those persons whose possessions were subject to confiscation according to the Decree Concerning the Treatment of the Property of Citizens of the Former Polish State, 17 September 1940. Section 1 of this decree provides: "The property of citizens of the former Polish State . . . shall be subject to confiscation."

expansion of Mannesmann in Nazi-dominated Europe. Aided by the experience the Deutsche Bank had gained through many years of foreign trade and with the advice, assistance, and often considerable financial backing of the Deutsche Bank or a Deutsche Bank subsidiary, this industrial affiliate of the Deutsche Bank acquired much foreign property in the countries occupied by Germany and in satellite countries within the sphere of German economic domination and even held "trusteeships" of property in Russia when Germany's armies were victorious in that country.

Mannesmann acquired most of its principal foreign subsidiaries following in the wake of Germany's aggression.

In Austria. Between 1934–1944, M/W Komotau took over about 52 percent of the shares of Trauzl A.G., Vienna, which had a share capital of RM 1.5 million. Most of these shares were bought from the Creditanstalt Bankverein, Wien. Between 1939–1944 alone, RM 867,817.44 were spent for such purchases.

In Czechoslovakia. Between 1939–1941, to strengthen its grip on the company, M/W purchased large blocks of shares of the Prager Eisen-Industrie Gesellschaft and its subsidiaries, at least part of which had been Jewish property acquired by the Boehmische Unionbank, Prague. These shares amounted to RM 1,358,150.35 and were then managed by Deutsche Bank's subsidiary, A.G. fuer Vermoegensverwertung, Berlin.

In 1939, Max Graber & Sohn A.G., Pressburg, a Jewish firm, was acquired by the M/W complex with the help of the Union Bank, Pressburg. This bank bought the shares for M/W because a German company could not appear on the Czechoslovakian market and, through a "gentleman's agreement" held all the shares in its name as trustee for M/W. The stock capital of the corporation was evaluated at Kr. 8,160,000 and renamed Mannesmann Roehren- und Eisenhandel A.G., Bratislava.

In 1940, the Boehmische Union Bank was instrumental in M/W's purchase of 51 percent of the Boehmische Montangesellschaft A.G., Prague, at nominal kronen 2,040,000.

In 1940, the Boehmische Union Bank instigated and arranged an agreement with President Kehrl, the sale to M/W of the Aryanized Metallwalzwerk A.G., Maehrisch-Ostrau, and its subsidiaries as well as the subsequent increase of the company's capital to kronen 28,000,000, in 1941.

In 1940, M/W purchased 48.9 percent of the stock capital of the Waagtaler Syenit Asbestzementschieferfabrik & Bergbau A.G. Puchov. Some of the stock bought was confiscated Jewish property then in the hands of the Creditanstalt Bankverein, Wien, a subsidiary of Deutsche Bank.

In Luxembourg. In 1941, when Germany had established herself in Luxembourg and Lorraine, the General Bank, Luxembourg, which was controlled by the Deutsche Bank, was instrumental in M/W's acquisition of three Luxembourg-Lorraine companies, namely: EMETA, Luxembourg, EIWAG, Esch-Alzig and subsidiaries, and Mequisa A.G., Hagendingen. The total cost of acquisition and investments amounted to RM 1,156,000. The controlling stock had been owned by Dr. Alfred Ganz, a Jew, who had "sold" his shares to a Swiss national for camouflage purposes in 1936. When M/W acquired his complex of corporations, Dr. Ganz had to renounce all future claims for repurchase later on.

In Holland. In 1942, H. Albert de Bary, Amsterdam, was instrumental in the purchase by M/W of part of the Van Leer combine located in Holland, France, and Belgium. The owner was Jewish and found it safer to leave his country now in the hands of the Nazis. Zangen was appointed by the Reichswirtschaftsministerium to liquidate the properties of B. Van Leer.

In France. In 1940, the M/W complex acquired factories, land and buildings, and machinery at Strasbourg. Part of the property taken over had been in Jewish, part in French hands and had been confiscated and sequestered by the Nazis. M/W's total expenditure for these acquisitions amounted to more than RM 18.5 million.

In Romania. In 1942, the M/W combine tried to purchase the controlling block of shares of Uzinele Metalurgica Unite Titan Nadrag Calan S.A.R., Bucharest, and to control the management of this corporation. Mr. Max Ausnit, a christened Jew, had been the owner of the stock. To show how M/W, with the knowledge and guidance of Mr. Roesler, the speaker of the Vorstand of the Deutsche Bank, attempted to realize its cartelization aims hand in hand with Germany's imperialistic Nazi ideals, the following lines are quoted from Exhibit II, Memo 20, of the Joint Special Financial Detachment U.S. Group Control Council, Control Commission for Germany (British Element), Duesseldorf:

> (From Mr. von der Tann's notes):

> Following the tendency discussed by the Reichswirtschaftsminister Funk with Mr. Zangen regarding a European combine of economical interests, especially also with Romania, we took for the industrial leadership of the Titan Nadrag Calan S.A.R., Bucharest, share capital Lei 500,000,000, almost the only really economical Romanian enterprise of the iron industry . . .

> We on our side have been in negotiations with the Prime Minister Mihai Antonescu since about one and a half years regarding a combine of interests as mentioned above by which we could take the lead . . .

> The matter of acquisition was amply discussed with Mr. Zangen and Mr. Roesler.

Even though this project did not materialize, it was recounted here because it is just as important to study the plans that miscarried, the schemes for which the days of Nazi domination were not long enough.

In the USSR. During 1942–1943, the M/W complex followed the German armies into Russia. The Nazi government commissioned M/W to become trustee and "guardian" for plants at Taganrog, Dnjepropetrowsk and Mariupol. Plans for future permanent acquisition of these projects did not materialize because the Russians soon drove the Nazi aggressors from Russia.

The industrial acquisitions of Mannesmann which were discussed above establish sufficiently the leading part of the Deutsche Bank and its network of branches abroad in securing for Mannesmann and ipso facto for the Deutsche Bank a prominent position in the Nazi–dominated economy of Europe. Exhibit II of the report on the Mannesmann Roehrenwerke, Duesseldorf, prepared by the Joint Special Financial Detachment, U.S. Group Control Council, Control Commission for Germany (British Element), Duesseldorf, contains a wealth of additional material and information which presents a detailed account of the foreign expansion of Mannesmann with the Deutsche Bank at its helm.

ACQUISITION, REPATRIATION, AND SALE OF FOREIGN GOVERNMENT SECURITIES

Purchases of participations in banking, commercial, and industrial enterprises in Eastern and Southeastern Europe for its own and customers' accounts were an important part of Deutsche Bank's participation in the spoliation of occupied Europe. Of lesser importance, but still considerable, was the acquisition of foreign government bonds, although the purpose here was to create free foreign exchange and to reduce German trade debts with neutral Turkey and the satellite countries of Bulgaria, Hungary, and Romania. These countries had been accumulating huge balances in their favor ever since 1941. The repatriation of their foreign bonded debt offered Germany some means to reduce her debts without requiring the delivery of goods, which became increasingly difficult for the hard-strained German war economy. The Deutsche Bank, which had been the agent of the respective governments in placing their foreign bonds in Germany and Western Europe, was predestined to assume a leading role in the repatriation of these bonds.

The Deutsche Bank served as the sole agency for the acquisition of Turkish loans for the account of the Turkish government. Only the period from 1942–1944 can be discussed, as files are not now available for the years 1938–1942, in which similar transactions took place. With the consent of the Ministry of Economics, purchases were made simultaneously in the occupied countries and in Germany. Turkey paid only a reduced price for her bonds, but she made it acceptable to the Germans by supplying a little over 20 percent in free foreign exchange. When Turkey withdrew its order for the repatriation of its type A bonds in May 1943, acquisition by the Deutsche Bank still continued and the bonds were sold in Switzerland. In the entire transaction, the price established by Turkey was considerably lower than the cost to the Deutsche Bank. The difference had to be made up by the Deutsche Golddiskontbank. All together, the Deutsche Bank spent RM 726,176.72 for which

Turkey paid: from blocked account	RM 167,024.00
in foreign exchange sfs 252,753.73	146,470.76
Sales in Switzerland amounted to sfs 55,786.85	32,328.44
The Deutsche Golddiskontbank contributed	380,353.52
	RM 726,176.72

Hungarian government bonds were bought up by the Deutsche Bank for repatriation from 1940 on. Purchases were made in Germany, Holland, and France in very substantial amounts, totaling about RM 160 million for the entire transaction.

Bonds acquired for the account of the Romanian government in Germany, France, Belgium, and presumably in other European countries amounted to about RM 50 million.

Bulgarian government bonds were repatriated from the same countries; total proceeds were about RM 3 to 4 million.

Yugoslavian bonds were bought up on the basis of agreements in 1939 and 1940 between the German and Yugoslavian governments prior to the German invasion of Yugoslavia. Total proceeds were in the vicinity of RM 50 million.

For the purchases in France, the Deutsche Bank utilized the small French banking firm La Gaze, Paris, until 1941, but upon instructions of the RWM in the succeeding years had to place its orders with the Westminster Foreign Bank Ltd., Paris, which the Berliner Handelsgesellschaft had chosen as its French office for the acquisition of foreign securities, foreign exchange, foreign currency, and gold. The Deutsche Bank effected payment for its purchases in France and Belgium through the Allgemeine Warenhandelsgesellschaft, Berlin. This company was a special agency of the Reichshauptkasse of the Reich Ministry of Finance and served as a vehicle for German purchases in the occupied countries.

Bulgarian as well as Turkish government bonds were acquired by the Deutsche Bank from the portfolio of Lippmann, Rosenthal & Co., Amsterdam, the notorious collecting agency of foreign securities from Jewish owners. The Deutsche Bank was the principal German banking connection of Lippmann, Rosenthal & Co. according to the summary on the activities of this Dutch bank submitted by Mr. Erbstoesser, a former manager of the Deutsche Golddiskontbank.

FOREIGN WORKERS' REMITTANCES

The fraudulent techniques connected with the German clearing system have been the subject of various studies. They are covered in the Trial Brief of the Office of the U.S. Chief of Counsel on the Spoliation of Western Europe, which makes at least two specific references to the misuse of occupation cost for the payment of foreign workers' remittances. On page 22, referring to Exhibit PS 3615, Ostrow Report, page 5, the Trial Brief states under the heading "France":

> The funds in account A were used for obviously nonoccupational purposes as follows: . . . A III Payment of support to dependents of laborers recruited in France for work in Germany June 1940 to end 1943 RM 1,500,000.

Occupation cost account B is similarly discussed on page 23:

> It is certain, however, that large sums were expended for such (nonoccupational) purposes.

Thus, a communication of the OKW to the Foreign Office of 6 November 1942, explaining the decrease in reserve for account B, states:

Allotments in favor of families of French workers working in Germany 1.5 million RM.

The study published by the Royal Institute of International Affairs, "Occupied Europe—German exploitation and its postwar consequences," explained:

Remittances sent home by foreign workers in Germany are credited in Reichsmark to the clearing account, but if the recipient at the worker's home is to benefit he or she must ultimately be paid by the local authority in the national currency which in turn is expended on national goods. The occupied country, therefore, in fact not only provides Germany with the worker but even has to pay part of his wages.

It is evident that this procedure was not clandestine, but known to the general public as the magazine *Die Deutsche Volkswirtschaft (German National Economics)* openly announced the following:

Germany's clearing debts (to foreign countries) have been further increased. However, this increase was due less to a change in the relation between imports and exports than to services in the field of war economics rendered by foreign countries. This applies first of all to the use of foreign workers in Germany; the savings from their wages, which have reached considerable amounts, have been transferred within the framework of clearing agreements. (page 21, No. 6 1943)

That the Deutsche Bank was given the almost monopolistic position for handling the remittance to their home countries of the savings made by foreign workers in Germany is indicative of the close working relationship between the Deutsche Bank and the Nazi government. The handling of these transfers developed into a sizable business.

Even the Dresdner Bank, which proved itself such a faithful servant of the Nazi regime, was relegated to a negligible role in this type of business. It only had charge of the transfers for Greek workers and such Slovakian workers as were employed by concerns other than the Hermann-Goering-Werke. For all others, except Russia which was handled by a government agency, the Deutsche Bank was the prescribed and exclusive channel of remittance.

The designation of Deutsche Bank as the official agency for this profitable business was sponsored by the RWM in agreement with the *Deutsche Arbeitsfront* (DAF, German Labor Front), the Reich Ministry of Labor and [Fritz] Sauckel, the Plenipotentiary for the Employment of Labor.

On the Deutsche Bank end, the acquisition of this business was largely accomplished by Director Weigelt who had long been associated with German expansionist circles. He first succeeded in having the Deutsche Bank appointed the sole transfer agency for Italian laborers who, in 1937, represented the first sizable group of foreign labor utilized in the speedup of Germany's production for war.

As Hitler's aggressive war engulfed more and more countries and ever increasing foreign labor forces were imported, frequently by force, Deutsche Bank's transfer business grew accordingly and covered the following countries in chronological order:

1937 Italy
1939 Bulgaria—Hungary
1940 Belgium—Denmark—France
1941 Finland—Norway—Serbia—Slovakia
1944 The Province of Lubliana.

The scope of the business transacted is shown by the following partial figures:

Country	Period	Number of Transfers Known to Have Reached Destination	Amounts Transferred
Italy	March 1941–May 1944	5,063,681	RM 756,583,806.55
Bulgaria	1942	130,933	RM 12,558,813.66
	1943	153,309	RM 17,117,527.79
Hungary	January–July 1944	17,628	RM 3,414,072.32
Belgium	total	3,348,129	RM 511,659,743.43
Denmark	1943	298,422	RM 36,044,700.60
France	total	3,851,969	RM 510,662,639.04
Finland	1943	505	RM 104,094.80
Norway	1941	1,372	RM 85,036.45
	1943	867	RM 176,817.62
Serbia	1942	34,184	RM 3,506,654.05
	1943	24,433	RM 3,040,004.83
Slovakia	1942	34,808	RM 2,653,745.32
	1943	14,688	RM 1,245,816.19
		12,974,928	RM 1,858,853,422.65

At first the bank charged RM 0.25 for each transfer regardless of amount but soon increased the rate to RM 0.60. That means, for instance, that the Deutsche Bank received RM 179,053.20 alone for the 298,422 transfers of savings during 1943 to Denmark, which had but a small labor force working in Germany. Accordingly the bank must have derived an income of close to 7.5 million RM alone from the transfers shown in the above schedule, which is far from complete and covers only part of the period involved.

In 1937 the Deutsche Bank set up a special department, "Foreign Workers," for these transfers. Lorenz Klebar, a *Prokurist* (chief clerk), headed the new department. Richard Haeussler was his immediate supervisor. "Foreign Workers" soon averaged 200 full-time employees and an unknown number of part-time workers.

The money a worker was permitted to remit was directly paid over to the Deutsche Bank by the employer.

In addition to the regular transfers of savings, which were limited to a certain amount per month, workers who were permitted to return to their native countries for good or on "leave," could also purchase a *Reisegutschein* (traveller's check) from the Deutsche Bank. (Employees of the Deutsche Bank accompanied the special trains taking the returning workers home.)

French workers could also buy at the Deutsche Bank an *Arbeiterscheck* (worker's check) for certain extra savings.

Payment to the beneficiary in the foreign country was effected through paying agencies designated by agreement between the Deutsche Bank and the German government. In Bulgaria and Slovakia, subsidiaries of the Deutsche Bank, the Deutsch-Bulgarische Kreditbank, Sofia, and the Unionbank, Bratislava, respectively, performed this function.

CLOAKING

The collaboration between the Deutsche Bank and the Nazi government in financing foreign trade and the spoliation of Europe does not embody all foreign operations where the bank worked "hand in glove" with the Nazis. Deutsche Bank's cloaking activities undertaken under the direction and with the assistance of the competent German authorities, which were heading for a war, are another form of such collaboration in the foreign field, primarily in neutral countries.

Already in 1936, but mainly immediately upon the outbreak of the war, Deutsche Bank attempted to camouflage all its foreign holdings.

In the course of cloaking its assets abroad, the Deutsche Bank undertook measures, presumably to protect itself against claims of people who were forced to leave Germany as a result of political, racial, and religious persecution. The letter of 19 September 1939 from the Deutsche Bank to the Reich Ministry of Economics stated:

> Special protective measures regarding customer deposits in USA were taken already in 1936 so that further measures are not necessary at the present time.

Apparently cloaking activities were familiar to the Deutsche Bank at the time war broke out.

It appears that the bank utilized several means to camouflage foreign assets and no definite pattern could be found. When Emil Puhl, vice-president of the Reichsbank, was questioned regarding German cloaking operations, he gave the following information:

> It was the general policy of the RWM to cloak German assets in neutral countries to prevent their seizure. Thus for example, the Deutsche Bank utilized its Dutch connections to distribute German holdings in Holland at the

outbreak of the war and thus prevent their seizure. The Export-Kredit Bank established by the Deutsche Bank in September 1939, was partially used for a similar purpose. Several companies were established for the purpose of dissociating German foreign holdings from their owners. There was no specific pattern employed to effect such cloaking. It depended primarily upon the individual cases. It was customary for large industrial concerns (Vereinigte Stahlwerke, Potash syndicate, Siemens) as well as the banks to maintain foreign subsidiaries established and officially managed according to the laws of the respective countries. Such companies were controlled by their German owners either through a majority of shares, through trusted representatives in the management, or through the special control of bookkeeping. These firms were utilized for the concealing of German interests abroad after the outbreak of the war. The banks through their affiliates in foreign countries established as native affiliates did not incur too many difficulties in transferring their openly German holdings to the respective affiliates.

The information now on hand regarding Deutsche Bank's cloaking activities at the outbreak of World War II falls under two headings: general measures and individual cases.

General Measures

Available correspondence between the Deutsche Bank and the Reich Ministry of Economics reveals the "Protective measures against confiscation by neutral and enemy Standstill creditors" taken at the outbreak of the war. The initial letter of 19 September 1939, signed by Hermann Abs and Alfons Simon (head of Foreign Department and chief legal adviser, respectively), informed the ministry of the following "protective" steps the Deutsche Bank took:

A) The Deutsche Bank transferred all *its stock and other securities* [emphasis in original] in the following countries to the A.G. fuer Vermoegensverwertung (see below):

Belgium	Yugoslavia
Bulgaria	Luxembourg
Denmark	Norway
Holland & Colonies	Finland
Italy	Latvia
Estonia	Mexico
Sweden	Argentina
Greece	Brazil
Switzerland	Chile
Protectorate	Uruguay
Slovakia	Venezuela
Guatemala	

Moreover, following a suggestion of the *Wirtschaftsgruppe Privates Bankgewerbe* (Economic Group Private Banking, part of the corporate organizations of the

Reich), the Deutsche Bank transferred to Berlin those securities depots in the above-named European countries, which formerly were held in the name of the Deutsche Bank and then transferred to the A.G. fuer Vermoegensverwertung.

B) The Deutsche Bank instructed their branches that all free foreign exchange *(freie Devisen)* which will be put at their disposal by customers outside of Germany be paid to the "Notenbanken" of the countries in question to the credit of the Reichsbankdirektorium, without naming the Deutsche Bank. In each such case, a statement regarding this transaction was to be mailed to the Deutsche Bank. This would prevent the confiscation of amounts incoming for the Deutsche Bank. The procedure was to be observed mainly for:

United States	Sweden
Holland	Norway
Switzerland	Denmark
Belgium	Finland

Deutsche Bank's own ("Nostro") accounts in the above countries were, as far as this was still possible, transferred to the national banks of the countries in question to the account of the Reichsbank. Later reports were to give detailed information regarding confiscation effected by England and Switzerland against Deutsche Bank's accounts and deposits with Swiss banks.

The Deutsche Bank was taking no measures to secure its accounts and incoming assets from the remaining European countries:

Italy	Romania
Yugoslavia	Bulgaria
Greece	Turkey
Spain	

A disposition in these countries could be made only through the clearing agreement.

INDIVIDUAL CASES

Accounts in Argentina. The September letter furthermore explains that Deutsche Bank's Argentinian peso account with the Banco Alemán Transatlantico (Deutsche Ueberseeische Bank, a subsidiary of the Deutsche Bank) was transferred to the Cia. Argentina de Mandatos S.A., Buenos Aires. This latter bank is one of the companies blacklisted by the U.S. government.

Accounts in Holland. In order to avoid the imminent confiscation of certain assets it had in Holland, the Deutsche Bank requested and immediately obtained official German permission to transfer its accounts with H.M.H. Albert de Bary & Co., Amsterdam, with the Amsterdamsche Bank, and with the Nederlandsche Handel-Maatschappij in Amsterdam and Rotterdam to the A.G. fuer Vermoegensver-wertung, its main cloaking agency.

The Deutsche Bank had an account of more than hfl. 2,000 with the Amsterdam branch of the French bank, Banque de Paris et des Pays-Bas, Paris. The Deutsche Bank had difficulties with the management of this account, and it requested and obtained official German permission to sell this account to a Dutch company, the N.V. Buitenlandsche Trust Maatschappij, so that the Deutsche Bank was able to bring a lawsuit against the Dutch branch of the French bank which had refused Deutsche Bank's disposition orders in regard to this account.

The main difficulty of the Deutsche Bank in Holland was to camouflage prior to the occupation of Holland the German character of H. Albert de Bary, its Dutch subsidiary, in order to keep it off the Allied blacklist. It became necessary to conceal Deutsche Bank's controlling interest in [that bank] which evidenced itself not only in the ownership of a majority of the share capital but in the fact that three of the seven members of the board of directors were Germans; blacklisting of the bank would have prohibited all foreign exchange transactions with France, and Great Britain, and de Bary would have lost its significance as a valuable German spearhead.

In order to "secure the position of de Bary as neutral bank," Abs and Simon proposed the renunciation of Deutsche Bank's right to vote and to receive dividends during the period of the war, as well as the reduction of German representation on the board of directors of de Bary from three to one.

To counteract the results of these steps, the following was agreed upon:

In regard to the renunciation of the right to vote, there was to be no change of by-laws during this period. To secure this, a special agreement was also made with the holding company in charge of hfl. 9 million of de Bary's stock (N.V. Gemeenschappelijk Bezit van andeelen Handel-Maatschappij H. Albert de Bary & Co. N.V.).

To compensate the bank's and Germany's loss of foreign exchange incurred by the cessation of the receipt of the dividends, Deutsche Bank again planned to draw on its credit of hfl. 2.5 million, which was granted in 1938, to the extent of the dividend.

The above measures were approved by the German Ministry of Economics, but a letter dated 11 April 1940, signed by Roesler and Simon, informed the Ministry that de Bary had been placed on the English and French blacklists in spite of all. This did not mean a serious loss to the Deutsche Bank and the Reich, as four weeks later Germany occupied Holland.

CLOAKING AGENCIES

The two main "cloaks" utilized by the bank in its camouflage activities were the A.G. fuer Vermoegensverwertung, Berlin, and the Export-Kreditbank A.G., Berlin, both subsidiaries of the Deutsche Bank. The first concentrated on cloaking of security and stock deposits, the latter on protecting from seizure the foreign credit balances and deposits of the parent bank and its customers.

Aktiengesellschaft fuer Vermoegensverwertung, Berlin. This corporation was founded in 1911 to finance building companies. When it was first utilized for cloaking is not known. The Deutsche Bank holds 100 percent of the entire capital of RM

1,200,000 of this corporation. Deutsche Bank's annual reports as far back as 1931 carry references to this company as a Deutsche Bank participation.

Director Alfred Kurzmeyer acted as president of the corporation.

In the period preceding the war the A.G. fuer Vermoegensverwertung was used as a cloak by Mannesmann to purchase Kronprinz shares at a total amount of RM 1,283,000, which exceeded the total capital of Vermoegensverwertung.

As a considerable number of Kronprinz shares were in the possession of Jews and Czech nationals, and as the purchase of these shares occurred after the Anschluss and after the Munich Agreement, it is more than probable that these shares were property expropriated from Jews or Czech nationals who did not cooperate with the Nazis.

This corporation attained its true importance in connection with the cloaking operations at the outbreak of the war.

The correspondence, discussed above, between the Deutsche Bank and the Reich Ministry of Economics regarding Deutsche Bank's security measures shows that the Deutsche Bank used the A.G. fuer Vermoegensverwertung as a cover firm for the protection of assets in neutral European and Latin American countries by transferring all their stock and security deposits in those countries to this corporation in September 1939.

The transfer was intended to prevent the confiscation of Deutsche Bank assets under the provisions of the Standstill Agreement, with which Abs was particularly well acquainted.

Export-Kreditbank A.G., Berlin. The Export-Kreditbank A.G., Berlin, was founded by the Deutsche Bank together with its main foreign subsidiary, the Deutsche Ueberseeische Bank (DUB) and the Allgemeine Deutsche Creditanstalt (Adca) in the second week of September 1939 immediately after the outbreak of war. The purpose of the new bank was the cloaking of the foreign credit balances and deposits of the founding banks and their German customers to prevent seizure.

The following excerpt regarding the Export-Kreditbank was taken from a letter dated 2 October 1939 from the Steel Union Export, Inc., Duesseldorf, Department East-Berlin, to its Export Sekretariat in Duesseldorf:

SUBJECT: *Foreign Balances*

> . . . we herewith inform you that we conferred with the Allgemeine Warenfinanzierungs-Gesellschaft m.b.H. . . . . The corporation was established to take charge of the foreign assets of companies which have to consider it important not to own any foreign assets and to perform the complete encashment. The management explained to us that a number of companies, which experienced difficulties from the Standstill Agreement, are already in contact with them and that they negotiate important transactions especially for a number of companies of the above mentioned kind.

> In this connection we inform you confidentially that on 5 Sept the Deutsche Bank also established a corporation (Aktiengesellschaft)

with a stock capital of RM 1 million under the name of EXPORT-KREDITBANK; officially the bank denies that this is a subsidiary. As directors for this corporation were appointed Count v.d. Goltz, whom you know from previous compensation business with England, and Director ALBERT SCHNEIDER, who several years ago once had been with the Deutsche Bank. The Deutsche Bank did not publish any circulars about this matter as they believe that they have to be very careful. But, on the other hand, they ask us to contact the company, which already achieved outstanding success, in case we are interested, and to get detailed information about this company, we ask you to get in touch with Director WUPPER-MANN of the Deutsche Bank in Duesseldorf.

For your information we are adding that Mr. Blessing, the former "General Referent" of the RWM, is represented on the board of directors. [emphasis in original]

In addition: Customers of the banks who had been dealing directly with foreign countries prior to the outbreak of war, also turned to the Export-Kreditbank for the protection of their export balances from seizure by creditors in countries at war with Germany. The same was true of German-owned enterprises in Polish Upper Silesia. The Export-Kreditbank thus fulfilled a vital function until most of the European countries were under German control, eliminating the danger of seizure of German assets from abroad.

CHAPTER XIII

Deutsche Bank Today

The outstanding position of the Deutsche Bank in the German financial and industrial structure and the active part it played in the fulfillment of the aggressive aims of the Nazi regime at home and abroad were discussed from a variety of aspects in the preceding chapters. The power of this largest general bank in Germany was rooted not only in the size of its assets but in its centralized structure, which enabled a small group of individuals to influence from Berlin the economic life of most communities in Germany and of several countries of Europe. Centralization made it comparatively simple for the Deutsche Bank's leadership to gear its vast machine to the attainment of the expansionist objectives of the Nazis, which bore close kinship to the Pan-Germanic tradition of this bank.

In the last year of the war the military situation deteriorated so rapidly that the Deutsche Bank was forced to decentralize its operations to some extent by establishing three regional evacuation offices (*Ausweichstellen*) in Hamburg, Wiesbaden, and Erfurt.

Nevertheless, the defeat of Germany neither decentralized the bank effectively nor eliminated from positions of influence those individuals who assisted the Vorstand in planning and executing the policies of the Deutsche Bank under the Nazi regime. On the contrary, the general agents and department heads of the Deutsche Bank who came to power after most of the Vorstand members were either arrested or removed from their positions by the Allies dedicated themselves during the first year of occupation to reestablish the Deutsche Bank's dominant position in German economy.

Investigation of the Deutsche Bank since the end of last year to date has revealed that the bank is again becoming a centralized institution contrary to U.S. policy. The focal point of centralization is Hamburg. Since the British Military Government permitted centralized banking operations in its Zone, it was quite logical, in view of the Berlin situation, for the top management of the Deutsche Bank to concentrate in Hamburg.

The U.S. policy with respect to decentralized banking has been known in the U.S. Zone since November 1945, and German banking circles have been advised to plan a banking system on that basis. The heads of the Deutsche Bank now working from the Hamburg branch strongly object to such U.S. policy according to a letter, dated 11 January 1946, from the *Fuehrungsstab* (head office of the Deutsche Bank, Hamburg 11, Alster-Wall 37-35), which was sent to the main branches of the Deutsche Bank in the British Zone and then on to branches in the U.S. and French Zones. This letter reads in part:

> We have learnt from our branch at Kassel that a committee has been
> set up there which concerns itself with the well-known proposals

(not decrees) by the U.S. Military Government regarding the decentralization of banking. At the request of the expert for banking in the Ministry of Greater Hesse this committee has worked out the following proposals aiming to break up the three big banks in the Greater Hesse area.

The managements of the banks were not consulted. They were informed, if at all, only subsequently of the view taken by the committee.

We regard such a procedure as entirely out of question as a treason to the own institution [*sic*], and as an altogether unimportant, but unfortunately damage-causing attitude on the part of non-authorized persons who lack an overall view. We hope that no persons connected with the Deutsche Bank have had any part in formulating these proposals.

No objections can be raised if managers of our branch establishments take part in discussing the decentralization of banking and in a given case do not decline to participate in committees, if after a serious examination they feel that they measure up to the difficulties involved in such negotiations and discussions. We expect, however, that each individual

1. regards the unity of German "economic space" and the overall interests of the Deutsche Bank as the guiding principles of his actions;
2. realizes that the decentralization question can only be finally dealt with by the legal representation of the Deutsche Bank. The legal representation is constituted by the Vorstand, which in such cases requires the authorization of the Aufsichtsrat. If and as long as the Vorstand is not able to act it is replaced by the Fuehrungsstab, which is represented at the head by the directors of the whole bank.

Seen from these viewpoints the procedure at Kassel cannot be condemned sharply enough. It goes without saying that selfish considerations by individual persons should have no part in such proposals.

The reputation and the credit of the Deutsche Bank are such a great asset of German business that everything has to be done to maintain this asset. When Germany is again integrated into world economy no twenty regional banks will be able to take the place of the Deutsche Bank. It is still more absurd to imagine that hundreds of local and Kreis banks should be able to do it.

This Fuehrungsstab has been in existence in Hamburg since April 1945. It originally consisted of Hermann J. Abs, Erich Bechtolf, and Clemens Plassman, all old

Vorstand members. First Abs was removed and subsequently Bechtolf and Plassmann. On 8 May 1945, Fritz Wintermantel, an old Vorstand member sought by the U.S. Military Government since November 1945, was appointed by the British authorities to head the Fuehrungsstab.

Directed by Wintermantel, the present Fuehrungsstab consists of Max Joergens and Ludwig Kruse, "Direktoren der Gesamtbank mit Generalvollmacht," who had general power to act for the entire bank, Victor-Albin von Schenk, manager of the Hamburg branch, and, since July 1946, Joachim Kessler, formerly with the Deutsche Bank in Berlin. This Fuehrungsstab is departmentalized like the Vorstand it is replacing. The following is the personnel in charge of the various departments:

Credits	Arnold Schwerdtfeger
Main Bookkeeping and Organization	Georg Steinmann
Personnel	Emil Gossmann
Secretariat and Syndicate Business	Dr. Ernst Wienands
Legal Department	Dr. Hans Paschke
Foreign Department	Dr. Johannes Feske

All but one of the department heads are from the former Berlin head office.

Dr. Walter Schmidt, manager of the Frankfurt branch of the Deutsche Bank, and Hermann Kaiser, of the central office, Berlin, branch of the Deutsche Bank, both stated that the Fuehrungsstab in Hamburg is responsible for all matters and functions formerly executed by the Vorstand in Berlin.

It has been approving loans above a minimum figure for all branches in all Western Zones. It has established a central cash deposit office for all branches of all zones in Hildesheim (British Zone). To coordinate the trading of securities in all zones the Fuehrungsstab in Hamburg is publishing a weekly bulletin called *Effektennachrichten (Security News)*. It has been setting the personnel policy for all branches in the Western Zones.

How personnel assignments and policy are set in Hamburg is explained in a statement supplied by Hermann Kaiser. On 14 June 1946 he stated:

> In relation to personnel policies there has to be added that the Fuehrungsstab in Hamburg endorses not only the employment of officials in the Western sector but also the suggestions regarding the employment of banking officials given by Berlin and other places, i.e., in regard to an opening in other branches in Munich, Baden-Baden, or Frankfurt.

On principal decisions of personnel policy, the Deutsche Bank not only issues directives from the Fuehrungsstab in Hamburg, it also acts in accordance with the other Grossbanken, the Dresdner Bank, and the Commerzbank. A memorandum of the Zentraldirektion West of the Dresdner Bank outlines the points of agreement between the "Big Three" including matters of personnel and cartellike arrangements for the opening of new branches. In regard to personnel these banks decided to keep their banking organizations strong by keeping as many employees as possible in contact with the bank. The agreement shows complete absence of consideration of denazification policies, which definitely affected the personnel structure of all banks.

Thus a list of certain branch managers of the Deutsche Bank in the three Western Zones of Germany indicated that five men had been NSDAP members before 1 May 1937 and therewith fall within the mandatory removal category, while twelve are in the discretionary removal category. None of these seventeen men has been removed from their jobs; all but one are heading branches located in the British Zone.

Fuehrungsstab directives are issued out of Hamburg as formal, mimeographed documents. They are headed as follows:

Deutsche Bank—Fuehrungsstab Hamburg
. . . .
For the management of the branches in the
British, American, and French Occupation Zones.

When it became apparent that the Deutsche Bank in the U.S. Zone did not undertake effective steps to comply with U.S. policy on the decentralization of banking, the Finance Division of the Office of Military Government informed the finance ministers of the three Laender in the U.S. Zone on 6 March 1946 that

It should be made clear to the branches of the former German branch bank systems that their head offices have been closed and that there are no longer head offices of these systems. Banks located in our Zone should not ask for and accept instructions from any other banking offices.

On 18 March 1946, the Finance Minister of Greater Hesse informed the banks about this directive of the Military Government, explained it carefully, and ordered them to take appropriate action:

It is demanded that measures be taken to fully explain to the bank branches located in Greater Hesse that their central offices have been closed and that the banks located in the zone occupied by the U.S.A. are not permitted to ask for instructions from other banking institutes or to receive them.

To clarify any remaining doubts as to whether the demanded decentralization of banks to "Land" level still permits the maintenance of branches or dependency from head offices, respectively from plenipotentiaries, in other "Laender" of the American Zone, it is expressly emphasized on the basis of given directives from Military Government that the Military Government demands reorganization on the level of the respective Land and not the zone (Laender).

All dependency in problems of personnel, credit, and general business organization are therefore not permitted and will have to be discontinued if existent.

The Deutsche Bank in Frankfurt forwarded a copy of this letter to their branches in Greater Hesse and designated the Frankfurt branch as the head branch for this *Land*. It also immediately informed the Fuehrungsstab. The Fuehrungsstab lost no time and dispatched the following telegram to the Frankfurt branch on 22 March 1946 to "clarify" and interpret the directive from the Finance Minister in Greater Hesse in the light of Deutsche Bank's centralized policy:

> Received your letter of 19th dealing with decentralization. Regulation of our Military Government only forbids bank-political instructions to any branch in another zone of occupation—The same appears from the minutes you sent with your letter of 14 Mar.—Hence instructions Wiesbaden of 18 Mar. concerning decentralization to a regional level is not supported by Military Government regulations. We assume that you and neighboring branches have pointed this out to the responsible authorities. If necessary get in touch with the highest local Military Government officials. Trying to send WERNER VOIGT and GEORG STEINMANN with proposals to conference in Stuttgart. (Steinmann is the head of Organization and Main Bookkeeping in Fuehrungsstab in Hamburg; Voigt, NSDAP member since 1940, headed the depositary in the Berlin central between 1941 and April 1945; he is now also employed by the Fuehrungsstab.)

In a letter dated 24 April 1946 director Willy Nuber, Commerzbank Nuernberg, reported to director Hans Erkelenz, Commerzbank Hamburg:

> The Deutsche Bank held a conference in Stuttgart of the managers of all important branches in the U.S. Zone.

Disregarding the directives of the Military Government and the Land Minister of Finance, the Frankfurt branch has continued to receive directives from the Fuehrungsstab in Hamburg and the bank has not been decentralized on a "Land" level. On 8 April 1946 the Commerzbank Nuernberg wrote to its Hamburg branch that:

> Kommerzienrat Maser of the Deutsche Bank (general agent of the bank, First Manager of Munich and Augsburg branches), Munich, has stated that he has appointed a general management for all the branches of the Deutsche Bank in the U.S. Zone, to which every branch in the three Laender would be responsible.

This fact becomes particularly important in view of official declarations from leading Deutsche Bank executives that there are independent Deutsche Bank units established for each of the three Laender of the U.S. Zone, none of which is directed from outside the given Land.

In overcoming communication and censorship obstacles to centralized operations, the Deutsche Bank established an illegal courier service covering Hamburg, Berlin, and cities in all four zones. The purpose of this courier service is the transmission of records, documents, money, securities, information, directives, instructions, and the like, which the bank does not wish to entrust to postal channels because of censorship and possible confiscation.

The Deutsche Bank is endeavoring to reopen its Berlin branches. Together with the Dresdner Bank, the Commerzbank, and the Berliner Handelsgesellschaft it formed a committee which submitted to the Berlin Magistrat a proposal to reopen the banks in Berlin. In its application "for permission to transact banking business in Berlin," dated 1 March 1946, the Deutsche Bank desires to resume all its former functions. To what extent the officials of the Deutsche Bank still consider their institution a centralized organization and even base their application for reopening the Berlin branches on this premise, is shown by the following excerpt from the application:

> It (the Deutsche Bank) maintains a large number of branches in all parts of Germany. Its business in the British, American, and French Zones of occupation was only temporarily interrupted at the end of the war and has been maintained since then to its full extent. All liabilities arising from new business in Berlin will form an obligation of the whole bank and its property.

Although the end of the first year of occupation found the Deutsche Bank in the Soviet Zone closed and the final fate of the Berlin branches undetermined, the Deutsche Bank was able to expand its branch network in the U.S., British, and French Zones.

Number of Branches of the Deutsche Bank

	End of 1944	Currently
American Zone	26	30
British Zone	85	88
French Zone	34	35
Total	145	153

The last complete balance sheet of the Deutsche Bank covers the year 1943–1944. . . . Following are the key positions which indicate the relationship between the main office and the branches:

(in RM billion)

	Berlin	West Zones	East Zone	Total for bank
Customers' deposits	2.7	5.5	2	10.2
Total assets	3.5*	5.9	2	11.4
Interbank accounts				
from West	+4.2	-4.2	-1.7	—
from East	+1.7			
Funds at disposition	9.4	1.7	.3	11.4
Accounts receivable	.66	.72	.21	1.59
Treasury bills	6.85	.59	.06	7.50

* Excluding interbank accounts

CHAPTER XIV

Profiles

The following section of this report contains biographical information on Vorstand and Aufsichtsrat members of the Deutsche Bank who were arrested and are [currently] in the custody of United States authorities. Included are reports on the following [five] members of the Aufsichtsrat and Vorstand of the Deutsche Bank:

> BRECHT, Gustav   RUMMEL, Hans
> PIETZSCH, Albert   SCHMID, Max
> . . .   SIEMENS, Hermann Werner von

Although Hermann Schmitz and Ernst Enno Russell are in U.S. custody, no biographical sketches were included in this report. Schmitz's activities as head of the I.G. Farben trust were the subject of exhaustive investigations by other U.S. agencies. Russell was too ill to be interrogated and remains under house arrest.

All profiles should be read in conjunction with the entire report on the Deutsche Bank, of which all the Vorstand and Aufsichtsrat members were responsible officials.

Since the information was obtained in the course of a financial investigation rather than in a series of industrial investigations, the profiles of those who were primarily industrialists are not complete.

GUSTAV BRECHT

(MEMBER OF THE AUFSICHTSRAT OF THE DEUTSCHE BANK)

SUMMARY

Gustav Brecht was president of the Vorstand of a lignite-, briquette-, and electricity-producing company, which was the largest single lignite producer in Germany. Brecht was appointed to the board of directors of some of the most important war industries, which were managed by prominent Nazis. He helped to establish two synthetic fuel producing corporations in preparation for World War II. His corporations employed slave labor and prisoners of war. He and his companies bought Aryanized property. He was given honorary positions by Nazi leaders. Under U.S. occupation he violated Military Government orders blocking his property.

The phenomenal upswing in Brecht's career after March 1933 shows that he was a participant and beneficiary in the Nazification of Germany.

Personal Data. Brecht was born 9 January 1880. He is a graduate of the School for Technology and Engineering (Technische Hochschule) at Berlin. Brecht's family consists of his wife, who is of Belgian origin, and his son Christoph, aged twenty-four, who holds an honorary, nonsalaried position in the local employment office. Two of Brecht's sons were killed since the outbreak of war. Brecht's last residence was Wiessee on the Tegernsee, Bavaria. He was arrested 15 November 1945 and is currently held at Civilian Internment Enclosure No. 91.

Principal Activity. Brecht's last full-time position and main occupation was President (*Vorsitzer des Vorstandes*) of the Rheinische A.G. fuer Braunkohlenbergbau und Brikettfabrikation, Koeln ("Rheinbraun"). This corporation produced briquettes, electric power, and 10–11 percent of all German lignite. Until 1939–40 it was the largest single German lignite producer. The Rhenish lignite district produced 30 percent of all German lignite.

Political Affiliations. Brecht claims never to have been a member of any party. He states he voted for the Deutsche Volkspartei, a right-wing party composed mainly of industrialists and professional people, many of whom later went over to the Deutsch-Nationale Volkspartei, which supported Hitler in 1933. His other political affiliations were:

> Member of Deutsche Arbeitsfront since 1934
> Member of NS Volkswohlfahrt (National Socialist People's Welfare)
>   1936–1942
> Member of National Socialist Bund of German Technical Science.

Baron von Schroeder has repeatedly characterized Gustav Brecht as a Nazi (Schroeder was on the board of directors of Rheinbraun, Brabag, and other boards of which Brecht also was a member). Schroeder also stated that Brecht was on very friendly terms with Gauleiter Grohe. Brecht claims that this is not true.

Connection with the Deutsche Bank. Gustav Brecht has been a member of the Aufsichtsrat of the Deutsche Bank since 1940. When the Deutsche Bank established district *Beiraete* (advisory councils) in 1935, as did the other large banks, Brecht was appointed a member of the one for his district, the Rhine-Westphalian territory, one of Germany's key districts for heavy industry.

Dr. Rolf Brecht, his brother, is an officer *(Prokurist)* of the Coblenz branch of the Deutsche Bank.

Gustav Brecht personally owns nominal RM 27,000 Deutsche Bank stock.

In all major financing transactions for the Rheinbraun and affiliated companies, Deutsche Bank headed the bank syndicates and participated with the largest quota (see details below).

Business Positions. Below is a chronological record of the positions held by Brecht after his entry into the field of industry. From this record it is evident that Brecht's success really started in March 1933. The following symbols are used in the listing below: B—grounds for blocking of accounts; R—grounds for mandatory removal from positions of authority; D—grounds for discretionary removal from positions of authority.

1925   Chairman of the Vorstand (President) of "Rheinbraun" (D). Two Deutsche Bank men were on the board of directors of this corporation as well as another industrialist, who also was a member of the board of directors of the Deutsche Bank. Immediately following the banking crisis of 1931, Rheinbraun purchased a substantial block of Deutsche Bank stock. (cf. Handelszeitung of *Berliner Tageblatt,* 17 July 1932)

In 1930 Rheinbraun received a RM 50 million loan and in 1940 another RM 50 million loan from banking syndicates. The Deutsche Bank was the leader of the syndicate in both cases.

The Abs family owned about 1 percent of Rheinbraun's capital stock (Hermann Abs was a member of Deutsche Bank's Vorstand and on the board of directors of Rheinbraun).

The Weidtmann family owned 1–2 percent of the capital stock. Mr. Herbst, former manager of the Deutsche Bank's branch in Koeln, was married to a Weidtmann daughter.

Between 1936 and 1944, the sales of this company increased from about RM 50 million to about RM 70 million per year.

Rheinbraun, through Roddergrube (see below), was controlled by RWE, the Rheinisch Westfaelische Elektrizitaetswerke (Rhenish Westphalian Electric Works).

RWE, Roddergrube, and Rheinbraun, according to Brecht, "were legally independent companies, but economically held together by mutual capital interests, dividend-guarantee contracts, and the same chairman of the board of directors in all three companies."

Koepchen, the "primus inter pares" of the RWE Vorstand, was also a member of the board of directors of the Deutsche Bank.

1925   Member of the Vorstand of REW, the Rheinische Elektrizitaetswerk im Braunkohlenrevier A.G., Koeln.

This company is a subsidiary of Rheinbraun and produces electric power. Its main customer is the city of Koeln.

F. Herbst, former manager of Deutsche Bank's Koeln branch, was on the board of directors of this subsidiary.

One hundred percent of REW stock was held by Rheinbraun.

Between 1936 and 1944, the sales of this company increased from RM 10 million to about RM 17 million per year.

1925   Member of the board of directors of the "Syndikat," the Rheinische Braunkohlen-Syndikat G.m.b.H., Koeln.

This corporation is a sales syndicate for all briquettes produced in the Rhineland district.

The chairman of the Vorstand of this corporation is on the district Beirat of the Deutsche Bank.

Between 1936 and 1944, sales increased from RM 100 million to almost RM 140 million.

Rheinbraun holds 36 percent; Roddergrube, 20 percent of Syndikat's stock.

1928   Member of the board of directors of Harpener Bergbau A.G., Dortmund. This is the largest independent coal mining enterprise in Germany and is controlled by Friedrich Flick. Flick had very close business relations with Goering, was one of Schacht's close friends, and is one of Germany's foremost steel and coal magnates. He acquired the bulk of his wealth during the Nazi regime.

Deutsche Bank's Vorstand member Kimmich and Kiehl from the Aufsichsrat of the Deutsche Bank were on the board of directors of this corporation.

Werner Carp, Aufsichsrat of Deutsche Bank, was also on the board of directors of this corporation.

1932   Member of the board of directors of "Zukunft," the Braunkohlen-Industrie A.G. Zukunft, Eschweiler. This company produces coal, briquettes, and electricity.

Kimmich and Koepchen, members of the board of directors of the Deutsche Bank, were on the board of directors of Zukunft. Meyer from Zukunft's Vorstand was on Deutsche Bank's district Beirat.

Eighty-five percent of Zunkunft's stock is controlled by RWE.

1933   Promoted to chairman of the board of directors of RWE.

1933   Promoted to vice-chairman of the board of directors of the Syndikat.

1933   Member of the board of directors of "Roddergrube," the Braunkohlen und Brikettwerke Roddergrube A.G., a producer of coal, briquette, and electric power, controlled by RWE, the Rheinisch-Westfalisches Elektrizitaetswerke.

Koepchen is on Roddergrube's Vorstand and also a member of the board of directors of the Deutsche Bank (see above). Abs, Vorstand member of Deutsche Bank, is on Roddergrube's board of directors.

In 1941 Roddergrube's RM 60 million loan was effected through a banking syndicate headed by the Deutsche Bank.

Roddergrube's sales between 1936 and 1944 increased from RM 40 million to RM 50 million per annum.

1934   Member of the Beirat (advisory council) of the Industrie und Handels-
(or 1935) kammer Koeln (R)—(Chamber of Commerce), which later became the Gauwirtschaftskammer. Since 1933 all members had to be approved by the NSDAP.

1934   Member of the board of directors of Humboldt-Deutz Motoren, a manu-
(to 1937) facturer of factory installations including installations for lignite companies. Brecht resigned from this position to become a member of the board of directors of this company's more important rival, the Maschinenfabrik Buckau R. Wolf A.G., Magdeburg.

1934   Member of the board of directors of the Koelner Glasversicherung, a small
(to 1938) subsidiary of the Colonia insurance company. Brecht resigned from this position to become a member of the Continent's largest life insurance company, the Allianz Lebensversicherung A.G., Berlin.

1934   Vice-chairman of the board of directors of Brabag (R), the Braunkohle-Benzin A.G., Berlin. This nationwide corporation was established as early as 1934 upon orders by Minister Schacht to produce synthetic fuel, one of the most important materials for warfare. Initial capital was RM 100 million. Brecht's Rheinbraun contributed 11 percent of the initial capitalization. Brecht remained vice-chairman even after "UK," the Union Rheinische Braunkohlen-Kraftstoff A.G., Koeln, closely connected with Rheinbraun, Roddergrube, etc. (see below), bought all Brabag shares belonging to Rheinbraun, Roddergrube and Zukunft. Brecht's co-workers in Brabag were Keppler, Baron v. Schroeder (succeeding each other as chairman), Rasche, Kranefuss, and Steinbrink—all members of the industrial and banking group around Heinrich Himmler, chief of the SS (Schutzstaffel). Brabag contributed RM 100,000 to the Special SS Fund put at Himmler's disposal by industry and banking.

      Brecht stated that Brabag's production and sales quadrupled between 1935 and 1944.

1935   Presided at annual meetings of "Verges" (Vereinigungsgesellschaft m.b.H. Rheinische Braunkohlen Bergwerke, Koeln), a holding company for the Rhine district's lignite mines, owned jointly by Rheinbraun and Roddergrube.

1935   Promoted to chairman of the board of directors of the Syndikat.

1935   Member of the district Beirat of the Deutsche Bank.

1935   Chief of the Bezirks-Gruppe Rheinische Braunkohlen-Bergbau (B) (District Group of Rhenish Lignite Mining).

1935   Deputy Chief of the Wirtschaftsgruppe Bergbau, Berlin (B) (Industrial Group Mining, Berlin). The latter was the top organ, the former a regional branch, of the mining section in the Nazi corporate organization of industry.

1936   Member of advisory council of Mineral Oelbau G.m.b.H., a consulting engineers company without a board of directors. This company was closely associated with Verges (see above) and UK (see below).

1936   Member of the board of directors of Felten und Guillaume Carlswerk A.G., Koeln-Muehlheim, a wire and cable concern with total assets amounting to over RM 128 million. Brigadier General Baron v. Schroeder (see Brabag, above) was chairman of its board of directors. This company contributed RM 20,000 to the special SS Fund put at the disposal of Himmler by industry and banking.

      Sippel from Deutsche Bank's Vorstand was a member of the board of directors of this company.

1937   Elected *Ratsherr* (councilman) (R, B) of the city of Koeln.

1937   Chairman of the board of directors of the newly established "UK," the Union Rheinische Braunkohlen-Kraftstoff A.G., Koeln. This corporation produced synthetic fuel and, like Brabag, was set up by order of the Nazi government as another step in the rearmament program. Rheinbraun provided 41 percent, Roddergrube 32 percent, Zukunft 9 percent of UK's initial capital of RM 45 million, which was doubled in 1940. The Deutsche Bank headed the banking syndicates for a bond issue of RM 60

million in 1940 and another one of RM 45 million in 1942 as well as a
bank loan of RM 50 million in 1943.

Rath represented the Deutsche Bank on UK's board of directors.

The production for 1943-44 amounted to 23,000 tons, for which about
RM 65 million was realized.

1937   Member of the board of directors of the Allianz Lebensversicherung A.G.
(or 1938) Berlin. This is the largest Continental life insurance company with insurance contracts in force totaling over RM 5 billion. It was managed by
Hilgard who had been introduced to Hitler in 1931. (As representative of
all German insurance companies and as head of Reichsgruppe
Versicherungen, Hilgard participated in a meeting with Goering,
Goebbels, Heydrich, and others, on the Jewish question following the
organized pogroms in 1938. At this meeting, it was decided the insurance
companies would make payments on their books but that such payments
would be immediately confiscated.)

Rummel, member of Deutsche Bank's Vorstand, also was on the board
of directors of this corporation.

1938   Appointed Wehrwirtschaftsfueher (war economy leader) (R, B), an honorary title bestowed upon important war industry executives by the Nazis.

1938   Member of the board of directors of Maschinenfabrik Buckau R. Wolf A.G.
Magdeburg, a large manufacturer of factory installations specializing,
among other products, in machinery for lignite mines and briquette factories.

Oswald Roesler, member of Deutsche Bank's Vorstand, is chairman of
the board of directors of this company.

1939   Vice-chairman of the newly organized Erft Bergbau A.G., Bruggen Erft.
This company is the Aryanized version of the former Hubertus
Braunkohle A.G., 50 percent of the capital of which was owned by the
Czech Jewish family Petschek. The Petscheks also owned about 1–2 per-
cent of the Rheinbraun stock; Brecht claims not to know the fate of these
Rheinbraun shares. But Brecht holds 3.33 percent of Erft's present stock.
Brecht stated that "Verges" (see above) and the Abs family each own close
to 50 percent of the Erft stock. Hermann Abs, member of Deutsche
Bank's Vorstand, is not only a part owner, but also on the board of direc-
tors of this briquette manufacturing company.

Annual sales amounted to about RM 4–6 million.

1940   Chairman of the Beirat of the newly founded RBT, the Rheinische
Braunkohlentiefbaugesellschaft G.m.b.H., Koeln, a company engaged in
experiments to increase coal production by working deep-level mines.
According to Brecht, this company, initially capitalized at RM 500,000,
never started production.

1940   Member of the board of directors of the Deutsche Bank, Berlin (R, B).

1941   Promoted to chairman of the board of directors of Erft.

1941   Vice-chairman of the Deutsche Braunkohlen Industrie Verein at Halle.

1941   As representative of the Rhine District, became member of Praesidium
Reichsvereinigung Kohle (Board of the Reich Association Coal) (R, B),
in Berlin, to which Goering called representatives from all districts or

syndicates. Brecht became supervisor of the department of Statistics and
Planning.

1945   In February, awarded the Ritterkreuz des Kriegsverdienst-Kreuzes I
(Knight's Cross of the Cross for Distinguished War Services, first class).
This was the highest decoration Hitler, Goering, and the Speer Ministry
awarded to particularly successful producers in war industry.

Slave Labor. Brecht's company Rheinbraun, its sister companies and subsidiaries,
counted up to 30 percent foreign workers among their working force. Roddergrube
had Polish prisoners of war, Rheinbraun employed French and Italian prisoners of
war. Rheinbraun and its related companies also employed Russian prisoners of war
(up to 12 percent of the total), and civilians from Belgium, Holland, Poland, Russia,
Italy, and other countries.

Aryanization. The Czech-Jewish Petschek family owned half of the stock of the
Hubertus Braunkohle A.G. which was Aryanized in 1939. Brecht first became vice-
chairman, then chairman of the new company and held 3.33 percent of its stock.

About 1943 Brecht bought for his own account RM 30,000 Berghuette Teschen
shares from the Koeln branch of the Deutsche Bank. This was former Bohemian
property and was offered by the bank as being for sale "for political reasons." Brecht
believes that these shares formerly were in Jewish hands.

According to information supplied by Rheinbraun itself, corporations of the
Rheinbraun concern acquired from "racially persecuted individuals" seventeen
pieces of real property, including a Jewish cemetery which was converted into coal
mining land. Similarly, corporations in the concern acquired from "racially persecuted individuals" as additional quota in the Rheinische Braunkohlen-Syndikat, a 48
percent interest in a coal distributing firm (of which 52 percent were previously
owned by the Rheinbraun concern) and the total assets of the above-mentioned
Hubertus.

Income. Between 1932 and 30 April 1945, Brecht earned RM 106,800 per annum
as president of Rheinbraun,

> RM 15,000–20,000 per annum in interest and dividends from personal
> assets,
> RM 40,000–60,000 per annum in fees for his different positions on
> boards of directors.

Assets. The assets, including outstanding claims, held by Mr. and Mrs. Gustav Brecht
total RM 870,101 taking security holding at the market value as of August 1945.

Brecht claims he does not hold any external assets.

Blocking Violation. Brecht violated the provisions of Law No. 52, General Order
No. 1 and probably willfully concealed assets. This has been reported to the appropriate enforcement agency.

Sources. The information contained in this report was obtained through interrogation, from questionnaires and reports submitted by Brecht and his principal industrial corporation, and from secondary source material.

Evaluation of Prisoner. As a witness, Brecht has been reluctant, inconsistent, and evasive.

CONCLUSION

Gustav Brecht held a high position in the financial, industrial, and economic life of Germany . . . and is deemed to have committed a crime against peace. . . . His detention is not subject to review.

Appendix. [Chart II] shows the integral relationship between the Deutsche Bank and the Rheinbraun concern. In every single company involved, Brecht is an interlocking director except in RWE.

Additional interlocking directorships between the Deutsche Bank and the coal, electricity, briquette, and synthetic fuel companies are shown by a dotted line, with the number of additional interlocks indicated.

Interlocks between the companies which do not involve the Deutsche Bank Vorstand or Aufsichsrat are now shown [ed. note: a typographical error; this should read "are not shown"] nor are interlocks with the Deutsche Bank on any level other than the Vorstand and Aufsichsrat.

Capital participations are shown by an unbroken line.

Brecht's personal participation is indicated by a solid circle.

Note: RWE, the top holding company, is interlocked with the Deutsche Bank, and Brecht has a capital participation in it. But Brecht is neither on the board of directors nor in the Vorstand.

This chart does not show the Brecht-Deutsche Bank interlocks in companies other than those connected with the RWE concern.

ALBERT PIETZSCH

(VICE-CHAIRMAN OF THE AUFSICHSRAT OF THE DEUTSCHE BANK)

SUMMARY

Albert Pietzsch is one of the most striking examples of a German industrialist who became a very early backer of Hitler and an active participant in Germany's scientific and industrial preparations for war. With Hitler's advent to power Pietzsch rose to high political prominence and office.

Personal Data. Albert Pietzsch was born 28 June 1874 at Zwickau, Saxony, Germany. From 1894 to 1898 he studied mechanical engineering at the Technical Institute, Dresden. In 1900 he began his career as an engineer and in 1910 he

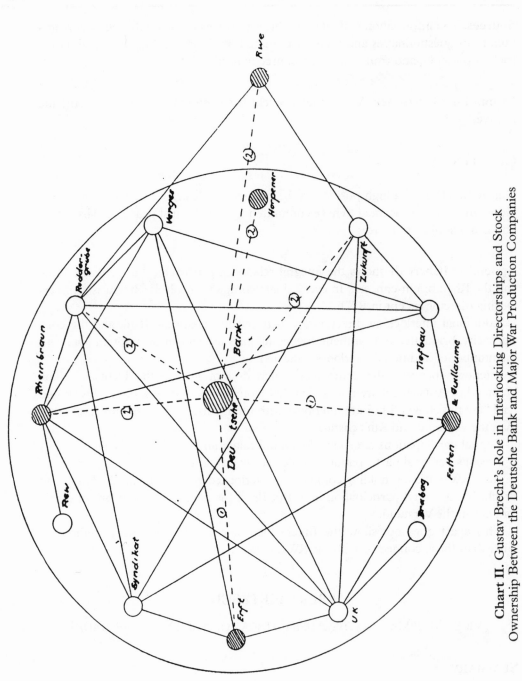

Chart II. Gustav Brecht's Role in Interlocking Directorships and Stock Ownership Between the Deutsche Bank and Major War Production Companies

founded the firm of Adolph Pietzsch, which later became the Elektro-Chemische Werke in Munich.

Pietzsch resided with his wife, Elfriede, and his two daughters, Irene Pietzsch and Renate Petersdorff, at Munich Solln, Terlanerstrasse 24. He was arrested at the end of October 1944 and is currently held at the Civilian Internment Enclosure No. 91.

Political Affiliations. Pietzsch held memberships and offices in the party and government organizations listed below: (symbols: A—grounds for mandatory arrest; B—grounds for blocking of accounts; R—grounds for mandatory removal).

> Member of the NSDAP since 1927. (R)
> Economic adviser to the deputy of the Fuehrer, Hess, 1934–36.
>   (A, B, R)
> President of the Reich Economic Chamber since 1936. (A, B, R)
> President of the Chamber of Commerce, Munich, from 1934 to 1943.
>   (B, R)
> Member of the "Wirtschaftsgruppe" Chemistry since 1934.
> Member of the NSKK.
> Member of the DAF since 1934.
> Member of the NSV since 1939.
> Member of the NS Bund Deutscher Technik.
> Member of the NS Altherrenbund.
> Member der Reichskammer der bildenden Kuenste.
> Wehrwirtschaftsfuehrer. (B, R)
> Special Plenipotentiary for the manufacture of hydrogen peroxide by
>   chemical process. (R)

Early Party Ties. Pietzsch made the acquaintance of Adolf Hitler after his release from prison in 1925 and became his ardent follower and close personal friend. In 1927 he joined the Party. Pietzsch was a financial supporter of the Nazi Party as early as 1925, opened up an office for Hitler in Munich, and also provided financial assistance to individual Party workers. His first contribution in 1925 amounted to RM 7,000, with further contributions of from one to several thousand marks from 1926 to 1932. From 1933 on, he contributed generously to the Adolf Hitler Fund; this fund eventually reached a total of RM 30 to 50 million per year. After Hitler's rise to power these contributions paid large dividends in increased personal power and influence. Pietzsch belonged to the close circle who, at an early stage, got to know Germany's aim for more power, secret armament, expansion and its unavoidable consequence: war.

Rearmament Conferences. In 1935, and then in 1936 and 1938, he participated in conferences with Goering. The first two dealt with the necessity of gaining the support of the industrialists for the rearmament program. As early as 1935 Pietzsch conferred with General Thomas, chief of the *Wehrwirtschaftsstab* (War Economy Staff) of the German High Command, about the integration of the organization of the German economy with the rearmament program of the OKW of the Nazi government, while the 1938 conference dealt with laws governing the Deutsche

Arbeitsfront. Pietzsch was trusted with matters the knowledge of which was confined to the highest of the government and Party officials. At the above-mentioned conference in 1938, the following personalities were present: all members of the Reich Cabinet, Martin Bormann, Himmler, and Pietzsch. As far back as 1933 Pietzsch participated in discussions between Hitler and members of his cabinet relative to the "Law for the Order of National Work," and in 1934 he attended conferences with Hitler and his government on matters of the budget. Pietzsch recalls a scene "which should have brought home to him Hitler's plan for huge rearmaments." Hitler suggested that 500 million RM should be added to the state budget for the increase of the Wehrmacht, and smilingly added: "This is small compared with what is yet to come."

Official Positions. In 1934 Pietzsch became the economic adviser to Deputy Fuehrer Hess. About the same time he resigned from his position as head of *Hauptgruppe V der gewerblichen Wirtschaftsorganisation* (Main Dept V of the trade economy organization) under the Ministry of Economics, in order to retain, in his own words, his "status as economic adviser to the Fuehrer's deputy in the spirit of the National-Socialist program which foresees the creation of an autonomous organization of the economy."

In 1936 Pietzsch was appointed President of the Reich Economic Chamber, one of the highest positions in Nazi German economy. The Reich Economic Chamber was the head office of the seven national branches of business organizations *Reichsgruppen* dealing with industry, handicraft, trade, banking, insurance, power, and tourist traffic. One of the functions of the head office was to consolidate the reports of the various branches in order to give an overall picture of the status of the German economy, its production and productive power. In his capacity as head of the Reich Economic Chamber, he participated in discussions concerning the establishment of liaison between German economy and the Oberkommando der Wehrmacht. These consultations go back as far as 1934. His files also disclose frequent correspondence with Generals Keitel and Thomas on this subject. In the spring of 1938 he submitted a report to General Thomas, the man in charge of the rearmament program for the army, on "The Integration of the Organization of Industrial Economy into the Preparation for Mobilization in the Event of War."

Propaganda Activities. During his career as an economist and politician, Pietzsch delivered many speeches and lectures and published some writings on "economic subjects." In 1938 he published a pamphlet "The Organization of Industrial Economy," commencing his tirade with the following sentence:

> The national socialist state claims the leadership in all walks of German life. Hence it is not possible for economy to go its own ways; it must subordinate itself to the state, its aims and needs. For this reason, the economic policy should never be a policy for itself but a part of the total state policy. . . . Economic policy, therefore, becomes one of the most important parts of the national socialist state leadership.

Industrial and Financial Connections. Pietzsch held the following posts and interests in industry and finance: (symbols: A—grounds for mandatory arrest; B—grounds for blocking of accounts; R—grounds for mandatory removal.)

Vice-Chairman of the Aufsichtsrat and member of the Working Committee of Deutsche Bank. (R, B)

Member of the supervisory board of the Deutsche Reichsbank. (R, B)

Founder and Manager of Elektro-Chemische Werke, Munich, since 1913. Manufacturers of highly concentrated hydrogen peroxide.

Member of the Aufsichtsrat of Siemens-Schuckert Werke, Berlin, since 1936. Manufacturers of electric machinery, instruments, and electrical appliances.

Member of the Aufsichtsrat of the Braunkohlen und Brikett Industrie A.G. (Bubiag) since 1939. Producers of brown coal, briquettes, bricks, electricity, and synthetic fuel. (R)

Member of the Aufsichtsrat of Loewenbrauerei Muenchen since 1936. Producers of beer.

Member of the Aufsichtsrat of Bayerischer Lloyd, Regensburg, since 1935. Danube shipping company (affiliated with Hermann-Goering-Werke).

Member of the Aufsichtsrat of Bavaria-Film, Munich, since 1936. Film producers.

Member of the Board of Directors of Buffalo Electrochemical Works, Buffalo, New York, since 1925. Producers of hydrogen peroxide (capital participation 11 percent).

Member of the Aufsichtsrat of "Société Produits Péroxydees," Paris, since 1932. Producers of hydrogen peroxide.

Member of the Aufsichtsrat of "Union Resinera Española," Santander, Spain, since 1924.

Capital participation in H. Walter Kommandit-Gesellschaft, Kiel. Manufacturers of gas turbines fueled by hydrogen peroxide.

Capital participation in Chemische Fabrik Gersthofen von Transehe & Co., K.G. Manufacturers of "B and C Stoffe" (new fuel for driving gas turbines mentioned below).

Capital participation in Otto Schickert & Co. Plants at Lauterbach and Rhumspringe for the manufacture of highly concentrated hydrogen peroxide as a propellant.

Capital participation in Krause-Linde-Pietzsch Gesellschaft, Munich. Distributors of machinery for concentrating fruit juice.

Capital participation in Honigmannfiltergesellschaft, Munich. Manufacturers of apparatus for cleaning chimney gases.

Connection with Deutsche Bank. Pietzsch's early contributions to the Nazi cause, his high office with the deputy of the Fuehrer and the Reich Economic Chamber, as well as his close personal friendship with the Nazi bigwigs gave him great political influence, which he well understood how to use.

In 1939 he was appointed to the Aufsichtsrat of the Deutsche Bank although the significance of his own industrial enterprises and their connections with the bank alone would not have warranted his nomination to the Aufsichtsrat of the bank. The

Deutsche Bank took him in solely, as Pietzsch put it, "as the man who, in the opinion of the directorate, could speak with the Party about the problems of the bank." In 1943 Pietzsch was made vice-chairman of the board, and as such sat on the important Working Committee, which was kept much more closely informed of the affairs of the bank than the full body of the Aufsichtsrat. When Party and government were pressing for stronger Party representation in the Vorstand of the Deutsche Bank, it was Pietzsch who was called into conference by Reich Minister Funk. A series of consultations between Funk, Pietzsch and the Deutsche Bank management resulted in the appointment to the Deutsche Bank Vorstand of Funk's nominee, Professor Hunke, an ardent Nazi.

Political Patronage. His appointments to the boards of Siemens-Schuckert and of Bubiag were also the result of his political contacts.

Of course, Pietzsch also appointed reliable Nazis to important posts in his own Reich Economic Chamber and, as he emphasized in correspondence, assigned them tasks of special importance.

Pietzsch's Principal Industrial Enterprise. Germany's drive for rearmament, aggrandizement, and war were wholly consistent with Pietzsch's political convictions, for rearmament and war would benefit him materially and make him an outstanding personality through his industrial contribution to the war effort.

Pietzsch was the founder and president of the Elektro-Chemische Werke in Munich, which produced concentrated hydrogen peroxide (H_2O_2) by a new electrochemical process. In peacetime this product is used in the textile industry in 30–40 percent concentration for bleaching purposes and as an antiseptic solution in a 3 percent concentration. Experiments of the Elektro-Chemische Werke resulted in the discovery that only a vacuum pump and steam were required to transform the seemingly innocuous bleaching fluid of 30 percent H_2O_2 into the basic propellant for many deadly weapons.

New Propellant for War Missiles. In 1933 Pietzsch assured Helmuth Walter, designer of V bombs, that it was possible to produce H_2O_2 in a 100 percent concentration in commercial quantities. Walter was also the inventor of a gas turbine which could be fueled with H_2O_2. Experiments were then undertaken for using highly concentrated H_2O_2 for various war purposes. According to a statement of Dr. Albert Pietzsch, as a result of the rapid development of these experiments, the Germans were able through the use of H_2O_2 to operate submarines under water up to twenty-six miles per hour, to develop a wakeless torpedo capable of traveling a distance of fifteen miles at a speed of sixty miles per hour and to begin the rocket propulsion of airplanes around 1936 or 1937. Later developments in jet propulsion, V-1 bombs, and V-2 rockets also made use of highly concentrated H_2O_2. How important for war use Pietzsch considered his discovery is clearly indicated by a letter written on 31 July 1933 to his collaborator engineer Helmuth Walter, stating that he was going to take this matter up with the Fuehrer personally that week.

Affiliated War Production Companies. After the completion of the experimental stage and acceptance of certain types of apparatus by the Reich, the H. Walter K.G. was organized in Kiel. Pietzsch participated in the financing of a large plant to manufacture the Walter-designed apparatus.

Along with the development of the above company a large plant had to be erected to furnish H_2O_2 to drive the apparatus built by the Walter company. Accordingly, a new firm, Otto Schickert & Company, was founded with a plant located at Lauterberg in the Harz mountains. Pietzsch had a 34.5 percent interest in this company.

During the course of the war, other new chemicals were developed for use in conjunction with H_2O_2. The H_2O_2 had been given the code name of "T Stoff" and two of the new chemicals were known as "B and C Stoffe." Following the usual pattern of establishing a new company, the Chemische Fabrik Gersthofen von Transehe & Company was organized and financed by Pietzsch in conjunction with others. The I.G. Farben leased the factory at Gersthofen near Augsburg and also delivered the necessary power and raw materials. All these plants manufactured close to 36,000 tons of 100 percent hydrogen peroxide per year, which was 90 percent of the world capacity.

American Affiliate. In 1925 Pietzsch also founded the Buffalo Electro-Chemical Works in Buffalo, New York, on whose board of directors he sat. The German group always maintained control over the production of this company. The importance of this control can be understood from the fact that the United States Navy from 1937 to 1944 unsuccessfully tried to obtain from American industry satisfactory H_2O_2 in highly concentrated form and that, to meet the navy's needs for the Pacific campaign, German production facilities were requisitioned after the conquest of Germany. This was the case in spite of the fact that thirty years ago the possibility of making 80 percent H_2O_2 and higher was already well known in Germany; in spite of the fact that an agreement providing for the free exchange of patent and process developments existed between the Buffalo Electro-Chemical Works in New York and the Elektro-Chemische Werke in Munich, the latter of which was already producing 70 percent and 80 percent concentrations in factory quantities around 1935; and in spite of the fact that various members of both firms visited each other's plants for technical and business reasons between 1935 and the outbreak of the war.

In the summer of 1944 the plans for the construction of the Walter apparatus and the process for manufacturing the fuels were sold to Japan for RM 37.4 million. For their shares Pietzsch's company, the Elektro-Chemische Werke, Munich, which is capitalized at RM 3 million, received 12 million; the Chemische Fabrik Gersthofen, with a total capital of RM 2 million, received 5.4 million; and the H. Walter & Company with a capital of RM 3.2 million, 20 million.

Income. The rise in Pietzsch's total income between 1930 and 1943 is illustrated below:

Year	Income
From 1930 to 1938—approx.	RM 150,000 per annum
1939—approx.	RM 190,000
1940—approx.	RM 250,000
1941—approx.	RM 310,000
1942—approx.	RM 310,000
1943—approx.	RM 360,000

Assets, External and Domestic. According to information contained in MGAF-1 report submitted to the Military Government, Pietzsch has total domestic assets of RM 1,022,000. Among his external assets are holdings of 510 shares of the Buffalo Electro-Chemical Co., Inc. the value of which is estimated at $51,000, and 32.5 shares of Sucro-Blanc S.A. Cuba, the value of which is reported at $12.00 per share. Another 350 shares of the Buffalo corporation estimated at $35,000 is held by Pietzsch as executor of the estate of his deceased daughter, Ingeborg Schickert, for the benefit of her minor heirs, Dorothea and Franziska, for whom a voting trust of some 22.5 shares of Sucro-Blanc is also held.

Sources. The sources of the preceding statements are personal files taken from the prisoner, files removed from his corporations, questionnaires, his own written statements, and personal interrogations, combined with information contained in a report by the Industrial Investigations Branch, Division of Investigation of Cartels and External Assets on the "Elektro-Chemische Werke."

Evaluation of Prisoner. Pietzsch has been evasive in his answers, tried to play down his political importance in Nazi Germany, and reluctantly admitted knowledge of early rearmament and an active part in the preparation for war only after documents were shown to him proving these points. He would then excuse his forgetfulness on his advanced age, the strenuous past years, and the weakening of his memory. In his written statements Pietzsch expounded lengthy political and economic theories of Hitler in his early years thereby trying to justify his early support of the Nazi cause.

CONCLUSION

Pietzsch held a high position in the financial, economic and political life of Germany . . . and is deemed to have committed a crime against peace. . . . His detention is not subject to review.

HANS RUMMEL

(MEMBER OF THE VORSTAND OF THE DEUTSCHE BANK)

SUMMARY

The Nazi Party's rise to power created for Rummel the opportunity to become a full member of the Vorstand of the Deutsche Bank in 1933, when Theodor Frank and Jacob Wassermann had to resign from the management of the bank in order to create vacancies for "Aryan" personalities. Rummel's adaptability to the new political trend soon bore fruit, and within a short period he became an influential figure among German bankers and industrialists, and, through his manifold directorships in German industry, was able to concentrate considerable economic power in his hands.

Personal Data. Rummel was born 9 March 1882 in Krautostheim, Mittelfranken. His permanent address was Berlin-Dahlem, Arnimallee 12.

He is currently held at the Civilian Internment Enclosure No. 91.

Position in the Deutsche Bank. As a member of the Vorstand, Rummel was in charge of the following departments:

> Internal Organization
> Main Bookkeeping
> Auditing
> Employees' Accounts
> Real Estate

He is an expert in matters of internal organization and in the branch cost accounting system. Rummel also supervised the operations of Deutsche Bank branches in the important districts of Bavaria and Wuerttemberg and therefore his Aufsichtsrat mandates were mainly located in these areas. Rummel's rise to influence in German industry began in 1934 when he was elected to his first Aufsichtsrat position, to which he added seventeen more within a short period. In 1940 Rummel became an Aufsichtsrat member of the Creditanstalt Bankverein, Vienna, the post-Anschluss subsidiary of the Deutsche Bank, a position which he held until 1942 when he was succeeded by Ritter von Halt.

Political Affiliations. Rummel became a member of the Deutsche Arbeitsfront in 1933 and of the NSV in 1934 but his questionnaire indicates that he was not a member of the NSDAP. There is no doubt, however, that he wholeheartedly cooperated with the Nazis in the expansion of German industry for rearmament and aggressive warfare.

He and his bank were also very generous in gifts and contributions to the Party and Party leaders. Besides the usual high contribution to the Adolf Hitler Fund, Winterhilfe, and so on, Rummel concurred in a proposal made by a Nazi Vorstand member of the bank to present an annual money gift of RM 75,000 to the Himmler Circle, and he personally signed the letters forwarding this contribution.

Financial and Industrial Connections. Listed below are Rummel's financial and industrial connections:

Member of the Vorstand	Deutsche Bank
Chairman of Aufsichtsrat	Bayerische Motoren Werke A.G. Munich
	Daimler Benz A.G. Stuttgart

	Vereinigte Kugellagerfabriken A.G. Schweinfurt
	Krauss-Maffei A.G. Munich
	Deutsche Tafelglas A.G. Fuerth
	Porzellanfabrik Lorenz Hutschenreuther A.G. Selb
	Gebr. Junghans A.G. Schrammberg
	Porzellanfabrik Kahla A.G. Kahla
	Elektrische Licht- und Kraftanlagen A.G. Berlin
Vice-chairman of the Aufsichtsrat	Stock & Co. Spiralbohrer A.G. Berlin
	Deutsche Telefon & Kabelwerke A.G. Berlin
Member of the Aufsichtsrat	Deutsche Hypothekenbank A.G.
	Freiherrlich von Tucher'sche Brauerei A.G.
	Heliowatt Werke A.G. Berlin
	Maschinenfabrik Augsburg-Nuernberg A.G.
	Wuerttembergische Metallwarenfabrik Geislingen
	Allianz Lebensversicherungs A.G.

Rummel acquired his first directorship in 1934, nine others in 1935, and seven more in 1936. At the end of the war Rummel still held eighteen directorships in German industrial corporations, of which nine positions were as chairman, two as vice-chairman, and seven as ordinary member of the board of directors.

Connection with War Industries. The companies in which Rummel served as a representative of his bank were, to a large extent, integral parts of the German war machine. They range in size and importance from such large concerns as Daimler Benz A.G., which in 1943 produced approximately RM 1 billion worth of trucks, tanks and airplane engines (as compared with a 1939 total of 225 million); Bayerische Motoren Werke A.G. (BMW), also a producer of trucks, tanks, and airplane engines; United Ball Bearing Works at Schweinfurt; and Siemens-Schuckert Werke, a vital part of the giant electrical trust, to smaller firms which also contributed their part to the German war effort.

The influence which Rummel exercised in these companies was considerable, amounting in some cases to complete control. Bayerische Motoren Werke (BMW), and Daimler Benz A.G. are examples of such wholly-dominated concerns. In these two companies the Deutsche Bank for many years exerted an influence far beyond not only normal bank-customer relations but far beyond the influence frequently exercised by German banks on industrial corporations through loans, stock ownership, interlocks and so forth. The Deutsche Bank has in effect been running these companies ever since the reorganization of BMW and Daimler Benz in 1925 and 1926, respectively. It was kept informed and consulted on all important affairs concerning the two companies as is evidenced in the voluminous files maintained by the Deutsche Bank. The Deutsche Bank, as a matter of course, provided the chairmen of the boards and determined all major policies in these firms. Rummel, who became chairman of the boards in 1943, after the death of his predecessor Emil Georg von Stauss, devoted a large part of his time to the affairs of these companies in order to keep them on the front line of war production. In addition Rummel served on either the Working or Finance Committee of fourteen other companies, and admitted that he took an "active interest" in most of them. This "active interest" amounted to considerable influence in matters of credits, production and labor problems.

Slave Labor. Almost without exception the corporations with which Rummel was connected were users of slave labor. Rummel's own estimate of foreign labor employed by each of his enterprises varied from "a few" to 60 percent of the total labor force. In most cases the percentage was substantial, and in only one case could Rummel definitely assert that no foreign labor was employed. The BMW, for instance, not only employed 10–12,000 foreign workers—60 percent of the total labor force—but it also employed prisoners of war and concentration camp inmates from Dachau at its plant at Allach only ten kilometers away. These facts were well known to Rummel from the BMW's reports, which contained, among other things, data on personnel, including concentration camp inmates and SS prisoners. In February 1944, after a directors' meeting at the BMW plant at Allach, the directors, including Mr. Rummel, personally inspected the halls where the concentration camp inmates worked.

Income. From the director's fees of eighteen corporations alone, Rummel received annual income of over RM 150,000, bringing his total income to about RM 400,000 per year.

CONCLUSION

Rummel held a high position in the financial, industrial, economic, and political life of Germany . . . and is deemed to have committed a crime against peace. . . . His detention is not subject to review.

MAX H. SCHMID

(MEMBER OF THE AUFSICHTSRAT OF THE DEUTSCHE BANK)

SUMMARY

Max H. Schmid has been a member of the Aufsichtsrat of the Deutsche Bank since 1940. His main industrial interests were in the field of paper manufacturing, airplane motors, and vehicle production. From 1933 until 1944 his income increased from RM 100,000 to RM 340,000.

Personal Data. Schmid was born 30 June 1891 in Hof/Bavaria. He claims Austrian citizenship. His wife—Lee Schmid née Roemer—was born in the United States and has U.S. citizenship. There is a daughter by prior marriage, Tatjana, age twenty-six, citizenship Austrian.

Schmid resided at Heidelberg, 6 Wilhelmstrasse. He was arrested 27 October 1945 and is currently held at the Civilian Internment Enclosure No. 91.

Political Affiliations. Schmid was a member of the Deutsche Arbeitsfront from 1933 on. He also belonged to the Weltwirtschaftliche Gesellschaft, Berlin. He claims that he was not a Party member.

Banking and Industrial Connections. Schmid's banking and industrial connections are as follows:

> Deutsche Bank, member of the Aufsichtsrat since 1940.
> Zellstoffabrik Waldhof Mannheim, president. Products: paper, pulp, alcohol, yeast.
> Natronpapier and Zellstoffabriken, Mannheim, vice-chairman of the board of directors. Products: paper and pulp product
> Papierfabrik Fockendorf, member of board of directors. Products: pulp and paper.
> Natron Papierindustrie A.G. Vienna, chairman of board of directors. Products: paper bags.
> DEGUSSA, Frankfurt, member of board of directors. Products: chemicals.
> O.Y. Waldhof A.G., Kexholm, Finland, chairman of board till 1944. Product: pulp.
> Neusiedler A.G. fuer Papierfabrikation, Vienna, member of board of directors. Products: pulp and paper.
> Bayrische Motoren Werke A.G., Munich, member of the board of directors. Products: airplane motors and tanks.
> Daimler Benz A.G., Stuttgart, member of the board of directors. Products: airplane motors, trucks, diesel engines.
> Deutsche Nileswerke A.G., Berlin, member of the board of directors. Products: heavy machine tools.
> Minimax A.G., Berlin, chairman of the board of directors. Products: fire extinguishers, chemicals (smoke screens).
> Riedel-De Haen, Berlin, vice-chairman of the board of directors. Products: pharmaceutical products, chemicals.
> Schnellpressenfabrik, Heidelberg, member of the board of directors. Products: printing machinery, machine tools.
> Heinrich Lanz A.G., Mannheim, vice-chairman of the board of directors. Products: agricultural machinery, gears for tanks.
> N.V. Transport, M'y, Rotterdam, chairman of board, transportation camp.
> N.V. Stevedoors M'y Neptunus, Rotterdam, vice-chairman of board, stevedore business.
> N.V. Cargadorsbedrien "Poswal," Rotterdam, vice-chairman of board, ship brokerage.
> Berlinische Feuerversicherung A.G., Berlin, member of the board of directors, insurance company.

Relations with the Deutsche Bank. Schmid at one time, as an industrial consultant of the Deutsche Bank, undertook the reorganization of various companies in behalf of the bank. It is from this connection that some of his industrial positions were derived, and in the case of several of the corporations the Deutsche Bank has additional representatives on the board.

Slave Labor. Schmid's main company (Zellstoffabrik Waldhof) employed 1–2,000 foreign workers out of a total labor force of 7,000. Most of the other corporations on whose board Schmid sat (Bayerische Motoren Werke and Daimler Benz A.G.), employed 12,000 (60 percent of total labor force) and 15,000 foreign workers, respectively. BMW also used prisoners of war and concentration camp inmates.

Acquisition of Nazi-confiscated property. In 1939 Schmid acquired a house in Vienna which was confiscated from a Polish citizen by the Treuhandstelle Ost.

Income and Assets. The following tabulation lists Schmid's income and assets:

Year	Total Income (in RM)	Directors' Fees (in RM)	Directors' Fees of Deutsche Bank (in RM)
1933	100,000	not stated	
1934	134,000	33,000	
1935	225,000	42,000	
1936	227,000	41,000	
1937	286,000	62,000	
1938	300,000	81,000	
1939	350,000	119,000	
1940	341,000	110,000	3,800
1941	355,000	99,000	5,700
1942	362,000	115,000	5,400
1943	346,000	102,000	5,800
1944	340,000	not stated	not stated

Internal assets: RM   272,860.00
                          RM 1,289,000.00 (wife)
                 Total RM 1,561,860.00

External assets: RM   83,000.00
                          RM   71,500.00 (wife)
                 Total RM   154,500.00

CONCLUSION

Schmid held a high position in the financial, industrial, economic, and political life of Germany . . . and is deemed to have committed a crime against peace. . . . His detention is not subject to review.

HERMANN WERNER VON SIEMENS
(MEMBER OF THE AUFSICHTSRAT OF DEUTSCHE BANK)

SUMMARY

Hermann von Siemens is the head of the Siemens Konzern, one of the largest combines in the electrotechnical field in the world. He was connected with Germany's leading companies in heavy industry and banking. The Siemens Combine spread over the globe from Japan to Argentina, from Sweden to Spain. Its web of foreign subsidiaries was an instrument of German espionage and Nazi propaganda activities. It exploited the working capacity of slave labor, concentration camp inmates, and prisoners of war. The men around Siemens had excellent connections with the Nazi Party, and the Siemens Combine could always count on the support of the Nazi Party and state while the Party could always count on large contributions from the Siemens Konzern.

Personal Data. Hermann von Siemens was born on 9 August 1885 at Berlin. He received his doctorate in physical chemistry in 1913. During World War I he served in the German army as a first lieutenant and entered the Siemens Combine immediately after his discharge.

Prior to his detection he was living at his country house Urschlau, in Ruhpolding, Upper Bavaria, with his family. His wife's maiden name is Charlotte Baroness von Malzahn. They have five children, Wendelin Arnold Oskar, Henning Friedrich Innozenz, Gundula Hertha Henrietta, Thiele Andreas, and Ruprecht. The three first-named children are studying at the University of Bonn at present.

Hermann von Siemens was arrested on 5 December 1945 and is currently in Civilian Internment Camp No. 91.

The Siemens Family. The Siemens family has always ruled the worldwide Siemens Combine; all members of the Siemens family, with the exception of Hermann, continue to direct and influence its activities.

Ernst von Siemens, cousin, at the present time supervises all Siemens establishments located in the American Zone of occupation.

Peter von Siemens, cousin, has been the head of the Argentinian Siemens house, Casa Loner, since about 1937.

Gerhard Pietschker, cousin, still is one of the three members of the Vorstand of Siemens-Plania.

Friedrich Siemens, cousin, still holds the position of vice-chairman of the board of directors of Siemens & Halske, principal company of the Siemens Combine.

Political Affiliations. Before 1933, Siemens was a member of the Deutsch-Nationale Volkspartei, the right-wing, conservative, and nationalistic party which helped Hitler to power. His other political affiliations were:

> Member of the Deutsche Arbeitsfront since 1934
> Member of the N.S. Volkswohlfahrt (National Socialist People's Welfare) since about 1942

Member of the Reichsluftschutzbund (Reich Bund for Air Raid
Protection) since about 1942

Member of Gauwirtschaftskammer, Berlin (District Chamber of
Economics), 1944–1945

Member of the N.S. Bund Deutscher Technik

Member of the N.S. Reichskriegerbund (National Socialist Veterans
Association)

Member of Deutsche Jaegerschaft (German Hunters)

Member of Vorstand of Foerderergemeinschaft der Deutschen
Industrie (Association of Sponsors of German Industry)

In the summer of 1944, he was awarded the (civilian) Kriegsverdienstkreuz I.
Klasse (Cross for Distinguished War Services, first class) by the Speer Ministry.

Siemens did not join many organizations himself. It was through his principal
associates that he maintained the industrial and political connections necessary for
success with the Party and state.

Positions in Industry and Finance. Hermann von Siemens is the head of the
Siemens Combine. Founded in 1847, the Siemens Konzern, together with AEG,
completely monopolizes the German electrotechnical field. . . .

Hermann von Siemens occupies the following key positions in industry and
finance:

(a) In the Siemens Combine:

Chairman of the Aufsichtsrat of Siemens & Halske, A.G., Berlin, the parent company of the Siemens Combine. Total assets of this company in 1942 amounted to
over RM 820 million.

Chairman of the Aufsichtsrat of Siemens-Schuckert Werke A.G., Berlin. Total
assets of this company in 1942 amounted to more than RM 800 million.

All operations of the Siemens Combine were directed through the above two
firms. In Germany alone, Siemens & Halske and Siemens-Schuckert had direct and
indirect interests of 25 percent or more in over one hundred firms, the share capital
of which ranged from RM 50,000 to RM 57 million.

He is also the chairman of the Aufsichtsrat of the Siemens-Plania Werke A.G. fuer
Kohlefabrikate, Berlin (Siemens-Plania Works for Coal Products, Inc.), which has a
capital of RM 22.5 million.

(b) In other companies:

It was not customary for a Siemens to sit on the boards of corporations outside
the combine. Such positions usually were delegated to Vorstand members. That
Hermann von Siemens was a member of the board of directors of the following corporations signifies an especially close relationship:

Vereinigte Stahlwerke, A.G., Duesseldorf, the huge steel trust which, even at the
time of its formation, accounted for one-third or two-fifths of total German heavy
industrial capacity. Three members of its directorate were on the board of directors
of the Deutsche Bank and seven had connections with the Siemens Combine.
Hitler's backer, Fritz Thyssen, was one of the principal figures of this trust. Vereinigte

Stahlwerke contributed RM 100,000 to the special SS Fund put at Himmler's disposal by industry and banking.

Mannesmann Roehrenwerke A.G., Duesseldorf, the leading tube and sheet metal combine with important coal interests, blast furnaces, rolling mills, and the like. It has twenty-one domestic and seventeen foreign trading companies, some of which were acquired through Aryanization and some in the wake of Germany's aggression. Georg Siemens, co-founder of the Deutsche Bank, together with Werner Siemens, the founder of the Siemens concern, were instrumental in establishing Mannesmann in the last decade of the nineteenth century. The ties between Siemens and Mannesmann remain close to this day. Siemens owns Mannesmann stock and two members of the Siemens family, Hermann von Siemens and Friedrich Siemens, vice-chairman of Siemens & Halske, are on the board of directors of Mannesmann. The interlocking relationship between Siemens, Mannesmann, and the Deutsche Bank is confirmed in the minutes of the 1937 General Stockholders' Meeting of Mannesmann, which lists Friedrich Siemens as "representative of the Deutsche Bank."

Friedrich Krupp A.G., Essen, Germany's biggest war production enterprise whose owner sponsored Hitler's rise to power. Alfred Krupp von Bohlen, at the same time, was a member of the Siemens-Schuckert board of directors.

Deutsche Bank, Berlin. Carl Friedrich von Siemens, Hermann's uncle and predecessor as head of the Siemens Combine, had been a member of the board of directors of the Deutsche Bank and a member of the bank's Working Committee until 1938 when Hermann took his place on the board of directors.

Relationship Between the Deutsche Bank and the Siemens Combine. . . . Tied to the House of Siemens from the day of its inception, the Deutsche Bank has perpetuated a close kinship with the Siemens concern through generations. Some of its manifestations were interlocking directorates, representations of eight-figure amounts of stock by Deutsche Bank at Siemens stockholders' meetings, Siemens ownership of Deutsche Bank stock, and the extensive use by Siemens of the facilities of the Deutsche Bank, its branches and affiliates. . . . A partial survey of the most recent interlocking directorships shows manifold links between the two.

Siemens & Halske A.G.

Oswald Roesler	Vorstand, D.B.	Aufsichtsrat, S. & H.
Hermann v. Siemens	Chairman, S. & H.	Aufsichtsrat, D.B.
Oskar Sempell	Vorstand, S. & H.	Aufsichtsrat, Deutsche Ueberseeische Bank
Ernst Kraus	Vorstand, S. & H.	Aufsichtsrat, Creditanstalt Bankverein, Vienna
Fritz Jessen	Vorstand, S. & H.	Advisory Council of Deutsche Bank for Berlin-Brandenburg district
Hermann Muenchmeyer	Aufsichtsrat, D.B.	Aufsichtsrat, S. & H.

Siemens-Schuckert Werke A.G.

Hans Rummel	Vorstand, D.B.	Aufsichtsrat, S-SW
Albert Pietzsch	Vice-chairman, Working Committee of D.B.	Aufsichtsrat, S-SW
Hermann v. Siemens	Chairman, S-SW	Aufsichtsrat, D.B.
Oskar Sempell	Vorstand, S-SW	Aufsichtsrat, Deutsche Ueberseeische Bank, Berlin
Hermann Reyss	Vorstand, S-SW	Aufsichtsrat, Deutsche Ueberseeische Bank, Berlin
Fritz Jessen	Vorstand, S-SW	Advisory Council of Deutsche Bank for Berlin-Brandenburg district

There are many additional interlocks between Siemens subsidiaries in Germany and the Deutsche Bank.

Interlocking directorships also appear between Siemens subsidiaries in foreign countries and Deutsche Bank subsidiaries and affiliates there, for example:

Elektrizitaets A.G., Pressburg, Czechoslovakia. Its manager, Friedrich Sobotka, is on the *Verwaltungsrat* (managing council) of Deutsche Bank's Slovakian subsidiary, the Union Bank, Pressburg.

Siemens Elektrizitaets A.G., Prague, Czechoslovakia. Its Vorstand chairman, Viktor Ulbricht, is a member of the board of directors of the Boehmische Union Bank, Prague, a subsidiary of the Deutsche Bank.

Compania Platense de Electricidad Siemens-Schuckert, Buenos Aires, Argentina. Alfred Hermann, the manager of the Deutsche Ueberseeische Bank in Buenos Aires, is on the board of directors of this Siemens subsidiary.

Wiener Kabel & Metallwerke A.G., Vienna, Austria. Ernst Kraus, chairman of the board of directors, is also a member of the board of directors of the Creditanstalt Bankverein, Vienna, which is controlled by the Deutsche Bank.

It is believed that a more complete investigation will disclose interlocking directorships, in addition to the ones named above, between Siemens subsidiaries and Deutsche Bank affiliates wherever the two met on foreign soil.

The large blocks of Siemens stock represented at stockholders' meetings by Deutsche Bank further confirm the close collaboration between the concern and the bank:

Year	Date of Meeting	Amount of Stock Voted by D.B.
1933	February 28	RM 13,334,300
1934	March 7	RM 13,185,200
1935	February 28	RM 12,919,900
1936	February 29	RM 14,000,000
1937	February 25	RM 13,711,600
1938	February 24	RM 12,317,200
1939	February 28	RM 15,190,000
1939	June 13	RM 16,543,100
1940	March 19	RM 14,406,000
1941	March 18	RM 14,028,000
1942	April 23	RM 14,605,500
1943	March 23	RM 42,050,000

While Deutsche Bank thus controlled a considerable number of Siemens votes, Siemens owned substantial blocks of Deutsche Bank stock.

In 1932 Siemens & Halske acquired an amount of nominal RM 2,000,000 Deutsche Bank stock to aid the Deutsche Bank in its crisis.

In 1936 Siemens & Halske acquired hfl. 250,000 stock of H. Albert de Bary & Co., Amsterdam (a Deutsche Bank subsidiary), which was sold to the Deutsche Bank early in 1942.

In 1937 Siemens & Halske bought nominal RM 2,000,000 Siemens-Schuckert nominal RM 1,000,000 Deutsche Bank stock.

The investment and commercial banking resources of the Deutsche Bank were always at the disposal of the Siemens concern.

❑ ❑ ❑

Following is a partial list of bond issues of Siemens & Halske and Siemens-Schuckert, in which the Deutsche Bank headed the syndicate.

```
1926—    $24,000,000
1930—RM 10,000,000
1938—  RM 9,000,000 (approx.)
```

During the war the Deutsche Bank extended guarantee facilities (performance bonds) to Siemens amounting to RM 10 million. Due to their liquid positions during the last ten years, the two main Siemens corporations maintained large credit balances with Deutsche Bank. On the other hand, whenever required, Deutsche Bank extended substantial loans to Siemens subsidiaries, e.g., a RM 50 million loan to the Telefunken Radio company during the war years. The bank also headed syndicates in connection with capital increases in the Siemens concern, such as the issue of new stock of Elektrische Licht- und Kraftanlagen A.G. in 1945.

The Deutsche Ueberseeische Bank, a subsidiary of the Deutsche Bank, served as the principal banking connection in the Latin American business of the Siemens concern. It facilitated the transfer of funds for purchases in Argentina and extended loan facilities for the same purpose and guarantees for Siemens delivery contracts.

Employment of Concentration Camp and Slave Labor. The Siemens Combine made extensive use of concentration camp inmates and foreign labor.

Siemens set aside special work halls where several hundred Berlin Jewesses labored until the Gestapo deported them. Workshops were set up for Siemens in concentration camps. There were "Siemens Commandos" in Buchenwald, in Oranienburg, and in Ravensbrueck.

Fifteen hundred female concentration camp inmates manufactured ammunition for Siemens & Halske in the Ravensbrueck workshops alone. They worked twelve hours daily. SS women guarded them and Siemens personnel supervised their work. The statements of an inmate of this concentration camp and of two employees of the Siemens plant within the camp speak for themselves. Some abstracts follow:

> This firm (Siemens) distinguished itself because all the inmates, women of all nationalities, looked especially miserable and were in a very poor condition. There was a possibility for Siemens to intervene with the camp management in order to get better food and decent barracks for the prisoners who had to do hard work . . . but nothing was done, no, on the contrary, the employees of the firm mistreated the prisoners and made life more difficult for them.

> The gentlemen from Siemens did not care how many lives were lost. Whenever the required job was not finished in time, the prisoners were beaten cruelly and this beating was ordered by Siemens.

> When a prisoner did not do [her] work the right way, but had to return the material given out, Mr. Boehnke [Siemens foreman] . . . made a report of sabotage to the SS supervisor . . . and the prisoner was sent to the penal barracks.

But Siemens did not only profit from cheap concentration camp labor, the employment of foreign slave workers also paid high dividends.

By the end of 1944 Siemens & Halske and its wholly-owned subsidiaries employed a total of about 220,000 workers of which 35,000 were foreign slave workers. Of this last figure, according to Siemens, about 20,000 were "Ostarbeiter" (workers deported from Eastern regions, mainly Russian territories, who were kept in special camps and had less liberty then the other foreign workers). Workers from France (many women), Holland, Denmark, Czechoslovakia, Italy, the Ukraine (mainly women), and Russian prisoners of war also toiled in Siemens plants.

Espionage. The far-flung operations of the Siemens Combine and the close ties with leading Nazi Party agencies lent themselves readily to espionage and Nazi propaganda activities.

Before the outbreak of the war, the Siemens Orient subsidiary covering the Near East and the crucial Suez area was headed by Willy van Meeteren, who is reported to have been one of the most active enemy espionage agents in Egypt. Several other officials of the Siemens Orient, among them Franz Waldman, chief engineer, and Frederico Biesler, in charge of correspondence and documents, are reported as particularly active Nazi propagandists.

Nazi Personnel Policies. The files of the Siemens Combine contain frequent references to anti-Semitic policies long before Hitler's rise to power. Three memoranda signed by von Witzleben, personnel manager and one of the men closest to Siemens, illustrate this point:

> 19 Sept. 38, Memo on conference with Count Wedel, Potsdam Chief of Police, states that the Siemens concern has always been attacked for its anti-Semitic attitude and that the percentage of Jewish employees in the Siemens concern has always been far below that of the German population.

> 12 Sept. 38, Inter-Office Memo: "A house like ours which, for decades, has been described by Jewry as a stronghold of anti-Semitism . . ."

> Inter-Office Memo to Drs. Jessen and Springer: "I availed myself of the opportunity to remind Mr. von Siemens of his planned visit with Mr. Streicher."

When Hitler's anti-Semitic laws made it impossible for Jews to work and live in Germany the Siemens concern also exploited the opportunities for expansion presented in Aryanizations. It availed itself of the services of the Deutsche Bank in the acquisition of the Aronwerke Elektrizitaets A.G., manufacturers of electric meters and radio receiving sets. Manfred Aron, owner of the majority of the nominal RM 8 million share capital, had been put under great pressure by the Party. Several times arrested by the Gestapo, he finally, in August 1935, consented to sell out. The Deutsche Bank took over the nominal RM 7,464,000 shares of the Aron family and resold them partly to Siemens, partly to the Siemens holding company, Elektrische Licht- und Kraftanlagen A.G. The name of the Aryanized firm was changed to Heliowatt Werke A.G.; Hans Rummel of the Deutsche Bank Vorstand became a member of the Aufsichtsrat of Heliowatt.

Shortly before the outbreak of the war, the Siemens concern acquired a considerable part of Mr. Koppel's share in the Osram G.m.b.H., the second largest manufacturer of electric lamps in the world. This company (total assets RM 172,542,000 in 1941) had been owned jointly by the Siemens Combine, AEG, and Koppel, a Jew.

In March 1942 the Siemens Combine instructed a bank to buy Hazemeijer shares out of Jewish-Dutch property, or enemy property.

The Men around Hermann von Siemens. The picture of Siemens would not be complete without mentioning the men he chose as his assistants. Hermann von Siemens did not need personally to become a member of many of the economic or political organizations set up and utilized by the Nazis because his assistants, in his stead, represented the House of Siemens in such organizations and maintained a strong and friendly relationship with the leaders of the Nazi Party and the government.

Three Siemens Vorstand members represented the Siemens interests in head organizations of the Speer Ministry: Lueschen, NSDAP member and SS major; Benkert, longtime NSDAP member; and Professor Kuepfmueller, NSDAP member and SS officer. Lueschen was the chairman of the Vorstand of Siemens & Halske and held several other high government positions (member of Reichsgruppe Industrie, member of German Wage and Price Control Board, member of Reich Committee for Increase of Productive Capacity).

Among the members of the Vorstand of the two key companies, Siemens & Halske and Siemens-Schuckert, alone, we find that

> five were Wehrwirtschaftsfuehrer
> three were members of advisory councils of Wirtschaftsgruppen (syndicates of economic groups within the Nazi corporate setup),
> four were chiefs of *Fachgruppen* (trade associations).

Siemens not only saw to it that his men were chosen to sit on Nazi committees, he also saw to it that men with good Party connections were members of the board or the Vorstand of his main companies. Pietzsch, von Stauss, and Bingel are such men.

An early NSDAP member, Hitler's personal friend and Hess's economic adviser, Albert Pietzsch became a member of the Siemens & Halske board of directors in 1938 to strengthen, by his own admission, the Siemens standing with the Party.

E. G. von Stauss until his death in 1942 represented the Deutsche Bank with Siemens & Halske. He was an NSDAP member, vice-president of the Reichstag, had good connections with Hitler, Schacht, and Dr. Goebbels, and was a personal friend of Goering.

Dr. Rudolf Bingel was promoted from a position at Siemens's Mannheim branch to a higher salaried and more important position in the Berlin head office about the time of Hitler's rise to power. Bingel was a member of the Keppler Circle, the economic group around Himmler.

Contributions to Nazi Funds. Only a few data are given here.

In the year 1934/35, the Siemens concern contributed RM 717,639.60 to Nazi causes. Of this amount RM 200,000 went to the *Winterhilfe* (winter aid) and RM 483,326.60 to the Adolf Hitler Spende.

By 1943/44, this amount had tripled. Out of a total of RM 2,227,402.25, RM 680,402 went to the Winterhilfe and RM 1,545,568 to the Adolf Hitler Spende.

RM 100,000 were given to the special SS fund put at Himmler's disposal by industry and banking. Dr. Bingel, one of Hermann von Siemens's closest assistants, presented this gift in the name of the House of Siemens.

Income. Siemens pleads inability to remember his full income. Siemens's main sources of income were his salary, bonus payments from Siemens works, dividends from Siemens & Halske shares and patents, and director's fees. The following are the rather moderate income figures furnished by Siemens himself:

1934—RM 130,000 per year
1935—RM 130,000 per year
1936—RM 130,000 per year
1937—RM 130,000 per year
1938—RM 130,000 per year
1939—RM 170,000 per year
1940—RM 170,000 per year
1941—RM 170,000 per year
1942—RM 170,000 per year
1943—RM 230,000 per year
1944—RM 220,000 per year

Assets. Siemens evaluates his property at RM 5,302,000 and claims not to own any external assets.

Evaluation of Prisoner. As a witness, Siemens has been very reluctant and evasive.

Remarks. The Decartelization Branch of the Economics Division of OMGUS in Berlin has completed an investigation of the Siemens Combine. Its report develops a detailed picture of the activities of the Siemens Combine both in Germany and abroad.

CONCLUSION

Hermann von Siemens held a high position in the financial, industrial, and economic life of Germany . . . and is deemed to have committed a crime against peace. . . . His detention is not subject to review.

PART TWO

OFFICE OF MILITARY GOVERNMENT FOR GERMANY (U.S.)

Finance Division
APO 742
Report on the Investigation of the DRESDNER BANK
1946
Prepared by the Financial Investigations Section

The following personnel participated, for varying periods, in the investigation of the Dresdner Bank:

Sidney L. Klepper	Irving Saxe
John Higby	Erna Uiberall
Helga Wolski	Norbert Heilpern
Saul Kagan	Paul Brand
Jules Schlezinger	Renee Brand
Wm. Schmeling	Emil Lang
Henry H. Collins	Patricia Clay

CHAPTER XV

Recommendations

It is recommended that:

1. Vigorous action be taken to effectuate the Dodge Plan for the decentralization of banking as quadripartite law.

2. The Dresdner Bank be dissolved and liquidated.

3. The Dresdner Bank and its responsible officials, including entire membership of the Aufsichtsrat and Vorstand and certain department heads and branch or affiliate managers be indicted and tried as war criminals.

4. The responsible officials of the Dresdner Bank be removed and banned from positions of importance in the political or economic life of Germany.

CHAPTER XVI

Summary

Investigation of the Dresdner Bank has revealed it to be an excessive concentration of economic power and a war criminal.

The Dresdner Bank has no American counterpart. It was a "universal" bank, engaging in commercial and investment as well as in branch banking. It controlled and voted huge blocks of shares of other corporations although owning only a small portion of them. It dominated established stock exchanges and maintained what was virtually a private stock exchange in its own bank. Its personnel had such interlocking connections with that of other financial and industrial institutions that together they formed a single economic entity.

The Dresdner Bank is the second largest commercial bank in Germany. [Although] on the verge of bankruptcy in 1931–1932 when it passed through two financial reorganizations, it emerged during the Nazi regime as an excessive concentration of economic power holding 14 percent of the total assets of all commercial banks in Germany, amounting to 8.6 billion Reichsmarks. During the six-year period between 1938–1944 alone, the Dresdner Bank's assets showed a threefold increase and its commercial deposits an increase of equal magnitude. The predominant position which the Dresdner Bank attained during the twelve yars of Nazi rule was the result of its ruthless exploitation of the opportunities for enrichment afforded by the Nazi regime, first within Germany and later in all the countries of conquered Europe.

The Dresdner Bank was closely integrated with the major enterprises of German industry and wielded a dominant financial control over entire key sectors of the German rearmament program. The interlocking connections and relationships existing between the Dresdner Bank and German industry become evident in the fact that the bank's nine Vorstand members held [among] them 195 directorships in major corporations, while Carl Goetz in addition held a greater number of directorships in heavy industry than any other figure in Germany.

The Dresdner Bank became the principal financial underwriter and banker of the entire military aircraft industry in Germany from its first establishment down to the last months of the war. It also from 1934 onward headed the banking syndicate that financed the first synthetic fuel combine, the Brabag, which embraced the entire lignite industry in Germany. It conspired in 1937 with Admiral Raeder of the German Naval High Command to procure and conceal large oil reserves in Mexico and Iraq for the supply of the German Navy in the event of war. It headed the banking syndicate which in 1937 financed the initial capitalization of the Hermann-Goering-Werke notwithstanding the fact that the latter was universally considered a poor credit risk. The Hermann-Goering-Werke, which became Germany's second largest steel producer, was created for the express purpose of assuring a plentiful supply of iron ore to the German rearmament program. As the principal banker of the Hermann-Goering-Werke during its expansion period, the Dresdner Bank on behalf of its client took over the eight largest coal, steel, machine tool, and armaments companies in Czechoslovakia, including the Skoda Works, directly after the annexation.

The Dresdner Bank emerged as the most active banking institution of Germany in the exploitation and spoliation of the economic resources of the countries of conquered Europe. Between the years 1937–1942 an eightfold increase in the number of its foreign affiliates took place. Its foreign operations became an integral part of the Nazi aim to dominate Europe, and its goals were defined by Goering, Funk, and other Nazi leaders to be:

1. to harness the economic resources of the conquered countries to the German war machine;
2. to integrate the economies of the conquered countries with that of Germany and to bring about permanent control of the industrial, commercial, and banking resources of these countries.

In Czechoslovakia, Poland, Belgium, Holland, and Luxembourg, the Dresdner Bank implemented these Nazi objectives by the ruthless acquisition and absorption of innumerable banking and industrial enterprises.

The Dresdner Bank together with its subsidiaries and affiliates was the leading agency in the forcible Aryanization of Jewish-owned businesses in Germany as well as in the conquered countries. It acquired many businesses, large and small, by having the Jewish proprietors tossed into jail or concentration camps where, on pain of death, they were compelled to transfer their interests to the Dresdner Bank. It also employed its Party and SS connections to locate businesses available for Aryanization; it supplied new "purchasers" to whom it granted the necessary credits to carry on and then collected fees in proportion to the value of its services.

The tremendous growth and expansion of the Dresdner Bank during the years between 1933–1942 were made possible by the closeness of its ties with the government, the Party, the SS and affiliated organizations. No other major commercial bank in Germany was as thoroughly Nazified in its policies, personnel, and practices as the Dresdner Bank. Three members of the Vorstand and the Aufsichtsrat were SS Brigadefuehrer and seven were members of the notorious Keppler or Himmler Circle. Three of the four most influential personalities at the Dresdner Bank were SS Brigadefuehrer Fritz Kranefuss, SS Brigadefuehrer Emil Meyer and SS Obersturmbannfuehrer Karl Rasche. During a nine-year period the Dresdner Bank supplied SS organizations with credits of tens of millions of Reichsmarks and out of its own treasury made contributions of 50,000 RM per year to the Himmler Circle for "Special Purposes."

Through its affiliates and subsidiaries, the Dresdner Bank acted also during the prewar years as an outlet for Nazi propaganda in South America, the Balkans, and the Near East, and many of its officials and employees in those countries played leading roles in these activities.

The Dresdner Bank employed its excessive power in the economy of Germany and of the conquered countries of Europe to participate in the execution of the criminal aims of the Nazi regime. It acted as an accessory to the perpetration of crimes against peace, war crimes, and crimes against humanity. The direct responsibility for these crimes lies with the Vorstand members of the Dresdner Bank who directed them, with the Aufsichtsrat members who approved and participated in them, and with the officials and employees who executed them.

CHAPTER XVII

Growth of the Dresdner Bank

The Dresdner Bank is the second largest German bank. It attained its position through absorption of smaller banks in Germany and through foreign expansion.

The Dresdner Bank was founded on 12 November 1872 in Dresden, with a capital of RM 24,000,000. By 1945 its expanded business required a capital of RM 190,000,000 including undistributed profits.

❑ ❑ ❑

The bank took a leading part in the foundation of the German Orient Bank (Deutsche Orientbank) and the German South American Bank (Deutsch Suedamerikanische Bank) in 1906. It established connections with the important banks of other countries, such as the Morgan bank in New York and with the Banque de Paris et des Pays-Bas.

World War I and the inflation that followed left the Dresdner Bank in a critical condition. The bank did not succeed in reaching the height of prosperity it had enjoyed in imperial Germany and the international financial crisis that began in 1929 shook the stability of the Dresdner Bank, along with the others. The year 1931 was the climax of the banking crisis in Germany and the German government had to step in. From that time until 1937, when the major banks were "reprivatized," 90 percent of the share capital of the Dresdner Bank was held by the government.

The Dresdner started its second period of expansion when it absorbed, with government blessing, Germany's fourth largest bank, the failing Darmstaedter Bank. After the merger, the institution had a capital of RM 150,000,000, 332 branches, RM 2,175,000 deposits, and the support of the government.

❑ ❑ ❑

The ties between the Dresdner Bank and the smaller and specialized banks are strongly evident in the considerable number of bankers representing mortgage and private banks on the Aufsichtsrat of the Dresdner Bank. Among these Robert Pferdmenges (of the Aryanized banking house Pferdmenges & Co., formerly Oppenheim & Co.), Josef Wiehen (Vorstand, Deutsche Central Boden Kredit, largest German mortgage bank), and Otto Kaemper (Vorstand of four mortgage banks) are outstanding.

The widespread control and influence of the Dresdner Bank over regional, private, and specialized banks proved themselves extremely useful in forming the underwriting syndicates which supplied the huge capital needs of the expanding armament industry.

While setting its domestic house in order the Dresdner Bank had not overlooked the foreign field and was steadily increasing the number of its foreign affiliations, adding the Societatea Bancara Romana in Bucharest and the Bank fuer Handel und Gewerbe in Danzig in 1929 and 1930. With the advent of Nazism the Dresdner Bank's rate of expansion was accelerated and its foreign operations became an integral part of Nazi Germany's plan to dominate Europe.

Austria was the first of the smaller countries which Hitler Germany planned to swallow. Intensive preparations and careful plans were made which culminated in the Anschluss on 11 March 1938. The Dresdner Bank, which had conspired with the Nazis to construct the military machine that made these plans possible, had its role to play. As the sole shareholder of the Mercurbank in Vienna, its influence was to be mobilized in the service of the economic integration that was to follow the political. The Dresdner Bank became an accomplice to the Nazi conspiracy against Austria.

Correspondence between Wilhelm Keppler, chief economic adviser to Hitler, and Carl Goetz, chairman of the Aufsichtsrat, clearly outlines the role assigned to the Dresdner Bank in the preparations for the acquisition of Austria. In a letter dated 13 July 1937, Keppler writes:

> Last week I attended political negotations in Vienna, and yesterday upon my return I discussed these matters with the Fuehrer. In the course of this conversation we discussed the economic strongholds *(Stuetzpunkte)* that Germany has in Austria. The Fuehrer expressed his definite view that we must maintain and expand those strongholds, especially the Mercurbank, and in that connection it is imperative to Aryanize this bank, for otherwise the desired goal will not be attainable.

❑ ❑ ❑

The next day, 14 July 1937, Carl Goetz expressed his understanding of the necessity of Aryanizing the Mercurbank in order to accomplish the aims of the Fuehrer in Austria:

> There is no doubt in our bank about the desirability of Aryanizing the Mercurbank and maintaining it as a German stronghold. There is always the problem of attaining this aim without affecting the considerable Jewish clientele of the bank. . . . I have assigned Dr. Meyer and Dr. Rasche from our Vorstand to get in touch with your office immediately. The specialists are in Berlin and a written report about the steps undertaken in this matter since the acquisition in 1932 are at the disposal of the above gentlemen. Heil Hitler.

When "Der Tag" arrived, the Dresdner Bank set out to build its stronghold in Austria into the main vehicle for penetration of Eastern and Southeastern Europe. That vehicle was the Laenderbank Wien, created through the merging of the Mercurbank with the Austrian subsidiaries of the Banque des Pays de l'Europe Centrale and those of the Zivnostenska Banka in Prague.

❑ ❑ ❑

Six months later the Dresdner Bank was prepared to share the spoils of the Sudeten annexation. It took over thirty-two Sudeten branches of the Boehmische Escompte Bank and four branches of the Zivnostenska Banka. This amputation weakened the Escompte Bank so greatly (loss of thirty-two of a total of thirty-eight branches) that its subsequent absorption into the Dresdner fold was a foregone conclusion. The occupation of Czechoslovakia in March 1939 formally completed the acquisition of this bank. (See [Chapter XXI], Dresdner Bank in Czechoslovakia.)

The military invasion of Poland and its Nazification under the General Gouvernement was a prelude to subsequent invasion by the Dresdner Bank. Before the end of 1939 it had opened branches in seven major cities, and by 1940 it had established two special banks for Poland—the Ostbank, Posen; and the Kommerzialbank, Cracow. The latter was controlled by the Laenderbank Wien, but was taken over in 1940 by the Dresdner Bank itself in order to coordinate all operations in Poland. (See [Chapter XXI], Dresdner Bank in Poland.)

On 12 October 1939, less than a month after the blitzkrieg in Poland, Emil Meyer, SS member of the Vorstand, had completed a visit to Poland for the purpose of establishing Dresdner Bank operations in that country.

❑ ❑ ❑

After May 1940 branches were opened in Eupen, Metz, Strasbourg, and other cities of the occupied territories.

The wealth of Belgium, Holland, and Luxembourg became the object of such a mad scramble among the banks that it necessitated mediation by Hjalmar Schacht.

This fight for supremacy in Belgium between the Deutsche Bank and the Dresdner Bank is described by Carl Goetz in a memorandum to Schacht:

> In May of this year (1940) during the German advances in Holland and Belgium I called during a conference the attention of Minister Funk to my long years of contact with Belgium. . . . I placed my services at his disposal, especially in the early period after the occupation of Brussels and Antwerp. Some time later when the Bank Department of the Ministry of Economics inquired which banks in Belgium we worked with, I stated that the Société Générale and the Banque de Bruxelles were close to us. After the occupation of Brussels we met several times with the leading officials of the Société Générale in connection with the taking over by us of the Eupen and Malmedy branches of the Société Général . . . Some time later, during a conference with Mr. Riehle of the Ministry of Economics (in charge of Banking Penetration), we were informed that the German banks must seek the closest economic integration of the Belgian economy with Germany. I suggested that the Ministry prevent competition of the large banks (Deutsche and Dresdner). I pointed out that such competition would be detrimental to the general German standing and not add to the prestige of German banking. In

the course of the discussion it was suggested that an arrangement be worked out whereby one bank will receive a preferential status in Holland and the other in Belgium.

This struggle for the spoils of the West was finally settled, and the Dresdner Bank established itself in Belgium through a "Stuetzpunkt" affiliate, the Continentale Bank. In Holland it maintained only a securities "purchasing" house, the Handelstrust West. (See [Chapter XXI], The Dresdner Bank in the Netherlands and The Dresdner Bank in Belgium).

At the same time the Dresdner Bank took over the control of the Internationale Bank in Luxembourg from the Banque de Bruxelles and Banque de l'Union Parisienne, thus transforming its former minority holding into complete control.

Germany's occupation of the Balkans brought to the Dresdner Bank the Kroatische Landesbank and increased its control over Societatea Bancara Romana.

It spread its influence to Greece by establishing the Griechische Deutsche Finanzierungs A.G. and a working agreement with the Banque d'Athenes. Bulgaria and Hungary were brought into its domain by acquisitions of sizable participations in the Bulgarische Handelsbank, Sofia, and the Ungarische Allgemeine Kreditbank, Budapest, formerly in French hands. Correspondence between the Dresdner and the Reich Ministry of Economics shows that the French themselves were made to pay the purchase price of these shares through the notorious Clearing Account No. 1006 at the Reichskreditkasse, for capital transfers from occupied countries.

The conquered areas of Russia and the Baltic states were served by a Dresdner Bank subsidiary called initially the Ostland Bank and later renamed the Handels- und Kreditbank, Riga.

Prior to the Russo-German war the Dresdner Bank fulfilled a mission of the German government in the Baltic States by "taking at the express desire of your Ministry (Ministry of Economics) an interest at the Dorpater Bank in Reyal (Estonia) in spite of the great risks we were aware of at that time." The Dresdner Bank was rewarded. It received almost a monopolistic banking status in Lithuania, Latvia, and Estonia.

Within five years (1937–1942) the Dresdner Bank increased eightfold the number of its foreign affiliates. This tremendous growth was largely a result of the bank's cooperation with Nazi Germany's military and political aggression.

❏ ❏ ❏

Analysis of the growth of assets, commercial deposits, savings deposits, number of branches and employees readily shows the tremendous development of the small banking house founded in Dresden in the early years of Bismarck's Germany. In the six-year period 1938–1944 the total assets of the Dresdner Bank tripled from RM 2,785 million in 1938 to RM 8,613 million in 1944. These figures represent about one-sixth of the total assets of all German commercial banks in this year.

A corresponding increase in the total deposits of the Dresdner Bank is evident in the same period. From RM 2,034 million in 1938, deposits grew to RM 6,176 million in 1944, a 300 percent increase. The figures on savings deposits are incomplete, but a sevenfold increase occurred during the same period (1938–1944).

❏ ❏ ❏

The number of employees of the Dresdner Bank rose from 11,157 in 1933 to 13,700 in 1943, but the figures for the war period include many soldiers, as they were still carried on the employment rolls. . . . These figures . . . were compiled from official Dresdner Bank statistics and by employees of the present staff from the partial records it has reassembled. The tripling of assets and deposits and the increase in the number of branches and employees reflect the increased power of the bank which enabled it to help execute the financial aims of the Nazi state in Germany and Europe.

The history and the statistics on the growth of the Dresdner Bank emphasize the fact that it was a concentration of financial power. The nerve center of these tremendous resources was in Berlin, the capital of Nazi Germany [and . . .] could instantaneously mobilize a tremendous economic power behind any desired project. The story of the operations of the Dresdner Bank, told in subsequent sections of this report, constantly reemphasizes the importance to Nazi Germany of this fact. . . . The Nazis found in this huge central institution an instrument shaped to their needs and they made full use of its potentialities.

CHAPTER XVIII

Organization of the Dresdner Bank

The general structure of the Dresdner Bank was in keeping with German law, but within that framework, there were divisions of duties necessitated by the complex and comprehensive financial business handled by it.

THE GENERAL MEETING

German corporation law provides for a general meeting of the stockholders once per year. . . .

THE AUFSICHTSRAT

Corresponding most closely to the board of directors of an American corporation, the Aufsichtsrat was the stockholders' agency for controlling the policies of the bank. It convened about twice a year and its chief functions were the supervision of the work of its executives, the appointment of the Vorstand members, and the approval of the periodic balance sheets. Because it held the power of appointment and removal from the Vorstand, the Aufsichtsrat was responsible for the actions of that body.[1] . . . The chairman of the Aufsichtsrat and Arbeitsausschuss since 1936, when he was transferred from the Vorstand, was Carl Goetz, the key personality of the bank. . . .

The [other] members of the Aufsichtsrat were representatives of the most important customers of the bank, and included prominent industrialists, outstanding political personalities, and others with whom the bank wished to maintain close and friendly relations. Although German corporation law limited the membership of the Aufsichtsrat to twenty, that of the Dresdner Bank, by special permission of the Ministries of Economics and Justice, consistently had twenty-five or more members on it.

THE *ARBEITSAUSSCHUSS* (WORKING COMMITTEE)

This was a small committee of Aufsichtsrat members who exercised a more active supervision of events than was possible for the larger membership. It met as fre-

---

[1] *Editor's note:* See the Deutsche Bank chapters for greater detail on the operations of the Aufsichtsrat, Vorstand and other aspects of corporate organization under German law.

quently as once a month and exercised the prerogatives of the Aufsichtsrat between sessions. . . . For example, any credits greater than RM 2 million had to have the prior approval of the Arbeitsausschuss.

THE VORSTAND

Corresponding most closely to the officers of an American corporation, this body had management responsibility for all of the bank's activities. It is the body which, together with Carl Goetz, chairman of the Aufsichtsrat, supervised the daily operations of the bank. . . .

The Dresdner Bank, unlike an American commercial bank, was a vertical combine that embraced the entire field of finance. It was a universal bank that performed all commercial or investment banking services needed by German industry. The bank had branches all over Germany and numerous foreign affiliates, all managed from a central office in Berlin.

❑ ❑ ❑

The Vorstand of the Dresdner Bank consisted of nine members; all of them were appointed after the Nazis came to power in 1933. They distributed among themselves the responsibilities and the direction of fourteen departments and forty-three geographical areas in which the Dresdner Bank was actively engaged. The dual division of operations by functional and geographical spheres explains the overlapping of jurisdiction among the Vorstand members.

Listed below are the nine members of the last Vorstand of the Dresdner Bank, the date each joined the Vorstand, and the departments and regions which each of them had under his direct supervision.

Alfred Busch
Member of the Vorstand since 1935
   (deputy from 1933)

Responsible for the following departments:	Syndicate Branch Supervision
Responsible for the following regions of Germany:	Saxony, Central Germany
Responsible for the following regions outside Germany:	Western Hemisphere, England, Spain

Alfred Hoelling
Member of the Vorstand since 1941
   (deputy from 1937)

Responsible for the following departments:	Main Office, Berlin, Branch Supervision Sub-Branches, Berlin
Responsible for the following regions in Germany:	Hamburg, Eastern Germany

Carl Luer
Member of the Vorstand since 1937

Responsible for the following department:	None
Responsible for the following regions in Germany:	Southwest Germany
Responsible for the following regions outside Germany:	Saar, Lorraine

Emil Meyer
Member of the Vorstand since 1935
　(deputy from 1933)

Responsible for the following department:	Aircraft Loans Legal, Affiliates, Foreign (since April 1944)
Responsible for the following regions in Germany:	None
Responsible for the following regions outside Germany:	Poland (Ostbank, Posen, and Commerzial Bank, Cracow), Slovakia (Kreditbank, Pressburg), Croatia (Kroatische Landesbank, Agram), Serbia (Suedbank, Belgrade)

Gustav Overbeck
Member of the Vorstand since 1941
　(deputy from 1937)

Responsible for the following departments:	Organization, main accounting, Auditing, Branch supervision
Responsible for the following regions in Germany:	Silesia
Responsible for the following regions outside Germany:	Sudeten

Hans Pilder
Member of the Vorstand since 1941
　(deputy from 1933)

Responsible for the following department:	Foreign
Responsible for the following regions in Germany:	None
Responsible for the following regions outside Germany:	Norway, Switzerland, Hungary, Italy, Albania, Egypt, Denmark, Bulgaria, Alsace, Greece, Romania, Turkey, France

Karl Rasche
Member of the Vorstand since 1935
   (deputy from 1933)

Responsible for the following departments:	Affiliates, Branch Supervision
Responsible for the following regions in Germany:	West Germany, Northwest Germany
Responsible for the following regions outside Germany:	Holland (Handelstrust West Amsterdam), Belgium (Contibank, Brussels), Luxembourg (Internationale Bank, Luzembourg), Protectorate of Bohemia and Moravia (BEB, Prague), Austria (Laenderbank, Vienna), Baltic states (Handels-Kreditbank, Riga), Sweden, Finland

Hans Schippel
Member of the Vorstand since 1933

Responsible for the following department:	Personnel
Responsible for the following region in Germany:	Northeastern
Responsible for the following region outside Germany:	Eastern Asia

Hugo Zinsser
Member of the Vorstand since 1941
   (deputy from 1933)

Responsible for the following departments:	Liquid funds, Securities trading
Responsible for the following region in Germany:	Southern

THE *LANDESAUSSCHUESSE* (REGIONAL ADVISORY BOARDS)

These bodies were formed for the explicit purpose of strengthening on a regional basis the ties between the Dresdner Bank and German industry. These boards, which acquired special significance when the size of the membership of the boards of directors *(Aufsichtsraete)* was limited as a result of the corporation law of 30 January 1937, were used as an additional means of establishing an interlocking between the Dresdner Bank and German industry. There were twelve district advisory boards of the Dresdner Bank, covering Greater Germany, with a total of some two hundred and fifty members prominent in politics, trade, and industry in the various regions.

CHAPTER XIX

The Dresdner Bank as
a Concentration of Economic Power

The Big Six [Berlin banks] dominated all of German banking. They dominated or influenced almost all sectors of German industry. Together with the Nazi Party and the Nazi state, the Big Six banks and German Big Business constituted Nazism.

The Dresdner Bank is the second largest bank in Germany, exceeded in size only by the Deutsche Bank. The Big Six constituted only 1 percent of the total number (650) of German commercial banks. They held, nevertheless, over 50 percent of the assets, and over 60 percent of the total deposits, excluding savings and interbank deposits. The Dresdner Bank alone held 14 percent of the total commercial bank assets, amounting to RM 8.6 billion.

When measured by number of employees (13,700 in 1943), Dresdner was exceeded only by the Deutsche Bank. When measured by branches (368 in 1941), again it was exceeded only by the Deutsche Bank.

The operations of the Dresdner Bank which are described in other chapters of this book were made possible by the fact that the Dresdner Bank constituted a gigantic concentration of economic and financial power.

Behind the German state there existed an organization of trusts and combines more flexible, more permanent, more closely knit than official government itself. It was, in effect, a second government. These industrial giants were the heart of all of German industry, setting the tempo of all German business. . . . Baron Kurt v. Schroeder, head of the association for German commercial banking, stated, "The influence of the big banks over German industry reached such a size that there was hardly a part of German industry which was not under their control."

The Dresdner Bank wielded its power over industry in manifold fashion. The methods used included partial ownership of share capital, representation of large blocks of shares at the annual meetings of industrial corporations, personal ties manifested through interlocking directorates, and, most important, the extension of loans and credits which enabled German industry in the 1933–44 period to expand and grow enormously in order to execute the aggressive plans of the Nazi regime.

A condensed analysis of each of the methods used by the Dresdner Bank will show that the sum total of the bank's influence on the activities of a given industry was strong enough to require that they share the responsibility for acts which fall within the definitions of crimes against peace, war crimes, and crimes against humanity, performed by any of these industrial concerns.

The direct ownership by the Dresdner Bank of the share capital of industrial firms was comparatively small, for the larger heavy industry concerns kept most of their stock in their own hands. Only in the 1931–1932 period, during the industrial reorganization following the world economic crisis, did the Dresdner Bank acquire considerable amounts of stocks, which came to the bank through the conversion of frozen loans into stock interests. The Dresdner Bank, however, did not desire to retain those sizable amounts of stock on account of the risk involved. Generally, the Dresdner Bank preferred to sell and distribute among its customers its industrial participations, reserving to itself the proxy voting rights at the annual meetings.

In Germany, it had always been the practice for most owners of stock in industrial concerns to deposit such stock with their banks and the banks have had the right to vote such shares at all legal meetings of the concerns involved. Dr. Otto Schniewind, former chief of the Banking Department in the Ministry of Economics (RWM), stated that through this practice the Grossbanken [six largest banks] have controlled the majority of votes of almost every industrial concern in Germany and thus definitely influenced the policy of practically every industrial concern of any size in Germany. A part of the stock which the banks voted was held in the bank's portfolio. A far larger part consisted of stock which the bank's customers had left with the bank for safekeeping. By keeping the stock within the circle of its own customers, the Dresdner Bank retained the voting power. . . . Thus the bank succeeded in minimizing risk on the one hand, and retaining its influence on a given industrial corporation on the other. Hans Rinn, the manager of the Syndicate Department of the main office of the Dresdner Bank until 1939 and subsequently manager of the Securities Trading Department, stated that most of the important stock transactions were done by the bank off the floor of the stock exchange—"We preferred to have such stock holdings distributed among our customers in order to retain some manner of control over the voting rights." Had the stock been sold to outsiders the measure of control over a corporation would have been lost.

The importance of retaining the voting rights becomes more significant in view of its being in most instances the key for the distribution of quotas among banks for large loans and credits involving syndicate transactions. Generally, in syndicate arrangements each bank's participation was governed or influenced by the extent of voting power in the corporation. In spite of certain governmental restrictions [under the Corporation Act of 1937] requiring the bank to procure written authorizations from its customers for exercising the voting rights at general meetings of industrial corporations, the bank continued to vote customers' stocks held in custody by the bank just as freely as before and written authorization by the customers became a mere matter of daily routine. Another factor that increased the bank's voting power was that frequently the collateral for a loan would consist of corporate shares. Naturally the bank voted these along with its other shares.

The close ties between the Dresdner Bank and industrial corporations expressed itself fully through interlocking directorates. The men who were influential in Dresdner Bank not only held tremendous financial power, they also wielded a concentrated and powerful control over German industry, assured by their presence on the boards of the industrial concerns.

[In 1944,] the total number of such positions held in other firms by Dresdner officials was 451 positions held by 34 men. These men controlled the major segments of the most important of German industries. Thus, together with the method of control over industry effected by the control of stock of industrial corporations, the Dresdner Bank, through its top officials, occupied a strategic position in the direction of Germany's industrial and economic policies.

❑ ❑ ❑

The Dresdner Bank actively sought to create this intricate network. In a letter dated 17 April 1942, Hans Rinn clearly shows this. The letter discusses the distribution of Schering A.G.'s RM 29,585,000 stock of which the Dresdner controls approximately 25 percent. In view of this he thought:

> We should investigate the possibility of establishing a closer connection with Schering, perhaps by taking a membership on the board of directors.

These memberships on the boards of industrial corporations were not mere honorary positions but a method of ensuring control of the policies of a corporation.

❑ ❑ ❑

A peculiarity of the organization of German business allowed a more extensive influence than superficially appears. *Aktiengesellschaft* (a pure stock corporation) could participate as a partner in G.m.b.H. (company with limited liability), which was in effect a limited partnership. Therefore, any control of an A.G. (stock corporation) would also extend to any G.m.b.H. (partnership) which the A.G. held. The Dresdner Bank used this device as fully as possible. For example, in the huge chemical complex known as the Deutsche Gold und Silber Scheideanstalt [DEGUSSA] there were a total of 42 separate business entities of which only 12 were A.G. and the remaining 30, G.m.b.H. The Dresdner Bank had representatives only on the boards of the key concerns but, through their partnership arrangements, automatically inserted its influence into all the concerns.

Since the large concerns frequently utilized the resources of more than one of the Grossbanken, it is sometimes difficult to specify that a certain corporation is exclusively controlled by a specific one of the Big Six.

However, certain definite alignments are apparent under closer scrutiny. The entire German aircraft industry was primarily the domain of the Dresdner Bank. The same holds true for Krupp, Wintershall, Brabag, and so on. The relationship between the Dresdner Bank and the German aircraft industry is discussed in Chapter XX, Air Rearmament.

There is no need to elaborate on the place of the Krupp family in German heavy industry and their part in planning and preparing Germany for World War I and II. The Dresdner Bank was the main banking connection of the Krupp concern. The close ties between the Dresdner Bank and Krupp date back to 1890. The only representative of a bank in the Krupp directorate was a member of the Vorstand of the Dresdner Bank. Until 1932 Henry Nathan represented the bank in the Aufsichtsrat of Krupp. Samuel Ritscher replaced him in 1932, and Carl Goetz, the leading personality of the Dresdner Bank, took Ritscher's place in 1937 when the latter was forced to retire from the bank management in view of the Nazi racial laws.

Krupp A.G. was always represented on the board of directors (Aufsichtsrat) of the Dresdner Bank. Up until 1937, when Alfred Krupp joined the Aufsichtsrat of the

Dresdner Bank, Buschfeld, Krupp's purchasing director, represented this concern. In 1939 a second member of the management of Krupp, Ewald Loeser, joined the Aufsichtsrat of the Dresdner Bank. It is significant to note that of the three members of the Management Committee of Krupp, two were on the Aufsichtsrat of the Dresdner Bank. The ties between Krupp and the Dresdner Bank manifested themselves also on a regional basis where [for example,] Busemann, the finance director of Krupp A.G., was a member of the District Advisory Board of the Dresdner Bank in Westphalia.

The Dresdner Bank was of the greatest service to the Krupp A.G. in subscribing to loans for the expansion of Krupp business and providing long-term credits for Krupp A.G. and its subsidiaries. In 1936 the Dresdner Bank subscribed to a loan of RM 53,800,000. In 1937, the Dresdner Bank placed at the disposal of the Krupp subsidiary, Krupp Treibstoffwerk, Essen (share capital RM 20,000,000), RM 10,000,000 to construct and manage a synthetic oil plant, based on the utilization of coal by-products. The purpose of this corporation was to "participate in similar (synthetic fuel) corporations, or acquire same." In 1939 the Dresdner Bank extended to Krupp a long-term loan of RM 40,000,000. The few loans described above constitute the major loans that Friedrich Krupp A.G. needed for its operations. The Dresdner Bank placed these funds at the disposal of Krupp.

The close cooperation between Krupp A.G. and the Dresdner Bank expressed itself not only in interlocking directorates and extension of loans. In 1937 when the share capital of the Dresdner Bank was transferred from governmental into private hands, Krupp A.G. acquired over RM 1,000,000 worth of Dresdner Bank shares.

The Dresdner Bank put at the disposal of Krupp the facilities of its foreign branches and affiliates. So, for example, was a RM 5 to 10 million credit placed by the Orient Bank in Turkey to secure Krupp export and import transactions with that country.

The head of the Krupp concern was included among the twenty-two defendants at the international war crimes trial at Nuremberg. The Dresdner Bank shares a major responsibility for the financing of Krupp activities.

The Dresdner Bank was intimately associated not only with Krupp, the leading heavy industry concern, but also with the Wintershall, the largest German potash concern, and after I.G. Farben, the largest chemical concern in Germany. The Dresdner Bank was the principal banking connection of Wintershall. At the annual meetings of Wintershall, the Dresdner Bank represented a sizable block of votes, between 15 and 20 percent.

The Dresdner Bank was represented on the board of directors of Wintershall by Henry Nathan up to 1932, by Carl Goetz up to 1935, and by Karl Rasche thereafter. The leading personality in Wintershall, Heinrich Schmidt, chairman of the Aufsichtsrat, was also a member of the board of directors of the Dresdner Bank. He combined in the board of directors the functions of a representative of a large industrial concern with political functions, being very close to Keppler and his group. Gustav Roemer, leading manager of Wintershall, was a member of the District Advisory Board of the Dresdner Bank in the Hessen-Nassau district.

The Dresdner Bank extended in the 1938–1942 period two RM 10 million loans each, and headed the banking syndicate which provided Wintershall with a RM 60 million loan.

For rearmament and contemplated warfare, oil would be required, much more than Germany naturally possessed. Synthetic methods of production was the goal. Therefore, as early as 1934, the Brabag (Braunkohle-Benzin A.G., Berlin) was created by order of H. Schacht, with participation of all German soft coal mines.

After his initial conference with the lignite producers, Schacht called Karl Rasche of the Dresdner Bank with the result that Rasche then formed a banking syndicate to aid in the financing of Brabag. The Brabag was from the beginning planned on a big scale, which made a corresponding amount of capital necessary. The testimony of Gustav Brecht, vice-chairman of Brabag, emphasizes the leading role assumed by the Dresdner Bank. RM 25,000,000 were extended by the banking syndicate led by the Dresdner Bank with a share of 25 percent. The chairman of the board of directors of Brabag was [Wilhelm] Keppler. Other members were [Fritz] Kranefuss, [Karl] Rasche, [Friedrich] Flick, managers and directors of the Dresdner Bank, all staunch Nazi adherents.

Although closely associated with the leading components of Germany's key industries, the influence of the Dresdner Bank extended much deeper, permeating all strata of German industry. The most important method used by the Dresdner to assure this influence over industry was that of extending loans and credits, which enabled the mushroomlike industrial growth and expansion in the 1933–1944 period.

An incomplete list of industrial loans extended under the leadership of the Dresdner Bank after 1933 gives some conception of the industrial influence of the bank.

Chemicals

Wintershall

Capital: RM 150,000,000 Loan: RM 50,000,000

Interlocking directors: Karl Rasche
Heinrich Schmidt

Deutsche Gold und Silber Scheideanstalt [DEGUSSA]

Capital: RM 35,600,000 Loan: RM 30,000,000

Interlocking directors: Wilhelm Avieny
Carl Goetz

Iron and Steel

Krupp

Capital: RM 160,000,000 Loan (1936): RM 53,800,000
Loan (1937): RM 10,000,000
Loan (1939): RM 40,000,000

Interlocking directors: Ewald Loeser
Alfred Krupp v. Bohlen u. Halbach
Carl Goetz

Mitteldeutsche Stahlwerke A.G.

Capital: RM 75,000,000 Loan: RM 29,400,000

Interlocking directors: Friedrich Flick
Alfred Busch

It is almost 100 percent owned by Flick.

Erzbergbau und Huettenbetrieb Goering Werke

Capital: RM 560,000,000 Loan: RM 25,000,000

The strongest figure in the Goering combine is Hellmuth Roehnert, a member of the Aufsichtsrat of the Dresdner Bank.

Roechling'sche Eisen und Stahlwerke

Capital: RM 36,000,000 Loan (1936): RM 15,000,000
Loan (1943): RM 25,000,000

Electrical

Lech Elektrizitaetswerke A.G.

Capital: RM 40,500,000 Loan: RM 5,000,000
Loan: RM 20,000,000

Controlled by RWE (Rheinisch-Westfaelisches Elektrizitaetswerke A.G.), which has interlocking directors Ernst Henke and Carl Goetz. Dresdner is also represented on the board of management.

C. Lorenz A.G. (Production of telephones and telephone apparatus and installations)

Capital: RM 9,500,000 Loan: RM 15,000,000

Interlocking directors: Albert von Forence of Dresdner heads the company board. The two enterprises have a common director in Emil Meyer.

Rheinisch-Westfaelisches Elektrizitaetswerke A.G.

Capital: RM 246,000,000 Loan: RM 25,000,000

RWE is the most powerful German public utility holding company.
Interlocking directors: Ernst Henke
Carl Goetz

Synthetic Fuel

Braunkohle-Benzin A.G.

Capital: RM 100,000,000 Loan: RM 40,000,000

Five bank officials held high positions in Brabag.
They are: Fritz Kranefuss, Karl Rasche, Heinrich Schmidt, Friedrich Flick, and Heinrich Koppenberg.

Gelsenberg-Benzin

Capital: RM 50,000,000 Loan: RM 55,000,000

The majority shareholder is a subsidiary of Vereinigte Stahlwerke.

Mining

Bergbau A.G., Lothringen

Capital: RM 20,000,000   Loan: RM 8,000,000

25 percent interest is held by Wintershall.

Interlocking directors: Gustav Overbeck
                        Heinrich Schmidt

Grube Leopold A. G., Bitterfeld (AEG)

Capital: RM 10,500,000   Loan: RM 5,330,000

Dresdner is connected with AEG through its interest in Gesfurel (Gesellschaft fuer Elektrische Unternehmungen) and through interlocking directors Friedrich Flick and August Goetz. The latter is deputy chairman of AEG's advisory board.

Coal

Gelsenkirchener Bergwerke

Capital: RM 200,000,000   Loan: RM 130,000,000

This is the largest unit in Vereinigte Stahlwerke.

The Dresdner Bank made available immense sums to the giants of German industry. In one given year, 1941, the bank extended the following huge credits:

AEG	—RM 39,290,000
I.G. Farben Complex	—RM 34,838,000
Hermann-Goering-Werke	—RM 125,000,000
Vereinigte Stahlwerke	—RM 39,000,000
Haniel Concern	—RM 35,000,000
Zentral Textiles	—RM 31,000,000
Junkers	—RM 32,000,000
Flick	—RM 38,553,000
To firms authorized by the Four Year Plan to procure raw materials	—RM 49,000,000

❏ ❏ ❏

One of the major methods for controlling other firms used by the Dresdner Bank was that of having its directors and managers receive positions in these firms after credits or loans were extended to the firm by the bank.

A striking example of the mechanics of this method may be seen in a letter from the Henschel Aircraft Company to Dr. Meyer of the Dresdner Bank which apprises him of the fact that he will be elected to the Aufsichtsrat of the aircraft company. However, his position in the Aufsichtsrat of the company will last only until the loan of RM 2,500,000 from the Dresdner Bank is repaid.

By this means the banks also obtained information about industrial and financial developments throughout the entire economy and were able to determine, or at least to influence, the policies adopted by the highly integrated German economy.

This influence indeed went far beyond Germany's borders since the bank officials held positions in numerous firms outside Germany and the German firms on which bank officials were represented also had connections abroad. In addition the Dresdner Bank owned outright or held the controlling interest in many banks outside the German border, each of which in turn had a network of branches and subsidiaries. All of these institutions exercised influence over the industries in their area. The measure of influence may be readily seen in the course of the negotiations in the spring of 1938 between the Dresdner Bank and Mr. Reuter of the Banque des Pays de l'Europe Centrale for the sale to Dresdner of the Banque des Pays' Austrian subsidiary, the Laenderbank Wien. One of the phases of the negotiation had to do with the disposition of the leaders and holders of positions of high rank in the industries controlled by the Laenderbank Wien. The Dresdner Bank by acquiring the Laenderbank thus gained the discretionary power to remove or replace officials in industries falling within the Laenderbank orbit.

Some idea of the extent of influence over industry in Austria which accrued to the Dresdner Bank by its absorption of the Laenderbank Wien may be seen in several of the Laenderbank participations and in examination of a partial list of interlocking directorates of Laenderbank officials.

In the Perlmooser Zementwerke A.G., the Laenderbank had a participation amounting to 30–40 percent of the capital stock. The share capital of the concern was RM 19,500,000 and assets of RM 36,000,000. The concern had sixteen plants throughout Austria.

In the paper mills Potschmuehle-Steyrermuehl A.G., the participation reached 25–30 percent of the capital stock of RM 12,000,000. This concern had about fourteen plants including paper mills, sulfate plants, electric works.

Director Wolzt of the Laenderbank was on the board of the following firms:

> Zellwolle- und Papierfabrik Lenzing, A.G. (paper mills)
>   Share capital RM 25,000,000 and assets of RM 41,382,341
> Litega Linoleum—Teppiche—Gardinen, A.G.
>   Share capital RM 1,500,000
> Allgemeine Elementar-Versicherungs A.G. (insurance)
>   Share capital RM 6,000,000 and assets of RM 26,227,726
> Steirische Magnesit-Industrie, A.G. (mining)
>   Share capital RM 2,400,000 and assets of RM 4,375,660
> Brucker Zuckerindustrie, A.G. (sugar)
> Leykam-Josefsthal A.G., Papierindustrie (paper and printing)
>   Share capital RM 12,000,000 and assets of RM 31,641,120
> Kremenetzki A.G. Gluehlampenfabrik (electrical products)
>   Share capital RM 2,500,000 and assets of RM 10,479,22

Director Wilhelm Lehr of the Laenderbank was on the board of the following firms:

> Waagner-Biro A.G. (steel mills)
>   Share capital RM 6,336,000 and assets of RM 25,435,292
> Gaskoks-Vertriebs-Gesellschaft m.b.H.
> Poelser Zellulose A.G. (cellulose)

Share capital RM 5,000,000 and assets of RM 9,745,247
Lihag, Landwirtschaftliche Industrie-u. Handels A.G.

Director Adolf Warnecke of the Laenderbank was on the board of the following firms:

Papierfabriken Potschmuehle-Steyrermuehl A.G. (paper and printing)
      Share capital RM 12,000,000 and assets of RM 11,504,025
Vorarlberger Zementwerke Loruens A.G. (cement)
      Share capital RM 2,733,300 and assets of RM 4,858,845
Perlmooser Zementwerke A.G. (cement)
      Share capital RM 19,480,000 and assets of RM 35,945,489
Gaskoks-Vertriebs-Gesellschaft m.b.H.
Julius Meinl A.G. (food importers)
      Share capital RM 8,000,000 and assets of RM 39,553,542
Vereinigte Lederwerke Franz Schmitt A.G. (leather and shoes)
      Share capital RM 1,000,000 and assets of RM 2,162,420
Vereinigte Lederfabriken A.G. (leather and shoes)
      Share capital RM 2,363,500 and assets of RM 3,491,352

As the Dresdner acquired banks and subsidiaries in the wake of German conquest, the number of industries over which it gained control in those territories mounted in geometrical progression. According to the deposition of Dr. Otto Schniewind, former chief of the Banking Department of the Ministry of Economics (RWM):

As a result of German expansion and occupation of foreign countries, the German banks were given an opportunity to acquire foreign assets. All of the big banks made use of this opportunity and took over interests in foreign banks in the wake of German occupation. The Dresdner Bank, probably because of its unusually close ties with the Party, benefited more in this respect than any of the other banks.

Using the same devices with which they were able to maintain influence over German industry they now extended that control to industries in lands overrun by the German hordes.

In 1939, after the occupation of Czechoslovakia, the Dresdner Bank acquired the BEB (Boehmische Escompte Bank) in Prague. Some of the most important industries which were participations of BEB and hence now under the influence of the Dresdner Bank were as follows:

Elbekosteletzer Zuckerraffinerie A.G., Prague
      Share capital—RM 10,000,000
      Assets—RM 123,317,728
      Approximate participation—35 percent

Vereinigte Carborundum Elektrik-Werke
      Share capital—RM 3,500,000
      Assets—RM 8,270,209
      Approximate participation—40 percent

Koenigshofer Zementfabrik A.G., Prague
Share capital—RM 9,600,000
Assets—RM 20,501,632
Approximate participation—20 percent

Poldi Huette, Prague
Share capital—RM 25,000,000
Assets—RM 79,417,490
Approximate participation—9 percent

"Sphinx" Vereinigte Emaillewerke A.G., Prague
Share capital—RM 3,700,000
Assets—RM 9,391,898
Approximate participation—40 percent

Zigarettenpapierfabrik Olleschau, Prague
Share capital—RM 3,500,000
Approximate participation—35–40 percent

Aktiengesellschaft fuer Spiritusindustrie, Prague
Share capital—RM 2,400,000
Assets—RM 4,314,933
Approximate participation—20–25 percent

Milchindustrie A.G., Prague
Share capital—RM 1,400,000
Assets—RM 3,682,891
Approximate participation—20 percent

Brosche A.G., Prague
Share capital—RM 1,800,000
Assets—RM 6,963,086
Approximate participation—20–25 percent

Holliner Spiritusfabrik, Prague
Share capital—RM 1,260,000
Assets—RM 6,063,000
Approximate participation—20–23 percent

In addition to these BEB participations there existed a great number of interlocking directorates between BEB officials and various Czech industries. A partial list to indicate the extent of these interlocks is as follows:

Director Novotny, BEB, Prague
Elbekosteletzer Zuckerraffinerie A.G. (sugar refineries)
Vereinigte Carborundum Elektrit-Werke (chemicals)
Poldi Huette, Prague (mining and steel mills)
Pilsener Aktienbrauerei, Pilsen (brewery)
Vereinigte Maehrische Zuckerfabriken, Olmuetz (sugar)
Melantrichverlag A.G., Prague (paper and printing)
Koenigshofer Zementfabrik A.G., Prague (cement)
A.G. fuer Spiritusindustrie, Prague (spirits)
Nordmaehrische Brauerei, Maher.-Schoenberg (brewery)

    Prager Eisenindustrie A.G., Prague (iron and steel)
    Moldavia Versicherungs A.G., Prague (insurance)

Director v. Luedinghausen, BEB, Prague
    Koenigshofer Zementfabrik A.G., Prague (cement)
    "Sphinx" Vereinigte Emaillewerke, A.G., Prague (metals)
    Waffenwerke Bruenn, Bruenn (munitions plant)
    Erste Bruenner Maschinenfabrik A.G., Bruenn (machinery and metals)
    Berauner Textilwerke A.G., Prague (textiles)
    Skoda Werke, Pilsen (munitions)
    Brosche A.G., Spiritus-Industrie A.G., Prague (spirits)
    Ringhoffer Tatra Werke, Prague (heavy machinery and metals)
    Milchindustrie A.G., Prague (food)

Director Dr. Hoelzer, BEB, Prague
    Roth Kosteletzer Spinnerei A.G., Prague (textiles)
    Zigarettenpapierfabrik Olleschau, Prague (tobacco)
    Inwald Glaswarenfabrik, Prague (glass and porcelain)
    Julius Meinl A.G., Prague (food)
    Kolliner Spiritus A.G., Prague (spirits)
    Fanto Werke A.G., Prague (chemicals)
    Berghuette, Prague (mining)
    Prag-Neusiedler Papierfabriken, Prague (paper).

This represents a very incomplete listing of interlocking directorates through BEB in Czechoslovakia and indicates the widespread influence Dresdner was able to gain over Czech industry merely through the acquisition of one bank.

BEB is not a unique case. It represents but one of many banks acquired by Dresdner. Through the medium of these bank acquisitions the magnitude of Dresdner influence on industry extended throughout all of occupied Europe.

Secondary influence was extended even further by reason of the fact that officials of firms controlled by the Dresdner Bank or its subsidiaries held positions in other firms so that there was an entire maze of interlocking positions which crossed political boundaries as if they were nonexistent, permeated entire economies, and penetrated to the four corners of the earth.

CHAPTER XX

OPERATIONS OF
THE DRESDNER BANK IN GERMANY

From 1933 on, the amassing of wealth, power, and holdings of the Dresdner Bank was intimately allied with the upsurgence of Nazism and Nazi activity. It is not amiss to say that each supplemented the policy of the other and each derived huge benefits from their close association. This partnership involved the use of the facilities of the bank in the economic mobilization of Germany's resources for war during the period 1933–1939. After 1939, the bank was rewarded for its services to the Reich by being allowed to participate in the spoliation of Europe.

This close association was fostered by the Dresdner's ties with the government, the Party, the SS, and affiliated organizations. The relationship between the bank and the offices of the government, particularly the *Reichswirtschaftministerium* (Ministry of Economics) and the Speer Ministry, was the working basis of this partnership. . . .

One opportunity for profit was the forcible Aryanization of Jewish-owned business in Germany. The Dresdner Bank was the leading banking agency in such Aryanization and it intensively engaged in this criminal method of implementing its assets. . . .

[As mentioned above, the Dresdner] conspired in 1937 with Admiral Raeder of the German Naval High Command to procure and conceal large oil reserves in Mexico and Iraq for the supply of the German fleet. . . . [It] became the principal financial underwriter and banker of the entire German military aircraft industry. It was the Dresdner Bank that headed the banking syndicate which financed the synthetic fuel combine, the Brabag. It was the Dresdner Bank that headed the banking syndicate which financed the initial capitalization of the Hermann-Goering-Werke, and it became the principal banker during the Hermann-Goering-Werke's expansion period.[1]

---

[1] The bank participated in the financing of all sectors of the rearmament field. . . . The available balance sheets of the Dresdner Bank between 1936–1943 show acceptances and bills, loans, and security holdings to be as follows:

	Acceptances and Bills	Loans	Security Holdings
1936	RM 544,896,274.55	RM 1,057,177,725.80	RM 244,882,543.03
1937	RM 734,496,732.81	RM 984,997,973.02	RM 245,123,156.51
1938	RM 671,726,999.05	RM 1,007,724,361.37	RM 221,715,054.31
1939	RM 675,917,144.03	RM 1,121,051,260.96	RM 202,704,882.23
1940	RM 676,738,606.39	RM 866,115,342.33	RM 209,813,239.19
1941	RM 702,308,450.51	RM 1,053,432,785.74	RM 211,410,295.20
1942	RM 851,685,652.56	RM 1,232,733,134.83	RM 220,254,983.53
1943	RM 825,341,994.86	RM 1,590,617,117.15	RM 206,743,101.05

Under "bills" the balance sheet includes any credit item which is rediscountable at the Reichsbank. Hence until 1939, when they no longer became acceptable, the notorious Mefo bills, the principal device for the financing of prewar rearmament in Germany, are included under this heading. . . .

❑ ❑ ❑

The credits supplied by the Dresdner Bank to industry cannot be specifically tabulated because of the destruction of records, but the total amounted to an immense sum to judge by the evidence available. In many cases the bank could not afford to make such advances unless they were guaranteed by the Reich. Examples of such credits are given in the section Air Rearmament. In extending these credits the Dresdner Bank acted as an agency of the government.

The following is a tabulation of the bank's holdings of government securities. Figures are from the balance sheet printed in the annual statement:

    1936 RM   274,288,809.96
    1937 RM   240,407,029.82
    1938 RM   429,792,138.79
    1939 RM   868,036,488.21
    1941 RM 2,583,795,334.84
    1942 RM 3,010,139,588.48
    1943 RM 3,564,494,439.96

Otto Schniewind, chief of the Banking Department of the Ministry of Economics until 1937, describes the role of the banks as principal holders of governmental securities in the following words:

> Unlike the First World War, when German securities were sold chiefly to the public, German debentures in this war were sold entirely to financial institutions, such as banks, insurance companies and savings banks. In this purchase of Government securities the Grossbanken (Dresdner and other Berlin banks), because of the tremendous assets at their disposal, were the chief factor.

In support of the rearmament program the Dresdner Bank in Berlin could further call on an immense chain of branches, subsidiaries, affiliates, associated private banks, and friends to help underwrite loans. . . . The credits granted amount to RM 1,530,759.

The Dresdner Bank was well qualified to play its part in accomplishing the objectives of Nazism. It was used to influence and support industry. The record of German industry in the period 1933–1939 speaks for itself. Its activities were integrated with the requirements of planning and conducting aggressive warfare.

The correspondence of the bank with the economic branches of the government and the Party is voluminous enough to permit the investigator to observe the manner in which it promoted the policies of the government within German industry. Companies engaged in the armament program could turn to the Dresdner Bank for a virtually unlimited drawing account.

The activities of the Dresdner Bank in Germany were so many and so varied, that not all of them can be set out in detail. Five fields which demonstrate the versatility of this huge universal bank have been chosen as examples and are presented in detail.

AIR REARMAMENT

At the time the Nazi regime seized power the German aircraft industry consisted of a few scattered, uncoordinated plants. In a few short years these were to be fashioned into the gigantic arsenal of the Luftwaffe that enabled it in 1939 to overwhelm all opposition in the air space over the battlefields of Europe. The primary importance accorded the development of this industry is easily understood in the light of the role of the airplane in Germany's blitzkrieg tactics. In a report on the growth of the Junkers plane manufacturing company, Heinrich Koppenberg, the general manager who was also a member of the Aufsichtsrat of the Dresdner Bank, emphasizes the importance of the big banks as the partners of Goering's Air Ministry in the creation of this arsenal—

> The attempt of the Air Ministry to interest . . . the banks was of little success [at first] . . . the aeroplane manufacturers who at that time existed in Germany were too unimportant and not strong enough with regard to capital to establish new plants or to enlarge their works.

> The Reich Air Ministry resolved to develop the existing airplane works and to establish new ones itself. At first, the financial backers, banks and other financial institutions, had to be induced to place at the disposal (of the plane manufacturers) the means for the necessary investments. . . . It was possible to obtain means for the establishment of manufacturing plants against the transfer of the guarantee (of the Reich) for deductions made for depreciation (of the plant).

The first loan made under this plan is discussed in a report on a meeting between representatives of the leading banks, General von Kesselring of the Air Ministry, and Wilhelm Keppler, Hitler's personal economic adviser, on 20 May 1935. . . . These partners knew that they were not engaged in any ordinary business transaction because the military Air Ministry, rather than the civilian air industry group of the Ministry of Economics, spoke for the government. The entire matter was handled with an extreme secrecy.

The manager of the Dresdner Bank's Bremen branch, who was in charge of disbursing the Focke-Wulf loan, states in an affidavit:

> . . . Aircraft credits were kept top secret, and only a small group of specially selected people worked on them. . . . The Bremen branch was excluded. . . .

The Dresdner Bank was represented at this meeting of May 1935 by Emil Meyer, an ardent Nazi, cousin of Keppler, and the head of its Special Department for Aviation Industry Loans. . . .

Evidently Meyer, with his excellent inner-circle NSDAP connections, foresaw the importance this field of financing would attain. That he was the spur to Dresdner's enthusiasm is indicated by the head of the Ministry of Economics Aircraft Industry Group, who wrote:

The only bank which could claim any merit (for the early financing of the industry), is the Dresdner Bank in the person of Professor Meyer.

At the first meeting of the partners in May 1935, while the other bankers were opposing the plans of the Air Ministry, his part is described as follows:

> Dr. Meyer, reporting on the negotiations conducted previously with the Air Ministry by the Dresdner Bank, stated that the Dresdner Bank was quite ready and willing to support the Air Ministry, only that as far as possible notice must be given for the banks to be able to mobilize their medium-term credits.

This unreserved support assured the success of the underwriting, and the Air Ministry from that date on considered the Dresdner Bank as a reliable partner in its conspiracy. In a report dated 18 September 1936, concerning the negotiations with the Air Ministry, the Dresdner Bank demonstrates its knowledge in confidential plans:

> *Heinkel* . . . Moreover, the Reich, jointly with Heinkel, is at present constructing a new aircraft plant at Oranienburg, spending about RM 22 million for this purpose. This plant is intended to be built up as a limited company with a capital of about RM 5 million.

> *Focke-Wulf* . . . The financial reorganization of this enterprise is being arranged. It is intended to increase the capital to RM 5 million. The funds necessary for the completion of the plant will be partially raised by credits from the banks.

> *Bayerische Flugzeugwerke* . . . Capital now RM 4 million. At present a large new plant is being built in Regensburg. The construction is first rate.

The extent of the bank's enthusiasm is clearly shown by the fact that in 1935 it had only twenty-two aircraft firms with which it wished to do business while it had fifty-two such firms in 1937. It wrote to the Air Ministry in 1937:

> With reference to our conference I am sending you a list of aircraft firms as we have them from our Statistical Department. With the greater number of these we already enjoy favorable business relations.

> You already know of my personal wish to aid in the expansion of the industry through operating credits granted by my institution. We want in every instance to help those firms to which the Aircraft Ministry gives priority.

> Therefore, I would like information from you which would specify such firms and we will undertake to establish connections with them.

The expansion of the industry's production facilities did not end its needs for money. On this subject [Heinrich] Koppenberg, in his report, writes:

> The Air Ministry . . . delayed more than the time stipulated for the payment
> of the amounts due . . . so that the industry . . . needed the assistance of the
> capital market and of the banks for running the enterprise. . . .

The records of the Dresdner Bank are incomplete, but some idea of the extent of
its loans for operating funds may be had from the statement of the Focke-Wulf
account in June, 1942, which totaled RM 19,750,000. But the conspiracy to violate
the Treaty of Versailles was fulfilled.

   These loans to the aviation industry were nominally made by the Luftfahrt
Bank, a subsidiary of the Reich Air Ministry, although the major portion of the
money was raised through syndicate participations of the big banks, such as the
Dresdner. The reason for the financing being channeled through the Air Ministry
organization was to enable those who were charged with determining and fulfilling
technical and permanent aircraft requirements to control the industry. Goering, in
a secret speech to the aircraft industry leaders in July 1938, declared just how
much control he had:

> Not for a second, and I mean second, would I hesitate . . . to intervene at
> once and to confiscate at once the whole business in case that the (the man-
> ufacturer) does not understand . . . by a stroke of my pen he would lose his
> business and his property.

The position of the Luftfahrt Bank is described by Hettlage, chief of the General
Division for Economics and Finance, in the Speer Ministry, as:

> Controlled and instructed by the Air Ministry, and was the agent in financial
> matters of the Air Ministry.

A letter to the Bank der Deutschen Luftfahrt dated 22 April 1942 from the
Dresdner indicates very clearly the relationship between the two institutions. The letter lists seventeen transactions in which the Dresdner is interested and contains statements such as the following concerning them:

> *Hansa Leichtmetal.* As you know we consider it very important to be includ-
> ed in the financing . . . should there be a question of financing in foreign
> countries . . . also participate . . .

> *Ringhofer Tatra-Werke.* We have made it clear that Rasche (of Dresdner Bank)
> will be able to exert his influence as president of the board of managers so
> that a credit extended . . . will be mutually handled by us and the
> Luftfahrtbank.

> *Focke-Wulf Flugzeugbau.* You informed me that the 12,000,000 Reichsmark
> credit will fall to us to the extent of RM 6,000,000.

Not content with expanding German production facilities, the Dresdner Bank
undertook the financing of the expansion of the air forces of Nazi Germany's Axis
associates. The bank had no doubts about the character of its job. A memorandum

of a meeting with the Air Ministry to settle details of supplying the Hungarian War Ministry states:

> Of course the Air Ministry would not be able to give a written obligation.

> Should the air force merely maintain its present extent, replacement orders will be very considerable since on an average the fleet must be entirely renewed every four years.

The contract for this transaction, as set out in a draft, provided that the Dresdner Bank finance the construction by Heinkel, Junkers, Focke-Wulf, and twelve other firms, of planes for the Hungarian War Ministry through a credit of RM 27,500,000.

This transaction was handled so successfully that in 1938, when the financing of Austro-Fiat was being negotiated, the Air Ministry official in charge reported:

> The Dresdner Bank in all these negotiations is absolutely backed by the Air Ministry, and both Secretary Milch and General Goering urgently wish the negotiations with the Austro-Fiat concerning credit to be brought to a favorable conclusion.

When the aggressive war was finally launched the Dresdner Bank naturally expected to profit. In a memorandum, dated September 1941, it listed the following transactions involving conquered countries of Europe in which it expected to participate:

> Large orders have been given to the Belgian aviation industry. Payment for these amounts to 59 million francs. Credits shall be given by our correspondent or by our bank.

> There are more important financings in the General Gouvernement (the annexed portion of Poland) in which, if desired, we can participate up to 50 percent.

> The Ostmaerkische Motorenwerke are intended to become the greatest German motor plant. Capital RM 150 million, and operating credits of RM 100 million . . . in his opinion, the amount of RM 40 million capital and RM 20 to 25 million operating credits would come under consideration. He—Rudorf—will safeguard our interests when the quotas are allotted—and refer these contractors to the Laenderbank, or rather Boehmische Escompte Bank, to place our affiliates in a position to carry out these credits.

> In Paris . . . huge credits to French aircraft firms and the accessories industry. Herr Rudorf agrees to let us participate in these credits.

> Herr Rudorf and Herr Parke are going to Brussels and there will establish a business relation with our affiliate.

> In Holland the gentlemen are recommending that our bank establish relations.

The story of the Dresdner Bank's part in the financing of Nazi Germany's aviation industry would be incomplete without further mention of Emil Meyer. He had been a minor executive in the Cooperatives Department of the Dresdner Bank, but with the advent of the Nazis to power in 1933, he became a figure of importance in the bank and established its Aviation Industry Credits Department. He was a Nazi with excellent Party connections and he was promoted rapidly. He was the link between the Dresdner and the Air Ministry and aviation industry. An interdepartmental letter of June 1936 of the Dresdner concerning Meyer's appointment to the advisory group of the Arado Flugzeugwerke states:

> Director Dr. E. H. Meyer was appointed member of the advisory board of the Arado Flugzeugwerke G.m.b.H., Brandenburg a.d. Havel by the Reich.

From the very beginning the Dresdner Bank was the partner of the Nazi state in the clandestine development of the German air forces. To show the completeness of the bank's identification with the growth of the Luftwaffe, it only remains to quote from a letter by the leader of the Dresdner Bank, Carl Goetz:

> The fact that by supporting the glider movement, we have been able, in a modest way, to do pioneering work for the Luftwaffe, gives great satisfaction to all of us and we shall be glad to serve the same cause in the future.

PROCUREMENT OF OIL

The Dresdner Bank with its subsidiaries and worldwide affiliates as a far-reaching and complex institution was able to accomplish a variety of financial and business tasks. It was the ideal partner for accomplishing missions with which the government did not wish to identify itself too closely.

The history of Germany's frantic efforts to secure the oil needed to man the war machine that was being so industriously constructed affords an insight into the diverseness of services the bank could provide. It provided the technical, political, legal, and financial wherewithal to secure oil reserves for the coming war. It played the role of diplomat negotiating with foreign governments. It was a promoter of corporations. It provided a geologist as part of its financial services. All these activities were directed toward getting the oil required by the Nazi rearmament program.

Oil was the most serious raw material deficiency facing a Germany preparing for war. The high commands of all three branches of the service were involved in overcoming this shortage, as were the Ministry of Economics and the Office for the Four Year Plan. Despite treaty limitations the German Navy prepared for war and recognized a need for oil reserves. In a report to Goering dated 9 September 1938, Admiral Raeder stated:

> the Navy can only fulfill its wartime tasks if in addition to the oil supply for current needs from Germany itself, reserves are maintained.

The same report further indicates that the Naval High Command was thinking of its future role:

> the oil installations as planned for Mexico could . . . if prepared in advance during peacetime . . . in wartime afford the Navy good possibilities for supply.

The Dresdner Bank became the partner of the German Naval High Command (OKM) in Germany's conspiracy to prepare for war. The Dresdner Bank accepted the assignment to locate oil fields in Latin America. In a report, Admiral Raeder defines the role of the Dresdner Bank in these words:

> The Naval High Command has engaged the Dresdner Bank for the purposes of camouflage, and from the financial aspect, to eliminate any risk of a loss of foreign exchange by the Reich, or for the Naval High Command to suffer any losses of Reichsmark.

The Dresdner Bank lent its aid to an early scheme (1934) in which a group of German businessmen, acting for the Ministry of Economics, participated in the exploiting of an oil concession in the Mosul fields of Iraq. Germany's limited foreign exchange prevented the group from meeting its obligations and it was forced to sell its participation. The bank, as trustee for the group, "made every effort to place the shares in Germany, an endeavor in which the German Naval High Command was interested" (interrogation of Hans Pilder, head of Foreign Department, Dresdner Bank).

The bank knew what these negotiations were about. Admiral Raeder wrote:

> as was done in reference to negotiations for participation in the Mosul oil fields, the Naval High Command likewise called in the Dresdner Bank for the purpose of camouflage.

Soon after the failure of this effort the Ministry of Economics permitted the Naval High Command to use £600,000 in foreign exchange, realized from the Mosul transactions, to finance oil concessions in the Americas. The project envisioned by the Navy required even closer cooperation and more delicate handling, but it had full confidence that this phase of Nazi Germany's preparation for war would be ably executed by the leader of the Mosul attempt. Admiral Raeder describes the duties in this transaction as follows:

> during the summer of 1937 the Naval High Command has directed the Dresdner Bank to establish the Gesellschaft fuer Ueberseeische Bergbauliche Unternehmungen. Its task will be to search for oil fields as directed possibly to prepare in detail the necessary contracts for concessions with the foreign governments concerns; to ascertain the geological and political risks involved in a foreign oil concession.

The two men principally concerned in carrying out the assignment for the bank were Karl Erk, a deputy manager of its Foreign Department, and Professor Bentz, of the Geology Institute, Berlin. The matter was handled by the Foreign Department of the Dresdner, and the salient developments are summarized in . . . [the] interrogations of Hans Pilder, the head of this department. This evidence briefly summarized reveals the following story.

The camouflage company was established in accordance with instructions, after Mr. Fetzer of the Naval High Command and the Dresdner Bank had worked out this plan. The Gesellschaft fuer Ueberseeische Bergbauliche Unternehmungen had a capital of RM 50,000 with the bank and an affiliate, the Treuhand Vereinigung, owning all the shares.

Five days after the formation of this company Erk and Bentz set out for Mexico. They received their instructions directly from the Naval High Command, but numerous entries in the books of the company show that cloaking of the Navy's interest was maintained by having all expenses paid by the company. The two agents also included visits to Colombia and Venezuela in their itinerary. They decided that Mexico most nearly met the demands of the Naval High Command for the following reasons:

> after examination of conditions . . . the result was that only in Mexico areas with large quantities of oil could be acquired in a relatively short time and with relatively small amounts of foreign exchange being necessary. . . .

> fields are offered which are not more than 60 km from oil shipping ports. [Mexico] is the only country where the influence of the American Standard Oil and Shell concerns has been effectively eliminated.

This negotiation for the armed forces of Nazi Germany might have been an unusual banking function, yet we find that

> Director Erk, as the representative of the Gesellschaft fuer Ueberseeische Bergbauliche Unternehmungen (Dresdner Bank) has drawn, and checked to the last detail, contracts for oil concessions with the Mexican government.

> As to the political risk I refer you to the memorandum of Bank Director Erk herewith attached. . . .

❑ ❑ ❑

The Naval High Command was not alone in its confidence in the Dresdner. The Ministry of Economics also joined in the search for an assured oil supply. It believed that Venezuela's need of a market for her coffee could be used as a lever for forcing oil sales. It wanted to pay for oil in Sondermark which the United States–owned Venezuelan oil companies would not accept.

To conduct negotiations it called on H. Wedekind, an official of the Dresdner Bank's South American subsidiary, the Deutsch-Suedamerikanische Bank. Wedekind's official report on his task describes its inception as follows:

> in April 1935 the Dresdner Bank in Hamburg and the Deutsch-Suedamerikanische Bank were called upon by the Ministry of Economics

(Dr. Schlotterer) to give an opinion as to ways in which it would be possible to procure crude oil from Venezuela; coffee also a raw material being of great importance for Germany is primarily bought from this country; payment must be effected in Sondermark.

The crux of the problem was paraphrased in these words:

now the question to be solved was how the necessary foreign exchange for Venezuelan oil purchase could at the same time be obtained from trade with Venezuela.

The importance of the role played by the bank in this undertaking cannot be over-estimated. Here we have a government ministry calling on a bank to negotiate the terms governing the entire commerce of Germany with Venezuela.

❏ ❏ ❏

The negotiations were carried on between the German banker and the Venezuelan Minister of Agriculture for a period of six months, from early November 1936 until March 1937. The major obstacle to an agreement was that "the oil companies (American) refused to deliver any oil to Germany" except for payment in gold. Germany could not make payment in anything except blocked marks. The pressure of the coffee growers was only sufficient to force a small increase in oil exports to Germany.

Wedekind had not obtained the quantities of oil the Nazis wanted; but he secured a promise from the Venezuelan government to try to get a cancellation of the present oil concessions.

❏ ❏ ❏

After Germany launched its war of 1939–40 and during the aerial Battle for Britain, oil was still the number-one supply problem. To obtain the greatest possible production from conquered Europe it was decided that oil activities were to be brought under one giant monopoly corporation called Kontinentale Oel. A report to the Vorstand of the Dresdner dated 22 January 1941 describes the inception of the plan as:

on the basis of a discussion between the Fuehrer and Reichsmarschall Goering which took place a little while ago [. . . A] new corporation is to include Germany's total interests in all oil questions (especially in so far as foreign participations are involved) . . . is intended for the purpose of a centralized direction, relating to this field, while the different production corporations will continue their work under their own legal status and management.

The plan contemplated the formation of a cartel. The report to the Vorstand of the Dresdner stated:

The production corporations already working in German territory (mainly Elveroth, Deca, Wintershall, Preussag, to which I.G. Farben, in a slightly different position, is to be added; for coal the Benzolverband and for lignite the Brabag) shall continue their German drillings and plants under their own management.

The holdings under the management of this contemplated company were to cover the entire continent of Europe. The report of the first meeting to the Dresdner Vorstand states:

At present it is intended to acquire the

Concordia   (22.5 millions required)
Columbia   (20 millions required)
Southeast interests of Wifo   (12 millions required);

furthermore, negotiations are pending concerning the Standard participations in Hungary (through the I.G. Farben–Standard connections).

The initial report to the Dresdner Bank Vorstand of 22 January 1941 indicates the immensity of the credit involved:

The present visible plans thus amount to about 100,000,000 RM. If they are to be carried out, it must be determined how to procure up to 70 millions. . . . The representatives who were present have been asked to discuss among themselves how to procure these. . . .

The "discussion" resulted in the large universal banks being again called on for heavy support in the financing of the Nazi war of aggression. Goering's letter of 8 March 1941 states that the necessary funds are to be supplied according to the following plan:

1. The original shareholders (i.e., the producing and processing firms) will be granted 50 votes and subscribe to pay 50,000,000 RM.
2. The banks for their own account will subscribe to 30 millions of the original shares, with single voting rights paying in 25 percent to begin with.
3. The banks will grant the corporation a credit of 40 millions.

The institution formed was more than a device for control of the present oil-producing companies. It was a monopoly corporation. The Dresdner's report of the 21 January 1941 meeting reads:

In order to secure the State guidance of the Konti, Reichsminister Funk in person is to take over the presidency of the corporation and State Secretaries Keppler and Neumann the deputy presidency.

The Aufsichtsrat of the new monopoly was an impressive group of the Nazi economic leaders that had directed the rearmament of Germany and hoped to profit by the war of aggression they had poured onto a peaceful world. Goering's letter lists twenty-eight. Among the more important are:

> Wilhelm Keppler—economist of the NSDAP Chancellery
> Fritz Kranefuss—a leader of the notorious Keppler Circle of industrialists and a member of the Aufsichtsrat of the Dresdner Bank
> Heinrich Buetefisch—I.G. Farben general manager
> Karl Rasche—the Dresdner Bank's leader in exploitation of Nazi conquests
> Karl Blessing—the Ministry of Economics chief for oil
> Dr. A. Bentz —who had formerly worked with the Dresdner on the Mexican oil transaction

The Dresdner Bank's share in this huge undertaking amounted to one-third of the total. The other banks were also to participate. In its annual report for 1941 the Dresdner boasts that it was the leader in this financing. The summary of the discussion in the Vorstand of the Dresdner Bank on 21 January reveals the aggressive nature of its seizure of the initiative:

> with regard to the preparatory work Deutsche Bank claims the leadership. I have suggested to Mr. Abs to concede to us the sharing of the leadership of the syndicate.

The suggestion was agreed upon, for a memorandum dated 9 March 1941 states:

> Abs agrees to the participation as of the time the public will have to be contacted.

The bank was expected to do more than merely aid in raising the capital needed to begin the new oil company. As had been done in the oil transactions previously discussed, the government intended to utilize the executives of the Dresdner Bank and its far-flung financial empire. A letter from Goering of 20 March 1941 states:

> The corporation after founding is to take over first the majority of shares of the Concordia, acquired from Belgian ownership, and then of the Columbia acquired from French ownership. Further plans concerning acquisitions of foreign undertakings will be reported at the first meeting.

Considering the ruthless methods used in acquiring the interests in concerns in the conquered territories, it may safely be presumed that the participating banks were intended to assume this duty. (See report on operations of the Dresdner Bank in the Netherlands and Belgium in Chapter XXI)

The Kontinentale Oel expanded further East. A report of the Ministry of Economics dated 22 July 1941, dividing up the exploitation of Germany's oil resources, assigns to Kontinentale Oel the rich Russian fields among others:

> The Kontinentale Oel A.G. has received a special assignment for the Russian mineral oil economy, which it will put to serving our oil needs, either in its own name or through subsidiaries.

In 1941 Stalingrad had not yet stopped the Wehrmacht and the Nazis could plan as conquerors. Therefore the Kontinentale Oel was instructed to establish special companies for the exploitation and management of various oil regions, including the Baltic states, Central Russia, Ukraine, and the Caucasus. The Reich government and the High Command considered this a task of top importance and priority. In a letter dated 22 July 1941 the Minister of Economics wrote:

> Referring to the order given you to carry out the measures to be taken concerning oil questions in Russia . . . I ask you to pursue the matter energetically from your end. You are authorized, in carrying out your duties, to refer to this order. If there are any difficulties which you are unable to overcome, let me know immediately so that I can take the necessary steps.

The Dresdner's contributions toward meeting the oil requirements of the Nazi military machine were continuous and varied. The annual report in the listing of the major financial transactions in which the bank "was proud to have had a leading share" cites a large number of loans to oil interests.

The records of the bank are incomplete; however, an idea of the extent of its loans in this war enterprise may be had from a partial list of the loans which it underwrote for corporations engaged in the production of synthetic fuel and oil.

1.	Deutsche Kontinentale Gas Gesellschaft, Dessau	1937	RM 25,000,000.
2.	Gelsenberg-Benzin	1937	RM 55,000,000.
3.	Krupp Treibstoff	1937	RM 10,000,000.
4.	Braunkohle-Benzin	1938	RM 120,000,000.
5.	Rheinisch Westfaelische Elektrizitaetswerke	1939	RM 25,000,000.
6.	Union Rheinische Braunkohlen Kraftstoff	1940	RM 60,000,000.
7.	Rheinische A.G. fuer Braunkohle etc.	1940	RM 50,000,000.
8.	Wintershall A.G.	1940	RM 60,000,000.
9.	Braunkohle- u. Brikettwerke Roddergrube	1941	RM 60,000,000.
10.	Essener Steinkohlenbergwerke	1941	RM 30,000,000.
11.	Sudetenlaendische Treibstoffwerke A.G.	1944	RM 109,000,000.

The Dresdner's partnership with the Nazi government in the quest for the oil needed to supply its military machine continued to the end. After the conquest of Southeastern Europe it employed its continent-wide network to bring the oil companies of the region under German control. A letter from Ludwig Schmidt, a Kontinentale Oel official, to Rasche of the Dresdner Bank clearly shows the value of these widespread banking connections:

> Upon my return from a long business trip through the Ukraine, where I had to build up the organization for distribution of mineral oil for interests of the Kontinentale Oel A.G., I found the following note. . . .

"The Swiss majority group has made use of its right of disposal in the administration and offered the chairmanship to a member of the Vorstand of the Dresdner Bank, Alfred Busch."

Perhaps you will recall from our days together in Prague that when creating the Protectorate the "B-V" was interested very much in the acquisition of "Fanto A.G.," Prague.

I think . . . the influence of your bank in the Prague enterprise has become stronger. . . . [We now] also have an interest in the acquisition of the Hungarian Fanto. . . .

Again in 1942 the Dresdner reporting the completion of a task on which Kontinentale Oel "placed very special importance" said:

We have learned from the Kontinentale Bank, Brussels, that it was able to acquire the 60 shares of subject stock from Mr. Waterkayn. . . .

That the German war machine ground to a halt through lack of oil was not due to lack of diligent participation in far-reaching efforts to secure it.

THE DRESDNER BANK AND THE HERMANN-GOERING-WERKE

The Hermann Goering complex was the third largest trust in Europe, ranking next to I.G. Farben and the Vereinigte Stahlwerke. It was the first and largest Nazi industrial combine created for one purpose only—to prepare Nazi Germany for its war of aggression by assuring a sufficient supply of iron ore, coal, steel, and the machines of a modern war. As Germany expanded to the East, South, and West, the Hermann-Goering-Werke expanded in the same directions. In the short period 1937–1941 the Hermann-Goering-Werke acquired five large corporations in Germany, four in Austria, two in the Sudetenland, six in the Protectorate of Bohemia and Moravia, three in Poland, two in Lorraine, and numerous small enterprises in the Soviet Union, combined under the Berg und Huetten Ost A.G.

The German Reich may have controlled the Hermann-Goering-Werke. However, when banking services were required it turned to the Dresdner Bank.

Otto Schniewind, chief of the Banking Department of the Ministry of Economics until 1937, says on this point:

An important example in this field (financing war firms) was the construction of the Hermann-Goering-Werke . . . an unprofitable concern and likely to be a poor credit risk. Despite this fact the Dresdner Bank took the lead in floating huge loans for the Hermann-Goering-Werke.

The Dresdner Bank cannot claim to have been an unwilling agent of a government corporation, however. In a letter to Hellmuth Roehnert, one of the most prominent executives of Hermann-Goering-Werke, Rasche wrote:

During our last discussion I mentioned the possibility of seizing an armament works located in Belgium. The enclosure will reveal further details.

When in the fall of 1937 the share capital of the Hermann-Goering-Werke was increased from RM 5 million to RM 400 million, the Dresdner Bank was empowered to procure the subscriptions of the steel industry to the share capital of the Hermann-Goering-Werke. The Dresdner Bank also headed a syndicate authorized to place RM 25 million of Hermann-Goering-Werke share capital.

Karl Rasche, the linking personality between the Hermann-Goering-Werke and the Dresdner Bank, executed "Special Missions" for the Reichsmarschall. In a letter dated 23 December 1943 to Gritzbach, chief of staff of Reichsmarschall Goering, Rasche prides himself that

> in the course of events (Sudeten crisis of 1938) Kehrl (of the Ministry of Economics) and I were given the authority by the Reichsmarschall to acquire and regroup such industrial concerns (Poldi Huette, Bruenn munition works), and I believe that we were able with good results to fulfill this assignment on the basis of his delegation of authority. You may see in all this to what extent we were active in this field (acquisition of foreign steel and mining establishments) precisely for the Hermann-Goering-Werke in a way similar to that in which we were active before in Germany in other situations.

The ties between the Hermann-Goering-Werke and the Dresdner Bank were further strengthened by the active participation of several leading personalities of the Hermann Goering complex in the Dresdner Bank Aufsichtsrat. The most important among these was Hellmuth Roehnert who was, next to Pleiger, the strongest figure in the Goering combine. Wilhelm Meinberg, director of eight Hermann-Goering-Werke subsidiaries, was also vice-chairman of the Working Committee of the Dresdner Bank, and Wilhelm Marotzke, director in the Office of the Four Year Plan for the Hermann-Goering-Werke, were instrumental in cementing the close relationship between the Dresdner Bank, its affiliates, and the Hermann Goering combine.

The correspondence files of the Dresdner Bank contain innumerable letters covering a variety of financial tasks which the Dresdner performed for the corporation. How far beyond normal banking practices this cooperation with Hermann-Goering-Werke took the bank may be judged from the fact that the Dresdner was one of the negotiators for the sale of a large French steel firm, S. A. des Hauts Fourneaux et Fonderies de Pont-a-Mousson Gewerkschaft Carolus Magnus, to the Hermann-Goering-Werke and that it acted as negotiator in settling claims arising out of the Goering acquisitions of Czechoslovakian holdings.

Karl Rasche's [postwar interrogation] on the Hermann-Goering-Werke describes, although sometimes in a vague fashion, the close relationship existing between the Dresdner Bank and the Hermann-Goering-Werke from the date of the latter's inception.

It is also evident from the Rasche letter to Gritzbach that the Dresdner Bank acted as the financial spearhead for the Hermann-Goering-Werke. Through its financial affiliates the Dresdner Bank secured the choice enterprises of every industry in the occupied and satellite countries of Europe. The acquisition of control of Skoda in

Czechoslovakia illustrates the role of the Dresdner Bank in the growth of the Hermann-Goering-Werke.

When in 1939 the Dresdner Bank acquired the Boehmische Escompte Bank, the Dresdner Bank took over its extensive industrial participations and turned them over to the Hermann-Goering-Werke. The Boehmische Escompte Bank retained the banking leadership for the Czechoslovakian enterprises incorporated into the Hermann-Goering-Werke. This bank handled capital increases, as well as the buying out of shares still in private industry, in order to give the Hermann-Goering-Werke the controlling interest, as the interrogation of Wilhelm Marotzke, director in the Office of the Four Year Plan for the Hermann-Goering-Werke, well substantiates. The report on the activities of the Dresdner Bank in Czechoslovakia discusses in detail the most important transactions on behalf of the Hermann-Goering-Werke in the Protectorate and Sudetenland. The Hermann-Goering-Werke in its operations in Czechoslovakia, "scarcely invited other banks" for example nonaffiliates of the Dresdner Bank.

Aryanization enters prominently into the methods used by the Dresdner Bank to expand the Hermann-Goering-Werke. A classic example is the acquisition of the Gewerkschaft Witkowitz Sudetenland. This large mining concern was 75 percent controlled by the Rothschild family and 25 percent by the Guthmann family. The Dresdner Bank negotiated the transfer of this mining concern to the Hermann-Goering-Werke. The date of payment was to be 1 October 1939. However, "as on the first of September 1939, the war had broken out, the agreement could not be fulfilled."

In Austria, the Laenderbank Wien, a Dresdner affiliate, was in close cooperation with Hermann-Goering-Werke Austrian subsidiaries through Hitschfeld, manager of the Laenderbank and member of the board of directors of the Hermann-Goering-Werke. Another Vorstand member of the Laenderbank, Wolzt, was a member of the board of directors of the Steyr-Daimler-Puch, a Hermann-Goering-Werke subsidiary.

The extent of financial assistance to the Hermann-Goering-Werke by the Dresdner Bank is also shown in the size of credits authorized by the Credit Committee of the Dresdner Bank to various Hermann-Goering-Werke subsidiaries in Europe. In 1941 alone the Dresdner Bank placed at the disposal of Hermann-Goering-Werke RM 123,614,000 through the following affiliates:

> RM 90,737,000 with Laenderbank Wien
> RM 19,000,000 with the Kommerzialbank, Cracow
> RM 13,877,000 with the Handels und Kreditbank, Riga.

The activities of the Dresdner Bank extended beyond the named banking tasks of supplying funds. Rasche, in describing the job to be done in the Protectorate by the manager of its affiliate, the Boehmische Escompte Bank, says:

> Since January 1st, while von Laedinghausen (the manager) was absent from Prague, important economic questions have come up for solution of which the continued presence of von Laedinghausen in Prague is necessary. Removals, capital increases, expansions and concentrations in the local (i.e.

Protectorate) industries, that are important to the war effort, require the presence of von Laedinghausen in particular concerns and in which he is one of the very few Germans.

In addition the rising political tension makes a strengthening of German influence necessary. Discussions are taking place at present regarding company management in which von Laedinghausen is greatly concerned.

Attached is a list of the concerns to which he is called.

Half the firms in the list are part of the Hermann Goering combine. The letter reveals the Dresdner Bank to be not in any impassive role of banker but as the active partner of Nazi Germany's huge arms firm.

The activities of Hermann-Goering-Werke as a leader in Nazi Germany's preparation for a war of aggression are properly the subject of an investigation of that concern. The Dresdner Bank as the most important support of the Hermann-Goering-Werke and as an aggressive partner in its activities in Germany and Europe must share responsibility for its activities, political, economic, and criminal.

ARYANIZATION OF GERMAN ECONOMY

Goering: Gentlemen! Today's meeting is of a decisive nature. I have received a letter written on the Fuehrer's orders by the Stabsleiter of the Fuehrer, Deputy Bormann, requesting that the Jewish question be now, once and for all, coordinated and solved one way or another. And yesterday the Fuehrer requested me once again by phone to take coordinated action in the matter. . . .

The meeting in which we first talked about this question and came to the decision to Aryanize German economy, to take the Jew out of it and put him into our debit ledger, was one in which, to our shame, we only made pretty plans which were executed very slowly.

If today a Jewish shop is destroyed, if goods are thrown into the street, the insurance companies will pay for the damages which the Jew does not even have—and furthermore goods of the consumer, goods belonging to the people, are destroyed. If in the future demonstrations are necessary and occur, I pray that they be directed so as not to hurt us.

For it is insane to clean out and burn a Jewish warehouse and then have a German insurance company make good the loss. And the goods which I need desperately, whole bales of clothing and whatnot, are being burnt; and I miss them everywhere. (From the stenographic report of the conference on the Jewish question under the presidency of Fieldmarshall Goering at the Air Ministry in November 1938)

Thus Goering summed up the economic aims of the Nazi regime in Aryanizing property in Germany.

Goering could not say of the Dresdner Bank that it had "only made pretty plans." From the very beginning it had aggressively seized every opportunity "to take the Jew out" of the German economy.

The Dresdner Bank gained for itself such a reputation in this field that firms intending to engage in Aryanizations solicited it for assistance, which they met with ready cooperation. This reply of the bank to such soliciting leaves no doubts as to its willingless to join in this dirty business:

> We took notice of your letter of March 22. The Dresdner Bank is very actively engaged in Aryanization problems and is, thanks to its connections, in a position to help you place the businesses (to be Aryanized) in proper hands. I shall be very happy to discuss this matter with you personally and request you to get in touch with me as soon as you arrive in Berlin.

The Dresdner Bank pursued its Aryanization activities in a manifold fashion. First came a series of acquisitions for the bank itself among which Aryanization of banking houses and some industrial enterprises are outstanding. Second—and most numerous—was the financing of Aryanizations coupled with selection of "targets," the appraisal of "targets," and the search for customers. The bank was able to utilize and exploit its reputation for political reliability in order to gain preference from the Ministry of Economics in allocations on a national scale and from the District Economic Adviser of the NSDAP (Gauwirtschaftsberater) on a regional and local level. Jewish holdings in Germany prior to 1933 were weak in heavy industry, stronger in private banking, and comparatively pronounced in the consumer goods industries, primarily in leather, shoe manufacturing, beer, cosmetics, and garment industries. This distribution of Jewish enterprises classified by industry is reflected in the kinds of business which were Aryanized.

The Dresdner Bank was probably unique in the exercise of political duress in Aryanizations as early as 1933–1934. At that time, it acquired control of the second largest brewery concern in Germany for the Dresdner Bank itself. The Engelhardt Brauerei A.G. was controlled by Mr. Ignatz Nacher. As it is evident from the affidavits [in a court case] Mr. Nacher was aware that he would be unable to continue directing his large brewery business and approached a small banking house, the Eidenschink, in Munich to explore the possibilities of selling his interests. By May 1934 an agreement between Nacher and the Eidenschink banking house was concluded.

To quote the affidavit of one of the partners of the Eidenschink banking house, Dr. Adolf Fischer:

> The Dresdner Bank, Berlin, learned about this agreement and in a very short time, due to the fact that the bank was interested in acquiring the business, had seen to it that Nacher was arrested under some pretext. Before I was in a position to find Nacher in jail, he was put under such pressure that he had to give to his lawyer an unlimited power of attorney for the disposal of his possessions. He was informed that he would not be set free if he did not sign this power of attorney. When I visited him in the jail, on Alexander Platz, this

power of attorney was already signed. After signing this power of attorney Nacher was released from jail.

It is quite apparent that someone got in touch with the Gauleiter of Berlin to see to it that Nacher placed his business in the hands of the Dresdner Bank. This conspiracy between the management of the Dresdner Bank and the leading Nazi authorities is further substantiated by the lawsuit which the Eidenschink banking house instituted against the Dresdner Bank, charging damages and breach of a legal contract. The partners of the Eidenschink banking house were summoned to Berlin at the time of this lawsuit and informed by the Gestapo that if they did not drop this matter they could expect to be arrested.

Excerpts from the records of the Dresdner Bank in 1936 show the results of this transfer of ownership from Nacher to the bank. Out of RM 100,000 worth of preferred stock, 92 percent was in the hands of the Dresdner Bank. Out of RM 12 million share capital, 5,556,000 was in the hands of the Dresdner Bank.

The new Aufsichtsrat of the brewery contained Karl Rasche, Overbeck and Baron du Four von Ference, all leading personalities of the Dresdner, as members. Karl Rasche was even made chairman of the brewery's Aufsichtsrat. The Dresdner appointed other members of the board. For instance, Karl Rasche brought into the direction of the brewery Paul Pleiger, an early Nazi supporter in the Rhineland, and subsequently the general manager of the Hermann-Goering-Werke.

In the field of private banking, those owned by non-Aryans became easy prey to the Nazi bankers. The Dresdner Bank led by taking over the private banking houses of Gebrueder Arnhold in Dresden and Berlin, S. Bleichroeder & Company, Berlin, Bank fuer Brauindustrie, Berlin, B. Simons & Co., Duesseldorf.

An example of Aryanization by the Dresdner Bank for its own benefit, and an extremely important and profitable venture, was the acquisition in 1938 of the banking firm, Gebrueder Arnhold and S. Bleichroeder, in conjunction with the Dresdner Bank affiliate, Hardy and Company. The firm of Gebrueder Arnhold was considered one of the soundest and best known of the small banks in Germany. The wealth of the Arnhold family amounted to about RM 15,000,000.

A letter by Dr. Walter Frisch, a partner of Arnhold, dated 9 October 1945, on the subject "The taking over of the business of Arnhold Brothers and S. Bleichroeder by the Dresdner Bank" indicates the circumstances under which the Dresdner Bank effected this acquisition and the motivation for such acquisition:

> Conditions had become unbearable for the Arnholds in Dresden, as the Gauleiter persecuted them in the meanest way and made their life miserable. . . .
>
> The Dresdner Bank approached us and offered to buy the Dresden branch. . . . The Dresdner Bank did not want to lose this opportunity for prestige reasons, inasmuch as valuable Saxonian interests were merged in the Dresden branch of Arnhold Brothers.
>
> One point which the Dresdner Bank refused to discuss was the question of how the Arnholds shall transfer their now tangible property. . . . The purchaser took care of the pensions except those of the Jewish employees. . . .

The later developments of stock exchange quotations in 1939 and during the war have resulted in benefits for the Dresdner Bank arising out of the transactions with Arnhold.

The bulk of Aryanization cases transacted by the Dresdner Bank were cases where the bank financed the Aryanization, found "appropriate" clients, and utilized its connections and its good standing with Nazi authorities to effect the Aryanization of Jewish business.

A very pointed case of that nature is the Aryanization of the I. & C. A. Schneider, Frankfurt a/M, a very large leather and shoe manufacturing business, whose annual sales in 1938 exceeded RM 20 million and whose net profits in the same year amounted to more than RM 2.5 million. The Dresdner Bank conducted this transaction, utilizing the economic section (Gauwirtschaftsberater) of the Nazi Party in Frankfurt. The sworn affidavit of Fred Adler, a naturalized American citizen residing in New York City, describes in detail the circumstances surrounding this Aryanization:

> We, my brother and I, the owners, were put under strongest economic and political pressure by the Nazis. This pressure was practiced on us with increasing force, and culminated in repeated threats on life and imprisonment if we did not yield. Particularly after the well-known pogrom of 9 November 1938, this pressure practiced upon us became unbearable, and we gave up our efforts towards either not selling or getting anything remotely equaling the true value of our enterprise. On 9 November 1938, I was arrested and put into the notorious Buchenwald camp. There I received official word from a representative of the above mentioned Commercial Department of the Frankfurt section of the NSDAP that I could not count on being ever released from Buchenwald unless my brother and I accepted the proposition embodied in the enclosed contract. Thus I accepted and after I had done so, I was released on 23 November 1938, and the contract, as per enclosure, was finally executed on 17 December 1938.

The contract signed under the threat of a return to the Buchenwald concentration camp provides for payment of less than 3 percent of the net worth of the I. & C. A. Schneider enterprise. Cases of this and similar nature can be cited covering all sorts of enterprises and ranging from small transactions to huge businesses.

A few items from the Dresdner Bank records suggest the magnitude of such operations.

> 1938—loan of RM 1,600,000 to Liedermann for Aryanizing the Goetze company in Silesia
> 1938—loan of RM 100,000 to Graf Dannersmark for Aryanizing the Vanag Eisen Giesserel
> 1938—loan of RM 1,048,000 to Grohag, store-buying corporation for the Aryanizing of stores
> 1939—loan of RM 300,000 to Robert Koch Stiftung for Aryanizing of Holz Industrie Witkowitz

> 1939—loan of RM 2,000,000 to Alfred Bonnecke for Aryanization of Anselm-Kahn, Neilbronn

The Dresdner Bank took full advantage of the laws passed by the Nazi government for the removal of Jews from the German economy and Jewish employees from positions in German business.

Thus no German bank today holds accounts of Jews on its books. All assets deposited by non-Aryans with German banks were confiscated under the Nazi regime. The establishment of the "legal bases" for such confiscation lagged behind the actual seizures. There are several ordinances on the basis of which the banks were used as a means for facilitating the theft of Jewish property.

The expropriation of Jewish firms fell within the official area of activity of the Gauwirtschaftsberater of the district in which the Aryanization took place. Walter Schieber, Wilhelm Avieny, and Karl Heinrich Heuser were among the directors of the Dresdner Bank who occupied these positions and whose functions therefore included the supervision and encouragement of the taking over of Jewish businesses.

The directors gained personally through Aryanization. Heinrich Koppenberg is among those who derived benefit through the taking over of Jewish property. In 1939 Koppenberg, general manager of Junkers, and member of the Aufsichtsrat of the Dresdner Bank since 1935, acquired from Mr. Strauss, a Jew, then in a concentration camp, the Argus Motorenwerke. The Dresdner Bank extended a RM 2,000,000 loan to complete this transaction.

It may also be noted here that one-third of the workers in this firm were slave laborers from France, Holland, Belgium, and Ukraine, and that the Ukrainian workers were kept in camps under guard.

The Dresdner Bank "cleansed" thoroughly its branches and affiliates of non-Aryan employees. It went a step further and made sure that the enterprises it controlled were free of Jewish employees.

An example of the thoroughness with which removal of Jewish employees was carried out in companies which were interlocked with the Dresdner Bank through directors or managers is contained in a letter of 21 February 1938 regarding the Mimosa Company, Dresden, found in the files of Busch, a manager of the Dresdner Bank and a director of the Mimosa Company. The letter states:

> In this company and its affiliated companies, all non-Aryans must immediately disappear.

The Dresdner Bank was an active force in executing the Hitler aim of eliminating the Jews from German life. The Dresdner Bank utilized its large funds to effect these Aryanizations. The Dresdner Bank utilized its political standing with the Party, the government, and the SS to assure that the bank and its customers profited to the greatest possible extent from this policy. The Dresdner Bank carried its experience in the field of Aryanization to the occupied and satellite countries of Europe.

The responsibility for acting as an accomplice in this flagrant crime against humanity rests with the Vorstand who directed these policies, with the Aufsichtsrat who approved them, and with the local managers and employees of the Dresdner Bank who executed these operations in the field.

NAZIFICATION OF THE DRESDNER BANK

The Dresdner Bank gave its full support to the Nazi Party, assisting in the maintenance and strengthening of this totalitarian dictatorship. From the Nazi rise to power in 1933 until the end of the war, a steadily increasing percentage of Dresdner officials were members of the Nazi Party and a large portion of the remainder gave a measure of direct support. The employment rolls of the bank were purged, financial support was given to a multitude of auxiliary and semi-official agencies of the Party, and loans were granted to these organizations.

The Dresdner enjoyed the dubious honor of being known as the "SS Bank." This sign of Party acclaim was well deserved.

A thorough Nazification of personnel followed the advent of Hitler to power. Accurate figures on the number of Dresdner employees who were Party members are not available. A report, compiled by the Berlin office of the bank on the basis of the partial records available, cites 219 persons who were removed for political reasons during the period 1933–1937. The attitude of the bank is clearly shown in the 1936 annual report on employees, which opens by saying:

> Furthermore we have given special one-year courses for selected members . . . by which the participants received a thorough education in banking and political points of view. . . . within our organization we made special efforts to promote feelings of unity and good fellowship. Our efforts were energetically supported by the confidence (Party block) men.

The practical implication of these words may be judged from the affidavit of Robert Stuck, manager of the Dresdner Bank's Bremen bank, on this point. He states in an affidavit that:

> we would also have come into difficulties with our chief office in Berlin in case we refused (to join the NSDAP).

Thorough education in "banking matters and political points of view" was required of the highest as well as the lowest. The Dresdner had three of its officials on Martin Bormann's Banking Committee. These were Heuser, Walter Schieber, and Wilhelm Avieny, all of whom were also members of the Working Committee of the bank. Kurt von Schroeder, head of the Industry Group Private Banks, in describing the formation of this banking committee says

> that this committee and its purpose of introducing leading officials of the Party into the major banks, had previously been discussed . . . with Goetz, Rasche, and Meyer, from the Dresdner Bank.

The Dresdner Bank not only complied with the Nazi racial "philosophy" itself, but saw that all the members of its vast chain of affiliates and subsidiaries did too. As early as August 1933, we find the Deutsch Suedamerikanische Bank writing:

We kindly inform you that we have carried out the Aryan paragraph of the above law (Aryan) in our German subsidiaries Berlin and Hamburg.

The percentage of Party members on its Aufsichtsrat ranged from 67 percent in 1933 to 84 percent in 1945. Carl Goetz, head of the Dresdner Bank, in an interrogation concerning the reasons for changes in this body, comments as follows:

> Kopher-Aschoff—he was dropped from the merged board (Darmstaedter-Dresdner) because someone had to be and he was an old-line Democrat.
> Bachem—he was manager of a socialist bank.
> Meindl—he went to the Laenderbank Wien . . . when we had to make room for some Party appointees.
> Loeser—Party troubles in Essen.

And similar comment is made with monotonous regularity as to the remainder.

From 1937 on the Vorstand had a total membership of nine and of this number five were Nazi Party members, four, while not members, were definitely acceptable to the strong SS group within the bank.

The SS Bank boasted of a complement of officers of the SS. The Aufsichtsrat and Vorstand alone had three Brigadefuehrer, one Standartenfuehrer, one Obersturmbannfuehrer, two Sturmbannfuehrer, and one Hauptsturmfuehrer among those whose membership are known.

The bank contributed in various ways to the host of auxiliary organizations of the NSDAP. No figures are available concerning the total of the contributions, but the annual reports mention the following organizations as receiving funds:

> Beihilfen zur Teilnahne an Erholungsreisen mit der NSG "Kraft durch Freude"
> Freizeitgestaltung
> Sportliche Gemeinschaften
> S.A.—Sportabzeichen
> Sportvereinigungen des Betriebes
> Segelflugsport
> Sport- u. Erholungsheim Gruenau
> Reichsberufswettkampf
> Leistungskampf deutscher Betriebe (Gaudiplome)
> Reichslehrgaenge zur Schulung des Nachwuchses (Reichsgruppe Banken)
> Musik u. Spielmannszug.

The history of Nazi blackmail has been well documented and one of the best known organizations is the notorious Keppler Circle, the group of industrialists and bankers around Himmler. The Dresdner Bank was represented in this select group by Rasche, Meyer, Kranefuss, Lindemann, Flick, Walz, and Roehnert. Lindemann, in an affidavit, says that Kranefuss, rather than Keppler, was the moving spirit of this group. That contributions were made as a business proposition is shown in this affidavit by Lindemann:

Helfferich added that it would be difficult for him to maintain friendly business relations with the NDL (Norddeutsche Linie) if Lindemann continued in such manner and reminded Lindemann that both HAL (Hamburg-Amerika Linie) were heavily dependent on government support.

The account books of the bank show a yearly contribution of RM 50,000 to this group. In making the 1944 donation Meyer wrote:

> I wish to inform you that the Vorstand of the Dresdner Bank has remitted today RM 50,000 to a J. H. Stein Bank in Koeln for special accounts.

> My firm is placing this amount at the disposal of our Reichsfuehrer (that is, Himmler, Reichsfuehrer of the SS).

In extending loans to the SS, the bank knew that the only sources for repayment were the loot and blackmail the SS extracted from Jews and political enemies of the Nazi regime, and later from inhabitants of the occupied countries.

The respectable bankers of the SS Bank viewed this sordid business nonchalantly. With respect to the approval of these "business" loans, the minutes of the Vorstand read:

> 21-7-38 Dr. Meyer reports that the leader of the SS Death's Head Band and concentration camp governing office advised. . . . In the SS budget submitted to the Reich Finance Ministry for approval, the amount in question (RM 20,000 per house) has been listed. In his (Meyer's) view the procurement of mortgages will not present any difficulties.

> 15-9-39 . . . changes in the board of directors of the Deutsche Ansiedlungs Bank planned by the Rasse und Siedlungsamt. In the judgment of the Vorstand we should try to get an official declaration for our indemnification, before giving our opinion about the changes mentioned.

> 27-3-39 Report on the request by the SS Gesellschaft Deutsche Erd- und Steinwerke A.G. for a credit of RM 5,000,000 (2,500,000 in the beginning) for one year. The Vorstand expresses the opinion that this request cannot be approved without the guarantee of the Reichsfuehrer of the SS in the usual form.

> 19-6-39 . . . the Gesellschaft zur Pflege Deutscher Kulturdenkmaeler (SS) has requested a loan of RM 2,000,000 at first, with the usual guarantee of the Reichsfuehrer of the SS . . . the present account with the Bank der Deutschen Arbeit is to be transferred to us in 1940 and maintained in our bank at a level of RM 1,000,000.

> 7-8-39 . . . after Mr. Goetz had been consulted, the Gotha Lebensversicherungs A.G. and the Allianz were contacted. In case the necessary approvals can be secured, these companies would be

prepared to take over this loan at a rate of 4 percent resp. 5 percent. The Reichsfuehrer of the SS agrees to pay 6 percent for this loan. It will be guaranteed in the same way as the present loan, by the usual declaration of the Reichsfuehrer of the SS.

The closing phrase of each credit report was a laconic "the Vorstand agrees." It is the Heil Hitler of the Dresdner Bank, approving of and participating in the organized brigandry of the SS.

CHAPTER XXI

Operations of the Dresdner Bank Outside Germany

The Dresdner Bank was not content with its dominant position in Germany proper but had branches and affiliates in every region of Europe, the Near East, and Latin America, where it served the Nazi cause.

In 1940 the annual statement said:

> The definite regulation of our economic relations to the territories more closely connected with the Reich, the further development of new forms for a European currency system, and the rebuilding of foreign trade will confront us with tasks which will require our whole power and attention. Thanks to our organization, consciously completed in this direction in the past decade, we hope to be able to render useful services to our customers and through them to the German economy.

The "definite regulation of our economic relations" meant the scouring of Europe for the controlling interests in the keys to European industry. The Dresdner Bank, its affiliates, and agents sought in every country to obtain, by any means possible, the property necessary for Nazi domination of Europe. The means included intimidation, black market, and the Gestapo.

The "useful services to our customers" included Aryanization of desirable firms, furnishing assistance in the Nazification of the industry of conquered Europe, furnishing economic intelligence, and acting as broker between the administrators of the conquered areas, Nazi businessmen, and the Nazi government.

The bank had "consciously completed its organization" as a part of the Nazi plan for exploiting Europe's conquered areas. When in 1944 the Four Year Plan Office handed Rasche the following order, it impressed the swastika seal of approval on the Dresdner as a partner. As a spearhead the bank had been so successful that when new areas were to be entered it was chosen as an agent for penetration. The order opens by saying:

> Within the limits of an extensive investigation of production possibilities, especially in the industrial field to increase rearmament efficiency, in Germany, allied and neutral countries, you are assigned, by order of the Reichs Minister for Rearmament to investigate the economic conditions of Sweden and Hungary. The enclosed publication by the Planungsamt, dated 16.9.43 will instruct you in your duties.
>
> Your duties are:

1. To discover the possibilities for developing unused or inefficiently used productive powers, and to ascertain the present industrial capacity.
2. To make reports and proposals as to the extent and in which way the experience of German specialists or the transfers of patents, etc., would result in additional war production.
3. To discover possibilities for particular individual business transactions in combination with third countries and additional export possibilities from occupied territories.
4. To report about the special political and economic situation, its possible improvement with consideration of the clearing and currency question.
5. To advise me of persons in foreign countries, who would be interesting as industrial business partners, or are especially influential in the economic and commercial rise (of their country), and especially those who are open-minded to the thought of European cooperative work in industry.
6. To report the general political, economic, and commercial situation with consideration of the above-mentioned points.
7. To observe generally the economic activities of enemy countries and their representatives, to report these facts, especially about measures taken to harm the German war economy such as "interference buys."
8. To call attention generally, to dangers that could harm the development of the German war economy. Your work will supplement the official reports and help me to finish my task and will have a direct effect on our economical warfare.

Current contact with you and cooperation in individual cases will be made through Karl Blessing, who has assumed the coordination and use of proposals made by the individual co-workers.

There was scarcely any need to brief the Dresdner, or Rasche, on their duties as economic fifth columnists. The following sections on espionage and propaganda activities, operations in Czechoslovakia, Poland, the Netherlands, Belgium, and the Baltic states show how experienced they were. This was the organization "consciously completed in this direction in the past decade" in operation.

THE DRESDNER BANK AS A NAZI ESPIONAGE AND PROPAGANDA AGENCY

The close ties between the Dresdner Bank, the Nazi Party, and the government agencies is also shown in the propaganda and espionage activities of the foreign branches and affiliates of the Dresdner Bank.

The Dresdner Bank cooperated in the dissemination of Nazi propaganda to foreign countries and important individuals who were influential in the banking and financial world. At the outbreak of the war, the Foreign Department of the Staff of the Deputy of the Fuehrer requested the cooperation of the banks by utilizing their foreign personal and business contacts to "enlighten" these people about the benefits of the Nazi regime in Germany. In response Carl Goetz prepared a partial list covering Holland, Switzerland, Romania, Luxembourg, Denmark, Belgium, Sweden, and the United States.

This was not the first time that Goetz participated in a propaganda campaign. A letter to him from C. H. Ehlers, 70 Pine Street, New York, New York, dated 3 May 1938, acknowledges receipt of a letter and a copy of the speech that Hitler delivered on 20 February 1938. Mr. Ehlers must have been an indoctrinated Nazi. In his letter he deplored the stupidity of the American people in retaining their firm belief in democracy.

An important propaganda battle waged by the Nazis took place in South and Central America. The Dresdner Bank maintained branches in Argentina, Brazil, Chile, Mexico, and Paraguay, and agents in Bolivia, Ecuador, Peru, and Venezuela through a subsidiary, the Deutsch-Suedamerikanische Bank.

All South American branches of the "SS Bank" cooperated with the NSDAP in furthering Nazi ideology. For example the Deutsch-Suedamerikanische Bank dismissed its non-Aryan Buenos Aires manager at the request of the NSDAP. Carl Goetz states that:

> We always had the interference of the Party. . . . I was approached by an official of the Reichskanzlei, Mr. von Gackwitz, who pressed us to dismiss Haase (the Jewish manager of the Buenos Aires branch).

Another example of the cooperation given the Nazi propaganda machine is revealed in the correspondence [concerning] . . . Carlos Meyer-Pelligrini, whose resignation from the Aufsichtsrat is the subject of discussion, was a prominent businessman. He had been a very helpful adviser to the Argentine branch of the Dresdner affiliate, Deutsch-Suedamerikanische Bank, for many years. The affiliate's letter to the Dresdner in summarizing his reasons for the resignation says:

> Dr. Meyer-Pelligrini writes in a very extensive letter to Mr. Leute (Buenos Aires branch manager), who sent us a copy, that the decision was very hard for him because he felt closely connected with Germany, but he considered that as a son of his father and as an Argentinian he would be involved in a conflict because of the actions and the program of the NSDAP which he did not hold to be proper, so he was drawing the conclusions.

The culminating circumstance which aroused Dr. Meyer-Pelligrini is described as follows:

> A circle has recently been formed here called "Amigos de Alemania" (Friends of Germany). It determined to organize a demonstration in honor of the German Ambassador during the presence of the English Willingdon mission. Among other persons Dr. Meyer-Pelligrini was summoned as a sponsor for the demonstration. . . . He continues in his letter saying that the party was allowed to demand of him, as a member of the Aufsichtsrat of the

bank, to join in actions which could not be harmonized with his neutral attitude as an Argentinian.

The Dresdner Bank's answer, as set out in a draft by Carl Goetz, emphasizes the completeness with which it had associated itself with the Nazi aims. The pertinent portion reads:

> Since I understand your decision has been prompted by political reasons, I have no other choice than to approve your resignation.

The close cooperation between the Dresdner Bank, its South American subsidiary the Deutsch-Suedamerikanische Bank (DSB) and the Nazi Party, and even the Gestapo is further substantiated in the dismissal in 1937 of Otto Egg, the manager of the DSB in Chile for "participation in the dissemination of Jewish refugee literature."

In South America the Dresdner Bank cooperated in the rearmament and war economy of the Nazi government by supplying intelligence. A letter of thanks to the Deutsch-Suedamerikanische Bank for information on Central and South America, by the I.G. Farben banking house, and the request that this be forwarded to NW 7, the Farben Intelligence Center, is an example of its cooperation.

Agencies of the Dresdner Bank in foreign countries served not only as centers of Nazi propaganda activities, but in several instances contained among their leading employees individuals engaged in espionage and generally subversive activities.

The close relationship between the Dresdner Bank and the Auslands-Organisation (AO) of the NSDAP under the leadership of Bohle is evident in an exchange of letters between the organization and the management of the Dresdner Bank:

> I shall attempt to contact Party Comrade Christians immediately, and in that fashion bring about an even closer cooperation between our affiliations abroad and the Auslands-Organisation of the NSDAP.

This pledge given by Emil Meyer to Bohle was accompanied by a list of Vorstand members in charge of banking affairs in foreign countries. Bohle was very happy to acknowledge this pledge.

Nazi propaganda activities in foreign countries were financed by the Dresdner Bank from Berlin, which also used its facilities to effect transfers of funds destined for Foreign Office and AO activities. An exchange of correspondence between Franz von Papen, former German ambassador in Turkey and master spy in World Wars I and II, and Carl Goetz deals with a Dresdner Bank contribution of RM 13,000 to the German School in Istanbul. The details of the transaction were worked out with the Foreign Office in such a fashion that the Turkish foreign exchange agencies would be in no position to identify this transaction. Undoubtedly considerable amounts of money were either directly contributed by the Dresdner Bank or transferred through Dresdner Bank channels for similar activities.

The Dresdner Bank always placed the leading personnel of its foreign branches and affiliates at the disposal of the Foreign Office. When diplomatic relations between Germany and Turkey were at the breaking point [near the end of World War II], the Dresdner Bank instructed its leading representative in Turkey, von Posth, to remain in Turkey in view of the desire of the Foreign Office to retain leading German economic representatives not only to look after German assets but also to lay the ground work for future German activities in Turkey.

The bank was most valuable in neutral and allied countries, for under the cover of routine banking activities and in the disguise of normal banking employees, German military intelligence and [a] fifth column could operate.

A classic example is provided by a glance at the activities of the Dresdner Bank in Egypt—the crucial Suez Canal area. Investigations of German espionage and propaganda activities in Egypt in the period 1933–September 1939 revealed that the Dresdner Bank was known to have been a center for Nazi activities, including espionage and propaganda in which the German employees were to a greater or lesser extent involved. The list of prominent Germans involved in operations on behalf of the Auslands-Organisation of the NSDAP, the German Foreign Office, and German Intelligence contains practically all the German employees of the Dresdner Bank in Egypt. The bank maintained branches in Cairo and Alexandria, although there was no sound commercial reason for these two branches, according to Rudolf Tofs, an employee of the Egyptian affiliate from 1934 to 1939.

The manager of the Dresdner Bank, Willy Lohmann, was closely associated with the internal organization of the Nazi Party in Egypt. He was the manager of the Dresdner Bank branch Alexandria and president of the *Deutsche Sportsverein* (German Sports Society).

Hans Sieber, the head of the Alexandria Nazi Party, was another leading employee of the Dresdner Bank. He attended to matters of administration for all Nazi groups in Alexandria and also maintained very close ties with the German Consulate.

The chief of the Exchange Department of the Dresdner Bank, Friedrich Wuelfkon, was the acting president of the Inspoltionsamt, Alexandria. . . .

Walter Bornecher, chief of the Portfolio Section of the Dresdner Bank, was an active Nazi organizer. . . .

The most prominent member of the German community in Egypt was Baron Richter, who was the director of the Dresdner Bank in Cairo. He was in constant touch with the German ambassador in Egypt, and is generally considered as a fanatical Nazi. Von Richter, by the admission of Hans Pilder, member of the Dresdner Bank Vorstand in charge of Foreign Operations, enjoyed the full confidence of the German political and diplomatic representatives in Egypt. He was appointed as head of the German Chamber of Commerce in Egypt.

Kurt Kunzel, Liquid Funds Section, was the leading Nazi organizer in Cairo, and eventually became commercial attaché of the German Consul in Beirut.

Typical of the Germans who used commercial or banking activities as camouflage for subversive and espionage activities is Ernst Otto, who came to Egypt in 1937 and was employed simultaneously by the Dresdner Bank and Bayer, [the] I.G. Farben Pharmaceuticals subsidiary. He was known to be one of the oldest members of the Nazi Party, specially trained in propaganda and engaged in espionage activities.

The treasurer of the Nazi Party in Egypt and of its Cairo section was the manager of the Dresdner Bank in that city, Harry Venske.

Another example of a prominent official of the Dresdner Bank and German espionage agent is Count Felix Czernin. Count Czernin was a director of the Continentale Bank S.A., Brussels—the Dresdner Bank spearhead in Belgium—a manager of a Sudeten branch of the Dresdner Bank, and a Vorstand member of the Laenderbank Wien. Count Czernin traveled extensively over Europe on behalf of the Dresdner Bank and reported his accomplishments to Karl Rasche. A report by Czernin dated 24 May 1944 deals with Hungary and describes vividly the process of Aryanization of the Hungarian economy. He describes in detail the effect of Aryanization upon Hungarian industry and banking, suggesting methods by which the Dresdner Bank can replace the Jewish banking and industrial interests in Hungary. Many of the activities of the Continentale Bank which are discussed in detail in the section The Dresdner Bank in Belgium were activities of Count Czernin. The above would not suggest that Count Czernin was anything else but an active, diligent official of the Dresdner Bank. However, an interrogation of Colonel Dehmel, Danzig Chief of the Intelligence Department of the German High Command until February 1944 and also of Intelligence Command, Prague, Reich Security Office of the SS, from February 1944 to the end of the war, disclosed that Count Felix Czernin was an agent of the German Counter Intelligence. He is listed as Czernin, Count Felix, alias Burger, Agent No. A-306.

THE DRESDNER BANK IN CZECHOSLOVAKIA

The bank in Czechoslovakia took the same leading part in formulating policies for organized fraud and robbery as it did in all other occupied countries. By obtaining a monopolistic delegation of authority from Goering, by utilizing close relations with the Nazi Party, and by milking dry Czech industry in Jewish hands, the bank was a foremost participant in the subjugation of the Czech economy.

In the process of economic conquest, the Dresdner Bank dealt with the government (the RWM and the Finance Ministry), and with the Party. It employed its affiliates in other countries. It applied pressure to the Protectorate authorities. It formed syndicates, it bought and sold shares, it acted as a depository custodian, and agent. It functioned as an economic intelligence agent, always planning in advance. It even arranged for passports.

The plan for the economic enslavement of Czechoslovakia was laid out along with the plans for the political conquest. Four days after the Munich pact, Carl Goetz was negotiating with the German Foreign Office about the acquisition of Czech banks, expressing the Dresdner Bank's special interests in the Boehmische Escompte Bank (BEB) and the Zivno Bank. These banks developed subsequently into the strongholds of the Dresdner Bank in Czechoslovakia.

Before war was officially declared, before the military conquest of Czechoslovakia was initiated, Goering handed Kehrl and Rasche their commissions to get Czech industry. Here is how Rasche tells his story, in a letter dated 23 December 1943 to Ministerial Direktor Gritzbach, Chief of Staff to Reichsmarschall Goering:

> The Poldi Huette A.G., Prague, which in its 50 years of existence has acquired a worldwide reputation, has since its inception had a comparatively

constant number of shareholders in Bohemia including the Boehmische Escompte Bank which worked with Poldi Huette at the time of its formation.

At the time of the return home to Germany of the Sudetenland in 1938, when the Boehmische Escompte Bank gave to the Dresdner Bank its Sudetenland branches, and when we could not foresee future developments, we attempted at the request of the German government offices even then to establish German influence over the industry of the Protectorate. We were successful in this and we acquired in trust for a certain German industrial group, which was yet to be ascertained, approximately 25 percent of the Poldi Huette shares and besides this the majority of the Bruenn Machine Works. In the course of events as you know, Kehrl and I were given a comprehensive delegation of authority by the Reichsmarshall for the acquisition and regrouping of such industrial concerns and I believe that we were able with good results to fulfill this assignment on the basis of his delegation of authority.

As you know out of these relationships grew in addition to the above-named also the Skoda shares, the Bruenner Waffen shares, and the group which is today under the name of Sudetenlaendische Bergbau A.G. You may see in all this to what extent we were active in this field precisely for the Hermann-Goering-Werke in a way similar to that in which we were active before in Germany in other situations. I may say frankly here that my personal activity in this connection has been condemned by other concerns.

With respect to the Poldi Huette, the goal at that time was to acquire gradually a greater and greater share of the stock and thus to bring the administration of this company securely into German hands. This was also accomplished by the formation of a syndicate. In addition to the above-mentioned 25 percent, other shares of various old holders were acquired so that by purchases on the open market and by the inclusion of acquired shares a majority of 51 percent in German hands was reached in 1939. At the end of 1939 and in the beginning of 1940 the further acquisition of shares for German industrial groups (Hermann-Goering-Werke were not so named openly at that time) was refused by both the Reichs Ministry and the Reichs Economics Ministry. At the same time our proposal to reacquire the shares (which appeared too expensive to the Reichs Finance Ministry) was similarly turned down. On 4 April 1940, the Hermann-Goering-Werke appeared openly in the pooling agreement.

The interrogation of Karl Rasche, 19 December 1945, further describes the efforts of the Dresdner Bank on behalf of the HGW. As soon as Dresdner Bank established a foothold in the Sudeten, it turned its main efforts to extending the Hermann-Goering-Werke into this new coal- and-iron rich territory. The principal companies acquired by the Dresdner Bank for the HGW were Sudetenlaendische Treibstoffwerke (fuel oil products), share capital RM 100,000,000. The Dresdner Bank executed this operation with the full consent of the Ministry of Economics. The lignite mines were held by the Czech-Jewish Petschek family. Karl Rasche, Herbeck, and Ansmann (the latter two from the Syndicate Department of the Dresdner Bank) incorporated these companies into the HGW combine, and when this company was consolidated with smaller lignite mines into the Sudetenlaendische Bergwerke (share capital RM 80,000,000; assets [1940] RM 140,129,844), Karl Rasche became the first chairman of the Aufsichtsrat. The Dresdner Bank and subsequently the BEB were established as the principal banking connections of these Sudeten companies and carried out the most important transactions on their behalf.

Karl Rasche's special mission on behalf of the Hermann-Goering-Werke was fully carried out and continued through the years by the BEB, the Dresdner Bank subsidiary in Bohemia.

❑ ❑ ❑

The report of the Dresdner Bank official on the acquisition of two Czech companies whose stock was held in France is informative. As a sideline he was promoting business for the Goering's Czech subsidiaries and is shown to be intimately connected with the management of the various plants of the huge armament combine. For example he states:

> The commanding admiral of France, represented by High Councillor Walbe, has upon my advice, sent a letter to the Isorel factory . . . he is not however in a position to make the formulae and specifications for the iron available . . . in my opinion, were it not for patents, these could be built by Skoda.
>
> Mueller . . . has offered, to send a machine to Prague for comparison. Then Skoda must work on an offer on these machines.

The condensed Dresdner Bank prospectus and correspondence introducing the Sudetenlaendische Bergwerke (Subag) shares on the stock markets of Berlin, Vienna, and Prague speak for themselves.

There were five principal components of the Hermann Goering combine in Czechoslovakia:

> The Poldi Huette (steel mills), share capital—K 250,000,000; assets—
>   794,174,903 (1942)
> Ferdinande Nordbahn (coal and coal products); share capital—
>   K 49,980,000; assets—K 509,895,187 (1940)
> Skoda A.G. (weapons, locomotives, machines), share capital—
>   K 687,500,000; assets—3,492,639,671 (1940)
> Waffenwerke Bruenn (small arms, explosives), share capital—
>   K 300,000,000
> Bruenner Maschinen A.G. (machines and power plant equipment),
>   share capital—K 65,000,000; assets—K 257,786,189 (1942)

The letter from Rasche to Gritzbach quoted above covers the role played by the Dresdner Bank in acquiring Poldi Huette for Hermann Goering. In the case of Ferdinande Nordbahn, the negotiations on behalf of the HGW were conducted by the Zivno Bank, and this company was incorporated into the HGW through the efforts of the Dresdner Bank affiliate. The jewel in the crown of Goering-Werke's far-flung possessions was the Skoda works—the largest European munitions facto-ry. It was the "great contribution" of the Dresdner Bank to assist actively in the acquisition of control by the HGW of the Skoda. Again, the Boehmische Escompte Bank, the Zivno Bank, and Rasche and Herbeck of the Dresdner Bank effected the transfer of control from Czech hands into German hands. The Waffenwerke Bruenn and Bruenner Maschinen were, to quote Karl Rasche, "brought into the Hermann-Goering-Werke group by the Dresdner Bank."

The means used to accomplish its aim mattered little to the Dresdner Bank. Sometimes a façade of legality was preserved. Blackmail, fraud, force, and pressure on the Protectorate government were all used as methods by the bank in conquered Czech provinces. Sometimes the transaction itself was dirty, as in the cases in which the Protectorate authorities would be approached to compel a businessman to go out of business. For instance, Werner Stenzel was a German machine-tool dealer who took the major portion of the foreign deliveries of the machine-tool division of Bata. He wanted to acquire that division. So Stenzel got in touch with his bank, the Dresdner, and discussed the matter with one of its officials, von Richter. Von Richter's memorandum on the meeting, dated 10 June 1942 [documents some of the intricacies of the takeover of a large business]:

> The firm Georg Stenzel & Co., a leading Berlin machine-tool company, is an old client of ours, with a considerable turnover [RM 13,000,000 2d half 1941; RM 7,8,00,000 1st quarter 1942, and very considerable property (at present RM 1,800,000)]. As of end of 1941 a capital of approximately RM 2,000 was indicated, in addition to owner's private property of several hun-dred thousand RM.
>
> Stenzel does considerable business with Bata's machine-tool division in Zlin.
>
> Stenzel estimates that it takes 70 percent (5 mill. RM) of the foreign deliver-ies of Bata's machine-tool division, and is anxious to effect a close relation-ship. In this connection a minority participation in the Podaiski machine-tool factory was effected.
>
> In case Bata should desire to separate itself from machine-tool production, Stenzel would be an interested party.
>
> Purpose of Stenzel's visit was
> (a)   to request us to ascertain, in the most discreet manner possible, whether Bata is considering cessation of machine-tool production.
> (b)   if not, whether such cessation could be suggested by Bata by the Protectorate authorities.
> (c)   to ask us if we are prepared to consider a combination with Stenzel & Co., which would facilitate a participation in the contemplated extension of the machine-tool industry.
>
> In response to (c) I answered that we unquestionably would be greatly inter-ested, if such project becomes concrete, and I can well imagine that we also would cooperate in effecting a solution which would make possible a partic-ipation by Stenzel in a company which might perhaps be organized together with other friends to incorporate Bata's machine-tool production. I pointed

out that the object apparently will become very large, and that therefore only a minority participation by Stenzel would be possible.

Stenzel believes he himself can answer (a), as he has excellent relations with Bata as his principal dealer for Germany; he also believes that if any sale suggestions were made to Bata, Bata would welcome a combination with Stenzel. Stenzel is therefore concerned that these questions are presented to the Bata management in the most discreet form possible—certainly without naming the name of Stenzel.

With respect to (b) Stenzel would appreciate most a discreet approach in that direction, as to whether the Protectorate authorities might approach Bata about the extension and making independent of the machine-tool production.

❑ ❑ ❑

Aryanization was one of the most common means of spoliation. It was in this connection that the bank dealt most frequently with the Gestapo. The relationship between the bank, its Czech affiliate, the Boehmische Escompte Bank, the Gestapo, the RWM, and the Protectorate are shown in the following brief notes, concerning the acquisition of the controlling interest in a Czech cement corporation:

TELEGRAM   4 MARCH 1942
TO: DRESDNER BANK, BERLIN
FROM: ESCOMPTE BANK PRAGUE

ACCORDING TO RECENT INVESTIGATIONS, 8,691 KOENIGSHOFER SHARES ARE STILL HELD BY JEWS. OF THESE 7,500 ARE BLOCKED BY THE GESTAPO AND APPROXIMATELY 1,000 ARE OWNED BY FOREIGN JEWS. WE NEED AN ADDITIONAL 5,200 SHARES TO COMPLETE THE 25 PERCENT FOR "SCHACHTELPRIVILEGS." A DECISION ABOUT THE SHARES BLOCKED BY THE GESTAPO HAS NOT YET BEEN RECEIVED. PURCHASE PRICE FOR FREE JEWISH KOENIGSHOFER SHARES AT 2.340—HAS NOT BEEN ACCEPTED BY THE GESTAPO AS YET. AFTER A SETTLEMENT WITH THE GESTAPO AND ACCEPTANCE OF SHARES WHICH ARE THE PROPERTY OF FOREIGN JEWS, 3,500 SHARES WILL BE FREE. NO JEWISH-HELD SHARES ARE SEIZABLE AT THIS MOMENT.

18 MAY 1942
TRANSMITTED BY MR. VON HEES, REICHSWIRTSCHAFTSMINISTERIUM.

THE REICHSPROTEKTOR INFORMED US THAT HE AGREED WITH THE SUDETENLAENDISCHE BERGBAU A.G. BRUEX, TO TAKE OVER 7,874 PIECES OF WESTBOEHMISCHE BERGBAUVEREIN SHARES DERIVING FROM JEWISH PROTECTORATE PROPERTY, AND TO SURRENDER AN APPROPRIATE AMOUNT OF KOENIGSHOFER ZEMENTFABRIK SHARES TO THE BOEHMISCHE ESCOMPTE BANK PRAGUE IN EXCHANGE . . . ADDITIONAL SHARES WILL PROBABLY BE AVAILABLE FOR THIS TRANSACTION IN THE NEAR FUTURE.
          [SIGNATURE ILLEGIBLE]

The simplicity with which national boundaries vanished within the Nazi economic Lebensraum is shown in the incident of the German firm seeking to acquire a

Slovakian firm by writing to the Austrian affiliates of the Dresdner Bank to suggest that the Hungarian Aryanization program be utilized. The German firm was the Lihag, the Landwirtschaftliche Industrie und Handels A.G., Pressburg. The Slovakian coal business was M. Schick, Pressburg. The Austrian affiliate of the Dresdner Bank was the Laenderbank Wien. The Hungarian affiliate of the Dresdner Bank was the Ungarische Allgemeine Kreditbank. On 6 June 1944, the German firm wrote to the Austrian Bank using the following typical reasoning:

> Since Schick has never operated in a clean business way (it disregards price controls), it has long been planned to confiscate subject firm, and its license has been withdrawn. But since Schick has influential Hungarian friends, these actions had to be postponed and the license returned.
>
> Would it not be possible in line with the confiscation of Jewish interests in Hungary, to assume the Slovakian interests of the Ungarische Allgemeine Kohlen A.G., and to confiscate the Jewish firm Schick?

In carrying out the program for penetration, the bank ran the gamut of functions. Some of the paragraphs above show how it welded together its foreign affiliates with the aid of the Reichs Ministry, the Party, the Protectorate, and how its customers were welded into a unit and driven in the direction of Nazi objectives. They show how it secured intelligence and participated in industrial Germanization. The bank was constantly acquiring participations. On 22 March 1939, immediately following the German occupation of Czechoslovakia, for instance, the "Kehrl-Rasche Group" "acquired" 130,528 out of a total of 296,840 shares, in addition to the 15,600 shares held by BEB and 15,600 held by the Zivnostenska Banka of Waffenwerke Bruenn A.G., share capital in 1937 120 million kroenen.

None of these functions were incidental. Their importance was recognized organizationally. A special section for Aryanization matters (*Arisierungsgruppe*) employing four people, constitutes one of the personnel units listed in the BEB's report on administrative expenses, dated 3 April 1941. Total administrative expenses incurred by the Aryanization section for the first half of 1940 were 164,900 kroenen. The monthly portion of this amount paid out as salaries increased from 16,600 kroenen in July 1940 to 16,900 kronen in December. As an apology for the fact that the statistical evaluation of administrative costs may not be entirely accurate, the explanation is given in the introduction of the report quoted above that this inaccuracy is due to the fact that

> the various divisions have been occupied for the most part with special tasks, such as the organic inclusion of the economy of the Protectorate into that of the economic sphere of Greater Germany and the exclusion of Jews from the economy.

The bank was a purchase and sales agent in connection with Jewish securities. The following is a listing taken from a BEB report on the monthly statement as of 31 August 1941, noting transactions during the month:

Our Assets (Nostro II)		(Jewish Securities)
	Purchases	*Sales*
Karborundum	K 100,000	
Koliner Spiritus	400,000	
Prager Eisen	100,000	
Pressburger Kabel	100,000	
Pressburger Magnesit	100,000	
Tarbouches	200,000	
Diverse	200,000	
Elbekosteletzer		150,000
Hellmann		750,000
Koenigshofer		300,000

It also acted as a custodian. A footnote to the listings of purchases of Jewish securities states that

> additional securities acquired from Jewish possession in the year 1941 appear in the sense that we function merely as custodians, and that (these securities) are listed under debtors in the amount of approximately 42,250,000 kroenen.

Although Aryanization activity was considerably less after 1942, the BEB's enthusiasm for this type of business had by no means diminished. Thus, for example, negotiations were carried on from March to June 1942 between the BEB, the Dresdner Bank, and the Gildemann Cigar Factory, Hamburg, a German concern which was eager to acquire an "Aryanizable object." The aid given Gildemann by the BEB in this connection left little to be desired.

The following chain of correspondence speaks for itself:

1. *Letter dated 12 March 42, from Helmut Ritter, Direktor, Gildemann Cigar Factory, Berlin, to Rasche:*

   Director Stitz-Ulrici, of the BEB, offered us the firm Waldes & Co., Prague, on Monday, via Franz Ploner of Rigele-Goering Bureau, who is very close to the Goering family and is also very well known to Reichsprotektor Heydrich, and who has been kind enough to transmit our request. Our interest in subject is foregone . . . It is therefore necessary that our Lehnert and Ritter visit Prague. We would appreciate it if you would assist us in securing the necessary passes.

2. *Cable dated 16 March 42, Boehmische Escompte Bank (BEB) to Rasche:*

   We are preparing the necessary affidavits for the passports.

3. *Letter 19 May 42, Ritter to BEB:*

   Referring to our letter of 6 May with enclosed list of 34 firms, we request information as soon as possible. We would appreciate it if your Stitz-Ulrici could come here with the desired information regarding the 34 firms. . . .

As it is evident from subsequent correspondence the 34 "Aryanizable" firms in question were the following:

Waldes & Co., Prague
A.G. fuer Textilindustrie, Koeniginhof a.d. E.
S. Katzau, Baumwollspinnerei, Babi
F. M. Oberlander und Hronower Baumwollspinnerei A.G., Hronow
Leo Czech & Co., Zementfabrik, Bruenn-Malmeritz
Josef Sochor, mechan. Weberei, Schlichterei und Druckfabrik,
        Koeniginhof a.d. E.
B. Spiegler & Soehne, Weberei, Hronow
Weiss & Soehne, Jutespinnerei und Juteweberei A.G., Koeniginhof, a.d. E.
Textilia A.G. Kaufhaus, Mahr. Ostrau
A. Landsberger, Baumwoll- und Flachsspinnerei, Baumwollweberei,
        Bleiche und Appreturanstalt, Friedek
Karl & Wilhelm Hellmann, mechanische Weberei, Koeniginhof
Leopold Strausky, Nached
Flachs u. Juteindustrie A.G., Epiel
M. Mandels' Soehne, mesch. Weberei, Koeniginhof
Hermann Hitschmann, mesch. Weberei, Grottau-Prague
J.L. Haurowitz, mesch. Weberei, Nachod
Mos. Low-Beer, Tuchfabrik, Bruenn
Gustav Jarotschek, Wollspinnerei, Tollstein
Theodor Korner, Holzindustrie, Prague
S.G. Goldschmidt & Soehne, Nachod
Ludwig Mueller, Neustadt
Alois Stranad & Co., Hemdenfabrikation und Textil-Handel, Kuttenberg
Neudecker Papierfabrik A.G., Neudeck
Heinrich Suchanek, amateurphotographische Artikel, Bruenn
L. Auspitz Enkel, Tuchfabrik, Bruenn
"Opp" A.G. Schokoladenfabrik und Zuckerwaren, Bruenn
Prager-Neusiedler Vereinigte Papier, Zellulose und Holzstoffabriken,
        A.G., Prag
Oderfurter Mineraloelwerke, Prag-Mahr. Ostrau
Lana-Rakonitzer Steinkohlen A.G.
M. Fichl's Soehne, Spiritus-Raffinerie u. Essigfabrik, Prague
Pardubitzer Spiritus-Raffinerie u. Essigfabrik A.G., Prague
Verlassenschaft Dr. Ed. J. Weinmann/Weinmannwerke Einziehungsmasse
        Hans/Stella/Frieda/Ella Weinmann Einziehungsmasse Petschek
Thonet-Mundus A.G., Moebelfabrik, Prague
Vereinigte Schafwollfabriken A.G., Bruenn

4.   *Cable dated 21 March, BEB to Rasche:*

>   Please inform Rasche that we are working on the report and
>   will have it ready in detailed form. Stitz-Ulrici (BEB) will be
>   in Berlin for discussion with Ritter.

5. *16-page letter dated 21 May 42, marked "Strictly Confidential," from BEB to Ritter:*

> We wish to note, first of all, that this list surprised us because it contained Aryanizable projects which have been familiar to us for a long time, which have for some time already been acquired, and which we will later discuss in detail. Unfortunately we do not in all cases have the specific information which you request. Specifically, we cannot inform you of the current production situation, and as to whether public contracts are held.
>
> 21 of the 35 listed firms (through an error only 34 were numbered) are textile firms, which are not interesting objects as most have been shut down or nationalized. Perhaps other firms available for confiscation, outside the realm of Aryanization, will be discovered in further discussions.
>
> Presumably some of the firms on your list were included because negotiations regarding purchase price are still under way, and new interested parties willing to pay higher prices may still be included. Purchase offers are handled by the Dejewification Commissioner *(Entjudungsreferat)* of the Reichsprotektor. The Dejewification Commissioner proposes purchasers to the Property Office. The Property Office then negotiates regarding the purchase price. . . .

This letter then continues with detailed descriptions of the status and desirability of the firms in which Ritter might be "interested," the majority of which are "Aryanizable" cases.

6. *Letter by Rasche dated 9 June 42:*

> We enclose the recommendation of the Chamber of Commerce for 2-month passport to the Protectorate which we procured for your honorable Mr. Ritter.

7. *Letter dated 17 June 42, BEB to Rasche:*

> We inform you that we had a discussion with Ritter yesterday. Ritter has had previous occasion to discuss with Dr. Hoelzer of our board of directors possibilities of acquiring firms in the Protectorate through Aryanization.
>
> As you know, we have given Ritter very detailed written suggestions in this matter . . . (discussion of bank's further aid to Ritter).
>
> At any rate we have done everything we can to support his efforts.
>
> The activity of Brinkmann is on the decrease, in view of the establishment of the tobacco monopoly, and ever larger

amounts of capital shall therefore become available. We will continue to make suggestions to the gentlemen within the scope of our activity.

So runs the monotonous routine of profitable dejewification. Another example of Aryanization, also in 1942, involves the acquisition of Herm. Pollack Soehne, a Bohemian textile factory, by the Brunauer Feinspinnerei und Weberei Gyger & Co. and the Deutsche Textil A.G., Berlin. The following are excerpts from a copy of a letter dated 28 February 1942 from the Reichsprotektor for Bohemia and Moravia (Heydrich) to the BEB:

The following is the result of discussions with the RWM.

The Neurod factory is already in Aryan hands, and must be excluded from plans.

The factories in Brunau & Boehmisch-Truebau are to be sold through the participating banks. The appropriate contracts are to be presented by the banks for approval by 1 May 42 at the latest. . . . For the benefit of the purchaser it may be stated in the contract that the sale will be considered for the purchaser by the Reichsprotektor as equal to a sale out of Aryan hands.

Firms listed have been designated to acquire subject company. . . . In case the sales are not completed by the specified time, the RWM will arrange that subject may then be sold through the banks. In this case, purchasers will require the approval of the RWM.

The proceeds of the sale of subject will first be applied to the banks' claims against H. Pollack. Ten percent will be applied against past taxes. Of the remaining sale proceeds, the banks will receive 1.5 percent of the sale price for services rendered to Pollack, including negotiations with Swiss banks, other interests, etc.

Sixty percent of the remaining sale price will go to the Reichsprotektor as an adjustment fee. The remaining 40 percent go to Polysamplex G.m.b.H., Prague & Participa A.G., Prague.

An interoffice memo dated 15 July 42, signed Kuehnen, reads:

The BEB has written to me regarding a decree from the Reichsprotektor to the Prague banks, as follows:

We are informed by the Reichsprotektor that the interest of the Jew Groedel in subject firm has fallen to the Reich, following certain decree. Therefore an acquisition on the basis of previous plans is no longer possible, and can only be effected through the Property Office. I have begun negotiations with the Property Office.

This decision is contrary to that of 28 February 42, in which the Reichsprotektor stated that the three factories would be sold through the interested banks.

This memorandum continues with a discussion of the desirability of intervening at a high government level, together with the Deutsche Bank's Prague affiliate, the Boehmische Union Bank.

An undated memorandum to Rasche lists the following on the agenda for Rasche's trip to Prague:

> To attempt to push through the declaration of Aryanization with the Reichsprotektor, since the banks have been the business owners of subject since 1931 (the debt goes back to this date).
>
> If this is impossible, to achieve a compromise by which all involved banks receive as great as possible a share of the sale proceeds. The Reichsprotektor has been insisting on taking 100 percent of the proceeds of the Aryanization for himself. The Prague banks have suggested that the proceeds be divided 60 percent to the Reichsprotektor and 40 percent to the banks.

In order to present a quick view of some of the bookkeeping aspects of Aryanization, the following items are mentioned.

An example of changes in the situation in the course of a month is contained in the listing of "Major changes between 31 July 41 and 31 August 41."

Debtors	Increase
Dividends on securities taken over from non-Aryans	K 5,700,000

Creditors	
Jewish Cultural Union	K 10,700,000
NSDAP–S.D. Management Division, Prague	K 2,100,000
Central Agency for Jewish Emigration	K 45,700,000

The problem of keeping the records straight in carrying out the program of mass seizures was approached dispassionately. The passage below is taken from the "Report on the Balance Sheets of the BEB as of 31 December 1940":

> In accordance with the order of November 1940, all non-Aryan deposit books were to be presented not later than 31 December 1940 for the purpose of being transferred to non-Aryan blocked accounts. Through this shifting of deposits—our deposit accounts were decreased by approximately 3,800 books and about K 125 million to the benefit of our current accounts.

Blocked accounts were taxed, serviced, and depleted. Following is a tabulation of fees used by the bank:

Prague	1939	1940	1941
Trustee Commission (probably involving primarily Jewish property)	K 800,000	K 600,000	K 70,000

Jewish Bookkeeping Fees *(Evidenzgebuehr)*	204,000	800,000	300,000

Bruenn Branch
("analogous to Prague, custodian   880,000
commission, and Jewish
bookkeeping fees")

The notes on the establishment of reserves show how in accordance with the wishes of the Gestapo relative to confiscated accounts, as well as with respect to a tax of 1.5 percent on all blocked accounts deducted from the account, the fees were set aside as reserves of the bank in 1941. The notes also contain the statement that "in recent times" no interest payments of any type were made to Jews, and money which could normally be used for such interest payments was likewise placed to reserves.

No matter how sordid the transaction, no matter how remote it was from what is normally regarded as the business of banking, the spoils that went to the bank were considerable. The profit derived from Aryanization in Czechoslovakia in 1940, for instance, amounted to K 1,279,000. In fact, in 1941, "the taking over of Jewish securities" accounted for 27 percent of the increase in BEB's portfolio (RM 4.1 million out of a total increase of RM 14.9 million).

The "favorable profit development" in the words of the BEB, which the bank was able to observe and feel as its very tangible benefits from exploitation in Czechoslovakia, was analyzed quantitatively by the Dresdner Bank. It noted how its Czech affiliate outstripped the Dresdner Bank itself in the rates of profiteering. The Dresdner Bank wrote:

> Business profits (of the BEB) rose from RM 2,921,000 (in the first half of 1941) to RM 3,644,000 (in the first half of 1942) or by approximately 25 percent, while profits of the mother institute increased by only 5 percent. . . . Deposits of clients and banks nearly doubled from 1940 to June 1942 (from RM 238 million to RM 437 million); increase for Dresdner Bank, approximately 33.3 percent.

Gross income on the basis of tables in the BEB files went from RM 10,992,000 in 1940 to 10,476,000 in 1941, to RM 15,803,000 in 1942, of which net profits rose from RM 3,652,000 to 5,988,000 to 8,341,000. The percentage of net profit to gross income thus rose from approximately 33 percent in 1940 to 57 percent in 1941.

While payments for "administrative fees for Jewish accounts and deposits" show an increase of from RM 67,000 in the first half of 1941 to RM 73,000 in the first half of 1942, the process of Aryanization was ruthlessly swift, so swift that by 1942 the field of Jewish property had been converted into a wasteland. In the dry statistical language of the Main Bookkeeping Division, it was stated:

> While during 1941, particularly in the first half of the year, the acquisition of Jewish securities showed a favorable result, the stock-exchange business was considerably less active in 1942. . . . The decrease in "other fees" (from

RM 219,000 to RM 126,000) is primarily due to the decrease in Aryanization and custodial fees.

But Aryanization was just one means to achieve the broader objectives of Nazi Germany in Czechoslovakia.

THE DRESDNER BANK IN POLAND

The story of Germany in Poland is so well known that it will not be repeated here in detail. A few documents have been selected merely to show how the bank took part in the exploitation of the country. It financed the depolonization of Poland; it financed the redistribution of property from Pole to Germany; it participated in the cartelization and concentration of industry in typical Nazi style; it financed the war in the East. It was a full-fledged partner of a Nazi economy engaged in its *Drang nach Osten.*

The aggressive forward planning of the Dresdner Bank did not omit Poland. When the Luftwaffe returned from its first mission to Warsaw, the presses were rolling with plans. In December 1939 the Dresdner Bank published an eighty-eight page booklet titled "People and Economy in Former Poland," from which the following is quoted:

> The purpose of the following information on folk and economy in former Poland is to serve for the personal instruction of our business friends interested in economic traffic with respect to the economic structure and significance of the new German economic sphere. As in our earlier brochures of similar nature ("Folk and Economy in the Sudetenland," "Folk and Economy in the Reichsprotectorate Bohemia and Moravia, and in Slovakia"), we have again provided descriptions of the most important industrial companies by branch and region of the economy.

> We and the Laenderbank Wien, together with all our branches and affiliated institutions, particularly in the new Eastern territories, are at your disposal for further information regarding all questions concerning the former Polish state.

For its activities in Poland, the Dresdner Bank used three instrumentalities:
1. The Dresdner Bank proper, both the head office in Berlin, and branches in Kattowitz, Bielitz, Lodz, Poznan, Sosnowitz, Koenigshuette, and Teschen. All the branches were opened in 1939–40, in the territories annexed from Poland.
2. The Kommerzialbank A.G., Cracow. This bank was owned by the Laenderbank Wien until 1940, when the Dresdner Bank took over the participation.
3. The Ostbank A.G., Posen, in that part of the territory annexed from Poland which was known as the "Warthegau" under German rule.

As an indication of the speed with which the bank prepared to take advantage of the new area opened to exploitation, the following quotations from the minutes of the Vorstand are informative:

5 Sept. 1939. Dr. Meyer mentioned the question of our affiliates in Kattowitz and Koenigshuette regarding the credit needs of the Olsa zones. It was decided to halt the liquidation of the affiliates immediately and to reopen them as soon as the necessary military and civilian permits are obtained.

28 Sept. 1939. Dr. Meyer reported on his conversation with the economic adviser of Reichsminister Frank concerning the occupied zone. We shall soon open affiliates in Cracow and Lodz, under guidance of our subsidiary the Cracow Laenderbank. In West Prussia and Posen we shall avail ourselves for the time being of our connection (Bank fuer Handel und Gewerbe) with the aim, to open affiliates for the large banking houses in case of release.

10 Oct. 1939. Dr. Meyer reported on his trip into the occupied zone. In Cracow we shall be represented by the Kommerzialbank, an affiliate of the Dresdner Bank and Laenderbank; it will open a branch in Tarnow. Opening other affiliates as for example in Gotenhafen was not handled.

What these instrumentalities conceived to be their duties and functions is succinctly stated by the Ostbank, A.G. in the opening paragraphs of a draft of its Annual Report for 1941:

The further development of the economy of the Warthegau proceeded, in the past years, with the goal, above all else, of reorganizing industries for war production in the most far-reaching sense.

The reprivatization (after confiscation by Reich agencies) of former Polish and Jewish businesses, begun in 1940 on the basis of commissorial administration, proceeded apace; the vigorous placement of Front Fighters (to these positions) is anticipated.

There can be no doubt that the inclusion of the new eastern areas will have great influence on industrial development, and that all branches of the economy will in the future have great tasks.

The Dresdner Bank through its affiliates in Poland pursued an extremely active Aryanization. The manner in which the bank took the initiative refutes the often-repeated plea that it was only attempting to assist a victim in making the best of an ugly situation over which the bank had no control. A series of letters between the Dresdner Bank in Berlin, the Boehmische Escompte Bank in Prague, and the Dresdner Bank branch in Kattowitz regarding the acquisition of a gas factory are as follows:

Letter dated 26 June 1942 from Rasche, Dresdner Bank, to Stitz-Ulrici, Boehmische Escompte Bank:

Dr. Kritzler, the secretary of Councilor Meinberg, asked me to name a business which would be available for his brother through Aryanization.

Letter 10 October 42, from Kattowitz branch to Dresdner Bank, Berlin:

Please inform us if you know of any person interested in the acquisition of a gas factory in Trzebinia costing approximately RM 700,000.

Letter 15 October 1942, Dresdner Bank to Kattowitz branch:

Arthur Kritzler (an official of the Hermann-Goering-Werke) brother of Councillor Meinberg, would be interested in such an acquisition. He will visit you to discuss details. Please inform me of the result of this discussion, in case Kritzler rejects this object, so that I might later recommend another party to you.

Letter 20 October 1942, Dresdner Bank Kattowitz to Dresdner Bank, Berlin:

Our Gleiwitz branch has discussed subject participation of Kritzler with Bergassessor Schorn of the Economic Group of Mining.

Letter 30 October 1942, Dresdner Bank to Kattowitz branch:

Today I learned that Kritzler is greatly interested in acquiring subject firm. I should appreciate it if you would take every step now to exclude other interested parties.

The web of branches and affiliates that the bank had spun over Europe enabled it to perform its function of penetration smoothly and efficiently. . . . If a target for economic conquest was in Poland, and part ownership of that target was in France or Belgium, the spearheads, branches, and affiliates went into action, always guided from Berlin. The skill of the bank in corporate finance was called in to effect cartelization, mergers, and combines.

The Dresdner Bank was a parent of many of Nazi Germany's monopoly corporations. For example, the Ost-Energie A.G. was founded in 1941 by the General Gouvernement for the express purpose of assuring "a strict and unified policy of electrical energy" and to coordinate all acquisitions so that they would be "only to the benefit of Ost-Energie A.G." Plans called for the acquisition through the Dresdner Bank of seven Polish electrical companies which had been listed in the booklet prepared by the Dresdner Bank on business in Poland. The following quotation from a letter dated 25 April 1942 from Dr. Zimmermann of the General Gouvernement, Cracow, to the Reich Ministry of Economics in Berlin is pertinent:

Subject: Purchase of shares of previously Polish electrical industries.

The General Gouvernement is interested in obtaining certain foreign shares of former Polish electrical companies for the Ost-Energie A.G. in Cracow to assure a uniform policy for power production as a base of assured supply for war-essential industries.

The following industries are of main importance:
1. Elektrizitaetswerke A.G. Teschenstochau
2. Elektrizitaetsgesellschaft G.m.b.H. Teschenstochau
3. Ueberland-Elektrifizierungs Ges.A.G. Teschenstochau
4. Elektrizitaetswerke Petriken A.G. Petriken
5. Elektrizitaetswerke Radom A.G. Radom
6. Elektrizitaetswerke Kielce A.G. Kielce
7. Elektrizitaetswerke fuer den Distrikt Warschau A.G.

It is, therefore, requested, that a permit be issued to the Dresdner Bank, Berlin, or its affiliate the Continentale Bank S.A.W.V., Brussels, to open negotiations with the foreign holding firms in question for account of the Ost-Energie A.G.

The explanation for this request is based on the necessity for improvements, which cannot be expected from the present shareholders, without prolonging the concessions which is out of the question, if foreign interference with rearmament interests is to be avoided. Investments by the Ost-Energie A.G. can only be made on the basis of obtaining those shares.

A defense problem is being considered so expeditious procedure is recommended.

The Dresdner Bank acted in a similar capacity on behalf of another monopoly corporation, the Kontinentale Oel A.G. An illustration of how the external assets of the French were mobilized to complete the concentration of a monopoly corporation, involving in this case the exploitation of oil resources, is found in a memorandum of 24 March 1942, in which Marty of the Dresdner Bank's Berlin office wrote:

By agreement with the German Armistice Commission we shall make available to the Kontinentale Oel A.G. the equivalent of RM 1,800,000 in French francs from Holland, for the acquisition of the Trzebinia Oel Refinery, Upper Silesia . . .

The integration of the bank with German industry in the exploitation of Poland is repeatedly reflected in correspondence between the Berlin office of the Dresdner Bank and the Kattowitz branch. In connection with the acquisition of Polish assets by the Hermann-Goering-Werke, for example, the Dresdner Bank advised its Kattowitz branch as follows, in a confidential letter of 7 December 1942:

With respect to the Zementwerke Schakowa, the interest of Hermann-Goering-Werke is a foregone conclusion. At present the acquisition of the Schakowa shares from Swiss possession is impossible because of Devisen considerations. Hermann-Goering-Werke have, with the consent of the Reich Ministry of Economics, solved the difficulty in an original manner by renting the Swiss shares for a yearly sum of sfrs. 50,000. 25 percent of the Schakowa capital has been acquired by the Hermann-Goering-Werke by other means. We have mentioned your interest in establishing a continuing relationship with Schakowa, in response to which Delius has promised to raise the question with the proper people. Also with respect to the RM 31 mill.—shares of Hydrierwerke Blechhammer assigned to Hermann-Goering-Werke, we have been negotiating for giving to the Dresdner Bank for safekeeping. The fact that the nucleus of the Upper Silesian coal property of Hermann-Goering-Werke arises out of the consortium of the Dresdner Bank is a significant justification for this. . . .

The manner in which the bank placed its financial resources in the same harness with Polish industrial capacity for the benefit of Germany's war machine is evident from the examination of nearly every document analyzed. For example, an undated draft of a letter from the Kommerzialbank to Stahlwerke Braunschweig G.m.b.H., an affiliate of the Hermann-Goering-Werke, states:

In the year 1940, in order to make possible the immediate resumption of war production in the Stalowa Wola mine which was seized by the OKH, we placed at your disposal a credit of zloty 1,000,000.

❑ ❑ ❑

An important part of the bank's loan business was represented by credits granted to assist German settlers to establish themselves. [At least] sixty loans for this purpose totaling RM 784,130 are [known]. The Warthegau Territory of the Ostbank was used to resettle politically reliable ethnic Germans, which accounts for the large number of debtors titled "Eheleute." These settlers were brought to western Poland by the *Deutsche Umsiedlungs Treuhand A.G.* (German Resettlement Trustee Corporation), the operations of which the Dresdner Bank, Berlin, and its subsidiaries in Poland financed extensively.

A list of credits above 500,000 zloty as of 31 August 1943 contains the item "Deutsche Umsiedlungs-Treuhandgesellschaft G.m.b.H., Contact Station Lublin," with a credit of zloty 6,000,000. The guarantee for this credit is described as: "our portion of 30 percent of the consortial credit of zloty 20,000,000–against credit assignment of the Dresdner Bank, Berlin, under custodianship of the Reichsfuehrer SS." The D.U.T. was instrumental in the "colonization" and "depolonization" of "German land" annexed by Germany during the war. It regulated all economic and financial questions regarding the confiscated property of millions of Poles who were forced out to make room for the German settlers.

The Kommerzialbank, Cracow, like the Ostbank derived the vast majority of its business from financing the German exploitation of Poland. A list of credits over Zl 500,000 outstanding on 31 August 1943 lists seventy-nine debtors of which forty-six carry a guarantee by a German firm. Loans totaling Zl 65,000,000 to a German monopoly corporation, the Landwirtschaftliche Zentralstelle, were used to strip Poland of the goods and raw materials needed by Nazi war industry. The major creditors and debtors of the Kommerzialbank are exclusively those monopoly corporations and government agencies which were created to exploit Poland.

Beskiden Erdoel Ges.	15 mill. zloty (increase in current a/c, June 1942)
Ost-Energie A.G.	5 mill. zloty (increase in current a/c, June 1942)
Plenipotentiary for the oil industry	13 mill. zloty (deposit, second quarter 1942)
NSDAP, Labor Division, General Government	3.5 mill. zloty (deposit second quarter 1942)
Textilhandelsgesellschaft m.b.H.	21 mill. zloty (increase in debit a/c)
Central Agricultural Office	5 mill. zloty (discount due)
Stahlwerke Braunschweig	RM 10.1 mill. (credit increase, first quarter 1944)
SS Economic Leader at the SS and Police Chief in the General Government	RM 8.8 mill. (creditor increase in assets, first quarter 1944)
Wehrmacht notes on behalf of industrial corporations	RM 13 mill. (third quarter 1943)

In implementing the overall German plan of domination and exploitation of Polish industry, the bank established its influence over whole segments of Poland's economy, working hand in hand with the Main Custodial Agency, East, the German office which managed the custodial administration of confiscated Polish and Jewish firms. In some cases, the competition from other banks, which were similarly eager to obtain as great a portion as possible of the spoils of exploitation, was encountered. Thus, the minutes of the meeting of the Aufsichtsrat of the Ostbank for 30 November 1940 includes the statement:

It will be of major importance to our business in the future whether the efforts of the Deutschland-Kasse to acquire control of the entire sugar industry and the potato-starch concerns Luban-Wronke by means of custodial administration of the former Polish shares are successful. The Deutschland-Kasse is being strongly supported by the Reich Food Office and the head of the Main Custodial Agency, East. In spite of this, we were able further to increase our influence on the sugar industry so that today two-thirds of all the factories in the Warthegau (including two outside of our region) are in our custody.

The management of the Kattowitz branch was aggressive in every phase of the weird business it was conducting. Some of its abuses, however, are more familiar. Numerous files of correspondence are available in which the branch requests the Berlin office of the Dresdner Bank to put pressure on the home offices of various firms to force the Polish branches of such firms to do business through the Kattowitz branch of the Dresdner Bank. A file of such correspondence [includes records of] the Vacuum Oil Co., A.G., Tschechowitz (placed under the Commissioner for Enemy Property), the Karpaten Oel A.G., Trzebinia (controlled 50 percent by

Kontinentale Oel A.G. and 50 percent by a group of other German oil interests), and the Erste Allgemeine Unfall- und Schadensversicherungs A.G., Vienna.

Nazi business was good in occupied Poland. Observations of the Main Bookkeeping Division in Berlin, dated 28 July 1942, state that "after the armistice in 1941," a considerable increase in creditors is to be noticed:

June 1941	119 mill. zloty
December 1941	121 mill. zloty
February 1942	131 mill. zloty
June 1942	174 mill. zloty

The report dated 2 September 1942, states that with respect to the Kommerzialbank:

> The vigorous expansion of the bank's business resulted in an increase of over 50 percent in the income of the credit business.

Profits rose from zloty 1,021,307 in the first half of 1941 to zloty 1,854,519 in the first half of 1942, and to zloty 2,222,511 in the second half of that year.

Business was good in Poland.

THE DRESDNER BANK IN THE NETHERLANDS

In the Netherlands, as in other countries, the Nazi state and the Dresdner Bank followed their carefully prepared plan for economic conquest, exploitation, and robbery. . . . An analysis of the bank's files reveals the completeness with which the bank cooperated with government and Party officials in capturing the finance and industry of Holland for the Nazi war machine.

Given the language and dates of declarations of economic policy in the Netherlands, it is difficult to distinguish those originating with the bank from those originating with the Reich. By first posing as collaborators with the Dutch, and then, two months later, by presenting a united Nazi front against the Dutch, by forcing German participation in management, by using every device possible to acquire domination, from ordinary purchase to robbery and ransom, the bank, through its own records, reveals how its role in subjugating the Dutch economy for the benefit of German industry and the Nazi war machine was not one forced upon it by the Reich, but as rather a part enthusiastically played for its own profits and for Nazism.

Only a month after the Wehrmacht had marched into Poland, long before the military invasion of Western Europe, the Dresdner Bank created its spearhead bank in the Netherlands. On 2 October 1939, the Handelstrust West N.V. was founded in Amsterdam with a capitalization of hfl. 100,000 worth of shares held by the Dresdner Bank.

Ostensibly, the main function of this institution was the encouragement and financing of Dutch exports to Germany, through clearing. Its real functions are revealed in its actions. And its actions were a fulfillment of Reich–Dresdner Bank statements of procedures for penetration.

The language of the Reich is clear:

> All attempts should be made to achieve the most all-embracing participation possible of German industry in the Netherlands. . . . Capital investments should be tied in with a significant influence over the management of the firm, and with infiltration of personnel. It is therefore necessary to review the inclinations of persons acquiring (businesses). Unreliable persons, particularly Jews, must be removed. Particular emphasis must be placed on the key areas of Dutch industry. . . . I request you to ascertain which interesting positions of the Dutch economy would be available for German participation, and to make such recommendations to me.

That is what the Reich Minister of Economics wrote in September 1940 in a confidential circular setting forth policies and procedures covering the investment of capital in Holland. A copy of this document was transmitted to the Dresdner Bank under confidential cover by the Economic Group Private Banks of the Ministry of Economics on 20 September 1940.

The Reich Minister of Economics reiterated and emphasized the policy of the state in a circular letter dated 20 September 1940, as follows:

> In order to increase the interconnection between the Dutch, Belgian, and French economy on the one hand, and the German economy on the other, and to strengthen the influence of German capital in the Netherlands and Belgium, I consider it important that German capital should participate in economically important Dutch, Belgian, and French firms. It is also desired that securities held in the Netherlands, Belgium, and France of foreign undertakings, particularly in the Balkans, be transferred to German ownership.
>
> I therefore intend to give German banks the possibility of acquiring securities in the Netherlands, Belgium, and occupied France for their own account.

The letter then gives detailed procedural instructions for transactions in the three subject countries.

This was one in a series of directives sent by the Ministry of Economics to the German banks regarding acquisition of securities in the Netherlands. They were marked top secret and sent to a list of twenty to thirty banks, which varied according to the subject matter but always included the Dresdner. As they contained particulars for carrying out the policy of the economic subjugation of Holland, copies were also sent to other interested governmental and Party groups such as the Commissar for the Netherlands, the Commercial Banks Section of the Ministry of Economics, the Reichsbank, the Office for the Four Year Plan, the Devisen Office, the Foreign Office, the Commissar for Finance and Industry, and the Reich Chamber of Commerce.

Discussions were held in the bank to determine the most effective procedures for the accomplishment of this objective of "all-embracing participation." Collaboration was decided upon. In a memorandum dated 6 December 1940, Georg Rienecker, an official of Handelstrust West N.V., wrote:

On the basis of discussions with Director Goetz, Dr. Rasche, and Dr. Pilder, unanimous agreement exists that our fundamental position must be along the following: We are in Holland as German business friends, who utilize representation in the form of the Handelstrust to care for our interests. . . . In all cases, there must be no competition with purely Dutch banks. . . . We must stand as partners never as opponents. The tasks of the Handelstrust West N.V. lie in the far-reaching protection of all interests of the Dresdner Bank . . . Examples: The Aryanization of the N.V. Gebr. Pappenheim's Tabakhandel was effected through us.

But that policy of collaboration is belied by the following statement:

The outlook does not appear to involve the strengthening of German influence through participations in the Dutch Grossbanken. On the contrary, the German banks will, rather, be approached to extend their *Stuetzpunkte* (literally, "spearheads") in such a way that the German banking front will present an overall strong position against the Dutch. . . . The overall plan is thus to establish a German united front in the banking field, which will be in a position to take away business from the Dutch banks on a commercial basis.

That was not written by a Reich official. It was written by the same bank official who described the Germans as partners of the Dutch. It was written only two months later, on 3 February 1941, in a letter to Rasche.

The necessary action to wean away business from the Dutch banks was taken. Application was made for permission to establish another Stuetzpunkt Bank in Holland—one in The Hague. This permission was granted on 15 December 1941, by the Reich Commissar for the Occupied Netherlands, who stated in part:

I declare myself in agreement with the establishment of a Stuetzpunkt in The Hague . . . (because) the business planned for The Hague will involve exclusively German clients who require banking assistance in connection with armament contracts.

Of course, any procedure for effecting transactions which would yield the desired results was used. On 16 June 1941, Dr. Knobloch, one of the three managers of the Handelstrust West N.V., wrote to Dr. Rasche, in connection with the flotation of a Dutch state loan:

Dutch and German banks will work together in effecting this flotation. It is clear that this loan may possibly be of a compulsory nature *(Zwangscharakten)*, since the time is not yet ripe for another policy.

In establishing policy on Aryanization, the Reich and the bank were merely particularizing policy on penetration and robbery. The bank's participation in the policy is borne out by the correspondence, discussions, and preliminary planning in which it engaged.

They refute the plea that the Aryanization deals which it engineered were merely normal business transactions, or actions forced upon it by higher authority. They reveal fraud, duress, and undue influence which tainted almost every transaction involving Jews. In implementing and carrying out the policy, which they helped conceive, they went far beyond the broad authorization of Nazi law, and attempted to collect ransom or extort funds, in the tradition of Nazi behaviorism.

For months before the passage of the "Aryanization Law," the banks had been engaged in preparatory work.

On 3 March 1941, Entzian of the Dresdner Bank noted in a memorandum:

> The law concerning enforced Aryanization is not to be expected for the next few days.

On 5 March 1941, Entzian made additional notations on the imminent Aryanization Law:

> The Aryanization Law will be an enabling act. Presumably it will not be published before 15 March 1941. In its implementation, procedure will be by branches (of industry). Firms earmarked for Aryanization will first be transferred to a custodial office. . . . The inclusion of the banks will be possible through their initiation and administration of negotiations for their clients.

In Holland, the bank was actively engaged on the policy level. On the same day that Entzian wrote his interpretation, Rienecker of the Handelstrust West N.V. wrote a memorandum regarding the Aryanization Law to Rasche, Entzian, Bardroff, Hobirk, and Kuehnen of the Dresdner Bank, and Dellschow of Handelstrust. It reads in part:

> At today's discussions in The Hague with Fischboeck (Germany's top Aryanization official in the Netherlands), I ascertained the following:

> The Law is an enabling act, which gives the Reich Ministry of Economics far-reaching authority. Its execution lies with the Supervisory Board, together with the Referent of the Reich Ministry of Economics, the (appropriate) Economic Group, the staff of Rudolf Hess, and the Armament Inspector.

> The Law will be entitled "Ordinance regarding establishment and changes of businesses and concerns" *(Verordnung betreffend Errichtung und Veraenderung von Unternehmen und Betrieben).*

> . . . The third and most important section concerns "businesses required to report" *(Anmeldepflichtige Unternehmen,* Jewish businesses).

> After indications of targets by all interested parties, final decisions will be made as to specifically which firms will go to which interested parties. The preparatory work which has been in process for months in the banking sector will be taken into consideration.

> It is recommended that the banks appear as fully empowered representatives for the German interests; and present their cases at the Planning Meetings.

> Once the Planning Meeting has established who shall acquire (a given business) . . . the sale price will be determined not by negotiation, but by the

establishment of a so-called fair price by a custodial office which will be created for this purpose by the Reich Commissioner for the Netherlands.

Ten days later Handelstrust West N.V. wrote to the Dresdner Bank:

The text of the Aryanization Law was published on 13 March. We cabled it immediately to Berlin.

At a meeting here in Amsterdam on 12 March the Reichskommissar declared that the dejewification of the economy here in Holland will be radically carried through. We can therefore count on much business for the Handelstrust in this area of activity in the near future.

The speed with which the Dresdner Bank took steps to translate policy into concrete transactions is almost startling. It implies painstaking preparation and planning, and a knowledge of European industry that could be had only by careful study. On the very same day that the Dresdner Bank received the cable from the Reich Ministry of Economics calling for an "increase in the interconnection between the Dutch, Belgian, and French economy on the one hand and the German economy on the other," and the strengthening of "the influence of German capital in the Netherlands," on the very day the cable was received notifying the banks of the possibility of acquiring securities in the Netherlands, Belgium, and occupied France, for their own account, the hand of the Securities Department of the Dresdner Bank in Berlin prepared a memorandum, implementing the cable by listing the firms whose securities it was especially desired to obtain for Germany:

(a) We have standing orders to acquire the following from Jewish-Dutch and enemy properties:

Hazemeijer shares	For Siemens
Heemaf shares	For Brown, Boverie & Cie. A.G.
Brocades shares	For Schering A.G.
Ned. Dok shares	For Stettiner Oderwerke
Nyna shares	For Ver. Glansstoff-fabriken
Verschure shares	For Ferrostaal A.G.
Stokvis and Zonen shares	For Ferrostaal A.G.
Lever shares	For Margarine Verkaufs Union
Jungens van den Bergh shares	For Margarine Verkaufs Union
Breda shares	For Klein, Schanzlin & Becker A.G.

(b) In addition we are negotiating for the acquisition of:

Chamotte Unie	For Didier
Blaaueholdenween	For Hochseefischerei Anderson & Co.

du Croc   For Joseph Voegele A.G.

Lija-on Gelatinefabr. "Delft"   For I. G. Farben

(c) We further request that (shares of the following Dutch firms) be reserved, since strong interest for these shares exists on the part of German firms, and the negotiations are more profitable if sizable blocks of shares are involved:

Wilton–Feyensord
Assurantie Nij. Nederland von 1845
Hollandische Druud-en Kabelfabriek
Internationale Viscose Cie.
Centrale Suiker Mij.
Reineveld Wasch, Fabr.
Automatic Screwwerke (intended for Torpedo Werke)
Nederlansche Handel Nij.
Hore Conserven Breda
Ned. Bankiestelling
Kronkert Motoren Fabriek.

The Aryanization Law had been passed in the middle of March 1941. Before the month ended, the Handelstrust West N.V. had established an Aryanization Division. It received a high priority in office space.

A memorandum dated 28 March 1941, stated:

Rooms on the first floor, adjoining the rooms of the Vorstand, are being reserved for the Aryanization Division.

Only a week after the passage of the law, Knobloch requested the Dresdner Bank for an experienced person to act as chief of the division. He wrote:

It appears indispensable, in order to preserve the immediate interests of the Dresdner Bank and to assure the successful protection for the German clientele, to set up a qualified gentleman, in addition to the energies now available, who will devote himself exclusively to this task (Aryanization). Only such a gentleman can be considered for this position, who has experience in this type of business. Remarks being made in Amsterdam banking circles indicate that the filling of this position is urgent.

The lucrative nature and importance of Aryanization transactions are not mentioned in the published annual reports of the bank. but it was well recognized by the management of the Dresdner Bank, and of the Handelstrust West. Thus, the Foreign Secretariat of the Dresdner Bank, in its report on the development of the Handelstrust West, for the first half of 1941, wrote:

In connection with the Aryanization of Dutch industry, inland clients made use of the Handelstrust West to a significant extent. Countless visitors from Germany, averaging 150 monthly, found advise *[sic]* and support [at the Handelstrust West].

The programmatic execution of the comprehensive plan with respect to Aryanization is characteristic of the bank's operation in all fields. Thus Rinn, head of the Securities Department of the Dresdner Bank, wrote on 3 September 1941:

the establishment (of provisions) regarding enemy property in Holland has been completed, with the result that large packets of Dutch bank securities are available. The possibility exists of assuring for ourselves unobtrusively positions in the Dutch banking field, especially with reference to Dutch banking securities in Jewish possession. This last group appears to be even larger (than previous estimates), so that in some cases a significant minority could be established.

And, on 19 January 1942:

The fact that Jewish shares are coming up for sale in the near future is particularly important since very significant amounts of Dutch Grossbanken securities are included among these properties.

Numerous examples are available in the files of cases in which both the Dresdner Bank and the Handelstrust acted as agents to advise German persons and firms desirous of obtaining the "best buys" of Aryanizable properties and to put Germans in touch with the proper parties.

Many transactions are also indicated in the files resulting in typical Aryanization cases, in which the bank arranged the purchase of non-Aryan businesses by Aryan Dutch firms, or, more often Germans. Documents regarding the proposed or effected Aryanization of the following firms include:

Bijenkorf Kaufhaus	fl.	10,000,000 (capital)
Papierhandlung Cats	fl.	3,828,620 (assets)
N.V. Centrale Suiker Mij.	fl.	500,000 (shares)
Polak & Schuard Essencifabrieken		
Staerkefabrik Honig		
Puddingfabrik Polak		

There were no extremes to which the Dresdner Bank would hesitate to go. It tried to branch out from the field of merely buying and selling property, into that of accepting payments of ransom from Dutch Jews imprisoned in concentration camps outside Holland and who held assets abroad. The correspondence in the case of Benjamin Soet [has been captured, for example].

In this case the Dresdner Bank wrote to the Reich Ministry of Economics that Swiss friends of Soet who was in the concentration camp at Mauthausen, Block XIV, Division A, Internment No. 1361, had deposited 20,000 Swiss francs with the Schweizerische Bank Gesellschaft with the provision that this sum would become available to the Dresdner Bank at the moment Soet appeared in person at the Swiss Consulate in Amsterdam. The Swiss francs would fall to the Reich; the equivalent would be paid out in Holland in gulden. The Handelstrust West informed Soet's Dutch friends that they would establish the necessary contact with government offices through the Dresdner Bank; and Schweizerische Bank Gesellschaft confirmed the deposit in Switzerland.

Negotiations with the Reich Ministry of Economics revealed that permission was required from the Judenreferat, as well as the Foreign Organization of the NSDAP. Apparently this permission could not be obtained. The disappointment of the bank was very businesslike, for Entzian had written on 8 August 1941 that although the sum of sfrs 20,000 was to fall to the Reich, "the Handelstrust expects an appropriate fee for its services."

A case involving the reverse circumstances—the Aryanization of a Dutch firm as the prerequisite to release by the Gestapo and a passport to America—is that of Isaac Keesing. One of the several memoranda dealing with this case, signed Stiller and dated 13 February 1941, states that:

> The passports to America for Isaac Keesing and relatives will be provided, as soon as the publishing and printing firm owned by Keesing's brother is Aryanized. The records are held by Oberfuerher Mueller of the Gestapo.

A letter from Rienecker of the Handelstrust transmitting a letter by Isaac Keesing to Rasche, dated 6 March 1941, concludes:

> I would appreciate it if you would follow this matter through (in Berlin).

This business, a far cry from orthodox banking, appeared easy and profitable. The institutionalization of the procedures of extortion is indicated in a memorandum of Knobloch, dated 3 April 1941:

> In response to my question regarding the interconnecting of passports for Jews with the Aryanization of their businesses, Major Lauritsch of the (Emigration Office) . . . told me that an Emigration Division would be established which would have sole responsibility for this.

Revolting as these Aryanizations are in themselves, however strong an indictment of the Dresdner Bank they may be, they were only a part of a plan for the economic subjection to Germany of the whole of the Netherlands.

Indicative of the Dresdner's desire to accomplish the influence of German capital in the Netherlands are the changes in management of the Handelstrust West in 1940. The bank's memorandum dated 6 December 1940 reads:

> According to the given statements, Herr Dr. Rasche took over from Dr. Pilder the active management of the business in the Netherlands and therewith also of the Handelstrust West. The operation of all current business affairs is done in the Foreign Secretariat, head Dr. Entzian. The operation of current stock exchange transactions is made directly with the exchange in Berlin. The operation of joint transactions *(Verflechtungsgeschaefte)* for Holland is performed in Berlin by the Syndicate Department (Mr. Kuehnen), but one copy of the proceedings is communicated to the Foreign Secretariat for information. From operation by the syndicate office are

excepted all joint transactions that are entered by Dr. Rasche and his Secretariat resp.

The men mentioned, Rasche and Entzian, formed the Dresdner's team for grabbing the prizes of an occupied area. They had already done this work in the East and were now ready to add the wealth of the West to their laurels.

The Dresdner with its network of "spearheads," branches and affiliates, had an enormous group of "clients" for any acquisitions of securities that it could obtain. Each of the sections of this chapter refers to instances in which the Dresdner acquired the controlling interest in a concern in some other European area by getting shares in Holland. A letter to the Ministry of Economics dated 4 February 1943, shows that these were constantly sought under standing orders of interested parties. This particular list names such outstanding armament firms as:

for the account of Siemens-Schuckert Werke A.G. Berlin
    fl. 150,000 N.V. etc.

Ferrostahl A.G. Essen
    fl. 113,000 Verschure & Co.'s etc.

Vereinigte Stahlwerke A.G. Duesseldorf
    fl. 141,000 Dok-en Werfmaatschappij etc.

Brown, Boveri & Cie. A.G.
    fl. 518,700
    fl. 35,700

This was a deliberate effort on the part of the bank to increase German influence in Dutch firms that were desirable or valuable to the war effort. In an interoffice memorandum dated 3 February 1943 Rinn of the Syndicate Department writes:

We now hold the view that these purchases are in the interest of German-promoted interlockings. This does not only apply to those securities which we gave to a definite client en bloc but also to such stocks as 6 percent and 7 percent. Unilever preferred stocks and banking selling stocks, which we widely distributed among our customers for similar reasons (to promote German interests).

The auditor's report for 1939 shows very clearly the purposes for which the Dresdner Bank first entered Holland and its subsequent transactions show that these remained its guiding principles. For example:

the Handelstrust West N.V. is only acting as agent. Credits are not granted. . . .

taking over the trust of outstanding debts, bonds, shares, stocks of goods, contract rights, etc. For this purpose in Berlin and Amsterdam considerable preliminary work has been done for a number of firms.

In close agreement with the German consulate general in Amsterdam, connections were taken up with the Dutch trade and manufacturing firms. . . .

Hereby (i.e. reports of Handelstrust) our Foreign Department is enabled to maintain a confidential information service within the bank (main office and its branches).

The Dresdner affiliate was working hand in glove with most of the Nazi authorities and agencies that overran Holland at the heels of the German Army. Numerous references in the correspondence files establish this fact and the auditor's report says:

the Handelstrust West N.V. in agreement with the consul general, the Ministry of Economics, the Ministry of Food and Agriculture, and the Reichsbank is acting as an agent.

The Dresdner Bank by charging Dutch security purchases to the clearing was acting against the Dutch people as a whole, not merely against a propertied class. An interoffice memo reporting on a talk with the Ministry of Economics makes the statement:

The preceding approvals are to be valid only for the purchase of French, Belgian, and Dutch stocks. . . . The purchase of Dollar bonds and German securities does not fall under this permission as the Ministry of Economics has no special interest at this time to repurchase German bonds by way of clearing.

The profit to Nazi Germany under the forced clearing agreements is well known and need not be repeated here.

The relations between the bank and Nazi Germany were happy and mutually profitable. The services extended to Nazi Germany by the Handelstrust West were appreciated, and the Dresdner Bank was rewarded for the sordid transactions of its affiliate not only in profits but also through official recognition.

The Handelstrust West N.V. was awarded in 1942, 1943, and 1944 the special diploma of the NSDAP in the Netherlands, which was extended by the Reich Commissar, Dr. Seyss-Inquart, personally.

Leader of the NSDAP
Netherlands

To the Handelstrust West N.V.
Amsterdam
I extend . . . for its achievements
the Diploma for outstanding accomplishments.

This award shall serve as recognition
for past achievements and as encouragement
for future work for National Socialism. . . .

THE DRESDNER BANK IN BELGIUM

Germany's official agent for most of the financial and industrial activities of National Socialism in occupied Belgium was the Continentale Bank, wholly owned by the Dresdner Bank. Through this spearhead instrument, the Dresdner Bank fulfilled the same functions for Germany in Belgium and reaped the same rewards for its services, as it did in other countries.

The Dresdner Bank, through the Continentale Bank, contributed vast sums to the German military machine directly, to such arms and appendages of the Wehrmacht as the Organisation Todt, the Four Year Plan Office, the Brussels Armament Office, and the like, as well as indirectly via credits to German war industries.

The Dresdner Bank, through the Continentale Bank, acted in accordance with Nazi procedures by financing purchases on the German-controlled Belgium black market, by disposing of Jewish property in cooperation with the Aryanized banking firm of Lippmann Rosenthal, which was employed as a depository for looted Jewish property; by carrying out the master plan for the industrial domination of Belgium through vigorously effecting "Penetration Purchases" of key Belgian securities; by acting hand in hand with the customs police, a Gestapo agency which policed foreign exchange transactions to assure that expropriation was total.

In all these operations the Bank risked nothing and gained everything since they were financed ultimately through clearing, the legal myth by which the Belgian people were forced to pay for their own despoliation.

Shortly after the war in the West was brought to an end by the fall of France the Nazi exploiters descended upon conquered Belgium. Among the first was the Dresdner Bank, which established an affiliate, the Continentale Bank S.A./N.V., Brussels and Antwerp. This bank had been formed by the Dresdner to serve as its agent in exploiting Belgium.

The following was the distribution of the stock capital of the Continentale Bank (bfrs 25,000,000) as of 1 November 1944:

Dresdner Bank Berlin	989 shares
Handelstrust West N.V., Amsterdam	250 shares
(Dresdner affiliate in Holland)	

The remaining eleven shares were scattered among officials of the Dresdner Bank and affiliates. In addition to its control through stock ownership, the purposes for which the bank had been established demanded German officials in the key positions. In a letter requesting draft deferment for an employee, the bank writes:

> As to German colleagues we have only some men in the leading positions while the remainder of the personnel are Belgian.

The Dresdner Bank established this branch in a foreign country for the purpose of integrating the German and Belgian economies to Germany's advantage.

❏ ❏ ❏

The German spearheads penetrating foreign economies had their duties prescribed for them long before the occupation. The establishment of this Belgian affiliate can be considered as the Dresdner's response to Goering's admonition:

> increase of German influence with foreign enterprises [is] necessary even now . . . that any opportunity be used to make it possible for the German economy to start its penetration, even during the war.

The annual report of the commissar at the National Bank (Belgium) for May 1940–41 further describes the task of German finance in Belgium as:

> It is desired to transfer to German hands important Belgian participations in foreign enterprises whose administration is located in Belgium. . . .

> The Reich Minister of Economics has given general permission to thirty-two German banks to obtain participation rights, particularly stocks in a limited quantity in Belgium.

> The first and main task of the German banking representation in Belgium is the creation of its business according to the interest and demands of the German economy.

During its brief life in conquered Belgium, the Continentale proved itself a worthy affiliate of the SS Bank. The military authorities of the occupying Nazi forces had suggested the establishment of the bank. It performed numerous financial services for the army. All the purchases and payments for services were charged against the clearing account between Belgium and Germany. However, as is stated in a letter of the Continentale Bank to the Devisenstelle:

> clearing transfers from the Reich required an unusually long time . . . advances on the clearing payments had to be made for several offices.

The correspondence [shows] one type of transaction that the bank handled for the Wehrmacht. By financing the Belgian firms during the interim period caused by the delays in clearing payments, it speeded up the repair work done by Belgian garages on Wehrmacht vehicles.

The bank also performed a similar service for other agencies operating in Belgium from Germany during the occupation period. A letter dated 31 January 1944 to the Devisenstelle records that the Reich plenipotentiary for iron and steel owed the bank bfrs. 660,964.04. Records of the bank now in possession of the Belgian authorities show other such customers, among them Organisation Todt, which built V-1 launching ramps in Belgium. At the time the bank evacuated Brussels this account showed a debit balance of bfrs. 10,984,000 covered by assigned invoices amounting to bfrs. 12,638,000.

Advances for Wehrmacht orders, in fact, constituted the largest part of the bank's business. As of 2 September 1944 loans outstanding totaled bfrs. 79,700,000, of which 36,700,000 were secured by assignments of claims (invoices) on German government agencies or German firms. (Figures obtained from books of Continentale

Bank now in possession of Belgian authorities.) The extent and importance of such transactions may be judged from the report of the Commissar at the National Bank of Belgium for August–October 1942:

> The big volume of loans in the interest of the armed forces economy as well as the advance payments in clearing (necessary in connection with shipping orders) led to a business expansion of these banks which stands in no relationship to the capital funds any longer.

In its commercial letter of credit business the bank also served the ends of the Nazi war economy.

The books of the Continentale Bank show numerous accounts opened on order of banks or commercial firms in Germany. They were in favor of procurers of products available in Belgium whether directly needed for the war or for indirect war use. The parent Dresdner Bank made extensive use of its affiliate in this connection and as of 30 June 1944, had credit lines totaling bfrs. 19,500,000 open with the Continentale Bank. The total amount of commercial letters of credit outstanding as of November 1943 was approximately 28,900,000, of which 28,200,000 were upon orders from Germany.

One such account stands on the books of the bank in the name of "Volk und Staat," a Nazi publishing house in Belgium. The credit was opened by order of the Dresdner Bank for Velhagon & Klasing and other German publishers. It amounted to bfrs. 409,000 and RM 58,000 during the period April 1942 to December 1943.

The Continentale also had extended a cash credit line of bfrs. 25,000,000 to the Zentral Textil G.m.b.H. of Berlin for "purchases of goods in Belgium." This loan was guaranteed by the head office of the Dresdner Bank.

A similar type of transaction was so-called guarantees by the bank, which in most instances were simply performance bonds. An account such as that of the Army Ordinance Office for the benefit of the Belgian Ford Corporation (under German administration) is of this type. The credit line amounted to RM 1,000,000 and was secured by assignment of the Ford Company's claims against the army. Guarantee accommodations in Belgian francs were also used at times to a maximum amount of bfrs. 12,500,000.

Another example of the use of a guarantee by a German firm is that of Krupp for the account of S.A. Ateliers de Construction de la Meuse. Over a six-month period in 1943 the guarantees furnished amounted to RM 916,000.

The *Verwaltung Juedischen Grundbesitzes* (Administration of Jewish real estate) maintained cash accounts, which on 2 September 1944, showed a credit balance of bfrs. 10,800,000 and also securities accounts with the Continentale Bank. Bank employees when questioned about why a real estate agency should have securities accounts offered the supposition that they had been deposited as surety for rental payments.

The Continentale Bank was a depository for various Party and governmental agencies. A number of them had substantial credit balances with the bank for example:

NSDAP, Antwerp	RM	10,000
The Deputy of the Four Year Plan	bfrs.	8,000,000
Armament Office Brussels representative	bfrs.	24,700,000
Armed Forces procurement agency	bfrs.	129,200,000
Pimotex (code name used to designate a branch of the Speer Ministry for Munitions and Armaments)	bfrs.	16,000,000
Enemy property	bfrs.	53,600,000

The Armed Forces procurement agency was a central office maintained by the occupation forces to channelize purchases in Belgium. It had been established because of a desire to put all purchases under the clearing, which could not be financed out of the occupation costs; many of its dealings were in the black market. The balance given above was that which existed on 31 August 1944, and of that amount bfrs. 125,000,000 had been received nine days previously from the Banque d'Emission and would be charged against the clearing.

The Armament Office was an agency of the army which engaged in the procurement of material that could not be obtained, or was in short supply in Germany. It too dealt with the black market.

The Deputy for the Four Year Plan was another German agency engaged in exploiting Belgian resources for the benefit of the German war economy.

The Pimetax account was involved in black market purchases. It was the agency for obtaining precious metals, diamonds, precision tools, and similar scarce items needed in Germany. On 2 September 1944 this agency had four accounts totaling bfrs. 16,000,000 of which bfrs. 2,500,000 were earmarked for Organisation Todt and HKP, and the remaining bfrs. 13,500,000 for German industrial firms.

The Reichkommissar for shipping also maintained an account at the Continentale Bank to facilitate clearing remittances to the Mittelmeer-Handelsindustrie Gesellschaft, representative for Belgium. These remittances were used to cover "rental" payments on Belgian ships which had been commandeered by the Germans. From 9 October 1943 to 25 July 1944 these remittances totaled bfrs. 25,000,000.

An equally important service which this extension of Nazi finance into a conquered country rendered was in the "increase of German influence with foreign enterprises," demanded by Goering. The objects closest at hand were of course desirable Belgian firms. The Continentale Bank first of all provided itself with a tool to accomplish this task in Hermann Prinsler. A series of letters asking for his deferment from army service throws a great deal of light on this portion of the bank's activity. In a letter the president of the Continentale says:

> He also worked on capital penetration and capital separation with the aim to return former German enterprises into German hands, or to obtain influence in Belgian corporations for German concerns. It was not limited to transactions primarily benefiting private enterprise, but extended to transactions important to the Reich and the war economy.

There is, for instance, at present an inquiry from a German official source about the possibility of acquiring French shares in Belgium. Such an inquiry can only be answered by a specialist who

1. knows what, if any, French securities are in Belgian hands,
2. is in a position to ascertain who owns such securities in Belgium,
3. has the necessary connections with the individuals and corporations in question to be able to negotiate with them for the surrender of such securities.

The last item especially is of great importance, as these negotiations can be conducted, only if the Belgian offices are convinced that they can speak freely. The performance of these transactions requires again a number of special skills, as it must be done in such a way that the transactions will not be known to the Belgian public.

The operations of the bank in the field of security acquisitions were quite extensive. The Dresdner Bank maintained an account earmarked for "penetration purchases," which, even at the end of the occupation of Belgium, totaled bfrs. 19,368,790.

"Certain special skills," such as were possessed by Mr. Prinsler, were undoubtedly valuable in the transaction outlined in the memorandum of 29 October 1943 from Rinn of the Dresdner Stock Purchase Department, the pertinent portions of which are as follows:

> Considerable lots of securities owned by Dutch Jews amounting to bfrs. 10 mill. are being offered for sale in Brussels. It was impossible for the entire liquidation to be handled by Contibank, because Messrs. Hoppe and Hofrichter desired the cloaking of the operation.

> In this connection it was also possible to include Dutch securities which have been bought previously and which were in the possession of the Contibank. I have, therefore, advised the people of the Contibank after the settlement of those securities to purchase successively small lots of Dutch securities, since those same securities are selling in Brussels about 35 percent below the market price in Amsterdam.

The directions of Reichsmarschall Goering as set out in the report of the Commissar at the National Bank of Belgium for May 1940–41 state that among the foreign interests to be acquired are:

> particularly enterprises are concerned which are located in the Balkans and in which a general German interest exists.

A creation of the Dresdner Bank, which had worked so diligently in creating the machine for conquest, could not fail to heed this patriotic call. Numerous transactions, some of which are covered in the sections on Eastern European countries, attest to this. In a letter dated 17 June 1944 the Continentale Bank describes one such transaction:

The Hermann-Goering-Werke are interested in an important armament enterprise located near the former Polish border and in which a Belgian financial group has a controlling interest. The purpose of the negotiations conducted here (in Belgium) is to acquire the participation of the Belgian group if possible. The Army High Command in Berlin is interested in this deal and whatever we propose to do has its approval.

An entry of bfrs. 3,900,00 as a guarantee to the Kreditbank voor Handel en Nijverheid, Brussels, disclosed an interesting story of the immensity of the profits to be obtained from Belgian securities transactions by a German firm operating in the favored position of a conqueror.

Securities sold on the Brussels Stock Exchange had to bear the exchange committee's certificate in order for the seller to be able to make "a good delivery." This was given only after the seller's title had been explained to the committee. Belgian law also required that a false title be made good, but allowed no recourse by a bank established in Belgium after 10 May 1940 against the person from whom the securities were bought.

A file memorandum of the Continentale Bank dated 27 April 1945 summarizes a transaction in which the bank sold certain securities on the Brussels exchange to the Kreditbank voor Handel en Nijverheid. These had been acquired in France by De Neuflize & Co., Paris, for a joint transaction with the Deutsche Golddiskontobank, at a price of bfrs. 20,000,000. To protect the Continentale Bank against loss, because it had acted as the seller on the Brussels exchange, the Golddiskontbank transferred its profit on the sale to the Continentale to be held as guarantee against loss because title to the securities was actually obtained through the German customs police. The sum transferred amounted to a 20 percent profit, not counting the share of the French company or the customs police.

[Captured] correspondence [shows] the Continentale Bank endeavoring to justify a similar transaction involving securities seized by the customs police. The German argument epitomizes the principle underlying the entire scope of the bank's operations in Belgium:

> The securities sold by the Continentale Bank have not only been confiscated by the customs police, but also legally confiscated for the benefit of the military administration . . . on the strength of forfeiture ordered by military courts in criminal proceedings for foreign exchange violations against the civilian residents of Belgium. Therefore, this concerns property of the military administration, i.e. Reich property.

Acquisition of Jewish-owned securities constituted a major activity of the Continentale Bank. Large sales were carried out by the Continentale Bank for the account of Lippmann, Rosenthal & Co., Amsterdam.

The firm of Lippmann, Rosenthal & Co. was described by Heinrich Friedmann, of the agency for liquidation of Jewish property in Holland, as having originally been a Jewish banking firm. It was Aryanized and used as a collecting agency and depository for all proceeds gained from the liquidation of Jewish firms. Belgian securities so obtained were delivered to the Continentale Bank for sale in the Belgian market.

The turnover in the account amounted to bfrs. 30,000,000 for the period January–August 1944. In a letter of 9 December 1944 Lippmann, Rosenthal & Co. of Amsterdam sent the Dresdner a list of Belgian and Dutch securities with a total value of several hundred million Belgian francs, which had been deposited with the Continentale and for which an accounting was desired now that the bank, retreating with the Wehrmacht, had withdrawn from Belgium.

The Continentale Bank even rendered personal services to its German officials and those of the Dresdner Bank in providing them with scarce "luxury" items obtained in the black market in Belgium. A special set of books attests to these operations. The accounts in these books show a turnover of bfrs. 470,000 for the period from January to August 1944. The commodities procured included cigarettes, cigars, soap, ham, cognac, coffee, and many other scarce articles. Among the "customers" named were Count Czernin, Gustav Overbock, Dr. Entzian, Karl Rasche, and an account named "Vorstand Kasino."

The Continentale Bank in Belgium proved itself a faithful replica of its German parent.

THE DRESDNER BANK IN THE BALTIC STATES

The Baltic states, which were the major components of a Nazi governmental unit known as the Ostland, were to act as a buffer to the East, according to German political thinking. A political paper, a copy of which had been sent to Rasche for comment, says of them:

> The Reich and Europe, when reorganizing the North-East, will have to start with the principle that in the future it must never be exposed to danger, whether political, nationalistic or military, from this region.

For this reason the economic reorganization of this region was much more under direct control of various governmental administrations than was true in other conquered areas. The Dresdner Bank [. . . was] called on to assist in the reorganization of this strategic area.

The bank was no stranger. It had had affiliates in Latvia and Lithuania until their occupation by Russia in 1940. Through the Libauer Bank and the Litauische Kommerzbank it had spearheaded German penetration in the area. For example the secret report of the Foreign Department for September and October 1937 describes a series of loans to be made to the government of Estonia, with a guarantee by the German Ministry of Finance, for building a phosphate plant, a fish meal plant, and other factories to process Estonian raw materials for the German market.

The extent to which the Dresdner Bank was acting as a government agency in its operations in the Ostland is clearly indicated by a memorandum of its Legal Department dated 5 April 1943. After discussing the form of the Reich government in the area, and property relationships, it describes certain "unique forms of organization for business concerns in the Ostland." These are

Monopoly corporations—controlled by Reich Commissar for the Ostland and to whom all profits accrue. Tobacco and spirits firms are typical monopoly corporations.

Self-administrative bodies—under the Reich Commissar for the Ostland who would be the actual debtor in case of a loan. The Latvian Forest Department is such a body.

Central economic offices—a dual form under control of both the Reich Commissar for the East and various Reich ministries. Such are the export agencies for flour and bread, grain, sugar, beverages, and livestock and meat.

East companies—founded in the form of a limited liability partnership but certain tasks have been assigned to the East Corporations within the scope of Germany's politico-economic goals and these have been expanded by decrees of the Reichsmarschall. As Reinbathe of the Ministry of Economics stated at a banking conference, the East Corporations should be viewed as in the service of the Reich. . . . Examples of such concerns are the holding company Central Trading Company East and under its control Eastland Fibre Company, Baltic Oil Company, Eastland Oil concern, Mining and Foundry Company of the Eastland.

Companies under trusteeship—"for the organization of the economy of the occupied eastern zone . . . the entire property of the U.S.S.R., its corporations, unions, etc., constitute a special property. This special property is administered by custodians appointed by the Reichs Commissar." The Latvian Barge Company and Eastland Realty Company are examples of this type.

The Dresdner was admitted to the Ostland very soon after it had been opened to exploitation by the Nazi army.

In a letter to the Ministry of Economics dated 25 August 1941, it proposed to establish the bank later known as the Handels- und Kredit-Bank, Riga. This letter stated that

Dr. Rasche has been in Riga and through conversation with Reich Commissar Lohse learned that it is desired that we soon open an affiliate of our bank which would extend its activities to the former Baltic States.

We wish to state that we consider it particularly important for the business of the Deutsche Ostland Bank A.G. (later changed to Handels- und Kredit-Bank) to extend to Reval, because at the express desire of your ministry we acquired an interest in the Dorpater Bank in Reval prior to the occupation of Estonia by the U.S.S.R., in spite of the great risks of which we were aware at that time.

The Ministry of Economics promptly replied, on 27 August 1941, granting the necessary permission to establish the bank.

The corporate charter dated August 29 was signed, the Vorstand and Aufsichtsrat had been determined, so that the new bank was ready for business by 11 October 1941.

The Handels- und Kredit-Bank functioned almost exclusively as an instrument to aid in the Nazi government's exploitation of the Ostland. The bank's statement of 31 January shows that 87.5 percent of the loans granted were to the "unique" concerns.

The remaining loans were granted to German concerns, or their affiliates, that were operating in the Ostland. A list, dated 31 August 1942, of all creditors of over RM 50,000 lists such prominent German firms as:

Siemens & Halske	RM 85,500
Olex, Deutsche Benzin- und Petroleum G.m.b.H.	RM 36,600
A.E.G.	RM 67,800
Mannesmannrohren und Eisenhandel Ostland G.m.b.H.	RM 53,400
Firma Georg Thalheim A.G.	RM 444,200

The following organizations included in the August list were political instrumentalities of the Nazi Party and state:

Deutsche Verlags- u. Druckerei-Ges. i/Ostland	RM 333,700
SS Frontarbeitbetrieb Stoedtner u. Poster	RM 121,300
SS Umsiedlungsstab	RM 150,000
Bala Barackenlager G.m.b.H. Kg.	RM 253,947.71
Deutsche Umsiedlungs Treuhand G.m.b.H., Danzig, Nebenstelle Kauen	RM 139,583.49

The true nature of the Dresdner's operations is shown by correspondence from Allgemeine Waren-Finanzierungs G.m.b.H. (a Dresdner-owned company) regarding the "natural restitution" to German interests of an Estonian cotton factory. The writer is requesting the Dresdner to use its influence with Kehrl (an influential figure in the Ministry of Economics) to have the property assessed with the Deutsche Umsiedlungs Treuhand. The property was valued by its owners at Kr. 54,400,000, which had been reduced by the Treuhand to Kr. 25,000,000 "and in accordance with the halving of true value" would be further reduced to Kr. 16,800,000.

Correspondence shows how the Dresdner by its financial support of the Trustee Companies was assisting in the robbery of the Ostland for the benefit of German industry. Hugo Stinnes and others through the Mitteldeutsche Zementwerke are proposing custodianship as a means of acquiring two Estonian cement companies. The plan is outlined in an interoffice memo dated 2 September 1942.

A trusteeship agreement has been cleared with the proper offices of the Reich Commissariat Ostland, valid until 1947, which covers the administration of subject firms. The agreement was concluded by the Rigaer Vereinigte Zementwerke und Baustoff G.m.b.H., which is to be provided with capital to RM 100,000. The two firms listed above will participate in this company. It is anticipated that the trusteeship contract will soon be supplanted by a conveyance effecting a transfer of the property of this company. The text of the trusteeship agreement will be made available to us by Mr. Kreyser.

The company has been assigned the task of administering the factories and doubling their capacity.

The money required to achieve this will amount to RM 5–6,000,000. . . . The interests forming this company have other cement holdings in the Gorka Company of Upper Silesia. Wepan, another cement factory, also expects to participate in the cement industry in occupied Russia.

Mr. Kreyser indicated that he would be gratified if the Dresdner Bank participated further in the development of this cement concern, and would place a man on the Aufsichtsrat, in order to be in constant touch with him.

A series of correspondence indicates the manner in which the Dresdner had identified itself with German business activity in the Baltic states. When the Ost Easer Gesellschaft needed some skilled help, such as bookkeepers and accountants, it wrote the Dresdner. Even Kehrl, of the Ministry of Economics, turned to it for help in finding a competent executive for one of the East companies. His request closes:

As the Dresdner Bank has particular experience in the field of the economy of the East territory and has a section concerned with business management, which has been built up over a number of years, I approached you with the request to aid me in the selection of personnel.

The Dresdner Bank promptly circularized its numerous branches and affiliates in connection with this request. Numerous other instances of such cooperation have been found in the files of the bank.

The practically monopolistic status of the Dresdner Bank in the Baltic states and its influence with the occupational administration is best illustrated in a series of letters from Solo Zuendwaren und Chemische Fabriken, A.G. (matches and chemical products) to the Dresdner Bank.

The Dresdner Bank was asked to secure entrance permission for the Solo to operate in Ostland territory.

This request is only another illustration of the power and influence possessed by the bank, and its exercise of nonbanking functions.

THE DRESDNER BANK IN OTHER COUNTRIES

The Dresdner Bank performed invaluable services in those states that were the nominal allies of Nazi Germany or neutrals. Assistance in these areas could not be as ruthless as in the conquered parts, but this versatile financial institution never failed to place its resources at the disposal of its partner, the Nazi state.

In the rearmament period very important sources of raw materials for Germany were the countries of South and Central America. The Dresdner's web of affiliates in strategic areas had extended to this zone through a subsidiary, the Deutsch-Suedamerikanische Bank. With branches in Argentina, Brazil, Chile, Paraguay, and Mexico and through agents in Bolivia, Ecuador, Peru, and Venezuela it served the interests of Nazi Germany. The Suedamerikanische Bank, speaking of its role in the economic structure of Nazi Germany, stated in 1936:

> Latin America is becoming increasingly important as a deliverer of raw materials to Germany. The German overseas banks are an indispensable support for German trade. A great portion of the upswing of German–Latin American trade relationship would have been impossible without the cooperation of the banks.

This was no idle boast as is evident from the credit files of the bank. A host of German firms operating in South America, as well as numerous native companies doing business with Germany, used the facilities of this bank. The minutes of the Credit Committee for 14 April 1937 show some of the firms dealt with and the extent of the credits granted. It will be noted that this one meeting alone granted substantial credits to such prominent armament firms as the Vereinigte Stahlwerke, Kloeckner Eisen, Bromberg & Company, and Metallgesellschaft.

❑ ❑ ❑

The cooperation of the Deutsch-Suedamerikanische Bank was valuable not only in South and Central America, but also in Spain, where an affiliate was maintained. A quotation from a memorandum, dated 5 January 1937, concerning Rowak, a corporation founded to assist Franco during the Spanish Civil War and afterward utilized by the Four Year Plan to expedite the import of wolfram and other badly needed raw materials, shows that the Nazi government actively sought the bank's help:

> At my conference today with the Foreign Organization, I obtained the following information regarding the Spanish corporation Rowag. Immediately after the formation of the corporation Major von Tagwitz invited the participation of the Deutsch-Suedamerikanische Bank. . . .

> The gentlemen (of the NSDAP) indicated that in their opinion it would be very desirable for the Dresdner Bank to have an official with Rowag, and asked if there was any intention of withdrawing Dr. Koehler.

The report of the Foreign Department of the Dresdner Bank for the month of June 1937 is marked top secret and contains notations by country of the transactions handled by the bank. Read in the light of later developments it shows both the extent of the bank's assistance to Nazi armaments for a war of aggression through the export-import trade and a varied list of services performed for the government itself. Among the transactions mentioned are:

> RM 350,000 each month to "Olex" Deutsche Benzin- und Petroleum G.m.b.H. Iranian oil development.

£30,000 to Mitsubishi Bank, London, for import of Manchurian soy beans.

£114,000 to Deutsche Oelmuehlen Rohstoffe G.m.b.H. to promote a barter deal with Norway.

Austrian schillings 700,000 to Alpenlaendische Bergbau (Krupp) to help in importing ore to Germany.

RM 50,000 monthly to Becker & Haag for import of Russian asbestos through Hungary.

Lei 50,000,000 through its Romanian affiliates to SOIA, S.A.R., with a guarantee by I.G. Farben.

RM 109,000 guarantee to Fried. Krupp, Grussonwerk to aid in a Polish transaction.

The actual declaration of war by Nazi Germany was not to be so timed that all foreign assets could be transferred from hostile areas. However all possible precautions against seizure were taken by the Dresdner Bank in order to save that portion of Germany's limited foreign assets entrusted to its care.

It found itself most exposed in that area in which its affiliate, the Deutsch-Suedamerikanische Bank, was operating. [Captured] correspondence sets out how, with typical Nazi disregard for law, this institution accomplished the protection of the foreign assets of itself and its customers. The means used constituted a fraud, as is shown in the following documents.

The Working Committee of the bank discussed the following on 1 October 1939:

The management reports that the bank intends to transfer its accounts with its overseas branches and with third parties to the a/c of the Auslands-Incasso-Bank G.m.b.H., which it controls, in order to prevent seizure by English and North American banks which have claims on the basis of Standstill Agreements. . . . The committee is in complete agreement, but recommends that capital of the branches be transferred not only to the Auslands-Incasso-Bank, but to more—perhaps three corporations—in order to make as difficult as possible any eventual seizure.

A "report on the current situation" of the bank dated 9 November 1939 states:

Our bank has not been particularly affected by seizures by the enemy states. The assets involved were for the most part transferred to neutral accounts in ample time. The same applies to New York, with respect to the overseas branches, with the exception of our Mexican branch, which happened to have a very large account with the Royal Bank of Canada at the outbreak of war. These assets were seized not only because of the interest of the Dresdner Bank in the amount of US $160,000. We have immediately taken energetic measures to effect the release of this seizure. . . .

Interesting light on the agent who effected cloaking operations is furnished by the following quotation from a letter of the Deutsch-Suedamerikanische Bank to the parent Dresdner Bank dated 13 December 1939:

We are pleased to inform you that our representative in New York, Herr A. de Chapeaurouge, has succeeded in negotiating satisfactorily all transactions connected with our assets located there. The seizures have been lifted, and the remaining assets have been transferred to neutral accounts. The Royal Bank of Canada has also released the $160,000 seized on account of Dresdner Bank interest.

In connection with the above, we would like to raise the question as to whether you see a possibility of having Herr de Chapeaurouge also work on behalf of the Dresdner Bank. . . . Our South American branches have been in complete contact with him since the outbreak of war . . . We have been paying him US $500 monthly, plus expenses. . . . We are very eager to assure his continued assistance. . . .

During [World War I] he represented the interests of our bank in a very proper and successful manner, until finally, long after the entry of the U.S. into the war, he was interned as one of the last Germans.

Meanwhile he has become an American citizen, so we need not fear an internment in case the USA should enter the [new] war against Germany.

❏ ❏ ❏

The Auslands-Incasso-Bank G.m.b.H. was not the only agency created by the Dresdner Bank for the cloaking of German assets in preparation for war.

A special company, the Allgemeine Waren-Finanzierungs Gesellschaft (Allwafinag) was established by the Dresdner Bank:

The corporation was founded in September (1939). Its managers are Dr. Entzian and Herr Dichler. Dr. Entzian is known to us as executive of the Dresdner Bank. The corporation was founded for the purpose of taking over foreign assets of firms who are in no position to own any assets abroad and of realizing such assets. . . . The management informed us that they are engaged in large transactions of that nature for a number of firms.

This letter goes on to criticize the Allwafinag and the Dresdner Bank for lack of secrecy in its operations:

The fact that the Dresdner Bank sent out circular letters about foreign trade offices and that the Allgemeine Waren-Finanzierungs Gesellschaft can be reached through the Dresdner Bank switchboard is bound to give foreign agents the impression that these two corporations are closely associated.

The funds thus safely cached were not lost to the Nazi war effort. For example, the manager of the Dresdner Belgian affiliate, the Continentale Bank, was proposing a transaction through Switzerland to use them. He had apparently engineered a three-cornered deal and needed to get some money to South America in order to save the Belgian share in a joint Swiss-Belgian venture in Brazil. He writes:

I have been considering the possibility of freeing an equivalent sum from the frozen assets in Brazil for this purpose and of having its equivalent amount paid to you through the German-Belgian clearing.

As the war progressed Nazi Germany, hemmed in by the blockade and locked in a desperate struggle, looked more and more to the Balkans for certain extremely important raw materials. Again it called on its trusted partner, the Dresdner Bank. . . .

The Dresdner Bank was well equipped to perform the task set, for its chain of affiliates and subsidiaries extended to the Balkans and it had connections in every country, Axis, occupied, or neutral, in the German sphere.

The most important of these was the Laenderbank Wien, established as a spearhead, since the economy of this region was naturally oriented toward Vienna. The acquisition of this bank is described in Chapter XVII, "Growth of the Dresdner Bank."

In Hungary the Dresdner Bank owned a participation in the Hungarian Allgemeine Creditanstalt. This bank had been acquired at the expense of the French. A small institution known as the Zipser Bank was also an agency of the Dresdner. The following notes of the Vorstand for 9 January 1941, concerning the establishing of the Dresdner in Hungary, are an interesting example of the integration of the bank with the Nazi fifth column, the *Volksdeutsche*:

> Report of the wishes of the ethnic Germans in Hungary (negotiations through the Volksdeutsche intermediary) to purchase the Mercurbank exchange office (of Laenderbank Wien), as a credit institute. The Vorstand agrees to the sale with the following reservations:
>   1. That we obtain the written promise of the Reich to inaugurate with full pressure an acceptance by the French government of a contract to "acquire" the shares of the Hungarian Credit Bank.
>   2. That Dresdner Bank will have priority in the purchase of other banks in Hungary, in the event the transaction for the Hungarian Credit Bank is not carried through.
>   3. That the Mercurbank assumes all Hungarian claims of Zipser Bank, which we intend to acquire.

The Dresdner had held a participation in the Societatea Bancara Romana for many years and used this in her efforts to increase Romanian capacity to export to Germany. The importance attached to this bank may be judged from the following, contained in a telegram dated 12 October 1942, from the Dresdner to Prager Credit Bank:

> However, by taking over these frozen 120 million Lei, the Bancara (Romanian affiliate) would damage the interest of German imports from Romania, as its assets must be available completely for the financing of the export of necessary foods and raw materials from Romania.

> The Ministry of Economics would never grant permission for the Bancara to use these assets for taking over debts in Romania which are realizable only on a long-term basis.

Conditions in Greece would not appear favorable for banking operations, as the German Army was hard-pressed to maintain itself there. Perhaps partly to assist it, the Dresdner Bank established a foothold in Greece. The Banque d'Athenes was not taken over by the Dresdner, though the latter had the foresight to obtain the agreement of the German government to do so when the war was over. Instead a corporation, the Griechisch Deutsche Finanzierungs Gesellschaft, was formed to handle commercial transactions between the two countries. The available records of the bank reveal few transactions with Greece. A report from Athens very briefly describes a few transactions engaged in by this company for the Dresdner Bank. The fact that the manager has been tried and sentenced as a collaborationist indicates the light in which the Greek people viewed the Dresdner's operations.

Yugoslavia, being a constant battleground, offered little attraction for even so voracious an institution as the Dresdner. It was prepared to step in when conditions became stable, for it had an interest in the Kroatische Landesbank and the Suedbank of Serbia.

The requirements of the German war machine were so high and the industrial capacity that could be spared for making goods to finance her barter trade so low that difficulties in paying for the excess of imports over exports were soon encountered. The dilemma is well described in a letter dated 15 January 1942 to the Ministry of Economics by one of its trade groups. Rasche received a copy of this for comment and correction, as the Dresdner evidently was commonly identified with the barter trade. The author notes:

> Our barter trade with all countries which still have valuable raw material or food is in grave danger. Romania, Bulgaria, Hungary, Croatia, Slovakia, Sweden, and Finland are exporting great quantities of goods to the Reich, for which they can receive no goods from us. The reason: Organization of our economy for war. . . . The inflation into which we ourselves are driving these countries . . . is crippling the willingness of the agrarian populations to deliver, and thus diminishes our own raw material and foodstuff supplies.

The soundness of these observations had been recognized, and an attempt made to meet them.

Already in 1940, the government called on the Dresdner and the Deutsche banks to head a syndicate which would finance German exports to Romania. Among the banks mobilized in this effort was the Dresdner's Austrian affiliate, the Laenderbank Wien. The sum of RM 200,000,000 in credit was actually used and the participating banks were pledged to raise more if needed.

To improve trade with Hungary, the Ministry of Economics decided to try and reduce Germany's clearing balance. This plan called for repatriating as many Hungarian securities as could be found in areas under German control. For this ambitious project Nazi Germany turned once more to the Dresdner. This was a task which would call into play the widespread branches and affiliates of the Dresdner Bank.

A Dresdner Bank memorandum dated 1 September 1942 shows the Dresdner as an extremely important agency in this matter. It summarizes their part in the following words:

Negotiations aiming at the resale to Hungary of Hungarian stocks held in Germany for the purpose of reducing the excess clearing balance, as is known, have been in progress for some time. The ground work of locating the German-held stocks has been done exclusively by us, together with the Laenderbank Wien in accordance with instructions received at the time from the Hungarian National Bank regarding acquisition of Hungarian securities circulating in Germany.

We forwarded, as desired, all the material to the Ministry of Economics for its negotiations with the Hungarians. We have since been in constant contact with the competent officials in the Ministry of Economics. . . .

While Germany searched for a scheme to solve her dilemma, she was seizing every opportunity to negotiate any barter that could possibly be arranged.

Rasche wrote to Count Felix Czernin of the Laenderbank Wien on 10 February 1944, that:

I have just established interest in Sweden for the formation of a Turkish-Swiss-Swedish trading corporation in which we could have a hidden interest.

A comprehensive eight-page memorandum marked "Highly Confidential," dated 26 April 1944, written by Hans Treue, director of the Hamburg branch of the Dresdner Bank, further discusses in detail plans for cloaking German interest in barter trade with Turkey, on the basis of conferences with Reinel of the Reichsbank, and Schulte-Schlutius and Landwehr of the Ministry of Economics (RWM).

These documents deal with the advisability of forming cloak corporations to handle barter trade between Turkey and Germany. Plans involved the establishment of a Slovakian cloak. The barter element was necessitated by recently instituted strict foreign exchange regulations between Germany and Turkey and the element of cloaking being necessary to avoid detection by the Allies:

In order to make the business appear Slovakianized, . . . the technical expression invented in this connection, . . . it would be handled through the Lihag in Pressburg (Landwirtschaftliche Industrie & Handels A.G.) . . . Furthermore, in order to assure that the banking connections would appear Slovakian, the Deutsche Handels & Kreditbank A.G. (a Dresdner Bank affiliate) located in Pressburg would be included. . . . (Not only for certain technical reasons) is it planned to entrust the business in Turkey to a German firm, but also the further reason appears that it is easier in this manner to cloak these transactions more effectively than if they were negotiated by a purely Turkish firm, since they will certainly arouse the interest of the enemies. For the implementation of these considerations, the thought has occurred to us to form in Turkey a Turkish firm closely related to the Laenderbank Wien, which should be the carrier of the barter trade with this country. It should appear from outside as a purely Turkish firm. (The modest capital planned for such a firm would not be sufficient for the larger transactions), and a banking guarantee in ample quantities would be necessary.

However, such cooperation might make illusory the most effective cloaking of the business, which is so especially in the interest of Germany. . . . It would also not be advisable to deal exclusively through Slovakia, since extensive dealings involving a relatively small country might awaken the attention of the enemy, but also to think in terms of developing the business through Switzerland and Sweden.

The implications of Germany's policy of international barter have always been completely clear to her economic leaders.

This policy involved deliveries to Germany of products from the rest of Continental Europe, theoretically in return for German products, but actually in return for nothing more than clearing balances credited to other nations, under a system euphemistically known as "barter" (*Kompensationsgeschaeft*). Such barter constituted merely another form of organized looting of Europe by Germany.

The Dresdner Bank, being fully aware of this fact, enthusiastically participated in its execution.

CHAPTER XXII

The Dresdner Bank Today

The Dresdner Bank today and the Dresdner Bank described in the preceding chapters bear a close resemblance to each other in their basic structure and approach to banking policies. The Dresdner Bank still controls a large portion of the wealth of Germany. As far as it could, it has maintained the chain of branches and affiliates that served so well in the building of the Nazi war machine. To run this plant it has a large proportion of the same people who carried out the policies of the bank for Nazi Germany. Economic conditions and the difficulties of communication in occupied Germany have reduced the scale of its operations, but the essential structure of a universal bank remains undisturbed. Steps to continue along the old lines of operations were taken by the management of the Dresdner Bank immediately after the zonal boundaries became known.

A circular sent to all branches within the Western Zones of occupation in July 1945 outlined plans for operation. The introductory paragraphs read:

> In an attempt to bring our institutions in the occupied West territories, that is to say, the American, English, and French Zones, to full activity for its task as a Grossbank in the German economy, we have erected various central departments under the name
>
> "Zentraldirektion West."
>
> All branches within the named zones will in the future circulars be called West Filialon. They (departments under Zentraldirektion West) will temporarily fulfill the functions of the corresponding departments of the former Berlin central office.

The Dresdner Bank followed the directives as outlined but due to the influx of leading Dresdner Bank officials from Berlin into the Western Zones some changes in the early post–V-E Day management (Vorstand) took place. A statement listing the present Vorstand and defining its functions was completed in Hamburg on 7 December 1945. It reads:

> According to the by-laws of the Dresdner Bank, the Vorstand consists of at least two members. Presently Director Hoelling is the only Vorstand member in a position to exercise his office. Under the present circumstances there is no practical possibility for another Vorstand member to exercise his functions. Upon the suggestion of the chairman of the Aufsichtsrat it was decided that the management of the bank is to consist of a board composed of the Vorstand member in office and four department chiefs of the bank.

Conferences among the undersigned concerning the execution of the above plan resulted in the following:

    1.   A "Geschaeftsleitung" (business management) is formed consisting of:

        Director Hoelling

        and the four gentlemen

        Director von Richter

        Director Rinn

        Director Schleipen

        Director Schobert

The objective of this "Geschaeftsleitung" is to take over the direction of operations of the Dresdner Bank in place of the complete Vorstand.

This statement carries the personal signatures of Richter, Rinn, Schleipen, and Schobert. Thus the present management looks to the old Vorstand and Aufsichtsrat as the source of authority and feels that its primary responsibility is toward the former stockholders.

The present management of the bank continues centralized operations embracing all aspects of banking direction including disposition of personnel, extension of loans, interzonal securities trading, and so on.

In order to successfully direct such operations the present management established three offices. One was in Hamburg to control all branches in the British Zone (Zentralstelle Hamburg), one in Frankfurt/Wiesbaden for the American and French Zones (Zentraldirektion West) and a Liaison Staff (*Verbindungsstab*) in Bochum in the British Zone.

The report of a meeting of the Zentraldirektion West held in Wiesbaden on Sunday, 20 January 1946, with the participation of Schobert, Schleipen, Goetz (chairman of the old Aufsichtsrat then under house arrest) states the following:

    1.   Mr. Schleipen reports that the present Zentraldirektion West, Bochum, was renamed to "Verbindungsstab Bochum." This also holds true for the French and American Zones because it is not desired, on the part of the Americans, that any influence from the British Zone be exerted on the business management active in the U.S. Zone, as was implied by the expression used so far.

It is interesting to note that the present leaders of the Dresdner Bank expect to satisfy U.S. policies for decentralization of banking by formal changing of office designations.

That the zonal separation is considered only a minor obstacle is fully evident in the statement of Hans Rinn, member of the Management Committee of the Dresdner Bank recently removed and prosecuted for violations of Laws No. 8 and No. 52.

He wrote on 10 January 1946:

As you probably know there was created a certain separation between the English Zone on one side and French-American Zones on the other.

—Both offices (Zentralstelle Hamburg and Zentraldirektion Frankfurt/ Wiesbaden) however work as closely together as before with the directorate at Bochum.

—It is understood that we remain in close contact with the gentlemen in the British Zone; for example, I am at present here in Hamburg for the purpose of conducting conferences regarding all pertinent questions.

Although the Dresdner Bank is closed in the Soviet Zone a special office is operating in Hannover (Verbindungsstelle Ost)

for all matters concerning the branches of our bank in the Russian-occupied Zone.

One of the main functions of the present management is to reemploy old personnel of the Dresdner Bank and utilize the discrepancies between the denazification policies of the Allied powers to shuffle individuals between Zones.

> 10. Mr. Schleipen further reports that in the matter of [Mr.] Reek, the British finance officer who permitted Mr. Roek to work in Bochum did not follow the American decision on the basis of which Roek was dismissed.

Significant in connection with reemployment of personnel is the absorption by the present Dresdner Bank of individuals who directed and executed operations of Dresdner Bank and its affiliates in the satellite and occupied countries of Europe since 1938.

Dr. J. Entzian, leading official of the Continentale Bank in Belgium, is currently heading the Foreign Department of the Liaison Staff in Bochum. Leonhard Stitz-Ulrici, whose activities on behalf of the Dresdner Bank in Czechoslovakia are discussed in another chapter, is currently employed by the Dresdner Bank in Frankfurt. Dr. Anspach, who was among the chief representatives of the Dresdner Bank in Slovakia and Poland, is in charge of credit operations of the Zentraldirektion West Frankfurt/Wiesbaden.

More cases of a similar nature can be cited.

Statistics on the denazification of Dresdner Bank personnel supplied by the Frankfurt branch indicate that there were 319 removals including 39 branch managers as of 20 February 1946. The managers of the Dresdner Bank branches in the French Zone in 1944 are still in office with the exception of one whose name does not appear on the list of present managers.

Centralized operations of the Dresdner Bank extend to the granting of loans to firms in the American, British, and French Zones thus giving the present management of the Dresdner Bank the opportunity to determine to a large degree the financing of economic reconstruction in those zones.

The minutes of the meetings of the management of the Dresdner Bank dated 4 January 1946 contain records of loans in amounts between RM 500,000–RM 3,000,000 each extended to nine firms in the British Zone and in amounts between

RM 100,000–RM 500,000 each to twelve firms in the same zone. The same meetings determined loans for the other zones. The French and American Zones were treated as a unit and loans to firms, irrespective of zonal location, were approved. Four loans ranging in amount from RM 500,000–RM 5,000,000 were granted along with 9 loans ranging in amount from RM 100,000–RM 500,000 to firms located in the French and American Zones.

The same exhibit throws an interesting light on the extent of control exercised by the management of the Dresdner Bank on industrial enterprises. This constituted one of the principal characteristics of the Grossbanken which made them excessive concentrations of economic power. The case in point is the statement made by the management of the bank in connection with the extension of a RM 1,500,000 loan to the NSU-Werke A.G. Neckarsulm (French Zone):

> As the Vorstand (of the NSU) has been dismissed, we took the necessary measures for the continuation of profitable operations.

That statement attains its true significance in light of the fact that at the last general stockholders meeting of NSU, 17 September 1943, the Dresdner Bank represented by proxy voting RM 6,687,700 out of a total of RM 8,000,000 or 84 percent of the share capital of this firm.

The centralized direction of operations by the Dresdner Bank in the three Western Zones was the major factor in the establishment of its predominant position in securities trading at present.

Hans Rinn, former member of the Management Committee and chief of Securities Trading of the Dresdner Bank, wrote on 19 January 1946:

> The business is developing in such fashion that we can say without exaggeration that the Dresdner Bank controls the entire securities trading business in the West and Southwest.

Some indication of the volume of trading in securities by the Frankfurt branch of the Dresdner Bank may be ascertained by its own figures. In the period from 1 January 1946 to 28 February 1946 this branch bought securities with the nominal value of RM 3,445,200 from other banks and individuals.

Inasmuch as securities generally carried higher quotations in Hamburg where the central offices of the Dresdner Bank are located, it is not surprising to note that a substantial portion of securities found its way from Frankfurt to Hamburg. In the same period from 1 January 1946 to 28 February 1946 securities with the nominal value of RM 983,800 were sold to Hamburg by the Frankfurt branch of the Dresdner Bank.

The Frankfurt branch of the Dresdner Bank is currently under investigation for the violation of United States Military Government Law 55 prohibiting trading in I.G. Farben stock after 29 January 1946. The Frankfurt branch delivered to Hamburg RM 170,000 worth of I.G. Farben stock after 29 January 1946. As late as February 27 this branch delivered to the Mainz branch of the Dresdner Bank RM 2,000 worth of I.G. Farben stock.

The Dresdner Bank of today is still a large bank. The records lost during the last days of the war have not been completely duplicated as yet. However, the bank estimates that the assets under control of the present management on 31 December 1945 amounted to RM 3,810,000,000. Of this total RM 1,450,000,000 are in the American Zone, RM 2,100,000,000 in the British, and 260,000,000 in the French [Zone].

The bank is currently operating a total of 128 branches in the three Western Zones, of which 15 are in the French, 73 in the British, and 40 in the American. The bank has about 2,800 employees in all three Western Zones.

The men who direct the bank today held responsible positions in the old Dresdner Bank. They assisted in formulating and executing policies of the bank under the Nazi regime.

In view of the past record of the Dresdner Bank such individuals cannot be entrusted with any responsibility for forming and influencing the economic and financial future of present Germany.

CHAPTER XXIII

Profiles

The following section of this report contains biographical information on those 1943–1945 Vorstand and Aufsichtsrat members of the Dresdner Bank who were arrested and are in the custody of United States authorities.

Since this information was obtained in the course of a financial investigation rather than in a series of industrial investigations, the profiles of those who were primarily industrialists are not complete.

All profiles should be read in conjunction with the entire report on the Dresdner Bank, of which all the Vorstand and Aufsichtsrat members were responsible officials.

Goetz, Carl	Schieber, Walter
Kisskalt, Wilhelm	Ullrich, Hans
Avieny, Wilhelm	Walz, Hans
Flick, Friedrich	Pilder, Hans
Koppenberg, Heinrich	Rasche, Karl
Lindemann, Karl	Schippel, Hans
Marotzke, Wilhelm	Zinsser, Hugo

CARL FRIEDRICH GOETZ

(CHAIRMAN OF THE AUFSICHTSRAT OF THE DRESDNER BANK)

SUMMARY

Carl Friedrich Goetz, chairman of the board of directors of the Dresdner Bank, takes rank as one of the foremost figures in German finance. Only Hermann Abs (Deutsche Bank), Otto Christian Fischer (of the Reichsgruppe Banken and the Reichs-Kredit-Gesellschaft), and Hjalmar Schacht of the Reichsbank have a comparable stature. He led the Dresdner Bank during the thirteen-year period between 1931–1944 out of the abyss of two financial reorganizations to the position of the second largest bank on the European continent.

This remarkable transformation in the fortunes and destinies of the Dresdner Bank took place under Goetz's leadership during the years of the Nazi regime. No other leading banking institution came to identify itself so intimately with the affairs of the Nazi Party, the Nazi government, and the SS, and no other banking institution exploited its political connections to such ruthless profit. The Dresdner Bank, directly or through its subsidiaries and affiliates, played an outstanding role in the financing of virtually every department of heavy industry which participated in Germany's preparation for war; it made extensive profits out of the Aryanization of properties and the exploitation of the economic resources of the countries in occupied Europe; its network of foreign subsidiaries was employed as an instrument of German espionage and Nazi propaganda activities. Goetz was no Party member himself, but the men around him enjoyed such excellent political connections that the Dresdner Bank came to be identified within Party and affiliated circles as the SS Bank.

Personal Data. Carl Friedrich Goetz commenced his banking career with the Wertheimer Bank at Frankfurt on Main where he had been born on 12 June 1885. From Wertheimer's he transferred his activities to the Banque Internationale of Brussels and passed the four years of World War I in an Allied internment camp. Upon his return to Germany after the war, he joined the Commerz Bank where he became a manager and afterward President of the Vorstand. He undertook the reorganization of the failing Dresdner Bank in 1931 and continued as its principal and most influential figure until the last months of the war.

Goetz was residing at Wolfratshausen, Bavaria, at the time of his arrest in November, 1945, and was taken to Frankfurt on Main for interrogation. He is at present at the Seventh Army Detention Camp.

Political Activity. Although not a member of the Nazi Party, Goetz's political reliability prior to the last months of the war never came into question since he worked hand in glove with the Party and affiliated organizations. To these organizations, he contributed freely of his time, effort, and money. He became a member in 1935 of the committee [establishing] the Nazi Party's Commission for Economic Policy. He [also] busied himself with the dissemination abroad of Nazi propaganda.

❑ ❑ ❑

Goetz made financial contributions to Party organizations of every description ranging from modest sums to SA detachments to contributions of RM 1,000 to the Ihueringen State Office for Racial Research. He was repeatedly thanked by his old and close friend, Gauleiter Fritz Sauckel, the director of the German slave labor program, for the extent of his cooperation and his magnanimous financial grants to the families of Party members who had fallen on the Eastern front.

Goetz was also a member of the following auxiliary organizations of the NSDAP:

Deutsche Jaegerschaft	1933
DAF	1934
NSV	1936
Luftschutzbund	1938

Industrial and Financial Connections. The roster of institutions in industry and finance with which Goetz identified himself as director or as chairman or vice-chairman is one of the most impressive and wide-ranging in the entire German economy. He was affiliated with the industries directed by Krupp, Flick, Voegler, Heinkel, and

Schmitz, which were front-rank producers for the German war machine. These companies included

1.	Armaments:	Fried. Krupp; Mauser Werke
2.	Steel:	Vereinigte Stahlwerke; Rheinische Stahlwerke
3.	Electrical:	Allgemeine Elektrizitaets Gesellschaft [AEG]
4.	Power:	Rheinisch Westfaelisches Elektrizitaetswerk A.G.
		Gesellschaft fuer Elektrische Unternehmungen
5.	Chemicals:	Wintershall; Salzdetfurth; Degussa
6.	Mining:	Harpener Bergbau; Rheinische Braunkohlenbergbau
7.	Machinery:	Adlerwerke

Goetz received the following annual fees from some of his principal connections:

Degussa	RM 20,000
Zellstoff Weldhoff	18,000
Mauser Werke	14,000
Fried. Krupp	10,000
Allgemeine Elektrizitaets Ges.	9,000
Vereinigte Stahlwerke	8,000
Balzdetfurth	8,000
Rheinische Braunkohlenbergbau	6,000
Rheinische Stahlwerke	6,000

These sums are far in excess of the 1,000–3,000 fees usually paid to a director whose sum of activity is restricted to attendance at two or three meetings per year. But then Goetz was no mere stuffed shirt of a director in these companies. He was a highly trusted adviser whose counsel on major questions of finance was in constant demand by policy-making officials.

Connections with the Dresdner Bank. Carl Goetz resigned his position as president of the Vorstand of the Commerz Bank in 1931 to accept the corresponding post at the Dresdner Bank. At the request of Reichs Chancellor Bruening, Goetz undertook this new responsibility during the banking crisis of 1931 when a merger of the failing Dresdner Bank and the bankrupt Darmstaedter Bank was carried out. The Reich government granted a large subsidy to the new institution but when the crisis continued to worsen, a second reorganization, carrying with it a second large government subsidy, took place in 1932. The coming to power of Adolf Hitler launched the Dresdner Bank on an era of prosperity which never abated during the remaining years of the Nazi regime.

During all the years of his affiliation with the Dresdner Bank Goetz remained the key personality and the dominant figure of that institution. He continued to tower over all the other staff members. The correspondence files reveal that he was consulted on every conceivable phase of operations of the bank and its affiliates, for not only was his grasp of German banking encyclopedic in scope but his understanding of foreign banking made his knowledge worldwide.

As president of the Vorstand between 1931–1936 Goetz exercised complete control over the Dresdner Bank and its policies. In 1936, Goetz, for reasons of internal organization, relinquished the presidency to become chairman of the Aufsichtsrat.

This new position weakened Goetz's authority in no way and he continued to enjoy an extraordinary status and complete control over the policies and personalities of the bank. Paragraph one of his contract with the Aufsichtsrat, dated 18 April 1936, states:

> Carl Goetz is obliged to devote his full time to the bank. He is to supervise constantly the entire scope of Vorstand activities, to strengthen business relations with the bank's customers, and to formulate policies and directives in the name of the Aufsichtsrat for the Vorstand to follow.

In addition to the authority extended by this contract all incoming members of the Aufsichtsraete of companies receiving credits from the Dresdner Bank as well as all banks and affiliates, which the Dresdner Bank might acquire in other countries, required the endorsement of Goetz.

Goetz also became at the same time chairman of the Arbeitsausschuss (Working Committee) of the Aufsichtsrat, a small committee which exercised a close supervision over all bank credits. Its approval of all credits larger than RM 600,000 extended by the bank, of the appointment of all managers of the bank and its principal affiliates and of every major participation of the Dresdner Bank in other banks, in industries, mergers, stock underwritings and the like, were required in advance.

Carl Goetz's position on the Aufsichtsrat and the Arbeitsausschuss was so predominant and his prestige so great that to separate the bank, its policies, and activities from its leading official becomes an impossibility. In speaking of himself that "he was the Dresdner Bank," Goetz was simply stating a fact obvious to all.

The Dresdner Bank and the SS. Three members of the Vorstand and the Aufsichtsrat of the Dresdner Bank were SS Brigadefuehrer and seven were members of the Keppler or the Himmler Circle. This Circle contributed to Himmler a fund of RM 1 million per year during nine years for "special purposes." The contribution of the Dresdner Bank to this fund came to RM 50,000 per year during the entire period and was given with the approval of the management. These sums were deposited at the J. H. Stein Bank at Koeln whence they were forwarded to the Dresdner Bank at Berlin. Through SS Brigadefuehrer Fritz Kranefuss, a Dresdner Bank director, these moneys were then paid over out of the Dresdner Bank account to Himmler.

The SS Economics Office, through SS Obergruppenfuehrer Pohl, also maintained close relations with the Dresdner Bank, which acted as the principal bank of this SS organization.

The Dresdner Bank extended large credits to various SS affiliates, including one of RM 2,000,000 in 1939 to the Gesellschaft zur Pflege Deutscher Kulturdenkmaler and another during the same year of RM 5,000,000 to the SS Gesellschaft Deutsche Erd-und Steinwerke. These credits, which received the prior endorsement of the Arbeitsausschuss, Carl Goetz, and the Bank Management, if scarcely to be justified as legitimate business loans, testify to the grounds whereby Nazi Party and affiliated circles came to refer to the Dresdner Bank as the SS Bank.

The Dresdner Bank as a Nazi Party Propaganda and Espionage Agency. The ties linking the Dresdner Bank and its subsidiaries to the Nazi Party and affiliated organizations were particularly close in the field of foreign propaganda and espionage. . . .

The Dresdner Bank, which was led by Carl Goetz, through its affiliates and subsidiaries was busily engaged in Nazi propaganda activities in South America, the Balkans and the Near East [as described earlier]. . . . The propaganda and espionage activities of the Dresdner Bank affiliates in Egypt between 1933 and 1939 [discussed in an earlier chapter] were of particular notoriety.

❏ ❏ ❏

Activities of the Dresdner Bank in the Countries of Occupied Europe. Between the years 1937–1942 the Dresdner Bank, contemporaneously with the formation and expansion of Greater Germany, enjoyed an eightfold increase in the number of its foreign affiliates. In the exploitation of the economic resources of the countries in occupied Europe the Dresdner Bank acted virtually as a rear echelon of the Wehrmacht.

1. Austria. The Dresdner Bank . . . was the sole shareholder of the Mercurbank of Vienna. . . .

   [As discussed earlier, Goetz was informed nine months before the 1938 Anschluss of Hitler's desire to use the Mercurbank as a "German stronghold" for economic domination of Austria and of Southeastern Europe.]
       Goetz . . . assign[ed] two "specialists" from the Vorstand, Dr. Meyer and Dr. Rasche, to work out the details.
       Directly after the Anschluss the Dresdner Bank merged the Mercurbank with the Austrian subsidiaries of the Banque des Pays de l'Europe Centrale and of the Zivnostenska Banka of Prague to form the Laenderbank Wien.
2. Czechoslovakia. Directly after the annexation of the Sudetenland the Dresdner Bank took over the thirty-two Sudeten branches of the Boehmische Escompte Bank. This amputation so weakened the Escompte Bank that it was taken over by the Dresdner Bank as a matter of course directly after the occupation of Czechoslovakia.
3. Poland. The Dresdner Bank opened branches in the seven major cities of Poland within fewer than three months after the conquest of the country had been completed. During the following year it opened two special banks for Poland—the Ostbank Posen and the Kommerzialbank, Cracow. The goal of these banks was stated to be "the reorganization of industry for war production," and "the reprivatization of former Polish and Jewish businessess."
4. Belgium. Shortly after the conquest of Belgium the Dresdner Bank established at Brussels and Antwerp an affiliate, the Bank Continentale with the mission to establish closer "integration" of the Belgian economy with the German. The affiliate worked to achieve this goal by means of penetration purchases of key Belgian securities by means of "clearing arrangements" whereby the bank did not have

to pay out in these transactions any of its own funds. It [meanwhile] extended vast credits to German war industries and military agencies [and . . .] engaged in large-scale Aryanizations of Jewish property in Belgium.

❑ ❑ ❑

5. Holland. The Dresdner Bank established in ["stronghold"] Holland after the conquest a Stuetzpunkt, the Handelstrust West . . . [This] mission was singled out with an award for "exceptional services in achieving the great aims of the National Socialist Movement."
6. Baltic Countries. The Dresdner Bank set up in these countries the Ostland Bank, later renamed the Handels und Kreditbank Riga. The Dresdner Bank thereby acquired a virtual banking monopoly in Lithuania, Latvia, and Estonia.

Between 1938–1944 the Dresdner Bank achieved an enormous expansion. Its assets and its commercial deposits showed a threefold increase and its savings deposits a sevenfold increase. This extraordinary and virtually unparalleled development in so brief a period was made possible in great part only through the ruthless exploitation by the Dresdner Bank, which was led by Carl Goetz, of the financial and industrial resources of the countries in occupied Europe.

Aryanization. . . . No German bank acted more ruthlessly than the Dresdner Bank in the seizure of Aryanized Jewish properties.

A typical example of the bank's methods in these cases is visible in the case of the Engelhardt Brauerei A.G., Germany's second largest brewery. [The Aryanization of this property, including the arrest of its owner by the Gestapo, was detailed earlier in this report.]

❑ ❑ ❑

The Dresdner Bank also did not neglect its interests in the Aryanization of private banks and led the way in the number of Jewish houses which it took over. These included Gebrueder Arnhold of Dresden and Berlin, S. Bleichroeder & Co., Berlin, Bank fuer Brauindustrie, Berlin, and B. Simons & Co., Duesseldorf.

In the bulk of the Aryanization cases with which the Dresdner Bank busied itself, it first employed its Party connections to locate available businesses for Aryanization; then it supplied new "purchasers" to whom it granted the necessary credits to carry on these businesses. For these undertakings it collected fees in proportion to the value of its services.

The case of I. & C. A. Schneider, Frankfurt a.M., a large leather and shoe manufacturer, is representative of these instances. . . . Through the agency of the Nazi Party's Gauwirtschaftsberater at Frankfurt, who also turned out to be a Dresdner

Bank director, the Jewish proprietors of the Schneider Company were imprisoned in Buchenwald. Their release was effected only after they had signed a contract for the sale of their business for a consideration of less than 3 percent of its net worth. For its services in the Schneider case the Dresdner Bank collected an honorarium of RM 40,000. . . .

The Dresdner Bank, which was led by Carl Goetz, its subsidiaries, and affiliates were the leading agencies in the forcible Aryanization of Jewish-owned businesses in Germany as well as in every country of occupied Europe.

❑ ❑ ❑

Income. As president of the Aufsichtsrat of the Dresdner Bank, Goetz's annual salary ran to RM 108,000. Bonuses, directorships in other companies, and investments brought his total annual income to RM 450,000. His total worth at the end of the war he estimates to be in excess of 1 million.

Sources. The information of Carl Goetz in this profile was obtained from Military Government questionnaires, interrogations, reports prepared by Goetz, and the correspondence files of the Dresdner and other banks with which he was identified.

Evaluation of Prisoner. Carl Goetz creates on the interrogator a particularly favorable impression at first for the keenness of his intellect, the wealth of his experience, and the breadth of his banking knowledge. In these qualities he towers head and shoulders above his colleagues not alone at the Dresdner Bank but of virtually all his fellow bankers in Germany.

Goetz is pleased to style himself as an anti-Nazi and relies heavily in this connection on the fact that in the autumn of 1944 the Gestapo charged him with complicity in the events of the 20th of July [the failed attempt to assassinate Hitler during 1944]. He explains that his arrest was delayed because of his indispensability to the operations of the Dresdner Bank in supplying money to the German war machine.

In the opinion of the Goetz interrogators there is no basis whatsoever for his claims of anti-Nazidom. To have retained his outstanding position during all the years of the Nazi regime would have been an impossibility unless the Party considered him completely reliable politically. In point of fact Goetz has proven himself an evasive and thoroughly unreliable witness who has been trapped in direct lies. Although a man of proved strength of memory on banking questions, he develops pernicious amnesia the moment that the unsavory transactions of the Dresdner Bank or of its officials or employees are touched upon.

CONCLUSION

Goetz held a high position in the financial industrial and economic life of Germany . . . and is deemed to have committed a crime against peace. . . . His detention is not subject to review.

WILHELM KISSKALT

(VICE-CHAIRMAN OF THE AUFSICHTSRAT OF THE DRESDNER BANK)

SUMMARY

Wilhelm Kisskalt typifies the man who became an early ardent supporter of Nazism not because of sincere belief in its principles, but out of sheer opportunism to advance his own personal benefits.

Personal Data. Wilhelm Kisskalt, age seventy-three, lives at Garmisch-Partenkirchen on Pflegerseestrasse 1. He was vice-chairman of the Working Committee of the Aufsichtsrat of the Dresdner Bank.

Subject was arrested on 29 October 1945, and is now under house arrest in his home.

Kisskalt was educated at the Universities of Wuerzburg and Berlin, and received the title of Privy Councillor of Law as well as the honorary degree of Doctor of Political Economy. His main occupation and field of interest is in insurance.

Political Activities. Wilhelm Kisskalt was a member of the NSDAP since 1933. Subject was a member of the following auxiliary organizations of the NSDAP:

DAF 1933
KDF 1933
NSKOV
NSV 1933
NS Rechtswahrerbund 1933
NS Altherrenbund 1933

Kisskalt claims that he joined the Party to protect his private insurance interests against attack from socialist elements with[in] the NSDAP. His actions, however, indicate other reasons. He made contributions to the SS Furtherance Movement.

Financial and Industrial Connections.

Dresdner Bank, Berlin	Deputy chairman of the Working Committe of the Aufsichtsrat 1938–1943
Bayerische Versicherungsbank, Muenchen	Chairman Aufsichtsrat 1924–1938
Hermes Kredit Versicherungs A.G., Berlin	Chairman Aufsichtsrat 1919–1945
Karlsruher Lebensversicherungs A.G., Karlsruhe	Vice-Chairman Aufsichtsrat 1931–1945
Muenchner Rueckversicherungs-Gesellschaft, Muenchen	Vice-Chairman Aufsichtsrat 1938–1945

Allianz Lebensversicherungs A.G., Berlin	Member Aufsichtsrat 1919–1945
Allianz Versicherungs A.G., Berlin	Member Aufsichtsrat 1919–1945
Berlinische Lebensversicherungs A.G., Berlin	Member Aufsichtsrat 1931–1938
Frankfurter Versicherungs A.G., Frankfurt	Member Aufsichtsrat 1931–1938
Union Hagel Versicherungs A.G., Weimar	Member Aufsichtsrat 1916–1938
Pilot Reinsurance Co., New York and Hartford, U.S.	Member Aufsichtsrat 1924–1938
Union Rueckversicherungs Gesellschaft, Zuerich	Member Aufsichtsrat 1924–1938
Schweizer National Versicherungs A.G., Basel	Member Aufsichtsrat 1913–1914
Wuerzburger Hofbraeu A.G., Wuerzburg	Member Aufsichtsrat

As vice-chairman of the Muenchner Rueckversicherungs-Gesellschaft (reinsurance company) he represented the interests of the largest reinsurance company in Europe on the board of the Dresdner Bank.

Income. Wilhelm Kisskalt's income:

1933	RM 250,000	1939	RM 150,000
1934	RM 250,000	1940	RM 140,000
1935	RM 250,000	1941	RM 130,000
1936	RM 250,000	1942	RM 120,000
1937	RM 250,000	1943	RM 120,000
1938	RM 250,000	1944	RM 110,000

Kisskalt's decrease in income results from his retirement. Subject estimates his assets to be worth RM 1,000,000.

Evaluation of the Prisoner. Kisskalt is an expert in the field of insurance and is very willing to volunteer information on the subject. His attempts to whitewash his early membership in the Party seem unsatisfactory.

CONCLUSION

Kisskalt held a high position in the financial, industrial, and economic life of Germany . . . and is deemed to have committed a crime against peace. . . . His detention is not subject to review.

WILHELM AVIENY

(MEMBER OF THE AUFSICHTSRAT OF THE DRESDNER BANK)

SUMMARY

Wilhelm Avieny is typical of the small Nazi raised to positions of prominence solely on the strength of his Party connections.

Personal Data. Wilhelm Avieny, age forty-nine, is a German citizen and lives at Lilienthal Allee 7, Frankfurt on Main. He was a member of the Aufsichtsrat of the Dresdner Bank.

Avieny was arrested on 23 April 1945 in Frankfurt a/M and is at present detained at the FIAT enclosure "Dustbin."

He was trained as an economist, but has been a second-rate executive for most of his business career.

Political Activity. Wilhelm Avieny has been a member of the NSDAP since 1931.

He was a member of the following affiliated organizations of the NSDAP:

> SS since 1933—Obersturmbannfuehrer since 1943
> Reichsbund der Deutschen Beamten from 1933–1939
> NSV since 1934

Avieny held several titles within the Nazi regime showing his good standing with the Party:

> Wehrwirtschaftsfuehrer (leader of the War Economy Program)
> Reichswirtschaftsrichter (judge of the National Economy Court)
> Gauwirtschaftsfuehrer (Regional Economic Adviser of Hessen-Nassau)
> Reichsgruppe Banken, Berlin Member Aufsichtsrat 1934–1945
> Reichsgruppe Banken, Bezirk Hessen, Regional Chief 1936–1938

Wilhelm Avieny's political activities took precedence over his business. Business associates have characterized him as being "a greedy, old Nazi who was a member for reasons of personal advantage—not to be trusted in any way." His Party honors and membership in affiliated organizations clearly show that he was considered reliable and deserving of reward for his services to the Party.

Avieny worked in the Race and Settlement Office of the SS.

As Gauwirtschaftsberater he was involved in the Aryanization of Jewish property. He was Ruestungsobmann of the Ruestungskommission XII at Wiesbaden and commander of the P.W. Cage in Oberursel for four weeks in 1939.

Financial and Industrial Connections. Avieny was associated with the following organizations:

Dresdner Bank, Berlin	Member of Aufsichtsrat 1943–1945
Deutsche Reichsbank, Berlin	Member of Aufsichtsrat 1943–1945
Nassau Landesbank, Wiesbaden	Member of Aufsichtsrat 1942–1945
Norddeutsche Affinerie, Hamburg (subsidiary of Metallgesellschaft) (Metal processing)	Vice-Chairman of Aufsichtsrat 1942–1945
"Sachtleben" A.G. fuer Bergbau und Chemische Industrie, Koeln (subsidiary of Metallgesellschaft) (Sulfur)	Chairman of Aufsichtsrat 1939–1944
Vereinigte Deutsche Metallwerke A.G., Frankfurt a/M (subsidiary of Metallgesellschaft) (Holding company)	Chairman of Aufsichtsrat 1941–1944
Unterwester Reederei A.G., Bremen (subsidiary of Metallgesellschaft) (Shipping)	Vice-Chairman of Aufsichtsrat 1939–1944
Deutsche Gold und Silber Scheideanstalt; vorm. Roessler, Frankfurt (I.G. Farben metal and chemical subsidiary)	Member of Aufsichtsrat 1940–1945
Neue Baugesellschaft Wayss & Freytag A.G., Frankfurt (Construction company)	Member of Aufsichtsrat 1940–1943
Vereinigte Aluminium Werke A.G., Berlin (Subsidiary of VIAG)	Member of Aufsichtsrat
Elektrizitaets A.G., vorm. W. Lahmeyer & Co. Frankfurt (Public utility)	Member of Aufsichtsrat 1940–1944
Telefonbau & Normalzeit G.m.b.H., Frankfurt (Public utility)	Member of Aufsichtsrat 1938–1940
Suedwestdeutsche Flugsbetriebs A.G. Rhein-Main, Frankfurt (Airline)	Vice-Chairman of Aufsichtsrat 1935–1944
Ernest Leitz G.m.b.H., Wetzlar (optics)	Member of Aufsichtsrat 1938–1945
Andreae-Noris Zahn A.G., Bremen (Pharmaceutical trade)	Member of Aufsichtsrat 1938–1945
Adam Opel A.G., Ruesselsheim (Cars, trucks)	Chairman Aufsichtsrat and member of Enemy Property Control Commission
Soehnlein Sekt Kellerei (Champagne)	Member of Aufsichtsrat 1938–1944

Wilhelm Avieny's principal business connection is Metallgesellschaft and affiliated companies. He obtained his position in this company when the Jewish management was ousted. Gauleiter Sprenger forced his appointment as a reward for Party service. In return he contributed substantially to the Gauleiter's Party treasury. He was not expected to run the business, as I.G. Farben also named Kissel, the son-in-law of one of its leading executives and a competent industrialist, as his assistant.

Similarly his banking connections derive from his Party status rather than any outstanding ability.

Rearmament and War Industry. As a leading member of a Farben concern, subject bears a large measure of guilt for the success of Nazi Germany's rearmament and the production of her factories for its war of aggression. His company, being a producer and fabricator of aluminum products, was closely associated with the expansion of the aircraft industry in Germany. Several of the companies of which Avieny was a member were extensive "employers" of slave labor.

Connections with the Dresdner Bank. Avieny's connection with the Dresdner Bank resulted from the fact that he was a member of the Martin Bormann NSDAP Banking Committee. He was made a member of the Personnel Committee where he could directly enforce the purge of politically and racially undesirable employees.

A secondary consideration was that he could furnish the Dresdner Bank a highly desirable interlocking directorate with an important I.G. Farben company.

Income. Between 1933 and 1943 Avieny earned the following sums:

1933	RM 18,000	1939	RM 60,000
1934	RM 23,000	1940	RM 60,000
1935	RM 26,000	1941	RM 72,000
1936	RM 30,000	1942	RM 78,000
1937	RM 30,000	1943	RM 90,000
1938	RM 30,000		

The increase in Wilhelm Avieny's income from RM 18,000 in 1933 to RM 90,000 in 1943 is remarkable in view of the unanimity with which his associates belittle his executive ability. It can only be a result of his Party standing and the fact that he was connected with so many concerns engaged in rearmament and war production. Avieny estimates his assets to be RM 300,000.

Sources. The information on Wilhelm Avieny was obtained from Military Government questionnaires, reports, and interrogations of prisoner and his associates.

Evaluation of Prisoner. Wilhelm Avieny is a very uncooperative witness and is overanxious to deny his Nazi past. He claims to know few details concerning most of the corporations with which he was associated.

CONCLUSION

Avieny held a high position in the financial, industrial, and economic life of Germany . . . and is deemed to have committed a crime against peace. . . . His detention is not subject to review.

FRIEDRICH FLICK

(MEMBER OF THE AUFSICHTSRAT OF THE DRESDNER BANK)

SUMMARY

Friedrich Flick is one of Germany's foremost steel and coal magnates, who acquired the bulk of his wealth during the Nazi regime. Friedrich Flick was a member of the Aufsichtsrat of the Dresdner Bank since 1922, occupying this position longer than any other member of the Aufsichtsrat.

Within the past fifteen years Flick built a personal empire comparable to those amassed over several generations by the Krupp and Roechling families. The Flick combine was the third largest producer of raw steel in Germany, exceeded only by Vereinigte Stahlwerke and Hermann-Goering-Werke.

Personal Data. Friedrich Flick was born on 10 July 1883 in Kreuztal near Siegen. He was educated at Siegen and Koeln where he graduated in 1907 from the Commercial Institute. He is a German citizen. His last residence was in Bad Toelz, Bavaria. He was arrested in June 1945, and is held at Pruengesheim Jail in Frankfurt.

Political Activities. Friedrich Flick belonged to the group of industrialists and financiers who to quote Walter Funk, "were in those days [1931–1932] convinced that the NSDAP would come to power in the not too distant future and that this had to be if communism and civil war were to be avoided."

Flick supported the Deutsche Nationale Partei, which joined hands with the Nazis in 1932 and whose influence among industrialists, higher civil servants, and the army paved the way for Hitler's advent to power. The first large-scale effort of German industrialists to directly finance the Nazi Party took place in February 1933 when, at a meeting in Goering's home, German heavy industry and banking created a RM 7,000,000 election fund for the crucial March 1933 election. Flick, by his own admission, contributed RM 100,000 to this fund which assisted Hitler in his final step toward controlling the German government.

Flick, like the other leading industrialists in the Ruhr and Rhineland, continued to support the Nazi Party, the SS, and contributed to various other collections which were placed at the disposal of prominent Nazi leaders. These political investments paid tremendous dividends in the expansion of the Flick empire under the Nazi regime. Flick had very early joined the Keppler Circle, the group of German industrialists and bankers associated with Himmler. Since 1936 he contributed RM 100,000 annually to the Special SS fund created by the Keppler Circle.

Flick maintained close personal relations with the higher Nazi leaders. He had personal interviews with Hitler and corresponded frequently with Goering. His friendship with Goering was greatly strengthened in 1938 when Flick transferred to Goering one-third ownership of the Harpener Bergbau and in return was able to acquire the Aryanized lignite mines of the Czech-Jewish Petschek family. Flick maintained his good standing with Goering by regular gifts primarily objects of art, of which the Reichsmarshall was so very fond.

Flick did not confine his financial support of the Nazi movement to the highest officials of the government and the Party in Berlin alone. He contributed approximately RM 50,000 and subsequently RM 100,000 to special projects of the Gauleiter of Saxony, Mutschmann. The first contribution was for the completion of a hunting lodge, the second for "social aims of the Gauleiter" (statement in Flick's Fragebogen to question 703). Together with Krupp and Thyssen, Flick financed the German Secret Service by running it as a private enterprise after the Versailles Treaty forbade its continuance and by hiring its director, Colonel Nicolai, as a private employee. Flick's formal membership in the NSDAP since 1937 is no indication of the extent of his activities and support of the National Socialists since the early 1930s.

Financial and Industrial Connections.

Dresdner Bank, Berlin	Member Aufsichtsrat 1922–1945
Harpener Bergbau A.G., Dortmund (Coal)	Chairman Aufsichtsrat 1934–1945
Essener Steinkohlenbergwerke A.G., Essen (Coal)	Chairman Aufsichtsrat 1936–1945
Anhaltische Kohlenbergwerke A.G., Halle-Berlin (Coal)	Chairman Aufsichtsrat 1938–1945
Hochofenwerk Luebeck A.G., Luebeck (Iron and copper products)	Chairman Aufsichtsrat 1937–1945
Mitteldeutsche Stahlwerke A.G., Riese a.d. Elbe (Iron products)	Chairman Aufsichtsrat 1926–1945
Saechsische Gusstahlwerke (Iron products), Doehlen	Chairman Aufsichtsrat 1938–1945
Maschinen u. Waggonfabrik Busch A.G., Bentzen (Electrical locomotives)	Vice-Chairman Aufsichtsrat 1934–1945
Linke Hoffmann Werke A.G., (Track vehicles), Breslau	Vice-Chairman Aufsichtsrat 1929–1945
Maximilianhuette Rosenberg (Iron)	Member Aufsichtsrat 1929–1945
Rheinische A.G. fuer Braunkohlen-bergbau u. Brikettfabrikation, Koeln (Coal, briquettes)	Member Aufsichtsrat 1928–1945

Schering A.G. Berlin (Chemicals)	Member Aufsichtsrat 1934–1945
Dynamit Nobel A.G. Troisdorf (Explosives)	Member Aufsichtsrat 1936–1945
Braunkohle-Benzin A.G. (Synthetic fuel) (Brabag)	Member Aufsichtsrat 1943–1945
Vereinigte Stahlwerke Duesseldorf (Coal)	Member Aufsichtsrat 1926–1945
Eisenindustrie zu Mendenschwerte, Schwerte (Iron)	Member Vorstand 1913–1915
Charlottenhuette Niederschelde (Iron)	Member Vorstand 1915–1934
Bismarckhuette Oberschlesien (Iron)	Member Aufsichtsrat 1920–1934
Kattowitz A.G., Kattowitz (Coal, steel)	Member Aufsichtsrat 1922–1934
Preussengrube Oberschlesien (Coal)	Member Aufsichtsrat 1922–1936
Oberschlesische Eisenindustrie (Steel), Gleiwitz	Member Aufsichtsrat 1922–1926
Linke Hoffman (Breslau)	Member Aufsichtsrat 1923–1927
Cosmopolite-Netherland (Metafine), Amsterdam (Finance Ind.)	Member Aufsichtsrat 1923–1936
Bochumer Verein, Bochum (Steel, coal)	Member Aufsichtsrat 1924–1927
Deutsch-Luxembourg (Coal, steel)	Member Aufsichtsrat 1924–1927
Gelsenkirchen Bergwerksgesell-schaft (Coal)	Member Aufsichtsrat 1924–1932
Vereinigte Oberschlesische Huettenwerke, Gleiwitz (Steel)	Member Aufsichtsrat 1924–1932
Alpine Montane Gesellschaft Wien (Steel)	Member Aufsichtsrat 1923–1933
Vereinigte Koenigs- & Laurahuette Oberschlesien (Coal and steel)	Member Aufsichtsrat 1927–1934
Veitscher Magnesitwerke, Wien (Magnesia)	Member Aufsichtsrat 1930–1935
Siegener Eisenindustrie (Iron)	Member Aufsichtsrat 1919–1937
Allgemeine Transportgesellschaft A.G., Leipzig (Construction of Transportanlagen)	Member Aufsichtsrat 1933–1934
Rombacher Huette G.m.b.H., Rombach (Iron)	Chairman Aufsichtsrat 1941–1945

Brandenburger Eisenwerke G.m.b.H., Brandenburg (Material for Panzer)	Chairman Aufsichtsrat 1938–1945
Montanverwertungs Gesellschaft G.m.b.H., Berlin (Government financing of war industries)	Member Aufsichtsrat 1941–1945
Spandauer Stahlindustrie G.m.b.H., Spandau	Chairman Aufsichtsrat 1942–1945
Berghuette Ost, G.m.b.H., Berlin (Official purchasing office)	Member Aufsichtsrat 1941–1945
Allianz Versicherungs A.G. Berlin (Insurance)	Member Aufsichtsrat 1936–1945
Deutsche Reichsbank Berlin	Beirat
AEG Allgemeine Electrizitaets Gesellschaft Berlin (Utility)	Member Aufsichtsrat 1926–1945
Sieben Planeten Dortmund (Coal and Iron Mines)	Member of the mining Vorstand 1934–1945
Siegener Maschinenbau A.G.	Vice-Chairman
Gewerkschaft Victoria Fortsetzung, Lullen Lippe	Member Vorstand

All of Flick's possessions and positions embrace the rearmament industry. In the early days of the Nazi regime Flick built his fortune on Germany's preparation for war. In 1935 his enterprises started secret production of ammunition shells. Flick's combine led Germany in the production of tanks. As early as 1933 he turned toward airplane production. Flick employed slave labor to a very great extent. About 40 percent of his employees were slave laborers, concentration camp laborers, and P.W.s, all working 60 to 70 hours weekly.

Aryanizations. Flick was quick to take advantage of the opportunities which the Nazi regime afforded. Several of his subsidiaries came to him by reason of the expropriation of Jewish property in Germany. Thus, for example, the Rawack, Gruenefeld A.G., Berlin, the Eisen & Stahlblech Handels G.m.b.H, Berlin, Hochofenwerke Luebeck A.G., Tureen & Jacobi G.m.b.H, Gassmann & Co., Berlin, were acquired within three to four years. Flick acquired several Jewish estates. In 1937 he became owner of an estate in Bad Toelz belonging to Ignatz Nacher the former owner of the Engelhardt Brewery, dispossessed by the Dresdner Bank in 1934. A few months after the occupation of Austria, in spring 1938, Flick acquired an estate in Steiermark belonging to the Gutmann family, formerly owners of the Witkowitz coal fields, expropriated by the Dresdner Bank for the Hermann-Goering-Werke. Flick was not satisfied with two estates and somewhat later he acquired the Baerfeld estate, valued at more than RM 4,000,000 belonging to Max Freidheim.

Relations with the Dresdner Bank. Flick was a member of the Aufsichtsrat of the bank since 1922. This fact is significant in view of the almost complete turnover of membership in the Aufsichtsrat after 1933. Although Flick divided the business of his numerous enterprises between the Deutsche and Dresdner banks, his personal relations were best with the Dresdner Bank according to the statement of Konrad Kaletsch, general manager of the Friedrich Flick enterprises. The Flick enterprises were greatly supported by the Dresdner Bank as statements of the financial standing of the Flick concern show.

Income. The total value of Flick's holdings approximate a billion Reichsmarks; seventy separate subsidiaries made up the network of his empire.

Evaluation of Prisoner. Flick is extremely evasive especially in matters pertaining to his political associations and benefits derived from the Nazi regime. The Flick combine is currently under investigation by a special team of the Economics Division, Office of Military Government. The findings of this investigation will undoubtedly disclose the full extent of Flick's power within German industry and his cooperation with the Nazi rulers.

CONCLUSION.

Flick held a high position in the financial, industrial and economic life of Germany . . . and is deemed to have committed a crime against peace. . . . His detention is not subject to review.

HEINRICH KOPPENBERG

(MEMBER OF THE AUFSICHTSRAT OF THE DRESDNER BANK)

SUMMARY

Heinrich Koppenberg is an engineer who has devoted his abilities to the development of the Nazi military machine. His most important work has been done in the aviation industry where he worked out many of the plans that mass-produced the planes by which the Luftwaffe wrought the defeat of so many European armies.

Personal Data. Heinrich Koppenberg, age sixty-six, is a German citizen and a member of the Aufsichtsrat of the Dresdner Bank. His main occupation is that of an executive for industrial plants.

Subject was arrested 5 December 1945, and is at present held at Pruengesheim Jail in Frankfurt.

Heinrich Koppenberg was trained as a mechanical engineer and has devoted his time to motors. This interest was later directed into the field of airplane development and manufacturing.

Political Activity. Heinrich Koppenberg was a member of the NSDAP since 1937. In addition the subject belonged to the following affiliated Nazi organizations:

NSFK—since 1937
DAF
KDF
NSV
NS Bund Deutscher Techniker—since 1933
NS Altherrenbund—since 1933
Deutsche Jaegerschaft—since 1933
Aero Club Berlin—since 1934
Rotary Club Dresden
Deutsches Museum Muenchen—since 1935
Wehrwirtschaftsfuehrer—since 1936

Koppenberg enjoyed an excellent standing with the Party. His being chosen as the person to acquire the large Argus Motorenwerke through Aryanization in 1939 is sufficient evidence of his Party reliability.

In addition he was given numerous tasks that would only be entrusted to a staunch believer in the expansionist aims of the NSDAP. Such a task was the leadership in organizing and increasing the production of the Norwegian aluminum industry in 1940.

A further proof is his presence at the periodic meetings of the fifty leading German aviation industrialists at which Goering transmitted his plans and orders for the secret construction of the military air arm.

His political standing is amply testified to by the fact that in 1937 Charles A. Lindbergh was allowed to enroll him in the "Institute of Aeronautical Sciences." He used this and connections with other American industries, such as Bendix, to bring to Germany American plane designers who gave Junkers the benefit of American experience and research.

Financial and Industrial Connections. Heinrich Koppenberg was associated with the following firms:

Dresdner Bank	Member Aufsichtsrat 1939
Nordische Aluminium A.G. (Aluminum)	Chairman Aufsichtsrat 1940–1942
Braunkohle-Benzin A.G. (Brabag) (Fuel)	Member Aufsichtsrat 1938–1940
Mitteldeutsche Stahlwerke A.G. (Iron, steel products)	Member Aufsichtsrat 1934–1945
Hanomag Hannover (Cars, tractors)	Member Aufsichtsrat 1934–1945
Auto Union A.G. (Cars)	Member Aufsichtsrat 1934–1945
Hansa Leichtmetallwerke A.G. (Light metal)	Member Advisory Board 1936–1945

Mineraloel-Bau G.m.b.H. (Construction firm)	Chairman Advisory Board 1931–1945
Duerener Metallwerke A.G. (Light metal)	Member Advisory Board 1936–1945
Linke Hoffmann A.G. (Railroad cars)	Member Aufsichtsrat 1936–1945
Waggon- und Maschinenfabrik, formerly Busch A.G. (Railroad cars)	Member Aufsichtsrat 1936–1945
Lettmetal Norsk	Member Aufsichtsrat 1941–1942
Eisenwerk-Gesellschaft Maximilianshuette Rosenberg (subsidiary of Mittelstahl)	Member Aufsichtsrat 1931–1933
Magdeburger Werkzeugmaschin-enfabrik (subsidiary of Junkers) Magdeburg	Member Advisory Board 1936–1941
ATG. Allgemeine Transport-anlagen G.m.b.H. (Mittelstahl) (Airplanes)	Member Aufsichtsrat 1933–1945
Pittler Werkzeugmaschinenfabrik A.G., Leipzig (Tools)	Member Aufsichtsrat 1938–1943
Deutsche Versuchsanstalt f. Luftfahrt, Berlin (Research Institute)	Chairman Vorstand 1935–1941
Maxhuette A.G. (subsidiary of Mittelstahl)	Member Vorstand 1930–1934
	Member Aufsichtsrat 1934–1940

All of Heinrich Koppenberg's industrial connections are with the armament industries and are mainly associated with aviation. He first became prominent through his success with ATG and transferred from there to the general manager-ship of the Junkers concern. His aluminum and oil interests arose because of the importance of their relationship to the development of the superior plane demand-ed by Goering, the research for which was intensively carried on by Junkers.

Connection with the Dresdner Bank. Koppenberg became a member of the Aufsichtsrat of the Dresdner Bank in 1939. He was chosen as a Nazi to replace a non-Party man and because of his extensive interests in aviation and related indus-tries. The Dresdner had at this time become heavily involved in the financing, "dar-ing financing" according to Hettlage, financial adviser to Speer Ministry, of numer-ous firms in this field. It had need of expert advice and assistance for the handling of these credits and therefore welcomed a man who was both a strong Nazi and had close ties with the Air Ministry, Goering, and the leaders of the industry.

Armament Activities. Since 1933 Heinrich Koppenberg was engaged in the build-ing of the Nazi war machine. He constructed the JU 88, the Stuka dive-bomber, which struck so effectively at the armies attempting to defend Europe. He was instrumental in obtaining for German use much technical information from American plane manufacturers prior to 1939.

He was one of the original developers of synthetic fuel on a large-scale production basis. He supervised the construction of plants for the government oil monopoly corporation and remained as an adviser during the war period. When the original plants proved the process feasible, Koppenberg became head of Oelbau, the engineering concern which created all of the synthetic oil plants in Germany.

Of even more potential war importance and certainly even more destructive than the Stukas at Rotterdam and Warsaw, was the V-1. Koppenberg, in his Argus Motorenwerke, was the man who perfected this lethal weapon so well known in London, Liège, Antwerp, and other cities. He first began to work on it in 1942 and had it ready for mass production early in 1944.

He participated in the Nazi exploitation of Europe as his plane factories expanded to various occupied countries in order to take advantage of materials, machinery, and labor in those countries.

All of the firms with which he was connected were employers of slave labor and prisoners of war. Subject has stated that in his own Argus firm one-third of the workers were slaves or prisoners of war working in the armament plant in violation of the Geneva prisoner of war convention.

Income. The following tabulation of subject's income does not clearly show the extent to which he profited from his Party affiliation and efforts on behalf of Nazi rearmament. In 1939 he acquired the very valuable Argus Motorenwerke, with several subsidiaries, from Dr. Strauss, a Jew, who was at the time in a concentration camp.

1930	approx. RM 150,000	1938	approx. RM 150,000
1931	approx. RM 150,000	1939	approx. RM 150,000
1932	approx. RM 150,000	1940	approx. RM 200,000*
1933	approx. RM 150,000	1941	approx. RM 200,000
1934	approx. RM 150,000	1942	approx. RM 200,000
1935	approx. RM 150,000	1943	approx. RM 200,000
1936	approx. RM 150,000	1944	approx. RM 200,000
1937	approx. RM 150,000		

Sources. This information has been obtained from interrogation of subject and business associates, and various reports which he has written covering different aspects of his industrial, financial, and political activities.

Evaluation of the Prisoner. Koppenberg's main interests were those of an executive engineer and researcher, so he is not too well informed on the financial affairs of many other firms and industries with which he was associated.

* After acquisition of Argus

He appears to be a thoroughgoing Nazi who underwent a change of heart after the decisive battles with Russia in 1942. He is on that account evasive when questioned on NSDAP matters and grasps at any slight evidence to show that he is not a true Nazi. This, of course, has slight weight against the record of his activity prior to 1942.

CONCLUSION

Koppenberg held a high position in the financial, industrial, and economic life of Germany . . . and is deemed to have committed a crime against peace. . . . His detention is not subject to review.

KARL LINDEMANN

(MEMBER OF THE AUFSICHTSRAT OF THE DRESDNER BANK)

SUMMARY

Karl Lindemann was an established German businessman prior to the Nazi rise to power. However, he associated himself with the Party and gave its aims his support to increase his personal power and gain.

Personal Data. Karl Lindemann, age sixty-five, a German citizen, resided at 76 Wachmann Strasse, Bremen. He is at present in the USFET G-2 detention camp.

Karl Lindemann has been connected with banking, export, and shipping interests since the beginning of his business career. Prior to 1926 he resided in China over a long period of time.

Political Activity.

> Subject joined the NSDAP in 1938
> Member of the Foerderungsgesellschaft fuer SS (Society for the
>   Furtherance of the SS) since 1938
> Member of the DAF since 1938
> Member of the NSV since 1936
> President of the Reichswirtschaftskammer since 1944
> President of the Foerderungsgesellschaft Institut fuer Weltwirtschaft

The mere listing of the NSDAP organizations to which subject belonged is not wholly indicative of the closeness of his alliance with the aims of the NSDAP. He was appointed to presidency of the Reichswirtschaftskammer by Walter Funk himself.

Lindemann was a member of the infamous Keppler Circle, that small group of businessmen who made immense yearly contributions to a fund used first by Hitler and later by Himmler and who, in return, obtained favors for themselves and their businesses.

Another important position held by Lindemann that attests his Party reliability and solidity was his membership in the delegation to negotiate German-Swiss trade agreements in 1943. These were concerned with increasing the imports of essential war materials.

Financial and Industrial Connections.

Dresdner Bank	Member Aufsichtsrat 1934–1945
Norddeutsche Kreditbank A.G., Bremen	Member Aufsichtsrat 1931–1945
Hamburg-Bremen Feuerversicherungs-Gesellschaft, Hamburg (Insurance)	Member Aufsichtsrat 1942–1945
Hamburg-Bremen Rueckversicherungs A.G., Hamburg (Insurance)	Member Aufsichtsrat 1939–1945
Deutsche Revisions & Treuhand A.G., Berlin (Trustee Syndicate)	Member Aufsichtsrat 1938–1945
Assecuranz Compagnie Mercur, Bremen (Insurance)	Member Aufsichtsrat 1937–1945
Norddeutscher Lloyd (Shipping)	Chairman Aufsichtsrat 1933–1945
Hamburg-Amerika Linie (Shipping)	Member Aufsichtsrat 1942–1945
Deutsche Amerika Linie	Member Aufsichtsrat 1942–1945
Atlas Werke A.G., Bremen (Iron, steel)	Chairman Aufsichtsrat 1933–1945
Wollgarnfabrik Tittel & Krueger und Sternwollspinnerei, A.G., Leipzig (Wool fabrics)	Vice-Chairman Aufsichtsrat 1931–1945
Norddeutsche Woll- und Kammgarnindustrie A.G., Delmenhorst (Wool fabrics)	Vice-Chairman Aufsichtsrat 1931–1945
Muehlheimer Bergwerksverein (Coal)	Member Aufsichtsrat 1936–1945
Norddeutsche Cementfabrik (Cement)	Member Aufsichtsrat 1939–1945
Vereinigte Industrie Unternehmungen A.G., VIAG (Holding company)	Member Aufsichtsrat 1937–1945
Deutsch-Amerikanische Petroleum A.G. (Fuel)	Member Aufsichtsrat 1934–1942
Unilever Concern	Member Aufsichtsrat 1940–1942
Deutsche Bank fuer Ostasien	Member Aufsichtsrat 1942–1945
Melchers & Co.	Partner 1913–1945
Reichsbank, Berlin	Beirat 1936–1945

Karl Lindemann's main industrial interests were in the shipping industry and he was an important figure in the two main German steamship lines, Hamburg-America and North German Lloyd. His main financial interests were in the importing firm of Melchers & Co. This concern had a branch in China and it was one of the most important German firms engaged in trade with the East.

The Deutsche Bank fuer Ostasien was founded for the financing of Japanese-German treaties for the purpose of exchange of German patents for war-essential raw materials from Japan.

Armament and War Industries. The importing firm in which subject was a partner was one of the important supports of the Nazi government in its program to obtain raw materials for the German industrial machine.

The Bank fuer Ostasien of which subject was a member of the Aufsichtsrat was founded by the Reich to facilitate trade between Germany and Japan so that both of these aggressor nations could supply deficiencies in their war material.

The VIAG was a huge holding company which directed the numerous armament industries founded by the Reich. Its range of activity extended into every field of armaments production and finance where supplementary state support was necessary if the desired output was to be obtained.

Lindemann was appointed to the Aufsichtsrat by Graf Schwerin Krosigk personally.

Connection with the Dresdner Bank. Lindemann was chosen as a member of the Aufsichtsrat of the Dresdner Bank in 1934. His association with Rasche in the Keppler Circle and the desire of the bank to obtain prominent Nazi businessmen for this body were the main reasons for his election.

Income.

1930	RM 50,000	1938	RM 125,000
1931	RM 50,000	1939	RM 250,000
1932	Loss of money through devaluation.	1940	RM 250,000
		1941	RM 300,000
1933	RM 15,000	1942	RM 300,000
1934	RM 15,000	1943	RM 300,000
1935	RM 80,000	1944	RM 300,000
1936	RM 100,000		
1937	RM 100,000		

As the above list shows, his political views paid him handsome dividends. Subject estimates his assets to be worth RM 800,000 at present, 500,000 of which is the value of his partnership in Melchers & Co.

Sources. The information herein has been obtained from Military Government questionnaires completed by subject and interrogations of him and business associates.

Evaluation of Prisoner. Lindemann appears to be well informed on financial subjects. He answered specific questions, but does not volunteer information. On political matters, he, like most Nazis, attempts to minimize any evidences of Party connections and activities.

Conclusion

Lindemann held a high position in the financial, industrial, and economic life of Germany, . . . and is deemed to have committed a crime against peace. . . . His detention is not subject to review.

WILHELM MAROTZKE

(Member of the Aufsichtsrat of the Dresdner Bank)

Summary

Wilhelm Marotzke offers a case history of an average German who obtained an extremely influential position in NSDAP political circles and derived great personal advantage from it. He was most active in rearmament and the expansion of the war industry of Nazi Germany.

Personal Data. Wilhelm Marotzke, age forty-nine, is a German citizen and lives at Duisburg. He is a member of the Aufsichtsrat of the Dresdner Bank, but his main occupation is that of an industrial executive.

Marotzke was first arrested by British field security and is now detained at the FIAT enclosure "Dustbin."

He studied law and economics as training for the civil service, which he entered in 1922. He advanced through the Reich and Prussian civil service until he finally obtained the rank of Ministerialdirigent.

Political. Wilhelm Marotzke became a member of the Nazi Party in 1937. He was a member of the following auxiliary organizations of the NSDAP:

> Allgemeine SS—Hauptsturmfuehrer—1937
> Obersturmbannfuehrer—1939
> Standartenfuehrer—1940
> NSV since 1933
> VDA
> Reichskolonialbund
> NS Reichskriegerbund
> NS Altherrenbund

Marotzke was identified with the NSDAP not only by his membership in the above organizations, but also through his membership in the select group comprising the Reich Ministry for Armament and War Production.

His Party ties were excellent. According to Hettlage, financial adviser to the Speer Ministry, he obtained the Kloeckner-Humboldt-Deutz concern as a reward for his Party services. This concern had been appropriated by the notorious Terboven and its owners put in a concentration camp. It then became Party spoils and was awarded to Marotzke.

Industrial and Financial Connections. The industrial and corporate connections of Marotzke fall into three groups:

The first group results from Marotzke's work in organizing the Nazi government's huge Hermann-Goering-Werke, an armament combine, under the Reichsminister for Armament and War Production. These concerns and his positions are as follows:

A.G. Reichswerke "Hermann Goering" (Holding company)	Aufsichtsrat 1940–1942
Reichswerke A.G. fuer Bergbau- und Huettenbetriebe "Hermann Goering" (Holding company)	Aufsichtsrat 1940–1942
Reichswerke A.G. fuer Waffen- und Maschinenbau "Hermann Goering"	Aufsichtsrat
Steinkohlengewerkschaft der Reichswerke "Hermann Goering" (Coal, coke)	Aufsichtsrat
Jugomontan	Aufsichtsrat 1937–1942
Alpine Montan A.G.	Aufsichtsrat 1938–1942
Sudetenlaendische Bergbau A.G. (Brux)	Aufsichtsrat 1939–1942
Sudetenlaendische Treibstoff A.G. (Processing lignite)	Aufsichtsrat 1939–1942
Ferdinand Nordbahn (Coal)	Aufsichtsrat 1939–1942
Mines de Bore	Aufsichtsrat
Ostdeutsche Steinkohlengewerk- schaft der Reichswerke (Coal)	Aufsichtsrat 1939–1942

The history of the Hermann-Goering-Werke shows that it was organized to increase the steel production capacity of Nazi Germany solely for the purposes of building the military machine necessary to fulfill the Nazi aims of conquest and exploitation. The first five of the corporations were the keystones of the Hermann-Goering-Werke empire. Some were small unprofitable German concerns, but in addition these also acted as holding companies for property acquired through Aryanization.

The last five companies were acquired during the conquest of Europe. Any means necessary to accomplish these acquisitions were utilized. The controlling stock interests would be confiscated through Aryanization, purchased from Belgian, Dutch, or French owners through clearing houses, and, in some instances, stolen by plain force.

The second category results from Marotzke's employment by the Kloeckner interests. This was a vertical steel-armament combine that had a tremendous and rapid growth during the period when the Nazi government was preparing for war. Similarly, as with the Hermann-Goering-Werke, many of the subsidiaries were acquired through Aryanization and expropriation. Marotzke's task was to repeat the success he had with the Hermann-Goering-Werke in making an efficient producer of an important war industry concern.

The concerns in this group are as follows:

Kloeckner Werke A.G. (Coal, steel and steel mag)	General director 1942–1945
Kloeckner Reederei und Kohlenhandels G.mb.H. (Coal)	Member Geschaeftsfuehrung 1942–1945
Kloeckner & Co. (Steel sales company)	Chairman Beirat and member of Aufsichtsrat 1942–1945
NV Montan, Amsterdam (Steel products sales company)	Aufsichtsrat 1943–1945
Kloeckner-Humboldt-Deutz A.G. (Motors—trucks, tractors)	Chairman Aufsichtsrat 1944–1945
Rheinische Chamotta und Dinaswerke (Stone averries)	Aufsichtsrat 1944–1945
Gewerkschaft "Victor" Rauxel (Wood gas, ammoniacal products)	Aufsichtsrat 1942–1944
Kloeckner-Deutz-Motoren A.G. (Plane motors)	Chairman Aufsichtsrat 1944–1945
Simmering-Graz-Pauker A.G. (Motors and machinery)	Chairman Aufsichtsrat 1943–1945

The third category consists solely of the Czechoslovakian shoe concern "Bata," which Marotzke in his capacity as chairman of the Aufsichtsrat from 1942 to 1945 reorganized to enable it to operate within an area that had changed from Czech to German control.

Connections with the Dresdner Bank. Wilhelm Marotzke's association with the Dresdner Bank dated from 1943. He was chosen as a Nazi member to replace a non-Party man and also to represent Kloeckner-Humboldt-Deutz-Humboldt with one of its valuable financial connections.

Rearmament Activity. Subject has since 1934, when he first became a member of the Reich Ministry of Economics, been a figure of growing importance in the Nazi armament industries. As one of the organizers of the Hermann-Goering-Werke, he worked with Speer, Goering, Koerner, Dr. Voss, Pleiger, Meiberg, Dr. Delius, Kehrl, and the others connected with the Four Year Plan in exploiting the Nazi conquest for the purpose of expansion of war industries. His entire career since 1933 has been spent in work designed to increase the production of armaments.

Income. The increase in annual income from RM 8,000 to RM 198,000 in the following list showing yearly income for the years 1933 to 1944, indicates that Wilhelm Marotzke's connections with the Party and war industries were extremely profitable.

1933	RM 8,000	1939	RM 16,000
1934	RM 9,000	1940	RM 17,000
1935	RM 10,000	1941	RM 17,000
1936	RM 11,000	1942	RM 132,000
1937	RM 13,000	1943	RM 196,000
1938	RM 14,000	1944	RM 198,000.

The subject has assets estimated to be worth RM 240,000.

Sources. Reports of interrogations, and writings of Wilhelm Marotzke which are available, are as follows:

> *Organization of Hermann-Goering-Werke*
> *Reorganization of Bata*
>
> *Fragebogen*
> *Economic history*
> *Family Corporation Connections*

Evaluation of Prisoner. Subject appears to be a straightforward and intelligent witness with considerable knowledge of financial matters. He will become evasive when questioned on the subject of NSDAP and its political ideology and of his part in implementing it.

Conclusion

Marotzke held a high position in the financial, industrial, and economic life of Germany, . . . and is deemed to have committed a crime against peace. . . . His detention is not subject to review.

WALTER SCHIEBER

(Member of the Aufsichtsrat of the Dresdner Bank)

Summary

Walter Schieber is the prototype of an ardent and convinced Nazi. He was an early member of the Party and has used his abilities in furtherance of its aims. He profited from his political associations, but he was more interested in achieving results for German rearmament than in personal gain.

Personal Data. Walter Schieber, age forty-nine, is a German citizen and resided at Bopfingen, Wuerttemberg. He was a member of the Aufsichtsrat of the Dresdner Bank.

Subject was arrested on 13 May 1945 and detained in prison enclosures at Garmisch-Partenkirchen and Augsburg. He is now at the FIAT enclosure "Dustbin."

Walter Schieber was trained as a chemist at the universities of Stuttgart and Jena. He began his career as a chemist for I.G. Farben, but after the Nazis came to power he rapidly advanced to a position of importance as head of the Nazi-sponsored Zellwolle und Kunsteide Ring, G.m.b.H. Berlin.

Political Activity. Walter Schieber joined the NSDAP in 1931. Subject was a member of the following auxiliary organizations of the NSDAP:

> SS Sturmfuehrer 1934–1939
>   Standartenfueher 1941
>   Brigadefuehrer 1943
> DAF since 1935
> NSV
> NS Bund Deutscher Techniker since 1938, Leiter Fachgruppe Chemie
>   1940–1945
> Deutsche Jaegerschaft since 1936

Walter Schieber received the following NSDAP special awards:

> Goldenes Parteiabzeichen 1939
> SS-Fuehrer ehrenhalber 1939–1943

Subject held the following positions which demanded absolute Party loyalty:

Todt Ministry 1939–1941	to organize of cellulose section in chemical industry.
Speer Ministry 1942–1944	to consolidate various war industries . . . member of special branch to produce wood gas generators
Gauwirtschaftsberater Thueringen	1937
Gasschutz Referent SS	1934

Walter Schieber is closely identified with the NSDAP as is shown by the number and variety of its auxiliary organizations of which he is a member, by the importance of his positions in these Nazi organizations, and by his rapid advancement in an NSDAP government-controlled combine.

Financial and Industrial Connections.

Dresdner Bank	Member Aufsichtsrat 1943–1945
Zellgarn AG, Litzmannstadt (Raw cellulose)	Member Vorstand 1941–1944

Thueringischen Zellwolle A.G. (Raw cellulose and coal yarn)	Member Vorstand 1935–1943 Member Aufsichtsrat 1944
Spinnfasen G.m.b.H., Kassel-Bettenhausen (Raw casein)	Member Vorstand 1938–1941 Member Aufsichtsrat 1942–1944
Schwaebische Zellstoff A.G. (Raw cellulose)	Rhin-Member Vorstand 1941–1943 Member Aufsichtsrat 1944
Lenzinger Zellwolle und Papierfabrik A.G. (Cellulose and paper)	Member Vorstand 1939–1944
Westfaelische Zellstoff A.G., Arnsberg	Member Vorstand 1941–1944
Adam Opel A.G.	Enemy property control custodian comm.

All of the above firms were established to assist in the accomplishment of the plans of the RWM for a self-sustaining economy, an essential of the war effort of Nazi Germany. Subject's Party connections were as helpful as his technical qualifications in gaining his position in these war-born concerns.

Walter Schieber was president of the Zellwolle und Kunstseide Ring in Berlin, a cellulose and synthetic fabric combine sponsored by the Reich Ministry for Armament and War Production. He was a principal member of the Aufsichtsrat or Vorstand of the principal concerns that comprised this war-important combine and was in control of the research activities and the technical operations of the processing units.

Connections with Dresdner Bank. Walter Schieber became a member of the Dresdner Bank Aufsichtsrat because of his influential NSDAP position and his important industrial connections. He was a member of Martin Bormann's NSDAP Banking Committee and because of this was elected to the Dresdner board replacing a non-Party member.

Rearmament Activities. Walter Schieber played an outstanding role in Nazi rearmament as a member of the Speer and Todt ministries. His work in building synthetic fabric and cellulose plants for I.G. Farben prior even to 1935 was a direct contribution to the Nazi war preparations. During the war years 1939–1942 his construction of cellulose plants in France, Belgium, Italy, Poland, and Russia materially increased Nazi Germany's production of this important munition item.

Income. The increase from RM 9,000 in 1933 to RM 55,000 in 1943, in the following listing of the subject's income during those years shows his participation in the profits of the Nazi rearmament and war industries.

1933	RM 9,000		1939	RM 40,000
1934	RM 12,000		1940	RM 45,000

1935	RM 15,000	1941	RM 45,000
1936	RM 16,000	1942	RM 55,000
1937	RM 18,000	1943	RM 55,000
1938	RM 25,000	1944	RM 45,000

Sources. Interrogation of subject and associates, writings of subject, and Military Government questionnaires.

Evaluation of Prisoner. Subject is well informed on technical subjects but not so certain concerning the financial aspects of the companies with which he is associated. He considers himself as a technician and is not communicative on political subjects.

CONCLUSION

Schieber held a high position in the financial, industrial, and economic life of Germany, . . . and is deemed to have committed a crime against peace. . . . His detention is not subject to review.

HANS ULLRICH

(MEMBER OF THE AUFSICHTSRAT OF THE DRESDNER BANK)

SUMMARY

Hans Ullrich was an able lawyer with a reputation that extended beyond the borders of Germany. He represented one of the leading German insurance firms. Both his reputation and ability were placed at the service of the Party and he became a member of the fifth column, cloaking the vices of Nazism with his own good name.

Personal Data. Hans Ullrich, age fifty-seven, is a German citizen and lives in Gotha at Schoene Allee 9. He was a member of the Aufsichtsrat of the Dresdner Bank.

Ullrich held degrees in law and political economy from the universities of Jena and Munich. Subject entered the Gothaer Lebensversicherungsbank A.G. in 1920 and quickly rose to the position of general manager.

Subject was arrested 8 April 1945 as a SHAEF personality and is at present confined at the FIAT interrogation and detention center, "Dustbin."

Political Activities. Hans Ullrich joined the NSDAP in 1934. Subject was a member of the following Nazi-affiliated or -dominated organizations.

SS	1935	Held rank of Sturmbannfuhrer
DAF	1934	
KDF	1934	
NSV	1934	

NSKOV	1934	
Reichs Kolonialbund		
NS Rechtswahrerbund	1934	
German Verein fuer		Deputy Chairman
Wirtschaftsversicherung		
Wirtschaftskammer	1935	Member Directorate
Thuringia		
Reichs Verein fuer	1924	
Privatversicherung		
Academie fuer Deutsches	1941	Chairman Committee for
Recht		Insurance Law

In addition to the large number of subsidiary Party organizations to which Hans Ullrich belonged, he has further identified himself with the Nazi Party and its aims. He voted for the NSDAP in 1933 and in 1937 incorporated Nazi "suggestions" into a proposed European automobile insurance code.

Financial and Industrial Connections.

Dresdner Bank	Member Aufsichtsrat 1930–1945
Thuringia Landesausschuss	Member 1930–1945
Mitteldeutsche Zentral Genossenschaftsbank	Member Aufsichtsrat 1927–1935
Deutsche Reichsbank	Member Beirat 1939–1945
Deutsche Hypothekenbank Weimar	Member Aufsichtsrat 1931–1945
Gothaer Allgemeine Versicherungs A.G.	Member Aufsichtsrat 1924–1945
Gothaer Lebensversicherungsbank 1920-1945	General Manager 1931–1945
Karolawerke A.G. (Chemicals)	Member Aufsichtsrat 1923–1945
Ullrich Sauer A.G. (Medical supply)	Member Aufsichtsrat 1924-1933
Gebrueder Heiler Metallwerke G.m.b.H.	Deputy Director 1922-1945

As a member of the Aufsichtsrat of one of Germany's largest casualty insurance companies, subject is guilty of the Nazi fraud practiced against the Jews after the 1938 pogrom. In a secret meeting with Goering the insurance companies agreed to pay the Jewish claims to save Germany's reputation but were to be repaid from the proceeds of a confiscatory tax levied against the victims.

Subject was a delegate to several international conventions and a member of the Comité Permanent des Congrès Internationaux d'Actuaires (insurance). Ullrich also made numerous contributions to various technical journals on insurance, both German and foreign.

Connection with the Dresdner Bank. Ullrich was originally elected to the Dresdner Aufsichtsrat to complete an interlocking directorate between the bank and his insurance company. As an influential personage in the political life of Thuringia he aided the bank in maintaining its influence in this region of Germany.

Income. The subject had an annual income of RM 63,000, which remained unchanged through the years 1931–1945. His assets are estimated at RM 550,000. Although Ullrich's income did not materially increase during the years 1933 to 1945 he profited from the Nazi regime in that his companies obtained insurance concessions in several conquered countries and thus laid the basis for profitable business when war risks and other abnormalities would not so greatly affect insurance companies.

Evaluation of Prisoner. Hans Ullrich makes an excellent impression and was obviously a good ambassador for Nazi Germany. He is well informed in his chosen fields of finance, law, and insurance. He makes the usual protestations of being unable to withstand political pressure in his activities and of being forced to acquiesce to Nazism.

CONCLUSION

Ullrich held a high position in the financial, industrial, and economic life of Germany . . . and is deemed to have committed a crime against peace. . . . His detention is not subject to review.

HANS WALZ

(MEMBER OF THE AUFSICHTSRAT OF THE DRESDNER BANK)

SUMMARY

Hans Walz is a successful German industrialist whose sound management of his company was of immense benefit to Germany in her war of aggression. He is a Nazi, of the Keppler Circle, and must accordingly have subscribed to the aims of this notorious group.

Personal Data. Hans Walz is sixty-four years old, a German citizen, and was a member of the Aufsichtsrat of the Dresdner Bank and of the Reichskredit-Gesellschaft. His present home is in Stuttgart, Hahnemann Strasse 1.

Subject was arrested on 1 November 1945 in Stuttgart and is now at the seventh Army Detention Camp 99, Butzbach.

Walz attended school in Stuttgart and upon completion obtained a leading position with Robert Bosch G.m.b.H., which position he held until 1942.

Political Activity. Hans Walz has been a member of the NSDAP since 1933. Subject was a member of the following affiliated organizations:

> SS—since 1934, highest rank held was that of Hauptsturmfuehrer
> NSKK—since 1933
> DAF—since 1935
> NSV—since 1935
> NSFK—since 1934
> Bund Deutscher Techniker—for about two years
> Deutsches Auslandsinstitut—until 1945
> Deutsches Rotes Kreuz—until 1945
> Reichsluftschutzbund—until 1945

Political

Chamber of Commerce and Industry, Stuttgart	Vice-President 1934–1937
Wuerttemberg Business and Industry Conference of Stuttgart	Vice-President
Wuerttemberg Economic Association of the German Labor Front	District Agent 1928–1933
Wuerttemberg Economic Company, Stuttgart	Deputy Chairman 1933–1937

Subject was also a member of the following associations:

Company for Promotion of World Economy, Kiel	Member Vorstand 1932 or 1933
Union for Improvement of the Peoples Education, Stuttgart	Member Vorstand 1917–1933
Academy for German Law, Berlin	Member 1931–1933

Hans Walz was solidly entrenched in the ranks of the Nazis. He held membership in two of its most rabid, nationalistic, and imperialistic organizations, the SS and the notorious Keppler Circle, to which he made a yearly contribution of several thousand Reichsmarks.

He was also a member of several regional labor and economic bodies. The membership in these organizations was carefully screened by Martin Bormann's Gauleiters and only politically trustworthy men could hope for appointment.

Financial and Industrial Connections.

Dresdner Bank	Member Aufsichtsrat 1941–1945
Robert Bosch G.m.b.H. (Electrical accessories for airplane automotors and diesel motors)	Managing Technical Director 1921–1945

Reichskredit-Gesellschaft A.G. Berlin	Member Aufsichtsrat 1941–1945
Wuerttembergische Bank, Stuttgart	Member Aufsichtsrat 1931–1936, 1938–1942
Handels und Gewerbe Bank Heilbronn A.G., Heilbronn	Member Aufsichtsrat 1941–1945
Victoria Feuerversicherungs A.G. Berlin	Member Aufsichtsrat 1939–1945
Victoria zu Berlin, Allgemeine Versicherungs A.G.	Member Aufsichtsrat 1939–1945
Victoria Rueckversicherungs A.G.	Member Aufsichtsrat 1939–1945
Treptow Teppichwerke A.G., Berlin (Rugs)	Chairman Aufsichtsrat 1939–1945
Otto Fischer A.G., Kirchheim/ Teck	Vice-Chairman Aufsichtsrat 1940–1945 Member 1925–1940
Kolb & Schuele A.G., Kirchheim/ Teck (Sheets)	Member Aufsichtsrat 1931–1945
Vermoegensverwaltung Bosch G.m.b.H. Stuttgart	Member Vorstand 1924–1945

Hans Walz's industrial connections are almost wholly centered in the Robert Bosch concern. This concern was one of the largest manufacturers of automotive and airplane motor parts and ignition systems in Europe. He was the general manager for this huge war-important industry.

Relation to the Dresdner Bank. Walz as a representative for Bosch became a member of the Aufsichtsrat of the Dresdner Bank in 1940 at the request of the bank.

Rearmament and War Industry. Hans Walz was an important figure in the rearmament of Nazi Germany. The Bosch concern was the holder of a number of basic patents, without which the motors for the Panzers, Stukas, and the machines for a blitzkrieg could never have been built.

This company was a huge concern and employed slave labor extensively. As a member of two special Labor Front associations, Walz was familiar with the conscripting of these unfortunates in the countries of occupied Europe.

Income.

1933	RM 74,000	1939	RM 159,000
1934	RM 150,000	1940	RM 126,000
1935	RM 125,000	1941	RM 143,000
1936	RM 231,000	1942	RM 137,000
1937	RM 165,000	1943	RM 188,000
1938	RM 158,000	1944	RM 173,000

A glance at the above listing makes obvious the benefit to Walz of his cooperation with Nazi Germany in preparing for its war of aggression.

Evaluation of the Prisoner. Walz has tried throughout the investigation to lean heavily on the association of Bosch with American industry. This, however, was apparently gained through cartel agreements. He is no banking authority but has considerable knowledge of his special field of industry. Because of his desire to disavow his Nazi connections he is an unreliable witness on any matter which he considers as implicating him in its activities.

CONCLUSION

Walz held a high position in the financial, industrial, and economic life of Germany . . . and is deemed to have committed a crime against peace. . . . His detention is not subject to review.

HANS PILDER

(MEMBER OF THE VORSTAND OF THE DRESDNER BANK)

SUMMARY

Hans Pilder is a specialist in foreign trade and banking. His abilities in these fields were at the service of the Dresdner Bank, which used them in accomplishing numerous of its complicated transactions to integrate the economy of Europe with that of Nazi Germany.

Personal Data. Hans Pilder, age sixty-one, resided at Berlin-Dahlem, Kronprinzenallee 34 and is a German citizen. He was a member of the Vorstand of the Dresdner Bank.

Pilder was arrested on 6 September 1945, being a SHAEF personality and is detained in a Third Army civilian internment camp.

Subject studied economics at the University of Berlin and received his Ph.D. in 1909 and then entered the Dresdner Bank. He served in its Egyptian branch until 1914. During World War I, he was purchasing agent for the army in Austria and Romania. After the armistice, he was appointed manager of the newly established branch of the Dresdner Bank in Bucharest and later was placed in charge of the Foreign Division of the bank.

Political Activity. Hans Pilder was not a member of the NSDAP, but made regular contributions to several affiliated organizations of the Party.

Financial and Industrial Connections.

Dresdner Bank	Member Vorstand 1931–1945
Deutsch-Suedamerikanische Bank	Beirat
Filmkredit Bank Berlin	Member Aufsichtsrat 1932–1938
Jugoslawischer Bankverein Belgrad	Member Aufsichtsrat 1940–1943
Mercurbank Wien/Laenderbank Wien	Member Aufsichtsrat 1936–1943
Ungarische Allgemeine Kreditbank Budapest	Member Aufsichtsrat 1941–1944
Gesellschaft fuer Industriebeteiligungen m.b.H.	Chairman Aufsichtsrat 1936–1945
Treuhand Vereinigung A.G. (Trustee)	Chairman Aufsichtsrat 1931–1945
Hamburgische Baukasse A.G. (Bank)	Chairman Aufsichtsrat 1926–1945
Societatea Bancara Romana, Bucharest	Member Aufsichtsrat 1935–1945
Banque d'Athenes, Athens	Member Aufsichtsrat 1942–1945
Industriefinanzierungs A.G. Ost (Financing corporation)	Member Aufsichtsrat 1936–1945
Nordstern Lebensversicherung A.G.	Member Aufsichtsrat 1930–1945
Deutsche Maizenwerke A.G. (Starches)	Member Aufsichtsrat 1930–1945
Vereinigte Jute-Spinnereien und Webereien, Hamburg (Burlap)	Member Aufsichtsrat 1921–1931
Buttergrosshandlung Eammonie A.G. Hamburg (Butter wholesale)	Member Aufsichtsrat 1931–1935
Baugesellschaft Norddeutschland G.m.b.H. Hamburg (Construction)	Member Aufsichtsrat 1921–1935
Fertie Kaufmann A.G., Berlin	Member Aufsichtsrat 1932–1936
Dyckerhoff & Wiedmann Baugesellschaft (Construction)	Member Aufsichtsrat 1932–1936
UFA Filmgesellschaft (Moving pictures)	Member Aufsichtsrat 1932–1943
Berliner Dampfmuehle, Berlin (Power mills)	Member Aufsichtsrat 1932–1937
Maschinenfabrik R. Wolff Bercken (Machinery)	Member Aufsichtsrat 1934–1937
Baumwollspinnerei, Ettlingen (Wool)	Member Aufsichtsrat 1931–1935

Mechanic Weberei, Sorau (Power loom weaving)	Member Aufsichtsrat 1931–1936
Gemeinnuetzige Wohnungsbau Gesellschaft, Hamburg (Construction)	Member Aufsichtsrat 1926–1932
Magdeburger Werkzeugmaschin-enfabrik (Tools)	Member Aufsichtsrat 1932–1936
Magnesitindustrie A.G., Pressburg (Heat-resisting stones)	Chairman Aufsichtsrat 1938–1945
Steirische Magnesit Industrie A.G. (Heat-resisting stones)	Chairman Aufsichtsrat 1941–1945
Veitscher Magnesitwerke A.G. (Heat-resisting stones)	Chairman Aufsichtsrat 1938–1945
Natronzellstoff & Papierfabriken A.G. (Paper)	Chairman Aufsichtsrat 1931–1945
Pittler, Werkzeugmaschinenfabrik A.G. (Tool machinery)	Vice-Chairman Aufsichtsrat 1932–1945
Deutsche Wollwarenmanufaktur A.G. (Wool yarn)	Vice-Chairman Aufsichtsrat 1935–1945
Norddeutsche Eiswerke A.G., Berlin (Ice, refrigeration plants)	Chairman Aufsichtsrat 1932–1945
Magnesit A.G., Suedost, Wien (Magnesia)	Vice-Chairman Aufsichtsrat 1941–1944
Kaufhaus A.G. (Kepa), Berlin (Department store supply)	Vice-Chairman Aufsichtsrat 1932–1945
Deutscher Eisenhandel A.G., Berlin (Iron, steel)	Member Aufsichtsrat 1933–1945
Charlottenburger Wasser & Industriewerke, A.G. (Water supply)	Member Aufsichtsrat 1932–1945
Julius Berger Tiefbau A.G. (Construction)	Member Aufsichtsrat 1935–1945
Norddeutsche Portland-Cement Fabrik (Cement)	Member Aufsichtsrat 1931–1945
Europaeische Tanklager and Transport A.G. (Fuel)	Member Aufsichtsrat 1941–1945

Subject's industrial connections result mainly from his being the interlocking director for the Dresdner Bank on a number of lesser corporations and those where his knowledge of foreign trade and banking would be helpful.

Connection with Dresdner Bank. Hans Pilder is an expert in foreign trade and banking and he was the principal executive for handling such matters for the bank. He was disliked on political grounds by the rabid Nazis like Rasche and therefore did not play an outstanding role. They, however, used his knowledge and abilities on many occasions. For example, he handled the negotiations for acquisitions of a controlling interest in the Laenderbank, Wien from the French Banque des Pays.

Rearmament and War Industries. Subject's specialty of foreign trade was used extensively during the frantic prewar efforts to obtain scarce raw materials. He was an adviser to the Deutsch-Suedmerikanische Bank, which financed a large portion of Germany's exports from South America.

Income.

1930	RM 150,000	1938	RM 240,000
1931	RM 150,000	1939	RM 240,000
1932	RM 150,000	1940	RM 240,000
1933	RM 150,000	1941	RM 240,000
1934	RM 150,000	1942	RM 240,000
1935	RM 170,000	1943	RM 240,000
1936	RM 240,000	1944	RM 240,000
1937	RM 240,000		

Associated as he was with the Dresdner Bank, he enjoyed a considerable increase in income under the Nazi regime.

Sources. Interrogation of subject and associates, reports which he prepared, and Military Government questionnaires.

Evaluation of the Prisoner. Hans Pilder is a cautious witness and all information has to be obtained by specific questions. He knows very little of purely political financial transactions and his loyalty to the bank makes him reluctant to divulge any details that he may know.

CONCLUSION

Pilder held a high position in the financial, industrial and economic life of Germany . . . and is deemed to have committed a crime against peace. . . . His detention is not subject to review.

KARL RASCHE

(MEMBER OF THE VORSTAND OF THE DRESDNER BANK)

SUMMARY

Dr. Karl Rasche, member of the Vorstand of the Dresdner Bank, is one of the leaders of the group who brought Nazi patterns of behavior into banking activity. He served as one of the key liaison men between the Dresdner Bank and the SS, the Nazi Party, and government so that the bank might function as an integral part of the Nazi war machine. It was Karl Rasche who, on behalf of the Dresdner Bank, was most active in carrying out the policies of the Party and the government for the plotting of aggressive war, for the economic penetration of Germany's neighbors, and for subsequent spoliation of the conquered areas. It was Rasche who was the Dresdner Bank's most ardent exponent of Aryanization policies.

The records of Rasche's activities are blackened by the use of duress, fraud, and robbery, and the utilization of the SS, Gestapo, and all the other ruthless Nazi agencies in order to accomplish his aims.

Personal Data. Karl Rasche was born in Westphalia on 25 August 1892. He attended secondary school at Iserlohn in Westphalia and studied law, political economy, and history at the universities of Muenster, Munich, Berlin, Leipzig, and Bonn. After finishing his studies he became an attorney in Duesseldorf and was active in several Westphalian courts. He later became a member of the board of directors of various West German companies.

In 1933 he became a member of the Management Committee of the Westphalian Bank, Bochum. Rasche became a deputy member of the Vorstand of the Dresdner Bank in 1934 and a full member in 1935. He was chosen because he already held the confidence of the Party leaders and could bring the bank into a closer working association with them.

His last permanent residence was in Schwalheim, Kreis Friedberg. Rasche was arrested on 21 November 1945 and is at present confined in Pruengesheim Jail, Frankfurt.

Political Activity. Rasche became a member of the NSDAP in 1940; Allgemeine SS since 1938, Obersturmbannfuehrer; DAF since 1933; NS Rechtswahrerbund since 1933; NS Reichsbund fuer Leibesuebungen since 1933.

Rasche was a thorough Nazi and had close personal and business ties with the leaders of the Party. Evidence of his close relationship to members of the Nazi hierarchy is readily revealed by glancing through his personal files, which contain interchanges of greetings and personal correspondence with such men as Generalfeldmarschall Kesselring, President of the RWM Hans Kehrl, SS Obergruppenfuehrer und General der Polizei Ernst Kaltenbrunner, Baldur von Schirach, Ministerialdirigent Dr. Landwehr, and so on. Rasche joined the notorious Keppler Circle, the group of industrialists and bankers around Himmler, at the Party Day in Nuremberg in 1936. This was the group that raised a million Reichsmarks a year for Himmler to use as he wished.

Rasche is unanimously characterized by his associates at the Dresdner Bank as a thorough Nazi for whom they do not even attempt the usual formal excuses.

Financial and Industrial Connections.

Laenderbank Wien, A.G.   Member Aufsichtsrat 1938–1945
(Dresdner affiliate)

Boehmische Escompte Bank, Prague (Dresdner affiliate)	Chairman Aufsichtsrat 1939–1944
Handels Kreditbank A.G., Riga (Dresdner affiliate)	Chairman Aufsichtsrat 1941–1945
Westdeutsche Bodenkredit A.G. (Building and loan bank)	Chairman Aufsichtsrat 1943–1945
Allgemeine Versicherungs A.G., Wien (Insurance)	Vice-Chairman Aufsichtsrat 1944
Gerling Konzern Lebensversicherung A.G. (Life insurance)	Member Aufsichtsrat 1938–1944
Engelhardt Brauerei A.G., Berlin (Beer)	Chairman Aufsichtsrat
Dyckerhoff Cement A.G., Amoeneburg (Cement)	Vice-Chairman Aufsichtsrat 1936–1945
Rhein-Kunstseide A.G., Krefeld (Rayon, staple fiber)	Vice-Chairman Aufsichtsrat 1939–1945
Eisen- und Huettenwerke A.G. Koeln-Beckum (Steel)	Member Aufsichtsrat 1938–1945
Muehlheimer Bergwerke-Verein (Coal)	Member Aufsichtsrat 1936–1945
Essener Steinkohlen A.G., Essen (Coal)	Member Aufsichtsrat 1938–1945
Accumulatoren-Fabrik A.G., Hagen (Accumulators)	Member Aufsichtsrat 1939–1945
Wintershall A.G., Kassel (Potash oil)	Member Aufsichtsrat 1937–1945
Metallgesellschaft A.G., Frankfurt (Metals)	Member Aufsichtsrat 1937–1945
Felten und Guillaume A.G., Koeln (Cables and electrical products)	Member Aufsichtsrat 1938–1945
Braunkohle-Benzin A.G., Berlin (Oil and oil products)	Member Aufsichtsrat 1940–1944
Kontinentale Oel A.G., Berlin (Oil products)	Member Aufsichtsrat 1940–1945
Poldi Huette A.G., Prague (Steel)	Chairman Aufsichtsrat 1939–1944
Perlmooser Cement A.G., Wien (Cement)	Chairman Aufsichtsrat 1938–1945
Tatrawerke A.G., Prague (Motorcars, railway carriages)	Chairman Aufsichtsrat 1943–1945
Bruenner Waffenfabrik A.G., Prague (Cranes, tools)	Member Aufsichtsrat 1939–1945
Skoda Werke A.G., Hannover (Arms, steam engines)	Member Aufsichtsrat 1940–1945
Doehrener Werke A.G., Hannover (Combing and washing wool)	Member Aufsichtsrat 1939–1944
Rheinmetall A.G., Duesseldorf (Locomotives, cannon sets)	Member Aufsichtsrat 1940–1945

The large number of companies in which Karl Rasche was a member of the Aufsichtsrat does not show the entire extent of his connections with German industry. An examination of his correspondence reveals that his ties with the Nazi leaders allowed him through them and through the Dresdner Bank to exert power over institutions with which he had no formal association.

The large number of corporations located in occupied territory is an accurate reflection of his activity in the exploitation of these areas.

Rasche obtained all his directorships after he joined the Dresdner Bank. In addition to these corporations in which the government had an interest, he was also in one or more owned by Flick, Stinnes, Farben, Otto Wolff, and others prominent in Nazi Germany's rearmament program.

Income.

1931	RM	60,000	1938	RM 160,000
1932	RM	70,000	1939	RM 200,000
1933	RM	50,000	1940	RM 240,000
1934	RM	70,000	1941	RM 300,000
1935	RM	50,000	1942	RM 330,000
1936	RM	70,000	1943	RM 320,000
1937	RM	120,000	1944	unknown

This listing of Karl Rasche's income, showing a 500 percent increase from RM 60,000 in 1931 to RM 320,000 RM in 1943, does not fully indicate the extent to which he profited from his nefarious activities in exploiting Europe.

Rearmament and War Industries. Karl Rasche was one of the most important financial figures in Nazi Germany's rearmament. By virtue of his Nazi convictions and his excellent standing in governmental circles he was instrumental in placing the huge resources of the Dresdner Bank behind such war potentials as synthetic fabrics, synthetic oil, steel, and expanding industrial capacity.

As early as 1934 when it was realized that Germany's natural oil resources would be insufficient to maintain and supply her contemplated war machine, a program was initiated by Hjalmar Schacht to produce synthetic fuel. A corporation, the Brabag (Braunkohle-Benzin A.G.), with the participation of all the German soft-coal mines was founded for this purpose. Inasmuch as Brabag was planned on a grand scale, Schacht summoned Rasche to a meeting to discuss the building of this new corporate structure. As a result of this meeting, the Dresdner Bank assumed the leadership of the banking consortium for the financing of Brabag.

After the Nazi hordes had overrun most of Europe, Hitler and Goering decided that in order to obtain the greatest possible production from conquered Europe, oil activities were to be brought under one giant monopoly corporation called Kontinentale Oel. Reichsminister Funk personally took over the presidency of this corporation, Karl Rasche became a member of the Aufsichtsrat, and the Dresdner Bank took the lead in the heavy support needed to finance the venture.

The Dresdner Bank acted as the financial spearhead for the Hermann-Goering-Werke. Through its financial affiliates the Dresdner was able to secure the choice enterprises of every industry in all the occupied and satellite countries of Europe. Karl Rasche was the linking personality between the Hermann-Goering-Werke and the Dresdner Bank.

Spoliation of Europe. Karl Rasche was ever in the forefront of the Dresdner's foreign economic penetration and exploitation of the economic resources of the countries of Europe.

Nine months before the Anschluss of Austria the Dresdner Bank was informed by Wilhelm Keppler, the Nazi Party economic adviser to Hitler, that the Fuehrer expressly wanted the Mercurbank (a subsidiary of Dresdner) strengthened and expanded as a German economic stronghold. . . . Karl Rasche was one of the two "specialists" from the Vorstand assigned to work out the details.

The "special skill" of Rasche [was] . . . put to full use in the subsequent penetration of Czechoslovakia. Goering himself commissioned Rasche and Kehrl of the RWM in 1938 to extend German influence over Czechoslovakian industry.

As soon as the Dresdner Bank established a foothold in the Sudeten it turned its main efforts into extending the Hermann-Goering-Werke into this new coal- and iron-rich territory. Lignite mines held by the Czech-Jewish Petschek family were incorporated by Karl Rasche into the HGW combine. This company was consolidated with smaller lignite mines into the Sudetenlaendische Bergwerke. Karl Rasche became the first chairman of the Aufsichtsrat. It was the "great contribution" of the Dresdner Bank to assist actively in the acquisition of control by the HGW of the Skoda Works. Again Rasche was active in affecting the transfer of control from Czech hands into German hands as he was in the cases of the Bruenner Waffen and Bruenner Maschinen.

Aryanization was one of the most common means of spoliation. It was in this connection that the bank through Rasche dealt most frequently with the Gestapo [including in the acquisitions of the Engelhardt Brauerei A.G. and Jewish-owned shares of the Koenigshofer concern, which were reported in earlier chapters].

When the Gildemann Cigar factory, Hamburg, was eager to acquire an Aryanizable project, Rasche arranged everything down to the smallest detail. He even secured affidavits for passports necessary for the would-be owners to visit Prague in order to see the firm, Waldes & Co., which they were to acquire.

Before the military invasion of Western Europe, the Dresdner Bank created its spearhead bank in the Netherlands. On 2 October 1939, the Handelstrust West N.V. was founded in Amsterdam. Ostensibly the main function of this institution was the encouragement and financing of Dutch exports to Germany. Actually its actions were a fulfillment of Reich policies for penetration. The Reich Minister of Economics in a confidential circular sent to the Dresdner Bank stated on 7 September 1940:

> All attempts should be made to achieve the most all-embracing participation possible of German industry in the Netherlands. . . . Capital investments should be tied in with a significant influence over the management of the firm, and with infiltration of personnel. It is therefore necessary to review the inclinations of persons acquiring (businesses). Unreliable persons, particularly Jews, must be removed. Particular emphasis must be placed on the key areas of Dutch industry.

This was one of a series of directives sent by the RWM for carrying out the economic subjugation of Holland.

Although previously Rasche had a share in shaping the bank's policy in the Netherlands, he was now placed in charge of carrying out these directives. The bank's memo dated 6 December 1940 reads: ". . . according to the given statements, Herr Dr. Rasche took over from Dr. Pilder the active management of the business in the Netherlands and therewith also of the Handelstrust West." The speed with which Rasche took steps to translate policy into concrete transactions was almost startling. There was an immediate effort to increase German influence in Dutch firms that were desirable or valuable. There was the taking over of outstanding debts, bonds, shares, stocks of goods, contract rights, and so forth. Connections were taken up with Dutch trading and manufacturing firms. The programmatic execution of the comprehensive plan with respect to Aryanization is characteristic of Rasche's operations in all fields. Scarcely a month after the Aryanization Law in Holland had been passed in March 1941, the Handelstrust West N.V. had established an Aryanization Division. Numerous examples are available in the files of cases in which the Handelstrust acted as agent in the purchase of non-Aryan businesses.

There were no extremes to which Rasche would hesitate to go. Not only buying and selling property, he also tried to exact ransom from Dutch Jews imprisoned in concentration camps outside Holland and who held assets abroad, such as in the case of Benjamin Soet, [reported in an earlier chapter].

In this case the Dresdner Bank wrote to the RWM that Swiss friends of Soet, who was in the concentration camp at Mauthausen, had deposited 20,000 Swiss francs with the Schweizerische Bankgesellschaft with the provision that this sum would become available to the Dresdner Bank when Soet appeared in person at the Swiss Consulate in Amsterdam. . . .

A case involving the Aryanization of a Dutch firm as the prerequisite to release by the Gestapo and a passport to America is that of Isaac Keesing. One of the several memoranda dealing with this case, signed Stiller, Rasche's personal secretary, and dated 13 February 1941, states that "the passports to America for Keesing and relatives will be provided as soon as the publishing and printing firm owned by Keesing's brother is Aryanized. The records are held by Oberfuehrer Mueller of the Gestapo. We might negotiate in the meantime with the Gestapo." . . .

The Handelstrust West under the management of Rasche was so successful in accomplishing its missions that it was singled out for an award for "exceptional services in achieving the great aims of the National Socialist Movement." These aims were further carried out in the Baltic states. Karl Rasche directed Dresdner Bank operations for Lithuania, Latvia, and Estonia. Here as elsewhere, the Dresdner Bank was helpful not only to government ministries and Reich corporations but also to private German firms who were eager to share in the spoils. Numerous cases are on record in which German firms approached the Dresdner Bank for assistance in "establishing a foothold in the East."

Rasche's experience and service in the execution of the long-range plans of the Nazi leaders for the economic subjugation of Europe were called upon once more in a secret task of international importance entrusted to Rasche by Goering.

A confidential letter of 22 January 1944 by Goering, as head of the Four Year Plan, to Rasche specifies his secret assignment. This mission was to survey and make recommendations concerning the economic situation in Hungary and Sweden. Attached to this letter is Minister Speer's order of 16 September 1943 creating the so-called *Planungsamt* (Central Planning Office). It was one of Rasche's functions, according to Goering's letter, to call attention to any dangers which might lie in the path of the German war economy and to contact reliable persons with political or economic influence "who are open-minded to the thought of European cooperative work." All of Rasche's efforts were to be characterized by the final aim of a uniform European economy fully dominated by the Third Reich.

Evaluation. Rasche is a fairly shrewd individual who is well aware of the fact that he cannot be convicted of perjury so long as he merely fails to remember and does not falsify. Despite the difficulties of recalling events which occurred five and six years ago, there is little doubt that Rasche is thoroughly familiar with many of the transactions concerning which documentary evidence has been found in his files. He avoids giving information, however, through the recourse of insisting that he cannot remember and when confronted with documentary evidence, attempts to limit his information to that contained in the document. He becomes very badly frightened and inconsistent and uncertain upon intensive interrogation supported by written exhibits.

The fact is plainly evident that he makes every effort deliberately to withhold information concerning events with which he is familiar.

CONCLUSION

Rasche held a high position in the financial, industrial, and economic life of Germany . . . and is deemed to have committed a crime against peace. . . . His detention is not subject to review.

HANS SCHIPPEL

(MEMBER OF THE VORSTAND OF THE DRESDNER BANK)

SUMMARY

Hans Schippel is a competent, though not outstanding executive, who after the advent of the Nazis to power in 1933 rose much more rapidly than his abilities warranted. He apparently had no real convictions and yet was of immense help to the Nazi conspiracy by his spineless, complacent acquiescence to their policy and doctrine.

Personal Data. Hans Schippel is sixty-six years old, a German citizen. He was the personnel executive and a member of the Vorstand of the Dresdner Bank. His present home is at See Strasse 40, Holzhausen, Post Utlig am Ammersee, Bavaria.

Subject was arrested 29 October 1945 and is now at Seventh Army Detention Camp 99, Butzbach. He has also been at the G-2 Division Interrogation Center in

Berlin.

Schippel finished his education at the University of Bremen in 1907, but already had begun to work as an accountant at the Reichsbank. From 1914–1919 he served as a foreign exchange specialist and after the war was appointed to the Ministry of Finance. He was successively Reichscommissioner of the Rentenbank, director of the Luebeck Branch of the Reichsbank, Reichstrustee of the Darmstaedter Bank and, finally, in 1933, became associated with the Dresdner Bank.

Political Activity. Hans Schippel has been a member of the NSDAP since 1937. Schippel was a member of the following affiliated organizations:

> NSFK—since 1937
> NSV
> DAF
> KDF

Subject received the "Foerdernadel" in gold of the N.S. Fliegerkorps on 29 November 1939 from General Christiansen.

Hans Schippel as a personnel executive for the Dresdner Bank contributed considerably to the nazification of this huge financial concern. He organized various recreational and educational activities for the bank's employees, which were mainly instruments for assimilation of NSDAP propaganda. The purge of the bank's employee rolls of politically and racially undesirable members, which began in 1933, was carried on under his department.

Financial and Industrial Connections. Schippel was associated with the following organizations:

Dresdner Bank, Berlin	Member Vorstand 1931–1945
Deutsche Bank fuer Ostasien, Berlin	Vice-Chairman Aufsichtsrat 1943–1945
Laenderbank A.G., Wien	Vice-Chairman Advisory Board 1934–1945
Deutsch-Asiatische Bank, Berlin	Member Aufsichtsrat 1925–1945
Rheinische Hypotheken Bank	Member Aufsichtsrat 1934–1945
Maschinenbau und Bahnbedarf A.G., Berlin	Chairman Aufsichtsrat
"Frankonia" Rueck- und Mitver-sicherungs A.G. (Insurance)	Chairman Aufsichtsrat 1935–1945
Saechsische Textil-Maschinenfabrik, Hartmann (Textile, machinery)	Chairman Aufsichtsrat 1941–1944
Wanderer-Werke A.G. (Typewriters, bicycles)	Chairman Aufsichtsrat 1934–1944
Koehlmann Werke, Frankfurt/Oder (Potato flour, starch)	Vice-Chairman Aufsichtsrat 1936–1945

Deutsch-Atlantische Telegraphen-Gesellschaft (Cable messages)	Vice-Chairman Aufsichtsrat 1936–1944
Schultheiss-Brauerei A.G. (Beer, mineral water)	Vice-Chairman Aufsichtsrat 1936–1944
Rabbethege & Giesecke A.G. (Sugar)	Member Aufsichtsrat 1936–1944
Deutsche Erdoel A.G. (Coal, fuel)	Member Aufsichtsrat 1936–1944
Deutsche Continental Gas A.G. (Gas)	Member Aufsichtsrat 1936–1944
Brown, Boveri & Cie. A.G. (Electrical appliances)	Member Aufsichtsrat 1936–1944
Kloeckner Werke A.G. (Coal, iron, steel)	Member Aufsichtsrat 1938–1944
Bayerische Motoren Werke A.G. (Autos, airplanes, and motors)	Member Aufsichtsrat 1935–1944
Daimler Benz A.G., Berlin (Cars, airplane motors)	Member Aufsichtsrat 1936–1944
Mansfeld A.G., Berlin (Coal, copper, coke)	Member Aufsichtsrat 1935–1944
Berliner Kraft & Licht A.G. (Electric power)	Member Aufsichtsrat 1938–1945
Beamtenversicherungsverein des Deutschen Bank- und Bankiergewerbes A.G., Berlin	Member Aufsichtsrat

Most of the subject's industrial connections arose from the practice of the Dresdner Bank to have a member on the Aufsichtsrat of corporations in which it had an interest. He could be relied on to carry on bank policy and therefore made an ideal man for this purpose.

Connection with the Dresdner Bank. Hans Schippel became associated with the Dresdner Bank in 1933. He was the director of the Personnel Department and supervised numerous small matters that were not specifically assigned to some other Vorstand member.

Armament and War Activities. Hans Schippel's efforts to promote Nazi propaganda constituted a support of the war plans of the Party. As a member of the Vorstand he went down the line in approving the immense loans and credits granted by the Dresdner Bank to finance the rearmament of Nazi Germany for its war of aggression.

Income. Subject . . . enjoyed a ninefold increase in income, most of it coming from industries engaged in war and rearmament activity. His income by years was:

1930	RM 36,000	1938	RM 300,000
1931	RM 36,000	1939	RM 300,000
1932	RM 36,000	1940	RM 300,000
1933	RM 36,000	1941	RM 300,000
1934	RM 36,000	1942	RM 300,000
1935	RM 100,000	1943	RM 300,000
1936	RM 300,000	1944	RM 300,000
1937	RM 300,000		

Sources. The information herein has been obtained from interrogations of subject and his business associates, and from Military Government questionnaires.

Evaluation of Prisoner. As a witness, subject is evasive on subjects touching on politics and is not too well informed concerning the details of transactions engaged in by the Dresdner Bank.

CONCLUSION

Schippel held a high position in the financial, industrial, and economic life of Germany . . . and is deemed to have committed a crime against peace. . . . His detention is not subject to review.

HUGO ZINSSER

(MEMBER OF THE VORSTAND OF THE DRESDNER BANK)

SUMMARY

Hugo Zinsser was a competent executive, but was not a leading figure in the Dresdner Bank. For the past six years he has been in the army. He served on the Eastern Front and in Poland and Czechoslovakia both in the conquest and subsequent exploitation of these areas.

Personal Data. Hugo Zinsser, age forty-six, is a German citizen and lived at Abegstrasse 11, Wiesbaden. He was a member of the Vorstand of the Dresdner Bank. Subject was arrested on 25 October 1945 and two days later was placed in the "Red Cross Hospital," Wiesbaden. He was recently moved to the Elisabeth-Krankenhaus in Bad Nauheim, at which place he is at present.

Zinsser was educated at Heilbronn attending the elementary school and *Realschule* (secondary school).

Political Activity. Subject never joined the NSDAP. He belonged to the following auxiliary Party organizations:

> DAF—since 1935
> NSV—since 1938
> Reichsluftschutzbund—since 1936

Financial and Industrial Connections. Zinsser was associated with the following organizations:

Dresdner Bank, Berlin	Member Vorstand 1934–1945
Pfaelzische Hypothekenbank	Member Aufsichtsrat 1936–1945
Hermes Kreditversicherungs A.G. (Insurance)	Member Aufsichtsrat 1936–1945
Diskonto Kompanie A.G., Berlin	Member Aufsichtsrat 1939–1945
Metallwarenfabrik vorm H. Wissner A.G. (War industry)	Chairman Aufsichtsrat 1941–1945
Chemische Farben von Heyden A.G. (Pharmaceutical products)	Chairman Aufsichtsrat 1943–1945
Gottfried Lindner A.G. (Railroad cars)	Chairman Aufsichtsrat 1937–1945
Oehringen Bergbau A.G. (Coal)	Chairman Aufsichtsrat 1939–1944
Plauener Baumwollspinnerei A.G. (Textile fabrics)	Chairman Aufsichtsrat 1934–1937
Chemische Werke Albert (Fertilizer, plastics)	Vice-Chairman Aufsichtsrat 1940–1945
Hugo Schneider A.G. (Ammunition)	Vice-Chairman Aufsichtsrat 1940–1945
G. Kaerger, Fabrik fuer Werkzeugmaschinen A.G. (Lathes)	Vice-Chairman Aufsichtsrat 1932–1945
Freiherrlich von Tucher'sche Brauerei A.G. (Beer)	Vice-Chairman Aufsichtsrat 1938–1945
Chemische Werke Aussig Falkenau G.m.b.H. (Salicylate)	Member Aufsichtsrat 1939–1945
Koenigsberger Zellstoff-Fabrik & Chemische Werke Koholyt A.G. (Cellulose, paper)	Member Aufsichtsrat 1934–1936
Pfaelzische Muehlenwerke (Mill products)	Member Aufsichtsrat 1938–1945
Riebeck'sche Montanwerke A.G. (Coal, mineral oil)	Member Aufsichtsrat 1939–1945
Reichelbraeu A.G. (Beer)	Member Aufsichtsrat 1936–1945
Radeberger Export Bierbrauerei A.G. (Beer)	Member Aufsichtsrat 1936–1945
Graschwitz Textilwerke A.G. (Yarn)	Member Aufsichtsrat 1937–1942
Hildebrand & Soehne Rheinmuehlenwerke A.G. (Mill products)	Member Aufsichtsrat 1933–1937
Feldmuehle, Papier- & Zellstoffwerke A.G. (Cellulose, paper)	Member Aufsichtsrat 1936–1945
Sueddeutsche Zucker A.G. (Sugar)	Member Aufsichtsrat 1934–1945

Zinsser was on the Aufsichtsrat of a great number of smaller companies with whom the Dresdner did a profitable business and wished to retain as clients. His banking connections were similarly for the benefit of his employer.

Connections with Dresdner Bank. Zinsser first entered the Dresdner Bank in 1915, becoming a manager in 1922. During the banking crisis of 1931 he was appointed vice-president of the Berlin head office. His sound judgment and diligent service during that critical time convinced the Aufsichtsrat of his worth, and, in 1935, he was made a deputy member of the Vorstand. He became a full member in 1941. He headed the Foreign Exchange department, the Liquid Funds department, and was in charge of the branches in southern Germany.

He was a competent executive for the bank, and faithfully applied the policies of the bank for the building of the Nazi war machine. He was promoted to full membership as an honorary gesture at the time he was in the army.

Income. Zinsser earned the following sums during the period 1930–1944:

1930	RM 18,000	1938	RM 180,000
1931	RM 18,000	1939	RM 195,000
1932	RM 21,000	1940	RM 204,000
1933	RM 26,000	1941	RM 216,000
1934	RM 38,000	1942	RM 206,000
1935	RM 114,000	1943	RM 206,000
1936	RM 140,000	1944	RM 205,000
1937	RM 174,000		

The increase in Zinsser's income was directly due to the rearmament and war production profits of the companies with which he was connected. He estimates his assets at present as being worth RM 400,000.

Sources. The information herein has been obtained from interrogations of Zinsser and associates, reports, and Military Government questionnaires submitted by Zinsser.

Evaluation of Prisoner. Zinsser's previous friends and associates characterize him as a reliable and industrious executive. He has been cooperative during interrogations, but his six years' absence because of his service with the army prevents him from having any considerable knowledge of details of transactions.

CONCLUSION

Zinsser held a high position in the financial, industrial, and economic life of Germany . . . and is deemed to have committed a crime against peace . . . His detention is not subject to review.

Index

Boldface numbers indicate pages where principal discussions appear.

Christopher Simpson is Associate Professor at American University's School of Communication in Washington, D.C. where he specializes in information literacy. He is the author of four books concerning genocide, international human rights law, and national security: *Blowback* (1987), *The Splendid Blond Beast* (1993), *Science of Coersion* (1994), and *National Security Directives of the Reagan and Bush Administrations* (1995). Simpson is also the editor of *Universities and Empire* (1998) and has written numerous articles for journals and professional publications, including a study on the development of international human rights law at the International Tribunal at Nuremburg. He now serves as editor of the Holmes & Meier Science and Human Rights Series.